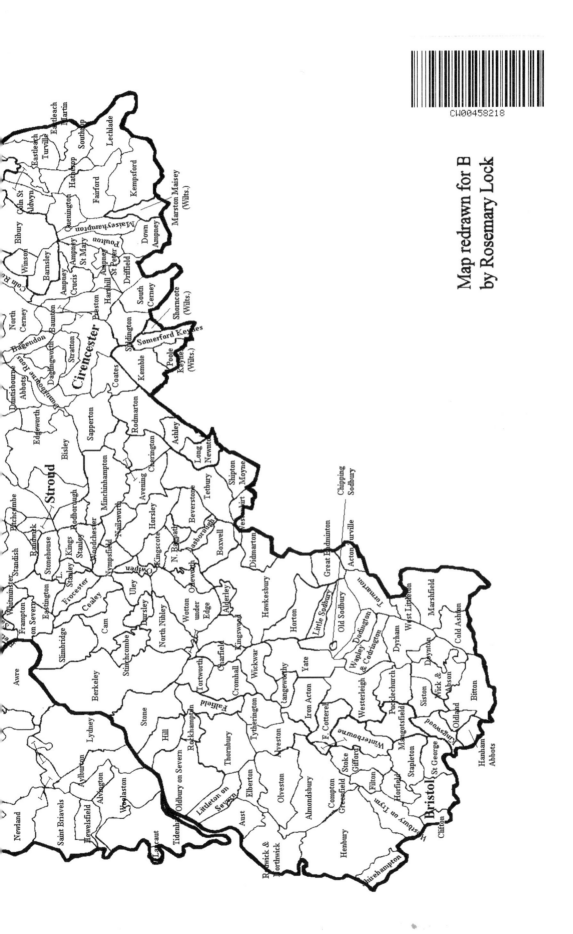

Map redrawn for B
by Rosemary Lock

The Bristol and Gloucestershire Archaeological Society
Gloucestershire Record Series

Hon. General Editor
Dr J D Hodsdon FSA

Volume 32

Dissenters' Meeting-House Certificates, 1672–1852

To the Right Rev.d Father in God Richard Lord
Bishop of the Diocese of Gloucester

These are to certify your Lordship that some of his Majesty's
Protestant Dissenting Subjects called Baptist intend to
hold a Meeting for the Worship of Almighty God at the
Dwelling house of Robert Gearing of Welford in the parish
of Kempsford in the County of Gloucester and therefore
pray that this Certificate may be duly registered in your
Court according to the Act of Toleration made in the first
Year of the Reign of King William and Queen Mary As
Witness our Hands this twelfth day of March one thousand
seven hundred and ninety nine.

Daniel Williams
James Andrews
John Smith
Will.m Hooke
Hen.y Thomson
Jacob Betterton
John Kent
Cha.s G. Thomson
Cha.s Hooke
John Thomas
Ben.n Thomas
John Purbrick

Molly Betterton
Priscilla Smith
Amelia Stephenson
Mary Bosbery
Mary Thomson
Jane Thomson
Sarah Gardner
Sarah Hooke
Ann Salis
Mary Hooke

Reg.d 16.th March 1799.

The names of twelve men and ten women Baptists, listed in separate columns, who in 1799 certified their intention to meet at a dwelling house in Welford [*see* entry **997**].   *GA*

DISSENTERS' MEETING-HOUSE CERTIFICATES AND REGISTRATIONS

FOR

BRISTOL AND GLOUCESTERSHIRE

1672–1852

Edited by Anthea Jones

Baptist Chapel, Hillesley (rebuilt 1824)   *photo: A Jones*

The Bristol and Gloucestershire Archaeological Society

2018

The Bristol and Gloucestershire Archaeological Society
Gloucestershire Record Series

© The Bristol and Gloucestershire Archaeological Society 2018

ISBN 978 0 900197 95 6

British Library Cataloguing in Publication Data
A catalogue entry for this book is available from the British Library

Produced for the Society
by 4word Ltd, Bristol
Printed in Great Britain

CONTENTS

†The Society is greatly indebted to Rosemary Lockie for adapting her online Gloucestershire parish map to the requirements of this edition.

PREFACE AND ACKNOWLEDGEMENTS

This volume originated in a suggestion by John Chandler, and it is a pleasure to acknowledge his support and unfailing stimulus once the project was underway. His expertise further led to consideration of Bristol's records and the Registrar General's Returns, adding considerably to the value of the volume.

Peter Barlow, Jan Mann and Anne Perkins volunteered to help with transcribing the Gloucestershire records, and their work is acknowledged with gratitude; their comments on the material have also been appreciated. Anne entered the large amount of information in the Registrar General's returns into a spreadsheet which has been exceptionally helpful in checking and supplementing the surviving local sources, she extracted relevant comments from some 19th century directories, and she created a spreadsheet of the information in Bishop Benson's survey of Gloucester diocese.

The decision to present the material by parish rather than by chronology has raised a number of issues of arrangement, but has yielded interesting insights into the presence and progress of dissent. The Forest of Dean, in particular, posed some problems, and I am grateful to Dr Nicholas Herbert for his comments. The final outcome is nonetheless the responsibility of this editor.

I am grateful to the director of Dr Williams Library, Dr David Wykes, for giving me access to the 'Evans list', and for his discussion of the material. Jonathan Barry made useful comments on an earlier draft of the Introduction, and drew my attention to comparisons between certificates and lists of nonconformist chapels in early Bristol Directories; he also led me to John Browning's paper read to the Royal Society, and gave other help on Bristol's in- and out-parishes, but as with the Forest of Dean, final presentation of the material is my responsibility.

Francis Boorman, recently a contributing editor, VCH Gloucestershire, made available his research into the Lay Feoffees in Cirencester. Alex Craven discovered the comment on the Cotswolds' lack of dissent in 1635, and he and John Chandler kindly provided images of meeting-house registrations. Sue Brown gave me a spreadsheet of Tetbury's inhabitants listed about 1737 (GA D566/Z/11). Averil Kear has been generous in sharing her knowledge of the Forest of Dean and giving permission for the use of two of her photographs.

I am pleased to acknowledge the financial help given me by the Bristol and Gloucestershire Archaeological Society for visiting Bristol Archives. The archivists there and in Gloucestershire Archives were unfailingly helpful in making sources available, answering queries, and reading some names; I would particularly mention the help given by Vicky Thorpe. James Hodsdon, as hon. General Editor of the Record Series, has been steadily encouraging and supportive.

Errors, misreadings, misunderstandings and omissions in the text remain my responsibility.

Anthea Jones
Cheltenham, June 2018

BIBLIOGRAPHY

Anon., 'Revd J Horlick', *Christian's Penny Magazine* (Aug 1858)

Ansell, W., *One hundred years of congregationalism in Cheltenham 1827-1927* n.d. [1927]

Austin, R., Obituary of Frank Step Hockaday (1856-1924) *Trans BGAS* 46 (1924) 379-83

Barry, J., 'The parish in civic life: Bristol and its churches 1640-1750', *Parish, Church and People. Local studies in lay religion 1350-1750* ed. S Wright (1988)

Beecham, K. J., *History of Cirencester* (1887, reprint 1978)

Bennett, James, *Tewkesbury Yearly Register* (1840, 1850).

Bettey, J., *From Catholic Devotion to Puritan Piety: Responses to the Reformation in the Avon Area 1530-1603* (ALHA Books No 11)

Bradley, James E., 'Nonconformity and the Electorate in Eighteenth Century England', *Parliamentary History* VI (1987)

Bright, Thomas, *The rise of Nonconformity in the Forest of Dean* (n.d.) [1955]

Browning, John, 'The number of people in the city of Bristol, calculated from the burials for ten years successive, and also from the number of houses', paper read to the Royal Society Jan. 25, 1753

Calendar of State Papers Domestic Series of the reign of Charles I 1635 ed. John Bruce Esq (1865)

Chandler, J. H. (ed), *Wiltshire Dissenters' Meeting-house Certificates and Registrations 1689-1852* (Wiltshire Record Society 40, 1985)

Dallimore, Arnold A., *George Whitefield: the life and times of the great evangelist of the eighteenth-century revival* (1970)

Day, Joan M., 'The Bristol brass industry: Furnace structures and their associated remains', *Journal of the Historical Metallurgy Society* 22/1 (1988)

Donaldson, B., *The Registrations of dissenting chapels and meeting-houses in Staffordshire 1689-1852: extracted from the return in the General Register Office made under the Protestant Dissenters Act of 1852* (15 and 16 Vic. c.36) (Staffordshire Record Society 1960).

Dresser, Madge, 'The Moravians in Bristol', *Reformation and revival in eighteenth century Bristol* ed. J. Barry & K. Morgan (Bristol Record Society 45 (1994)

Evans, D.E., *As mad as a hatter! A history of Nonconformism in Dursley. Puritans and Whitefieldites in the history of Dursley and Cam* (1982)

Evans, M J Crossley, 'Methodism in late 19th-century Bristol : as exemplified by the life, preaching engagements and writings of Joseph Perry Distin', *Trans BGAS* 124 (2006)

Fendley, John (ed), *Bishop Benson's Survey of the Diocese of Gloucester 1735-1750* (Gloucestershire Record Series 13, BGAS 2000)

Field, Clive D., 'Zion's people: who were the English Nonconformists?' part 1, *The Local Historian* (40, May 2010)

Gell, R & T Bradshaw, *The Gloucestershire Directory* (1820)

Hayden, R. (ed), *The Records of a Church of Christ in Bristol, 1640-1687* (Bristol Record Society 27, 1974)

Hine, G. R., *History of the Methodist churches and chapels in the Gloucester circuit from the time of John Wesley to 1970* (1971) (GA D2689/1/6/6)

Hodsdon, James (ed), *An Historical Gazetteer of Cheltenham* (Gloucestershire Record Series 9, BGAS 1997)

Hodsdon, James (ed), *The Court Books of the Manor of Cheltenham 1692-1803* (Gloucestershire Record Series 24, BGAS 2010)

Horn, Joyce M., *Fasti Ecclesiae Anglicanae 1541-1857*: Volume 8, Bristol, Gloucester, Oxford and Peterborough Dioceses (London, 1996)

[Hunt, E.], Hunt & Co's Directory & Topography for the cities of Gloucester & Bristol (1849)

Jenkins, Rhys, 'The copper works at Redbrook and at Bristol', *Trans BGAS* 63 (1942)

Jones, A. E., 'Protestant dissent in Gloucestershire: a comparison between 1676 and 1735', *Trans BGAS* 101 (1983)

Judge, G. H. Bancroft, *Origin and progress of Wesleyan Methodism in Cheltenham and district* [etc]. (Cheltenham, 1912)

Kirby, Ethyn W., 'The Lay Feoffees: A Study in Militant Puritanism', *The Journal of Modern History*, 14, No. 1 (Mar., 1942)

Kirby, I. M., *Diocese of Bristol : a catalogue of the records of the bishop and archdeacons and of the dean and chapter* (Bristol Corporation 1970)

Kirby, I. M., *Diocese of Gloucester: a catalogue of the records of the Dean and Chapter including the former St Peter's Abbey* (Gloucester County Council 1967)

Lacock, R., 'Quakers in Gloucester: the first fifty years, 1655-1705', *Trans. BGAS* 125 (2007)

Lewis, Cherry, 'David Mushet and his contribution to the 'map that changed the world', *The Local Historian* 47 (October 2017)

Lewis, Samuel, *A topographical dictionary of England* (1831)

Little, Bryan (ed), *Sketchley's Bristol Directory 1775* (Kingsmead reprints, Bath 1971).

Matthews, W., *The new history, survey and description of the city and suburbs of Bristol or Complete Guide* (1794).

Minchinton, W. E., 'Bristol – Metropolis of the west in the eighteenth century', *Transactions of the Royal Historical Society,* 5th series, iv (1954)

Moore, J. S., *The Goods and Chattels of our forefathers* (1976)

Morgan, K. (ed) [i], 'The John Evans list of dissenting congregations and ministers in Bristol 1715-1729', *Reformation and revival in eighteenth century Bristol* ed. J. Barry & K. Morgan (Bristol Record Society 45 (1994)

Morgan, K. (ed) [ii], 'Methodist Testimonials collected by Charles Wesley in 1742', *Reformation and Revival in Eighteenth-Century Bristol* ed. J. Barry & K. Morgan (Bristol Record Society 45, 1994)

Mortimer, R. (ed), *Minute Book of the Men's Meeting of the Society of Friends in Bristol 1667-1686* (BRS 26, 1971)

Mortimer, R. (ed), *Minute Book of the Men's Meeting of the Society of Friends in Bristol 1686-1704* (BRS 30, 1978)

Munden, A. (ed), *The religious census of Bristol and Gloucestershire 1851* (Gloucestershire Record Series 29, BGAS 2015)

Pierce, Sylvie, *History of Cambray Baptist Church 1843-1993* (1993)

Pigot's Directory of Gloucestershire 1830

Ralph, Elizabeth (ed) 'Bishop Secker's Diocese Book', *A Bristol Miscellany* (Bristol Record Society 37, 1985).

Ripley, P., 'Village and town: Occupations and Wealth in the Hinterland of Gloucester, 1660-1700', *Agricultural History Review* 32 (1984)

Rivers, J., *The law of organised religions: Between Establishment and Secularism* (OUP 2010)

Royal Comission on the Historic Monuments of England, *An Inventory of Nonconformist Chapels and Meeting-houses in Central England. Gloucestershire* (HMSO 1986)

Rudder, S., *A new history of Gloucestershire* (1779 reprinted Stroud 1977)

Skea, Kinda, The Ecclesiastical Identities of Puritan and Nonconformist Clergy, 1640-1672, Thesis submitted for the degree of Doctor of Philosophy at the University of Leicester February, 2015

Smith, A H, *The Place-Names of Gloucestershire* (1964)

Spurrier, Lisa (ed), *Berkshire Nonconformist Meeting-house Registrations 1689-1852* (Berkshire Record Society 9, 2005)

Stanley, John, 'Was John Skinner ejected in 1662', *Trans Baptist Historical Society* 3.2 (1912)

Stephens, L., *Cirencester Quakers 1655-1973* (Cirencester Preparative Meeting n.d.) [1973]

Tonks, W. C., *Victory in the Villages The history of the Brinkworth Circuit* (1907)

Turner, G. Lyon, *Original records of early Nonconformity under persecution and indulgence* (3 vols, 1911)

Urdank, A., *Religion and Society in a Cotswold Vale: Nailsworth, Gloucestershire 1780-1865* (University of California, 1990)

Victoria History of the county of Gloucester:
  Vol. 2 (ed) W. Page (1907)
  Vol. 4 (ed) C. R. Elrington (1988)
  Vol. 5 (ed) N. Herbert (1996)
  Vol. 7 (ed) C. R. Elrington (1981)
  Vol. 8 (ed) C. R. Elrington (1968)
  Vol. 10 (ed) R. B Pugh (1972)
  Vol. 11 (ed) N. M. Herbert (1976)
  Vol. 12 (ed) A. R. J. Jurica (2010)
  Vol. 13 (ed) J. H. Chandler and A. R. J. Jurica (2016)

Victoria History of the county of Wiltshire: Vol. 18 (ed) Virginia Bainbridge (2011)

Vinter, D., *The Friends Meeting-house, Frenchay* (Dursley 1963)

W.W., 'History of the Baptist Church at Cheltenham', *Baptist Magazine for 1818* (10) (London 1818)

Watts, M. R., *The Dissenters I. From the Reformation to the French Revolution* (Clarendon Oxford, 1978)

Watts, M. R., *The Dissenters II. The expansion of Evangelical Nonconformity* (Clarendon Oxford 1999)

Welch, Edwin (ed), *Bedfordshire chapels and meeting-houses: Official Registration 1672-1901* (Bedfordshire Historical Record Society 75, 1996)

Whiteman, A. (ed), *The Compton Census of 1676 A critical edition* (British Academy 1986)

Willis, A. J., 'Dissenters' Meeting-house Certificates, 1702-1844', *A Hampshire Miscellany* 3 (Folkestone, 1965)

Youngs, F. A. jr, *Guide to the Local Administrative Units of England* (1979)

MSS

'A Memorial of Nonconformity elicited by the Centenary Services of the Rodborough Tabernacle' [Sermons, papers and addresses] (1866) (GA D4248/14/7)

Horlick, John, *A visit to the Forest of Dean* (c.1832 with additions up to 1850) (GA D2297/1)

ABBREVIATIONS

BA	Bristol Archives
BGAS	Bristol & Gloucestershire Archaeological Society
BRS	Bristol Record Society
EP	Bristol Episcopal Records (held at Bristol Archives)
GA	Gloucestershire Archives
GDR	Gloucester Diocesan Records (held at GA)
LT	G. Lyon Turner (*see* Bibliography)
ODNB	Oxford Dictionary of National Biography
RCHM	Royal Commission on the Historical Monuments of England
RG 31	RG 31/2 and 31/6: Registrar General, Returns of Dissenters' Meeting-house registrations 1852 (TNA)
TNA	The National Archives, Kew
VCH	Victoria County History (*see* Bibliography)
Wilts MHC	*Wiltshire Dissenters' Meeting-house Certificates* (ed J. Chandler; *see* Bibliography)
WRS	Wiltshire Record Society
f.	folio (where there is no pagination)
/r	recto (right side of folio)
/v	verso (reverse side of folio)

(Photographs on the following six pages are all by Anthea Jones, with the exception of the Jesus Rock and the Mitcheldean Independent Chapel, by Averil Kear.)

Friends' Meeting Houses are generally the oldest dissenters' buildings still in use, though they have been extended. Broad Campden *above* (a small house purchased in 1663) and Nailsworth *below* were two of the 19 Quaker meetings registered at the Gloucester Quarter Sessions at Easter 1690 [**494**, **1224** and Appendix 1].

with kind permission of the Trustees of Gloucestershire Area Quaker Meeting

Dissenters sometimes met for religious worship in town halls or market houses, sometimes in the open air. Minchinhampton market hall was registered for meetings in 1746 [**1164**] and 1802 [**1170**].

Richard Stiff was noted for his outdoor preaching in the Forest of Dean (*see* lxv), reputedly making use of the striking 'Jesus Rock' near Danby Lodge, Yorkley.

Baptists were meeting in Chipping Sodbury in 1672 [**506**]. The Baptist chapel in Hounds Lane, built in 1819, replaced a smaller chapel on the same site [**511**]. In 1971 it was replaced by a modern building on High Street.

The Baptist church in Sherborne Street, Lechlade, was registered in 1817 [**1041**], and continues in use. William Fox esq., lord of the manor, a Baptist and founder of the Sunday School Society, was amongst the first trustees.

Originating in an 1835 meeting [**462**], this church in Russell Streeet, Cheltenham, was built by Primitive Methodists *c*.1836 [**465**]. Congregationalists met there in 1847, followed by Baptists, who re-named it to recall a short-lived meeting in 1840 in the Railway Schoolroom in Gas Green [**471**].

'Mount Pleasant Union Church 1813' is recorded above the central window of the former chapel on the outskirts of Falfield. It was descibed as 'An upper room over an outhouse belonging to William Dorney, yeoman', when registered [**800**]. It was rebuilt in 1843; the school was added in 1848.

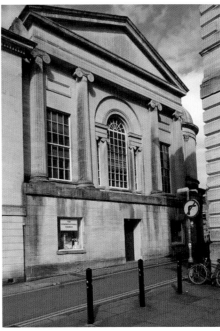

left Wotton-under-Edge Tabernacle, said to be built in 1852 (but note registration of the Tabernacle in 1842 [**2017**]) replaced Rowland Hill's meeting house (possibly registered in 1771 [**2006**]). It was closed and sold in 1973. *right* Stroud Congregational chapel [**1660**] was built in 1835–7, at right angles to the Subscription Rooms erected the previous year. Both reflected Stroud's new status as a parliamentary borough. The meeting room is above the school room.

Cinderford Methodist church on Littledown Hill, known as 'Wesley', was registered in 1850 by Aaron Goold [**696**]. He favoured an ecclesiastical style which became more usual in the later 19th century. Goold had registered an earlier meeting house in Cinderford in 1829 [**679**].

Mitcheldean Independent chapel, later Congregational, of 1822, was registered by John Horlick in 1847 [**1212**]. Mitcheldean Independents had earlier registered meetings in Ruardean [**1486 & 1487**]. It is now Forest Gate church, having been taken over by Mitcheldean Christian Fellowship in 1977.

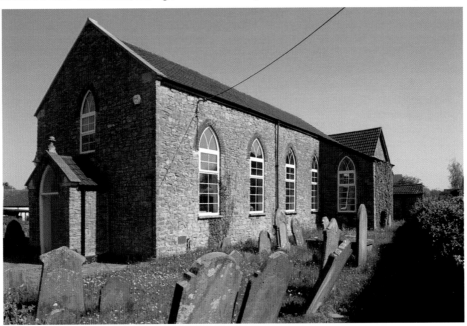

The Congregational church in Charfield Green was built in 1847 but registered in 1851 [**406**]. A building had been registered in 1834 by Independents and Baptists in Charfield Green [**404**], with a minister from Kingswood. The church has been well restored thanks to the endowment of land which was sold in exchange for necessary building works.

EXAMPLES OF CERTIFICATES *(see also pp lxxiii–lxxvi)*

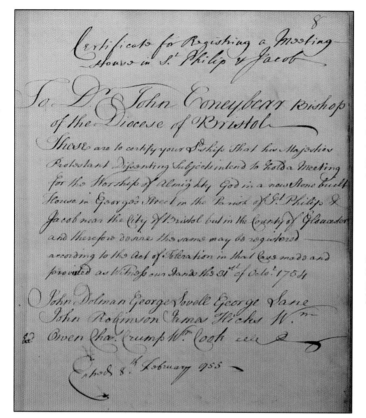

left The new stone-built house in George's Street in St Philip & St Jacob was described as 'near the City of Bristol but in the County' [**82**]. The parish church was in the city.　　*BA*

below The certificate [**38**] for registering the Seaman's chapel in Bristol harbour.　*BA*

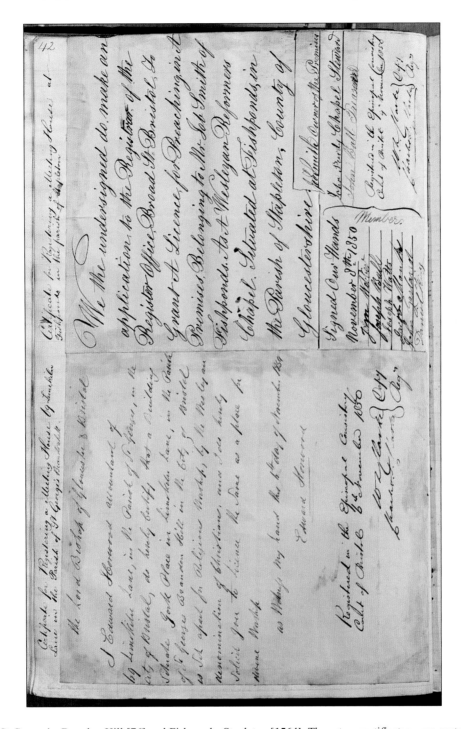

St George's, Brandon Hill [**76**] and Fishponds, Stapleton [**1564**]. These two certificates were pasted into the Bristol register sideways on the page. Edward Horwood used unusual wording 'I do hereby solicit you to licence the [building]'. The Fishponds certificate probably contains the signatures of the three officers.

BA

Registration of the Music Hall in Park Street Avenue, Bristol [71] for Protestant dissenters 'holding the true Christian faith as declared in the first XIX articles of the Church of England'. *BA*

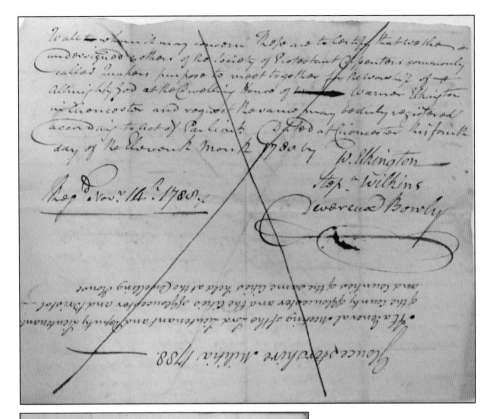

above A copy of a Cirencester certificate [**550**] made by the registrar or his clerk on a scrap piece of parchment on which the first few words of a record of a meeting about the Gloucestershire militia was written It was crossed through once entered in the Act Book.   *GA*

left An original certificate for Wickwar [**1897**] bearing the certifiers' signatures. It was retained in the diocesan archives but apparently not registered. A replacement a few weeks later was registered, but two signatories were different.   *GA*

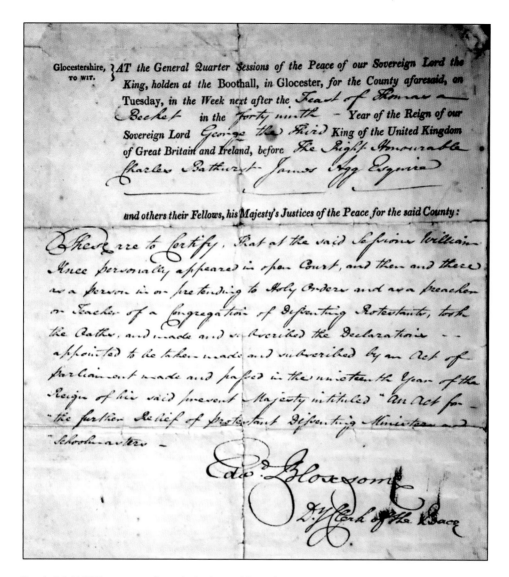

Randwick [**1453**]: an unusual survival of a certificate for a man in Holy Orders who was minister of a dissenting congregation, taking oaths of allegiance and supremacy, but being freed of the obligation to subscribe to the Thirty Nine Articles of the Church of England.   *GA*

INTRODUCTION

This edition gives details of all certificates and registrations of Protestant dissenters' meeting-houses, as far as official records survive, for both Bristol and Gloucestershire. They span the period from 1672, when there are records of applications to the Crown for licences under Charles II's Declaration of Indulgence, to 1852, when by Act of Parliament the licensing of a congregation wishing to meet for religious worship outside the Church of England was transferred from diocesan or Quarter Session authorities to the Registrar General. It thus complements the publication of equivalent records for Wiltshire (1985), Bedfordshire (1996), and Berkshire (2005),[1] as well as the more limited coverage of Staffordshire (1960)[2] and the diocese of Winchester (1965).[3]

The records offer insights into the history of those parishes where a dissenting congregation was formed, and name many of the inhabitants involved in the enterprise. They also contain evidence of nonconformist evangelising, a minister sometimes certifying meetings in several places; Joseph Everard was a signatory to no fewer than 22 meetings, spread quite widely through Gloucestershire [see **197**].[4] Meeting-house trustees sometimes came from other parishes. The certificates can confirm or amplify local records, and help to illustrate the progress of the different denominations. The date of chapel building can often be verified, and may be seen to follow from an earlier meeting in a private house. Meetings might be in single rooms, private houses, chapels or a miscellany of other buildings adapted for the purpose; the informality of meetings in private houses contrasted with the formality of the Church of England. By the 19th century congregations had become larger, organisation had become more formal, and the number of chapels built increased rapidly.

I. ARRANGEMENT OF MATERIAL

Because of the interest in the development of dissent in particular places and communities, the Bristol and Gloucestershire material has been arranged by parish and where relevant by chapelry, when specified.[5] There are three exceptions, where a chronological order has been followed: the cities of Bristol

---

[1] See respectively Chandler, Welch and Spurrier.
[2] Donaldson.
[3] Willis.
[4] Possibly more than one individual of this name was involved.
[5] The Gloucester diocesan survey of 1735 by Bishop Benson (Fendley, 2000) is taken as the source for chapelries. In the same year, Bishop Secker surveyed Bristol diocese (*see* xlvi below). Statistics of dissent are generally collected by parish but meeting-house certificates usually identified the chapelry and/or parish. The Religious Census of 1851 (Munden, 2015) also provided clarification.

and Gloucester, and the Forest of Dean. The two cities contained numerous parishes, some very small, and city boundaries often cut across more ancient parish territories. The resulting out-parishes have been linked with the city parishes to which they belonged, rather than separating the 'in' parts from the 'out'.

There were 17 ancient parishes in Bristol and the extra-parochial Castle precincts. Two ancient parishes had significant areas outside the city: St James and St Philip & St Jacob. The parish of St James, in the north of Bristol, covered a large city area and contained important early dissenters' chapel sites like Broadmead Baptist Chapel, the first nonconformist chapel in Bristol, Quakers Friars and Lewins Mead. Development in the equally large out-parish, which was in Gloucestershire but in the purlieus of Bristol city, started in the later 18th century with prosperous housing like Brunswick and Portland Squares, reaching into the parish of Westbury-on-Trym. St Paul's parish was created in 1794, taking in a large part of the out-parish, but a small out-parish area remained in St James's until the redrawing of the city boundary in 1835.[1] Three-quarters of the registrations of dissenters' meetings in St James's were for that part of the parish in the city; all registrations in St James's parish have been brought together in the sequence of city of Bristol entries.

The other ancient parish divided by the city boundary was St Philip & St Jacob.[2] It had a relatively small area adjacent to the non-parochial Castle precincts on the east side of the city, and an extensive out-parish in Gloucestershire, wrapping round the eastern side of Bristol; the part containing the settlements of Upper and Lower Easton remained outside the city after 1835. The out-parish was the site of manufacturing and grew substantially in the later 18th and early 19th centuries. St George's parish was created in the eastern part of St Philip & St Jacob in 1756, some 40 years before St Paul's, indicating earlier and more intensive development than in St James's out-parish;[3] the district of Holy Trinity in the north-east was designated in 1834. The majority of dissenters' meeting-house certificates relate to the out-parish. All registrations have therefore been collected together under the ancient parish name with the heading 'city of Bristol and County of Gloucester', immediately following the entries for the city of Bristol.

There were 11 ancient parishes in the city of Gloucester, and, as in Bristol, the boundaries of the borough cut across them. But there were also extra-parochial areas: Littleworth, North Hamlet, South Hamlet and the vill of Wotton, which were intermingled with six hamlets attached to Gloucester churches: Barton Street, Kingsholm, Longford, Tuffley, Twigworth and Wotton. Altogether they covered an area of more than 5,000 acres (2023 ha). All had 'boundaries of great

---

[1] The boundaries of the old and new borough in 1835 are given in BA/07706.

[2] In many records the name of the parish appears as 'St Philip & Jacob', but modern usage generally favours 'St Philip & St Jacob', which is the form adopted here.

[3] The civil parish of St George was created in 1785 'from parts of several parishes and later called Easton St George to distinguish it from St George Brandon Hill': Youngs, 166; Smith, (3) 100; BA EP/A/45/2 457–60; see eg **59**, **62**, **88**.

complexity'; most of the area was brought into the borough in 1835.[1] The meeting-house certificates often but not always specified the situation of each with respect to the 'out-parish' or extra-parochial place and as population and settlement increased in the 19th century, dissenting meetings were established in many of them. These areas, with the exception of Twigworth which was made a parish in 1844, have been included under the heading of Gloucester city.

The third exception to the arrangement by parish is the Forest of Dean. For most of the period concerned here, the largest part of the Forest was extra-parochial, and was administratively in the hundred of St Briavels; dissenters in the small and scattered Forest settlements often described their meeting place as in St Briavel's hundred. By the end of the 18th century many small settlements had a meeting. Boundaries were undefined, and as in the relevant volume of the VCH,[2] dissent is dealt with in one sequence under the heading 'Dean Forest (extra-parochial), the parish of St Briavels, and detached parts of Newland parish'. Some place-names could refer both to extra-parochial areas within the Forest and to portions of land physically separate from but attached to a particular parish; Newland had 22 detached portions, some very small.[3] The settlement names of meetings in these detached portions are given in the certificates, and these are all included under Dean Forest in order to maintain the settlement as the focus. The exception is Coleford which at this period was in Newland and in the hundred of St Briavels, but had become a market town in 1661, and was a clearly defined and sizeable settlement; it was given separate treatment in the Victoria County History and it has been separately listed here. St Briavel's parish, as the centre of the hundred, is included under Dean Forest, as it is not always clear whether the parish or the hundred was being indicated; moreover the parish has varied in extent many times and the modern parish is 'the product of a complex history.'[4]

In the last decades of local registration, there were changes in the organisation of the extra-parochial Forest, but certificates specifying the new units are not separated from the run of Dean Forest material. The Church of England began to build churches in the Forest from 1816 and to create parishes.[5] The first were Berry Hill, Harrow Hill near Drybrook, and Parkend. In 1842, the main part of the extra-parochial area of the Forest of Dean was divided into two townships for poor law purposes, East Dean and West Dean.[6] Christchurch ecclesiastical parish was formed in 1844 from parts of West Dean; Lydbrook parish was formed in 1852 from parts of English Bicknor, Newland, Ruardean and East and West Dean.

II. CONTEXT
The Legislative Background
Groups dissenting from the tenets of the Church of England had met during the

---

[1] *VCH Glos* 4, 1, 382.
[2] *VCH Glos* 5.
[3] *VCH Glos* 5, 197.
[4] *VCH Glos* 5, 248.
[5] Munden, 410–11.
[6] *VCH Glos* 5 378.

1650s, after the abolition of the Church of England, and allegiances had become firm. After the Restoration, Charles II was in sympathy with dissent, including Roman Catholicism, but his first parliament was determined to re-establish the Church of England, especially in view of the continuing existence of the parliamentary army with its adherence to strong Puritan beliefs, and the small rebellion in London by some Fifth Monarchists who would establish the kingdom of Jesus. Over the next several years the so-called 'Clarendon Code' tried to suppress nonconformity.

From 1660, clergy could be accused of sedition, which led to some being ejected from their livings; other acts made it difficult for those who had adopted the Solemn League and Covenant to remain within the restored Church of England.[1] The *Corporations Act* of 1661 required members to take certain oaths and to have taken communion in the Church of England within the past year, which automatically excluded Quakers who refused to swear on the Bible. In 1662 the *Quakers Act* forbade assemblies of more than five persons, other than members of the same household, and punished the refusal to take an oath. Other parts of the Clarendon Code included the *Conventicles Acts*, 1664 and 1670, which extended the provisions of the Quakers Act to all dissenters. The threat of fines or imprisonment did not prevent dissent continuing in clandestine meetings.

The *Act of Uniformity*, passed in 1662, 'determined the shape of the law for 170 years'.[2] It reimposed the requirement for clergy to assent to the Book of Common Prayer, which included the Thirty-nine Articles formulating the tenets of the Church of England. Some 2,000 clergy refused to accept the Prayer Book in its entirety and were ejected from their church livings. To prevent them staying in the communities they had been attached to, an act in 1665 prohibited them from coming within five miles of their former parish, or a corporate town, unless they took an oath. The location of many meeting-houses over the next 200 years, and of numerous nonconformist ministers, substantiates the general perception that towns were the most important centres of dissent.

Charles II attempted to use his royal prerogative to issue a *Declaration of Indulgence* in 1672 suspending the penal laws and instituting a system of licensing of ministers and preachers and of the houses or buildings where they wished to gather in 'conventicles' outside the Church of England (and Roman Catholics to meet in their own houses). The attempt at toleration was short-lived. Parliament annulled the Declaration and reimposed the penal laws, strengthened by the *Test Act* in 1673 requiring oaths and communion annually for officers of the Crown and in 1678 by requiring a declaration against transubstantiation as a sure method of excluding Roman Catholics.

Dissenters and Anglicans found common cause when James II came to the throne with his personal commitment to Roman Catholicism. Toleration for Protestant dissenters was a condition of the agreement by William of Orange in 1688 to invade England, which led to the flight of James, and to William's

---

[1] Skea, ch 6.
[2] 14 Cha II, c.4; Rivers, 13.

acceptance of the throne jointly with his wife Mary, James II's daughter. The provisions of the *Toleration Act* of 1689[1] generated the bulk of the material relating to organised Protestant dissent. The Act relieved Trinitarian dissenters, ministers and schoolmasters from assenting to three of the Thirty-nine Articles, and Anabaptists from accepting infant baptism, and suspended the penal laws against them for meetings for religious worship so long as the meeting was public and certified to the Bishop of the Diocese or to the Archdeacon of that Archdeaconry or to the Justices of the Peace at the General or Quarter Sessions, and was registered in the bishop's or archdeacon's court or recorded at the Quarter Sessions; the registrar or clerk of the peace was required to give a certificate of the same if asked, for which the fee was to be no more than 6d. (2½p). The act may have applied to some 300,000 dissenters in England.[2]

The Toleration Act was modified several times over the next 160 years. Having suffered severe penalties for decades, Quakers were now allowed to affirm rather than swear an oath if demanded by the justices of the peace, in the event of holding a religious meeting; in 1695 this was extended to all cases where oaths were required and the Act was made permanent in 1715. The loophole of taking communion once a year in order to hold civil office was closed in 1711 by the *Occasional Conformity Act*, while the *Schism Act* 1714 prevented dissenters from keeping a school; both were repealed in 1719.[3] From 1726 a series of *Indemnity Acts* was passed exonerating dissenters from penalties for serving in a public office without swearing the oaths. In 1779 dissenting teachers and preachers were relieved of the necessity of accepting the Thirty-nine Articles (Roman Catholics shared this relief from 1791).[4] The oaths continued to be required in some cases, as for William Knee in Randwick in 1809 [*see* **1453**]. In 1813 an act removed the requirement to accept the Articles referring to the Trinity and so gave Unitarians relief.[5] A few certificates refer to Unitarian beliefs.

The *Places of Religious Worship Act* 1812[6] made an important concession to dissenters. It was no longer necessary to register meetings of fewer than 20 Protestant dissenters in addition to the occupier of the meeting-house and his family. It has been called 'the Little Toleration Act'. It probably made a substantial difference to the number of registrations; the bishop of Peterborough in 1824 commented that actual numbers of meeting-houses used for religious worship were quite different from the numbers certified because the 1812 Act allowed small congregations to meet without a licence.[7] The meetings had to be 'public', made known and not behind locked doors. A maximum fee for registration of 2s. 6d. (12½p.) was stipulated. There were still fines for those permitting unregistered meetings, preaching or teaching on their premises, but

---

[1] 1 W&M, c. 18.
[2] Rivers, 15.
[3] 10 Ann, c.7; 12 Ann, c.7; 5 GIII, c.9.
[4] 19 GIII, c.44; 31 GIII, c.32.
[5] 53 GIII, c.160.
[6] 52 GIII, c.155.
[7] Parl. Papers, 1824 vol 18, sections 21 and 25.

Quakers were exempt from this act (the provisions of the 1812 act were extended to Roman Catholics in 1832). Diocesan registrars and clerks of the peace were to inform each other annually of registrations carried out but the requirement does not seem to have been heeded until some years later. The Deputy Clerk of the Peace in Bristol complained in 1836 that 'I have ascertained that several [meetings] have been certified to the Bishop's Court … which do not appear to have been returned to the Sessions',[1] and the Gloucestershire Deputy Clerk of the Peace similarly noted that 'many [meetings] have been certified to the Bishop's or Archdeacon's court but I have no account of them.'[2] A few of the forms returned by the bishop to the registrars between 1845 and 1851 survive in Gloucester Quarter Sessions records.[3]

The election to parliament in 1830 of a reforming Whig majority led to the introduction of privileges attached to registration; until then it had been a necessity to avoid penalties. The *Poor Rate Exemption Act* in 1833[4] exempted buildings 'exclusively appropriated to public religious worship'. In 1836 the *Marriage Act*[5] allowed marriages in a registered building provided 20 householders certified that it had been used for a year as a usual place of worship; this left its mark on some certificates. Quakers and Jews were exempt from registration, but it was still necessary to have a registrar or other suitable person present to ensure the marriage was properly registered.

Some bishops had resented the implication that, by agreeing to register meetings, they approved of dissenting beliefs, Roman Catholic beliefs, Mormon or even socialist beliefs. They pressed for a change. By the 1852 *Places of Religious Worship Certifying Act*[6] the Registrar General became the licensing authority. Returns were requested by the Registrar General on 29 June 1852 of all local registrations up to the date of the act (30 June 1852). Clerks of the peace and diocesan registrars had to search their records and enter the information on printed forms, which were stored in the Registrar General's office but have now been transferred to The National Archives.[7] A report and statistical tables were submitted to parliament and printed as a parliamentary paper.[8] By no means all records of registrations had survived, while some records have been lost since these returns were made, so that on occasion they are the sole source of information. Surviving records in Bristol and Gloucestershire, however, correspond closely with the returns.

The 1852 Act was in force for only three years; in practice it had proved

---

[1] Parl. Papers 1836 vol 40.
[2] GA Q/CR 31/1 (a copy of the return).
[3] GA Q/RNp4.
[4] 3 & 4 GIV, c.30, s.1.
[5] 6 & 7 GIV, c.85, s.18.
[6] 15 & 16 V, c.36.
[7] TNA RG 31: General Register Office: Places of Religious Worship Certifying Act 1852: Returns.
[8] Dissenters' places of worship. List of Returns made to Registrar General of the number of certified places of religious worship of Protestant dissenters; with an analysis and summary of the said returns. Parl. Papers 1852–53 (156) vol 78.

onerous. Dissenting congregations possibly thought that, even if already licensed, they had to apply again. In 1855 the *Places of Worship Registration Act*[1] replaced it, and is still the principal act governing registration. From this time congregations could choose whether to register, and to have the privileges which had been introduced in the 1830s. For the first time it was possible to de-register a licensed meeting-house.

A few Roman Catholics took advantage of the new toleration extended to them. Thomas Fox, of the parish of St Augustine, Bristol, wrote on 4 Aug 1840

'I certify that a room or rooms attached to the new church now building, under the bank in the parish of St Augustine in the city of Bristol is to be used (until the consecration of the said new church) for the worship of Almighty God by members of the One Holy Catholic and Apostolic Church and I request that this certificate may be registered.'

On 1 January 1841 Thomas Fox wrote again, requesting that his certificate for worship in the new church be registered.[2] A second Roman Catholic church, Holy Apostles in Clifton, was certified by William Joseph Vaughan, clergyman, on 9 June 1851.

The bishop of Gloucester's Visitation Book, compiled in 1825, includes references to four Roman Catholic chapels, at Beckford, Cheltenham, Hartpury and Hatherop, and a Roman Catholic family at Hampnett. When the clerk of the peace for Gloucestershire replied in 1836 to a request for information on Roman Catholic meetings, he only knew of Hartpury, but thought there were Roman Catholic chapels in Cheltenham and Gloucester.[3] The Gloucester records note registrations of three Roman Catholic meetings, in Chipping Sodbury, Kemerton and Woodchester (1839, 1844 and 1850). Roman Catholic registrations are not included in this volume. Protestant dissenters often referred to 'religious worship in their own way' but one group, meeting in the Club Room adjoining the *Compasses* inn in St Philip & St Jacob's parish, wrote of their wish to meet for public worship 'free from the errors of the Church of Rome.' [**94**].

The dioceses of Bristol, Gloucester, and Gloucester and Bristol
When constituted in 1541, the diocese of Gloucester took parishes from the sees of York, Worcester and Hereford to cover the county as it then was, though former Hereford diocese parishes remained in the Archdeaconry of Hereford.[4] The following year, the diocese of Bristol was created, covering the city of Bristol's 17 ancient parishes (the area of Castle precincts remained extra-parochial). The diocese was enlarged with 15 south Gloucestershire parishes abstracted from the new Gloucester see; they formed the deanery of Bristol, although remaining under the archdeacon of Gloucester. To make the bishopric more viable, Dorset parishes were removed from the diocese of Salisbury and

[1] 18 & 19 V, c.81.
[2] BA EP/A/45/3 8; 26.
[3] GA Q/CR 31.
[4] Section based on *VCH Glos* 2, 48–51; Horn; and Kirby 1967, 1970.

attached to Bristol. This was not geographically a practical arrangement for the bishop but survived until 1836. Bristol diocese records generally indicated in which city parish, as well as in which rural Gloucestershire parish, each dissenters' meeting was to take place. If the information was not in the certificate itself, the registrar entered it as a heading. In the returns to the Registrar General in 1852, most meetings in the city were simply said to be in Bristol.

TABLE 1. GLOUCESTERSHIRE PARISHES IN THE
DIOCESE AND DEANERY OF BRISTOL IN 1542

Almondsbury	Henbury with Aust	Out-parish of St Philip & St Jacob
Clifton	Horfield	Stapleton
Compton Greenfield[1]	Littleton	Stoke Gifford
Elberton	Mangotsfield	Westbury-on-Trym
Filton	Olveston with Alveston	Winterbourne

The *Liber Regis* (1786) confirms the list, except that Elberton, and Henbury with Aust, were then in the deanery of the Town of Bristol.

The administrative structure of the city and county of Bristol and of the diocese remained stable until the 1830s, by which time the population was expanding into all the areas surrounding the city, including across the River Avon. The 1832 Reform Act led to a new boundary for the parliamentary constituency of the city, and three years later the Municipal Corporations Act 1835[2] extended the city and county boundary to match the parliamentary constituency. Bristol was enlarged to include the main part of Clifton (a further part was added in 1844); part of the tithing of Stoke Bishop in the parish of Westbury-on-Trym, including the Redland area; the out-parish of St James, by this time largely in the new parish of St Paul; what remained of the former out-parish of St Philip & St Jacob after the creation of the parish of St George and the district of Holy Trinity; and the northern part of Bedminster, formerly in Somerset. One certificate for St Philip & St Jacob for 24 February 1848 [**115**] spelled out the changes: 'house and premises in Bread Street in the parish of St Philip & St Jacob, late in the county of Gloucester but now in the city and borough of Bristol'; one for Bedminster, dated June 1828 [**2043**] was entered by mistake in the Bristol Register of Records and was crossed out with a statement of the error.

Church reform followed hard on the heels of municipal reform. In 1836 Bristol and Gloucester dioceses were united, and described as the diocese of Gloucester and Bristol. The Dorset parishes were returned to their former diocese of Salisbury. In 1837 a group of Wiltshire parishes in Cricklade and Malmesbury deaneries, which had been in Salisbury diocese, was attached to the see of Gloucester and Bristol, as also was the parish of Bedminster in Somerset which

---

[1] Rudder noted 'Compton Greenville'.
[2] 5 & 6 Wm. IV., c.76.

had been in the diocese of Bath and Wells.[1] The dissenters' certificates reflect the changing composition of the dioceses. Six for Dorset parishes between 1774 and 1799 are in the Bristol diocesan Register of Records, although most Dorset meetings were more conveniently registered by the local archdeacon and he made the 1852 return to the Registrar General. Similarly after 1836 two Wiltshire certificates were entered in the Bristol Register of Records by the two deputy registrars and 40 Wiltshire registrations were entered in the Gloucester diocesan act books. Meetings in south Gloucestershire continued to be recorded in the former Bristol act books, as noted specifically by dissenters from Fishponds in 1850 who made 'application to the Registrar of the Register Office, Broad Street, Bristol, to grant a licence for preaching' [**1564**].

The boundaries of Gloucestershire
A decade after these administrative adjustments, the process of rationalisation was extended to the counties. From 1844 onwards numerous changes have been made to Gloucestershire's boundaries. Registrations of dissenters' meeting-houses in parishes which have been transferred from other counties are not included in this volume, but those for Gloucestershire parishes transferred to other counties are included. The criterion has been to make available all Protestant dissenters' meetings recorded in the Diocesan and Quarter Sessions archives of Bristol and Gloucestershire, including meetings in parishes now outside the two counties.

TABLE 2. PARISHES TRANSFERRED FROM GLOUCESTERSHIRE TO OTHER COUNTIES

(i) in the certificate period

from Gloucestershire	*to*
Shenington	Oxon 1844
Sutton-under-Brailes	Warws 1844
Little Compton	Warws 1844
Widford	Oxon 1844
Minety	Wilts 1844
Lea	Herefs 1844

(ii) since the certificate period

from Gloucestershire	*to*	*from Gloucestershire*	*to*
Admington	Warws 1935	Hinton-on-the-Green	Worcs 1931
Ashton-under-Hill	Worcs 1931	Kemerton	Worcs 1931
Aston Somerville	Worcs 1931	Marston Sicca [Long Marston]	Warws 1931
Beckford	Worcs 1931		
Childswickham	Worcs 1931	Pebworth	Worcs 1931
Clifford Chambers	Warws 1931	Preston-on-Stour	Warws 1931
Clopton	Warws 1935	Quinton	Warws 1935
Cow Honeybourne	Worcs 1931	Welford-on-Avon	Warws 1931
Dorsington	Warws 1931	Weston-on-Avon	Warws 1931

---

[1] 6 & 7 Will. IV c. 77; Orders in Council 5 Oct. 1836, 19 July 1837.

TABLE 3. PARISHES TRANSFERRED TO GLOUCESTERSHIRE FROM OTHER COUNTIES

(i) before the end of the local registration period

to Gloucestershire	from
Alstone & Little Washbourne	Worcs 1844
Icomb (Church Icomb)	Worcs 1844
Kingswood (near Wotton-under-Edge)	Wilts 1844
Poulton	Wilts 1844

(ii) after local registration ceased

to Gloucestershire	from	to Gloucestershire	from
Ashley	Wilts 1930	Long Newton	Wilts 1930
Blockley	Worcs 1931	Poole Keynes	Wilts 1897
Chaceley	Worcs 1931	Redmarley d'Abitot	Worcs 1931
Cutsdean	Worcs 1931	Somerford Keynes	Wilts 1897
Daylesford	Worcs 1931	Staunton	Worcs 1931
Evenlode	Worcs 1931	Teddington	Worcs 1931
Kemble	Wilts 1897		

The registration process

From 1689 until 1852 there were three stages in securing permission for a Protestant dissenters' meeting. Firstly one or more of those involved signed a paper certifying their intention of meeting for religious worship, specifying the place, whether private house or purpose-built meeting-house, but later in the 18th century on occasions a chapel; this certificate or petition was presented either to the Justices of the Peace at their Quarterly session, or to the diocesan authorities, the bishop or the archdeacon. Provided these officials offered no objections, the certificate was registered and a licence issued, often in the form of an endorsement on the original certificate.

Five men, Independents, in 1779 stated the date of their first meeting: they *'intended to assemble (with others who may choose to do the same) on Monday the fifth day of this instant April for the publick worshipping of Almighty God in the dwelling house of Thomas Jones (being one of us the subscribers) at Woodford in the tithing of Alkington in the parish of Berkeley'* [236]. Certifiers quite often asked that the registration should be recorded (in a few cases this possibly did not happen), and many asked for a certificate of registration, as the Toleration Act had suggested they could, which the clerks to the Quarter Sessions referred to as a licence.

The details in the certificate were entered in the authority's records in a standardised format in the Quarter Sessions Act books and verbatim in the diocesan records. Few original certificates signed by the minister and/or his congregation have survived, unlike the rich archive of 19th-century certificates in Wiltshire.[1]

---

[1] Where about 1000 examples survive in Wiltshire and Swindon Archives: Chandler, xxiv.

The licence or certificate was valued:

> 'To the Worshipful the bench of Justices, their humble petitioners sheweth:
> That the Dwelling house of Francis Hoskinson in the parish of Horsley was
> licensed above 30 years ago for a Baptist Congregation there to assemble and
> there to worship God according to the laws of the land but the Licence being
> Lost and we being willing to act according to law do petition your worships to
> grant us a new Licence there to meet and you will highly oblige your Humble
> petitioners and servants. 14 July 1746. Francis Hoskines, John Marttin,
> Nathaniel Mildwaters, William Hoskins.' [**958**]

That same congregation had to apply again 10 years later:

> 'We whose names are hereunder subscribed do in the name of many others of
> His Majesty's loyal subjects under the denomination of Baptists meeting in the
> parish of Horseley under your cognizance humbly petition a licence for the
> houses and place where we meet to worship God in according to the dictates of
> our conscience, having by some accident lost a former licence to us granted for
> that purpose, which favour will be gratefully received by us that continue to
> pray for the protection and happiness of His Majesty's person and government.'
> 5 June 1756. Samuel Bowen, George Haines, Thomas Powell, James Loakier,
> Daniel Cook. [**959**]

Without a procedure for de-licensing a house, it remained a legal meeting place
although no longer used as such; a new tenant or owner might not share the views
of his predecessor, and the meeting moved elsewhere. The series of registrations
in some parishes suggests that this happened, as was the case with Goatacre in
Wiltshire:

> 'Holding services here from the earliest period, our church was only able to
> build a home for itself in 1867 ... After years of wandering, as in other places,
> from cottage to cottage.'[1]

In a single instance, the Gloucester Diocesan registrar noted that permission had
been given to cancel a licence for a meeting near Colford in Newland parish in
1789 [**605**].

III. SOURCES

Early records from the reign of Charles II

G Lyon Turner in his volume detailing early Protestant nonconformity extracted
the Episcopal Returns for 1665, 1669 and 1676 from the Tenison manuscript, and
the records relating to Charles II's Declaration of Indulgence in 1672.[2] The two
earlier returns do not include the diocese of Gloucester, and the third, known as
the Compton Census, which was an attempt by the Church of England to estimate
how far the re-establishment of the church had succeeded by 1676, is in print; it
gives some information on the number of dissenters at a time when dissenters'
religious meetings were illegal.[3] The Bishop of Bristol made a return (dated 1666)

---

[1] Tonks, 153.
[2] Vol 639 in Lambeth Palace Library; LT.
[3] Whiteman.

of nonconformist ministers 'who are now inhabiting within the city of Bristol, contrary to the late Act of Parliament' and appended a list of 11 names which is set out here at the beginning of the Bristol entries.[1]

Notes of applications for licences in 1672 survive in quite substantial numbers in the National Archives, including for Bristol and Gloucestershire, together with Entry Books which include notes of licences issued.[2] Over the whole country 3,500 licences for meetings were issued; they remained valid until formally cancelled in 1675.[3] Eleven related to Bristol and 148 to Gloucestershire, either for a meeting-house or for a preacher, teacher or minister; the houses licensed were often occupied by the preacher.[4] More than one note may relate to the same minister or house; there are no fewer than 13 for the three Congregational ministers in Tewkesbury. Forty-three places in Gloucestershire (in both Bristol and Gloucester dioceses) are named and 84 meetings; two (Painswick and Thornbury) were mistakenly said to be in Herefordshire, and two cannot be placed. A few licences for a 'General teacher' were not related to any specific house.

One Owen Davies applied for and received licences for Congregational teachers and meetings in 20 places in Gloucestershire. One application containing 14 ministers' names and four houses, is headed 'These Ministers underwritten being of the Congregational persuasion living in the County of Gloucester do humbly crave Licence for the excercise of their Ministry in the houses herein mentioned according to his Majesty's gracious Declaration'. [5] Owen Davies received these Licences. Just possibly he may have been the dissenting preacher in Mitcheldean who took the oaths of allegiance and supremacy in 1715 in order to continue to preach [**1205**].[6] The licences are summarised under the relevant parishes.

Florid petitions from Bristol and Cirencester have survived. The Bristol petition is set out at the beginning of the entries for Bristol county and city [**2**], and that for Cirencester is set out below in its original form with some editorial amendments.

> 'Endorsed : 'Indulgence, Cirencester. Weavers hall there'.
> 'To the Kinges most excellent Majesty Charles the 2d by the grace of God Kinge of Great Brittaine France & Ireland, Defender of the fayth etc:
> The humble Addresse of yr Majestys thankefull subjects
> In and about the Brough or Borrow of Cirencester in the County of Gloucester
> Most humbly sheweth
> That whereas It has pleased the lord in whose hand the hearts of Kinges are

---

[1] LT, I 182.
[2] SP/29/320 and 321. LT I 195–299 are from TNA SP 29/320 and 300–409 from TNA SP 29/321 (State Papers); these originals were not paginated but the 'pieces' were numbered; SP 44/38A. LT I 419–585 are from TNA SP 44/38A (Entry Books) and these records were paginated
[3] Spurrier, vii–viii. Spurrier printed the wording of the printed form for applications.
[4] The entries are not always easy to interpret. Many entries in a list were prefaced by 'the like', implying that the last fuller entry, for instance a licence for a preacher in his own house, applies to all the following entries. The spelling of personal names and place-names can also be difficult.
[5] LT I 71, 401.
[6] GA Q/SO/4.

gratiously to incline your sacred Majesty's heart, to emitt your most gratious Declaration for the indulgeinge your non-conformeinge subjects not only by inhibiteinge all ways of coercion by your Regall power suspendinge all penall lawes in matters Ecclesiasticall out against your humble subjects but also, by concedinge us out of your sovraigne clemency to have publiq places allowed for the worship of the great God, as also lycence for our teachers that may be helpfull to us in our devotion and finally our eternall salvation, and also to take us under the winges of your royall protection in our peaceable behaviour toward your sacred majesty's person and governent and all others, by which unparrelled act of grace, you have made our hearts to leape and our soules to singe for joy of heart. And have layd such a sense of your royall condescention and indulgence upon us if we canot but now, always and in all places acknowledge and celebrate the most worthy deeds done to us your poore subjects, and as men raysed out of the grave from every corner of the land, stand up and call your Majesty blessed - and doe also resolve in the strength of divine grace to acquitt our selves, with that moderation, fidelity & peaceablenesse as also to keepe soe close to the rules layd downe in your Majesty's most gratious declaration that your Majesty shall never have cause to repent of this famous act of grace toward us, farre exceedinge the noblest acts of all your predecessors, an act worthy only of the grandour of your Majesty's Royall Spirit.

And in obedience to your Majesty's most gratious Declaration and that we may reape the fruit thereof, we your Majesty's most humble subjects doe wth all submission implore and begge your Majesty's allowance of the weavers-hall for our meetinge place in Cirencester, as also your Royall approbacion of Mr James Greenwood who is of the Presbiterian perswasion for our teacher, as also that he may have your Majesty's gratious permission & lycence According to your Majesty's sayd gratious declaration to preach in any other place allowed by your Royall Authority as opportunity may be offered. And your humble petioners shall pray for your Majestys prosperity, length of days, and life for evermore'.

John Paine	*William Eisworth*
Walter Harbert	*John Blissett*
Anthony Archer	*Giles Coates*
Thomas Dickes	*Isaac Lawrence*

There are no records of petitions to James II following his Declaration of Indulgence, but when news of it reached Gloucestershire, some dissenters in Nailsworth at once prepared to acquire a site and build a meeting-house - the Forest Green Congregational meeting-house.[1]

Quarter Sessions records
Bristol Quarter Sessions records for the registration period have been lost, but a

---

[1] Urdank 86. See below **193**.

large number of Gloucestershire Order Books have been preserved, and contain information on dissenters' meetings between 1689 and 1800.[1] At the back of the third Order Book there are brief details of 140 licenses, starting with the Trinity sessions of 1689, immediately following the Toleration Act (which became law on 24 May) and continuing to 1711; the list is not entirely chronological. It appears to have been compiled at a date approximately contemporary with the latest sessions records in this volume, as the handwriting is similar. The information was arranged in columns: place, description of premises, often naming an owner or occupier of a house, denomination, and session at which registered. By 1690, the Quakers had already established 20 meeting-houses (with no personal owner specified), and these were all listed together; more were added later in this period. Four are for places in south Gloucestershire in Bristol diocese. [*see* Appendix 1]

Further Quarter Sessions volumes followed a formula for registration which gives only occasional hints of the idiosyncrasies of individual applications or petitions. It started with 'It is ordered by this court' and ended with 'according to the petition for that purpose filed and allowed' or 'pursuant to a petition and request'. The first full record of licensing a meeting-house was for Minchinhampton at the Trinity sessions 1723 [**1158**]:

> '*It is ordered by this Court that the dwelling house of Samuel King situate in Minchinhampton in this county in a street there called the Westend be lycensed and allowed for the protestant dissenters called Independents to assemble and meet in for the worship of God according to the petition for that purpose filed and allowed and that Richard Rawlins be lycensed and admitted to be the teacher or preacher there.*'[2]

For the next 50 years, the formula was the same.

The fourth volume also contains a list of those, including dissenting ministers and teachers, who took oaths of allegiance and supremacy and abjuration between November 1715 and April 1716, and a few Quakers who affirmed. The oaths were required following George I's accession on 1 August 1714, the first Jacobite rebellion, and the act passed in 1715 'for the further security of his Majesty's person and government, and the succession of the crown in the heirs of the late princess Sophia, being protestants; and for extinguishing the hopes of the pretended Prince of Wales, and his open and secret abettors'.[3] There is a gap in the Gloucestershire record of dissenters' meetings between 1711 and 1723, so that the 35 dissenters taking the oaths are useful evidence of continuing dissent. The Evans list of dissenting congregations at approximately the same date named 39 places with a resident minister, of whom 15 were noted as taking the oaths, but neither names nor places in the two sources completely correspond.[4] Eleven

---

[1] See Table 4.
[2] GA Q/SO/4 455.
[3] 1 Geo I c.13.
[4] Dr Williams's Library 706.E.22. Dr Evans collected information on the numbers of dissenters and those who were qualified to vote in parliamentary elections to strengthen the case for the repeal of the Schism Act.

dissenting ministers made their subscription at Bristol between 1714 and 1716.[1]

Amongst Gloucestershire Quarter Sessions papers are 21 original certificates or petitions. They contrast with the formula in the Act Books. The earliest, signed by the applicants, is for Stow-on-the-Wold in 1736 [**1606**].[2]

'County of Gloucester

These are to certify his Majesty's Justices of the peace for the said county at their General Sessions held at the Boothall in the city of Gloucester for the county aforesaid That we whose names are subscribed together with other his Majesty's well-affected subjects being protestant dissenters do meet for the performance of religious worship at the house of Mr Thomas Sandford in Stow which house we desire may be registered (for the purpose aforesaid) as required in an act of parliament made in the first year of the reign of the late King William & Queen Mary by the last clause of the said act. In witness whereof we have hereunto set our hands the 25th day of July in the year of our Lord 1736.' Thomas Rooke, William Franks, Anthony Fletcher, William Hall, Robert Perry, Joseph Marsh.

The entry in the Order Book, Trinity session 1736, is briefer:

'It is ordered by this court that the dwelling house of Mr Thomas Sandford situate in the town of Stow on the Wold in this county be licenced and allowed for His Majesty's protestant dissenting subjects called Baptists residing in and near the said town to assemble and meet together in for the worship of Almighty God in their way pursuant to their petition for that purpose filed & allowed.'

The information that the congregation was Baptist must have been obtained orally. The names of the certifiers were not recorded in the Order Books until the late 18th century. Four surviving certificates do not appear to have been entered in the Act Books.

When in 1836 the House of Commons asked for a 'Return of the number of Licensed dissenting meeting-houses and Catholic chapels in England and Wales', the Deputy Clerk of the Peace in Bristol replied that 'Since the year 1800, only three Dissenting meeting-houses have been registered at the general quarter sessions of the peace for this city and county'.[3] The deputy clerk of the peace of Gloucestershire replied

'The Register in my office of the dissenting places of Worship in this county commences in 1689 and ends in 1800. In between those years the number of places of worship registered was 186 but none since.'[4]

The tally of Gloucestershire licences found is 194. The last meeting registered at the Quarter Sessions was in Kemerton in 1800. As the Deputy Clerk observed in 1852, meetings could be registered with the Bishop's Registrar 'at any time but

---

[1] Morgan [i], 69. Only the surname is recorded for nine of the names, but one repeated surname with a Christian name may mean the total was 12.

[2] GA Q/SR/1736/C 18; Q/SO/6 f80v.

[3] A return of the number of registered dissenting meeting-houses and Roman Catholic chapels in England and Wales (Parl. Papers 1836)

[4] GA Q/CR 31/1.

with the Clerk of the Peace only four times a year viz at each Quarter Sessions'.[1]

Seven returns by the registrar of Gloucester diocese to the Quarter Sessions for the period 1845–51 have fortunately been preserved amongst the Quarter Sessions records, as neither original certificates nor diocesan registrations have survived after the beginning of 1847. Following the entry in the Diocesan Act Book for May 1846 there is a note that the return had been made to Gloucester Quarter Sessions 6 January 1847. A minimum of information was entered in columns on printed forms, but these forms help to complete the record, giving description of the place of meeting, where situate, date of registration and by whom certified.

Tewkesbury had its own Quarter Sessions courts from 1605, and order or sessions books survive from 1774. Eight meeting-house certificates were registered, one in 1777 and seven between 1806 and 1839. The format of these records was not the same as in the county, and varied from entry to entry; the last three were recorded without the name of a certifier but the 1852 return to the Registrar General did include a certifier's name. [1731-1733] The clerk may have had a different source to work from, or, as these three were registered in 1839, he may actually have known who was responsible.

TABLE 4. SUMMARY OF GLOUCESTERSHIRE AND TEWKESBURY QUARTER SESSIONS REGISTRATIONS AND CERTIFICATES IN GLOUCESTERSHIRE ARCHIVES

Reference	no of Gloucestershire registrations	Period
Q/SO/3 Order book	140	1689–1711
Q/SO/4 do	8	1723–24
Q/SO/5 do	16	1724–33
Q/SO/6 do	9	1734–40
Q/SO/7 do	7	1741–46
Q/SO/8 do	7	1753–60
Q/SO/9 do	1	1771
Q/SO/10 do	3	1782–88
Q/SO/11 do	2	1790–96
Q/SO/12 do	1	1800
Q/SR sessions papers	21	1736–1800
Q/RNp/4 Diocesan returns	136	1845–51
QT/SO/1 Order book	1	1777
QT/SO/2 do	4	1806–24
QT/SO/3 do	3	1839

---

[1] TNA RG 31/6 f.75.

Diocesan records: Bristol diocese

Diocesan records are the only official source of registrations for Bristol, and in the 19th century for Gloucestershire. Bristol diocesan registrations are in four 'Register of Records' volumes in which entries are interspersed with other ecclesiastical business, and one volume called 'List of certificates'.[1] The first registration is dated January 1755 and this is also the first in the 1852 return to the Registrar General. Eight folios of volume 1 were numbered, but from folio 8 the volume is paginated; the first registration was on folio 7 verso, but in the index at the back is given as page 8. Thereafter the volumes are all paginated. Volumes 2 and 3 include some interesting maps and details of new ecclesiastical districts. All were well-written, and until the amalgamation of the dioceses of Bristol and Gloucester appear to be transcripts of original certificates; headings state 'Certificate' above the entry and give brief details of location and denomination, information which is not always in the certificate itself. The date when the certificate was registered is noted against each. The last few certificates in volume 3, from the beginning of 1847, and most in volume 4 are original certificates pasted onto the pages, with a few loose sheets bound in. There were 74 registrations for South Gloucestershire parishes before 1837, and 28 between 1839 and 1851. A separate 'List of certificates of registration of buildings to be used as dissenters' meeting-houses' covers the years 1762 to 1808. It matches the registrations in the first two Registers.

TABLE 5. SUMMARY OF BRISTOL DIOCESAN REGISTRATIONS IN BRISTOL ARCHIVES

	No of registrations[2]	Period
EP/A/45/1 Register of records	47	1755–1808
EP/A/45/2 do	94	1808–40
EP/A/45/3 do	35	1840–49
EP/A/45/4 do	36	1849–52
Total	212	
EP/A/43/4 List of certificates	46	1762–1808

Diocesan records: Gloucester diocese

The General Act Books of the bishop of Gloucester contain registrations of dissenters' meeting-houses from 1724 until 1847, with just one before 1724, in 1701/2 for the out-parish of St Philip & St Jacob, in the Archdeaconry of Gloucester [**80**]; most meetings in this parish were registered with the bishop of Bristol.

Entries in the Act Books are interspersed with records of other ecclesiastical business, with the exception of the last volume which contains nothing but dissenters' meeting-house registrations; 39 entries for 1824 were copied from GDR/344 into GDR/350.[3] In the first two volumes, meetings were recorded in

---

[1] See Table 5.
[2] Registrations include 6 for Dorset, 6 for Somerset (as it was before 1836), and 2 for Wiltshire.
[3] See Table 6.

English while clerical institutions were in Latin. Thereafter English was used throughout. Four volumes are paginated in blue crayon, probably the work of F S Hockaday who rescued and worked on the diocesan records for 16 years.[1] The numbering, in blue crayon, is not always very distinct. In one volume the meetings were all written at one end of the volume turned upside down, and the routine bishop's acts were entered at the other end;[2] it was paginated throughout from the end containing ecclesiastical business, so that the page references to registrations are in the reverse order to the dates on which they were made. One volume is not paginated, but the folios are numbered in ink.[3]

The act books were usually laid out with a wide margin on the left-hand side in which the subject of the entry is briefly noted. Some early certificates had the rubric in Latin, 'Certificator loci pro cultu divino' (certifier of the place for divine worship) or a variation; the next volume initially employed the description 'a faculty for divine worship', but thereafter 'certificate', with in the later 18th century an occasional return to 'faculty'. Some indicated the denomination. A few certificates have no rubric. Rubrics appear to have been added later than the entry itself; in a significant number of cases the place noted in the rubric is where the certifier lived, information usually included at the beginning of the certificate, instead of the place where the meeting was to be held. Rubrics mainly identified a parish or chapelry, but occasionally a township.

The registry clerks appear to have copied the form of words used in the petition or certificate. Certificates usually had the date when they were signed, but the registration date was not generally noted before 1771. Certificates were probably returned to the applicant(s) endorsed as licensed, with the date. They became more verbose as time went on; early certificates were usually brief and to the point (*see* **590**, **1037**), but later certifiers were frequently precise about requesting the registering and recording of their meetings, and specifying the maximum payment which could be asked for a diocesan registry copy of the entry.

Forty-seven original certificates survive amongst the diocesan records.[4] Most appear to be copies made by the Diocesan Registry clerk rather than the signed originals, sometimes made on scraps of paper or parchment; one certificate, for 1788, was written on one side of a piece of parchment, and another on the reverse side where there is also the beginning of a militia list.[5] [*see* p xxi] The copies were sometimes endorsed 'Ent' [entered] and sometimes the date of entry was added which is presumed to be the date of registration. Most are crossed through, suggesting that the contents had been recorded in the act book, but 13 were not copied, all but one for the later months of 1802; the returns to the Registrar General do not contain these registrations either. A small number of certificates are amongst the records of individual nonconformist churches.

---

[1] For the work of Frank Step Hockaday, see Austin, 379–83.
[2] GDR/334B.
[3] GDR/344.
[4] GDR/ N2/1 and N2/2.
[5] GDR N2/1 24.

TABLE 6. SUMMARY OF GLOUCESTER DIOCESAN REGISTRATIONS
AND CERTIFICATES HELD IN GLOUCESTERSHIRE ARCHIVES

	No of registrations	Period
GDR/248 Act book	1	1701
GDR/279a do	21	1724–31
GDR/284 do	66	1732–57
GDR/292A do	73	1755–89
GDR/319A do	111	1784–1803
GDR/334B do	411	1803–21
GDR/344 do	149	1821–24
GDR/350 do	598	1824–47
GDR/N2/1 diocesan papers	45	1780–1838
GDR/N2/2 do	2	1788–1802

Parliamentary returns: attempts to gauge the extent of nonconformity
At the behest of Viscount Sidmouth, in 1809 the House of Lords requested information on licensed preachers and places of worship over the years 1760 to 1808; the return was laid on the table in the House of Lords in 1810 and led to Sidmouth requesting a more comprehensive return from diocesan and Quarter Sessions authorities of Church of England churches and chapels and dissenting places of worship over this same period, in parishes with a population of 1,000 and upwards. The surviving Bristol volume of registrations between these dates was doubtless drawn up to answer this request.[1] An Abstract of the returns was arranged by diocese.[2] From the returns it appeared there were more dissenting chapels and meeting-houses than Church of England churches and chapels. Bristol diocese had 58 churches and 71 dissenting places of worship in 41 parishes with populations of 1,000 or more; Gloucester diocese had 46 churches and 76 dissenting places of worship in 36 parishes. The following year Sidmouth proposed to introduce a bill limiting ignorant or profligate people, 'coblers, tailors, pig-drovers and chimney-sweepers' from teaching, which might have curbed the growth of dissent; his view was countered by Lord Holland who thought persons in inferior situations of life 'as entitled to preach those religious opinions which they conscientiously believed, as those who received the rich endowments of the church'.[3] The bill was defeated.

  In 1821 a further return was called for covering the years 1809–20, and in April 1824 a return for the years 1800 and 1824. Some of the 1821 returns have survived locally, as in Leicestershire; the 1824 returns were published the same

---

[1] BA/EP/A/43/4. *Hansard House of Lords Debates* 27 Feb 1810 vol. 15 c653; http://hansard.millbanksystems.com/lords/1810/feb/27/toleration-of-dissenters.
[2] Abstract of the total number of parishes in each diocese of England and Wales containing a population of 1,000 persons and upward, the number of churches and chapels therein, number of persons they will contain, and the number of dissenting places of worship therein House of Commons Accounts and Papers 1812 (256) vol. 10.
[3] House of Lords debates 9 May 1811 vol 19 cc1128–33.

year.[1] It is clear that the basis of each return could vary significantly. The number of Church of England churches and chapels in Gloucester diocese had increased from 321 in 1800 to 329 in 1824. Five dwelling houses were licensed in 1800 and one chapel, but only three registrations for 1800 have been found, and 12 dwelling houses in 1824 which matches the registrations up to early April. In Bristol diocese there were 16 churches in the city in 1800, together with two chapels, and 16 churches and four chapels of ease in the Gloucestershire parishes in the diocese; there was also a Church of England chapel at the Hotwells for which no deed of consecration could be found. One chapel of ease had been added in the city parish of St Augustine and one in Stapleton by 1824. However, Bristol clerks interpreted the request idiosyncratically and recorded the number of licences issued from February 1755 to September 1799, total 21, and for the years 1800 to 1824, total 69, a neat summary of the early 19th century increase in dissent. These figures exactly match those found in the records. A comment was appended to this return:

'There are several dissenting Chapels in Bristol which do not appear to have been ever licensed unless they were at the Quarter Sessions of which the Registrars of the diocese have no account'.

Returns were again required in 1829 but have not survived, except as local copies in some archives.[2] An 1836 return was published and provides numbers returned by the clerks of dioceses, quarter sessions and corporate cities and towns. The Bristol diocesan registrar commented that 119 meeting-houses and places of worship had been registered from the year 1755 inclusive to the present day 'including those of Dissenting and Roman Catholic … in this part of the diocese' (Bristol city and south Gloucestershire but not the Dorset parishes), and drew attention to the nature of most of the registrations:

'the larger number consists of rooms in houses and private dwellings which have been used as Dissenting places of worship temporarily and on different occasions. It has been thought proper to include those in the return though they do not strictly come under the denomination of meeting-houses.'

Gloucester city's town clerk could do no better than to record the denominations of meeting-houses: Catholic, Baptist, Unitarian, Wesleyan, Independent, Lady Huntingdon, Quakers, with Jews 'not licensed'. Tewkesbury's clerk of the peace stated that there were 'five licensed Dissenting meeting-houses but no Roman Catholic chapel in this borough'. The two deputy registrars of Gloucester diocese stated that the 'Number of Dissenting meeting-houses registered from the passing of the act 52 Geo 3 (i.e.1812) up to the present time was 770; the like of Roman Catholic chapels none.' This count exceeds by nineteen the number found in

---

[1] Leicestershire, Leicester and Rutland Record Office QS95/1/3/1; A return of the number of churches and chapels of the Church of England in each diocese in England and Wales in 1800 and 1824, also the number of licences issued in each diocese of places of worship dissenting from the Church of England in 1800 and 1824; Parl. Papers, 1824 vol 18, sections 21 and 25, p.209, 280, 286, 301, 304, 306.

[2] For example in Wiltshire and Swindon Archives (Chandler, xxix), and in Leicester and Rutland Record Office, QS95/2.

existing sources.

Following the creation of the General Register Office, a commission was appointed in 1838 to enquire into dissenters' registers.[1] As a result, many were deposited with the Registrar General. The list in the Commissioners' report is an interesting account of organised chapels and denominations, and gives dates of foundation. Most registers recorded baptisms, some recorded burials, and only a few recorded marriages. The chapel in Bristol, formerly the Mayor's chapel, St Mark the Gaunt, was categorised as a foreign protestant church, founded in 1687 and dissolved in 1814; it was the only Bristol register noted. Registers of a French chapel at Stonehouse started in 1692 and ended in 1791, and this, too, had been dissolved. Fifty-eight dissenting chapels with registers were noted in Gloucestershire, the majority for the three denominations: Presbyterian, Independent and Baptist; 13 were Wesleyan Methodists, two Calvinistic Methodists, three the Countess of Huntingdon's Connexion.

Parliamentary returns: the Places of Religious Worship Certifying Act 1852

The details of registrations required by this 1852 Act were entered on printed forms with headings for the name or description of place of worship, the parish or place and the county, the denomination, the name, residence and rank or profession of the certifier and the date of Registry or Record.[2] In 22 cases these summary records give information not available in the certificates, or for the few registrations in 1852.

The Bristol diocesan returns as from 'the Diocese of Gloucester & Bristol at Bristol', correspond exactly with the Registers of Records. The Gloucestershire returns do not completely match either Consistory Court or Quarter Sessions records. Returns may have been compiled from sources no longer available, possibly the clerk's copies of the original certificates or volumes now lost; the list at the back of the first relevant Quarter Sessions book is not in the same order as the return to the Registrar General. In some returns the place of residence of the certifier is given instead of the meeting place, following the rubric in the original act book, and the date is sometimes when the certificate was signed rather than when it was registered. The name of the first signatory of a certificate only was entered, ignoring other named certifiers who were often the trustees of the chapel concerned. Nonetheless the reliability of the 1852 Returns is remarkable; the clerks who made the returns searched conscientiously, and neatly summarised the information.

---

[1] Report of the Commissioners appointed to inquire into the safe custody and authenticity of registers or records of births or baptisms, deaths or burials, and marriages in England and Wales other than the parochial registers (Sessional Papers of the House of Lords 1837–38) 1838 (46).
[2] See Table 7.

TABLE 7. RETURNS TO THE REGISTRAR GENERAL IN THE NATIONAL ARCHIVES

TNA reference	Folios	Source of registrations
RG 31/2	109 to 126	Bishop of Gloucester
RG 31/2	128 to 130	Bishop of Gloucester and Bristol
RG 31/6	72 to 75	Gloucester Quarter Sessions
RG 31/6	107	Tewkesbury Quarter Sessions

An analysis of these returns was published in 1853.[1] It detailed denominations, but three-quarters of the registrations gave no denomination at all or from 1824 said simply 'Protestants'. 'Temporary' registrations were distinguished from those considered more permanent because described as 'Building, Cemetery, Chapel, Church, Edifice, Meeting, Meeting-house' or had names such as 'Bethel, Ebenezer, Salem etc'. Early usage was to call a building used for a meeting a 'house' whether a private house, or, as in the case of the Quakers, a building used solely for a religious meeting. In Gloucestershire, of 1,882 entries only 339 were categorised as 'permanent', bearing out the comment by the Bristol Registrar on the frequency of houses or rooms.

The majority of the 'permanent' buildings were registered in the 19th century, which was a period of enthusiastic chapel building in architecturally distinct styles. The earliest reference to a chapel in Gloucestershire is in 1776 in Frampton upon Severn, described as 'Brethertons Chappel' for the Independents [808]. A Congregational chapel is said to have been built in 1760 but registrations in Frampton in 1756 and 1757 are for houses [806, 807].[2] Comparison between the Gloucestershire records and the survey of existing Nonconformist chapels by the Royal Commission on the Historical Monuments of England (RCHM) shows that buildings originally described as 'meeting-houses' later become 'chapels'. A building in Stow-on-the-Wold, for example, is described as the 'present chapel built in 1852 on the site of the former'; it was the 'new erected house' when registered at the Easter 1700 Quarter Sessions [1604].[3]

The table opposite summarises chronologically locally-recorded registrations and the few certificates returned to the Registrar General for which no local source has been found. Not included are the dissenting preachers, teachers or ministers who took the oaths of allegiance, supremacy and abjuration. The table highlights the surge in registrations in the 19th century, starting after the end of the Napoleonic Wars, evident in Bristol as in Gloucestershire and nationally.

[1] *Dissenters' places of worship. List of Returns made to Registrar General of the number of certified places of religious worship of Protestant dissenters* Parl. Papers 1852–53 (78). Dorset and Wiltshire parishes have been excluded from the analysis presented here.
[2] *Nonconformist chapels and meeting-houses* (RCHM, 1986) 82.
[3] *Nonconformist chapels and meeting-houses* (RCHM) 94.

TABLE 8. CHRONOLOGICAL SUMMARY OF REGISTRATIONS AND CERTIFICATES FOR DISSENTERS' MEETINGS IN BRISTOL AND GLOUCESTERSHIRE[1]

| | Bristol diocese | | | Gloucester diocese | | | | |
	Bristol city	South Glos (parishes in Bristol diocese)	RG record only	Gloucester city	Glo'shire	RG record only	Totals	RG31/2 /6 & /8
1672	11	1		6	67		85	
1689–1700		4			71	1	76	72
1701–20		8			60		68	62
1721–40		3		5	70	1	79	67
1741–60	1	3		2	69	1	76	70
1761–80	1	3		1	55		60	59
1781–1800	3	9		3	103		118	109
1801–20	21	43		6	388		458	442
1821–40	24	40		31	565		660	662
1841–52	18	42	1	13	233	18	325	334
TOTALS	79	156	1	67	1681	21	2005	1877

Other sources of information on dissenters 1715–1825: the Evans list

Dr John Evans was a Presbyterian minister of the Hand Alley congregation in London and probably also the secretary to the Committee of the Three Denominations, Presbyterian, Congregational and Baptist.[2] In 1715 he collected statistics from 17 named correspondents all over the country in order to estimate the voting strength of the dissenting 'interest', with the aim of influencing parliament to modify the disabilities of dissenters. Correspondents usually specified the number of 'hearers', the denomination, and the number qualified to vote in parliamentary elections; there is information from Bristol and Gloucestershire. Evans also made notes of ministers' names, and added further information in the next few years as ministers moved or died.[3] Some entries are ambiguous; a few are crossed out; a few cover two places. The concept of

---

[1] The Registrar-General's returns and analysis reflect the changes in county boundaries in 1844. The small difference from the analysis of sources above was the result of two parish registrations attributed to Gloucestershire but originally registered in another county.
[2] Watts 1978, 267.
[3] Dr Williams's Library 706.E.22.

'hearers' is flexible; it possibly included occasional conformers, and the numbers are nearly all rounded to the nearest 50, but an intensive study of surviving dissenters' baptismal and burial registers has strongly supported the inherent reliability of the numbers.[1] The Evans list is particularly useful for its picture of nonconformity in Bristol at a period when registrations of meeting-houses are not available.

The Evans list has led to the conclusion that dissent was more urbanised than in the population at large.[2] Where both population and congregations were small, the loss of even one family could make the survival of a meeting problematic, whereas towns could draw on a larger, geographically concentrated population to sustain the charges of a meeting-house; also, town-dwellers were not dependent on Anglican gentry for employment as might be the case in agricultural parishes. On the other hand, the towns described in the Evans returns appear to have been centres from where nonconforming ministers travelled to preach in the surrounding area.

Other sources of information on dissenters: Diocesan surveys
In 1735, the newly-instituted bishops of Bristol (Thomas Secker) and of Gloucester (Martin Benson) each made surveys of their dioceses, including numbers of dissenters in each parish; both have been published.[3] Benson required more precise information about numbers than Secker, but both asked for information on denominations and probably on meeting-houses.

The survey of his diocese carried out in 1825 by the newly-instituted bishop of Gloucester, Dr Christopher Bethel, also provides information on dissenters.[4] The last question (no. 17) in Bishop Bethel's survey asked what dissenters' meetings there were in the parish and of what denomination. Parliament asked for returns of meeting-house registrations in 1824, but Bethel's enquiry seems to have been related to his interest in his new diocese. He did not ask for numbers. These returns were summarised in a dedicated book which has not hitherto attracted much attention, and the answers to Question 17 appear as Appendix 2.

IV. THE DISSENTING DENOMINATIONS
'Old Dissent'
'Old Dissent', sprung from the experience of the Civil War, was categorised as Presbyterian, Independent, Baptist and Quaker. Between 1689 and 1711, Gloucester Quarter Sessions registered 42 Presbyterian meetings, 1 Presbyterian and Independent, 41 Quaker, 15 Anabaptist, 6 Baptist, and 4 Independent; 31 other registrations were described simply as 'Protestant Dissenters' or not given any specific description.[5] Presbyterians in the Evans list accounted for more than half of all dissenters in Gloucester diocese, and nearly half in Bishop Benson's

---

[1] Watts 1978, 493–512.
[2] Watts 1978, 285–9.
[3] Ralph 21–76, with notes added following visitations in 1766 and 1784 by later bishops; Fendley.
[4] GDR/383.
[5] Q/SO/3, 520–522.

survey in 1735, with 21 meeting-houses, more than any other denomination. Evans added 20 Seventh Day Anabaptist hearers meeting in Aston on Carrant to the four main divisions of dissent, and Benson was informed of some Sabbatarian meetings.

The Presbyterians had the initial advantage that in 1646 parliament had attempted to establish a Presbyterian church to replace the episcopal Church of England which was being dismantled. Presbyterianism relied on ordained and educated ministers and a parochial framework, and there had been a chance that it could have been comprehended within a church settlement in the late 17th and early 18th centuries. The congregational principle of the Independents contrasted with the Presbyterians; each congregation appointed its minister, and was a 'gathered' church of true believers; its adherents became known more generally as Congregationalists.[1] The Quakers took the congregational principle even further, eschewing a ministry and any form of ritual, but relying on 'prophesying' or extempore prayer. The Baptists were defined by their belief that only an adult could accept the faith and strictly should be baptised by total immersion, even if already baptised as an infant. But there was disagreement over whether adult baptism was essential for full participation in the church's communion, which led to dissension and splits into different varieties of the Baptist persuasion.

Ministers appointed to churches during the Commonwealth, but deprived of their livings for non-conforming views after 1660, were a focus for dissent. A recent study identified 57 men who had served as ministers or teachers in Gloucestershire, and were ejected between 1660 and 1662.[2] Bristol clergy had increasingly adopted Puritan attitudes and practices and 'many of them were to become leaders of the early separatist congregations';[3] in 1666 11 Presbyterian Nonconformist ministers were living in Bristol 'contrary to the late Act of Parliament' [the Five Mile Act 1665]. Some ejected clergy moved from other counties, like Henry Collett [**1714**] who may have moved from Suffolk to Tewkesbury, while some stayed close to their forbidden town.

James Forbes is a good example, inaugurating a dissenting meeting in the bishop of Gloucester's cathedral city. He was born and educated in Scotland but after coming to Oxford, in 1654 he was appointed preacher or lecturer in Gloucester cathedral. He also became the pastor of a congregational church which met in the great hall of Edward Fletcher's house near the little cloister in the cathedral precincts. Forbes was ejected in 1660. He applied in 1672 for a licence apparently as a Congregational minister, and possibly also in Stinchcombe as an Independent [**815**, **1575**]. His ministry in Gloucester was interrupted several times by imprisonment and persecution; he was described by the bishop as 'once a Presbyterian, afterwards an Independent, but always a sectary, in Cromwell's time, and ever since'. Forbes sought to bring together the different nonconformist groups, he opened his vast library to other ministers, and he educated young men

---

[1] Watts 1978, 266, 291.
[2] Skea; Munden, 13.
[3] Bettey, 3–4, 22, 37, 40; Hayden, 17–19.

for the ministry. There is no record of the registration of the meeting-house in Barton Street built in 1699, where James Forbes continued to preach until his death. His last sermon to ministers in Gloucestershire was delivered at Stroudwater on 19 June 1711, and in 1712 his funeral sermon was preached by Isaac Noble, the congregational minister in Bristol who was responsible for the returns of dissenters in Bristol to John Evans.[1]

Nicholas Billingsley is another example. He had been admitted as vicar of Weobley, Herefs., in 1657, but was ejected in 1662. He settled in Abergavenny, and in 1664 subscribed to the Thirty-Nine articles in order to become the master of the school, shortly afterwards being ordained deacon. Three years later he was offered the vicarage of Blakeney in the parish of Awre, a living of the Haberdashers' Company, but refused on conscientious grounds, agreeing instead to be the curate. Although he then subscribed, his behaviour was unconventional, and he was suspended more than once and resigned in 1689. He stayed in the village, and established a Presbyterian meeting in his own house [**320**]; it was said there were 200 in his congregation who subscribed to his maintenance.[2] He died in Bristol in 1709. Dissent became well-established in Blakeney; a second unconventional minister was there in the 19th century, Isaac Bridgman, an energetic evangelist, who is described below.

Dissenting groups were not tightly defined; what they shared was a major objection to the episcopal rule of the Church of England and there was co-operation and movement of ministers and congregations between them. Ministers preached to congregations nominally not of their persuasion. Congregations were differentiated as much by style as theology;[3] certificates frequently refer to the wish to worship 'in our way'. Many throughout the period simply described themselves as Protestant Dissenters. The Tucker Street meeting in Bristol, for example, was variously regarded as Presbyterian or Independent, and the first minister of Lewins Mead chapel in Bristol was said to be of the 'presbyterian persuasion' [**2**], but Lewins Mead was described in 1936 as 'The Meeting-house of the Ancient Society of Protestant Dissenters assembling in Lewin's Mead for the worship of Almighty God'. Buildings were shared, like a 'commodious room' fitted up for religious worship in Cinderford in 1829 by a union of Baptists, Independents and Methodists [see **679**].

Without the controlling influence of the Church of England on doctrine, there was scope for variety in the detail of religious belief. The Baptists experienced particularly strong disagreements. Particular Baptists, Strict Baptists, Welsh Baptists and Seventh-day Baptists all made returns to the Religious Census. They had grown steadily through the period, but the large number of registrations in the 19th century (at least 100 were for Baptist meetings) was partly the result of congregations splitting. The establishment in 1836 of the Salem chapel in

---

[1] ODNB, 'Forbes, James (1628/9–1712)'; VCH *Glos* 4, 319. After Forbes' death a group seceded from his church, establishing an Independent meeting which became a centre of evangelical revival. The chapel became Presbyterian in 1716, and Unitarian by the later 18th century.
[2] ODNB, 'Billingsley, Nicholas (bap. 1633, d. 1709)'.
[3] Morgan 1994 [i], 65–7; Barry, 158, 160; BA 39461/PM/14.

Cheltenham [**466**], for example, was the result of some members of the congregation rejecting the very strict principle of adult baptism by total immersion of the Bethel chapel members [**443**].[1] Another example is 'The loving Baptist brethren of Arlington in Bibury', calling themselves 'Particular or Calvinistic Baptists'. They claimed they had been having the Lord's supper administered in Arlington and had two deacons even though members of the Fairford church. A Memorandum dated February 1839 in their new church book recorded that they applied for their 'dismission' because they 'feared entanglement in the disgraceful quarrel that exists at Fairford church'. The Arlington congregation had leased property in 1832, in order 'conveniently to exercise the forms of their religious worship', and then in 1839 rebuilt the meeting-house. Possibly they took over the first meeting-house in Arlington licensed in 1747 for Independents [**251**].[2] There were 44 members of the Baptist chapel in 1840.

As well as differences in theological opinions, population growth was another factor in the increase in dissenting meetings, making it viable for some congregations to set up more local meetings. A few people attending the Baptist meeting in Shortwood in Horsley came from Avening, and occasionally met locally in a private house there as it was more convenient, though not apparently registered; it may not have been thought necessary to register it because the main meeting was licensed. In 1819, the Avening group asked to have a local Baptist meeting recognised. A tablet in the chapel records that it was erected in 1805 and enlarged 1821 [**199**].[3]

Presbyterians, Independents and Baptists had combined to fight for religious freedom in the early 18th century and were still regarded as one group, 'The Three Denominations', by the Commissioners who collected information on dissenting registers. The tradition of the common dissenting interest had strong political significance. The Bristol Dissenters Committee held a general meeting for delegates from the Associations of Protestant Dissenters of Somerset, Gloucestershire, Monmouth and the city of Bristol on 23 February 1790 'in order to unite into one District' in the way that dissenters in Birmingham had proposed, and agitate for release from political disabilities. The Bristol delegates were drawn from five congregations in the city.[4] A record of meetings at Stokes Croft School House, Clifton Down Congregational chapel, survives from 1788-95, mainly notes concerning dinners.[5] Co-operation was a natural response to official disapproval or intolerance, and probably declined as toleration became widely accepted.

---

[1] W.W., 378; Pierce, 10.
[2] GA D2751/3; Kelly's *Directory* (1910) gives date of first meeting-house as 1747 and the rebuilding 1839.
[3] Urdank, 294–5; Watts 1999, 156–7.
[4] BA 39399/CD/A/3a.
[5] BA 39461.

The Methodists

The growth of Methodism, although it had its origins in the evangelising work of Charles and John Wesley and George Whitefield in the earlier 18th century, was only widely observable in registrations in the 19th century after the break was made from the Church of England. Wesley and Whitefield saw their mission as reviving rather than replacing the Church of England.

George Whitefield had been a devoted member of John and Charles Wesley's Holy Club in Oxford, but he became convinced of Calvinistic principles and broke with the Wesleys who accepted an Arminian theology.[1] The trust deed of Dursley Tabernacle in 1764, inspired by Whitefield, stated specifically that it was for 'people who profess themselves to be of Calvinistic Principles in connection with the said George Whitefield according to the doctrines contained in the Articles of the Established Church and are commonly called Methodists'.[2] Whitefield travelled widely throughout England and Scotland, as well as crossing the Atlantic 13 times to preach in Georgia, and has been considered the finest preacher of the religious revival. While his influence was less widespread than John Wesley's, he inspired the erection of a small number of Tabernacles; the first certificate for Bristol dated January 1755 related to the Tabernacle in Penn Street in the parish of St James [**12**]. The Countess of Huntingdon made him her chaplain and through her Whitefield's influence was extended.[3] The Countess also did not wish to break from the Church of England. Her name was used directly in certificates in relation to only two chapels, one in Bristol [**50**] and one in Gloucester [**829**], but the minister of the Countess of Huntingdon's chapel in Ebley certified a meeting in Cainscross in 1826 [**1601**] showing that there was one in her connexion there although there is no specific surviving record. Whitefield died in 1770.

Registrations show there were Calvinist Methodist meeting-houses called Tabernacles inspired by Whitefield at Blakeney [**327**, **328**], Cheltenham [**467**], Dursley [**733**, **734**], North Nibley [**1310**], Rodborough [**1472**], Westerleigh [**1871**] Wick [**1890**] and Wotton-under-Edge [**2017**]. His name is preserved in 'Whitefield's Tump' on Minchinhampton Common, the remains of a long barrow where he preached [*see* **1176**]). The Gloucester diocesan survey in 1825 mentions Whitefield's name in connection with meetings in Bitton, Frampton Cotterell, North Nibley and Rodborough; in the last place, 'a large chapel capable of containing 1200'. John Rees, minister of Rodborough Tabernacle, followed Whitefield's example as an energetic evangeliser, and established ten meetings altogether, in Avening, Minchinhampton, Miserden, Rodborough, Stroud and Woodchester.[4]

[1] Watts 1978, 400.
[2] Evans, D.E., 71.
[3] Watts 1978, 448.
[4] Watts 1999, 611: the Calvinistic Methodists were the last to give up itinerancy.

For John Wesley the break from the Church of England began in 1784 when he ordained clergy for the newly independent American adherents and then for Scotland; it became formally acknowledged only in 1795.[1] It was significant that Methodist groups described themselves as 'Societies'.[2] The first certificate using the specific term 'Methodist' was for a meeting near Coleford in 1789 [**605**]. There was not another until 1796 [**1946**] and this referred to the 'Methodists' chapel' in Winterbourne. It may imply that registration was not deemed necessary before the break from the Church of England. But from 1805 there was a steady flow of Methodist applications: nearly 200 were recorded in Bristol and Gloucestershire. Certificates show the result of the efforts of particular Methodist ministers like James M. Byron [*see* **166**] who certified six meetings, Daniel Campbell [*see* **179**] eleven, John Chettle of Gloucester [*see* **178**] five, Isaac Denison of Little Dean [*see* **608**] seven, Charles Clay of Kingswood Hill in Bitton [*see* **120**] nine, and Joseph Preston, the Primitive Methodist from Brinkworth [*see* **254**] nine; Joseph Everard has been noted above for being a signatory to 22 meetings. Most did not specifically state that they were Methodists in the certificates they signed, but the late John Wesley's [New] Connexion was referred to in eight registrations in 1810 and 1811.

Methodist congregations were divided on the importance of the Calvinistic belief in the salvation of the elect, and the movement split into several different sections. The Methodist New Connexion started in 1797, and a branch in Siston (Warmley tower) registered a meeting in 1811 [**1529**]; the Primitive Methodists began in 1811 and first registered a Gloucestershire meeting in 1839 in Lydbrook [**678**]; the Bible Christians began in 1816 and were meeting in Drybrook in 1837 [**683**]; John Knight of Ruardean was responsible for a Bible Christian meeting in Dymock [**750**] and one in Woodside, Wollaston, registered twice [**1989, 1990**]. No certificates refer specifically to the Wesleyan Association which started in 1834 although two made returns to the Religious Census, one in Cheltenham which also had a branch meeting, and one in St George's near Bristol.[3] A small group known as the Tent Methodists registered two meetings in Tetbury in 1823 [**1705, 1706**]. A congregation of Wesleyan Reformers was meeting in Fishponds in Stapleton in 1850 [**1564**: *see* illus., xix], one year after that Methodist group was formed.

The Moravian church (the Church of the United Brethren) came to Bristol in 1739 as a result of John Wesley's invitation to a Moravian evangelist, and John Cennick, who had been engaged as schoolmaster for the school which Whitefield and John Wesley built in Kingswood, became a Moravian as a result of his disagreement with the Wesleys' theology. Cennick bought houses in Kingswood and Tytherton to further his evangelism, and built another school and a chapel in Kingswood in 1757. He, and Mr and Mrs Marston, who lived in Bristol, 'went forth preaching in fields, barns, and dwelling houses, according to circumstances'.

---

[1] Watts 1978, 448; *http://www.methodist.org.uk/who-we-are/history/separation-from-the-church-of-england* accessed 30 September 2016; ODNB, 'Wesley, John (1703–1791)'.
[2] Munden, 17.
[3] See Munden, 19–20, 16.35, 16.36, 2.31.

In Bristol, a house was provided for a Moravian minister in Great Gardens in Temple parish in 1748, and meetings were held in a hired room in Redcliff Street. A more permanent home was purchased and developed in Blackfriars in St James's parish; in 1756 the foundation stone was laid for a chapel of the Holy Trinity, completed the following year. The early Moravian churches were not apparently registered; as an episcopal church it was not significantly nonconformist and it had a small amount of influence in Bristol and in Gloucestershire.[1] The churches in Upper Maudlin Street, Bristol, and Kingswood made returns to the Religious Census, as did the minister of a Moravian chapel in Brockweir, Woolaston, which had been erected in 1832 [**945**] and the minister of a chapel at Broom's Green in Dymock, built in 1837 [**747**]. A chapel in Apperley in Deerhurst, built in 1750, was taken over by the Methodists before 1845, with the burial ground.[2]

V. The Pattern of Dissent
Early Dissenting communities prior to 1755
Bristol

Bristol was early a significant centre of dissent. Even before the Reformation, reforming ideas had taken hold of some of the clergy, reaching Bristol from the continent through the widespread trading links of the port, and there was little resistance to the changes of the Reformation period. Episcopal oversight was not strong. Before the Reformation, the town was divided between the diocese of Worcester, controlling parishes north of the Avon, and the diocese of Bath and Wells, controlling parts of Bristol south of the Avon. It was still weak after the creation of Bristol diocese; the new bishopric was poorly endowed, and frequently did not have long-lasting or resident bishops.[3]

Eleven Presbyterian ministers were living in Bristol in 1665, and at least 11 applications for licences were made to Charles II in 1672, possibly more, as four were grouped together, and related to Templecombe as well as Bristol. The Compton Census four years later provides a minimum tally of 600 dissenters in the city. Returns in Bristol Record Office give a total of 620, representing about 11% of the inhabitants aged over 16, but returns from three parishes are missing.[4] Only fully committed dissenters may have been counted, not those who were occasional attenders in an Anglican church. Nonetheless the local returns suggests that one in three of the inhabitants in the extra-parochial Castle Precincts were dissenters, and in the parish of St Philip & St Jacob two-fifths of the small population.

It is unfortunate, therefore, that registrations of dissenters' meetings in Bristol after the Toleration Act are not available until the mid-18th century and then only from the bishop's court and not from Quarter Sessions; if at all similar to

---

[1] C, E. M., *A short sketch of the work carried on by the ... Moravian Church ... in the west of England and south Wales from 1740* [by E.M.C.] (Leeds 1886, 1887); see also Dresser, 45.
[2] *Nonconformist chapels and meeting-houses* (RCHM) 80–1.
[3] *VCH* 2, 42; Barry, 154.
[4] Whiteman, 550–1 (BA/EP/A/43/1); Morgan 1994, 66.

Gloucestershire, the Quarter Sessions would have licensed most of the meetings in this early period. There is one docket from Quarter Sessions in 1737 which refers to a meeting-house in Shannon Court off Corn Street in the heart of Bristol, certified by Joseph Whitehead and built at his own expense.[1] The histories and records of individual churches provide information about the more important dissenters' meetings, but, with a few exceptions, the numerous and often transient groups which met in private houses cannot be traced.

The record of the Quakers in Bristol commenced in 1654, and the Men's Meeting met regularly from 1667, keeping minutes of their meetings. Their records state that their two meeting-houses were registered on 12 August 1689.[2] Similarly, a history of the Broadmead Baptist church, written initially by Edward Terrill, and continued by other members of the congregation, suggests that the Baptist congregation was formed by 1640, a date probably a little earlier than in fact was the case. Terrill's account of the persecution in 1670 following the Second Conventicle Act is vivid. The bishop of Bristol arranged for congregations to be turned out of their meeting-houses, and the trained band 'was called out each Sunday for a number of weeks to nail up the doors'. The Broadmead congregation met in lanes and highways for several months and then moved to Edward Terrill's Garden House near Lawford's Gate. This was the boundary of the city, and they presumably met on the further side of the gate, in the Gloucestershire part of the parish of St Philip & St Jacob.[3] The Baptists established a permanent site in Broadmead, Union Street, in 1671, and another Baptist congregation bought a site at the Pithay about 1699.[4] Another early example is the Lewins Mead congregation, which dated its origin to 1672 [see **2**] and when a lease, dated 18 December 1706, was given to three trustees, a maltster, a grocer and a salter, it referred to an earlier lease of a building in Lewins Mead made on 12 July 1687, perhaps in response to James II's attempt at toleration. These were not poor men's meetings: members were able to rent or buy sometimes quite extensive property.

The Evans list, and Bishop Secker's Diocese Book, started in 1735, help to bridge the gap in registrations. Isaac Noble sent John Evans details of five large meetings in the city, suggesting a total of 6,200 hearers. In addition Noble observed that there was 'a great body of Quakers', the number supposed to be about 2,000, making 8,200 hearers; if accurate, as much as a fifth of Bristol's population could be regarded as nonconformist. The meeting-houses recorded by Evans would appear to have been centres for adherents, with a permanent minister, while house meetings may also have existed quite widely in the city. The claim could be made that 'Bristol was one of the great centres of Nonconformity in the west'.[5]

---

[1] BA InfoBox 15/79.
[2] Mortimer, ix, xiii.
[3] Hayden, 64.
[4] BA 39461/D/1; *Nonconformist chapels and meeting-houses* (RCHM) 62; and see the schedule of deeds BA 28410/32 including one of 1678 relating to Castle Green Meeting-house.
[5] Bradley, 241–2.

TABLE 9. BRISTOL DISSENTERS ABOUT 1715[1]

Presumed meeting place	Approximate no. of 'hearers'	Denomination
Castle Green	500	Independent/Congregational
Lewins Mead	1600	Presbyterian
Tucker Street	500	Presbyterian/Independent
Pithay	1200	Baptist
Broadmead	4 or 500	Baptist
[Friars and Temple Street]	2000	Quaker

Bishop Secker did not require incumbents to give actual numbers of dissenters; some obviously made their returns more precise, some were content with indications like 'many'.[2] Six Bristol parishes were categorised as having 'many': St James's parish where there were three meeting-houses, 'all licensed', three Presbyterian ministers and two Anabaptist teachers; St Philip & St Jacob with 'many Presbyterians and Quakers', and 20-30 families of foreigners sent for by the Quakers to their Brass works at Baptist Mills; 'many Protestant dissenters' in St Mary Redcliffe, where the meeting-house in Tucker Street was noted; and many in the small parish of St Augustine, in St Peter's and in St Thomas's.

Secker included in his diocese book the number of houses in each parish drawn from a census of 1712 taken by the Bristol Corporation of the Poor, and a second series of figures in 1735 when he became bishop. St James was more populous than any other city parish, with 682 houses in 1712, and 1407 in 1735. It was also physically a large parish with plenty of land available for development and it continued to grow, so that by 1784 Bishop Wilson noted that there were about 2,500 families. St Philip & St Jacob in-parish had 263 houses in 1712 and 330 houses in 1735. The inhabitants joined with the Justices of the Peace in 1724 to request Gloucestershire Quarter Sessions to appoint 12 new petty constables to supplement the two tithing men and one constable. It was claimed the peace could not be kept because of 'the numerous buildings lately erected and the many inhabitants now inhabiting'.[3] Amongst the new buildings was a brass works at Crew's Hole.[4] A few years later the inhabitants petitioned parliament for the right to build a workhouse because of the large population, many of whom were out-of-

---

[1] Based on Morgan (i), 70–1.
[2] Ralph, *passim*.
[3] GA Q/SO/5 7.
[4] Jenkins, 156.

work, and to drive out vagrants.[1] By 1766 Bishop Newton noted that there were 400 families in the in-parish and 850 in the out-parish. It was a notable centre of dissent; 45 meetings were licensed between 1755 and 1852. Numbers of burials between 1741 and 1750 were greater in the parishes of St James's and St Philip & St Jacob than in any other Bristol city parish,[2] and might suggest a population of at least 9,800 in St James's and 12,200 in St Philip's.[3] Numerically they were likely to have more dissenters than smaller parishes.

There is no official record of early Methodist meetings in Bristol. John Wesley was preaching in Bristol in 1739, and in May laid the foundation stone of his first dedicated accommodation, the New Room, near St. James's churchyard in the Horsefair; it was completed the following year, the oldest Methodist building anywhere, and was used not only for society and preaching meetings but to accommodate visiting preachers, as a pharmacy for the poor, and for education.[4] Charles Wesley became the regular minister. But George Whitefield had preached in Bristol two years before this, and he persuaded John Wesley to follow his example of open air preaching.[5] Both men travelled widely to evangelise though Charles Wesley followed this example less keenly; he settled in Bristol and lived there for some 30 years after giving up itinerant preaching.[6] The open-air places where Methodists attracted some of their largest audiences in Bristol were Rose Green, Temple Backs, the Bowling Green, and the Brickyard on St Philip's Plain. They also preached indoors, for example Newgate in Little Wine Street, the prison in Bristol that witnessed many visits by the Methodists, and the Weavers' Hall, near Temple church, a meeting place of one of the Bristol religious societies with which George Whitefield had been associated.[7] All three preached in Clifton and St. Nicholas's churches, a reminder that at this stage 'The People called Methodists,' as they styled themselves, were an adjunct to the Church of England and not a nonconformist denomination. John Wesley's organising abilities nonetheless created the basis for a successful Methodist church.[8]

George Whitefield's early evangelising was in Kingswood; the forest or chase was in the parish of Bitton, close to Bristol but in the diocese of Gloucester. He first preached in the open air to the colliers on 17 February 1739 on Hannam Mount on Kingswood Hill, and they gradually warmed to his message. He described the effect of his preaching, moving the Kingswood colliers to tears so that there were 'white gutters . . . down their black cheeks'. He began to collect money to open a school for the miners' children, but then persuaded John Wesley to take over the work.[9] In 1742 he commissioned a Tabernacle to be built in which

[1] Journal of the House of Commons vol 221 p656, 684 (1731).
[2] Browning.
[3] Assuming burials at the rate of 30 per thousand. St Philip & Jacob 3661; St James 2945.
[4] ODNB, 'Wesley, John (1703–1791)'.
[5] ODNB, 'Whitefield, George (1714–1770)'.
[6] ODNB, 'Wesley, Charles (1707–1788)'.
[7] Morgan [ii], 78.
[8] Watts 1978, 448–9.
[9] Dallimore, 47; ODNB 'Whitefield, George'; Watts 1999, 399.

people could come to hear him preach, the name reflecting the intended temporary nature of the building. The Kingswood Tabernacle still stands, though in a very dilapidated state.[1] It was presumably the 'large building called "the late Revd Mr Whitfield's Room" at Kingswood in the hamlet of Oldland' referred to in a certificate in 1796 [**1348**], 'used as a place of worship for dissenters of the Independent denomination'. The first surviving Bristol diocesan registration is for The Tabernacle in Penn Street in St James's parish, Bristol [**12**].

South Gloucestershire

For the 14 south Gloucestershire parishes in the diocese of Bristol,[2] there is only one early indication of dissent, in Horfield [**949**], and there are no known returns in the Compton Census. Eleven meetings were registered at Gloucestershire Quarter Sessions in the years after the Toleration Act, but it no doubt became more convenient for dissenters to register with the bishop of Bristol. There is good evidence that seven of the 14 parishes in the diocese contained a measure of dissent.

Dissenters in Elberton applied to the Michaelmas Quarter Sessions in Gloucester in 1689 to register Jonathan Tovey's barn' [**771**]; the Quakers in 'French Hay' (Winterbourne), King's Weston (Henbury), and Olveston all had meeting-houses registered at the Easter sessions 1690 [**928**, **1354**, **1937**]. These three Quaker congregations applied again for registration in 1707 [**929**, **1356**, **1941**] for new-built houses, suggesting that the use of an existing house was a temporary measure. In 1701 a 'new erected house' was registered in Tockington (Olveston) for Presbyterians [**1355**], and in 1704 three private houses were registered in Winterbourne [**1938**, **1939**, **1940**], which became a considerable centre of dissent.[3]

There is a gap in registrations after this, although Thomas Tyler, a dissenting minister, took the oath of allegiance and William Baker, a Quaker schoolmaster, affirmed his loyalty to George I before the Gloucestershire Justices on 7 December 1715. They were both of Frenchay in Winterbourne parish [**1942**, **1943**]. Frenchay and Hallen, both in Winterbourne, were the only south Gloucestershire places in the Evans list. Joseph Tyler was the minister in Frenchay, which returned 200 hearers. Against Hallen is the comment 'most colliers' but no minister was named and no number of hearers. The same information was recorded for Kingswood (in Bitton). As the colliers were unlikely to be voters in parliamentary elections, their numbers were not important to the compilers of the Evans list. Four licences were issued at later Gloucester Quarter Sessions: a Presbyterian meeting in a private house in Hambrook (Winterbourne) in 1724 [**1944**]; a Baptist meeting in a private house in Mangotsfield in 1725 [**1119**]; a meeting in the Quaker workhouse in St Philip & St Jacob out-parish in 1738 [**81**], and in a private house in Stoke Gifford in 1743 [**1582**].

---

[1] Edward Green, 'George Whitefield at Kingswood'. Restoration is planned:
www.buildingconservation.com/articles/georgewhitefield/georgewhitefield.htm, accessed 16/9/2016.
[2] Abbots Leigh was also in the diocese but was in Somerset.
[3] Ralph, 62.

 Bishop Secker's Diocese Book indicates that 11 south Gloucestershire parishes contained dissenters, though in most no meeting-house was mentioned; Presbyterians and Quakers were the predominant denominations. Secker's informants confirmed the nonconformist nature of Winterbourne, saying there were 'many' Presbyterians and Quakers and a meeting-house for each; the Presbyterians were said to be declining but the Quakers increasing. In Mangotsfield and Olveston there were 'many' Presbyterians and some Quakers. In Elberton and 'Littleton or thereabouts' there were said to be 15 dissenting families. Small numbers of Presbyterians and many Quakers were noted in Almondsbury, especially on the estates of the Bristol Chamber; there were a few dissenters in Clifton, in Filton there was one Quaker, in Westbury-on-Trym two families were Quakers, in Henbury a few Presbyterians and Quakers, and in Stapleton five Presbyterian families and one Quaker. About Stapleton Secker's informant was unusual in commenting that 10 occasionally 'come from Bristol from which two Presbyterians, two Quakers and one Anabaptist'. Dissenters walked considerable distances to attend a meeting, as did ministers and evangelisers in their mission work who certified meetings where they preached.[1] Certificates requesting registration named those interested in the meeting, not necessarily inhabitants of the parish where it was to be held. An example from Gloucester diocese points to the same characteristic; Bishop Benson's respondent for the Quaker meeting-house in Stoke Orchard, which had been licensed in 1690 [**1584**], noted: 'five men, Meeting, from other places in a poor thatched house'.[2]

Gloucestershire within Gloucester diocese
Nonconformity was spread widely in Gloucestershire, though more notable in the towns than the countryside. Applications for licences were made to Charles II in 1672 by men in 49 or 50 parishes (two places were not given) out of the 276 in the diocese in 1735, or 318 including chapelries[3] and in the Compton Census there were some dissenters in 178 parishes out of the 288 making returns, nearly two-thirds, and a total of 3,834 dissenters, perhaps 6% of the estimated population.[4] Amongst the 26 places about 1715 with the highest numbers of dissenters are the market towns of Stroud, the highest number of dissenters of any place in the Evans list (500 Independents and 400 Anabaptists), Cirencester (600 Presbyterians and 150 Anabaptists), Gloucester (400 Presbyterians and 250 Independents), Tewkesbury (350 Presbyterians and 150 Anabaptists), Tetbury (250 Presbyterians) Cheltenham (200 Anabaptists) and Painswick (200 Presbyterians). Bourton-on-the-Water (500 Anabaptists) and Nailsworth (450 Independents) were also notable.

---

[1] Members of the Congregational Bristol Itinerant Society (founded 1811) walked between 10 and 16 miles to preach in villages around Bristol. Evans, M. J. C., 152, quoting G H Wicks' history of the society. *See* lxxi belo. The Baptist Itinerant Society likewise regularly walked great distances.
[2] GA GDR/285 B(1) *sub* Bishop's Cleeve.
[3] The same number of parishes and chapelries was recorded in 1735 and 1825 by Bishops Benson and Bethel.
[4] Using Whiteman's suggested population total of 65,085: Whiteman lxxxiv.

Quarter Sessions and diocesan records contain 272 registrations of meetings in the period 1689-1755 in 98 parishes, about a third of the diocese. Ten or more certificates were registered in each of the parishes of Bisley, Bitton, Cheltenham, Painswick, Tetbury and Wotton-under-Edge; Painswick registered no fewer than 17. However, a well-established meeting-house needed only one licence. Cam had three certificates registered by 1715, but no more until 1807; it was one of the places where the Evans list recorded a large number of 'hearers' (800 Presbyterians).

Although small compared with Bristol, Gloucester city was also an early centre of nonconformity. Six licences were obtained in 1672: one for James Forbes in Sampson Bacon's house, three more for houses in the city for Congregational meetings and two for Longford, an out-parish area divided between St Mary de Lode and St Catherine.[1] Seven meetings were licensed in the following years up to 1755. The presence of the bishop might have encouraged incumbents of the city's parishes to deter dissenting meetings. George Whitefield, despite being born in the Bell Inn in Gloucester, ordained deacon by Bishop Benson in Gloucester cathedral and priest by Bishop Benson in Christ Church Oxford, was not allowed to preach from the pulpit in St Michael's church on weekdays,[2] and the Presbyterian Samuel Jones was forced to move his Academy to Tewkesbury. Jones established a school or Academy in Barton Street, Gloucester, in 1708 in the house of Henry Wintle, a trustee of the nearby Presbyterian meeting, to give prospective ministers a religious education as they were unable to attend an established university; he had a reputation for oriental learning.[3] Thomas Secker attended the Gloucester Academy but later accepted the tenets of the Church of England, becoming Archbishop of Canterbury, so did Samuel Butler, the future bishop of Durham. Jones is named as a Presbyterian minister in Tewkesbury in the Evans list with 350 'hearers', his house was attacked by a mob in 1715,[4] and after his death in 1719 some students were taken on by Jeremiah Jones, minister of the Independent meeting at Forest Green, Nailsworth.

The two main market towns of Cirencester and Tewkesbury were early centres of dissent. Cirencester was established as a Puritan stronghold early in the 17th century. It was one of the market towns targeted by the group of 12 Puritan trustees, formed in 1625 and known as the Lay Feoffees, who were Calvinist in opinion; they bought impropriations and used them to fund lecturers and Cirencester was one of their first acquisitions. The Cirencester lecturer was probably the man 'of a notorious Inconformity ... hunted from one Diocess to another'. He met with the hostility of the incumbent curate, who stimulated a legal attack which led to the disbanding of the feoffees.[5] Nonetheless there were five petitions from Cirencester for licences in 1672, and the following year

[1] VCH Glos 4, 382.
[2] VCH Glos 4, 319–20.
[3] ODNB, 'Jones, Samuel (1681/2–1719)'; 'Jones, Jeremiah (1693/4–1724)'; VCH Glos 8, 165–6.
[4] VCH Glos 4, 319; Bennett, 2, 442.
[5] Kirby, E.W. (1942), 12.

Quakers leased land and built a meeting-house, to which 48 Friends contributed.[1] Quakers and Baptists had meetings licensed immediately after the Toleration Act [**540, 541**]. Dissent persisted strongly thereafter.

Tewkesbury, like Cirencester, was a poorly endowed curacy which attracted curates and lecturers of Puritan views. The curate in 1628 was later suspended and the minister in 1650 was an Independent. Another minister, a Presbyterian, was one of the 64 who in 1648 signed the *Gloucestershire Ministers' Testimony*,[2] in effect a manifesto, and in 1678 yet another curate was suspended. Quaker and Baptist meetings were established in the Commonwealth period and three Congregational ministers applied for licences in 1672.[3] Tewkesbury was remarkable for the number of nonconformists in the Compton Census, three quarters of the population, but only two meeting-houses were licensed in the period 1689-1755 [**1716, 1717**]. Both towns illustrate the importance of non-conforming clergy in creating strong dissenting communities.

Stroud, the place with the largest number of 'hearers' in the Evans list, is documented as a very active centre of nonconformity towards the end of the 18th century. Technically a chapelry in the large parish of Bisley until the 1720s, Stroud was served by chaplains (though often called curates) until becoming a perpetual curacy. There were Puritan churchwardens in the late 16th century, but the curate at the Restoration subscribed to the Act of Uniformity and it is significant that a small number of nonconformists was returned in the Compton Census (as also in Bisley). Nonetheless two ministers ejected at the Restoration, William Becket and Daniel Capel, came to live in Stroud, suggesting a tolerant attitude amongst inhabitants. Becket, a congregational minister, had been licensed in Winchcombe in 1672 [**1907**]; in 1690 he was minister to the Presbyterian congregation in Tewkesbury which was to build the first chapel in the town, but was also said to be a minister in Stroud. Daniel Capel, ejected rector of Shipton Moyne, a Congregational minister, was not subsequently recorded in Stroud; he died in 1679.[4]

Bishop Benson's survey might suggest that dissent had declined in the 20 years since the Evans list was made. Evans recorded nearly 8,500 dissenters in 33 places, without Quakers. Benson's survey recorded 5,414, possibly 4.3% of population calculated from his returns; 62 places had 10 or more dissenters, which probably meant more than one family, and 27 had 40 or more; 17 out of 27 named were market towns or boroughs.[5] Dissenting numbers generally were lower than in the Evans list, 100 in Stroud, 210 in Tewkesbury and 220 in the city of

[1] Stephens, 1.
[2] Skea, 86.
[3] *VCH Glos* 8, 155.
[4] Skea, 242; *VCH Glos* 11, 140.
[5] Ashchurch, Avening, Bibury, Bisley, Bitton, Bourton-on-the-Water, Cam, Cheltenham, Cirencester, city of Gloucester, Dursley, Fairford, Horsley, Kingswood (Kingswood Abbey), Marshfield, Minchinhampton, Painswick, Little Rissington, Chipping Sodbury, Stow-on-the-Wold, Stroud, Tetbury, Tewkesbury, Thornbury, Uley, Wickwar, Wotton-under-Edge.

Gloucester, where dissenters were about 4% of the population;[1] only in Cirencester was the figure close to Evans, 700 dissenters, the highest of any place in the diocese and possibly nearly 16% of the town's population.[2] The listing by household of the population of Tetbury parish, probably made in order to supply Bishop Benson with information, is a warning not to place too much trust in individual totals; 3115 people were initially recorded, subsequently corrected to 2216, which matches the listing.[3] Individual families' allegiances were specified, and it is interesting that 41 families were split between different denominations and 17% of households contained at least one dissenter.

As well as ministers' personal allegiances influencing returns of dissenters numbers, another important factor in comparing the Evans returns with Bishop Benson's survey is that the first appears to relate to places where ministers were centred and the second relates clearly to parishes. Nailsworth, where there were 450 hearers in the Evans list and five ministers named between 1716 and 1725, was divided between three parishes: Avening, Horsley and Minchinhampton, none named in the Evans list [*see* map, p305]. Quakers were holding meetings in members' houses here in 1660, and the Privy Council complained of conventicles in Colliers Wood in 1669.[4] Following Charles II's Declaration of Indulgence a barn was licensed in Nailsworth as a Presbyterian meeting place and also a house [**1223**]. Quakers, Independents and Presbyterians all obtained licences from the Quarter Sessions between 1690 and 1715 [**1224-1229**]. By contrast, Nailsworth was not named in Benson's survey, but returns were made of 75 dissenters in Avening, 550 in Horsley and 127 in Minchinhampton; many no doubt attended Nailsworth meetings. Similarly 'Chalford Bottoms' in the Evans list with 500 hearers was not a parish but was in Bisley; a meeting-house had been built in 1696 [**392**], and the Presbyterian minister in the Evans list, Theodore Westmacott of Chalford, subscribed to the oaths of allegiance and supremacy in 1715 [**393**]. Benson's survey recorded just 70 dissenters in Bisley parish.

The pattern of dissent 1755–1852
In each area the social composition of dissent was not very different from that of the population in general. Where manufactures and artisanal crafts were most common, providing relative independence for many, the areas were characterised by most nonconformity. Dissent was early associated with the textile trade; it is estimated that 40% of the Quakers in Bristol and Gloucestershire were in the clothing trades in the years immediately before the Toleration Act. The next most common occupations amongst dissenters were the 'mechanic trades' like smiths, blacksmiths and carpenters. These characteristics continued to be evident in the

[1] Jones, 131–45. Population figures were not given on a uniform basis, and have been calculated allowing 4.5 to a family and 5 to a house where these were specified, and an average size where a range was returned, but not adding in a figure for those places where no population figure was given.
[2] GA D566/Z/11 contains a figure of 3797 inhabitants in Cirencester.
[3] GA D566/Z/11.
[4] *VCH* XI, 211; Urdank, 85–6, 92.

18th and 19th centuries.[1]

Bristol at the beginning of the 18th century was the country's second largest city, the economic and social focus of south Gloucestershire and indeed of a wider region. The population had doubled by 1801 to 41,000 inhabitants in the city, or 64,000 in the whole urban area including the parishes of Clifton, Mangotsfield and Stapleton; by 1831 the city had 59,000 inhabitants and the urban area 104,000.[2] Clifton experienced much the fastest growth. It was suggested by F. M. Eden in 1797 that Bristol was 'not more a commercial than a manufacturing town'.[3] However, in 1831 only a small number of men (aged 20 and above) were regarded as employed in manufacturing, while close to half were employed in retail trade or in handicraft, suggesting a great many small-scale enterprises.

The city had a number of well-established meeting-houses. *Sketchley's Bristol Directory* 1775 noted 14 nonconformist meetings amongst the public buildings of the city: three Baptist and three Quaker, two Presbyterian, and one each for Independents, Moravians, Wesley's Room, Whitefield's Tabernacle, the French chapel and 'Dissenters'.[4] Two or three of these can be verified from registrations. One is the Quaker 'workhouse' just outside the city in the out-parish of St Philip & St Jacob; the Quakers had applied to Gloucester Quarter Sessions for a licence for the workhouse 'as a meeting-house for the exercise of religious worship' in 1738 [**81**], one of the few early Bristol meetings for which the registration survives, and one for which the original certificate also survives. Licences for Whitefield's Tabernacle [**12**] and probably the predecessor of Dolman's chapel [**82**] are also recorded. Meetings were located in certificates by street names, and can be difficult to identify. Matthews's *Complete Guide* of 1794[5] described the actual buildings, and named 18 meeting-houses including the French chapel and the New Jerusalem or Swedenborgian church, one of only two in Gloucestershire in 1851 (the other was in Chalford). Directory compilers included only the more obvious chapel buildings and ignored house meetings.

Areas outside the city's boundaries were not well-supplied with established churches, experienced considerable development, and were notable for the number of meeting-house registrations. Twenty-nine were in St James and St Paul's, and a few certificates in the parish of Westbury-on-Trym were effectively in the purlieus of Bristol city; 47 were in St Philip & St Jacob and St George, and 21 in Clifton, the first dated 1788 [**563**]. Clifton in 1831 was pre-eminently a professional area; noted for the spa as well as being a favoured residential area, it is in this respect comparable with Cheltenham, also surprisingly non-conformist.

St Philip & St Jacob and St George's were notable for some larger industrial enterprises. Evans' list named a 'cupilo' in Kingswood, a reverberatory furnace

---

[1] Watts 1978, 271, 348–9, 353–4, 360; Watts 1999, 306, 313, 317–8, 493, 601, 735 (table 27); Lacock, 280.
[2] Minchinton, 297–313.
[3] Quoted by Minchinton, 301.
[4] Little, 121–2.
[5] Matthews, 79–80.

dated to the late 17th century, formerly used for lead smelting, and a second one 'near Bristol', possibly the one at Conham; the Bristol Brass Company built a works at Crew's Hole before 1712, both in the out-parish of St Philip & St Jacob.[1] Rudder in 1779 noted that the parish of St George supplied Bristol with most of its coal and also had two copper works and a glass house for the manufacture of bottles. He had an unfavourable view of the revel held on the anniversary of St George's church foundation, celebrated 'with all the solemnities of an old pagan festival; that is drunkenness, gluttony, riot, debauchery, cursing and swearing, scolding and fighting, fiddling and dancing, Bacchanalian songs, and midnight impurities'.[2] It was not surprising that the Wesleys and George Whitefield saw a need for evangelism in the area. Matthews's *New History*[3] mentioned the large iron foundries in St Philip's parish, a steam engine for boring cannon, and considerable lead works. Hunt's *Directory* in 1849 noted 'The great western cotton works in St Philip's & St Jacob are an assemblage of colossal buildings, erected for the manufacture of cloth;' 1,500 pairs of human hands were 'daily put in requisition' and six engines were constantly employed. There was an iron foundry on the same premises.[4] This parish had the most nonconformist licensed meetings of any in Bristol diocese.

Of 126 certificates for Bristol parishes, only 50 identified a denomination: 17 Baptist (including one Primitive Baptist), 14 Independent, 14 Methodist (including two Primitive Methodist), two Quaker, one Countess of Huntingdon, one Christian Revivalist, and one Rational Religionists. The floating chapel in the Harbour was not denominational. As Hunt's *Directory* observed, 'there are chapels for almost every body of dissenters', and noted 36, including three newer meetings not apparently licensed, one each of Moravian, Unitarian and Welsh Calvinist.

Industry was important in south Gloucestershire, especially in those parishes bordering Bristol and on the coal field, and in the 1831 census the majority of men were working in manufacturing, as artisans or in retail trade, and as labourers not in agriculture. The growing industrial and domestic demand for coal in the Bristol region assured employment not only for miners but also for carters, carriers, and especially blacksmiths needed to service the pumps which enabled deeper seams of coal to be mined.[5] There was also a widespread felt hat industry. It was an area of small owner-occupiers. 'The typical farmer was an owner-occupier or long leaseholder utilising only family-labour on moderately sized farms'. A manorial survey of Westerleigh in 1801 recorded a big preponderance of land-holdings of 1 to 10 acres; this was also a parish where coalminers probably formed a third of the population.[6] Small farms encouraged or necessitated dual occupations. There was an early application for a meeting-house

---

[1] Jenkins, 145–6, 153–4, 162, 164; Day, 24–5. The name 'The Cupilo' was applied to another lead smelting works near Bristol, probably on the Somerset side of the river Avon.
[2] Rudder, 459.
[3] Matthews, 40.
[4] Hunt, 7.
[5] Moore, 33.
[6] Moore, 13, 14, 17.

in Westerleigh [**1862**], and nine in the period 1755–1852, also one early licence [**1438**] and three later ones from the chapelry of Pucklechurch. Other industrial parishes were keenly nonconformist; Stapleton was noted for both coal mining and quarrying and for hatting; Winterbourne was noted for quarrying and for iron works. There is no early evidence of dissent in Stapleton, but 13 meetings were registered between 1779 and 1851; 25 meetings were registered in Winterbourne, including eight early ones at Gloucestershire Quarter Sessions. Coal mining and copper smelting were important in Kingswood in Bitton. Ten certificates were registered in Bitton after 1755 and by 1825 it had become the largest centre of nonconformity in Gloucester diocese, with no fewer than nine meeting-houses 'besides innumerable preaching houses [in] Kingswood', where there was a 'scattered population'.

In the rest of the county, within the diocese of Gloucester, an outline of the pattern of dissent can be seen by comparing the number of parishes with dissenters in each deanery in the surveys of 1735 and 1825. Dursley, Fairford and Stonehouse deaneries were most disaffected in 1735, with nearly two thirds of parishes having some dissenters, and in 1825 Dursley and Stonehouse again had most parishes containing dissenters, but Fairford was no longer notable. Instead, dissent had taken hold in the Forest deanery, which reflected the growth in settlements and population. By contrast, less than half the parishes in deaneries in the north Cotswolds and the Severn Vale had dissenting meetings in either 1735 or 1825. The pattern of dissent echoes the agricultural regions into which the county was divided. The terrain of a parish, which might make the journey to the parish church long and inconvenient, also encouraged inhabitants of small rural communities in the deeply-folded valleys of the Stroud area or the Forest of Dean to set up local religious meetings.

Dursley and Stonehouse were described by Rudder as in the 'clothing country',[1] and nonconformity and the textile industry were strong in both deaneries. Stroud was the centre of the industry by the beginning of the seventeenth century, as well as of nonconformity. There were eight licences before 1755 and 44 between 1755 and 1852, amongst the highest number in any parish in the county.[2] In the same period there were 36 certificates for Minchinhampton, and 30 each for Painswick and Bisley with Chalford chapelry (listed separately), all parishes noted in this period for the textile industry. The 1831 census confirms the strong manufacturing and artisanal nature of the area; three quarters of employed men of 20 years and above were in these two categories, and in Cam, Minchinhampton, Dursley, Stroud, Uley and Wotton-under-Edge between a half and two thirds.

There is much evidence of important links between dissent and those involved in the textile industry. Nailsworth in Stonehouse deanery, already prominent as a centre of nonconformity in 1715, had at least 14 cloth mills. The trustees of the plot of ground on which the Forest Green Congregational meeting-house stands included three clothiers, two dyers and a maltster. The 1716 trust deed of the

---

[1] Rudder, 60.
[2] *VCH Glos* 11, 120.

Baptist meeting-house at Shortwood, part of Nailsworth in Horsley parish, named seven broadweavers, one clothworker and one mason, and one clothier of Trowbridge; no licence for a Baptist meeting in Nailsworth is recorded but in Horsley one is dated 1708 and one 1733 [**955, 956**]. A bitter strike of weavers in 1825 divided Shortwood Baptist chapel congregation; some joined the strike, and while it lasted the union attracted members away from the chapel.[1] Bishop Bethel's survey recorded three Baptist meetings in Avening, three (Quaker, Baptist, Wesleyan) in Horsley and four (one Baptist, three Wesleyan) in Minchinhampton, some of which were in practice in Nailsworth.

Cam Independent chapel was built in 1702 on land donated by clothier William Hicks, and amongst the trustees were John Phillimore of Cam fulling mill, John and Thomas Pope, clothiers, and Nathaniel Hicks, owner of Upper Cam corn and fulling mill, but the new built house licensed in 1704 [**382**]was said to be for Presbyterians.[2] The trustees of the schoolhouse in Dursley in 1740, given for the education of the children of Protestant dissenters by Joseph Twemlow, the Presbyterian minister of Cam in 1715 [**383**], included three clothiers and three broadweavers.[3] The house of Robert Clissold, broadweaver, in the tithing of Sheepscombe in Painswick, was licensed in 1741 [**1383**]. A 'Gig man' in Huntingford Mill, Wotton-under-Edge, registered a meeting in his house in 1818 [**2009**], three clothiers of the parish of Kingswood certified a meeting in 1821 [**1036**] and David Apperley of Cainscross, clothier, certified houses in Nailsworth in Avening [**1238**], Alkerton in Eastington [**760**], Dewbridge in King's Stanley [**1025**] and Cainscross in Stonehouse [**1602**] between 1842 and 1845.

Clothing mills are referred to in several 19th-century certificates. A large upper room in the north east end of the clothing factory in the occupation of Messrs Cooper and Wathen in the parish of Stonehouse was certified in 1807 [**1591**]; a meeting was to be held in Fromebridge Mills in the parish of Frampton upon Severn, 1820 [**809**]; meetings were certified in Badbrook Mill, Stroud [**1640**], and in Dye House Mills in Minchinhampton in 1832 [**1178**]; in 1827 [**1405**] some Independents begged respectfully for a licence for a 'house or building and premises' occupied by Matthew Rice at Small's Mill in Painswick; meetings in a workshop at Charfield Mills in 1834 [**405**], and in a house at Framilode Mills in the parish of Saul, 1836 [**1502**] were certified. However, a sign of the depressed state of trade in 1851 was the certificate for a room in a void mill and premises in Sheepscombe (Painswick) [**1416**].

Dean Forest's mineral wealth and woodland led to the development of 'a strong industrial element': places such as Ruardean, Littledean and Clearwell (in Newland parish) had 'miners, ironworkers, quarrymen, charcoal burners, and makers of barrel staves and hoops, trenchers, shovels and cardboard'.[4] Applications for licences had been made to Charles II from ministers in Littledean

---

[1] Urdank, 238.
[2] Evans, D.E., 34.
[3] Ibid, 41, 42.
[4] *VCH Glos* 5, 91.

[**1067**], Newland [**1271**] and Ruardean [**1484**, **1485**], and the Evans list had included Blakeney in Awre (Presbyterian), Coleford in Newland (Anabaptist) and Mitcheldean (Independent). Later-18th and early-19th century expansion of coal mining and iron working led to significant population expansion and corresponding expansion of nonconformist meetings.[1] There are almost no certificates for places in the extra-parochial area of the Forest until the early 19th century but 63 meetings were registered to be held in the Forest from 1802 to 1852. Few Forest certificates mention occupations; a house in the occupation of a coal miner in Ruardean was registered in 1808 [**1489**], and of an iron-master of Lydbrook in 1823 [**659**]; a workshop in the occupation of a carpenter, at Bradley Forge near Ayleford, noted as extraparochial, was registered in 1823 [**660**]. Newland, Coleford and Clearwell, Littledean and Ruardean continued to be vigorous centres of nonconformity. Bishop Bethel's informant in 1825 reported Newland had 'many' dissenters: 'Baptists, Wesleyans, Ranters, Bryanites, Bridgeman'; 14 Forest deanery parishes had congregations described as Methodist or Wesleyan Methodist.

The isolated small settlements in the Forest gave ample scope for nonconformist evangelisers, although Revd Horlick, in his manuscript account, kept from the time he arrived as a young preacher in 1800 until his death in 1858, was fair-minded enough to acknowledge the hard work of some Anglican clergy who built churches and schools, and even offered cottage lectures, like Myles Dixon, stipendiary curate of Coleford. John Horlick was an example of the missionary zeal of nonconformist ministers. He was ordained as an Independent minister in Ruardean in 1801 and was also minister in Mitcheldean. He certified three meetings [**1096, 1212, 1489**] and possibly one in Gloucester towards the end of his life [**868**]. The son of Robert Horlick, serge and flannel weaver in Painswick, he was educated by Cornelius Winter, minister of the Independent church in Painswick [**1392, 633**] who was a disciple of George Whitefield, had been to America with him and was there when he died.[2] Horlick was a member of a notable family of proselytisers, Robert and Thomas Horlick certified two meetings in Painswick [**1389, 1390**]; Robert Horlick also certified a meeting in Bisley [**282**] and Daniel Ellis Horlick and Cornelius Winter a meeting in Cranham [**633**].

Richard Stiff was a remarkable dissenting evangeliser and signed eight certificates. He was born in Dursley and in 1779 signed a certificate there [**731**]. In 1783 he went to live in Blakeney, and invited gospel ministers to come and preach in his house, working long hours in order to give them a small pecuniary reward.[3] On certain Sundays Stiff went to 'some sequestered spot in the Forest where himself and some of his family took their station under the extended branches of one of the trees, for the purpose of reading the word of God' [*see* illus., xiii]. He became a

---

[1] *VCH Glos* 5, 303, 330–3, 342–4.
[2] *VCH Glos* 10, 84; GA SR3.44GS; 'Revd J Horlick', *Christian's Penny Magazine* (Aug 1858) 215–9; Evans, D.E., 84.
[3] GA D3397/1 (Horlick, 'A visit to the Forest of Dean').

preacher, and preached three times on Sundays, walking 17 miles to do so. He was reputed to have a strong Gloucestershire accent. A house shared by Richard Stiff and Richard Craduck was certified in 1795 [**325**] by William Bishop, an Independent minister in Gloucester, and one of a group of ministers who about that time formed a Missionary Society to work in the Forest. Stiff joined with Robert McAll, the minister of the Countess of Huntingdon's chapel in Gloucester,[1] another member of the Missionary Society, in certifying a meeting in the Lea Hamlet in 1797 [**641**], and with Isaac Skynner, minister, in Lydney in 1804 [**1108**]. These certificates illustrate the fluidity of denominational labels. His last certificate was signed in 1805 [**1070**]. After nearly 40 years of evangelism in the Forest, in 1816 he was buried in the grounds of Dursley Tabernacle.[2]

Another evangeliser in the Forest, Isaac Bridgman, was a curate of unconventional views, who was forced to leave his church, Holy Trinity, at Harrow Hill in the Forest after being accused of insulting Henry Berkin, the reader and preacher, instigating a riot, consorting with the lower classes, being anecdotal and controversial in his preaching, and bringing contempt on the Anglican Prayer Book. He had considerable local support and the support of Rowland Hill.[3] He was 'of Ruardean' when he certified a meeting in Lydbrook in 1823 [**659**], one in Awre [**210**] and one in Newnham [**1292**], but then moved to Wood Side Cottage near Blakeney (in Awre). He built the Tabernacle at Brain's Green in Blakeney, registered in August 1823 [**327**]; as was the practice in Rowland Hill's chapels, at first the Book of Common Prayer was used, but in 1825 the chapel congregation opted to become Independent. Bridgman registered further houses in Awre [**211**], Newnham [**1293**] and Bradley Forge [**660**], all in 1823. The following year another house in Awre was registered [**212**], and in 1827 yet another [**213**]. In these cases, a small congregation may have moved from cottage to cottage.

The area least affected by nonconformity extended both north and south of Gloucester, and can be characterised as the Severn Vale and the Cotswolds. In the 18th century the Severn Vale was noted for dairying, market gardening and cider-making. In 1735 less than a quarter of the parishes in the deanery of Gloucester had any dissenters, but as elsewhere they had increased by 1825, when nearly half had some. Although lacking the international trade which contributed to Bristol's commercial success, and less than one quarter of Bristol's size at the beginning of the 18th century, Gloucester was by some margin the largest place in the county, a traditional shire town with an important function in inland trade.[4] During the 18th century the population increased a little; in 1801 it was 7,600, but it expanded faster in the early 19th century, stimulated by the proposed Gloucester and Berkeley canal. By 1831 it had reached 12,000 within the city, with another 4,200 in the adjoining hamlets; development of land outside the city was not yet

---

[1] *VCH Glos* 5, 400.
[2] Bright, 15–6, 49; *VCH* 5, 44, 171, 399–400.
[3] Munden, 30.
[4] Ripley.

substantial.[1] The occupational structure in the city in 1831 was remarkably similar to Bristol, with the retail trades and handicrafts employing over half the men of 20 years and over. St Michael had the most meeting-house registrations, followed by St Mary de Lode; these parishes included part of Barton Street which was outside but integral with the city, and was the road from Over Bridge to Upton St Leonards.[2] The hamlet of Longford continued to be a centre of nonconformity, to which the lack of clear parochial authority, and development on the road northwards out of Gloucester, contributed. The small amount of development in the rest of the out-parish and extra-parochial areas at this period meant that they did not match the population expansion of the extensive out-parishes of Bristol's churches. Over the whole period 1672–1852, 67 dissenting congregations applied for a licence in Gloucester; 54 were certified between 1755 and 1852. In 1735 Gloucester had three meeting-houses and in 1825 six.

The Cotswolds between Cirencester and Stow-on-the-Wold, in the deaneries of Cirencester, Stow and Winchcombe, were least affected by dissent. This area could be categorised as 'champion' country, where the upland supported arable husbandry as well as sheep. As early as 1635 the report of Sir Nathaniel Brent, Vicar General to Archbishop Laud, contained the aside about the area around Moreton in Marsh that 'These parts are more free of schism than drunkenness'.[3] Nonconformity was largely limited to towns throughout this generally agricultural area. Cirencester was notable in 1735 but by 1825 Cheltenham had seven dissenting chapels whereas Cirencester and Tewkesbury each had four. In the years 1672 to 1852, 62 certificates were applied for in Cheltenham, 27 in Cirencester and 24 in Tewkesbury. The numbers are roughly proportionate to the population. The rapid increase in Cheltenham's population and the prevalence of dissent casts as interesting light on the social background of newcomers to the town and contrasts with the impression given by the several proprietary churches which were built in the 19th century.

The Religious Census 1851
The Religious Census provides an overview of nonconformity in 1851, listing dissenters' chapels and their denominational allegiance. Only a few private houses were returned and the census therefore appears to lead to an underestimate of the extent of dissent; it is likely that no census forms were sent to such meetings in the first place. A total of 453 meeting-houses made returns within the county of Gloucester and the city of Bristol as they were constituted in 1851.[4] Although denominations were not always stated, the impact of Methodism was outstanding; 45% of dissenting chapels were Methodist of one grouping or

---

[1] *VCH Glos* 4, 102, 124.
[2] *VCH Glos* 4, 412 (map).
[3] *Calendar of State Papers Domestic Series of the reign of Charles I 1635* ed John Bruce Esq (1865) xli.
[4] Table D & F, Census 1851 of Religious Worship, ccxlii & ccliv: Munden 406. The total and the table of denominations exclude Bedminster and those parishes not in Gloucestershire in 1851 although in registration districts based in the county; they also exclude the two Swedenborgian 'New Jerusalem' churches, one in Bristol and one in Chalford.

another. Although Bristol had been the first place to have a Methodist meeting, not many more had been opened in the city by 1851. The Religious Census, on the other hand, shows how active the Methodist evangelisers had been in south Gloucestershire, where 71 meetings were described as belonging to one of the variant Methodist denominations. Methodism had also made progress in the rest of the county; in the 16 parishes in Stroud registration district there were 22 Methodist congregations and in the Forest of Dean 26.

The Baptists of various allegiances were the next most numerous. In a number of places buildings were shared. Independent congregations had been steadily established throughout the registration period, and are seen as particularly successful, returning very large congregations at some of their chapels, notably in Bristol: the Tabernacle in Penn Street [12] returned a total congregation of 614, Gideon chapel in Newland Street [27] 560, Brunswick Square chapel [54] 600, and Highbury chapel [63] 1,047.[1] The Quakers' emphasis on marrying within the faith had tended to reduce their numbers from generation to generation and they did not generally proselytise. From 41 meeting-houses registered in the early years they declined to only 10 in Gloucestershire and one in Bristol in 1851. The economic success of individual Quakers was not matched by the success of the denomination. The number of Presbyterian congregations had also declined through the 18th century, and although one meeting house was registered in Wotton-under-Edge in 1837 [2015] and a house meeting in 1845 [1958] in St John's, Frenchay (previously in Winterbourne), no Presbyterian church was returned in Bristol or Gloucestershire in the Religious Census.

TABLE 10. SUMMARY OF PROTESTANT DISSENTING DENOMINATIONS IN
BRISTOL AND GLOUCESTERSHIRE IN THE 1851 CENSUS

Denomination	Number of meetings
Baptist	100
Congregational	2
Countess of Huntingdon & Calvinistic Methodist	12
Independent	79
Independent & Baptist	3
Independent & Congregational	13
Methodist	202
Miscellaneous	21
Non-denominational	6
Quaker	12
Unitarian	6
TOTAL	*456*

---

[1] Munden, 1.23–1.31.

Bristol had 68 meeting-houses or chapels in a much-enlarged municipal borough area, or 30 in the old city of Bristol, including the Seamen's floating chapel, and there were 76 dissenters' meeting in the south Gloucestershire parishes formerly in Bristol diocese, three of which were in a room rather than a chapel; only two parishes had no dissenting meetings. St Philip & St Jacob with 13 meetings and St George with 12 remained, as earlier, most strongly nonconformist;[1] Clifton with eight and Winterbourne with nine had significant dissenting populations, and 18 returns were made from Bitton.

Dissent was still prevalent in the clothing areas of Gloucestershire. Dursley and Stroud registration districts had 67 nonconformist meetings; Bisley had nine, more than were returned in other parishes in the area, Stroud had seven. In the Severn Vale, Cheltenham, with a population half that of Bristol, had 18 dissenting places of worship; the city of Gloucester, only a quarter the size of Bristol, had 11. The registration districts in the north of the county had the fewest, matching the relatively small numbers of certificates registered. The returns suggest that certificates and registrations do substantiate generalisations on the prevalence of dissent in particular areas.

Overall, a big increase in dissent is evident between 1825, when Bishop Bethel surveyed Gloucester diocese, and the 1851 census returns. It appears that many who had met in private houses in 1825 had built chapels by 1851, and in the intervening quarter century a significant number of new meetings had been established, followed by chapel building. In 1825 there were 164 chapels and 50 houses or rooms used for meetings, and dissenters in 120 of the 318 parishes and chapelries (two fifths). In 1851, in the same area of Gloucester diocese, there were 318 dissenting chapels and eight meetings in houses, in 158 parishes.[2]

Some incumbents replying to the 1851 census noted that dissent was not parochial. The vicar of Frampton-on-Severn commented that 'No reliance can be placed on the return from the dissenting place of worship in this parish. More than half of the congregation are collected from the parishes of Saul, Fretherne etc and the very same persons attend elsewhere on the very same Census day to swell the ranks of dissent in other parishes'. In fact it appears from the returns that on census Sunday dissenters were not swelling the meeting in Frampton-on-Severn.[3] The minister of Shortwood Baptist Meeting-house drew attention in a long note to the scattered nature of his congregation, 'so that generally not many more than about half of the persons who really belong to the congregation . . . are present at one and the same time'.[4]

---

[1] One entry for Ebenezer chapel, one for Lower Easton chapel, and one for Baptist Mills chapel in St Philip & Jacob or St George's are duplicated in the Bristol returns: Munden.
[2] Analysis using Munden.
[3] Munden, 5–6.
[4] Munden, 229.

VI. CONCLUSIONS

There is a large amount of evidence in the dissenters' meeting-house certificates and registrations between 1689 and 1852. It is clear that in many places, dissent was a movement of house-churches, informal and flexible. Meetings might be held in the kitchen, in an upstairs room, or in a barn. In the early years, dissenters chose not to advertise their existence by building a prominent meeting-house in a main street; only the 'ever-reckless Quakers' built a meeting-house and rebuilt it if it was pulled down.[1] Early meeting-houses were modest, like the Quaker meeting-house in Broad Campden, converted from two bays of housing. A house in Blakeney was adapted for the growing Baptist congregation by making a gallery of the upper room and a large timber-framed house in Tewkesbury, adapted by the Baptists in the same way, survives as a notable example, but most such alterations have disappeared.[2] There was a change in attitude in the 19th century, evident in the imposing and ecclesiastical-style chapels which were built in many places. In a number of cases the certificates and registrations allow the progression from house meeting to chapel building to be tracked. Chapel-building went with greater freedom to advertise their dissent, with political protest, and with growing formal organisation. It also appears as a sign of social status as it had been for traditional Church of England squires and gentry. Denominational rivalry has also been suggested as a spur to chapel building.[3]

Despite the evidence presented here, it is apparent that many meetings and chapels were either not registered, or the certificates and registrations are lost, in addition to the obvious loss of Bristol records. The Gloucester diocesan registrar drew attention to one such loss: he noted in May 1809 'Treddington cert registered May 1809 but by mistake sent out before it was copied' [**1776**]. It seems possible that many meetings were so informal that registration as places of 'religious worship' did not appear necessary. It was also the practice for branch meetings to be established, as in Arlington in Bibury, mentioned above, and this may have seemed to obviate the need to register the subsidiary meeting. Only where there was a diligent or authoritarian clergyman or justice of the peace were the people at such meetings punished, the Quakers particularly. There are later examples. A cottager in Cheltenham who allowed a prayer meeting to take place in his cottage in 1811 was fined £20 by the justices of the peace because the meeting was not licensed, and when he could not pay the fine, was put in prison; those attending the meeting were each fined 5s.[4] Another reason for non-registration may have been that when a chapel was built on part of a site where a house meeting had been registered, even if many years earlier, it was not seen as

---

[1] Watts 1999, 303.
[2] *See Nonconformist chapels and meeting-houses, Gloucestershire* (RCHM 1986) 98–100. Horlick 'A visit to the Forest of Dean'.
[3] Watts 1999, 601, 603–4: 'Even the Primitive Methodists were abandoning their cottages and converted barns for purpose-built chapels'.
[4] Ansell, 5.

necessary to apply again for a licence.[1] Some meetings may not have been considered as 'dissenting' from the Church of England in their theology and these may not have been deemed to fall within the provisions of the Toleration Act.

In many places there were early dissenting congregations, but then no extension of nonconformity until the early 19th century, when the striking spread of dissent fuelled the concern of the bishops about the condition of the Church of England. Population growth, changes in economic structure, the work of individual evangelisers and increases in literacy all contributed. Dissenting organisations were important entrepreneurs of literacy, opening Sunday schools before organising religious meetings; teaching the young brought their families into the dissenting community; preaching meetings, which probably did not need the permission of the authorities, were established in school rooms. The history of the congregational church in Pucklechurch started with the establishment of a 'Sabbath school' in 1816 by the Bristol Itinerant Society, which had been founded in 1811 to open Sunday schools in villages surrounding Bristol and distribute religious tracts; the school moved from cottage to cottage and not until 1841 was a formal 'church' founded and another four years passed before the Itinerant Society was able to buy a piece of land and erect a chapel.[2] None of these events is recorded in certificates.

Dissent was individualistic; it demonstrated the personal decisions of those who joined with other like-minded men and women to meet and worship 'in their own way'. Almost two-thirds of the members of dissenting congregations were women and considerable numbers were certifiers of meetings.[3] It was not uncommon for some members of a household to attend the Anglican church and others a dissenting meeting.[4] The tendency for dissenting congregations to split and create new meetings also demonstrates evident individualism. In the nineteenth century, however, ministers were largely reponsible for submitting certificates for registration, suggesting less democratic foundations of these later dissenting groups.

Dissenters' meetings were a basic challenge to the authority of church and parish. The parochial framework was intentionally not relevant to a dissenting congregation, and their lack of formal organisation on the pattern of the Church of England was one of the reasons they incurred the hostility of the clergy and of people like Lord Sidmouth. The greater formality and administrative oversight of the 19th century altered the nature of dissent.

---

[1] For a possible example see entry **1674**.
[2] GA D8697 1/1: Pucklechurch Congregational Church Book. *See also* lvii above.
[3] Field, 94–100; Watts, 1978, 357, suggests weekday meetings during the hours of daylight tended to exclude men who were at work then.
[4] See for example GA D566/Z/11, a listing of households in Tetbury with numbers attending Presbyterian, Baptist or Quaker meetings; 41 households were split between denominations.

EDITORIAL METHOD

Some editors of dissenters' meeting-house certificates and registrations have opted for a simple calendar, as in the Bedfordshire volume; others offer a full transcript, as in Berkshire. The Wiltshire volume lies mid-way between the two, and the present edition too is a compromise, as explained further below.

Applications for licences started by addressing the 'Honourable Justices of the Peace at the General Quarter Sessions', or with a salutation to 'the Right Reverend and Father in God', naming the bishop concerned, and sometimes also naming the Archdeacon. These prologues have generally been omitted. The citation of the Toleration Act is also omitted or occasionally shortened where the form is of interest, as when the writer of the petition of 1738 from the 'out parish' of St Philip & St Jacob near Bristol cited very precisely 'an act of parliament passed the 24th day of May Anno 1689 in the first year of the reign of the late King William & Queen Mary' while the apothecary of Kemerton in 1800 simply referred to 'the Toleration Act'.[1]

All meetings recorded here were of groups of Protestant dissenters. References to 'His Majesty's Protestant Dissenting subjects' or 'Protestants dissenting from the Church of England' and similar descriptions are omitted, but occasionally the word 'dissenters' is needed to complete the sense of what follows. A denomination was often not recorded, the fact that the meeting was of Protestant dissenters being sufficient to comply with the Toleration Act. Where it is known that a minister belonged to a particular dissenting church, this information has been used to suggest that other meetings in which the minister was concerned were of that same denomination, and is indicated in square brackets. Legalistic verbiage such as 'do hereby', or, referring to the names of the certifiers, 'are hereunder subscribed' and similar phrases, are omitted or abbreviated. The certifiers' names are all given. Where their names were included in the text and were repeated below as signatories to the certificate, the names have not been repeated. Abbreviations, including of Christian names, have generally been expanded except where the expansion is uncertain. The location of meetings has been given in the original spelling, in inverted commas where not the standard spelling, but references to the county and diocese are generally omitted.

The dating of entries is not straightforward. Meetings of the Justices of the Peace took place four times a year and were dated by reference to the church's calendar: Epiphany (6 January), Easter (movable, March/April), Trinity (8 weeks after Easter, May/June) and Michaelmas (25 September). Until 1 January 1752 the year ran from 25 March to 24 March; dating by Epiphany and dates between 1 January and 25 March before 1752 record the Old Style year, and an indication of the New Style year is added.

With these caveats, the Gloucestershire text follows closely the wording in the original, and deviations are indicated in square brackets. Where unusual wording exists it has been given verbatim within inverted commas. The attempt has been

---

[1] GA Q/SR/1738/D 1; Q/SR/1800/B 15.

to give the full flavour of each entry and all relevant information, together with the many variations of phraseology, while condensing the entries to avoid much repetition.

Each entry here is preceded by an index number, the location in township or chapelry (where given) and parish, the date of the certificate and, in round brackets, the date of registration. The order is determined by registration date, or if not available then by certificate date. The text follows, and the names of the certifiers. Finally the source is given in round brackets, indicating volume number and page or folio number. Reference to Bristol or Gloucestershire Archives is not given for each entry, but Tables 4, 5, and 6 in this Introduction are the guide. The same format has been used to give the information in Lyon Turner's transcripts of licences under the Declaration of Indulgence of Charles II.

This edition provides an account of all surviving registrations of dissenters' meeting-houses or certificates requesting registration in the Bristol, Gloucester, and Gloucester and Bristol diocesan records and in Gloucestershire Quarter Sessions Order Books and papers. The registrations for Wiltshire parishes brought into the diocese of Gloucester and Bristol in 1836 were published in Chandler (1985); for the sake of completeness, most are listed with references to the published volume, with a small number transcribed in more detail.

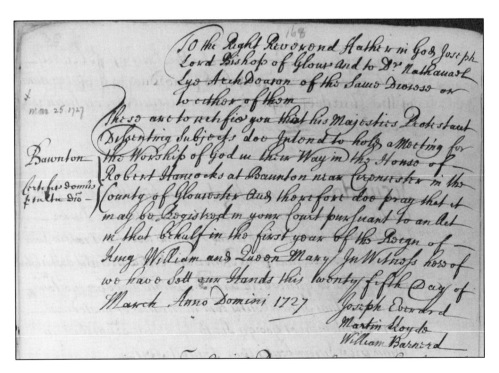

This certificate for Baunton [**225**] was one of the first to be registered by the bishop of Gloucester and includes the Latin rubric 'Certific[atio] domus pro cultu di[vin]o'. *GA*

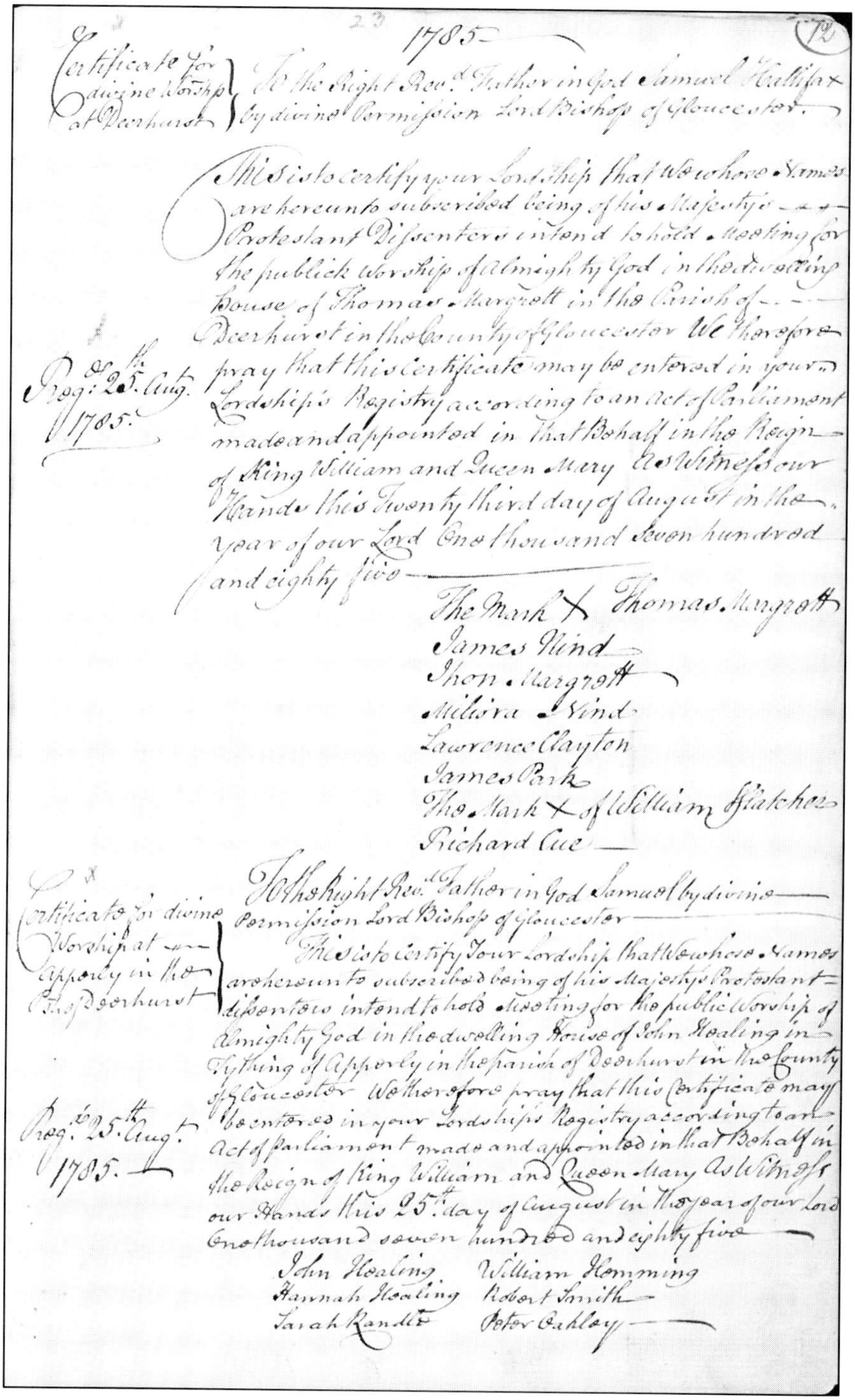

23

1785 — 72

Certificate for divine Worship at Deerhurst

To the Right Revd. Father in God Samuel Hallifax by divine Permission Lord Bishop of Gloucester.

This is to certify your Lordship that We whose Names are hereunto subscribed being of his Majesty's Protestant Dissenters intend to hold Meeting for the publick Worship of Almighty God in the dwelling House of Thomas Margrott in the Parish of Deerhurst in the County of Gloucester We therefore pray that this Certificate may be entered in your Lordship's Registry according to an Act of Parliament made and appointed in that Behalf in the Reign of King William and Queen Mary As Witness our Hands this Twenty third day of August in the year of our Lord One thousand Seven hundred and eighty five

Reg: 25th Aug. 1785.

The Mark X Thomas Margrott
James Hind
Jhon Margrott
Milsira Hind
Lawrence Clayton
James Park
The Mark X of William Fletcher
Richard Cue

Certificate for divine Worship at Apperly in the Parish of Deerhurst

To the Right Revd. Father in God Samuel by divine Permission Lord Bishop of Gloucester

This is to Certify Your Lordship that We whose Names are hereunto subscribed being of his Majestys Protestant Dissenters intend to hold Meeting for the public Worship of Almighty God in the dwelling House of John Healing in Tything of Apperly in the parish of Deerhurst in the County of Gloucester We therefore pray that this Certificate may be entered in your Lordships Registry according to an Act of parliament made and appointed in that Behalf in the Reign of King William and Queen Mary As Witness our Hands this 25th day of August in the year of our Lord One thousand seven hundred and eighty five

Reg: 25th Aug. 1785.

John Healing — William Hemming
Hannah Healing — Robert Smith
Sarah Randle — Peter Oakley

Two certificates [**702**, **703**] were written and registered on the same day in 1785 for different meetings in dwelling houses in the parish of Deerhurst. Two men in Apperley were unable to sign their names.

GA

The meeting in Lapley [**584**], in Coaley parish, was to be held in a dwelling house, 'the kitchen part of which is intended to be set apart for the same purpose in future'. *GA*

A rather pompously worded certificate [**1139**] for an Independent meeting in Marshfield refers to worship 'according to the dictates of our own Consciences and without any Molestation'.   *GA*

THE CERTIFICATES

BRISTOL CITY & COUNTY

The following list is of Presbyterian Nonconformist ministers living in Bristol 'contrary to the late Act of Parliament' (i.e. the Five Mile Act, 1665, which forbade a minister from living in the place from which he had been ejected, or where there was a corporation):

> *Mr Chroughton [Troughton, see **10**], Mr Ewins [Thomas Ewins, first minister of Broadmead church 1650], Mr Hazard [Matthew Hazard, ejected 1662 from St Mary Redcliffe and St Ewen's], Mr Taylor, Mr Voyle, Mr Blindman [Richard Blindman], Mr Hubbert, Mr Jennett, Mr Brock, Mr Griffin, Mr Paul [John Paule, ejected from St Paul's]. List endorsed Bristol 1666. (LT/182)*

The details of at least 11 nonconformist meetings for which application for a licence was made in 1672 following Charles II's Declaration of Indulgence are noted here. Although not preaching in Bristol, a licence was also requested for Dr Francis Cross of Bristol, Doctor of Physick, a Presbyterian, to preach in a house in the possession of Thomas Ford in Pensford, Somerset. (LT/361)

All registrations for meetings in the parish of St James and St Paul are included here. For St Philip & St Jacob see 'City of Bristol and County of Gloucester' immediately following the Bristol sequence. See Introduction, xxiv.

1 Bristol. 1672. *Congregational.* Application for Mr John Thompson, teacher in Bristol, 'of the congregational perswasion'; the meeting place in Castle Street there, belonging to the house of Mr Thomas Harris; licence recorded 16 Apr 1672. (LT/230, 433)

2 [St James], Bristol. 1672. *Presbyterian.* 'Licence desired' for the house of John Lloyde lying on St James Back, Bristol, to be a Presbyterian meeting place and for John Weekes to be a Presbyterian teacher in John Loyde's house. (LT/239, 240)

The petition is set out below.

> Bristol. 1672. Endorsed : 'Indulgence. Citty of Bristoll'.
>
> To our dread Sovereign Charles the Second by the grace of God King of England Scotland France and Ireland defender of the faith etc.
>
> The humble petition of your Majesty's faithful subjects in your city of Bristol. Most humbly showeth:
>
> That with many others of your Majesty's true hearted, non-conformist subjects in England who in every corner of the land, do sing for joy of heart, we also some of your Majesty's most faithfull subjects in Bristol, in the name of many more of our neighbours, do rise up, and call your Majesty blessed for your unparallelled grace expressed in your late declaration of Indulgence to us.
>
> Humbly praying your Majesty for the benefit of this gracious Indulgence in your city of Bristol, and that the house of Mr John Loyde, lying on St James Back in the said city, may be allowed to Mr John Weekes, of the Presbyterian persuasion, whom we have chosen for our teacher there; for which your Royal grace as we shall every way be obliged to aquit our selves with such moderation, fidelity, and peaceablenes as never to give your Majesty any cause of offence, so we shall continue to pray for your

1

Majesty's prosperity in length of days, and life for ever more. [Autograph signatures] John Tucker, Richard Payne, Michaell Pope, Hugh Whyte, William Salmon, William Willoughby. (LT/244)

Note. Revd John Weekes was the first accredited minister of the Ancient Society of Protestant Dissenters at Lewins Mead [*see* **16**] (BA/39461/PM/14). The original licence was preserved at the chapel at Clifton Down built 1868.

3 Bristol. 1672. Four licences, for Bristol and 'Temple Combe', received 18 Apr 1672 by Joshua Churchill. (LT/246)

4 Bristol. 1672. *Congregational.* Application by Mr Jeremy Holwey 10 May 1672 for [his] house in 'Cornstreet in Bristoll' for one that is licensed of the congregational persuasion. (LT/328)

5 Bristol. 1672. *Presbyterian.* Licence recorded 10 Jun 1672 to Sam Winney to be a Presbyterian teacher in his house at 'Glastry, Bristol'. (LT/501)

Note. Lyon Turner (819) quotes Calamy's record that Samuel Winney lived in Bristol, but was ejected from Glastonbury.

6 Bristol. 1672. *Congregational.* Licence rcorded 5 Sept 1672 to Enock Gray of the city of Bristol to be a Congregational teacher. (LT/553)

7 St James. 1672. *Presbyterian.* Licence recorded for the house of Simon Tovy of St James parish in Bristol. (LT/560)

Note. A comment in LT/III 839 says Simon Tovy was 'a decided Baptist'. Simon Tovey's house was noted as a meeting-house in the 1670 Hearth Tax return [information from Jonathan Barry].

8 Bristol. 1672. *Presbyterian.* Licence recorded 5 Sept 1672 for the house of John Ceager in the city of Bristol. (LT/560)

9 Bristol. 1672. *Presbyterian.* Licence recorded 5 Sept 1672 to Andrew Jifford [Gifford] of the city of Bristol, Presbyterian teacher. (LT/560)

Note. A comment in LT/3, 839 claims that Andrew Jifford was a Baptist; he himself altered the denomination given in the Licence.

10 Bristol. 1672. *Congregationl.* Licence recorded 30 Sept 1672 to William Troughton to be a Congregational teacher at his own house in 'Phillip Street 'in the city [of] Bristol. (LT/562)

11 Bristol. 1672. *Presbyterian.* Licence recorded 28 Oct 1672 to Francis Fuller of the city of Bristol to be a general Presbyterian teacher. (LT/561, 572)

12 St James. 20 Jan 1755. We [named below], intending to hold a meeting for the worship of God at a house known by the name of the Tabernacle, situate in Penn Street in the Old Orchard in the parish of St James in the city of Bristol, desire it may be registered. Francis Labee, Nathaniel Wathen, William Robert Comfort, John William, William Small, Thomas Britton, Jos Shewring, Samuel Johnston, Abel Dagger, Francis Collins snr, Godfrey Fownes, Daniel Drake. (EP/A/45/1/8)

13 [Temple]. 13 Nov 1764 (20 Nov 1764). *Independent.* We [named below] being willing and desirous that the house called the Tuckers Hall in Temple Street in the city of Bristol may be appropriated and confirmed as a place of religious worship of Almighty God for dissenters commonly called Independents, being well affected to His Majesty King George III, have hereunto set our hands this 13 Nov 1764. Samuel Holloway, James Norton, Humphry Rendell, Thomas Nevitt, John Tyly, William Hughs, David Lloyd, John Yeates, Charles Henry, James Doyle, George Tizard. (EP/A/45/1/52)

14 St James. 6 Aug 1779 (14 Aug 1779). *Independent.* We whose names are hereunto subscribed being part of a congregation of dissenters hereby certify that an house situate in the 'Quakers Fryers' in the parish of St James in the city and your lordship's diocese of Bristol, commonly called the Bakers Hall, is intended or set apart for a meeting place of a congregation under the denomination of Independents. We therefore request and desire the same may be registered. William Brooksbank minister, Robert Hesketh, George Thomas, Philip Marks, Thomas Hillier, Thomas Dale, Richard Jones, Samuel Rees, William Morrill. (EP/A/45/1/106)

15 Temple. 6 Aug 1785. We [named below] certify that we have reared and set apart a room situate in Temple Street in the parish of Temple, otherwise Holy Cross, in the city and diocese of Bristol, over an Almshouse commonly called the Clothworkers Company's Almshouse, as a place of a meeting for religious worship and pray that the said room may be recorded. Joseph Hoskins, John Wall, John Browne, William Browne, Benjamin King, John Withington, Rees Harris, John Evans, John Parker, John Arnold, Joseph Gatward, Mary Ann Goodman, Ann Pile jnr, Mary Pill. (EP/A/45/1/156)
Note. Date 'entered' was not noted. RG/31/2 has registered 6 Aug 1785.

16 St Michael and St James. 27 Aug 1791 (1 Sept 1791). We, Thomas Wright and John Prior Estlin, whose names are hereunto subscribed, being ministers, teachers and preachers in a congregation of [dissenters], and several other persons whose names are also hereunto subscribed, being part of the said congregation, certify that a new erected building in a street or place called 'Lewin's Mead', within the several parishes of St Michael and St James in the said city of Bristol and in your Lordship's diocese, is intended and set apart for and to be used as a place of meeting for religious worship . We therefore desire that the same may be registered. Thomas Wright, Thomas Prior Estling [*sic*], ministers, teachers and preachers in the above congregation, Richard Bright, James Harvey, John Wright M.D., John Edge, Joseph Hall, I G Harris, Arthur Palmer, Thomas Andrewes, John Fry jnr, Levi Ames, George Gibbs, Robert Bruce, R Hall, Orton Smith, Brooke Smith, William Inman, L J Jardine, George Webb Hall, Jo Lloyd; witness Arthur Palmer Attorney at law Bristol. (EP/A/45/1/245-46)
Note. This was the second Meeting-house of the Ancient Society of Protestant Dissenters in Lewin's Mead, erected on the site of the first Meeting-house of 1694. In the early 19th century it was regarded as Unitarian, although Rules and Regulations agreed in October 1936 were still using the traditional name. (BA/3946251/PM/14; *Nonconformist chapels* (RCHM), 70-2) [*See* **2**]

17 St James. 24 Jun 1795 (27 Jun 1795). We [named below] desire that the chapel newly erected in King Street in the parish of St James in the city may be registered among the records of the Bishop's court as a chapel set apart for the worship of God and religious exercise for dissenters. Jon Crowther, Robert Chidgey, William Hunt, James Ewer, Robert Boley. (EP/A/45/1/265).

18 St Augustine the Less. 30 Oct 1802. We [named below] humbly request that the place set apart for the worship of Almighty God in St Augustine's Place in the parish of St Augustine the Less in the city of Bristol may be registered and a certificate thereof granted. Thomas Young minister, Isaac Amos, Thomas Stevens, William Gardener, Thomas Taylor, Thomas Pickett, Christopher Slade, Thomas Blinsman. (EP/A/45/1/332–3)

19 St John the Baptist. 20 Feb 1804 (3 Mar 1804). *Independent.* We [named below], dissenters of the Independent denomination, have set apart a dwelling house, in the occupation of John Gregory, carpenter, in Christmas Street in the parish of St John the Baptist within your lordship's diocese for the worship of Almighty God and we pray the said dwelling house may be registered and a certificate granted us. Thomas Curtis minister, Samuel Westlake, James Westlake, William Heard, John Sears, John Wall, William Penney, John Gregory. (EP/A/45/1/345)

20 St James. 17 Oct 1804 (10 Nov 1804). *Independent.* We [named below] dissenters of the Independent denomination, have set apart a dwelling house in the occupation of Samuel Westlake, 'taylor', in Montague Street, in the parish of St James within your lordship's diocese for the worship of Almighty God and we pray the said dwelling house may be registered and a certificate granted us. Thomas Curtis minister, Thomas Gwyther, William Heard, John Sears, J S Fox, James Berry, Samuel Westlake. (EP/A/45/1/351)

21 St Stephen. 10 Nov 1804 (21 Nov 1804). We [named below] being part of a congregation of [dissenters] certify that part of a dwelling house in King Street within the parish of St Stephen in the city of Bristol, in the occupation of John Seilly, is set apart for and to be used as a place of meeting for religious worship. We therefore desire that this same may be registered. William Pealy, Jonathan Hands, Charles Stowe, Philip van Dyk, William Francis, J Ellis, A Smith, Samuel Dean minister, S Whittingham, John Eager, George Lewis, Henry Roberts, J N Cossham, Evan Lewis. (EP/A/45/1/352)

22 St Paul. 1 Aug 1805. *Independent.* Those [named below] wishing to meet for the worship of Almighty God in a place situate in 'Corlo Hill Street' [Callowhill Street] in the parish of St Paul, Bristol, known by the name of Providence chapel of the denomination of dissenters called 'Independants', earnestly request your Lordship to permit the same to be registered and to grant a certificate of the same. John Hues, Bettey Coombe, Jane Musgrove, Mary Emans, Eliza Duggan, Lydia Evans, Sarah Phillips, Hester Williams, Mary Lansdown, L W Underwood minister, Jeremiah Grant, Walter Duggan jnr, Joseph Blake, Jacob Hambly, Bartholomew Coombe, Enoch Lloyd, Shamis Hall, Henry Newman, Margaret Bell. (EP/A/45/1/357)
Note. Difficult & small writing. William Sherring built Callowhill Meeting-house before 1758 (BA/5918/18).

23 St Stephen. 9 Jan 1806 (10 Jan 1806). In pursuance of an act of parliament' issued forth in the first year of K W & Q M' [*sic*] We [named below] desire the house of Thomas Jeffery Safford in the parish of St Stephens in the city of Bristol may be registered among the records of the city as set apart for the worship of God and religious exercise. Thomas Jeffery Safford, Samuel Williams, William Burleigh, Ely Mills minister, Richard Hurley. (EP/A/45/1/358)

24 [St Mary Redcliffe]. 29 Oct 1808 (3 Nov 1808). *Independent.* In virtue of an act of parliament, passed in the reign of King William & Queen Mary for the toleration of Protestants dissenting from the Church of England, it is requested that a room formerly possessed by Mr Long, teacher in the house of Mrs Sadgebar, No. 6 'Redclift' Street, Bristol, be registered as a place of public worship of Almighty God for dissenters of the Independent denomination for the benefit of legal toleration according to the intent of the aforesaid act. John Dove, William Heard, George Smith, Ann Sadgebeer, proprietor of the house. (EP/A/45/1/420)

25 St James. 19 Oct 1809 (28 Oct 1809). In pursuance of an act of parliament we [named below] desire that the Drawing Room in the house of Miss Elizabeth Lorain in Union Street in the parish of St James in the city of Bristol may be registered among the records of this city as a room set apart for the worship of God and religious exercise. Elizabeth

Lorain, H Perkins minister, John Viner, William House, John Parkinson, Stephen Allen. (EP/A/45/2/20)

26 St Leonard. 11 Nov 1809 (17 Nov 1809). We [named below] being part of a congregation of dissenters, certify that the front room of the second story of a dwelling house in Baldwin Street in the parish of St Leonard, now in the occupation of Frederick Young, is set apart as a place of meeting for religious worship. We desire that the same may be registered. Frederick Young. Benjamin Baker, John Hyatt, Thomas Smith, Henry James, Charles James Fox, John Bond, John Baker, John Hill, James Griffiths, John Johnson, Francis Bird. (EP/A/45/2/21)

27 St Paul. 30 Nov 1809 (9 Dec 1809). We [named below beg leave to acquaint your Lordship that Gideon Chapel in the parish of St Pauls in the city is intended for the worship of Almighty God. We pray that the chapel may be registered and a certificate granted. John Pearce, Archibald Rankelor, George Ridout, William B Wiltshaw, dissenting minister, John Hughes, Robert White, Thomas Howland. (EP/A/45/2/28-9)

28 Temple. 17 Mar 1810 (21 Mar 1810). We [named below] being part of a congregation of dissenters humbly certify that a certain new erected building situate standing and being in a certain street or place called 'The Counter Slip', near Temple Street within the parish of Temple, otherwise Holy Cross, in the city of Bristol is set apart as a place of meeting for religious worship. We desire that the same may be registered. Joseph Seymour minister, William Tyler, deacon, Richard Alcock, Daniel Driver, Thomas Wire, Soloman Leonard, Isaac Leonard, J Tommas, E C Shoard, Robert Shoard, William Watts, Thomas Overbury, Samuel Rennolds, Jacob Riddle, Peter Copley, John Bingham, Thomas Phillips, George Gould, Jeptha Riddle, George Kelson, William Hicks, William Cherry, William Davies. (EP/A/45/2/29-30)

29 Temple. 12 Apr 1813 (21 Apr 1813). We [named below] being part of a congregation of dissenters certify that the lower room or ground floor of a dwelling house in Water Lane in the parish of Temple, otherwise Holy Cross, now in the occupation of James Glyde, is to be a place of meeting for religious worship. We desire that the same may be registered. Minister presiding William Rennolds; John Spears, John Wall, Michael Pratten, John King, Moses Reynolds James Blackstock, James Glyde. (EP/A/45/2/63)

30 St Stephen. 20 Dec 1814 (20 Dec 1814). I Christopher Slade residing in Bath Street in the parish of St Thomas in the city and county of Bristol, carrying on the trade of saddler, certify that a building known by the name of the Assembly Room in Princes Street in the parish of St Stephen, in the city and county of Bristol, is forthwith to be a place of religious worship and request you to register the same. (EP/A/45/2/91)

31 [Castle Precincts]. (5 June 1817). We [named below] have taken a room of Messrs Mark & Benjamin Pratten, for the worship of God, situated at No 78 [Castle Street as in heading] in the city of Bristol. We request a licence that we may worship as peaceable subjects without molestation. Mark Pratten; witness Charles Pratten; William Payne, William Rogers, Joseph Wallis, James Brooks, Philip Loader, William House. (EP/A/45/2/106-7)

32 St Nicholas. 8 Aug 1817 (8 Aug 1817). We [named below] certify that a room in the parish of St Nicholas in Nicholas Street in the city of Bristol, in the possession of Mr Wayland, Redcliff Street, Bristol, is to be a chapel for religious worship and we request that this certificate may be registered. Thomas Wayland, Thomas Thorp, Thomas Lane, James Thornton. (EP/A/45/2/108)

33 [St Mary Redcliffe]. (2 Jan 1818). We [named below] have taken a room of Mr James Wansborough, 142 Redcliffe Street in the city of Bristol, for the worship of God. We request of your Lordship a licence that we may worship God as peaceable subjects without molestation. James Wansborough, Joseph Wallis, William House, Charles Pratten, John Sage, William Pyne, Philip Leader. (EP/A/45/2/109)

34 Kingsdown, St James. 3 June 1819 (4 Jun 1819). We [named below] certify that a house, 36 St James' Place, Kingsdown, in the out-parish of St James, the property of James Weekes esq, Westbury, occupied by H C Howells, is forthwith to be a place of religious worship and I request you to register the same. H C Howells, E Bath, H James. (GDR/334B/260)

35 St Augustine the Less. 1 June 1819 (8 June 1819). We [named below] certify that a building in Great George Street, in the parish of St Augustine the Less in the county of the city of Bristol is to be used as a chapel for religious worship and we request that this certificate may be registered. Thomas C Cowan, Peter Shorland, Thomas Combes, Thomas H Cook. (EP/A/45/2/120)
Note. RG/31/2 has certifier 'Edward Cowan'.

36 St James. 5 June 1819 (10 July 1819). We [named below] certify that a house at the bottom of Grangers Court otherwise Aldens Court, 'Broad Mead' [Broadmead] in the parish of St James in the city of Bristol, the property of Joseph Alden, saddler, Broad Mead, is to be a place for the worship of God and we require you to register the same. H C Howell, E Bath, John Williams. (EP/A/45/2/121)

37 St James. 25 Sept 1819 (2 Oct 1819). We [named below] certify part of a dwelling house in Silver Street in the parish of St James in the city of Bristol, now in the occupation of Evan Lewis, pawn broker, is to be a place of meetings for religious worship and we request the same may be registered and require a certificate thereof. Joseph Enoch, minister, William Stewart, Jonathan Hands, George Smith, William Brison, John Docksey, David Harris, Thomas Short, Rees Hughes, Thomas Lane, James Marychurch, Robert Turner, Evan Lewis, James Farr. (EP/A/45/2/123)

38 Bristol Harbour. 27 Feb 1822 (28 Feb 1822). We [named below] 'beg leave to certify that a ship has been fitted up as a place of worship called the Seaman's chapel and now lying in the Bristol Harbour and which is requested to be registered in the Bishop's court in the city of Bristol.' Thomas Roberts, Stephen Prust, Alexander S Corrick, James Rees, William Tapsel, John Jenkins, Robert May, G C H Ashmead, John Foster, W D Price, T Butter, Thomas Price. (EP/A/45/2/148) [*see* illus., xviii]

39 Castle Precincts. 1 Jan 1823 (2 Jan 1823). *Welsh Independent.* We [named below] certify that a building called the Welsh Independent chapel in Lower Castle Street within the Castle Precincts is to be a Meeting-house for religious worship by dissenters of the denomination of Independents and request that the certificate may be registered. Herbert Herbert, Josiah Francis, John Jones, Enoch James, Evan Davies, John Griffiths. (EP/A/45/2/176)

40 St James. 30 Nov 1822 (3 Jan 1823). We [named below] certify that part of a dwelling house in the Horse Fair in the parish of St James within the city of Bristol, now in the occupation of Joseph Enoch, schoolmaster, is to be a place of meeting for religious worship and we humbly request that the same may be registered and require a certificate thereof. Joseph Enoch, minister, Thomas Jones, Thomas Hooper, Richard Harris, John

Williams, John Wright, Samuel Winterson, W W Walker, James Marychurch, A G Hunt, Emanuel Billinge, William Lane. (EP/A/45/2/177)

41 St John [the Baptist]. 13 May 1823 (14 May 1823). I Samuel Smith of the city of Bristol, gentleman, certify that a late messuage or dwelling house heretofore used as a chapel or place for religious worship, now in the occupation of Samuel Slack and William Slack, in a court called Taylors Court in the parish of St John in the city of Bristol, bounded on the westward side by a warehouse late in the occupation of Messrs Stanton & Co but now void and on the eastward side by a warehouse, in the occupation of Jonathan Nash, is to be hereafter a place or chapel for religious worship. (EP/A/45/2/178)

42 St Paul. 10 June 1823 (11 June 1823) *Baptist*. We [named below] certify that a building in Stokes Croft in the parish of St Paul in the city of Bristol called the Baptist Academy, now the property of the Bristol Education Society, is to be a Meeting-house for religious worship by dissenters of the denomination of Baptists and we request that this certificate may be registered. A Livett jnr, J E Ryland, James Livett. (EP/A/45/2/178-79)

43 St James. 19 July 1824 (19 July 1824). I James Bonser of Stroudwater in the parish of Stroudwater in the county of Gloucester certify that a room and premises at Bridewell Lane in the parish of St James in the county of Bristol, now in [my] holding and occupation, are to be a place of religious worship and I request you to register the same and request a certificate thereof for which shall be taken no more than 2 shillings and 6 pence. (EP/A/45/2/197)

44 St Augustine [the Less]. 3 Nov 1824 (5 Nov 1824). *Baptist.* We [named below] 'humbly and respectfully solicit your Lordship to grant a Licence for Zion chapel built for the sole purpose of worshiping God as Protestant Baptists situated in [heading states St Augustine's Back] St Augustine's parish in the city of Bristol'. George Gray, minister, Thomas Pasmore, deacon, Maudlin Lane, George Edy, William Tilly, George Webb, William Wells, John Heath. (EP/A/45/2/203)

45 St Paul. 10 Jan 1828 (18 Jan 1828). I Joseph James of the city of Bristol, painter, certify that a room in my dwelling house, being No 5 in Orange Street in the parish of St Paul in the city of Bristol, is forthwith to be a place of religious worship and I require you to register the same and request a certificate thereof. Joseph James; witness W Weston, Robert Cox, John Johns. (EP/A/45/2/237)

46 St Paul. 17 Jan 1828 (18 Jan 1828) I Sarah Stone of the city of Bristol, widow, certify that a room in my dwelling house, being No 14 Wilder Street in the parish of St Paul in the city of Bristol, is forthwith to be a place of religious worship and I require you to register the same and request a certificate thereof. Sarah Stone (mark), John Price, John Stone, George Read; witness John Palmer, Thomas Rogers. (EP/A/45/2/238) *5002*
Note. The names of John Price etc follow Sarah Stone's on right hand side of page, and the two witness names are on the left hand side.

47 St James. 18 Feb 1829 (25 Feb 1829). *Baptist.* We [named below] certify that a building in King Street in the parish of St James in the city of Bristol 'in the possession or occupation of a Society of Protestants commonly called Baptists' are intended to be used as a chapel, vestry and school room for religious worship and we request that this certificate may be registered. Thomas Roberts, minister; deacons: Joseph Whittuck, John Hart, Thomas Clark, Isaac Stephens, Thomas Pewters . (EP/A/45/2/257–8)

48 St Mary Redcliffe. 1829 (2 Oct 1829). I Thomas Piercy of the parish of St Mary Redcliffe in the city of Bristol certify that a house in [my] occupation in the same parish is forthwith to be used as a place of religious worship and I require you to register the same and request a certificate thereof. (EP/A/45/2/267)

49 St Mary Redcliffe. 5 June 1830 (7 June 1830). We [named below] certify that a chapel lately erected in Coronation Road and Bedminster Parade in the parish of St Mary Redcliffe in the city of Bristol is about to be used and occupied as a chapel or place for divine worship and request that your Lordship will cause the same to be registered. John Hare, Robert Leonard, James Livett. (EP/A/45/2/269-70)

50 St Augustine [the Less]. 15 Aug 1831 (5 Aug 1831). *Countess of Huntingdon's Connexion.* We [named below] beg to inform your Lordship that it is our wish and intention to use the building lately erected at the bottom of Lodge Street in the parish of St Augustine in the city of Bristol (hereafter to be named the Countess of Huntingdon's Chapel) as a place of worship for Almighty God and I shall feel obliged by its being enrolled in your Lordship's court. William Lucy, John S Lewis, Charles Carpenter, James Stallard, E W Slade, Joseph Holdway, William Collings, William Wilkins. (EP/A/45/2/311)

51 Temple. (24 July 1833). *Christian Revivalists.* We [named below] request that premises in Bear Lane in the parish of Temple or Holy Cross in the city of Bristol, now occupied by the Revd Thomas Piercey as tenant and preacher, be registered in a regular form for that purpose under the name or title of the Christian Revivalists. Members of the society of the above chapel: James Johnson, landlord, Thomas Piercey preacher, Joseph Day assisting preacher; John Knaggs, Christopher James, William Fackrett, Joseph Wite, Benjamin Lapping, Thomas Rowe, Joseph Wilson, Theodore James, William Jones, Lewis Hiley, Robert Winter, Richard Waldron, Joseph Spraggs. (EP/A/45/2/397)

52 [Castle Precincts]. 7 Aug 1833 (10 Aug 1833). We [named below] part of a congregation of dissenters, certify that a room on the ground floor of a house in Castle Green, in the occupation of Mr Brennan, is set apart and to be used a a place of meeting for religious worship. We desire that the same may be registered. Members: S Merrifield, James Tucker, Betsy Merifield, Dinah Tucker (mark); V F D Arey Brennan, minister; M A S Parker, H W Parker deaconesses. (EP/A/45/2/397-98)

53 [Castle Precincts]. 1 Aug 1834 (1 Aug 1834). We [named below] part of a congregation of dissenters, certify that a room on the first floor of a house, No 61 Castle Street, in the occupancy of Revd V F D A Brennan, is set apart and to be used as a place of religious worship. We desire that the same may be registered. Ann Ellis, Thomas Hemmings, Mary Hemmings, William W Ellis, V F D A Brennan, pastor, M A F D A Brennan. (EP/A/45/2/403)

54 St Paul. 4 September 1834 (8 Sept 1834). We [named below] being part of a congregation of dissenters, humbly certify that a new erected building in or near a certain square called Brunswick Square in the parish of St Paul in the city of Bristol, is set apart and to be used as a public place of meeting for dissenters. We desire that the same may be registered. Robert Fletcher, William Armstrong, John E Linell, Alfred Day, Luke Arnold, George Davies. (EP/A/45/2/383)

55 St Stephen. 21 Jan 1835 (21 Jan 1835). I Thomas King of the parish of St Stephens in the city of Bristol certify that a room in my dwelling house, No 44 Prince [*sic*] Street, city of Bristol, is forthwith to be a place of religious worship and I require you to register the same and request a certificate thereof. Thomas King, Thomas Morris, Samuel Morris, William Harris, James Owen. (EP/A/45/2/415)

56 St Paul. 29 Apr 1835 (29 Apr 1835). We [named below] part of a congregation of dissenters, certify that a newly erected building called Brunswick chapel, in or near Brunswick Square in the parish of St Paul in the city of Bristol, is set apart and to be used as a public place of meeting for dissenters. We desire that the same may be registered. Robert Fletcher, William Armstrong, John E Linell, Samuel Ware, George Davies, Joseph Rider. (EP/A/45/2/422)
Note. The original of this certificate - identical in wording and signed – is in BA/38030/16, endorsed as registered 29 Apr 1835 and on back 'Brunswick Chapel. Bishop of Bristol Licence, obtained on the completion of the chapel. 29 Apr 1835'.

57 Temple. 1 May 1835 (1 May 1835). I George Underhill certify that a room in my house, No 108 Temple Street, Temple parish, city of Bristol, is to be a place of religious worship and request you to register the same and request a certificate thereof. George Underhill, Thomas Stephens, G W Gerrard, Philip Palmer. (EP/A/45/2/423)

58 St James. 30 Oct 1837 (30 Oct 1837). We [named below] part of a congregation of dissenters humbly certify that a building called Broadmead Meeting-house, in a street called Broadmead in the parish of St James in the city of Bristol, is set apart and used as a public place of meeting for religious worship. We desire that the same may be registered. Isaac Leonard, A Livett, Samuel Cary, R B Sherring, D Walters, Joseph Ash. (EP/A/45/2/548)

59 St Paul. 18 Sept 1839 (19 Sept 1838). I William Parry, of Upper Easton in the parish of St George in the county of Gloucester, certify that a dwelling house and premises at Houlston Street in the parish of St Paul in the city of Bristol, now in the holding and occupation of Mr James Hole, glazier, are to be used as a place of religious worship and I request you to register the same and request a certificate thereof for which shall be taken no more than 2 shillings and 6 pence. William Harvey, James Hole. (EP/A/45/2/592)

60 St Thomas. 9 Mar 1840 (9 Mar 1840). I William Harris of the city of Bristol certify that a house and premises in Thomas Street in the parish of St Thomas in the city of Bristol, now in my holding and occupation, is to be a place of religious worship and I request you to register the same and request a certificate thereof for which shall be taken no more than 2 shillings and 6 pence. William Harris, William Chilton, Peter M Evans. (EP/A/45/2/596)

61 St James. 16 Dec 1840 (17 Dec 1840). *Rational Religionists.* We John Field and Charles Brown of the city of Bristol certify that a house and premises in [our] occupation in Broadmead in the parish of St James in the city of Bristol is forthwith to be a place of religious worship by an assembly or congregation of Protestants called Rational Religionists and we require you to register the same and request a certificate thereof. William Chilton, William Harris, John Field, Charles Brown. (EP/A/45/3/25)

62 St Thomas. 3 Dec 1843 (23 Dec 1843). *Primitive Methodist.* I Edward Bishop of Upper Easton in the parish of St George in the county of Gloucester certify that a room and premises at 34 Thomas Street, in the parish of St Thomas in the city of Bristol, now in the holding and occupation of the Primitive Methodist Society, are to be used as a place of religious worship and I request you to register the same and request a certificate thereof for which shall be taken no more than 2 shillings and 6 pence. (EP/A/45/3/246)

63 St Michael. 13 May 1844 (14 May 1844). We [named below] certify that a building known by the name of Highbury Chapel on St Michael's Hill in the parish of St Michael in the city of

Bristol is used and occupied as a place of divine worship and we request your Lordship will cause the same to be registered. Richard Ash, Samuel Nowell, H O Wills. (EP/A/45/3/267)

64   Castle Precincts. 12 Aug 1844 (13 Aug 1844). I Richard Rawle of the city and county of Bristol certify a room in Castle Green in the Castle Precincts in the city and county of Bristol known as No 20 Castle Green is forthwith to be a place of religious worship and I request you to register the same and request a certificate of the same for which no more than 2 shillings and 6 pence is to be charged. Richard Rawle, Reubin Williams, owner, John Knowles, David Webb, Job Salter, Joseph Crook, William Irwin, John Roberts. (EP/A/45/3/271)

65   St Paul. 18 Apr 1845 (26 Apr 1845). *Baptist.* We [named below] certify that buildings in King Street in the parish of St Paul in the city and county of Bristol, in the possession or occupation of a society of protestants commonly called Baptists, are to be used as a chapel, vestry and school room for religious worship, and we request that this certificate may be registered. George Henry Davis, pastor; Thomas Clark, George C Ashmead, George Thomas, William Hamley, James Skinner, William Cross, Charles K Whittuck, deacons. (EP/A/45/3/358)

66   St Augustine [the Less]. 8 Oct 1845 (8 Oct 1845). I William Dimock of the city of Bristol certify that a room and premises at No 3 Lodge Street, in the parish of St Augustine, and now in [my] holding and occupation, are to be a place of religious worship and I request you to register the same and request a certificate thereof. (EP/A/45/3/372)

67   Wilder Street, Bristol. 21 July 1847. *Baptist.* Providence Chapel. William Hicks. (RG/31/2/f.129/v)
Note. No record has been found in Bristol Register of Records.

68   St Paul. (7 Dec 1848). We [named below] certify that a building formerly used as a workshop in York Street in the parish of St Paul in the city of Bristol is about to be used and occupied as a place of meeting for nonconformists and we request that you will cause the same to be registered. Joseph Stancomb, John Jewry, Henry Branscombe, Charles Ware, Francis Gillman, John Thompson, James Thompson, Henry Naish. (EP/A/45/3/468)
Note. Original signatures on sheet pasted in.

69   St Augustine [the Less]. (29 May 1849). We [named below] certify that a building known by the name of the Albert Rooms in College Green in the parish of St Augustine in the city of Bristol is used and occupied as a place of divine worship and we request you will cause the same to be registered. Minister J Panton Ham, W H Kembale, William Hughes. (EP/A/45/3/510)
Note. Loose sheet with signatures.

70   St Nicholas. (26 July 1849). We [named below] certify that a building known by the name of the Coopers Hall, King Street, in the parish of St Nicholas in the city of Bristol, is to be used and occupied as a place of divine worship and we request you will cause the same to be registered. J Panton Ham, minister, Charles Carpenter, Walter Hughes. (EP/A/45/3/516a)
Note. Loose certificate bound in and paginated later. Signed.

71   St Augustine the Less. 13 Aug 1849 (20 Aug 1849). 'Whereas a statute commonly called the Toleration Act was made in the first year of the reign of William and Mary [and] confirmed by 10 Anne c2 and by 52 George III c155. Now in compliance with the conditions of the aforesaid acts we [named below] certify that a building known as the Music Hall in Park Street Avenue in the parish of St Augustine the Less in the city and county of Bristol is to be used as a place of divine worship by Protestant dissenters 'holding the true Christian faith as declared in the first XIX articles of the Church of England' and we the undersigned on behalf of the said congregation notify the same in order that the aforesaid building may be registered. Robert Aitchison, Cotham Terrace, Bristol, George Woodfall, Preston Villa, Clifton, John Withy, 12 Frederick Place, Clifton'. (EP/A/45/3/520)

Note. Original sheet pasted on last page in volume 3 and signed. [*see* illus., xx]

72 [St Nicholas?]. 27 Feb 1850 (28 Feb 1850). *Wesleyan*. I Joseph Wood, Wesleyan minister residing at No 12 St James's Square, in Bristol, certify that a Wesleyan chapel called Ebenezer in Old King Street in the city of Bristol is used and is henceforth to be used as a place of religious worship and I require you to register the same. (EP/A/45/4/5)

Note. Certificate pasted in. Original signature but Wood did not write the certificate - there are others in this hand signed by different people.

73 St James. 19 June 1850 (20 June 1850). We [named below] certify that a building formerly used as a chapel, and now lately used as an ironmongery warehouse by Mr Timothy Bromhead, in Barton Street in the parish of St James, is about to be used and occupied as a place of meeting by certain Christians. We request that you will cause the same to be registered. John Jewry, Joseph Stancomb, Henry Naish. (EP/A/45/4/29)

Note. Loose sheet bound in with page 29 but not paginated.

74 [St Paul]. 29 Aug 1850 (31 Aug 1850). *Baptist*. We [named below] certify that a room in a dwelling house, No 42 Milk Street, in the city of Bristol, in the occupation of John Bavus is to be used and occupied as a place of divine worship by a congregation of Baptists 'Decenters', and we request you will cause the same to be registered. W S Short preacher, John Nott, Henry Thomas. (EP/A/45/4/34)

Note. Pasted in book and possibly original signatures.

75 Castle Precincts. 21 Sept 1850 (21 Sept 1850). *Wesleyan Methodists*. I, Samuel Mountain, certify that premises now held by me in No 57 Castle Street in the parish of Castle Precincts is forthwith to be a place of religious worship by a congregation of Wesleyan Methodists and I request you to register the same and request a certificate hereof. (EP/A/45/4/35)

Note. Pasted in book; original signature, if Mountain wrote the certificate. The Castle precincts were extra-parochial until 1858. (Youngs 165).

76 St George, Brandon Hill. 6 Nov 1850 (6 Nov 1850). *Wesleyan*. I Edward Horwood, accountant, of 69 Lime Kiln Lane, in the parish of St George in the city of Bristol, certify that a building, York Place, Lime Kiln Lane, in the parish of St George, Brandon Hill, in the city of Bristol, is set apart for religious worship by the Wesleyan denomination of Christians, and I solicit you to license the same as a place for divine worship. (EP/A/45/4/42) [*see* illus., xix]

Note. This is the first of four certificates pasted in two to a side turned sideways in the volume. Probably written and signed by Horwood.

77 St Augustine the Less. 14 Jan 1851 (15 Jan 1851). Whereas a statute commonly called the Toleration Act was made in the first year of the reign of William and Mary [and] confirmed by 10 Anne c2 and by 52 George III c155. Now in compliance with the conditions of the aforesaid acts we [named below] certify that a building, No 14 College Green, in the parish of St Augustine the Less in the city and county of Bristol is to be used as a place of divine worship by Protestant dissenters 'holding the true Christian faith' and we the undersigned, on behalf of the said congregation, notify the same in order that the aforesaid building may be registered. Robert Aitchison, Cotham Terrace, Bristol, George Woodfall, Preston Villa, Clifton. (EP/A/45/4/48)

Note. Almost identical wording to **71** of 20 Aug 1849 except no mention of 19 articles. Certificate pasted in. Signed.

78 St Thomas. 31 Oct 1851 (1 Nov 1851). I Joseph Manning of the city and county of Bristol certify that a large room, No 34 Thomas Street, in the parish of St Thomas in the city and county of Bristol and now in [my] holding and occupation, is forthwith to be a place of religious worship and I require you to register the same for which shall be received no more than 2 shillings and 6 pence. (EP/A/45/4/99)
Note. Certificate pasted in and signed if written by Manning.

79 St Luke. 16 Mar 1852 (16 Mar 1852). *Wesleyan Methodists.* I Sydney Sprod [Spratt] certify that a building erected by me at Barton Hill in the parish of St Luke in the city of Bristol is forthwith to be a place of religious worship by a congregation of Wesleyan Methodists and request you to register the same and request a certificate thereof. Sydney Spratt. (EP/A/45/4/127)
Note. One of 3 loose sheets bound in together and paginated but not pasted in. Clearly signed.

CITY OF BRISTOL AND COUNTY OF GLOUCESTER
ST PHILIP & ST JACOB
All meetings in the parish of St Philip & St Jacob, whether in-parish or out-parish, are gathered together here, including those for the parish of St George and the district of Holy Trinity, both drawn out of St Philip & St Jacob. The ecclesiastical district of Holy Trinity was created in 1834. See Introduction xxiv.

80 St Philip & St Jacob. 29 Nov 1701 (12 Feb 1701/2). We [named below] humbly certify to your Lordship that the dwelling house of Mr Gabriell Wayne, and being in the parish of 'St Phillipp and Jacob' in the county of Gloucester, is a fit and convenient place for the Protestant nonconformists living there and in other adjacent parts to meet together, and we pray that the same may be registered as such in the Consistory Court of the diocese of Gloucester. Thomas Wright, Edward White, Richard Leaker, Samuel Fox, Gabriel Wayne, William Vaughan, John Mitchell, Richard Lewis, William Wheeler. (GDR/248 154-5)

81 St Philip & St Jacob. 3 Oct 1738 (registered Michaelmas 1738, Q/SO/6/f.142v). *Quaker.* 'We whose names are subscribed request the Justices of the Peace at their general Quarter sessions for the county of Glocester to be held at Gloster the 3rd Oct 1738 To register a house commonly called the Quakers workhouse at the bottom of a street called New Street near Bristol in the county of Glocester as a meeting-house for the exercise of religious worship in the way of the Protestant dissenters called Quakers, and to grant a certificate thereof which will oblige your petitioners.' Thomas Frank, Thomas Daniels, N Champion, Jona[tha]n Nelsen. (Q/SR/1738/D1)

82 St Philip & St Jacob. 31 Oct 1754 (8 Feb 1755). These are to certify your Lordship that dissenters intend to hold a meeting for the worship of Almighty God in a new stone built house in George's Street in the parish of St Philip & St Jacob near the city of Bristol but in the county of Gloucester, and therefore desire the same may be registered according to the act of Toleration in that case made and provided. John Dolman, George Lovell, George Lane, John Robinson, James Hickes, William Owen, Charles Crump, William Cook. (EP/A/45/1/8) [*see* illus., xviii]
Note. The address of 'Dolman's chapel' was Eugene Street in 1842, *see* **113**.

83 St Philip & St Jacob. 8 July 1765 (9 July 1765). *Independent.* We [named below] commonly called Independents do hereby certify that we have reared and set apart a new built house in Lamb Street in the out-parish of St Philip & St Jacob in the county of Gloucester as a place of meeting for religious worship and pray that the said house may be recorded. George Tizard, I Luwelland, Moses Underwood, Joseph Hughes, William Tayler, James Squire, Henry Purrier, Richard Champion. (EP/A/45/1/53)

84 Pile Marsh, St George. 6 Dec 1795 (12 Dec 1795). *Independent.* The undersigned inhabitants of Pile Marsh in the parish of St George in the county of Gloucester and diocese of Bristol showeth That it is their desire that the house of David Williams in the village above named may be registered among the records of the Bishop's court as a house set apart for the worship of Almighty God according to the manner of that denomination called Independants. In testimony to the faith of the above we subscribe our names. David Williams (mark), Mathew Davis, Robert Henderson, William Thomas, S W Davis, Roger Davis, Charles Chrichley, James Iles, William Haw, Andrew Haynes. (EP/A/45/1/266)

85 St George. 9 Aug 1803 (15 Sept 1803). We [named below] certify to your lordship that the house with the appurtenances belonging to Harford & Company's Brass Works at 'Screws Hole' in the parish of St George in the county of Gloucester is to be a place of meeting for religious worship and I request you to direct the same to be registered. John Ryland, Henry Page, Thomas Powell, Robert Dix, James Battens, Henry Curtis, Emanuel Thorn. (EP/A/45/1/344)

Note. The modern place-name does not have an initial 'S' [*see* **122**] but it is clear in this record.

86 St Philip & St Jacob. 12 Apr 1805 (13 Apr 1805). We [named below] being part of a congregation of dissenters certify that a certain building in West Street within the parish of St Philip & St Jacob, Gloucestershire, and in your lordship's diocese of Bristol, is set apart for and to be used as a place of meeting for religious worship. We therefore desire that the same may be registered. Ely Stiles minister, William Smith, William Shenton, Benjamin Thresher, Samuel Hemmings, Daniell Triblett, Samuel Evans, Richard Burnes. (EP/A/45/1/356)

87 St George. 22 Sept 1807 (9 Dec 1807). We [named below], the minister and part of a congregation of Protestants dissenting from the Church of England certify that a certain new erected building standing and being in a certain place called Dendridge in the parish of St George, Gloucestershire, and diocese of Bristol is set apart for and to be used as a place of religious worship. We therefore desire that the same may be registered. Israel Passco, Victory Purdy, Abraham Palmer, John Purdy, James Bitton, William Minting, Edmund Jones, Richard Lewton, Joseph Jenkins, Robert Dix. (EP/A/45/1/410)

88 Lower Easton, St George, nr Bristol. 21 July 1808 (9 Aug 1808). [*Primitive Methodist: as p33; see note*]. We [named below] being part of a congregation of dissenters, certify that a certain building newly erected in the township of Lower Easton in the parish of St George, Gloucestershire, is to be set apart as a place of religious worship of Almighty God. We desire the same may be registered. H Hobbs, Henry Collings, Thomas Sanders, James White, M Randole, William Horwood, Thomas Taylor, L B Lorwile. (EP/A/45/2/1)

Note. Munden, 2.29, has return from Primitive Methodist chapel erected 1808.

89 St Philip & St Jacob. 27 June 1810 (29 June 1810). In pursuance of an act of parliament we [named below] desire that the garden and a small tenement erected thereon, now in the occupation of Daniell Niblett, [West Street stated in heading], in the parish of 'St Phillip & St Jacob' in the county of Gloucester in the diocese of Bristol and county of the same city may be registered among the records of this city as a place set apart for the worship of God and religious exercise. Daniell Nibblet, Samuel Hall, James Hall, William House, James Tyler, Isaac Dole. (EP/A/45/2/30-1)

Note. Careful registering of the parish which crossed the city and county boundary.

90   St George. (11 Dec 1811). We [named below] intend to hold a meeting for the purpose of worshipping Almighty God in a room in the house of John Jones in the parish of St George's near Bristol, pray that your Lordship will be pleased to register the same. John Bullock, Anthony Bretherton, W B Wiltshaw, William Barnes. (GDR/334B/358)

91   St George. 2 Dec 1811 (19 Dec 1811). *Independent.* We [named below] dissenters of the Independent denomination have set apart the lower rooms or ground floor of a tenement or dwelling house, now in the occupation of Samuel Ford, in the parish of St George, Gloucestershire, for the worship of Almighty God and pray that the apartment of the tenement or dwelling house be registered. Samuel Ford (mark), Thomas Lewis, W Duggan jnr, Thomas Haskins, Thomas Davis, George Wosage, William Thomas, James Powell, William Clark, John Johnson, Thomas Edwards, minister. (EP/A/45/2/60)

92   St Philip & St Jacob. 8 Mar 1817 (3 Apr 1817). *Baptist.* We [named below] certify that a building in the out-parish of St Philip & St Jacob, Gloucestershire, in the possession or occupation of Thomas Harse, is to be a meeting-house for religious worship by dissenters of the denomination of Baptists and request that this certificate may be registered. Thomas Harse, John Tozer, William Clark, William George Harris, Thomas John, Benjamin Pratten. (EP/A/45/2/107)

93   St Philip [& St Jacob]. 6 Feb 1819 (13 Feb 1819). We [named below] certify that a part of a dwelling house in Bread Street in the parish of 'St Phillip's' within the city and diocese of Bristol, now in the occupation of Philip Morgan, smith, is to be a place of meeting for religious worship and we request that the same may be registered. Phillip Morgan, John Rew, Joseph Roberts, John Lewis, Charles Browning, William Chilcott, R Whereat, Mary Stone, Sarah Roberts, Elizabeth Browning. (EP/A/45/2/115)

94   St Philip [& St Jacob]. 31 Dec 1822 (1 Jan 1823) 'It being our desire to meet for public worship (free from the errors of the Church of Rome) in a Club Room adjoining the Inn known by the sign of the *Three Compasses* in Jacob Street, 'St Philipp's' Bristol (with due allegiance to His Majesty George George the Fourth), we are desirous of having the above-mentioned room licensed for the above purpose'. John Philipps, William Morgan, Daniel Davies, William Jones. (EP/A/45/2/175)

95   St Philip & St Jacob. (5 Dec 1823). We [named below] certify that a house, in the possession of John Chapple, in Matthias Court, Avon Street, in the parish of St Philip & St Jacob is to be used for religious worship. John Chapple, William Pring, John Dark. (EP/A/45/2/196)

96   St Phillip & St Jacob, Bristol. 7 Jan 1828 (7 Jan 1828). *Baptist.* We [named below] certify that a building in the parish of St Phillip & St Jacob in the county of Gloucester is to be used as a chapel for religious worship by dissenters of the denomination of Baptists and request that this certificate may be registered. Henry Tripp, William Parsons, James Skinner, Richard Thompson, Thomas Underwood. (EP/A/45/2/235-36)

97   St George. 9 May 1828 (10 May 1828). *Baptist.* We [named below] certify that a dwelling house in the parish of St George in the county of Gloucester, in the occupation of Henry Plummer, shoemaker, is to be used for religious worship by dissenters of the denomination of Baptists and request that this certificate may be registered. William Parsons, John Radford, Thomas Underwood, Henry Plummer. (EP/A/45/2/238-39)

98 St Philip [& St Jacob]. 16 Nov 1828 (16 Nov 1828). *Baptist*. We [named below] certify that a building in the parish of St Philip in the county of Gloucester, in the possession or occupation of Lucy Davis, is to be used as a chapel for religious worship by dissenters of the denomination of Baptists and request that this certificate may be registered. Samuel Nicholl, Lucey [*sic*] Davis, John Kingdon, George Smith. (EP/A/45/2/254).

99 St Philip & St Jacob. 25 July 1829 (8 Aug 1829) *Baptist*. We [named below] certify that a building in the out-parish of St Philip & St Jacob in the county of Gloucester and diocese of Bristol, in the possession or occupation of Thomas Davis, is to be used as a chapel for religious worship by dissenters of the denomination of Baptists and we request that this certificate may be registered. Samuel Davis, John Radford. (EP/A/45/2/266)

100 St Philip [& St Jacob]. 1829 (26 Oct 1829). This is to certify that a front room on the ground floor of a dwelling house in the occupation of Mr Nicholas Carwood in the Plain at St Philip's had been taken by me for the purpose of preaching the Gospel and holding meetings for prayer and the reading the Scriptures on the Sabbath and at other times as most convenient under the Act of Toleration. John Leifchild, Nicholas Carwood, John Watson. (EP/A/45/2/268)

101 St Philip & St Jacob. 27 Oct 1829 (28 Oct 1829). Mr Samuel Gould of the city of Bristol, linen draper, John Evans of the said city, hatter, and John Roberts of the said city, tobacconist, certify that two rooms in a dwelling house belonging to Mrs Morle and at No. 7 Avon Street in the out-parish of St Phillip & St Jacob in the county of Gloucester is to be forthwith used as a place of religious worship and we require you to register the same. S Gould, John Evans, J Roberts; witness James Cooper. (EP/A/45/2/268-69)

102 St Philip & St Jacob. 8 Oct 1830 (9 Oct 1830). *Baptist*. We [named below] certify that a building in Jacob Street in the parish of St Philip & St Jacob in the city of Bristol, in the occupation of Alexander Pinney, is to be used as a chapel for religious worship by dissenters of the denomination of Baptists and we request that this certficate may be registered. Benjamon Pratten, James Clift, James Livett, Alexander Pinney. (EP/A/45/2/273)

103 St George. 9 June 1831 (9 June 1831). *Baptist*. We certify that a buiding in the parish of St George in the county of Gloucester is to be used for religious worship by dissenters of the denomination of Baptists. We request that the certificate may be registered. John Curtis, Thomas Underwood, James Clift. (EP/A/45/2/319)

104 St Philip & St Jacob. 29 June 1831 (1 July 1831). *Baptist*. We [named below] certify that a dissenting chapel lately erected [Russell Street named in heading], near the top of Thissell Street in the out-parish of St Philip & St Jacob in the county of Gloucester, and fronting the east, together with a large room adjoining on the north side, and so connected with the chapel as to form a line with it in front, are to be used for religious worship by dissenters of the denomination of Baptists and we request that this certificate may be registered. Benjamin Pratten, James Clift, David Waller. (EP/A/45/2/310)

105 St Philip & St Jacob. 24 Mar 1832 (26 Mar 1832). *Baptist*. We [named below] certify that a dwelling house in the Dings in the out-parish of St Philip & St Jacob in Kingsland Road on the south side, the property of William Clap and in the occupation of John Gillies, is to be used for religious worship by dissenters of the denomination of Baptists and we request that this certificate may be registered. Thomas J Crisp, Thomas Gough, William Tayler. (EP/A/45/2/346-47)

106 [St Philip] Gloucestershire [as in heading]. 23 Aug 1833 (23 Aug 1833). We [named below] part of a congregation of dissenters, certify that a front room on the first story of a house in the occupation of Joseph Guest, in a place commonly called No. 5 Broad Plain, is set apart and to be used as a place of worship. We desire that the same may be registered. David Powell, minister, James Clift, John Evans, John F Evans. (EP/A/45/2/399)

107 St Philip & St Jacob. 30 Nov 1833 (30 Nov 1833). We [named below] part of a congregation of dissenters, certify that a house now known by the name of Providence Chapel in Bread Street in the parish of St Phillip & St Jacob is set apart and to be used as a place of worship. We desire that the same may be registered. Richard Lewis, John Godwin, James Clift, John Evans, David Powell, minister. (EP/A/45/2/401)

108 St Philip & St Jacob. 15 Jan 1835 (22 Jan 1835). *Baptist.* We [named below] part of a congregation of dissenters, certify that a room in No 9 Ann Street in the parish of St Philip & St Jacob in the county of Gloucester is to be used as a chapel for religious worship by dissenters of the denomination of Baptists and we request that this certificate may be registered. Henry Cuzner, T S Cuzner, Samuel Hopkins, George Saunders. (EP/A/45/2/416)

109 St Philip & St Jacob. 15 July 1835 (15 July 1835). We [named below] of the city of Bristol certify that a chapel in Anvil Lane called Avon Chapel in the out-parish of St Philip & St Jacob in the county of Gloucester is forthwith to be a place of religious worship by a congregation of dissenters, of which we the undersigned form a part, and we require you to register the same. Jacob Riddle, James Weeks, Isaac Withers, John Haines, Henry Edwards, Daniel Gibbs. (EP/A/45/2/473)

110 Holy Trinity district, St Philip & St Jacob [as in heading], Bristol city. 4 Feb 1840 (6 Feb 1840). *Independent.* We [named below] certify that a dwelling house in the occupation of Jarrett Bucknell, known as No 8 Lamb Street in the Holy Trinity district parish in the borough of the city of Bristol, is to be used for religious worship by dissenters of the denomination of Independents and we request that this certificate may be registered. Robert Jarrett Bucknell, George Kovichich, George Woolley. (EP/A/45/2/594)

111 St Philip [& St Jacob]. 6 Mar 1841 (29 Mar 1841). *Wesleyan Methodist.* We [named below] certify that a house in the occupation of Thomas Gready and known as Barton Hill House, Barton Hill in the parish of St Phillips in the borough of the city of Bristol is to be used for religious worship by dissenters of the denomination of Wesleyan Methodists and we request that this certificate may be registered. Thomas Gready, Henry Curnock, Sidney Sprod, Cyrus Offer. (EP/A/45/3/34-5)

112 St Philip & St Jacob, Bristol city. 21 Dec 1841 (8 Jan 1842). *Independent.* We [named below] certify that a dwelling house in New Street without Lawfords Gate in the parish of St Philip & St Jacob in the borough of the city of Bristol, in the occupation of Mary Clark, widow, is to be used for religious worship by dissenters of the denomination of Independents and we request that this certificate may be registered. John Martin, George Koverchick, Mary Clark. (EP/A/45/3/118)

113 Holy Trinity district, St Philip [as in heading], Bristol Borough. 21 Dec 1841 (8 Jan 1842). *Independent.* We [named below] certify that a separate building or chapel called 'Dolmans chapel' in Eugene Street without Lawfords Gate, in the district parish of the Holy Trinity in the borough of the city of Bristol is to be used by dissenters of the denomination of Independents and we request that this certificate may be registered. John Martin, George Koverchick, R J Bucknell. (EP/A/45/3/119)

Note. John Dolman was the first signatory to a certificate in 1754. *See* **82**.

114 Holy Trinity and St Philip & St Jacob. 20 Oct 1846 (20 Oct 1846). *Primitive Baptist.* I James Hale certify that a chapel in the occupation of James Allen in Eugene Street in the district of Holy Trinity and parish of St Philip & St Jacob (without) in the city and county of Bristol is forthwith to be a place of religious worship by dissenters called Primitive Baptists and I require you to register the same and request a certificate thereof. Thomas Allen, James Hole, minister, Henry Breeding, William Parfery, John Webb, John Jones, Thomas Fry, Thomas Parfery, Charles Smith, William Elliot. (EP/A/45/3/404)

115 St Philip & St Jacob. 24 Feb 1848 (24 Feb 1848). I George Halliday of the city of Bristol certify that house and premises in Bread Street in the parish of St Philip & St Jacob, late in the county of Gloucester but now in the city and borough of Bristol, now in [my] holding and occupation, is to be used forthwith as place of religious worship and I request you to register the same for which shall be received no more than 2 shillings and 6 pence. (EP/A/45/3/454)
Note. Loose sheet bound in and paginated and probably written by signatory.

116 St Jude. 2 Aug 1848 (11 Aug 1848). *Independent.* We [named below] certify that a house or building lately used as a dwelling house in Great Ann Street without Lawford's Gate in the district parish of St Jude in the borough of the city of Bristol, in the possession of Christopher Godwin, clothier, is to be used for religious worship by dissenters of the denomination of Independents, and we request that this certificate may be registered. George Kovachick, Charles Rower, Chris Godwin. (EP/A/45/3/463)
Note. Loose sheet but better written than earlier examples. Like them, original signatures. St Jude created 1844 from Holy Trinity. (Youngs 166)

117 [St Philip & St Jacob]. 27 Feb 1850 (28 Feb 1850). *Wesleyan.* I Joseph Wood, Wesleyan minister residing at No 12 St James's Square, in Bristol, certify that a Wesleyan chapel called St Philips between Redcross Street and Old Market Street in the city is used and is henceforth to be used as a place of religious worship and I require you to register the same. (EP/A/45/4/6)
Note. Certificate pasted in. Original signatures.

118 St Philip & St Jacob. 13 May 1850 (13 May 1850). *Wesleyan Methodist.* I Samuel Baldwin certify that a building erected by me on my premises on Lawrence Hill in the parish of St Philip & St Jacob is forthwith to be a place of religious worship by a congregation of Wesleyan Methodists and I request you to register the same and I request a certificate hereof. (EP/A/45/4/26)
Note. Certificate pasted in and original signature.

119 St Philip & St Jacob. 4 Oct 1850 (9 Oct 1850). *Wesleyan Methodist.* I George Brewer certify that a house taken by me, No. 1 Britannia Place, Jacob Street, in the parish of St Philip & St Jacob, is forthwith to be a place of religious worship by a congregation of Wesleyan Methodists and I request you to register the same and request a certificate hereof. (EP/A/45/4/37)
Note. Certificate pasted in; signature.

120 Redfield, St George. 7 Nov 1850 (8 Nov 1850). *Wesleyan Methodist.* I Charles Clay of Kingswood Hill in the parish of Bitton certify that a building at Redfield called the Wesleyan Methodist chapel, near the turnpike road leading from Bristol to Kingswood Hill in the parish of St George <is used and henceforth to be used as a place of religious worship and I require you to register the same and request a certificate thereof.> (EP/A/45/4/43)

Note. One of four certificates pasted sideways on facing pages. Hand-written form: the bracketed section written by a different hand whereas first part filled in by a less neat writer, possibly the signatory. Nearly identical to next certificate, but location of chapel described differently.

Charles Clay of Kingswood Hill was minister of seven Methodist chapels in 1851. *See* Munden: Bitton 20.6, Hanham Street, Bitton 20.7, Cock Road, Bitton 20.14, Kingswood nr Bristol 20.16, Longwell Green, Bitton 20.17, Soundwell, Mangotsfield 20.33, and Redfield chapel, St George's 2.26. There is a certificate for Soundwell, Bitton, see **311**. For Charles Clay *see* **121**, **122**, **312**, **894**, **1128**, **1351**, **1352**, **1563**.

121 St George. 7 Nov 1850 (8 Nov 1850). *Wesleyan Methodist.* I Charles Clay of Kingswood Hill in the parish of Bitton certify that a building at White Way called the Wesleyan Methodist chapel, near the turnpike road leading from Bristol to Kingswood Hill in the parish of St George in the county of Gloucester <is used and henceforth to be used as a place of religious worship and I require you to register the same and request a certificate thereof.> (EP/A/45/4/44)
Note. Nearly identical to previous certificate, but location of chapel described differently.

122 St George. 7 Nov 1850 (8 Nov 1850). *Wesleyan Methodist.* I Charles Clay of Kingswood Hill in the parish of Bitton in the county of Gloucester certify that a building at Crew's Hole Way called the Wesleyan Methodist chapel in the parish of St George in the county of Gloucester <is used and henceforth to be used as a place of religious worship and I require you to register the same and request a certificate thereof.> (EP/A/45/4/44)
Note. Also two certificates pasted side by side (*see* comment on **120**). Signed by Charles Clay who filled in part of the certificate.

123 St Philip & St Jacob. 9 Nov 1850 (9 Nov 1850). *Wesleyan Methodist.* I Edward Millard certify that premises now held by me in No 10, Hampton Place, Baptist Mills, in the parish of St Philip & St Jacob without, is forthwith to be a place of religious worship by a congregation of Wesleyan Methodists and I request you to register the same and request a certificate thereof. (EP/A/45/4/45)
Note. Certificate pasted in and signed.

124 St George. 6 Jan 1851 (8 Jan 1851). We [named below] certfy that a building known as a British School Room, [Two Mile Hill in heading], in the parish of St George is to be a place of religious worship and we require you to register the same and request that this certificate may be registered. George Brain, J C Newman, George Fenton, George Lovell, John Hooke, James Iles, Joseph Burgess. (EP/A/45/4/47)
Note. Certificate pasted in. May be signatures.

125 St George. 1 Jan 1851 (10 Feb 1851). We [named below] certify that a place fitted up as a chapel at Whiteway in the parish of St George is to be a place of religious worship and we require you to register the same and we request that this certificate may be registered. J C Newman, Daniel Flook jnr, Edwin Weight, Aaron Watkins, William Masters, Isaac Stibbs, Joseph Bateman, Daniel Earl, Thomas Watkins, George Flook, Robert Barratt, John Hulbert. (EP/A/45/4/52)
Note. Certificate pasted in and signed.

126 St George. 29 Mar 1851 (29 Mar 1851). We [named below] certify that a room called the 'Whitehouse' at Crew's Hole in the parish of St George is to be a place of religious worship and we require you to register the same and request that this certficate may be registered. Edward Lawrence, John Martin, Richard James, John Wooley, Francis Martin, 'William Rutler'. (EP/A/45/4/54)
Note. Initial letter of last surname very difficult to read. Certificate pasted in and signed.

GLOUCESTERSHIRE

Entries are from the records of Gloucestershire Quarter Sessions (Q), Bristol diocese (EP), Gloucester diocese (GDR) and the combined diocese of Gloucester and Bristol (EP or GDR).

ABENHALL

127 Abenhall. (Michaelmas 1695). *Presbyterian.* William Vaughan's house called the Bear [?Beer] House. (Q/SO/3/521)

Note. The very small parish of Abenhall contained part of Mitcheldean, and the Evans list brackets the two together under the Independent minister Owen Davies; congregation of 120. *See* **1205** for Owen Davies, who may have been the man who applied to Charles II for many licences in 1672.

ACTON TURVILLE

128 Acton Turville. (11 Apr 1825). We [named below] certify that we intend to set apart the dwelling house of Richard Baker in the parish of Acton Turville for the service and worship of Almighty God and we request that this our certificate may be recorded and the entry thereof certified. Richard Baker, W Underwood, Charles Webber, Moses Stinchcomb, William Hannam, W Brooks. (GDR/350/38)

129 Acton Turville. (5 Sept 1832). We [named below] intend to set apart one room attached to the dwelling house of Isaac Evans in the parish of Acton Turville for the service and worship of Almighty God. And we request that this our certificate may be recorded, and the entry thereof certified. James Goulter, James Pinnill, John Tanner, Richard Baker, John Pinnell, Thomas Brookman, Edward Ralph (mark). (GDR/350/132)

130 Acton Turville. 28 Aug 1838 (31 Aug 1838). *Baptist.* We the undersigned certify that a building newly erected in the parish and village of Acton Turville, known by the name of Ebenezer Chapel, is intended to be a place for the worship of Almighty God by the denomination of dissenters called Baptists and is required to be licenced. Richard Baker, James Goulter, John Bidnell, Charles Davis, Joseph Milliner. (GDR/350/229)

ALDERTON

131 Alderton. 9 Nov 1785 (23 Jun 1785; registration GDR/319A/21). 'This is to certify your Lordship that some [dissenters] intend to hold a meeting for the worship of Almighty God in the dwelling house of Thomas Slatter in the parish of Alderton. We therefore pray that this certificate may be entered in your lordship's registry according to an act of parliament made in that behalf in the reign of King William and Queen Mary.' Thomas Slatter, Joseph Taylor, John Welles, Daniel Wells, Benjamin Beckett, John Williams. (GDR/N2/1)

132 Alderton. 1 Mar 1809 (3 Mar 1809). *Methodist.* We [named below] beg leave to certify that a house in the occupation of John Grimmet, farmer, in the parish of Alderton, is intended to be a place for the worship of Almighty God by dissenters called Methodists and I request that the same may be registered and a certificate of the same given. John Grimmet, William Harding, John Ewins, John Millington, Charles Grizell, William Green. (GDR/334B/406)

133 Alderton. 5 Dec 1821 (8 Dec 1821). I Robert Bromiley, minister, certify that a building, in the occupation of Robert Stevens in the village and parish of Alderton is intended forthwith to be a place for religious worship and I require that you will register the demand according to an Act. (GDR/344/page 2 from rear)

Note. RG/31/2 has identical details but dated 5 May 1821.

134 Alderton. 29 Oct 1822 (2 Nov 1822). I Joseph Allen, minister, certify that a building, in the occupation of John Evins in the village of Alderton is intended forthwith to be a place for religious worship by a congregation of Protestants and I require that you will register the same. 'Dated at Kemerton Gloucestershire.' (GDR/344/38v)

135 Alderton. 2 Dec 1822 (7 Dec 1822). I Joseph Allen, minister, certify that a dwelling house in the occupation of Edward Ballard in the village and parish of Alderton is intended forthwith to be a place of religious worship and I require that you will register the same according to the provisions of the Act. (GDR/344/40v)

136 Alderton. 20 Nov 1824 (22 Nov 1824). I James Roberts of Alderton certify that my house in the parish of Alderton is intended to be a place of religious worship and I require you to register the same and request a certificate thereof. Witness J Hills, B Wheeler. (GDR/350/24)

137 Alderton. 15 Apr 1833 (17 Apr 1833). [*Methodist: see* **140**]. I Richard Bartlett of the parish of Alderton certify that my house in Alderton is intended forthwith to be a place of religious worship and I require you to register the same and request a certificate thereof. Witness Thomas Ashwood, George Sexty. (GDR/350/139)

138 Alderton. 28 Apr 1834. I Thomas Day of the parish of Alderton certify that my house in Alderton is intended forthwith to be a place of religious worship and I desire you to register the same and request a certificate thereof. Witness Thomas Slatter, John Oakley. (GDR/350/151)

139 Alderton. 12 Nov 1834 (13 Nov 1834). [*Methodist: see next entry*]. I Joseph Slatter of the parish of Alderton certify that my house in Alderton is intended forthwith to be a place of religious worship and I require you to register the same and request a certificate thereof. Witness William Townshend, George Sexty. (GDR/350/160)

140 Alderton. 20 Apr 1836 (21 Apr 1836) *Methodist*. We, the undersigned trustees of a Methodist Chapel at Alderton, certify that [it] is intended forthwith to be a place of religious worship and we require you to register the same and request a certificate thereof. George Sexty, William Townshend; witness William Cooke, Joseph Townshend. (GDR/350/194)
Note. Munden, 15.29, dates chapel to 1833. *See* **137**.

ALDSWORTH
Aldsworth was a chapelry in Bibury parish.
141 Aldsworth. 25 Aug 1742. Some [dissenters] intend to hold a meeting for the worship of Almighty God at the house of Mrs Anne Wane, widow of the parish of 'Alsworth' and therefore we pray that the said house may be duly registered. William Maysey, John Higgins, Jeremiah Hewer, William Bayley. (GDR/284/142)

142 Aldsworth. 16 July 1754 (registered Trinity 1754, Q/SO/8/f.91v). *Independent*. 'We [named below] do humbly certify to . . . the General Quarter Session of the peace held at Gloucester for the said county the 16 day of July 27 GII by the grace of God King of Great Britain in the year of our Lord 1754 that His Majesty's Protestant dissenting subjects called Independents do intend to hold a meeting for the worship and service of God in their way in a house [Q/SO/8/f.91v has 'the house of William Adams'] in the parish of Aldsworth in the said county which we humbly desire may be recorded at the said sessions pursuant to the statute in that way made and provided.' William Adams, John Greenwood, John Kimber, William Pearce. (Q/SR/1754/C 13)

ALMONDSBURY
Diocese of Bristol from 1542

143 Almondsbury. 12 Feb 1801 (11 Mar 1801). These are to certify that some [dissenters] intend to hold a meeting for the worship of Almighty God in a house in the occupation of Thomas Hall in the parish of Almondsbury. We therefore pray that this certificate may be registered. Thomas Hall [RG/31/2 has John Hall], John Hicks, Luke Jain, Daniel Harding, Samuel Rosser, Robert Hicks (EP/A/45/1/288)

144 Almondsbury Hill, Almondsbury. 11 Feb 1808 (25 Mar 1808). We [named below] desire that a room or meeting-house, erecting and building on a spot of ground purchased of Mr John Hill situate at Almondsbury Hill in the parish of Almondsbury may be registered as a meeting-house set apart for the worship of God and religious exercise. John Hill, John Powell, Thomas Davis (mark), Benjamin Smith, James Hokins, William Kerslike (mark), William Hokins. (EP/A/45/1/414)
Note. Munden, *Religious Census* 4.5: chapel erected about 1810.

145 Almondsbury. 19 May 1808 (27 May 1808). *Methodist.* We [named below] beg leave to certify to your lordship that a room in a house occupied by James Hopkins, sawyer, in the village of Almondsbury, is set apart for the worship of Almighty God by a congregation of dissenters commonly called Methodists, and we request that the same may be registered and a certificate given accordingly. James Hopkins, John Powell, Arthur Parker, John Tyler, Ann Batten, John Boulton. (EP/A/45/1/419)

146 Redwick, Almondsbury. 2 Apr 1835 (3 Apr 1835). I John Scott of Bristol, minister, certify that a chapel at Redwick in the parish of Almondsbury is intended forthwith to be a place of religious worship and I require you to register the same and request a certificate thereof. (EP/A/45/2/420)

ALVESTON
Alveston was annexed to Olveston parish. In the diocese of Bristol from 1542

147 Alveston. 28 Apr 1798 (10 May 1798). We [named below] certify that we intend on Sunday 13 May to meet and assemble for the purpose of publicly worshipping of Almighty God in the dwelling house of Abraham Pullen in the parish of Alveston in the county of Gloucester and diocese of Bristol, which dwelling house we intend to use for that purpose in future, and we desire the same may be registered. William Jones, Abraham Pullen, William Reed, James Eley, Thomas Child, John Greenwood. (EP/A/45/1/279).

148 Alveston. 28 Mar 1804. These are to certify that we [named below] with others intend to hold a meeting for the worship of Almighty God in the dwelling house of James Lackington esq in the parish of Alveston and pray it may be registered. Valentine Ward minister, J Lackington, gent, John Crowther, gent, R Martin, gent, James Higgs, William Hobby, gent, John Cullimore. (EP/A/45/1/347).

149 Alveston. 6 Jan 1805. These are to certify that we [named below] with others intend to hold a meeting for the worship of Almighty God in a chapel lately fitted up by James Lackington esq in the parish of 'Alvistone' and desire it may be registered. James Lackington, gent, Valentine Ward, minister, John Crowther, gent, Ed. Thurston, gent, Richard Martin, gent, George D Dermott, James Higgs, William Hobby, gent, John Cullimore. (EP/A/45/1/353).

150 Alveston Down, Alveston. 20 May 1808 (3 June 1808). *Methodist.* We [named below] beg leave to certify that a room in a house occupied by James 'Broye', labourer, on Alveston Down in the parish of Alveston is intended to be used for the worship of Almighty God by a congregation of dissenters commonly called Methodists and request that the same may be registered and a certificate of the same given accordingly. James Bovey (mark), John Olive, William Olive, Richard Bovey, Henry Barrett, Ann Doward, Abraham Tilley, Elizabeth Doward, Mary Stephens, William Jones, John Callimore, John C? Doward. (EP/A/45/1/419-20)

151 Alveston. 10 Mar 1811 (1 May 1811). *Wesleyan.* Whereas we [named below] dissenting from the Church of England, and in the connection of the late Revd John Wesley, deceased, have appropriated and set apart the newly erected building called the Methodist Chapel in the parish of Alveston for the worship of Almighty God, we request that the same may be registered. Edward Dunn, John Cullimore, John Oliver, William Stephens, James Burse, Isaac Thomas, Henry Barrett, Richard Burse, William Oliver. (EP/A/45/2/42)

152 Earthcott Green, Alveston. 23 July 1819 (30 July 1819). *Independent.* We [named below], dissenters of the Independent denomination, have set apart a tenement or dwelling house, occupied by John White, at Earthcott Green in the parish of Alveston for the worship of Almighty God, and pray that the said tenement may be registered. Thomas Edwards minister, John White, Samuel Colborn, Benjamin Angell, Joseph Thornwell, Thomas Parker, John Thornwell, Thomas Kethro, George W Sage. (GDR/334B/257)

153 Earthcott Green, Alveston. 18 May 1831 (21 May 1831). *Wesleyan.* I Paul Orchard of Thornbury, Wesleyan minister, certify that a house at Earthcot Green in the parish of Alveston is intended forthwith to be a place of religious worship and I require you to register and record the same and require a certificate thereof. (GDR/350/115)

154 Earthcott Green, Alveston. 6 Aug 1831 (13 Aug 1831). *Methodist.* We [named below] of the Methodist denomination have set apart a tenement belonging to Mr John Savery at Earthcott Green in the parish of Alveston for the worship of Almighty God and we request that the said tenement may be registered in your court and a certificate granted us. John Simpson, minister, John Savery, Thomas Parker, Jabez Pullin, James Brashar. (GDR/350/117)

155 Ridgeway, Alveston. 25 Nov 1841 (26 Nov 1841). I George Wood Rodway of Stroud Road, Gloucester, minister, certify that a house at Ridgeway in the parish of 'Alvestone' now occupied by George Thomas, is forthwith to be a place of religious worship and I request you to register the same and request a certificate thereof. (GDR/350/284)

ALVINGTON
Alvington was a chapelry in Woolaston parish.

156 Alvington. (12 July 1806). This is to certify that the house of Edward Martin in the parish of Alvington is intended to be a place of publick worship. We [named below] request that the same may be registered and a 'License' granted. Edward Martin, Richard Parry, John Davis, Mary Martin, William Cooke, John Smith, Benjamin Goodwin, John Cooke, William Hughes. (GDR/334B/426)

157 Alvington. 22 Dec 1817 (23 Dec 1817). I Daniel Edwards, officer of excise, certify that a building, messuage or tenement together with both front and back courts 'where I reside at', as well as the adjoining tenement thereto (William Cooke, farmer, owner), at

Alvington in the parish of Alvington, are intended forthwith to be a place of religious worship and I require you to register the same. (GDR/334B/288)

158 Alvington. 16 Nov 1818 (23 Nov 1818). I Daniel Edwards, officer of excise, certify that a certain building, messuage or tenement together with its back court thereof '(commonly called Libes) where I reside at', Edward Harris, farmer, owner, at Alvington in the parish of Alvington, is intended forthwith to be a place of religious worship and I require you to register the same. (GDR/334B/270)

AMPNEY
159 Ampney St Peter. 7 Oct 1809 (11 Oct 1809). This is to certify that we [named below] intend to hold a meeting for the worship of Almighty God in the dwelling house of Edward Carter in the parish of 'Amney Peter'. We pray that this certificate may be entered in your Lordship's Registry.Thomas Morgan, John Rogers, Richard Savoury, John Vizard, Edward Carter. (GDR/334B/397)

160 Ampney [?Crucis]. 18 Nov 1835 (19 Nov 1835). *Wesleyan*. I William Jackson, Wesleyan minister of the town of Cirencester, certify that a house in the village and parish of Ampney is intended forthwith to be a place of religious worship and I require you to register the same and request a certificate thereof. (GDR/350/183)

ARLINGHAM
161 Arlingham. (Michaelmas 1708). *Presbyterian*. Sarah Daniels house. (Q/SO/3/520)

162 Arlingham. 14 Jan 1809 (19 Jan 1809). These are to certify that some dissenters intend to hold a meeting for the worship of Almighty God in a house belonging to Thomas Hooper in the parish of Arlingham. We pray that this certificate may be registered. Thomas Hooper, Charles Rowles, John Weight, John Savage, T Pinder, William Hardwick, John Ely, George Pegler, Elijah Morgan. (GDR/334B/409)

163 Arlingham. 16 Nov 1812 (21 Nov 1812). This is to certify that we [named below] intend to use the dwelling house of Ann Carter, widow, and also the garden court and premises adjoining, belonging to the said Ann Carter, for the public worship of Almighty God. The said house etc [*sic*] are in the parish of Arlingham. We pray that the premises and garden may be duly registered. William Worthington, Ann Carter, John Bird, John Savage, William Carter, John Eley, William Ely. (GDR/334B/350)

164 Arlingham. 25 Mar 1816 (29 Mar 1816). I Stephen Hopkins of the parish of 'Woottonunderedge' certify that a room or floor belonging to Thomas Jones, adjoining his dwelling house in the parish of Arlingham is intended forthwith to be a place of religious worship and I require you to register the same and request a certificate thereof. Signed in the presence of J Rickards. (GDR/334B/321)

165 Arlingham. 24 Sept 1819 (25 Sept 1819). I certify that the premises occupied by Richard Taylor in the parish of Arlingham will hereafter be used as a place of religious worship. John Pyer, minister. (GDR/334B/254)

166 Arlingham. 24 Feb 1821 (24 Feb 1821). [*Methodist: see note*]. I, W Wheeler of the city of Gloucester, linen draper, certify that a chapel erected in the parish of Arlingham is intended forthwith to be a place of religious worship and I require you to register the same and require a certifcate thereof. James M Byron, minister, W Wheeler. (GDR/334B/226)
Note. J M Byron was noted as a Methodist minister in Hine 5-6. He was in the Gloucester circuit 1804-5 and again 1811-20. *See also* **173**, **1247**, **1720**, **1828**, **1855**.

167 Arlingham. 2 Aug 1834. I John James Waite of the city of Gloucester, gentleman, certify that a house called the Reddings in the parish of Arlingham in the occupation of John Campbell esq is intended to be forthwith a place of religious worship and I desire you to register the same. (GDR/350/155)

168 Friday Street, Arlingham. (26 Dec 1849). Chapel. John Irving. (Q/RNp/4)

169 Arlingham. (14 Oct 1851). House occupied by David Taysume. John Campbell. (Q/RNp/4)

ASHCHURCH
The parish included the tithings of Aston on Carrant, Fiddington, Natton and Newton, and Pamington.
170 Ashchurch. 1672. *Congregational*. Licence recorded 25 July 1672 for the house of 'Richard Davisen at Ash Church'. (LT/540)

171 Natton, Ashchurch. 16 Sept 1746. [*Seventh Day Baptist: see note*]. Some [dissenters] intend to hold a meeting for the worship of Almighty God at a house fitted for that purpose at Natton in the parish of Ashchurch and desire the same may be registered. Samuel Wells, Benjamin Purser, Thomas Pope, Benjamin Hudson. (GDR/284/176)
Note. Munden, *Religious Census* 17.29: return from Seventh Day Baptists at Natton stating licensed for divine worship 1748.

172 Aston on Carrant, Ashchurch. 20 July 1775 (24 July 1775). *Baptist*. Some [dissenters] called Baptists intend to hold a meeting for the worship of Almighty God at the dwelling house of Joseph Stratford of Aston on Carrant in the parish of Ashchurch and therefore pray that this certificate may be duly registered. Joseph Stratford, William Stratford, Samuel Purser, Thomas Dobbs, Thomas Alsop, William Nind, John Osbaldeston, John Stratford, John Turner, James Nind, Benjamin Grove: John Ryland, Thomas Beale, Thomas Sowley, Joseph Farley (mark), Isaac Stratford, James Toveye (mark). (GDR/292A/184)

173 Aston on Carrant, Ashchurch. 20 May 1819 (21 May 1819). [*Methodist: see* **166**]. I George Robinson of Tewkesbury certify that an orchard, a part of an orchard called Bloxhams Orchard at Ashton [Aston upon Carrant] in the parish of Ashchurch, belonging to Mr Edward Robinson, is intended forthwith to be a place of religious worship and I require you to register the same and require a certificate thereof. George Robinson, James M Byron, minister. (GDR/334B/261)

174 Aston on Carrant, Ashchurch. 2 May 1821 (5 May 1821). I Robert Bromley, minister, certify that a house, in the occupation of Thomas Knight in the hamlet of Aston upon Carrant in the parish of Ashchurch is intended forthwith to be a place of religious worship and I require that you will register the same. (GDR/334B/223)

175 Ashchurch. 26 Dec 1843 (1 Jan 1844). I Joseph Earnshaw of the borough of Tewkesbury certify that a dwelling house in the parish of Ashchurch, in the occupation of William Page, day labourer, is intended forthwith to be a place of religious worship and I desire you to register the same and request a certificate thereof. (GDR/350/327)

176 Ashchurch. 28 Oct 1845 (31 Oct 1845) *Wesleyan*. I Joseph Earnshaw of the borough of Tewkesbury certify that a building called the Wesleyan Chapel in the parish of Ashchurch is intended forthwith to be a place of religious worship and I require you to register the same and request a certificate thereof. (GDR/350/362)

ASHLEWORTH

177 Ashleworth. (Michaelmas 1691). *Quaker*. Daniel Dobbins house. (Q/SO/3/522)

178 White End, Ashleworth. 17 Feb 1815 (17 Feb 1815). [*Methodist: see note*]. I John Chettle of Gloucester, minister, certify that the house of William Lane of White End in the parish of 'Ashelworth' is intended forthwith to be a place of religious worship and I require you to register the same and request a certificate thereof. (GDR/334B/330)
Note. See Hine 5-6 for John Chettle, Methodist minister. *See also* **904**, **1057**, **1442**, **1790**.

179 Ashleworth. 7 Dec 1816 (12 Dec 1816). [*Methodist: see note*]. I Daniel Campbell of Gloucester, minister certify that the house of Robert Chandler in the parish of 'Ashelworth', is intended forthwith to be a place of religious worship and I require you to register the same and request a certificate thereof. (GDR/334B/308)
Note. Daniel Campbell was a Methodist minister in the Gloucester Circuit in 1815-17 (Hine 5). *See also* **332**, **375**, **835**, **836**, **990**, **905**, **1249**, **1317**, **1765**.

180 Ashleworth. 14 June 1821 (15 Jun 1821). [*Methodist: see* **166**]. I James Byron minister in Gloucester certify that the dwelling house of William Dance of the parish of Ashleworth is intended forthwith to be a place of religious worship and I require you to register the same and request a certificate thereof. (GDR/334B/220)

181 Ashleworth. 25 Apr 1837 (25 Apr 1837). I John Coxhead of the parish of St John in the city of Gloucester, certify that a dwelling house and premises in the parish of Ashleworth, now in the holding and occupation of William Gough, are intended forthwith to be a place of religious worship and I request you to register the same and request a certificate thereof for which shall be taken no more than two shillings and six pence. (GDR/350/207)

182 Ashleworth. 26 Jan 1839 (30 Jan 1839). *Wesleyan*. I Thomas Moss of Gloucester, preacher of the Gospel, certify that a dwelling house in the occupation of William Dance, labourer, in Ashleworth is intended forthwith to be a place of religious worship and I require you to register the same and request a certificate thereof. Thomas Moss, Weslyan minister. (GDR/350/235)

ASHTON-UNDER-HILL

The impropriation of Ashton-under-Hill was annexed to Beckford and so sometimes styled a chapelry. Ashton-under-Hill and Beckford were transferred to Worcestershire in 1931.
183 Ashton [-under-Hill?]. (1672). *Congregational*. Licence recorded for the house of 'John Harison' of 'Ashdon' in Gloucestershire. (LT/576)
Note. One John Harrison, yeoman of Ashton-under-Hill, left a will in 1693.

184 Ashton-under-Hill. 28 May 1822 (1 June 1822). I Joseph Allen, dissenting minister, certify that a house, now in the occupation of William Hicks in the village of 'Ashton-underill in the parish of Ashton underill' is intended forthwith to be a place for religious worship by a congregation of Protestants and I require that you will register the same. Dated at Kemerton, Gloucester this 28th day of May 1922. Joseph Allen (mark), Edward Robinson. (GDR/344/31v)
Note. Minister made mark.

185 Ashton-under-Hill. 21 July 1835 (27 July 1835). *Wesleyan.* I John Wevill of the Borough of Evesham and county of Worcester, Wesleyan minister, certify that the dwelling house of Elizabeth Print of the parish of Ashton under Hill is intended to be forthwith a place of religious worship and I require you to register the same and request a certificate thereof. (GDR/350/177-8)

186 Ashton-under-Hill. (29 Apr 1850). Building messuage or tenement occupied by Charles Garritt. William Edwards. (Q/RNp/4)

ASTON BLANK *or* COLD ASTON
187 Aston Blank. 24 Jan 1780 (4 Mar 1780). We intend to meet for the worship of Almighty God in the dwelling house of William Bosbury, farmer, in the parish of Aston Blank and therefore pray that this certificate may be registered. John Bubb, 'Robeart Weake, Robeart Pinchis, Jos.h [Joseph] Hall', Samuel Perry, William Perry, Jeremiah Greening. (GDR/292A/226)

188 Cold Aston. 3 Nov 1828 (29 Nov 1828). I James Osborne of the parish of 'Cold Ashton' certify that a dwelling house in my possession at Cold Ashton is set apart for the public worship of God and I request you to register the same. Witness John Turner. (GDR/350/96)
Note. This certificate could have been for Cold Ashton in the south of the county but there are no other certificates for that place.

189 Aston Blank. 29 May 1845 (7 June 1845). *Baptist.* This is to give notice that a room at Aston Blank, the property of John Hanks of Naunton, is intended henceforth to be used as a place of public worship by dissenters of the Baptist persuasion and we request that the room be registered in the office of the Registrar of the diocese. Isaac Wood, Robert Comely, James Cubitt, David Stait. (GDR/350/359)

ASTON SUBEDGE
190 Aston Subedge. 3 Jan 1818 (15 Jan 1818). I Joseph Wheatley of Aston Subedge certify that my house in Aston Subedge is intended forthwith to be used as a place of religious worship and I require you to register the same and request a certificate thereof. (GDR/334B/287)

191 Aston Subedge. 11 November 1822 (28 Nov 1822). *Methodist.* I William Jones of Evesham in the county of Worcester, Wesleyan Methodist minister, certify that the dwelling house of Samuel Farley of Aston Subedge is intended forthwith to be a place of religious worship. And I require you to register the same and request a certificate thereof. (GDR/344/39v)

192 Aston Subedge. 11 Apr 1835 (17 Apr 1835). *Wesleyan.* I John Weevil of Evesham, Wesleyan minister, certify that the dwelling of Thomas Pitt at Aston Subedge is intended forthwith to be a place of religious worship and I require you to register the same and request a certificate thereof. J Wevill, Thomas Pitt. (GDR/350/170)

AVENING
See also Nailsworth, part of which was in Avening
193 Avening. (Epiphany 1689/90). At the Forest Green. (Q/SO/3/522)

194 Avening. (Michaelmas 1699). *Anabaptist.* 'Jo:' Giffin's house [RG/31/6 has Joseph Griffin]. (Q/SO/3/521)

195 Avening. (Epiphany 1702/3). *Presbyterian*. Abraham Hicks's house. (Q/SO/3/521)

196 Avening. 11 Dec 1731. These are to certify you that [dissenters] intend to hold a meeting for the worship of God in their way in the dwelling house of John Lennard of Avening. We therefore pray it may be recorded. Martin Lloyd, Martin Lloyd jnr, James Smith (GDR/279a/252)

197 Avening. 17 Dec 1743. These are to certify your Lordship that [disseenters] intend to hold a meeting for the worship of God at the dwelling house of Calvin Sansum in the parish of Avening and desire the same may be registered. William Hogg, William Hopson, Joseph Everard. (GDR/284/157)
Note. For Joseph Everard *see* Introduction and **225**, **323**, **422–3**, **434**, **625**, **821–4**, **931**, **1161**, **1213**, **1379–80**, **1417**, **1624**, **1677**, **1744**, **1825**, **2003**.

198 Avening. 8 Jan 1772 (1 Feb 1772). [Dissenters] intend to hold a meeting for the worship of Almighty God at the dwelling house of Martha Perrin in the parish of Avening and desire the same may be registered. William Franklin, William Tindal Sansum, William Hogg, John Mansfield. (GDR/292A/155)

199 Avening. Apr 1804 (2 May 1804). [*Baptist: see note*]. This is to certify that a meeting-house lately erected in the parish of Avening near the turnpike road leading from Minchinhampton to Tetbury is intended to be a place of worship. We request that the same may be registered and a certificate granted. John Blackwell, Thomas Earl, Cor[neliu]s Blackwell, James Niblett, Abraham Cox (GDR/334B/439)
Note. The tablet in the Baptist chapel records that it was built in 1805 (possibly the date of dedication) and enlarged in 1821 (Munden, 10.75).

200 Avening. 16 July 1821 (18 July 1821). I certify that the premises occupied by Hester Poulton in the parish of Avening will be hereafter used as a place of religious worship. Adam Nightingale, minister. (GDR/334B/216)

201 Avening. 19 Sept 1821 (19 Sept 1821). I Christopher Griffin of Coaley certify that a certain piece of pasture land situate in Forest Green in the parish of Avening, near to the dwelling house of Robert Day, now in the occupation of Robert Teakle, is intended forthwith to be a place of religious worship and I require you to register the same and request a certificate thereof. (GDR/334B/213)

202 Avening. 22 Nov 1821 (22 Nov 1821). I certify that the premises occupied by Jacob Burford in the parish of Avening will be hereafter used as a place of religious worship. Christopher Griffin, minister. (GDR/334B/211)

203 Avening. 17 Dec 1821 (19 Dec 1821). This is to certify that an house in the occupation of William Smith, near Inchbrook in the parish of Avening, is intended to be a place of religious worship and require you to register the same. John Rees minister of Rodborough Tabernacle, William Marling, William Smith. (GDR/334B/211)

204 Forest Green, Avening. (26 Jan 1822). *Independent*. We the trustees [named below], certify that we have erected last year, 1821, a new Independent Chapel at the Forest Green in the parish of Avening and that it will be hereafter appropriated as a chapel for religious worship. The names of the trustees viz. Thomas Osborn jnr, Thomas Day, John Bird jnr, John Hill, William Edge, Nathaniel Ludlow, John Evans, Thomas Hervey, Thomas Cook, Jacob Burford snr, James Teakel, Joseph Burford, Jacob Burford jnr, Philip Cave. (GDR/344/15v)

Note. Munden, 10.72, 10.73: Congregational or Independent chapel, Lower Forest Green, Nailsworth, erected 1821; Independent chapel, Upper Forest Green, Spring Hill, Nailsworth, erected 1821.

205 Avening. 23 Sept 1823 (13 Oct 1823). I Daniel Smith of Avening in the parish of Avening hereby certify that a dwelling house and premises at Avening and now in the holding and occupation of Daniel Smith, are intended to be a place of religious worship and I request you to register the same and request a certificate thereof for which is to be taken no more than two shillings and sixpence. (GDR/344/115r)

206 Avening. 15 Oct 1835 (22 Oct 1835). I Richard Rigsby of Nagshead [Nags Head] in the parish of Avening certify that my dwelling house at Nagshead is intended forthwith to be a place of religious worship and I require you to register the same. Richard Rigsby (mark). (GDR/350/182)

207 Avening. 25 Nov 1844 (26 Nov 1844). We [named below] certify that a room in a dwelling house in the parish of Avening, called the dwelling house of William Whiting, is intended to be used for religious worship and we request that this certificate may be registered. John Ludlow, James Huish (mark), Nathaniel Ludlow (mark), William Whiting. (GDR/350/352)

208 Avening. 10 Aug 1845 (11 Aug 1845). We [named below] certify that a house in the parish of Avening, the property of Sarah Hall, is intended to be a place of religious worship and we request you to register the same and request a certificate thereof. (GDR/350/360)
Note. No signatures listed.

AWRE
Blakeney, which see, a chapelry in Awre, by the 18th century was the effective centre of the parish; it had a chapel by 1551.
209 Viney Hill, Awre. 7 Oct 1817 (11 Oct 1817). I Joseph Hunt of Monmouth, minister, certify that the house of Ann Prout, 'Vine Hill' in the parish of Awre is intended forthwith to be a place of religious worship and I require you to register the same and request a certificate thereof. Joseph Hunt, Thomas Jenkins, Benjamin Rickitts, George Morse. (GDR/334B/292)

210 Awre. 27 May 1823 (28 May 1823). [*Independent: see Introduction*]. I Isaac Bridgman of the parish of Ruardean certify that the barn of Richard White snr, situated about and a mile from the parish church of Awre, is intended forthwith to be a place of religious worship and I require you to register the same and request a certificate thereof. (GDR/344/63r)
Note. For Isaac Bridgeman *see* Introduction lxvi and **211–3**, **327**, **659–60**, **1292–3**.

211 Awre. 23 Aug 1823 (25 Aug 1823). [*Independent: see Introduction*]. I Isaac Bridgman now residing at the Wood Side Cottage near Blakeney certify that the house of Mr Thomas Brown in the parish of Awre is forthwith to be a place of religious worship and I require you to register the same and request a certificate thereof. (GDR/344/112v)

212 Awre. 12 July 1824 (13 July 1824). [*Independent: see Introduction*]. I Isaac Bridgman now residing in Blakeney in the parish of Awre certify that a house, now in the occupation of Mr William Sanders near to the village of Blakeney is intended forthwith to be a place of religious worship and I require you to register the same. I request a certificate thereof. (GDR/344/134v)
Note. For Isaac Bridgman *see* **210**.

213 Etloe, Awre. 19 Mar 1827 (19 Mar 1827). [*Independent: see Introduction*]. I Isaac Bridgman of Woodside Cottage near Blakeney certify that a dwelling house and premises at Etloe in the parish of Awre, now in the holding and occupation of John Morgan, are intended to be a place of religious worship and I request you to register the same and request a certificate thereof. (GDR/350/63)

Note. For Isaac Bridgman *see* **210**.

214 Awre. 9 Apr 1835 (10 Apr 1835). *Baptist.* We [named below] certify that a building in the parish of Awre recently erected is intended to be used as a chapel for religious worship by dissenters of the Baptist denomination and we request that this certificate may be registered. Thomas Shaw, William Virgo, James Chorley. (GDR/350/169)

Note. Registration date unclear.

215 Awre. 7 Aug 1845 (8 Aug 1845). I Joseph Hyatt of the city of Gloucester certify that a dwelling house in the parish of Awre occupied by Joseph Merrett, wharfinger, is intended to be forthwith a place of religious worship and I require you to register the same. Joseph Hyatt. (GDR/350/360)

AYLBURTON
Aylburton was a chapelry in Lydney parish.

216 Aylburton. (22 Jan 1807). This is to certify that there is a building in the occupation of John Smith, William Parry and William Burnal in 'Aylberton' that is intended to be used for a place of public worship. We [named below] request that the same may be registered. John Cooper, William Cooper, William Hughes, William Roberts, S Huntley, Mary Dyer (GDR/334B/425-4)

217 Aylburton. 10 Feb 1819 (15 Feb 1819). *Wesleyan.* I Joseph Hunt of Monmouth, Wesleyan minister, certify that the house belonging to Elizabeth Stevens and Mary Dyer, and occupied by Robert Jenkings, situated in 'Aleburton' in the parish of Lydney is intended forthwith to be a place of religious worship and require you to register the same and request a certificate thereof. (GDR/334B/266)

218 Aylburton. *Baptist.* 16 Nov 1840 (17 Nov 1840). We whose names are underwriten certify that a building in the tithing of Aylburton and parish of Lydney, in the possession or occupation of John Hillman, is intended to be a chapel or meeting-house for dissenters of the denomination of Baptists and request that this certificate may be registered in the Commissary's Court of your Lordship. E E Elliott, Thomas Nicholson, John Trotter. (GDR/350/263)

BADGEWORTH
Shurdington was a chapelry in Badgeworth parish; Little Witcombe was a township.

219 Badgeworth. (Easter 1690). Thomas Lawrence's barn. (Q/SO/3/522)

220 Little Witcombe, Badgeworth. 22 July 1778 (1 Aug 1778). We being [dissenters] intend to hold a meeting for the worship of Almighty God in the dwelling house of William Smith, cordwainer, at Little Witcomb in the parish of Badgeworth and therefore pray that this certificate may be registered. Samuell Elbridge, William Smith jnr, Henry Bubb, John Ball, Thomas Wiggel, William Hogg. (GDR/292A/211)

221 Little Shurdington, Badgeworth. 27 Oct 1825 (2 Nov 1825). We the undersigned certify that a house and garden in the tithing or hamlet of Little Shurdington in the parish of 'Badgworth', in the possession of Joseph Shill as yearly tenant, is intended forthwith to be a place of religious worship and we request you to register the same. John Timbrell, John Blackwell (mark), George Blackwell, William Smith, Joseph Shill (mark). (GDR/350/48)

222 Shurdington, Badgeworth. 12 Aug 1836 (12 Aug 1836). I Mark Cunningham of Leckhampton certify that a dwelling house in the occupation of Baynham Coopey in the parish of Badgeworth in the village of Shurdington is intended forthwith to be a place of religious worship and I require you to register the same and request a certificate thereof. (GDR/350/198)

BARNSLEY

223 'Barnsly in Britwell Barrow Hund in county of Gloucesr' [Brightwells Barrow]. 6 Jan 1741/42 (registered Epiphany 1741/2, Q/SO/7/f.19r). [*Presbyterian: see note*]. 'We whose names are under writen do desir you to grant us a licence to licence a house to worship God in that we may enjoy the Liberty of Conscienc. We would have the hous of David Larner licenced at the Generall Quarter Sesions held at the Boothall in Gloucester. David Larner, William Larner, Robert Wake Rowland, Drew Larner, Richard Allaway, John Keen, Jestinin Mors'. (Q/SR/1742/A 8)
Note. Poor handwriting and spelling but reasonably legible. [*see* illus., 306] Quarter Sessions Order Book records certificate for Mr David Larner's house for 'Presbyterians to assemble and meet together in for the worship of Almighty God in their way'.

224 Barnsley. 21 Dec 1786 (30 Dec 1786; registration GDR/319A/58). This is to certify that we [named below] intend to hold a meeting for the worship of Almighty God in the house of James 'Shermer' in the parish of Barnsley. We therefore pray that this certificate may be entered in your Lordship's registry. James Shurmer, John Shurmer, William Larner, John James, Edward Larner. (GDR/N2/1)
Note. Dates as entered on back of very small piece of paper and very small handwriting.

BAUNTON

225 Baunton. 25 Mar 1727. These are to certify you that [dissenters] intend to hold a meeting for the worship of God in their way in the house of Robert Hancocks at Baunton near Cirencester and pray that it may be registered. Joseph Everard, Martin Lloyd, William Barnerd (GDR/279a/168). [*see* illus., lxxiii]
Note. 'Bawnton' in rubric. For Joseph Everard *see* **197**.

BECKFORD

In Worcestershire since 1931. Ashton under Hill, which see, was sometimes styled a chapelry of Beckford because the impropriation was annexed to Beckford.
226 Beckford. 1672. *Presbyterian*. Licence recorded 5 Sept 1672 to 'John Humpherys' of Beckford, and for [his] house. (LT/559)

227 Grafton, [Beckford]. (Epiphany 1692/3). *Quaker*. Daniel Dobbins house. (Q/SO/3/522)
Note. RG/31/6 has 'Grafton, Beckford'.

228 Beckford. (Easter 1700). *Presbyterian*. Benjamin Bayley's house. (Q/SO/3/521)

229 Grafton [Beckford]. (Easter 1709). *Presbyterian*. Alice Baylis house. (Q/SO/3/520)

230 Beckford. 5 September 1822 (6 Sept 1822). I Joseph Allen of Kemerton, dissenting minister, certify that a farmhouse in the parish of Beckford, now in the occupation of Thomas Barnett, is intended forthwith to be a place of religious worship and I require you to register the same. (GDR/344/36v) *Note.* Rubric states Kemerton.

BERKELEY

The large parish of Berkeley contained the chapelry of Stone, which see, the tithings of Alkington, Hinton and Ham, and the hamlets of Breadstone and Hamfallow.

231 Berkeley. 1672. *Presbyterian*. Licence recorded for the house of Eliza Bayly of 'Berkly'. (LT/581)

232 Berkeley. (Epiphany 1702/3). *Presbyterian*. 'Marg' Alcott's mill house. (Q/SO/3/521)

233 Berkeley. (Epiphany 1702/3). *Presbyterian*. Richard Clark's house. (Q/SO/3/521)

234 Berkeley. (Michaelmas 1705). *Presbyterian*. William Hawks's house. [RG/31/6 has Hawke's] (Q/SO/3/521)
Note. William Hawkes of Berkeley, dissenting preacher, took oaths of allegiance and supremacy on 6 Dec 1715. (Q/SO/4/[8]) Named in Evans list.

235 Alkington, [Berkeley]. (Epiphany 1708/9). *Presbyterian*. A new erected house. (Q/SO/3/520)

236 Woodford, Alkington, Berkeley. 1 Apr 1779 (3 Apr 1779). *Independent*. 'We [named below] being protestants dissenting from the Church of England and called or known by the name or denomination of Independents do hereby certify your Lordship that we intend to assemble (with others who may choose to do the same) on Monday the fifth day of this instant April for the publick worshipping of Almighty God in the dwelling house of Thomas Jones (being one of us the subscribers) at Woodford in the tything of Alkington in the parish of Berkeley . . . And that the said dwelling house will from henceforth be used for the same sacred purpose which we hereby desire may be registered in your Lordship's Ecclesiastical Court.' Thomas Jones, Daniel Long, Joseph Heaven, William Oldland, William Mower. (GDR/292A/219)
Note. Date specified for first meeting.

237 Berkeley. (15 Dec 1804). These are to certify that we [named below] with others intend to hold a meeting for the worship of Almighty God in the dwelling house of Mr Samuel King in the town of Berkeley and pray that it may be registered. Mr Williams, Valentine Ward, Samuel Howell, Mr Hardwicke, James Warner. (GDR/334B/435)

238 Berkeley. (6 Dec 1806). We [named below] certify that a building called Berkeley Chapel and the dwelling near to the chapel, now in the 'tenor' and occupation of John King, cordwainer, and all the ground and premises to the distance of one hundred yards round about the said chapel in the borough of Berkeley, is appropriated to the publick worship of Almighty God and request the same may be registered and a certificate thereof. Thomas Allen jnr, George Hopkins, William Baker, Thomas Allen (mark), George Smith, John Smith, John Neale, William Smith, William Worthington. (GDR/334B/426-5)

239 Halmore Green, [Hamfallow], Berkeley. 24 June 1809 (27 June 1809). These are to certify that some dissenters intend to hold a meeting for the worship of Almighty God on the piece of ground around the Great Elm on Halmore Green in the parish of Berkeley. We pray that this certificate be registered. William Worthington, Thomas Trinder, George Cornock snr, George Cornock, Thomas Stinchcome, William Hardwick. (GDR/334B/400)

240 Breadstone, Berkeley. (26 Oct 1809). We [named below] certify that the dwelling house of Richard Brain of Breadstone in the parish of Berkeley, labourer, is appropriated for the public worship of Almighty God and we require the same may be registered and a certificate of the same given. George Cornock, Thomas Stinchcomb, Hester Knight,

Robert Price (mark), William Worthington, John Womorsley, Samuel Lear. (GDR/334B/396)

Note. Samuel Lear certified five meetings in the north Cotswold area. *See* **409**, **886**, **926**, **1848**.

241 Alkington, Berkeley. 3 Aug 1815 (8 Aug 1815). I Stephen Hopkins of 'Woottonunderedge' certify that the house of John Organ in the tithing of Alkington in the parish of 'Berkley' is intended forthwith to be a place of religious worship and I require you to register the same and request a certificate thereof. (GDR/334B/327)

242 Michaelwood Common, Berkeley. 6 Mar 1820 (28 Mar 1820). I William Croome of White Hall on Michael Wood Common in the parish of Berkeley, labourer, certify that the tenement occupied by me is intended occasionally to be a place of religious worship and I require you to register the same. (GDR/334B/244)

243 Hinton, [Berkeley]. 3 Feb 1821 (3 Feb 1821). [*Wesleyan Methodist*]. I Richard Tyndall of Chipping Sodbury, schoolmaster, certify that a tenement in the parish of Hinton, now occupied by Charles Watkins, is intended forthwith to be a place of religious worship and require you to register the same. (GDR/334B/228)

Note. Rubric names Chipping Sodbury. It is assumed that Hinton is in Berkeley parish rather than Dyrham; Lewis 1 (1831) 395 noted that 'there is a place for Wesleyan Methodists' in Hinton tithing in Berkeley parish.

244 Berkeley. 31 May 1832 (1 June 1832). I William Jarman Cross of Thornbury, minister, certify that it is intended to use the Town Hall in the town of Berkeley for the purpose of religious worship, which is intended to contain a congregation exceeding 20 persons. (GDR/350/128)

245 Bevington, [Ham], Berkeley. 29 May 1841 (15 June 1841). I James Darke of the parish of Berkeley certify that a cottage in Bevington in the parish of Berkeley, in the occupation of Thomas Nash, is to be a place of religious worship and I request you to register the same and request a certificate thereof for which shall be taken no more than two shillings and six pence. (GDR/350/282)

246 Berkeley. 29 Apr 1844 (21 May 1844). [*Independent: see note*]. I James Darke of the parish of Berkeley certify that a building called Union Chapel in Salter Street, Berkeley, is intended to be a place of religious worship and I request you to register the same and request a certificate thereof for which shall be taken no more than two shillings and six pence. (GDR/350/342) *4288*

Note. Munden, 4.41 has return from Union chapel, Independent; foundation stone laid in 1835 and opened for worship 1836.

BEVERSTON

247 Beverston. (Easter 1700). *Presbyterian.* 'Beaverston, Jo: Shipway's house'. [RG/31/2 has Joseph]. (Q/SO/3/521)

BIBURY

The parish included Ablington and Arlington, and the chapelry of Winson, which see.

248 Bibury. (Easter 1706). *Independent.* Thomas Pooles house. [RG/31/6 has Poolett] (Q/SO/3/520)

249 Bibury. 21 Dec 1715. John Holtham of Bibury, dissenting preacher, took oaths of allegiance and supremacy and made, repeated and subscribed the declaration against transubstantiation of 30 Charles II. (Q/SO/4/[10])

250 Arlington, Bibury. (Epiphany 1730/31). *Independent*. It is ordered by this court that [dissenters] called Independents living in about the parish of Bibury be and hereby are licensed to meet in the dwelling house of Mr Thomas Marchant in Arlington in the parish of Bibury. (Q/SO/5/f.150v)
Note. Rubric has 'Independents Meeting-house Bibury'.

251 Arlington, Bibury. 12 Jan 1746/47 (Michaelmas 1746). *Independent*. 'We [named below] do certify his Majesties Justices of the Peace held at Gloucester for the said county the 12 day of Jan in the twenty-first year of the Reign of our soveraigne Lord George the second by the Grace of God King of Great Britain etc Anno domini 1747 That His Majesty's Protestant dissenting subjects called Independents do intend to hold a meeting for the worship and service of God in their way in a house erected for that purpose in Arlington in the parish of Bibury in the county, which we humbly desire may be recorded at the sd. Sessions.' Richard Acock, Thomas Hignell, William Pearce, Joseph Brindle, John Greenwood, John Munden, Thomas Collett. [Endorsed] Michas 1746' (Q/SR/1748/A)
Note. Petition endorsed on back 'Michaelmas 1746' and 'Epiphany sessions entered'; not in QS order book or in RG/31/6.

252 Arlington, Bibury (Trinity 1754). *Independent*. New built house. (RG/31/6 75)
Note. Record not found in Quarter Sessions Order Book.

253 Arlington, Bibury. 6 Dec 1760. *Independent*. Some [dissenters] called Independents intend to hold a meeting for the worship of Almighty God in a house in a place called the Row in Arlington in the parish of Bibury and now in the possession of one John Shurmur and therefore desire the same may be registered. Samuel Acock, John Shurmur, John Barns, Joseph Barnns, Thomas Savery. (GDR/292A/16)

254 Bibury. 8 Mar 1842 (11 Mar 1842). [*Primitive Methodist: see note*]. I Joseph Preston of Brinkworth, Wilts, certify that a house and premises at Bibury, now in the holding and occupation of William Davis, are intended to be a place of religious worship and I do hereby request you to register the same and request a certificate thereof for which shall be taken no more than two shillings and six pence. Witness E Preston. (GDR/350/292)
Note. Joseph Preston and J Excell were the two 'missioners' from Brinkworth who travelled into Gloucestershire, visiting Tetbury first. (Tonks 55) *See* **255**, **557**, **716**, **1001**, **1190**, **1482**, **1527**, **2052**.

255 Ablington [Bibury]. [*Primitive Methodist: see* **254**] 8 Mar 1842 (11 Mar 1842). I Joseph Preston of Brinkworth, Wilts, certify that a house and premises at Ablington in the parish of Ablington, now in the holding and occupation of Samuel Spencer are intended to be a place of religious worship and I request you to register the same and request a certificate thereof for which shall be taken no more than two shillings and six pence. Witness E Preston. (GDR/350/292)

BISHOP'S CLEEVE
Stoke Orchard, which see, was a chapelry in Bishop's Cleeve.
256 [Bishop's] Cleeve. 1672. *Congregational*. Application by Owen Davies for licence to 'Josua Steed', minister, of Cleeve, at his own house; licence recorded 29 May 1672 to 'Josuah Heed' to be a congregational teacher in his house in 'Cleve, Gloucestershire Congregational meeting' and for his house; licence received for Joshua Steed 1 June 1672. (LT/372, 388, 497)

257 Gotherington, Bishop's Cleeve. 1802 (22 Oct 1802). We [named below, dissenters] have set apart the house of Richard Williams in the hamlet of Gotherington in the parish of

Bishop's Cleeve for the worship of Almighty God and humbly request it may be registered. Richard Gower, John Harris, James Trenfield, John Fisher, Thomas Croswell, Charles Nind, John Reeve, Richard Williams (mark). (GDR/N2/1)
Note. No record in Diocesan Act Book or RG/31/2.

258 Gotherington, [Bishop's Cleeve]. (15 Mar 1809). *Methodist.* We [named below] certify that a house in the occupation of John Hall, tailor, in the hamlet of Gotherington in the parish of Bishop's Cleeve is to be used for the worship of Almighty God by dissenters commonly called Methodists and require that the same may be registered and a certificate given accordingly. William Kent, Charles Nind, Peter Roberts (mark), John Hall, Thomas Barsell, Thomas Creswell. (GDR/334B/406-05)

259 Woodmancote, Bishop's Cleeve. (12 Jan 1811). This is to certify that we [named below] have taken a house in the village of Woodmancote in the parish of Bishop's Cleeve, the property of William Gyde of Cheltenham. And we certify the same at the request and by the desire of the said William Gyde and several others to the intent that the same may be registered 'as a place of Divine Service and public dissenters' and a certificate be given. John Jeffries Church, William Gyde, George Hopkinson, Henry Fyffe, Ebenezer Bradshaw, B Drayton, N A Cesar, George Gibbs, Samuel Fisher. (GDR/334B/368)

260 Woodmancote, Bishop's Cleeve. 28 Aug 1822 (7 Sept 1822). We [named below] certify that a house in Woodmancote in the parish of Bishop's Cleeve, the property of Charles Parker, is intended to be forthwith a place of religious worship and we request you to register the same. Samuel Etheridge, Charles Parcker (mark), John Fowler Spencer, John Cull, William Hobbs, George Arkell, John Stanton (mark), Thomas Stanton (mark), William Jackson, James Pitt. (GDR/344/37r)

261 Gotherington, Bishop's Cleeve. 4 Dec 1822 (7 Dec 1822). We [named below] certify that a house, outhouse, garden and court in Gotherington in the parish of Bishop's Cleeve, the property of George Okey, is intended to be forthwith a place of religious worship and we request you to register the same. George Okey (mark), Charles Nind, William Velender, William Prise, James Hyett, William Hobbs jnr, William Tombs, William Hobbs snr, Aron Pools, George Arkell. (GDR/344/40r)

262 Woodmancote, Bishop's Cleeve. 2 Apr 1825 (6 Apr 1825). We the undersigned being dissenters and householders beg leave to inform your Lordship that we intend opening a newly erected chapel or building for the purpose of divine worship at Woodmancote in the parish of Bishop's Cleeve and request that it may be registered. Robert Summerfield, William Jackson, Samuel Etheridge, John Cull, William Surman, William Barnes, Hester Etheridge, Henry Lucy. (GDR/350/37)

263 Bishop's Cleeve. 26 June 1828 (28 June 1828). We [named below] certify that a room or house and piece of 'grownd' in the hamlet in the parish of Bishop's Cleeve, property of 'Hanah' Harris, is intended forthwith to be a place of religious worship and we request you to register the same. Hannah Harris, Isaac Hobbs. (GDR/350/90)

264 Gotherington [Bishop's Cleeve]. 6 June 1834. We certify a building erected on ground granted by Hon. Augustus Henry Berkeley, Lord of the Manor, intended to be a Chapel. John Fowler, William Harman, William Hobbs, John Tayler, Thomas Roberts, John Reeve, Richard Williams, William Jacksons. (GDR/350/153)

265 Bishop's Cleeve. 16 Oct 1834 (16 Oct 1834). I James Gill of Cheltenham certify that a messuage of John Price, schoolmaster in the parish of Bishop's Cleeve, is intended forthwith to be a place of religious worship and I require you to register the same and request a certificate thereof. (GDR/350/158)

266 Bishop's Cleeve. 3 Nov 1834 (5 Nov 1834). I James Smith of Cheltenham certify that a dwelling house in the parish of Bishop's Cleeve, occupied by William Jones, labourer, is intended to be forthwith a place of religious worship and I request you to register the same. Witness Samuel Franklin, James Hughes. (GDR/350/159)

267 [Bishop's] Cleeve. 6 Mar 1841 (11 Mar 1841). *Wesleyan.* I John McOwan of Cheltenham, Wesleyan Minister, certify that a house occupied by Thomas Staite in the village of Cleeve is intended forthwith to be a place of religious worship and I hereby require you to register and record the same and request a certificate thereof. (GDR/350/275)

268 Bishop's Cleeve. 6 Nov 1844 (7 Nov 1844). *Countess of Huntingdon's Connexion.* These are to certify that we [named below] on behalf of ourselves and others have erected a building in the village and parish of Bishop's Cleeve named 'Cleeve Chapel' and intended to be used for the purpose of public worship or divine service, and we request that the said chapel be registered and duly entered in the records of the Consistory court and that a certificate thereof be given to us. Leonard James, minister of Countess of Huntingdon Connexion, Cheltenham; W Sheldon, surgeon, Cheltenham; William Vizier, Cheltenham; James Downing, draper, Cheltenham; Jonas Radford, engraver, Cheltenham. (GDR/350/349)

BISLEY

Chalford, which see, was a chapelry in Bisley; Bussage became a parish in 1848 and Oakridge in 1849.

269 Bisley. (Trinity 1724). *Baptist.* It is ordered by the court that the dwelling house of William Verinder, tallow chandler, near Steven's Bridge in the parish of Bisley be and is hereby licensed and allowed for [dissenters] called Baptists to assemble and meet together for the worship of God in their way according to their petition for the purpose filed and allowed. (Q/SO/5/f.12r)

Note. Rubric has 'Bisley Meeting-house'.

270 Bisley. (Michaelmas 1739). *Quaker.* It is ordered by this court that the dwelling house of Mr Richard Champion, now in the occupation of Thomas Davis, in the parish of Bisley be licensed and allowed for [dissenters] called Quakers to assemble and meet together in for the worship of Almighty God in their way. (Q/SO/6/f.167r)

271 Oakridge Lynch, Bisley. 3 Sept 1742. These are to certify your Lordship that some [dissenters] intend to hold a meeting for the worship of God at the house of Giles Davis 'in that part of Okerridge Linch called the Wherr Corner in the parish of Bisley'. Therefore we pray your Lordship that it may be registered. Thomas Jenkins, William Hogg, Jonathan Gardner (mark), Giles Davies [*sic*], Aaron Davies (mark). (GDR/284/132)

272 Eastcombe, Bisley. 26 Oct 1742. These are to certify your Lordship that some [dissenters] intend to hold a meeting for the worship of Almighty God at the house of James Young in a place called 'Eastombs' in the parish of Bisley and therefore we pray your lordship that the said house may be registered. James Young, William Gardner (mark), John Cornott, T Jenkins. (GDR/284/142)

273 Oakridge Lynch, Bisley. 3 Jan 1743/44. These are to certify your Lordship that some [dissenters] intend to hold a meeting for the worship of God in the dwelling house of Daniel Jew in Oakridge 'Linch' in the parish of Bisley and 'prays' that it may be registered. John Rudhall, Nathaniel Brock, Samuel Bale. (GDR/284/157)

274 Bisley. 14 Aug 1744. *Baptist.* These are to certify your Lordship that some [dissenters] known by the name of Baptists intend to hold a meeting for the worship of God in the dwelling house of John Cook of Averiss Green in the parish of Bisley and pray it may be registered. Nathaniel Cotes, William Cook, William Jones. (GDR/284/164)
Note. Since 1842 Averiss Green has been in Chalford.

275 Bisley. 14 Feb 1746/47. *Baptist.* These are to certify your Lordship that some [dissenters] known by the name of Baptists intend to hold a 'stated meeting' for the publick worship of God in a house bought of Mr Edward Cordrey (lately inhabited by Thomas Smith) near the wood originally known by the name of Bullings Frith or (now) the Coppice Gate, in the parish of Bisley and therefore 'prays' your Lordship that it may be duly registered. John Cook, Samuel Hide, Joseph Waer, Thomas Hide. (GDR/284/178)

276 Bisley. 27 May 1760. *Baptist.* Some [dissenters] of the Baptist denomination 'intends' to hold a meeting for the worship of Almighty God in the dwelling house of Thomas Woodfield in the parish of Bisley and desire that the same may be registered. Thomas Woodfield, Thomas Jelleman (mark), Thomas Skinner, Thomas Jones. (GDR/292A/15)

277 Bisley. 31 Aug 1762. Some [dissenters] intend to hold a meeting for the worship of Almighty God at the dwelling house of William Sansum in the parish of Bisley and desire the same may be registered. James Workman, Henry Bestall, John Hall. (GDR/292A/56)

278 Bisley. 28 Mar 1763. Some dissenting from the Church of England intend to hold a meeting for the worship of God in their way in the dwelling house of David Price in the parish of Bisley. We therefore pray that this may be recorded. William Lloyd, John Hall. (GDR/292A/57)

279 France [Lynch], Bisley. 16 Dec 1771 (17 Dec 1771). These are to certify that [dissenters] intend to hold a meeting for the worship of Almighty God at a place commonly called France Meeting-house in the parish of Bisley and desire the same may be registered. Henry Ballinger, William Lloyd, Edward Taylor. (GDR/292A/154)

280 Bisley. 8 Jan 1772 (1 Feb 1772). These are to certify that [dissenters] intend to hold a meeting for the worship of Almighty God at the dwelling house of William Davis in the parish of Bisley and desire the same may be registered according to a clause in the Act of Toleration. Richard Piercy, Thomas Pincott, William Hogg. (GDR/292A/156)

281 Bisley. 22 Oct 1775 (11 Nov 1775). Some dissenting from the Church of England intend to hold a meeting for the worship of Almighty God in the dwelling house of John Baglin in the parish of Bisley and therefore pray that this may be recorded in your court. William Walker, Daniell Gilman, Maurice Roc: David Price, John Sansum, John Beglin. (GDR/292A/192)

282 Bisley. 28 Sept 1777 (11 Oct 1777). Some [dissenters] intend to hold a meeting for the worship of God in their way in or at the dwelling house of John Bidmead in the parish of Bisley. We therefore pray that this may be recorded. Robert Horlick, William Neale, Thomas Waren, Stephen Watkins, Stephen Pinfold. (GDR/292A/206)

283 Oakridge, Bisley. 18 Mar 1784 (20 Mar 1784; registration GDR/292A/259). These are to certify that some [dissenters] intend to hold a meeting for the worship of Almighty God at the house of Tho [edge torn] Pacey 'scituate' in a place called Oakridge in the parish of Bisley. Therefore we pray your lordship that the said house may be registered in your court. Thomas Peacey, John Innell, Thomas Taylor, Thomas Joiner [Jones in GDR 292A]. (GDR/N2/1)
Note. A very worn page and crossed through vertically many times.

284 Oakridge, Bisley. [9 Apr] 1809 (11 Apr 1809). These are to certify that some dissenters intend holding a meeting for the worship of Almighty God in a building erected for this purpose in the village of 'Oakeridge' in the parish of Bisley. We pray that this certificate be registered. William Restall, Thomas Crook, John Whiting, Reubin Phelps, James Blackwell, William Cook. (GDR/334B/402)
Note. Licence printed in GA D3931/2/9/7/4, where the date of the certificate is recorded (but a reading of the name of William Restall is given as 'William Drestalk').

285 Bisley. 1 Mar 1811 (5 Apr 1811). *Particular Baptist.* We [named below] being dissenters of the Particular Baptist denomination, desiring legally to meet for the religious worship of Almighty God in the dwelling house of Mrs Eleanor Sollars at 'Burage' [?Bussage] in the parish of Bisley request that the same may be registered as appropriated to the said purpose. Simeon James, Benjamin Brinkworth, Samuel Gardener, Mary Gardener, John March, Richard Webb, John Fawkes, Eleanor Sollars, Thomas Davis, Francis Fawks, James Crook, 'Phebe' Williams. (GDR/334B/366)

286 Bisley. 22 Dec 1814 (24 Dec 1814). I Michael Cousin of Stroud, minister, certify that a meeting-house in the parish of Bisley is intended forthwith to be a place of religious worship and require you to register the same and request a certificate thereof. (GDR/334B/333)

287 Tunley, Bisley. 5 Nov 1816 (12 May 1817). I Henry Hawkins of Eastcomb, minister, certify that a building or kitchen at Tunley in the parish of Stroud, in the occupation of Robert Phelps, labourer, the proprietor, is intended forthwith to be used as a place of religious worship and require you to register the same. Witness William Hurst. (GDR/334B/297)

288 Hilcombe, Bisley. 16 Apr 1818 (18 Apr 1818). I Henry Hawkins of Eastcombe in the parish of Bisley, minister, certify that a building or stone kitchen at Hilcombe in the parish of Bisley, now in the occupation of James Whiting, is intended forthwith to be used as a place of religious worship and require you to register the same. Witness Jacob Aldum. (GDR/334B/282)

289 Bisley. 13 Nov 1819 (13 Nov 1819). We [named below] certify that a building in the parish of Bisley, erected for the purpose, is intended forthwith to be a place of religious worship and require you to register the same and request a certificate thereof. Samuel Nichols minister, James Davis, Jacob Lewis. (GDR/334B/252)

290 Eastcombe, Bisley. 18 Feb 1820 (22 Feb 1820). I Henry Hawkins of 'Eastcombs' in the parish of Bisley, minister, certify that a building or kitchen in the parish of Bisley, now in the occupation of Giles Driver, labourer, is intended forthwith to be a place of religious worship and require you to register the same. Witness Jacob Aldum. (GDR/334B/246)

291 Bisley. 8 Feb 1825 (9 Feb 1825). We the undersigned certify that a house in the occupation of Mr Richard Teakle at Hilleigh in the parish of Bisley is intended forthwith to be a place of religious worship, and we desire you to register and record the same and request a certificate thereof. Richard Heath, Isaac Baglin. (GDR/350/32)

292 Bisley. 4 May 1825 (1 May 1825). I John Burder of Stroud, minister, certify that the house owned and inhabited by Sarah Tranter at Helcomb [Elcombe] in the parish of Bisley is intended to be used forthwith as a place of religious worship and I hereby request you to register the same. (GDR/350/38)
Note. Dates as entered. John Burder certified 13 meetings, *see particularly* **1655***, also* **357**, **358**, **634**, **1296**, **1634**, **1636**, **1644**, **1648**, **1650**, **1652**, **1656**, **1657**.

293 Bisley. 13 July 1825 (16 July 1825). I Robert May of the parish of Bisley, labourer, certify that a building or kitchen in the parish of Bisley, now in my occupation, is intended forthwith to be a place of religious worship and I hereby require you to register the same. Witness Peter Cornock, Stephen Fry (mark), R May. (GDR/350/42)

294 Bisley. 4 Feb 1828 (2 Aug 1828). I William May of the parish of Bisley, labourer, certify that a messuage, tenement or dwelling house at 'Custam Scrubbs' [Custom Scrubs] in the parish of Bisley, now in my own occupation, is intended forthwith to be a place of religious worship and I hereby require you to register the same. (GDR/350/92)
Note. Custom Scrubs, a small common, was the site of a Primitive Methodist chapel in 1840 (*VCH Glos* 11, 37; Munden 10.38).

295 Oakridge, Bisley. 18 Feb 1835 (5 Mar 1835). *Wesleyan.* I Paul Orchard of the town of Stroud certify that a chapel at Oakridge in the parish of Bisley is intended forthwith to be a place of religious worship and I require you to register the same and request a certificate thereof. Paul Orchard, Wesleyan minister. (GDR/350/166)

296 Bussage, Bisley. 12 Feb 1841 (12 Feb 1841). I Samuel Watkins of Bussage in the parish of Bisley certify that my house and premises at Bussage, now in [my] holding and occupation, are intended to be a place of religious worship and I request you to register the same and request a certificate thereof for which shall be taken no more than two shillings and six pence. (GDR/350/274)

297 Bussage, Bisley. 9 Aug 1844 (10 Aug 1844). We [named below] certify that a building at Bussage in the parish of Bisley, in the possession or occupation of Francis Fawkes, is intended to be a chapel for religious worship and I request that this certificate may be duly registered. Francis Fawkes, John Pincott. (GDR/350/346)

298 Tunley, Bisley. (15 Apr 1850). Chapel. Thomas Webb. [RG/31/2 has of Stroud]. (Q/RNp/4)

BITTON

The large ancient ecclesiastical parish of Bitton had four tithings: Bitton, Hanham, Oldland and Upton. Hanham was a chapelry, and became a parish in 1842 and Oldland was also a chapelry (and became a parish in 1861); both are listed separately. Kingswood, a village in Oldland tithing, became a parish in 1821; no certificates were registered for this Kingswood. Kingswood parish near Wotton-under-Edge, although surrounded by Gloucestershire, was in Wiltshire until transferred to Gloucestershire in 1844, and is listed below.

299 Bitton. *Presbyterian.* 1672. Licence recorded 5 Sept 1672 to Thomas Hardcastle of 'Bittin' in Gloucestershire to be a Presbyterian teacher. (LT/560)

300 Bitton. (Epiphany 1699/1700). *Independent.* 'Jos: Roswell's house'. [RG/31/6 has James Rodwell]. (Q/SO/3/521)

301 Bitton. (Michaelmas 1702). *Presbyterian*. A new house on Jeffreys Hill. [RG/31/6 has Jefferies Hill] (Q/SO/3/521)

302 Bitton. (Trinity 1705). The Goal house, T Baylis's. (Q/SO/3/521)

303 North Common, Bitton. 3 Oct 1760 (registered Michaelmas 1760, Q/SO/8/f.246v). *Presbyterian*. We [named below] Protestant subjets dissenting from the Church of England, certify that we intend to make use of the house of John Pincher, on the North Common in the parish of Bitton as a place of meeting for religious worship, and pray that the said house may be recorded at the sessions, as a place of meeting for [dissenters] '(Presbyterians)'. John Pinker, Isaac Jefferis (mark), Samuel Herver (mark), Edward Monk, William Brown, Emerson Gerrish, Thomas Brain, Joseph Pencock, Robert Miledge. (Q/SR/1760/D/18)

Note. The signatures are mainly rather illiterate. The document is endorsed in scratchy writing in the left-hand bottom corner 'House of me Jno Pincker in the North Common' but he had two goes at his surname: crossed out is 'Pinker'. In the text a 'c' is inserted before the 'h', but the 'k' is very distinct in the signature.

304 Bitton. (8 Feb 1794). We [named below] signify to the 'Register' of the Bishop's Court that a house in the occupation of Mr John Jewson in the parish of Bitton is intended to be a place for the religious worship of God. And we desire the Register of the Bishop's Court to record the same. John Jewson, Jane Jewson, James Evans. (GDR/319A/164)

305 Bitton. (9 Jun 1794). We [named below] signify to the Register of the Bishop's court that a house in the occupation of Mr John Hopes in the parish of Bitton is intended to be a place for the religious worship of God and we desire the Register to record the same. John Hopes (mark), Stephen Matthews, Thomas Proctor, Ann Palmer, John Terris. (GDR/319A/183)

306 Bitton. 27 Jan 1810 (3 Feb 1810). We [named below] have set apart and appropriated for the public worship of Almighty God a room known by the name of 'the New Room' on the premises of Henry Hill Budgett in the parish of Bitton and request that the same may be registered and a certificate granted. Robert Britton, H. H. Budgett, Thomas Tindey, Thomas Edwards, William Wragge, George Shadford, William Stephens, Joseph Hobbs. (GDR/334B/395-94)

307 Bitton. 2 Apr 1811 (15 Apr 1811). These are to certify that some dissenters intend to hold meetings for the worship of Almighty God in the dwelling house of James Middleton in the parish of Bitton. We pray that this certificate be registered. James Middleton, J Pinder, Ann Hussey, M Hussey, James Roberts, Jonas Felden, Ann Felden, Samuel Whyatt. (GDR/334B/366)

308 Bitton. 29 Mar 1812 (4 Apr 1812). These are to certify that some dissenters intend to hold a meeting for the worship of Almighty God in a room known by the name of the New Room on the premises of George Clark in the parish of Bitton. We pray that this certificate be registered. H H Bugett, Robert Britton, Joseph Hobbs, James Roberts, Samuel Webb, George Clark, James Olds, John Pool. (GDR/334B/353)

309 Warmley, Bitton. 7 May 1835 (8 May 1835). *Methodist*. I Jonathan Woodington of the parish of Siston certify that a new building, Warmley Methodist Chapel in the parish of Bitton, is intended forthwith to be a place of religious worship and I require you to register the same and request a certificate thereof. (GDR/350/173)

310 Kingswood Hill, Bitton. 29 July 1844 (7 Sept 1844). *Wesleyan*. I James Heaton of Kingswood Hill in the parish of Bitton, certify that a building newly erected at Kingswood Hill called the Wesleyan Methodist Chapel, near turnpike road leading from Bristol to Marshfield, is forthwith to be a place of religious worship and I require you to register the same and request a certificate thereof. (GDR/350/348)

311 Soundwell, Bitton. 4 May 1846 (15 May 1846). Wesleyan. I Wiliam Davis of Kingswood Hill in the parish of Bitton, certify that a building newly erected at 'Sundwell' called the Wesleyan Methodist School Room and Preaching House, near turnpike road leading from Kingswood Hill to Downend in the parish of Bitton is intended forthwith to be a place of religious worship and I require you to register the same and request a certificate thereof. (GDR/350/386)
Note. Munden, *Religious Census* includes several Wesleyan Methodist chapels in Bitton but only one at Soundwell which was in Mangotsfield. *See* **120**.

312 Bitton. (9 Nov 1850). *Wesleyan Methodist chapel*. Charles Clay. (Q/RNp/4)
Note. For Charles Clay *see* **120**.

BLAISDON
313 Blaisdon. 9 Feb 1818 (10 Feb 1818). I James Wood of Norfolk Buildings near the city of Gloucester certify that a dwelling house in the parish of Blaisdon in the Hundred of 'Wesbury', occupied by William Harper, carpenter, is intended forthwith to be used as a place of religious worship and request you to register the same. (GDR/334B/284)

314 Nottwood, Blaisdon. 19 February 1822 (20 Feb 1822). I, Robert Jennings of the city of Gloucester, printer, do hereby certify that a dwelling house at 'Notwood' in the parish of Blaisdon occupied by Robert Burcher, labourer, is intended to be forthwith a place of religious worship; and I request you to register the same. (GDR/344/17v)

315 Nottwood, Blaisdon. 2 Feb 1828 (4 Feb 1828). I William Lawry, minister, certify that the dwelling house of Samuel Burcher [of] 'Notwood' in the parish of Blaisdon is intended forthwith to be a place of religious worship and I hereby require you to register the same and request a certificate thereof. William Lawry, Samuel Burcher (mark). (GDR/350/82)

316 Blaisdon. 28 May 1842 (28 May 1842). I John Rowe of Gloucester, Local Missionary, certify that a messuage, now in the occupation of John Dobbins, mason, in the parish of Blaisdon is intended forthwith to be a place of religious worship and I require you to register the same and request a certificate thereof. (GDR/350/298)

317 Blaisdon. 28 Mar 1844 (28 Mar 1844). *Baptist*. I Henry Clement Davis of Blaisdon, Baptist minister, certify that a messuage, now in my occupation, in the parish of Blaisdon is intended forthwith to be a place of religious worship and I require you to register the same and request a certificate thereof. (GDR/350/354)
Note. Entry out of order, following Dec 1844.

BLAKENEY
Blakeney was a tithing in Awre parish, and had a chapel by 1551; it was created a parish in 1853. (VCH Glos 5, 17, 22, 43). By the 18th century the village was the effective centre of the parish. The chapelry extended beyond the boundaries of the tithing into Etloe tithing in Awre (see 213).
318 Blakeney. (Michaelmas 1691). Ansel Naish's house. [RG/31/6 has Anselm Nash] (Q/SO/3/522)

319 Blakeney. (Michaelmas 1691). James Bayly's house. (Q/SO/3/522)

320 Blakeney. (Michaelmas 1691). [*Presbyterian: see note*]. Nicholas Billingsley's [house], Clerk. (Q/SO/3/522)
Note. The Evans list names Nicholas Billingsley, Presbyterian minister. *See* Introduction, xlviii.

321 Blakeney [RG/31/6 has Awre]. (Michaelmas 1691). Edmond Browne's. (Q/SO/3/522

322 Blakeney [RG/31/6 has Awre]. (Epiphany 1693/4). *Presbyterian and Independent.* 'Phillip' Pace's house. (Q/SO/3/522)
Note. This entry for Blakeney and the one following for Falfield **799** are difficult to disentangle.

323 Blakeney. (8 June 1727). [*Presbyterian: see note*]. These are to certify that [dissenters] intend to hold a meeting for the worship of God in their way in the dwelling house of David Thomas, minister in the town of 'Blackney' in the parish of Awre and pray that it may be registered. Joseph Everard, Nathaniel Brock, Martin Lloyd, William Lodge. (GDR/279a/171)
Note. David Thomas was named as Presbyterian minister of Blakeney in 1727 in the Evans list which indicates that the congregation about 1715 may have numbered 100. For Joseph Everard *see* **197**.

324 Blakeney. 5 Jan 1793 (2 Mar 1793). These are to certify that we [named below] with others intend to hold a meeting for the worship of Almighty God in a building in the village of Blakeney and desire it may be registered in your Lordship's Court. Richard Cue, D Williams, Richard Stiff, W Harding, S Harding, T Stiff, Joshua Halin. (GDR/319A/146)
Note. For Richard Stiff *see* Introduction, lxv–lxvi; he certified six more meetings in the Forest. *See* **325**, **641**, **642**, **1069**, **1108**, **1070**.

325 Blakeney. 30 July 1795 (3 Aug 1795). [*Independent: see Introduction, lxvi*]. We [named below] certify that an house in the occupation of Richard Craduck and Richard Stiff in the tithing of Blakeney in the parish of Awre is intended to be a place of religious worship and we request that it may be registered William Bishop, minister, Richard Stiff, Richard Craduck, John Smith. (GDR/319A/211-2)
Note. For Richard Stiff see **324**.

326 Blakeney. (19 Mar 1818). This is to certify that there is a building in the possesson of Thomas Gilbert and Daniel London in Blakeney that is intended to be a place of public worship. We [named below] request that the same may be registered. Daniel London, James Waters, Henry Powell, Thomas Gilbert, George Imm, James Martin. (GDR/334B/283)

327 Blakeney. 23 Aug 1823 (25 Aug 1823). I Isaac Bridgman now residing at the Wood Side Cottage near Blakeney certify that a new building called Blakeney Tabernacle situated near the Wood Side, Blakeney, in the parish of Awre, is intended forthwith to be a place of religious worship and I require you to register the same and request a certificate thereof. (GDR/344/112v)
Note. VCH *Glos* 5, 44 places this chapel at Brains Green. For Isaac Bridgman *see* **210**.

328 [Blakeney] Awre. (26 Nov 1850). *Independent.* Building called the Tabernacle or Independent chapel. Richard Watts White. (Q/RNp/4)
Note. RG/31/2 locates the chapel in Blakeney and *VCH Glos* 5, 44 on the Ayleford Road in Blakeney; it was a replacement for the earlier Tabernacle.

BLEDINGTON
329 Bledington. 27 July 1847 (4 Aug 1847). These are to certify that a house in the parish of 'Bleddington', now in the occupation of John Benfield, is intended to be forthwith a

place of religious worship and we the undersigned request that the same may be registered. John Benfield, William Davis, William Stayte, Joseph Miles. (GDR/350/388)

330 Bledington. (2 Apr 1852). *Wesleyan.* Chapel. Sam Cooke, Chipping Norton, Wesleyan Minister (RG/31/2)

BODDINGTON
331 Hayden [Boddington]. (Easter 1707). 'Heyden', Elizabeth Halling's house. (Q/SO/3/520)

332 Barrow, Boddington. 19 Oct 1816 (19 Oct 1816). [*Methodist: see note*]. I Daniel Campbell of Gloucester, minister, certify that the house of William Turner of the Barrow in the parish of 'Bodington' is intended forthwith to be a place of religious worship and I require you to register the same and request a certificate thereof. (GDR/334B/311)
Note. For Daniel Campbell *see* **179**.

333 Barrow, Boddington. 13 Nov 1819 (13 Nov 1819). [*Methodist: see* **166**]. I James Byron of Gloucester certify that the now dwelling house of Samuel Hay 'of Barrow of the Bodington' is intended forthwith to be a place of religious worship and require you to register the same and require a certificate thereof. (GDR/334B/251)

334 Hayden, Boddington. 14 June 1821 (15 Jun 1821). I, Oliver Watts, minister, Hayden Villa, certify that a dwelling house in the parish of Boddington, the property of James Barnes, builder, Hayden Villa, and occupied by [me] and James Barnes, is intended forthwith to be a place of religious worship and request you to register the same. (GDR/334B/218)

335 Barrow, Boddington. 13 Oct 1840 (13 Oct 1840). I Daniel Browett of the parish of Leigh certify that the house of James Hopkins and premises at the Barrow in the parish of Boddington, now in [his] holding and occupation, are intended to be a place of religious worship and I request you to register the same and request a certificate thereof for which shall be taken no more than two shillings and six pence. (GDR/350/259)
Note. Rubric is 'Leigh' but the house is in Boddington.

336 Boddington. (9 Mar 1850). Room in a house occupied by Henry Freeman. Henry Freeman. (Q/RNp/4)

BOURTON-ON–THE-HILL
Moreton-in-Marsh, which see, was a chapelry annexed to Bourton-on-the-Hill.
337 Bourton-on-the-Hill. 21 Dec 1715. Robert Greening of Bourton-on-the-Hill, dissenting preacher, took oaths of allegiance and supremacy and made declaration against transubstantiation. (Q/SO/4/[10])

338 Bourton-on-the-Hill. 18 May 1821 (21 May 1821). This is to certify that a barn at Bourton on the Hill, in the occupation of John Wheatcroft, is intended to be a place of religious worship and request that the said barn be registered and a certificate granted accordingly. Daniel Wright, John Wheatcroft, Crescius Smith. (GDR/334B/222)

339 Bourton-on-the-Hill. 10 Feb 1835 (13 Feb 1835). I James Morish of Moreton-in-Marsh certify that a dwelling house and premises at Bourton-on-the-Hill, now in the holding and occupation of William Brain of Bourton-on-the-Hill, the property of Ralph Gardner of Bourton, are intended to be used as a place of religious worship and I request you to register the same and request a certificate thereof for which shall be taken no more than two shillings and six pence. Witness Ralph Gardner, William Brain, Joseph Russell. (GDR/350/164)

340 Bourton-on-the-Hill. 15 Feb 1840 (17 Feb 1840). I Francis H Green of Moreton parish certify that a dwelling house in the occupation of Thomas Jennings in the parish of Bourton-on-the-Hill is intended forthwith to be used as a place of religious worship and I request you to register the same and request a certificate thereof. (GDR/350/250)

BOURTON-ON-THE-WATER

Clapton, which see, was a chapelry; Lower Slaughter, which see, was a parish annexed to Bourton-on-the-Water.

341 Bourton [on-the-Water?]. 1672. *Congregational.* Licence recorded for the house of Giles Lawrence in 'Burton', Gloucestershire. (LT/525)
Note. Giles Lawrence also had a house licensed in Broadway. (LT/525)

342 Bourton-on-the-Water. 1672. Application by Owen Davies for licence to Mr Driver at Bourton-on-the-Water in Gloucestershire, 'a village'. (LT/243)

343 Bourton-on-the-Water. 1672. *Congregational.* Application for licence to John Dunce, preacher, at Giles Lardner's house, 'Burton on the Water'; licence recorded 10 Aug 1672 for John Dunce to be a general teacher. (LT/372, 548)

344 Bourton-on-the-Water. (Trinity 1689). 'Jo:' Johnson's barn [RG/31/6 has Jos.]. (Q/SO/3/522)

345 Bourton-on-the-Water. (Epiphany 1689/90). Thomas Collett's house. (Q/SO/3/522)
Note. Thomas Collett of Bourton-on-the-Water, dissenting preacher, took oaths of allegiance and supremacy on 21 Dec 1715. (Q/SO/4/[10])

346 Bourton-on-the-Water. (Trinity 1701) *Baptist.* A new erected house. (Q/SO/3/521)
Note. Joshua Head of Lower Slaughter, who took oaths of allegiance and supremacy, was named as Anabaptist minister at Bourton-on-the-Water [**1102**] in Evans list.

347 Bourton-on-the-Water ['Bourton sup acqua' in rubric]. (Epiphany 1723/4). It is ordered by this court that the dwelling house of John Collett in Bourton-on-the-Water be licensed for [dissenters] called [blank] to assemble and meet together in for the worship of God in their way. (Q/SO/4/471)

348 Bourton-on-the-Water ['Bourton sup acqua' in rubric]. (Epiphany 1723/4). It is ordered by this court that the dwelling house of Thomas Kite lying and being in Bourton-on-the-Water be licensed for [dissenters] called [blank] to assemble and meet together in for the worship of God in their way. (Q/SO/4/472)

349 Bourton-on-the-Water ['Bourton sup acqua' in rubric]. (Epiphany 1723/4). It is ordered by this court that the dwelling house of Andrew Paxford in Bourton-on-the-Water be licensed for [dissenters] called [blank] to assemble and meet together in for the worship of God in their way. (Q/SO/4/471)

350 Bourton-on-the-Water. (Michaelmas 1735). *Baptist.* It is ordered by this court that the dwelling house of Richard Strange and William Fox in the parish of Bourton-on-the-Water be licensed and allowed for [dissenters] called Baptists to assemble and meet together 'in pursuant to their petition for that purpose filed and allowed'. (Q/SO/6/f.60v)
Note. RG/31/6 has these two men entered in separate houses.

351 Bourton-on-the-Water. 22 Aug 1829 (22 Aug 1829). I Thomas Brindle of the parish of Bourton-on-the-Water certify that my dwelling house and premises in Bourton-on-the-Water 'is' intended to be a place of religious worship and I request you to register and record the same and request a certificate thereof for which shall be taken no more than two shillings and six pence. Witness William Hood. (GDR/350/104b)

352 Bourton-on–the-Water. 25 July 1831 (25 July 1831), I John Fox of the parish of Bourton-on-the-Water certify that my room called the Assembly Room is intended to be used as a place of religious worship and I hereby require you to register the same and request a certificate thereof for which shall be taken no more than two shillings and six pence. Witness Benjamin Newmarch. (GDR/350/116-7)

353 Bourton-on-the-Water. 10 Mar 1843 (8 Mar 1843). I Job Teale of the parish of Bourton-on-the-Water certify that a building called Zion Chapel at Bourton-on-the-Water is intended to be a place of religious worship and I request you to register the same and request a certificate thereof. (GDR/350/317)
Note. Dates as entered.

354 Bourton-on-the-Water. 24 Feb 1845 (25 Feb 1845). I John M Collard certify that one room in the house belonging to Mr John Fox at Bourton-on-the-Water is intended to be a place of religious worship and I require you to register the same. (GDR/350/357)

355 Bourton-on-the-Water. 13 Oct 1846 (13 Oct 1846). I John M Collard certify that one room in a house belonging to Mr John Painter at Bourton-on-the-Water is intended to be a place of religious worship and I require you to register the same and require a certificate thereof. (GDR/350/380)

BOXWELL
Leighterton, which see, was a chapelry in Boxwell.
356 Boxwell. 10 June 1821 (15 Jun 1821). We, 'X Sarah Robbins', James Hathaway certify the tenement now occupied by Sarah Robbins in the parish of Boxwell is intended occasionally to be a place of religious worship and require you to register the same. (GDR/334B/219)

BRIMPSFIELD
357 Birdlip, Brimpsfield. 21 July 1820 (22 July 1820). I John Burder, minister of the town of Stroud, certify that a building at Birdlip in the parish of Brimpsfield, owned by Giles Tombs, and at present unoccupied, is intended forthwith to be a place of religious worship and I require you to register the same. (GDR/334B/238)
Note. For John Burder *see* **292** & **1655**.

358 Birdlip, Brimpsfield. 30 Mar 1821 (4 Apr 1821). I John Burder, minister, certify that a building owned by Mr Richard Welsh at Birdlip in the parish of Brimpsfield is intended forthwith to be a place of religious worship and I require you to register the same. (GDR/334B/225)
Note. A second certificate on the opposite page of the Act Book (*see following*) registered on 14 Apr, appears to relate to the same property but places it in Cowley, and may be a correction of the previous certificate; a small part of Birdlip was in Cowley parish. For John Burder *see* **292** & **1655.**

359 Birdlip, Cowley. 13 Apr 1821 (14 Apr 1821). I John Burder, minister residing at Stroud, certify that a building at Birdlip in the parish of Cowley, owned by Richard Welsh

and known by the name of Cowley Manor house, is intended forthwith to be a place of religious worship and request you to register the same. (GDR/334B/224)
Note. For John Burder *see* **292 & 1655**.

360 Caudle Green, Brimpsfield. 28 Jan 1825 (29 Jan 1825). I Thomas Davis of Winstone, gentleman, certify that a building or meeting-house at Caudle Green in the parish of Brimpsfield is intended forthwith to be a place of religious worship and I hereby desire you to register the same. Witness E Harding. (GDR/350/31)
Note. Davis was a missionary of the Particular Baptist chapel at Eastcombe (*VCH Glos* 7, 149) *see* **285**.

361 Birdlip, Brimpsfield. 20 June 1834 (23 June 1834). I Benjamin Leach of Cheltenham certify that a building at Birdlip in the parish of Brimpsfield, late in the occupation of Joseph Seabright, is forthwith to be a place of religious worship and I desire you to register the same. Witness James Hughes, John Cox. (GDR/350/154)
Note. Staverton added in pencil over 'Leach'.

362 Birdlip, Brimpsfield. 14 Jan 1842 (14 Jan 1842). *Baptist.* I Samuel Franklin of Cheltenham certify that a new Baptist Chapel in the village of Birdlip in the parish of Brimpsfield is intended to be forthwith a place of religious worship and request you to register the same. (GDR/350/289)

363 Caudle Green, Brimpsfield. 9 May 1846 (9 May 1846). I John Johnson of Cheltenham certify that the house and premises of William Day at Caudle Green in the parish of Brimpsfield, now in [his] holding and occupation, are to be a place of religious worship and I request you to register the same and request a certificate thereof for which shall be taken no more than two shillings and six pence. (GDR/350/375)

BROADWELL
364 Broadwell. 12 July 1742 (registered Trinity 1742, Q/SO/7/f.39v,). *Baptist.* 'We [named below] do hereby humbly request that the house of Robert Perry of Broadwell . . . be licenced for the worship and service of Almighty God (by his majestty's loyal Protestant dissenting subjects of the Baptist perswasion.)'. Thomas Rooke, John Morse, William Read, Robert Perry, Joseph Marsh.
[Endorsed on the back] 'I have sent by the bearer 2 shillings six pence with humble service, from yr friend and servt. Stow July 12 1742.
PSS If you have noe conveniency to send it I will order Thos Rooke the newsman to call for it Jos Marsh'. (Q/SR/1742/C/18)
Note. This is the only certificate with an endorsement of this sort.

365 Broadwell. 24 Oct 1821 (7 Nov 1821). I William Day of Broadwell, gent., certify that my dwelling house at Broadwell is intended forthwith to be a place of religious worship and I require you to register the same and request a certificate thereof. (GDR/334B/212)

366 Broadwell. 1 Nov 1831 (19 Nov 1831). I Thomas Hodgkins of Broadwell in the parish of Broadwell certify that my house and premises at Broadwell, now in [my] holding, are intended to be a place of religious worship and I request you to register and record the same and request a certificate thereof for which shall be taken no more than two shillings and six pence. Thomas Hodgkins, Boaz Tripp, Jonas Jeys (mark). (GDR/350/120-1)

367 Broadwell. 18 Dec 1839 (7 Jan 1840). I Francis H Green of the parish of Moreton certify that a dwelling house iin the occuaption of William Day in the parish of Broadwell is intended forthwith to be a place of religious worship and I request you to register the same and request a certificate thereof. (GDR/350/248)

368 Broadwell. 5 Nov 1840 (21 Dec 1840). I Francis H Green of the parish of Moreton certify that a dwelling house in the occupation of William Day snr in the parish of Broadwell is intended forthwith to be a place of religious worship and I request you to register the same and request a certificate thereof. (GDR/350/267)

BROCKWORTH

369 Coopers Hill, Brockworth. 8 July 1814 (8 July 1814). [*Methodist: see* **178**]. I John Chettle of Gloucester, minister, certify that the house of Richard Organ of Cooper's Hill in the parish of Brockworth is intended forthwith to be a place of religious worship and I require you to register the same and request a certificate thereof. (GDR/334B/336)

370 Brockworth. 10 July 1826 (21 July 1826). We the undersigned certify that a house and garden in the parish of Brockworth, in the possession of Joseph Shill as yearly tenant thereof, is intended to be forthwith a place of religious worship and we request you to register the same. Joseph Shill, minister, William Smith, George Blockwell, John Bardell, Edward Hyett, John Timbrell. (GDR/350/57)

371 Brockworth. (29 Apr 1851). Building called Bethel chapel. Richard Cordwell. (Q/RNp/4)

BROMSBERROW

372 Bromsberrow. (Easter 1702). Jo Stock's house. [RG/31/6 has Joseph Hock's]. (Q/SO/3/521)

373 Bromsberrow. 6 Nov 1733. These are to certify you that [dissenters] in the parish of Bromsberrow intend to hold a meeting in their way in the dwelling house of John Stock and therefore pray that it may be registered. Benjamin Hunt, John Haynes, John Stock, James Lawrence, John Coundley. (GDR/284/28)

374 Bromsberrow. (24 Nov 1848). *Wesleyan.* Chapel. John Smedley. Bromsberrow Heath. (Q/RNp/4)

BROOKTHORPE

375 Brookthorpe. 29 Nov 1817 (29 Nov 1817). [*Methodist: see* **179**]. I Daniel Campbell of Gloucester, minister, hereby certify that the house of William Davis in the parish of 'Brookthrop' is intended forthwith to be used as a place of religious worship and I require you to register the same and require a certificate thereof. (GDR/334B/289)

376 Brookthorpe. 27 Nov 1820 (27 Nov 1820). I Samuel Pitt, tailor of Whiteshill, certify that a dwelling house in the parish of Brookthorpe, occupied by John Mills, is intended to be forthwith a place of religious worship and I request you to register the same. (GDR/334B/230)

BUCKLAND

377 Buckland. 27 Mar 1813 (6 Apr 1813). I William James, labourer, certify that a building messuage or tenement in the parish of Buckland, being myself occupier and Thomas Phillips esq proprietor, is intended forthwith to be a place of religious worship and I require you to register the same. William James (mark), Benjamin Rastall, Samuel Rastall, William Leach (mark). (GDR/334B/346)

378 Buckland. 6 Jan 1818 (2 Feb 1818). I Benjamin Rastall of Buckland, weaver, certify that a building, messuage or tenement in the parish of Buckland, being my property and in my possession, is intended forthwith to be a place of religious worship and I require you to register the same. Witness Samuel Restall. (GDR/334B/285)

379 Laverton, Buckland. 30 June 1828 (4 July 1828). I James Whitworth of Evesham, minister of the Gospel, certify that a building in the hamlet of Laverton in the parish of Buckland, at present occupied by Richard Gibson, is intended forthwith to be a place of religious worship and I require you to register the same and request a certificate thereof. (GDR/350/91)

BULLEY
Bulley was a chapelry in Churcham parish.
380 Bully. (30 Oct 1812). This is to certify that the public worship of God is established by some dissenters in a house belonging to Joseph and Elizabeth Richardson in the parish of Bully, which we desire may be registered. Richard Moody, Mary Moody, John Dickinson (mark), Elizabeth Humpidge, Elizabeth Richardson (mark), Thomas Attwood. (GDR/334B/351)

CAM
381 Cam. (Trinity 1703). *Presbyterian.* James Sanacher's house. (Q/SO/3/521)

382 Cam. (Epiphany 1703/4). *Presbyterian.* A new built house for Presbyterians. (Q/SO/3/521)

383 Cam. 2 Nov 1715. [*Presbyterian: see note*]. Joseph Twemlow, dissenting preacher at Cam, took oaths of allegiance and supremacy. (Q/SO/4/[3])
Note. Joseph Twemlow was the Presbyterian minister in Evans list (ordained in 1707).

384 Newnham Quarry, Cam. 22 Sept 1807 (26 Sept 1807). We [named below] do make known to your Lordship that a house situated at Newnham Quarry in the parish of Cam, in the occupation of Richard Cox, is appropriated and set apart for the purpose of worshipping God and performing religious duties therein and we desire that the same may be registered. William Marsh, John Cox, Stephen Brown (mark), W B Wiltshaw, minister, Sarah Gabb (mark). (GDR/334B/420)
Note. In this entry it is not clear whether William Marsh or W B Wiltshaw is the minister, but the next entry (for Spinkham Bottom, North Nibley **1309**) places 'minister' clearly above W B Wiltshaw's name.

385 Lower Cam [Cam]. 17 June 1817 (19 Jun 1817). We, Thomas Griffith, minister of Cam, and James Holloway, smith, of Lower Cam in the parish of Cam, certify that a part of a tenement in the occupation of James Holloway, smith, in the parish of Cam, consisting of one room situate over the dwelling apartments of James Holloway, is intended forthwith to be used as a place of religious worship and we require you to register the same. (GDR/334B/296)

386 Cam. 6 Sept 1817 (6 Sept 1817). I Thomas Griffith, dissenting minister of Cam, and Thomas Trotman, weaver of the parish of Cam, certify that a part of a tenement in the occupation of Thomas Andrews, labourer of the parish of Cam, formerly used as a malthouse and the court which adjoins the same, are intended forthwith to be used as a place of religious worship and we require you to register the same. Thomas Griffith, Thomas Trotman. (GDR/334B/294-3)

387 Cam. 15 Aug 1818 (23 Oct 1818). I William Underwood of parish of Cam, farrier, certify that a messuage or tenement in the parish of Cam, in the occupation of Ann

Rodway, widow, forthwith is intended to be used as a place of religious worship and I require you to register the same and request a certificate thereof. Witness John Walsh. (GDR/334B/274)

388 Cam. 8 May 1819 (8 May 1819). I Dennis Potter of the parish of Cam certify that a field, belonging to Samuel Holloway in the said parish, is intended forthwith to be a temporary place of religious worship and require you to register the same and request a certificate thereof. (GDR/334B/262)

389 Cam. 16 Mar 1826 (18 Mar 1826). We [named below] inhabitants of Cam certify that a place of worship has been erected in the parish of Cam, near the corner of a parcel of ground called Rowley, in which divine worship will be 'regarly' and duly performed: William Homer, minister, Samuel Holloway, William Underwood, Thomas Hadley. (GDR/350/54)

390 Cam. (3 Aug 1827). We [named below] inhabitants of the parish of Stinchcombe certify that a house near the Quarry in the parish of Cam, formerly in possession of William Hale, labourer, but now void, will henceforth be used as a place of religious worship. Thomas Ashton, minister [RG/31/2 has of Stinchcombe], John Morgan, Thomas Collis, Thomas Stephens. (GDR/350/71)

391 Cam. 22 Apr 1828 (22 Apr 1828). I John Hampton certify that a dwelling house in the parish of Cam, occupied by me, is intended to be forthwith a place of religious worship and I request you to register the same. (GDR/350/87)

CHALFORD
Chalford, one of the nine tithings in Bisley, was early provided with a chapel and became a parish in 1842. It had about 2,000 inhabitants in 1779 (Rudder 289)

392 Chalford, Bisley. (Trinity 1696). *Presbyterian*. A new erected house. (Q/SO/3/521)

393 Chalford, Bisley. 6 Dec 1715. [*Presbyterian: see note*]. Theodore Westmacott of Chalford, dissenting preacher, took oaths of allegiance and supremacy. (Q/SO/4/[8])
Note. Westmacott was the Presbyterian minister in the Evans list.

394 Chalford Lynch, Bisley. 29 Oct 1742. These are to certify your Lordship that some [dissenters] intend to hold a meeting for the worship of God at the house of John Cornett in a place called 'Chalford-Linch' in the parish of Bisley and therefore we pray your Lordship that the said house may be registered. James Young, John Cornott, Robert Davis his mark, T Jenkins. (GDR/284/143)

395 Chalford, Bisley. 14 Mar 1812 (25 Mar 1812). These are to certify that some dissenters intend to set apart for the public worship of Almighty God a building belonging to William Togwill in the village of Chalford and parish of Bisley. We pray that this certificate may be registered. William Smith, William Jones, Timothy Twissell, Robert Lamburn, William Jeffres, James Wood. (GDR/334B/355)

396 Chalford, Bisley. 3 July 1819 (3 July 1819). We [named below] certify that a certain building at Chalford in the parish of Bisley, now occupied by Mrs Mary Innell, is forthwith to be a place of religious worship and require you to register the same and require a certificate thereof. Samuel Nichols, Mary Innell, John Lewis. (GDR/334B/258)

397 Chalford Lynch, Bisley. 29 Dec 1823 (29 Dec 1823). I James Bonser of Stroud certify that a chapel and premises situate in the parish of Bisley, known by the name of Chalford Lynch, now in [my] holding and occupation, are intended to be a place of religious worship and request you to register the same and request a certificate thereof for which shall be taken no more than two shillings and sixpence. (GDR/344/126r)

Note. Rubric is Stroud.

398 Chalford Lynch, Bisley. 17 Dec 1824 (23 Dec 1824). I James Bonser of Stroud certify that a chapel and premises at Chalford Lynch in the parish of Bisley, now in the holding and occupation of James Bonser, are intended to be a place of religious worship and I hereby require you to register and record the same, and request a certificate thereof, for which shall be taken no more than two shillings and sixpence. (GDR/350/26)

399 Chalford, Bisley. 2 Apr 1844 (6 Apr 1844). I John Coxhead of Stroud certify that a room and premises at Chalford in the parish of Bisley, now in the holding and occupation of Samuel Hoare, are intended to be a place of religious worship and I request you to register the same and request a certificate thereof for which shall be taken no more than two shillings and six pence. (GDR/350/338)

400 Chalford [Bisley]. (12 Oct 1850). House occupied by William Wall. William Wall [RG/31/2 has of Horsley, and registration 1 Nov 1850] (Q/RNp/4)

401 Chalford Hill [Chalford, Bisley]. (29 Mar 1852). House. John Gardner [of] Chalford Hill. (RG/31/2/f.126/r)

CHARFIELD
402 Charfield. 17 Sep 1792 (25 Sep 1792). We [named below] certify that we intend to meet for the worship of Almighty God in the house of Joseph Limbrick of Charfield. Therefore pray that this certificate may be registered in your Lordship's Registry. Joseph Rodway, Thomas Limbrick, Joseph Limbrick, Thomas Lords (mark), William Pullin, Thomas Halls, Daniel Rowles, Daniel Wilkins, Moses Amos, Daniel Rodway, William Thomson, Joseph Limbrick jnr, William Boulton. (GDR/319A/141)

403 Charfield. 31 Aug 1816 (11 Sept 1816). I Stephen Hopkins of 'Wottonunderedge' certify that the dwelling house of Thomas Butterworth of the parish of Charfield is intended forthwith to be a place of religious worship and I require you to register the same and request a certificate thereof. Witness Stephen Waterer. (GDR/334B/314)

404 Charfield. 14 Mar 1834 (14 Mar 1834). *Independent & Baptist.* This is to certify that a building in Charfield Green in the parish of Charfield occupied by Tara Earl is intended to be used by a congregation partly of the Independent and partly of the Baptist denomination and I hereby request you to register the same. James Griffiths, minister, Kingswood. (GDR/350/147)

405 Charfield. 14 Mar 1834 (14 Mar 1834). *Independent & Baptist.* This is to certify that a building at Charfield Mills in the parish of Charfield, occupied as a workshop by Samuel Long esq., is intended to be used by a congregation partly of the Independent and partly of the Baptist denomination and I hereby request you to register the same. James Griffiths, minister, Kingswood. (GDR/350/148)

406 Charfield. (23 Oct 1851). Chapel. Stephen Walter [RG/31/2 has of Charfield]. (Q/RNp/4) [*see* illus., xvii]

CHARLTON KINGS
407 Charlton Kings. (Easter 1690). William Welch's house. (Q/SO/3/522)

408 Charlton Kings. (Easter 1690). Richard Kench's house. (Q/SO/3/522)

409 Charlton [Kings]. (10 Dec 1810). We [named below] beg leave to certify that the dwelling of Lawrence Dyer in the parish of Charlton is set apart for the worship of Almighty God and request the same may be registered. Samuel Lear, George Margrett, Lawrence Dyer, John Freeman, John Fisher, Oliver Watts. (GDR/334B/370)
Note. For Samuel Lear *see* **240**.

410 Charlton Kings. 26 July 1822 (26 July 1822). I Oliver Watts of Charlton Kings, minister of the Gospel, certify that a house in [my] occupation in Charlton in the parish of Charlton together with one hundred yards of ground situate in front of the said above house are intended forthwith to be a place of religious worship and I do hereby require you to register and record the same. (GDR/344/33v)

411 Charlton Kings. 15 Mar 1826 (17 Mar 1826). I William Gardner of Cheltenham certify that a dwelling house in Charlton Kings occupied by John Freeman, shoemaker, is intended to be forthwith a place of religious worship and I hereby request you to register the same. (GDR/350/53)

412 Charlton Kings. 14 Sept 1827 (15 Sept 1827). I William M Gardner of Northfield Terrace, Cheltenham, certify that a building named Charlton Chapel in the parish of Charlton Kings is intended to be forthwith a place of religious worship and I hereby request you to register the same. (GDR/350/72)

413 Charlton Kings. 10 Mar 1828 (10 Mar 1828). I Thomas Cornett of Cheltenham certify that a dwelling house in the parish of Charlton Kings, occupied by John Bridgeman, shoemaker, is intended forthwith to be a place of religious worship and I request you to register the same. (GDR/350/84)

414 Charlton Kings. 19 Sept 1833 (11 Jan 1834). I James Smith of Cheltenham certify that a dwelling house in the parish of Charlton Kings, occupied by John Bridgman, shoemaker, is intended forthwith to be a place of religious worship and I hereby request you to register the same. James Smith, James Hughes, William Williams (GDR/350/143)

415 Charlton Kings. 19 Aug 1836 (8 Oct 1836). I John James, labourer, of Charlton Kings certify that the dwelling house and premises, now in [my] holding, are to be a place of religious worship and I request you to register the same and request a certificate thereof for which shall be taken no more than two shillings and six pence. John James (mark). (GDR/350/201)

416 Charlton Kings. 6 July 1837 (7 July 1837). *Wesleyan.* I Jonothan Turner of Cheltenham, Wesleyan minister, certify that a dwelling house at Charlton Kings in the occupation of William Langford is intended forthwith to be a place of religious worship and I require you to register the same and request a certificate thereof. (GDR/350/210)

417 Charlton Kings. (16 May 1851). Schoolroom now occupied by Joseph Hobbs. James Russell. (Q/RNp/4)

418 Charlton Kings. 25 May 1852. Building. John Thurston [of] Gloucester. (RG/31/2/f.126/v)

CHEDWORTH
419 Chedworth. (Trinity 1701). *Quaker.* Thomas Robert's house. (Q/SO/3/521)

420 Chedworth. 16 Nov 1743. These are to certify your Lordship that some [dissenters] intend to hold a meeting for the worship of God at the house of Joseph Humphreys in the parish of Chedworth therefore we pray that it may be registered. Joseph Humphreys, minister, Henry Wilson, Samuel Wakefield, Lawrence Dyer. (GDR/284/156)

421 Chedworth. 29 Aug 1744 (3 May 1745 'entered'). These are to certify your Lordship that some [dissenters] intend to hold a meeting for the worship of God at the house of John Lifely in the parish of Chedworth and pray that it may be registered. John Humphreys, minister, Henry Wilson, John Lifely, William Wilson, Daniel Wilson, Lawrence Dyer. (GDR/284/166)

422 Chedworth. 18 June 1750. *Congregational (Independent).* These are to certify your Lordship that some [dissenters] of the Congregational persuasion but commonly called Independents intend to hold a meeting for the worship of God in a house built for that purpose on a place called and known by the name of the Lime Kiln Hill in the parish of Chedworth and therefore desire the same may be registered. Joseph Everard, John Wickham, Nathaniel Brock, Samuel Ball. (GDR/284/206)
Note. For Joseph Everard *see* **197**.

423 Chedworth. 27 Mar 1805 (30 Mar 1805). *Independent.* This is to certify that the meeting-house lately erected in the village and parish of Chedworth is intended to be opened as a place of public worship for dissenters of the Independent denomination. We request that [it] may be registered. Stephen Phillips, minister, Robert Coles, Charles Barton, Thomas Poole, William Wilson. (GDR/334B/433)

424 Chedworth. 25 Oct 1844 (26 Oct 1844). I Thomas Boulton of Cirencester certify that a house and premises at Chedworth, now in the holding and occupation of John Trotman, are intended to be a place of religious worship and I request you to register the same and request a certificate thereof for which shall be taken no more than two shillings and six pence. (GDR/350/349)

425 Chedworth. (10 Mar 1852) House. Anthony Webb [of] Chedworth. (RG/31/2/f.126/r)

CHELTENHAM

426 Cheltenham (Easter 1690). *Quaker.* Meeting-house. (Q/SO/3/522)

427 Cheltenham. (Easter 1697). *Anabaptist.* William Ballinger's house. (Q/SO/3/521)

428 Cheltenham. (Easter 1698). *Anabaptist.* 'Jo:' Ballingers house [RG/31/6 has Joseph]. (Q/SO/3/521)
Note. The manuscript history of Cheltenham Baptist church, 'The Church Book belonging to Salem Church', in the church's ownership, notes that the meeting-house 'was recorded at the general Quarter Sessions at Gloucester in the month of February in the year 1703 (see the certificate among the writings)'. If 1703 is new style the session would have been Epiphany 1702/3 and if old style Epiphany 1703/4. John and William Ballinger were trustees together with John Ashmead of Gloucester.

429 Cheltenham. (Trinity 1702). *Anabaptist.* 'Jos:' Kear's house. [RG/31/6 has Joseph Sheare]. (Q/SO/3/521)

430 Cheltenham. (Michaelmas 1703). *Quaker.* A new erected house lying towards 'Alston'; 'Jo:' Drewett's certificates [RG/31/6 has Joseph]. (Q/SO/3/521)
Note. The new meeting-house was on the south side of the High Street - 'towards Alston'. Daniel Hayward and John Drewett had reported to the Monthly Meeting at Gloucester in June 1702 that Cheltenham friends were building a new meeting-house and asked for financial assistance from the meeting (D1340/A1/M1).

431 Cheltenham (Epiphany 1703/4) *Quaker.* A new built house for Quakers (Q/SO/3/521)

432 Cheltenham. (Michaelmas 1710). *Anabaptist*. Edward Nicholls' house. (Q/SO/3/520)

433 Cheltenham. 8 Oct 1726. *Independent*. This is to certify that [dissenters] called Independents intend to hold a meeting for the worship of God in their way in the house of Margaret Milton, widow, in the town of Cheltenham, on the west side of the street near the dwelling house of William Gibbs and pray that it may be recorded. Martin Lloyd, John Weston, Joseph Everard. (GDR/279a/151)
Note. For Joseph Everard *see* **197**.

434 Cheltenham. 15 July 1729. *Independent*. These are to certify you that [dissenters] known by the name of Independents intend to hold a meeting for the worship of God in their way in the dwelling house of Mr William Brooks in the east end [RG31/2 has place-name 'East End'] of the town of Cheltenham and pray that it may be registered. Martin Lloyd, Joseph Everard, Godfrey Fownes. (GDR/279a/216)
Note. For Joseph Everard *see* **197**.

435 Cheltenham. [1730?; entry between 15 July 1729 and 6 Aug 1730]. *Presbyterian*. 'We [named below] (being dissenters from the Church of England but Presbyterians) humbly desire that a house newly erected in the town of Cheltenham, near the middle of the town of the Northside of the same and on the backside of the *Bull Inne*, between the houses of Nathanael Macock and a garden of Mr Ashmead belonging to Mr William Brook, [mercer], and Nathanael King [of Shurdington, yeoman] and John Weston and others, may be licensed for to hold a meeting for the service of God in their way.' William Brooks, John Weston, John Gilliam, Nathaniel King. (GDR/279a/239)
Note. Cheltenham Court Book 1565 (1731) is the surrender by Nathaniel Macock to the first and last of the certifiers above of a strip of ground in the backside of Nathaniel Macock and near the house in which Macock lived between the Bull backside and land of Maycock, running north-south close to the foundation of a recently demolished wall. A later transfer (*Court Book* 1749, 2138) to a number of men assumed to be trustees, the first named being John Meylett clerk, of this same piece of land states that it was taken out of the garden of Nathaniel Macock, on which a meeting-house has since been erected.

436 Cheltenham. 20 Feb 1781 (28 Apr 1781). We with some others intend to hold a meeting for the worship of Almighty God in a house set apart for this purpose, the property of Mr Richard Hooper in Cheltenham and pray it may be registered. Thomas Pope, John Ballinger, John Millward, William Hogg. (GDR/292A/233)

437 Cheltenham. 16 June 1812 (18 June 1812). We [named below] certify that a tenement or dwelling house in the town of Cheltenham, the property of Mr Seward, landscape painter, lately or heretofore called Sadlers Wells, is designed to be used and occupied as a place of divine and public worship, and we request that the same be duly registered and a certificate thereof given. Charles Campbell, Samuel Reed, book binder, James Hiam, Benjamin Jubb, George Hunt, George Fern, William Bliss, minister. (GDR/334B/352)

438 Cheltenham. 6 Aug 1816 (7 Aug 1816). *Independent*. We [named below] certify that a building lately erected in North Place near Portland Street, Cheltenham, is intended forthwith to be a place of religious worship for [dissenters] commonly called Independents, and request the same to be registered. Thomas Snow, David Withington, Arthur Parker, Henry Gamble, Samuel Banfield, Thomas Smith, Edward Tanner. (GDR/334B/317)

439 Cheltenham. 26 Mar 1817 (27 Mar 1817). We [named below] certify that the house called Selkirk Villa [RG/31/2 has 'Selkiel Villa'] in the parish of Cheltenham, is intended to be a place of religious worship and we request the same be registered. Thomas Snow, Edward Turner, Thomas James, Samuel Banfield, Joseph Green. (GDR/334B/300)

440 Cheltenham. 22 May 1818 (22 May 1818). We [named below] certify that [the] building lately erected in Gydes Terrace, Cheltenham, is intended to be a place of worship and religious instruction and request the same to be registered. Edward Turner, Thomas Snow, Samuel Banfield, Nathaniel Colt, Joseph Green. (GDR/334B/280)

441 Golden Valley, Cheltenham. 22 Sept 1819 (29 Mar 1820). I George Gillard of the parish of Cheltenham certify that a house, occupied by John Smith, 'Hamplet' in the Golden Valley in the parish of Cheltenham, is intended forthwith to be a place of religious worship and I require you to register the same and request a certificate thereof. (GDR/334B/244)
Note. Dates as entered.

442 Cheltenham. 21 Jan 1820 (24 Jan 1820). These are to certify that the undersigned, together with others, propose and intend to meet for public worship in a room over the public market house in the town of Cheltenham. We request that the room may be registered and a certificate be given to us. William Walton, Hugh H Williams, Benjamin Wells, W Gyde, James Potter, W Bastard. (GDR/334B/248)

443 Cheltenham. 12 Sept 1820 (13 Sept 1820). [*Baptist*]. 'These are to certify that we [named below] in connection with others have on the behalf of and for the use of ourselves and others lately built and erected a certain chapel or meeting-house adjoining a certain street called Chapel Street in the town of Cheltenham, to be called or known by the name of בית אל i.e. Bethel Chapel and request that the same may be registered and entered as a place of public worship and that a certificate of the said entry be given to us either seperately or that the same be inserted underneath by the Registrar or his deputy. Signed by us on the behalf of the Trustees and congregation, being ourselves such and part of the same.' William Walton, Hugh H Williams, Samuel Banfield, Thomas James. (GDR/334B/234)
Note. For Bethel chapel see Introduction, xlix.

444 Cheltenham. 25 July 1821 (27 July 1821). We [named below] inhabitants of the town of Cheltenham certify that a room in the New Bath Road, being part of a house in the occupation of Benjamin Mayer, is intended for the purpose of religious worship. Charles Griffiths, Arthur Parker, Richard Billings, Mathew Davies, James Hughes, Francis Hewlings. (GDR/334B/215)

445 Cheltenham. 4 July 1822 (5 July 1822). I Paul Rose, dissenting minister of Cheltenham, certify that a room in Gloster Place in the parish of Cheltenham, [my] property, is intended to be forthwith a place of religious worship and I request you to register the same. (GDR/344/33r)

446 Cheltenham. 18 July 1822 (20 July 1822). I Thomas Dowty of Cheltenham, minister of the Gospel, certify that a house in the occupation of Edwin Boheim, coal merchant, in Worcester Street in the parish of Cheltenham, is intended forthwith to be a place of religious worship and I require you to register the same and request a certificate thereof. (GDR/344/33r)

447 Cheltenham. 4 July 1823 (14 July 1823). I Paul Rose, dissenting minister of Cheltenham, certify that a house and yard in the parish of Cheltenham, [my] property, is intended to be forthwith a place of religious worship and I request you to register the same. (GDR/344/110r/110v)

448 Cheltenham. 18 Aug 1824 (27 Aug 1824). I George Oakley certify that a dwelling house occupied by me [in] Stanhope Street in the town and parish of Cheltenham is intended forthwith as a place of religious worship and I require you to register and record the same, and request a certificate thereof. Witness John Pilley. (GDR/344/136v)

449 Cheltenham. 9 Oct 1824 (11 Nov 1824). I William White of Cheltenham certify that a house in the aforesaid parish [Cheltenham], the property of the aforesaid [*sic*] Thomas Bryan, is intended forthwith to be a place of religious worship and I request you to register and record the same. (GDR/350/21)

450 Cheltenham. 21 Sept 1826 (22 Sept 1826). I Edward Vaughan of the parish of Cheltenham certify that my dwelling house and premises in Cheltenham in Milsom Street are intended to be a place of religious worship and I hereby request you to register and record the same and request a certificate thereof for which shall be taken no more than two shillings and sixpence. (GDR/350/58-9)

451 Cheltenham. 18 Feb 1828 (19 Feb 1828). I William M Gardner of Northfield Terrace, Cheltenham, certify that a building denominated Union Chapel in Upper Bath Street, Cheltenham, is intended forthwith to be a place of religious worship and I request you to register the same. (GDR/350/83)

452 Cheltenham. 4 Dec 1828 (5 Dec 1828). I Joseph Glover, of No 271 High Street, Cheltenham certify that a room in the above mentioned dwelling is intended forthwith to be a place of religious worship and I request you to register the same. (GDR/350/96)

453 Cheltenham. 16 Feb 1829 (17 Feb 1829). We Benjamin Newmarch and Augustus Eves, proprietors of a room in a house, No. 9 Portland Street, Cheltenham, certify that the above room is intended to be forthwith a place of religious worship and request you to register the same. (GDR/350/99)

454 Cheltenham. 3 June 1829 (4 June 1829). We [named below] being householders beg leave to inform your Lordship that we intend opening a house, being No 51 Stanhope Street, Cheltenham, for the purpose of divine worship and request that it may be registered. David Banbury, Samuel Ockford, Joseph James. (GDR/350/102)

455 Cheltenham. 7 Sept 1830 (9 Sept 1830). I Thomas Osborne of Cheltenham, minister of the Gospel, certify that a building on the Bath Road, Cheltenham, is intended forthwith to be a place of religious worship and I require you to register the same and request a certificate thereof. (GDR/350/111)

456 Cheltenham. 7 Dec 1830 (7 Dec 1830). We [named below] inhabitants of the town of Cheltenham humbly certify that a room in a dwelling house, No 190 High Street, in the occupation of William Henry Cooper, is intended to be opened for religious worship. William Henry Cooper, Catherine Cooper, Ed. Young, Sarah Pyrie, Thomas Young, Jane Down, W J Stratford. (GDR/350/112)

457 Cheltenham. 28 May 1832 (1 June 1832). We [named below], inhabitants of the town of Cheltenham, humbly certify that a chapel in Union Street, Bath Road, Cheltenham, is intended to be opened for religious worship. John Cull, John Ross, Thomas Young, Richard Slader, Job Parker, S Parker, Joshua Cull. (GDR/350/129)

458 Cheltenham. 10 July 1832 (14 July 1832). We [named below] inhabitants of the town of Cheltenham humbly certify that a building in St George's Place, Cheltenham, is intended to be opened for religious worship. Thomas Butt, Laurel Cottage; John Addis, Milsom Street; George Compton, King St; Thomas Calcot, 'Stanup' [Stanhope] St; Thomas Wall, Bath Rd; Solomon Syms, Regent St; George Beckett, 'Stanup' Street; Henry Read, Bath Road; John Price, Regent Street; Thomas Croker, Barton Street; Charles Miles, nr Workhouse; Robert Young, Grove Street. (GDR/350/130)

459 Alstone, Cheltenham. 27 Dec 1833 (28 Dec 1833). [*Baptist*]. I James Smith of Cheltenham certify that a dwelling house at Alstone in the parish of Cheltenham, occupied by Samuel Gibbons, slater and plasterer, is intended forthwith to be a place of religious worship and I hereby request you to register the same and request a certificate thereof. Witness William Hexter, George Arkell snr. (GDR/350/143)

460 Cheltenham. 25 Mar 1834 (27 Mar 1834). [*Unitarian*]. I G B Brock of the city of Gloucester, dissenting minister, certify that a house in High Street, Cheltenham, No 380, occupied by Thomas Furber, jeweller & silversmith, is intended forthwith to be a place of religious worship and I require you to register the same and request a certificate thereof. (GDR/350/148)
Note. Thomas Furber re-established a Unitarian church in Cheltenham, which moved to the Mechanics' Institute (**463** below) and then built a chapel (**476** below). *VCH Glos* 15 (forthcoming)

461 Cheltenham. Aug 1834. I Thomas Dover of Cheltenham certify that a dwelling house near Lansdown in the parish of Cheltenham is intended forthwith to be a place of religious worship and I request you to register the same. (GDR/350/156)

462 Cheltenham. 6 Mar 1835 (7 Mar 1835). I James Gill of Cheltenham certify that a room in Union Street, Somers Town, in the parish of Cheltenham is intended forthwith to be a place of religious worship and I require you to register the same and request a certificate thereof. (GDR/350/167)

463 Cheltenham. 17 Mar 1835 (19 Mar 1835). [*Unitarian; see* **460**]. I G B Brock, dissenting minister of the city of Gloucester, certify that a building in Cheltenham, No 105 Albion Street, now and for some time past used for the purpose of a Mechanics Institute, is intended forthwith to be a place of religious worship and require you to register the same and request a certificate thereof. (GDR/350/167)

464 Cheltenham. 30 Sept 1835 (1 Oct 1835). [*Baptist*]. I James Smith of Cheltenham certify that a room called Clarence Gallery in the parish of Cheltenham is intended to be forthwith a place of religious worship and require you to register the same. Witness Charles H Channon, Samuel Fisher. (GDR/350/179)

465 Cheltenham. 22 Feb 1836 (25 Feb 1836). I James Morish of Cheltenham certify that a chapel and premises in the parish of Cheltenham, now in the holding and occupation of Richard Boulton and [me], are intended to be a place of religious worship and I request you to register the same and request a certificate thereof for which shall be taken no more than two shillings and six pence. James Morish, James Boulton. (GDR/350/191) [*see* illus., xv]

466 Cheltenham. 19 Feb 1836 (27 Feb 1836). [*Baptist*]. I James Smith of Cheltenham certify that a building called Salem Chapel in Regent Street in the parish of Cheltenham is intended to be forthwith a place of religious worship and request you to register the same. James Smith, John Whitmore, Samuel Fisher (GDR/350/192)
Note. For Salem chapel, see Introduction xlviii-xlix and 478.

467 Cheltenham. 1 Sept 1836 (1 Sept 1836). I Mark Cunningham certify that a chapel or meeting-house called the Cheltenham Tabernacle in Clare Street, Bath Road, Cheltenham, is intended forthwith to be a place of religious worship and I require you to register the same and request a certificate thereof. (GDR/350/204)

468 Cheltenham. 28 Sept 1837 (30 Sept 1837). I John Smith certify that an uninhabited room in Commercial Street, Cheltenham, is intended forthwith to be a place of religious worship and request you to register the same. (GDR/350/216)

469 Cheltenham. 3 June 1840 (6 June 1840). I Samuel Ockford of Cheltenham certify that the building, No 27 St Georges Place, in the parish of Cheltenham is intended forthwith to be a place of religious worship and I require you to register the same and request a certificate thereof. (GDR/350/254)

470 Cheltenham. 12 Aug 1840 (13 Aug 1840). *Wesleyan.* I John McOwan, Wesleyan minister, certify that a chapel recently erected in St George Street, Cheltenham, is intended forthwith to be a place of religious worship and I require you to register the same and request a certificate thereof. (GDR/350/256)

471 Cheltenham. 14 Aug 1840 (15 Aug 1840). I James Smith of Cheltenham certify that a building called the Railway School Room in the Gas Green in the parish of Cheltenham is intended to be forthwith a place of religious worship and I request you to register the same. Witness John Whitmore, Charles H Channon. (GDR/350/257)

472 Cheltenham. 18 Dec 1840 (18 Dec 1840). I William Leader [signature like 'Loader'], dissenting minister, certify that a dwelling house, No 62 St Paul's Street North, occupied by [me] in the parish of Cheltenham, is intended to be forthwith a place of religious worship and I request you to register the same. (GDR/350/266)

473 Cheltenham. 5 May 1841 (15 May 1841). I Theodore Curtis of Cheltenham certify that a building occupied by the members of the Mechanics Institution in Cheltenham is intended to be a place of religious worship and I request you to register the same and request a certificate thereof for which shall be taken no more than two shillings and six pence. (GDR/350/280)

474 Alstone [Cheltenham]. 9 Sept 1842 (9 Sept 1842). I Thomas Smith of Cheltenham certify that a house, occupied by Thomas Brown, in Queen's Retreat in the hamlet of Alstone in the parish of Cheltenham is intended to be used as a place of religious worship and request you to register the same and request a certificate thereof for which shall be taken no more than two shillings and six pence. (GDR/350/302)

475 Cheltenham. 17 Nov 1843 (17 Nov 1843). I Samuel Clutterbuck of Cheltenham certify that a dwelling house at No 16 in Albion Street in Cheltenham is intended forthwith to be a place of religious worship and I request you to register the same and request a certificate thereof. (GDR/350/323)
Note. Date and place identical in RG/31/2 but certifier named as Thomas Mann.

476 Cheltenham. 19 Mar 1844 (19 Mar 1844). [*Unitarian: see* **460**]. T Lewis, dissenting minister of Cheltenham, certify that a building on 'Bays Hill', near the Royal Well Terrace in Cheltenham, is intended forthwith to be a place of religious worship and I require you to register the same and request a certificate thereof. (GDR/350/353)

477 Cheltenham. 17 Apr 1844 (17 Apr 1844). I Sarah Smith of Cheltenham certify that my house and premises at No 5 Elm Street in the parish of Cheltenham, now in [my] holding and occupation, are to be place of religious worship and I request you to register the same and request a certificate thereof for which shall be taken no more than two shillings and six pence. (GDR/350/340)

478 Cheltenham. 8 June 1844 (8 June 1844). *Baptist.* I John Whitmore of Cheltenham certify that a house or building called Salem Chapel in Clarence Parade, Cheltenham, is intended to be forthwith a place of religious worship by dissenters of the denomination of Baptists and I request you to register the same. Samuel Fisher, grocer, 299 High Street; C H Channon, carpenter, Chapel House; John Whitmore, Town Surveyor. (GDR/350/342)
Note. For Salem, *see* **466**.

479 Cheltenham. 3 Jan 1846 (5 Jan 1846). *Wesleyan.* I William Penington Bergess of Cheltenham, minister of Gospel, certify that a building called Bethesda Wesleyan Chapel in Great Norwood Street, in the borough of Cheltenham, is intended forthwith to be a place of religious worship and I require you to register the same and request a certificate thereof. (GDR/350/367)

480 Cheltenham. 24 Aug 1846 (25 Aug 1846). I James Ballinger of Cheltenham certify that a room in the premises of No 230 High Street, Cheltenham, now in [my] holding and occupation, are intended to be a place of religious worship and I request you to register the same and request a certificate thereof for which shall be taken no more than two shillings and six pence. (GDR/350/378)

481 Cheltenham. 2 Nov 1846 (2 Nov 1846). I James Bayliss of Cheltenham certify that the house or building at No 2 Queen Street in the parish of St Peters, Cheltenham, 'are' intended to be a place of religious worship and I require you to register the same and request a certificate thereof. (GDR/350/384)

482 Cheltenham. (10 Jun 1848). Room at No 11 Pittville Street. James Ballinger. (Q/RNp/4)

483 Cheltenham. (24 Jun 1848). Temperance Hall, 230 High Street. James Bayliss. (Q/RNp/4)

484 Bath Road Cheltenham. (23 Sep 1850). Room adjoining the County's Retreat. John Steele. (Q/RNp/4)

485 Cheltenham. (26 May 1851). Dwelling house, 396 High Street occupied by Richard Edwards. Richard Edwards. (Q/RNp/4)

486 Cheltenham. (19 Dec 1851). 186 High Street, house of William Harper. William Harper. (Q/RNp/4)

487 Cheltenham. (12 Jun 1852). Chapel. R Bulgin. (RG/31/2/f.126/v)

CHILDSWICKHAM

488 [Childswickham?]. 1672. *Congregational.* Application by Owen Davies for William Smith [Congregational minister] at William Coombes' house in 'Wickam'; licence recorded for William Smith congregational teacher and for William Coombe's house 10 June 1672; received by Owen Davies 12 June 1672 for 'William Coomebs' house. (LT/372, 401, 509, 510)

489 Childswickham. 26 Mar 1813 (5 Apr 1813). I Thomas Weston of Childswickham, labourer, certify that a certain building, messuage or tenement in Childswickham, being myself occupier and Thomas Phillips esq proprietor, is intended forthwith to be a place of religious worship and I require to register the same. Thomas Weston (mark). Witness James Drew, John Morris. (GDR/334B/347)
Note. RG/31/2 has 'barn'.

490 Childswickham. 13 Jan 1843 (19 Jan 1843). We [named below] certify that a building in the parish of 'Childs Wickham' is to be used as a chapel for religious worship by dissenters of the denomination of Independents and request that this certificate may be registered. Richard Phipps, farmer, Joseph Rogers, miller, John Paine. (GDR/350/311)

CHIPPING CAMPDEN
Chipping Campden originally referred to the planned market town or borough, while Campden parish contained several townships, including Broad Campden, as well as the borough. 'Campden' was used quite often for the parish, but it has become conventional to call it Chipping Campden.

491 [Chipping] Campden. 1672. *Congregational.* Application [by S Ford] for licence to Mr Thomas Worden. A house for him in Broadway in Worcestershire and in 'Camden' in Gloucestershire, Congregational; Mr Thomas Worden also listed in note by Will Owen for house in 'Cambden'. (LT/218, 371)

492 [Chipping] Campden. 1672. *Congregational.* Licence recorded for the house of Sam Horsman of 'Cambden'. (LT/577)

493 [Chipping Campden]. (Michaelmas 1689). [RG/31/6 has *Anabaptist*]. 'Cambden', William Davison, minister. (Q/SO/3/522)
Note. 'Cambden' bracketed with Willersey.

494 Broad Campden [Chipping Campden]. (Easter 1690). *Quaker.* Meeting-house. (Q/SO/3/522) [*see* illus., xii]

495 Chipping Campden. (Trinity 1695). *Presbyterian.* 'Chiping Cambden', Mary Wells' house. (Q/SO/3/522)

496 Chipping Campden. 21 Dec 1715. [*Independent: see note*]. Samuel Knight of 'Chiping Cambden', dissenting preacher, took oaths of allegiance and supremacy and made declaration against transubstantiation. (Q/SO/4/[10])
Note. In the Evans list, Samuel Knight was the Independent minister.

497 Chipping Campden. 28 Sept 1724. *Presbyterian.* These are to certify there is a meeting of dissenters called Presbyterians for the worship of God at a new house built for the purpose in Chipping Campden and this our certificate we humbly desire may be registered in either of your courts. Samuel Knight minister, Nehemiah Griffotts, James Williams, Samuel Coombs. (GDR/279a/78)
Note. Rubric states 'Campden Cert^{um} Loci divini Cultus' [certificate of a place of divine worship]; this is the first of the run of registrations in the bishop's court.

498 Chipping Campden. (Epiphany 1771). *Quaker.* It is ordered by this court that the house of Jeffery Berrington licensed for Quakers to assemble and meet together pursuant to a petition and request. (Q/SO/9/f.121r)

499 Chipping Campden. 25 Nov 1808 (30 Nov 1808). *Methodist.* We [named below] of the Methodist persuasion desire that the house of William Robins, the property of George Manton in the town and parish of Chipping Campden, be licensed as a place for the public worship of Almighty God. William Robins (mark), Mary Allcock, Susannah Manton, Joseph Stanley, Susannah Dyer. (GDR/334B/411-10)

500 Chipping Campden. 30 Jan 1819 (10 Feb 1819). I James Stanley of Chipping Campden certify that my dwelling house at Chipping Campden is intended forthwith to be a place of religious worship and require you to register the same and request a certificate thereof. (GDR/334B/267)

501 Broad Campden, Chipping Campden. 2 Apr 1821 (13 Apr 1821). *Baptist.* This is to certfy that a house in the village of Broad Campden and parish of Chipping Campden, in the occupation of Richard Taylor, is intended forthwith to be a place of religious worship by dissenters of the Baptist denomination, and we require you to register the same. George Jayne, minister, Richard Taylor (mark), Richard Smith. (GDR/334B/224)

502 [Chipping] Campden. 22 Mar 1822 (27 Mar 1822). I James Standley of Campden, minister, certify that the house of William Holmes esq in the parish of Campden is intended forthwith to be used as a place of religious worship and I require you to register the same. (GDR 344/32r)
Note. Registered promptly but 'entered' 2½ months later. 'Rec'd by W E. Howsell'.

503 Chipping Campden. 7 Feb 1824 (19 July 1824). I Ann Cox of 'Chippen' Campden certify that my dwelling house at Chipping Campden is intended forthwith to be a place of religious worship and I hereby require you to register the same, and request a certificate thereof. (GDR/344/135r)
Note. Dates as entered.

504 Broad Campden, [Chipping] Campden. 15 Sept 1829 (26 Sept 1829). *Baptist.* We [named below] give notice that the house in the occupation of Richard Saunders of Broad Campden in the parish of Campden will be used henceforth for preaching the Gospel by a congregation of the Baptist denomination and we require you to register the same and request a certificate thereof. William Elliott, Francis Davis (GDR/350/104b)

505 [Chipping] Campden. 3 Jan 1846 (5 Jan 1846). I Thomas Williams, minister, of Chipping Campden, certify that a dwelling house and premises at Chipping Campden, now in the holding and occupation of [—] Manton of Chipping Campden, are to be a place of religious worship and I request you to register the same and request a certificate thereof for which shall be taken no more than two shillings and six pence. (GDR/350/366)
Note. See **499** for George Manton.

CHIPPING SODBURY
Chipping Sodbury was a chapelry in Old Sodbury parish.
506 Chipping Sodbury. 1672. *Anabaptist.* Licence recorded 5 Sept 1672 for the house of John Kibble of Chipping Sodbury. (LT/558) [*see* illus., xiv, and see **511**]

507 Chipping Sodbury. 1672. *Baptist.* Licence recorded 5 Sept 1672 to Sam Webb to be a Baptist teacher att 'Chipping-Sudbury'. (LT/559)

508 Sodbury [Chipping?]. (Easter 1690). *Quaker* meeting-house. (Q/SO/3/522)

509 Chipping Sodbury. (Michaelmas 1698). *Quaker.* 'Chiping Sodbury', Mans house. (Q/SO/3/521)

510 Chipping Sodbury. (Michaelmas 1699). *Anabaptist.* 'Chiping Sodbury', Nathaniel Bennett's house. (Q/SO/3/521)

511 Chipping Sodbury. (Trinity 1709). *Baptist.* 'Chiping Sodbury', A house in Hounds Lane. (Q/SO/3/520) [*see* illus., xiv]

512 Chipping Sodbury. 11 Oct 1799 (17 Oct 1799). 'In pursuance of an act of parliament issued forth in the first year of the reign of K.W. and Q.M.' we [named below] desire that the house of John Howell of Chipping Sodbury be registered as a house set apart for the worship of God in religious exercise.' William Hunt, William Pring, William Stephens, Charles Power, John Parker, John Howell. (GDR/319A/283-4)

513 Chipping Sodbury. 3 Jan 1800 (13 Jan 1800; registration GDR/319A/289). 'In pursuance of an act of parliament issued forth in the first year of the reign of K W and Q M' we [named below] desire that the house of William Pring of 'Chippen Sodbury' be registered among the records of the bishop's court as a house set apart for the worship of God in religious exercises.' Stephen Salliss, John Hook, Thomas Smith, James Summers, William Pring, William Hunt. (GDR/N2/1)

514 Chipping Sodbury. 21 Oct 1818 (24 Oct 1818). I Richard Tyndale of Chipping Sodbury, school master, certify that a certain room of a messuage in the parish of Chipping Sodbury, occupied by Horam Ford and belonging to William Ford, is intended forthwith to be a place of religious worship and I require you to register the same. Richard Tyndall, John Vick, Charles Power. (GDR/334B/274)

515 Chipping Sodbury. 17 Oct 1835 (23 Oct 1835.) I William Wigley of Mangotsfield certify that a dwelling house and premises at Chipping Sodbury in the parish of Sodbury, now in the holding and occupation of George Melsom, are intended to be a place of religious worship and I request you to register the same and request a certificate thereof. (GDR/350/183)

516 Chipping Sodbury. 29 Mar 1852. House. Daniel Mossop [of] Hawkesbury. (RG/31/2 f.126/r)

CHURCHAM
Bulley, which see, was a chapelry in Churcham.
517 Churcham. 4 Apr 1814 (5 Apr 1814). [*Baptist: see note*]. I Thomas Powell of the city of Gloucester, 'accomptant', certify that a building, a meeting-house on Birdwood Common in the parish of Churcham, the property of Mr John Elliott, is intended forthwith to be a place of religious worship and I require you to register the same. Thomas Powell, G B Drayton. (GDR/334B/339)
Note. George Box Drayton, a Baptist, certified seven meetings and became a Baptist minister. *See* **523**, **833**, **838**, **849**, **1094**, **1095**.

518 Churcham. 28 Jan 1817 (1 Feb 1817). We [named below] residing in the parish of Churcham or in adjacent parts are desirous of meeting for religious worship in the house of William Pool in [Churcham]. We request that your Lordship would order that an entry be made in your Court that we design to meet together in the kitchen of the said house for the purpose herein specified. William Burston, Joseph Green jnr, Richard Hart, William Sandford, William Pool. (GDR/334B/306)

519 Over, Churcham. 18 Apr 1835 (18 Apr 1835). I James Grimes of the city of Gloucester certify that a dwelling house in the hamlet of Over in the parish of Churcham, now in the occupation of William Preene, is intended to be forthwith a place of religious worship and I request you to register the same. (GDR/350/171-2)

CHURCHDOWN
520 Churchdown. 26 May 1746. These are to certify your Lordship that some [dissenters] intend to hold a meeting for the worship of God in their way in the dwelling house of Thomas Smyth, shoemaker, in the parish of Churchdown and 'desires' it may be registered. John Harmar, John Summers, Richard Jones. (GDR/284/172)

521 Hucclecote, Churchdown. (19 Apr 1790). This is to certify that we with some others intend to hold a meeting for the worship of Almighty God in a house set apart for that purpose, in the occupation of John Dance, in the hamlet of Hucclecote in the parish of Churchdown and pray it may be registered in your Lordship's court. William Hulbart Ballinger, Richard Harris, William Smith, John Daniel, John Cree. (GDR/319A/100)

522 Churchdown. 11 Nov 1814 (11 Nov 1814). I Thomas Parks of the city of Gloucester, tailor, certify that a certain part of a messuage in the parish of Churchdown, belonging to and occupied by Mrs Elizabeth Arkell, is intended forthwith to be a place of religious worship and I require you to register the same. (GDR/334B/335)

523 Hucclecote, Churchdown. 7 June 1817 (7 Jun 1817). [*Baptist: see note*]. I Thomas Flint, minister of the city of Gloucester, certify that a building in the hamlet of Hucclecote in the parish of Churchdown, that is the barn of William Dauncey, is intended forthwith to be used as a place of religious worship and require you to register the same. Witness G B Drayton. (GDR/334B/296)
Note. Thomas Flint was a Baptist minister (VCH Glos 4, 321). For George Box Drayton *see* **517**.

524 Hucclecote, Churchdown. 11 Sept 1817 (12 Sept 1817). I William Bishop, dissenting minister in the city of Gloucester, certify that a dwelling house in the hamlet of Hucclecote in the parish of Churchdown, occupied by George Underwood, blacksmith, is intended forthwith to be a place of religious worship and I require you to register the same. (GDR/334B/293)

525 Churchdown. 29 Apr 1820. [*Methodist: see* **166**]. I James Byron, minister of Gloucester, certify that the dwelling house of Thomas Yeates in the parish of Churchdown is forthwith to be a place of religious worship and require you to register the same and request a certificate thereof. (GDR/334B/241)

526 Hucclecote [Churchdown]. 6 Sept 1820 (9 Sept 1820). I James Wood of Norfolk Buildings [Spa, South Hamlet] in the county of Gloucester certify that a dwelling house in the hamlet of Hucclecote, occupied by Sarah Keylock, widow, is intended to be forthwith a place of religious worship and request you to register the same. (GDR/334B/235-34)

527 Chosenhill, Churchdown. 4 Mar 1822 (4 Mar 1822). We [named below] certify that the dwelling house and premises, now occupied by Ann Affield, 'inn Chozen in the parish of Churchdown' is opened for the public worship of Almighty God and we request the same may be registered. Ann Affield, Thomas Price, Thomas Purnett, Thomas Berry. (GDR/344/19r)

528 Churchdown. 24 Aug 1824 (24 Aug 1824). I Francis Collier of Gloucester, minister of the Gospel, certify that a dwelling house in the occupation of Richard Holford in the parish of Churchdown is intended forthwith to be a place of religious worship and I hereby require you to register the same, and I request a certificate thereof. (GDR/344/136r)

529 Hucclecote [Churchdown]. 27 Aug 1831 (27 Aug 1831). I Job Bown of the city of Gloucester certify that a dwelling house in the parish of Hucclecote occupied by Daniel Smart is intended to be forthwith a place of religious worship and I hereby request you to register the same. Daniel Smart (mark). (GDR/350/118)

530 Churchdown. 8 May 1833 (11 May 1833). I James Byett of the city of Gloucester certify that a dwelling house in the occupation of John Benfield in the parish of Churchdown is intended forthwith to be a place of religious worship and I require you to register the same and request a certificate thereof. (GDR/350/140)

531 Hucclecote [Churchdown]. 1 Mar 1834 (1 Mar 1834). *Wesleyan.* I John Geden of the city of Gloucester, Weslyan minister, certify that a messuage, now in the occupation of Sarah Cooke of Hucclecote in the parish of Churchdown, is intended forthwith to be a place of religious worship and I hereby require you to register and record the same and request a certificate thereof. (GDR/350/147)

532 Hucclecote, Churchdown. 9 Oct 1842 (9 Oct 1842). I Richard Colwell of the parish of Churchdown and the hamlet of Hucclecote certify that a dwelling house in my occupation in Hucclecote is intended forthwith as a place of religious worship and I require you to register the same and request a certificate thereof. (GDR/350/303)

533 Churchdown [RG/31/2 has 'Hucclecote']. (8 Apr 1848). *Wesleyan.* Building, Wesleyan chapel. Edward Jennings. (Q/RNp/4)

534 Hucclecote, Churchdown. (24 Nov 1848). *Wesleyan.* Hucclecote Wesleyan chapel. John Smedley (Q/RNp/4)

CIRENCESTER
535 Cirencester. 1672. *Presbyterian.* Licence desired by Mr Francis Benson for James Greenwood to be a Presbyterian teacher in Weavers Hall, Cirencester, and for the Weavers Hall to be licensed for a Presbyterian meeting place; licence received by James Innes jnr 22 May 1672. (LT/240, 245, 369)
Note. See text of petition (LT/245) in Introduction, xxxiv–xxxv.

536 Cirencester. 1672. *Presbyterian.* Licence recorded for Thomas Greenwood, a place called 'the 2 ices' [Gosditch] in Cirencester. (LT/404)
Note. LT/2/818 suggests 'the Recess'; Gosditch is the probable reading. The origins of a Presbyterian chapel in Gosditch Street are 'uncertain' but by 1690 the ejected vicar of Tideswell was pastor and the former chapel building is of the late 17th century (which became Unitarian in the 19th century). (RCHM *Nonconformist Chapels and Meeting-houses* 79).

537 Cirencester. 1672. Licence recorded for the house of the Widdow 'Joaane Palteeres' of Cirencester. (LT/581)

538 Cirencester. 1672. *Baptist.* Licence recorded 9 Dec 1672 for Giles Watkins of Cirencester, a Baptist teacher. (LT/581)
Note. The Baptists in Cirencester trace their history to 1651 when about 40 people met together 'under the pastoral care of Mr Giles Watkins, a highly respectable tradesman of the town' (Beecham 140). *See* **540**.

539 Cirencester. 1672. *Baptist.* Licence recorded 9 Dec 1672 for John Oates to be a Baptist teacher at Cirencester. (LT/581)

540 Cirencester. (Epiphany 1689/90). [*Baptist: see* **538** *above*]. Giles Watkins' house. (Q/SO/3/522)

541 Cirencester. (Easter 1690). *Quaker.* Meeting-house. (Q/SO/3/522)

542 Cirencester. (Easter 1709). *Anabaptist.* The Weavers Hall. (Q/SO/3/520)
Note. The Weaver's Hall was the subject of a Presbyterian application for a licence to Charles II. *See* **535**.

543 Cirencester. 25 Nov 1715. John Keeling of Cirencester [*Presbyterian: see note*], dissenting minister, took oaths of allegiance and supremacy; Daniel Flaxney, Quaker, made solemn declaration of fidelity at Cirencester. (Q/SO/4/[7])
Note. John Keeling was the Presbyterian minister in the Evans list.

544 Cirencester. Epiphany, 10 Jan 1715/16. James Lovell, William Freeman, Richard Dowell, all of Cirencester, dissenting ministers, took took oaths of allegiance and supremacy. (Q/SO/4 [13])

545 Cirencester (Easter 1724) *Baptist.* William Field, licensed preacher. (RG/31/6/f.74/r)
Note. No record found in Quarter Sessions Order Book.

546 Cirencester. (Easter 1735). *Baptist.* It is ordered by this court that the Weavers Hall in St Thomas Street in the town of Cirencester be licensed and allowed for [dissenters] called Baptists to assemble and meet together in for the worship of Almighty God in their way. (Q/SO/6/f.43v)

547 Cirencester. 15 Feb 1757. *Baptist.* This is to certify all whom it may concern that we [named below] desire a licence for the house of Robert Gillespie in Gloucester Street within the borough of Cirencester for a place of publick worship for the use of Protestant dissenters commonly called Baptists. William Webb, John Wavell, Joseph Waters, Thomas Dawson, Henry Wavel, Jane Freeman, George Waters, William Cobb (mark), Daniel Elliots, John Gillman. (GDR/284/233)
Note. This page is crossed through. No return to RG.

548 Cirencester. 6 Dec 1769. *Independent.* Some [dissenters] commonly called Independents humbly request that an outhouse of James Haddock, glover, in Black Jack Street, Gosditch Ward in the parish of Cirencester, be recorded as a place for public worship of Almighty God. James Haddock, Thomas Payne, John Hiles, John Carter, William Welsted. (GDR/292A/138)

549 Cirencester. 24 Feb 1786 (28 Feb 1786; registration GDR/319A/51). 'This is to certify that we [named below, dissenters] intend to hold a meeting for the worship of Almighty God in the dwelling house of Thomas Atkins in the borough of Cirencester. We therefore pray that this certificate may be entered in your Lordship's Registry.' Thomas Atkins, Joseph Stevens, Thomas Blake, William Ludlow, Thomas Mace, William Wood. (GDR/N2/1)

550 Cirencester. 4 Nov 1788 (14 Nov 1788; registration GDR/319A/87). *Quaker.* 'To all whom it may concern. These are to certify that we the undersigned and others of the Society of Protestant dissenters commonly called Quakers purpose to meet together for the worship of Almighty God at the dwelling house of Warner Elkington in Cirencester and request the same may be duly registered.' W Elkington, Stephen Wilkins, Devereux Bowly. (GDR/N2/1) [*see* illus., xxi]
Note. Parchment written one way up is this certificate for a Quaker meeting and the other way up a neat start to Gloucestershire Militia 1788, while on the other side is a certificate for Maiseyhampton (28 July 1788) *see* **1149**, suggesting these are copies made on scraps of paper before entries were made in the Act Books. Both sides are crossed through.

551 Cirencester. 17 Nov 1790 (26 Jan 1791). This is to certify that we [named below] intend to hold a meeting for the worship of Almighty God in the dwelling house of Richard Savory in the borough of Cirencester. We therefore pray that this certificate may be entered in your Lordship's Registry. Richard Savoury, Thomas Blake, William Ludlow, Joseph Brookes, Thomas Mace, Joseph Stevens. (GDR/319A/120)

552 Cirencester. 4 Sept 1809 (5 Sept 1809). These are to certify that we [named below] intend to hold a meeting for the worship of Almighty God in a house erected for that purpose in the borough of Cirencester. We pray that this certificate may be entered in your

Lordship's Registry. John Rogers, William Hall, William Hall jnr, Thomas Morgan, Edward Herbert. (GDR/334B/398)

553 Cirencester. 2 Mar 1824 (10 Mar 1824). [*Methodist: see* **1399**]. I James Blackett, minister of [blank], certify that a dwelling house in the occupation of James Simpson in Cirencester is intended forthwith to be a place of religious worship and I hereby require you to register the same and request a certificate thereof. (GDR/344/130r)

554 Cirencester. 18 May 1830 (22 May 1830). *Independent.* We [named below] certify that a building in Castle Street, Cirencester, in the occupation of William Flux, is intended to be a chapel for religious worship by dissenters of the denomination of Independents and request that this certificate may be registered in the 'Commissaries' Court. William Flux, Jerome Clapp, W Smith. (GDR/350/109)

555 Cirencester. 16 June 1837 (24 June 1837). *Baptist.* We [named below] certify that a building in Coxwell Street in the parish of Cirencester is to be a chapel for religious worship by dissenters of the denomination of Baptists and request that this certificate may be registered in the Commissary's court of your Lordship. Daniel White, George Hoare, John Legg, P H White, W Hopwood, William Brasington. (GDR/350/209)

556 Cirencester. 22 Sept 1838 (24 Sept 1838). I John William Peters of Quenington certify that a room known by the name of 'the Music Room' in a house in my occupation in the town of Cirencester is intended forthwith to be a place of religious worship and require you to register the same. (GDR/350/231)

557 Cirencester. 2 July 1839 (4 July 1839). *Primitive Methodist.* I Joseph Preston of Brinkworth, Wilts, certify that a room and premises in Dyke Street in the parish of Cirencester, in the holding and occupation of the Primitive Methodist, are to be a place of religious worship and I request you to register the same and request a certificate thereof for which shall be taken no more than two shillings and six pence. Witness John Goodwin. (GDR/350/244)
Note. 'Dyke Street' is clearly written, perhaps referring to the Fosse Way.

558 Watermoor, Cirencester. 29 Oct 1844 (29 Oct 1844). I Charles Darkin of the town and parish of Cirencester certify that a house in the 'Water-moor' in the said parish, now in the occupation of Edward Mutlow, is intended forthwith to be a place of religious worship and I request you to register the same and request a certificate thereof. (GDR/350/349)

559 Watermoor, Cirencester. 6 Feb 1847 (6 Feb 1847). I Charles Darkin 'at the town and parish of Cirencester' certify that a house in Watermoor in the parish of Cirencester, now in the occupation of Edward Mutlow, is intended forthwith to be a place of religious worship and I request you to register the same and request a certificate thereof. (GDR/350/387)

560 Cirencester. (19 Aug 1848). Room and premises in Coxwell Street. George Lee [RG/31/3 has 'minister']. (Q/RNp/4)

561 Cirencester. (17 Oct 1851). Rooms of William Wills, Coxwell Street. Robert Esam Farley and William Wills. (Q/RNp/4)

CLAPTON
Clapton was a chapelry in Bourton-on-the-Water parish.
562 Clapton. 6 Nov 1797 (15 Nov 1797). We [named below] certify that we intend to meet for the worship of Almighty God in the dwelling house of Stephen Roffe of Clapton and

pray that this certificate may be registered. Thomas Uppadine, William Palmer, Samuel Palmer, Robert Humphris. (GDR/319A/257)

CLIFTON

In Gloucestershire, and Bristol diocese from 1542.
Part of Clifton was drawn into the city and county of Bristol in 1844.

563 Clifton. 30 Aug 1788 (30 Aug 1788). *Independent.* We [named below] being part of a congregation of dissenters certify that an house or building lately erected near Dowry Square within the parish of Clifton in the county of Gloucester and your lordship's diocese and intended to be called Hope Chapel, is intended or set apart for a meeting place for a congregation of dissenters under the denomination of Independents. And we desire the same may be registered. Thomas Grove minister, James Fry, Josiah Greethead, J G Strachan, Robert Langford, W Skinner, James Power, William Tozer, Philip Parry. (EP/A/45/1/163)

564 Clifton. 26 May 1802 (4 Jun 1802). We [named below] certify to your lordship that a certain dwelling house in or near the Hotwell Road in the parish of Clifton and diocese of Bristol, which dwelling house is now in the occupation of Thomas Davis, cooper, is intended to be used as a place of meeting for religious worship and we request that the same may be registered. Mary Stone, Ann Baker, Eliza Crook, Ann Crook, Hester Crook, Thomas Davis, J H Browning, George Smith, Josh Robbins, Henry Tull, Thomas Norman. (EP/A/45/1/292).

565 Clifton. (14 Nov 1815). 'We the undersigned, in consequence of the inclement weather, being frequently prevented from meeting with our Christian Friends & Brethren in Bristol with whom we have been accustomed to worship, and being desirous of assembling together in the lower room of the house of Mr Thomas Birch, No 2 Little Gloucester Place, Clifton, the front entrance to which is down a flight of steps, the back entrance by an avenue, the back of Portland Place, and there as Protestants and peaceable subjects to worship the Supreme in a Scriptural way, believing the Bible to be our sure guide, we therefore pray your protection and licence for the same in the name of the right Reverend the Lord Bishop of Bristol, that we might worship God without fear of molestation.' Sarah Best, Mary Warren, Elizabeth Perrin, Hannah Langster, Jane Brown, Solomon Phillips, J Palmer, S Colly, Mr Thomas Birch, John Reed, R Kemp, Sarah Herring, Mary Fouler. (EP/A/45/2/100-1)

566 Clifton. (13 Apr 1816). We [named below] have taken a loft belonging to Messrs J & S Barton, coach makers, for the worship of God, in Love Street, Clifton, Gloucestershire, and request a licence for the same that we may worship God as peaceable subjects without molestation. Joseph Wallis, James Brooks, Phillip Loader, John Lewis, William Rogers, William Davis, David Denham minister. (EP/A/45/2/102)

567 Clifton. 14 Aug 1820 (15 Aug 1820). *Independent/Calvinist.* To the Right Revd Lord Bishop of the diocese of Gloucester.
'May it please your Lordship
We the undersigned being householders and inhabitants of the parish of Clifton in the county of Gloucester and members of the Protestant denomination of Christians called Independents otherwise Calvenists begs leave to approach and inform your Lordship that in the dwelling house of John Lewis, one of the undersigned signatories hereof, situate in the Hotwells Road in the parish & county aforesaid a large room is fitted up intended for the public worship of Almighty God to be called The Pilgrims Lodge and feeling desirous

of acting in unison with the excellent and mild Laws of Toleration with which we are blest as a nation and enjoy as individuals do feel it incumbent upon us as a duty to lay before you in few words our object and humbly solicits that the Pilgrims Lodge may be registered as a regular place of public worship in and at the Registrar's Office and on our receiving from your Lordship a Certificate Licence or what is proper for our Authority to act upon and which we desire by the earliest post in order to make our necessary arrangements we shall feel ourselves honoured by your Lordship's attention to the subject matter and Petition of your most obedient and very humble servants.' Thomas Hobby, John Rew, John Lewis. (GDR/334B/237)

568 Clifton. 24 Jan 1824 (24 Jan 1824). I Samuel Williams of the parish of Clifton in the county of Gloucester, undertaker, certify that a room, part of a house at Clifton, is forthwith to be a place of religious worship and I require you to register the same and request a certificate thereof. (EP/A/45/2/196)

569 [Clifton]. Hull of a vessel in the harbour of Bristol called the 'Clifton Ark'. 1 Jun 1824 (14 Oct 1828). We request that the ship *Mary,* late of New York, now called the Clifton Ark, may be registered for divine worship. John Rew, James Poole, John Brooking, J W Tucker, Thomas Price, Thomas Baker. (EP/A/45/2/253)

570 Clifton. 17 Dec 1830 (18 Dec 1830). I the undersigned desire to inform your Lordship that a number of protestants do meet together for religious worship in No 4 Harly Place in the parish of Clifton. I do accordingly request your Lordship to certify and register the same. Thomas Willliam Carr. (EP/A/45/2/318)

571 Clifton. 2 Feb 1832 (4 Feb 1832). We [named below] assembling for public worship in a room, in the occupation of Mr John Hands in the Hotwell Road, humbly petition the bishop that he would grant a 'license' for the room. William Duffett, John Davis, Daniel Rew, Thomas Stock (mark), Thomas Hopkins, Rowland Morgan, John Hands, Ann Hands, Jane Sawer, Frances Morgan, Ann Virley, Emma Williams. (EP/A/45/2/346)

572 Lime Kiln Dock, Clifton. 24 Apr 1832 (25 Apr 1832). We [named below] assembling for religious worship in the house of Jonathan Chidley at Lime Kiln Dock, parish of Clifton county of Gloucester, humbly petition the bishop that he will be pleased to grant a licence for the above room. T Chudgleigh, S Lepey, William Duffett, M Estmay, H Cook, I Chudgleigh, A Wade, R Williams, M Mills, T Reed, D Reed. (EP/A/45/2/371-72)
Note. Ink fading and initials difficult to read.

573 Clifton. 24 Apr 1832 (25 Apr 1832). We [named below] assembling for religious worship in the house of Mr Thomas Reed in the parish of Clifton and county of Gloucester, humbly petition the bishop that he will be pleased to grant a licence for the above room. T Reed, M Mills, R Dugmore, D Reed, W Carter, William Duffett, H Carter, I Berry, A Redmore, G Osberne, H Perrot, J Little, J Morton, J Riddle. (EP/A/45/2/371)

574 Hotwell Road [?Clifton]. 5 Nov 1832 (6 Nov 1832). We [named below] intending congregation to assemble in William Duffett's school in Love Street, Hotwell Road, for religious worship, humbly petition the bishop to grant a licence for the above room. William Duffett, Sarah Gibbons (mark), Hh. Duffett (mark), Thomas Burbidge, Stephen Hobbs, Dorothea Lee, Robert Macer, Eleanor Rowell, Thomas Huxtable, Sarah Goodland. (EP/A/45/2/372)

575 Jacobs Wells, [Clifton]. (16 Nov 1832). We [named below] assembling for religious worship in a room in the occupation of Mr Matthews, Jacobs Wells, county of Gloucester, petition the bishop to grant a 'license' for the above room. William Duffett, John Hands (mark), Joseph Albert, William Thomas, Benjamin Fox, George Eastaway, Samuel Griffin, Jonathan Chudgleigh, James Chudgleigh, James Chembery, Richard Owens, John Simes, Charles Trott. (EP/A/45/2/376)

576 Durdham Down, Clifton. 8 Feb 1833 (2 Mar 1833). *Independent.* We [named below] dissenters of the Independent denomination, have set apart a building or chapel at Durdham Down in the parish of Clifton in the county of Gloucester for the worship of Almighty God and we pray that the chapel may be registered and a certificate granted us. William Lucy minister, William Burleigh, Durdham Down, John Thorn, Durdham Down. (EP/A/45/2/385)
Note. Certifiers often stated the county, but in view of Clifton becoming part of the city and county of Bristol for parliamentary elections, stating the county has some resonance.

577 Clifton. 14 Nov 1833 (14 Nov 1833). I William Howard Rogers of High Street, city of Bristol, draper, certify that a building in Hotwell Road in the parish of Clifton is forthwith to be a place of religious worship and I require you to register the same and request a certificate thereof. 'Will Rogers'; witness James Wood, druggist, Bristol. (EP/A/45/2/400)

578 Durdham Down, Clifton. 2 Apr 1835 (3 Apr 1835). I John Scott of Bristol, minister, certify that a chapel at Durdham Down in the parish of Clifton is intended forthwith to be a place of religious worship and I require you to register the same and request a certificate thereof. (EP/A/45/2/421)

579 Clifton Down, Clifton. 6 Mar 1850 (9 Mar 1850). I (named below] certify that a building known by the name of Crofton House on 'Clifdon Down' in the parish of Clifton, in the city and county of Bristol, is to be used and occupied as a place of divine worship and I request you to cause the same to be registered. Mary Way. (EP/A/45/4/7)
Note. Possibly original signature.

580 (nr) Durdham Down, Clifton. 6 Feb 1851 (6 Feb 1851). I William Priestley Sibree of the city of Bristol, gentleman, certify that a newly erected building in or opposite Caroline Row near to Durdham Down in the parish of Clifton in the city and county of Bristol called Highbury Schools is to be a place of religious worship and I require you to register the same and request a certificate thereof. (EP/A/45/4/50)

581 Clifton. (6 Mar 1852). We [named below] certify that a building at the north end of Waterloo Place in the parish of Clifton, in the city and county of Bristol, is used and occupied as a place of divine worship and we request your Lordship will cause the same to be registered. Minister J Panton Ham, John Soper, John S Willway, Thomas F Osborne. (EP/A/45/4/125)
Note. One of a number of late certificates bound in or pasted into the Act Book, and paginated. Signed.

582 Durdham Down, St John the Evangelist, Clifton. 6 Mar 1852 (6 Mar 1852). *Wesleyan Methodist.* I Corbett Cooke, Wesleyan minister of the parish of St James in the city of Bristol certify that a building known by the name of the Wesleyan Chapel on Durdham Down in the parish of St John the Evangelist is forthwith to be a place of religious worship and I require you to register the same and require a certificate thereof. (EP/A/45/4/126).
Note. St John the Evangelist was consecrated on 27 Apr 1841 and a district created out of Clifton and Westbury-on-Trym by Order in Council, 12th November 1841. (BA sub P.St JC)

583 Granby Hill, Clifton. 23 June 1852 (23 Jun 1852). *Wesleyan Methodist.* I Isaac Knight certify that a building rented by me at Granby Hill in the parish of Clifton in the city of Bristol is forthwith to be a place of religious worship by a congregation of Wesleyan

Methodists and I request you to register the same and request a certificate thereof. Isaac Knight, Richard Zell householder, Edward Boucher householder, Christopher Watkins householder, Thomas Sellinger householder, Christopher Davies householder. (EP/A/45/4/144)

COALEY

584 Lapley, Coaley. 24 Dec 1795 (26 Dec 1795). 'We [named below] . . . certify that we intend on next Lord's Day viz 27 Dec to meet and assemble for the public worship of Almighty God in a dwelling house at a place called Lapley in the parish of Coaley, now in the occupation of Mr Thomas White, the kitchen part of which is intended to be set apart for the same purpose in future, which we desire may be registered in your Lordship's Court.' J Thomas, Samuel Joyner, John Underwood, William Rowles. (GDR/319A/228) [*see* illus., lxxxv]

585 Coaley. 6 Feb 1802 (10 Feb 1802). 'We (being the obedient subjects of the king) dissenting from the Church of England as established by law humbly request that the house now occupied by Thomas Nichol in the parish be registered in your Lordship's office for divine worship. James Sabine, minister, William Griffin, Thomas Nicholls. (GDR/N2/1)
Note. No record in Diocesan Act Book or RG/31/2.

586 Coaley. 4 Mar 1805 (9 Mar 1805). We [named below] certify that we intend on the tenth day of this Instant March, being the Lords day, to meet and asemble for the public worship of Almighty God in the dwelling house of Mr John Underwood in the parish of Coaley, and where we intend to meet for that purpose in future, and which we desire may be registered in your Lordship's court. J Thomas, John Underwood, Samuel Joyner, Samuel Harding, William Summers. (GDR/334B/434)

587 Coaley. 27 June 1807 (4 July 1807). We [named below] certify that we intend on the 8th day of July next ensuing to meet and assemble for the public worship of Almighty God in part of the dwelling house of Mr Samuel Joyner in the parish of Coaley, which place is to be used for that purpose in future, which we desire may be registered. J Thomas, Samuel Joyner, Charles Whittard, John Underwood, Samuel Harding. (GDR/334B/421)

588 Coaley. (29 Nov 1808). We [named below] certify that the house of William Palmer in the parish of Coaley is appropriated for the public worship of Almighty God and we require that the same may be duly registered and a certificate granted. William Palser, William Lewis, Daniel Griffin, William Holder, Daniel Jollyman, Thomas Palsor [*sic*]. (GDR/334B/412)

589 Coaley. (30 Nov 1808). We [named below] certify that we have set apart a building or chapel in the parish of Coaley of which we are trustees, for the public worship of Almighty God and require that the same may be registered and a certificate of the same be granted. William Hardwick, William Lewis, Joseph Watts, Richard Harmer, Jonas Smith, Daniel Jillymer (trustees). (GDR/334B/410)
Note. All trustees named in text signed.

590 Coaley. 23 Mar 1822 (23 Mar 1822). 'I hereby certify that the premises occupied by Samuel Tickel situate in the parish of Coaley in the diocese of Gloucester will be hereafter used as a place of religious worship.' Samuel Park, a minister. (GDR/344/21r)
Note. Extreme economy of certificate.

591 Coaley. 25 Aug 1832 (25 Aug 1832). We the undersigned inhabitants of Coaley parish certify that a house in the parish at the lower end of the village, now occupied by John Webb, hedge tool maker, will henceforward be a place of religious worship. Joseph Hunt, minister, George Lewis, Thomas Jellyman, Robert Camm, Micah Jellyman. (GDR/350/132)

592 Tickshill, Coaley. (26 Apr 1851). Dwelling house occupied by James Smith. 'Ticks Hill'. James Smith. (Q/RNp/4)

COATES

593 Coates. 1 Dec 1802 (11 Dec 1802). *Independent.* 'This is to certify that a house in the occupation of John Savage is intended to be a place of worship for Protestant disssenters of the Independant denomination. We therefore request that the said house may be registered and a certificate granted accordingly. William Weaver minister, John Savage, John Lawrence, Jonathan Cole, William Wall. (GDR/N2/1)
Note. No record in Diocesan Act Book or RG/31/2, but see following registration.

594 Coates. (11 May 1804). *Independent.* This is to certify that a house in the occupation of Richard Liddington in the parish of Coates is to be a place of worship for dissenters of the Independent denomination. We request that the house may be registered and a certificate granted accordingly. William Weaver, minister, Richard Shipway snr, Thomas Gegg, Richard Shipway jnr, Richard Liddington, Jonathan Cole, William Wall. (GDR/334B/438)

595 Tarlton, Coates. 14 Sept 1813 (13 Oct 1813). I John Appleyard of Cirencester, minister of the Gospel, certify that a dwelling house, the property of and occupied by Thomas Gegg, in the village of Tarlton in the parish of Coates, is intended forthwith to be a place of religious worship and I require you to register the same and request a certificate thereof. (GDR/334B/343)

596 Coates. 22 June 1829 (24 June 1829). *Baptist.* We [named below] certify that a house in the parush of Coates in the possession or occupation of John Allen, is intended to be a place of religious worship by dissenters of the Baptist denomination and we request that this certificate may be registered in the Commissary's court. George Hoare, William Gray, Daniel White. (GDR/350/103)

597 Coates. 25 Feb 1846 (26 Feb 1846). I David Kent of Cirencester certify that a house and premises at Coates, now in the holding and occupation of John Bramble, are intended to be a place of religious worship and I request you to register the same and request a certificate thereof for which shall be taken no more than two shillings and six pence. (GDR/350/370)

COBERLEY

598 Coberley. 11 February 1822 (13 Feb 1822). I Henry Hawkins of Eastcombe in the parish of Bisley, minister, do hereby certify that a building or kitchen situate in the parish of 'Cubberley' and now in the occupation of Henry Moss, labourer, is intended forthwith to be a place of religious worship. And I hereby require you to register the same. Witness Henry Hawkins jnr, Stroud. (GDR/344/17r)

599 Coberley. 25 Aug 1823 (30 Aug 1823). I Henry Hawkins of Stroud, gentleman, certify that a building or meeting-house at 'Cubberley' in the parish of Withington is intended forthwith to be a place of religious worship and I hereby require you to register the same. Witness C Meadows. (GDR/344/113r)

COLEFORD

Coleford was the principal town in the parish of Newland, and had a chapel in 1489 (VCH Glos 5, 133), in ruins by the mid-17th century; it was also the name of one of the three tithings in the parish. It was granted a market in 1661 and became the principal settlement on the west side of the Forest.

600 Coleford. (Michaelmas 1689). [*Presbyterian: see note*]. 'Colford', Richard Benfield's house. (Q/SO/3/522)
Note. RG/31/6 has 'Coleford, Newland' and '*Presbyterian*'.

601 [Coleford]. (Easter 1690). *Quaker.* 'Cover in Newland', Meeting-house. (Q/SO/3/522)
Note. RG/31/6 has registration Easter 1689 - possibly old style date. 'Coverd' or 'Cover' was the popular name for Coleford, *see* **603** and *VCH Glos* 5, 117.

602 Coleford. 23 Jan 1715/16. William Davis of 'Colford', dissenter, took oaths of allegiance and supremacy.
Note. About this date the Evans list recorded 50 'hearers' who were Anabaptists.

603 Coleford. 1753 (registered Trinity 1753, Q/SO/8/f.72v). *Quaker.* 'We and others of the Kings Protestant subjects calld Quakers desires the Market House in Coleford, commonly called Coverd, in this county may be recorded for a meeting for the service and worship of Almighty God.' William Humphris, John Wilkins, John Gainer. (Q/SR/1753/C 25)

604 Coleford. 1 Apr 1786 (5 Apr 1786; registration GDR 319A 52). *Baptist.* Whereas we with some other [dissenters] called by the name of Baptists intend to hold a meeting for the worship of Almighty God at the house of John Stock in the town of Coleford in the parish of Newland [we] pray it may be registered in your Lordship's court. Paul Birt, Richard Alcock, James Phillips, John Alcock, John Trotter, William Trotter, Joseph Preston, Samuel Thomas, John Harris, Edward Scotney. (GDR/N2/1)

605 Coleford. 9 Jan 1789 (14 Jan 1789; registration GDR/319A/92). *Methodist.* 'Whereas we with some [dissenters] called by the name of Methodists do intend to hold a meeting for the worship of Almighty God at a room erected for that use and purpose near the town of Coleford in the parish of Newland', [we] pray it may be registered. Richard Trigg jnr, George Dow, John Parry, Thomas Teague, Henry Tomkins, George Williams, James Grindall, W Grindell, Henry Miles, Mary Worgan. (GDR/N2/1)
Note. Crossed through. GDR/319A/92 has certifiers George Dew, James Grindale, W Grindale. It also contains an endorsement written sideways against the entry: 'This licence was delivered up to the Bishop to be cancelled which his Lordship accepted & cancelled the same by consent of the parties etc alive who obtained it. Revd Gardner Reg.'.

606 Coleford. 13 Jan 1800 (14 Jan 1800). *Baptist.* We [named below], dissenters commonly denominated Baptists, being desirous of meeting for the purpose of 'worshiping' Almighty God in a house we have lately erected for that purpose in the town of Coleford, we request that the said house be registered in your court. William Bradley, George Harris, William Harris. (GDR/319A/290)
Note. William Bradley was a Baptist minister, 'one of the miners of the Forest' and also an early geologist. He drew a 'beautiful cross-section' of the Forest of Dean coal basin (although also described as simplistic). Lewis, C, 272-73.

607 Coleford. 8 Sept 1815 (9 Sept 1815). I James Ball of Coleway Lane End in the tithing of Coleford certify that my dwelling house as aforesaid in the parish of Newland is intended forthwith to be a place of religious worship and require you to register the same and request a certificate thereof. (GDR/334B/326)

608 Coleford. 18 Nov 1824 (20 Dec 1824). [*Wesleyan Methodist: see note*]. I Isaac Denison of Little Dean certify that the dwelling house of James Smith, Coleford in the parish of Newland, is intended forthwith to be a place of religious worship and I request you to register the same. (GDR/350/25)

Note. Isaac Denison was a missionary sent by the Wesleyan Conference, preaching in Cinderford, Drybrook, Lydbrook and Parkend, and also outside the Forest (*VCH Glos* 5, 314, 402). *See* **609**, **665**, **667**, **669**, **812**, **1076**.

609 Coleford. 18 Nov 1824 (20 Dec 1824). [*Wesleyan Methodist: see* **608**]. I Isaac Denison of Little Dean certify the dwelling house of Joshua Chivers, Coleford, in the parish of Newland, is intended to be a place of religious worship and I require you to register, and request a certificate thereof. (GDR/350/25)

610 Coleford. 14 Jan 1834. I John Williams in the tithing of Coleford certify that my dwelling house in the parish of Newland is intended to be a place of religious worship and I require you to register the same and request a certificate thereof. (GDR/350/144)

611 Coleford. 5 July 1837 (8 July 1837). *Baptist.* We [named below] certify that a building in the town of Coleford in the parish of Newland, in the possession or occupation of Revd John Fry and others, known by the name of Coleford Baptist Meeting-house, is to be a chapel for religious worship by dissenters of the denomination of Baptists and we request that this certificate may be registered in the Commissary's court of your Lordship. Peter Teague, James Thomas, J T Thomas. (GDR/350/211)

612 Coleford. 6 Sept 1842 (7 Sept 1842). I Nicholas Hawley of Coleford in the parish of Newland certify a newly erected Chapel in the town of Coleford is forthwith to be a place of religious worship and require you to register the same. (GDR/350/301)

613 Coleford. (9 Nov 1850). Room belonging to John Holder. Samuel Wesley. (Q/RNp/4)

614 Coleford. (9 Jan 1852). Public Room. J N Thomas, East Dean. (RG/31/2/f.126/r)

615 Coleford. (19 Feb 1852). Chapel. William Shaw, Coleford. (RG/31/2/f.126/r)

COLESBOURNE

616 Colesbourne. 16 Feb 1816 (16 Feb 1816). I Henry Hawkins of Eastcomb in the parish of Bisley, minister, certify that a building or barn in the parish of 'Colesborn', now in the occupation of Esau Rodway, is intended forthwith to be a place of religious worship and I require you to register the same. Henry Hawkins, Richard Whittard. (GDR/334B/323)

617 Colesbourne. 21 Oct 1819 (23 Oct 1819). I Henry Hawkins of Eastcombs in the parish of Bisley, minister, certify that a certain building or kitchen in the parish of 'Colesbourn', now in the occupation of William Peachy, tailor, is intended forthwith to be a place of religious worship and I require you to register the same. Witness Henry Hawkins snr. (GDR/334B/253)

618 Colesbourne. 15 Dec 1831 (21 Dec 1831). I James Smith of Cheltenham certify that a dwelling house in the parish of Colesbourne, occupied by John Smith, labourer, is intended forthwith to be a place of religious worship and I request you to register the same. James Smith, Benjamin Leach, James Hughes. (GDR/350/123)

619 Colesbourne. 27 Aug 1846 (28 Aug 1846). I Samuel Franklin of Cheltenham certify that a dwelling house in the parish of 'Colsborn', occupied by Jacob Chaplin, labourer, is intended to be forthwith a place of religious worship. Now I request you to register the same. (GDR/350/379)

COLN ROGERS

620 Coln Rogers. 16 Dec 1810 (20 Dec 1810). This is to certify that we [named below] intend to hold a meeting for the worship of Almighty God in the dwelling house of Aaron Smith in the parish of Coln Rogers. We therefore pray that this certificate may be entered in your Lordship's Registry. John Rogers, Thomas Turfery, Robert Coles, Charles Barton. (GDR/334B/370)

621 Coln Rogers. 26 Dec 1817 (3 Jan 1818). I John Rogers of Cirencester, licensed teacher, certify that a barn, in the occupation of Mr Charles Barton, in the parish of Coln Rogers is intended forthwith to be used as a place of religious worship and I request you to register the same and request a certificate thereof. John Rogers, minister, Charles Barton, Justinian Hathaway, Thomas Turfery. (GDR/334B/287)

COLN ST ALDWYNS

622 Coln St Aldwyns. (Trinity 1702). *Quaker.* 'Coln Allwins', Gil Phettiplace's house, Quaker. [Fettiplace; RG/31/6 has Giles Phettyplace]. (Q/SO/3/521)
Note. George Fox attended a meeting at Giles Fettyplace's manor house in 1677. (*VCH Glos* 7, 54)

COMPTON ABDALE

623 Compton Abdale. 9 Oct 1834 (9 Oct 1834). I James Smith of Cheltenham certify that a dwelling house in the parish of Compton Abdale, occupied by Jane Harris, is intended to be forthwith a place of religious worship and request you to register the same. Witness Charles Channon, James Hughes. (GDR/350/157)

624 Compton Abdale. Mar 1846 (16 Mar 1846). I Richard Skinner of Cheltenham certify that the house of William Panter and premises at Compton Abdale, now in [his] holding and occupation, are intended to be a place of religious worship and I request you to register the same and request a certificate thereof for which shall be taken no more than two shillings and six pence. (GDR/350/373)

CORSE

625 Corse. 14 Apr 1747. These are to certify your Lordship that some [dissenters] intend to hold a meeting for the worship of God at the dwelling house of Henry Fudger in the parish of Corse therefore pray it may be registered. Martin Lloyd, Joseph Everard, John Wickham. (GDR/284/181) *Note.* For Joseph Everard *see* **197**.

626 Corse. (13 Feb 1850). Room in a house belonging to John Roberts. John M Collard. (Q/RNp/4)

COW HONEYBOURNE

Cow Honeybourne was a chapelry in Gloucestershire in the parish of Church Honeybourne in Worcestershire; it had once had a chapel which was in ruins bfore 1735.
627 [Cow] Honeybourne. (Trinity 1695). *Presbyterian.* 'Honiborne'. Elizabeth Peters house, Presbyterian. [RG/31/6 has barn]. (Q/SO/3/522)

628 Cow Honeyborne. (17 Feb 1804). We [named below] have set apart the house of Mr Luke Heath of 'Cowhoneyborne' for the worship of Almighty God and humbly request it may be registered. Luke Heath, Joseph Chambers, Thomas Cotterell, William Gould, William Dowty, Thomas Chambers. (GDR/334B/441)

629 Cow Honeyborne. 2 Oct 1812 (14 Oct 1812). *Methodist.* This is to certify that the Methodist Chapel in the village and parish of Cow Honeyborne is set apart for the worship of God by the ministers and people in connection with the late Revd John Wesley, and we require that [it] be registered. John Hodgson, John Collett, Thomas Thompson, Joseph Chambers, Robert Chambers, William Dowty, William Gould. (GDR/334B/352)

COWLEY
See also Birdlip, Brimpsfield 358.
630 Cowley. 5 June 1741. These are to certify your Lordship that some [dissenters] intend to hold a meeting for the worship of God in their way in the dwelling house of Richard Panting, in the parish of Cowley, therefore do pray that it may be registered. Martin Lloyd, Martin Lloyd junior, Jacob Lumbard (GDR/284/117)

631 Cowley. 17 Feb 1831 (18 Feb 1831). I John Moss of Cheltenham certify that a dwelling house in the parish of Cowley, occupied by John Draper, shopkeeper, is intended to be forthwith a place of religious worship and request you to register the same. (GDR/350/114)

632 Bolton Lane, Cowley. (24 Jun 1851). Building. Joseph Bloodworth. (Q/RNp/4)

CRANHAM
633 Cranham. 22 Mar 1793 (26 Mar 1793). [*Independent: see lxv*]. These are to certify that we [named below] with others, intending to meet together for the worship of Almighty God in the dwelling house of Mrs Priscilla King in the parish of Cranham, desire that this may be recorded in your Lordship's Registry. Cornelius Winter, Benjamin Clift, Daniel Ellis Horlick, Thomas Simms, Henry Clift, Joseph Chandler, William Smith, Thomas Smith, William Hulbart, George Browning, 'Pricilla King'. (GDR/319A/146)

634 Cranham. 21 July 1820 (22 July 1820). I John Burder, minister of the town of Stroud, certify that a building in the parish of Cranham, occupied by William Green, is intended forthwith to be a place of religious worship and require you to register the same. (GDR/334B/239)
Note. For John Burder *see* **292 & 1655**.

635 Cranham. 2 Jan 1840 (2 Jan 1840). I John Moss of Cheltenham certify that a chapel at Cranham is forthwith to be a place of religious worship and I request you to register the same. (GDR/350/248)

CROMHALL
636 Cromhall. 2 Oct 1819 (17 Nov 1819). We [named below] who live in the parish of Cromhall certify that the new-built building, erected on the ground, the property of Mr Samuel Long and opposite to the residence of Mr Baker in the public road, is intended to be used as a place of religious worship and we require you to register the same. George Pick, Thomas Daniel, James Summers, James Aslam. (GDR/334B/251)

DAGLINGWORTH
637 Daglingworth. 16 Apr 1818 (18 Apr 1818). I Henry Hawkins of Eastcombs in the parish of Bisley, minister, certify that a building or stone kitchen in the parish of Daglingworth, in the occupation of Robert Hillman, is intended forthwith to be a place of

religious worship and I require you to register the same. Witness Jacob Aldum (GDR/334B/282)

638 Daglingworth. 27 Apr 1828 (10 May 1828). *Baptist.* We [named below] certify that a building in the parish of Daglingworth, in the possession or occupation of John Page, is intended to be a place of religious worship by dissenters of the denomination of Baptists and we request that this certificate may be registered in the Commisssary's Court of your Lordship. Daniel White, Thomas Moss, Richard Moss, George Hoare. (GDR/350/88)

DEAN FOREST (EXTRA-PAROCHIAL), THE PARISH OF ST BRIAVELS, AND DETACHED PARTS OF NEWLAND PARISH

Dean Forest was largely extra-parochial, and was administratively in the hundred of St Briavels, see Introduction, xxv. St Briavels hundred included the parishes of Abenhall, English Bicknor, Flaxley, Hewelsfield, Littledean, Mitcheldean, Newland, Ruardean, and Staunton, which see.

Included under this heading: Cinderford and Ruspidge, Lydbrook and Parkend, and detached portions of Newland including Bream (partly a chapelry in Newland parish) and Bream's Eaves, Ellwood, Joyford, Pillowell, Whitecroft and Yorkley. Lea Hamlet or Lea Bailey are also included here. The larger part of Lea parish was a chapelry annexed to Linton parish in Herefordshire, but there were ten detached portions of land in Newland parish known as Lea hamlet or Lea Bailey, which adjoined Forest woodland of the same name and Lea parish, while three small parts were in the hundred of St Briavels - they were transferred to Herefordshire in 1844. In the 1880s some detached portions were transferred to Herefordshire and in 1965 Lea Bailey Inclosures, formerly extra-parochial, were transferred. (VCH Glos 5, 87, 195).

639 St Briavels parish. 6 Oct 1746 (registered Michaelmas 1746, Q/SO/7/f.128r). *Presbyterian.* These are to certify your Worships that some [dissenters] of the Presbyterian denomination intend to hold a meeting at the house of Thomas Byrkin in the parish of St Briavels and therefore we pray your Worships that the said house may be registered in your Court.' Thomas Jenkins, Thomas Gay, Samuel Trotman, Thomas Byrkin. (Q/SR/1746/D/4)

640 Whitecroft, Newland. 19 Aug 1787 (Trinity 1787). *Independent.* All [those named below, [dissenters] commonly called Independents and householders in the parish of Newland, certify to this court that we intend to set apart a dwelling house, now or late in the occupation of Samuel Baker, at a place called 'White Croft' in the parish of Newland for the service and worship of Almighty God in our way. 'And we humbly request that this our certificate may be entered and enrolled among the records of the court of quarter sessions for the county aforesaid and a licence thereupon granted according to the form of the statute in that case made and provided'. William Dobbs, Benjamin Bennett (mark), Anthony Roberts, William Ellaway (mark), William Davis, George Phipps (mark), Samuel Morse, William Williams. (Q/SO/10/f.265r)
Note. Names written in a different or much larger hand but not signatures. Long endorsement about adjournment of the Trinity sessions at the Kings Head in the city of Gloucester on Saturday 25 Aug 27 GIII [1787] at which 'the certificate (by order of that court) entered and inrolled of Record in the said court pursuant to the statute in that case made and provided.'

641 The Lea hamlet. 23 July 1797 (5 Aug 1797). We the undersigned request your Lordship to cause to be registered in your court the house of which Thomas Teague is now tenant in 'the Lea hamlett near Littledeane' as a place of divine worship. Robert McAll, minister, Thomas Teague, James Williams, Richard Stiff, Richard Craduck. (GDR/319A/255)
Note. Robert McAll was minister of the Countess of Huntingdon's chapel in Gloucester. *See also* **1289** and Introduction, lxvi.

642 Bream, St Briavels hundred. 24 Apr 1802 (8 May 1802). *Independent*. This is to certify that an house in the occupation of William Adams of Yorkley in the tithing of Bream in the hundred of 'St Briavells' is intended to be a place of worship for dissenters of the Independent denomination. We therefore request that the house may be registered. Richard Stiff, James Ashwell, William Adams, Nathaniel Wakeford. (GDR/319A/311)
Note. For Richard Stiff *see* **324**.

643 Brockweir, St Briavels parish. 31 Mar 1812 (7 Apr 1812). We [named below] have set apart and appropriated for the public worship of Almighty God a dwelling house in the occupation of George Williams in 'Brockwear' in the parish of 'St Brevils' and request that the same may be registered and a certificate thereof granted. George Williams, John Right, John Phillips, Josh Malton, James Darby, Richard Lewis, Catherine Jenkins. (GDR/334B/353)

644 Lydbrook. 11 May 1813 (15 May 1813). I William Woodall of the town of Monmouth, minister of the gospel, certify that a chapel in Lydbrook in the parish of 'Bickney' [Bicknor] is forthwith to be a place of religious worship and I require you to register the same and request a certificate thereof. Witness John Tyler (GDR/334B/81)
Note. The rubric has Bickney crossed out and 'Lidbrook' inserted. 'Bickney' was alternative spelling for 'Bicknor'.

645 'The [Lea] Baily', St Briavels hundred. 12 Apr 1814 (16 Apr 1814). We [named below] intend to meet for divine worship in a house, now in the occupation of Mr Moses Hiles, at a place called 'the Baily in the hundred of St Brevels' and we request that the same may be registered. W Williams, Cornelius Jayne, Moses Hiles. (GDR/334B/338)

646 St Briavels parish. 10 Apr 1815 (14 Apr 1815). I William Woodall of the town of Chepstow, minister of the gospel, certify that a dwelling house in the parish of 'St Brevalls', in the occupation of Benjamin Wogan, is intended forthwith to be a place of religious worship and I require you to register the same and request a certificate thereof. William Woodall, John Williams, John Phillips, John Symonds. (GDR/334B/329)

647 Pillowell, Newland. 4 Oct 1816 (10 Oct 1816) *Wesleyan Methodist*. This is to certify that, in the house of William Elway of Pillowell in the parish of Newland, the religious worship of Almighty God is intended to be performed by those commonly called Wesleyan Methodists and we require that the same may be registered. William Brocklehurst, minister, James Jones, John Martin, Samuel Nash. (GDR/334B/313)
Note. See **672** registration of a meeting in 1827 in Pillowell but not in the parish of Newland.

648 Lea [St Briavels hundred]. 1 Oct 1818 (2 Oct 1818). [*Baptist or Particular Baptist: see note*]. I William Williams, dissenting minister of Ryeford [Herefordshire], certify that a messuage, now in the occupation of Mr William James, carpenter, in the parish of the Lea is intended forthwith to be a place of religious worship and I require you to register the same. William Williams, James Turner, Moses Hiles. (GDR/334B/275)
Note. A register of baptisms between 1787 and 1837 in the Particular Baptist Ryeford chapel in Weston under Penyard survives (http:/www.archersoftware.co.uk/igi/fs-hef.htm). *See also* **785**, **1252**, **1253**.

649 St Briavels. 27 Jan 1819 (4 Feb 1819). *Wesleyan*. I Benjamin Taylor of the town of Chepstow in the county of Monmouth certify that the dwelling house of William Tuder, called the Green Farm, at 'St Briavells' is intended forthwith to be a place of religious worship and I require you to register the same and require a certificate thereof. Benjamin Taylor, Wesleyan preacher. (GDR/334B/268)

650 Cinderford, Dean Forest. 20 Apr 1819 (20 Apr 1819). *Independent*. This is to certify that a messuage or tenement at 'Sinderford' in the Forest of Dean, now in the occupation of John Cooper, is intended to be opened as a place of worship for dissenters of the Independent denomination. We request that the said messuage or tenement may be registered. Nathaniel Wakeford, John Cooper (mark), James Wood (mark); witness G Wakeford. (GDR/334B/263)
Note. RG/2 gives G Wakeford as the certifier.

651 Ellwood, St Briavels hundred. 7 May 1821 (12 May 1821). I Richard Cullis of Ellwood in the hundred of St Briavels certify that my dwelling house is intended forthwith to be a place of religious worship and I hereby require you to register the same. (GDR/344/15)
Note. Heading reads: 'Ellwood Certificate in the Forest of Dean'.

652 Bream, Newland. 18 June 1821 (22 Jun 1821). I Thomas Smith of Bream in the parish of Newland certify that my dwelling house and premises 'is' intended forthwith to be a place of religious worship and require you to register the same and request a certificate thereof. (GDR/334B/218)

653 [Soudley], Dean Forest. 11 July 1821 (13 July 1821). We certify that a messuage or tenement situate at 'Soudlow' [RG/31/2 has 'Soundlow'] in the Forest of Dean, in the occupation of William Williams, is intended forthwith to be a place of religious worship and request you to register the same. Joseph Pearce, Nathaniel Wakeford; witness William Cooper. (GDR/334B/217)

654 Dean Forest, St Briavels hundred. 16 Mar 1822 (23 Mar 1822). [*Methodist: see note*]. I George Robinson of Ledbury certify that the dwelling house of Robert Meredith in the Forest of Dean, hundred of St. Briavels, is intended forthwith to be a place of religious worship and I require you to register the same and request a certificate thereof. (GDR/344/21r)
Note. Horlick, c.1831, attributes the rise in the Methodist cause to the Revd George Robinson, who began preaching in a tent; thereafter interest kept up principally by travelling preachers.

655 Pope's Hill, St Briavels hundred. 2 Apr 1822 (5 Apr 1822). We certify that the messuage or tenement at Pope's Hill in the hundred of 'St Briavells', in the occupation of William Elton, is intended forthwith to be a place of religious worship and we request you to register the same. William Elton (mark), Nathan Wakeford, William Cooper, John Thomas. (GDR/344/21v)

656 [Soudley] St Briavels hundred. 2 Apr 1822 (5 Apr 1822). We hereby certify that the messuage or tenement at 'Souderlow in the hundred of St Briavells' [Soudley], in the occupation of John Davis, is intended forthwith to be a place of religious worship and we request you to register the same. John Davies (mark), Nathaniel Wakeford, William Cooper, John Thomas. (GDR/344/21v)

657 Joyford, Dean Forest. 30 Aug 1822 (2 Sept 1822). I George White of Joyford in the Forest of Dean certify that my dwelling house in the hundred of St. Briavels is intended forthwith to be a place of religious worship and I require you to register the same and request a certificate thereof. (GDR/344/36v)

658 Berry Hill, St Briavels hundred. 5 Sept 1822 (7 Sept 1822). I Thomas Webb of 'Burry-hill' in the Forest of Dean certify that my dwelling house as aforesaid in the hundred of 'St Briaveles' is intended forthwith to be a place of religious worship and I require you to register the same and request a certificate thereof. (GDR/344/37r)

659 Lydbrook, Ruardean. 26 May 1823 (28 May 1823). I Isaac Bridgman of the parish of Ruardean certify that a house now in the occupation of Mr James Russell, ironmaster, Lydbrook, in the parish of Ruardean, is intended forthwith to be a place of religious worship and I require you to register the same and request a certificate thereof. (GDR/344/63v)
Note. For Isaac Bridgman *see* **210**.

660 Bradley Forge, Dean Forest. 20 July 1823 (25 July 1823). I Isaac Bridgman of the parish of Awre certify that a workshop, now in the occupation of Mr. Samuel Hewlett, carpenter, and situated at Bradley Forge in the Forest of Dean near Ayleford, extraparochial, is intended forthwith to be a place of religious worship and I require you to register and record the same and request a certificate thereof. (GDR/344/111v)
Note. The rubric refers to Awre. For Isaac Bridgman *see* **210**.

661 Lydbrook, Ruardean. 13 Oct 1823 (7 Nov 1823). [*Baptist: see note*]. I Thomas Wright of 'Lidbrook', dissenting minister, certify that a chapel recently erected at 'Lidbrook' in the parish of Ruardean is intended forthwith to be a place of worship and I hereby require you register the same. (GDR/344/117v)
Note. Thomas Wright built a small chapel in Lydbrook using money from Goff's charity which was applied to establishing Baptist missions. (*VCH Glos* 5, 397)

662 Lydbrook. 29 Nov 1823 (29 Nov 1823). I John Taylor of 'Gloster' certify that the dwelling house of Robert Wall at 'Lidbrook' is intended forthwith to be a place of religious worship and I require you to register the same and hereby request a certificate thereof. (GDR/344/119v)

663 Joyford, Newland. 20 Jan 1824 (26 Feb 1824). I George Smith of Joyford in Newland certify my dwelling house, garden and appurtenances thereto are intended forthwith to be used for religious worship and I require you to register the same and request a certificate thereof. (GDR/344/129v)

664 St Briavels parish. 14 Aug 1824 (27 Aug 1824). *Independent.* We [named below], dissenters commonly called Independents, certify that there is a house, the property of Mr James Bird in the parish of 'St Brevals', intended henceforth as a regular place of religious worship and we request that the same be registered. David Thomas, James Bird ('is mark'), Benjamin Evans, W Morris. (GDR/344/136v)

665 Dean Forest, St Briavels hundred. 11 Oct 1824 (11 Oct 1824). *Wesleyan Methodist.* I Isaac Denison of 'Little Dean' certify that the Wesleyan Methodist chapel in the Forest of Dean, Hundred of St Briavels, is intended forthwith to be a place of religious worship and I require you to register the same, and request a certificate thereof. (GDR/344/138v)
Note. Rubric has 'Littledean'.

666 Whitecroft, Newland. 25 Oct 1824 (29 Oct 1824). *Wesleyan.* I John Mason of Monmouth certify that a building called the Wesleyan Chapel at Whitecroft in the parish of Newland is intended forthwith to be a place of religious worship and I require you to register the same, and request a certificate thereof. (GDR/344/139r)

667 Lea Bailey, St Briavels hundred. 18 Nov 1824 (20 Dec 1824). [*Wesleyan Methodist: see* **608**]. I Isaac Denison of Little Dean certify that the dwelling house of George Higg of Lea Bailey in the hundred of 'St Brevils' is intended forthwith to be a place of religious worship and I require you to register the same, and request a certificate thereof for which shall be taken no more than two shillings and six pence. (GDR/350/26)

668 St Briavels village. 8 Mar 1824 (12 Mar 1825). I James Hulin of the village of 'Saint Brevials' certify that the dwelling house now in my occupation in the said village is intended forthwith to be a place of religious worship and I require you to register the same, and request a certificate thereof. James Hulin, David Thomas, minister. (GDR/350/34)

669 St Briavels hundred. 7 May 1825 (7 May 1825). [*Wesleyan Methodist: see* **608**]. This is to certify that the dwelling house of Jonathan Hodges in the hundred of 'St Brevills' is intended forthwith to be a place of religious worship and [to] require you to register the same and request a certificate thereof. Isaac Denison. (GDR/350/40)

670 St Briavels hundred. 20 Sept 1825 (21 Sept 1825). [*Congregational: see* **671**] I John Parkyn, minister, certify that a house in the Forest of Dean in the hundred of 'St Brevells', occupied by John Dean, is intended forthwith to be a place of religious worship and I require you to register the same and request a certificate thereof. John Parkyn, minister, John Dean (mark), occupier. (GDR/350/46)

671 Dean Forest, St Briavels hundred. 8 Mar 1826 (9 Mar 1826). *Congregational*. I John Parkyn, minister, certify that a dwelling house in the Forest of Dean and hundred of 'St Brevails', in the occupation of Jane Broadstock, is intended forthwith to be a place of religious worship and I require you to register the same and request a certificate thereof. Jane Broadstock (mark), Richard Matthews (mark), John Parkyn. (GDR/350/53)

672 Pillowell, St Briavels hundred. 30 June 1827 (5 July 1827). I James Elway of Pillowell in the hundred of 'St Briavells' certify that my dwelling house in the hundred of 'St Breavells' and now in [my] occupation is intended to be a place of religious worship and I request you to register the same and request a certificate thereof. Witness Thomas Elway, Edward Bergak. (GDR/350/69)
Note. Pillowell was largely extra-parochial but a small part was in Newland parish. (*VCH Glos* 5, 197). *See* **647**

673 Yorkley, Newland. 24th Apr 1827 (5 July 1827). I Richard Dobbs of Yorkley in the hundred of 'St Breavels' certify that my dwelling house in the parish of Newland is intended forthwith to be a place of religious worship and require you to register the same, and request a certificate thereof. Witness James Johnson, Joshua Harrison. (GDR/350/68)

674 Bream, Newland. 8 July 1827 (12 July 1827). I Edward Gardener of Bream in the parish of Newland certify that my dwelling house, situate as aforesaid, now in [my] holding and occupation, is intended to be a place of religious worship and I require you to register the same, and request a certificate thereof for which shall be taken no more than two shillings and six pence. Witness Edward Bergak, George Morgan. (GDR/350/70)

675 Lydbrook. 17 Mar 1828 (7 Apr 1828). I Charles Waver of 'Lidbrook' in the Forest of Dean certify that my dwelling house and premises at Lidbrook (Forest) in the hundred of St Briavels, in [my] holding and occupation, are intended to be a place of religious worship and I request you to register the same and request a certificate thereof for which shall be taken no more than two shillings and six pence. (GDR/350/86)

676 Parkend, St Briavels hundred. 21 Apr 1828 (22 May 1828). I William Tippins of Parkend in the hundred of St Briavels certify that the dwelling house and premises at Parkend (Forest) in the hundred of St Briavels, now in [my] holding and occupation, are intended to be a place of religious worship and I request you to register the same and request a certificate thereof for which shall be taken no more than two shillings and six pence. William Tippins (mark). (GDR/350/89)

677 St Briavels parish. 24 Oct 1828 (31 Oct 1828). *Baptist.* I Joseph Burroughs, Baptist minister, of Llandogo, Monmouthshire, certify that a building in the parish of 'St Brivals', now in the occupation of William Jenkins, is intended forthwith to be a place of religious worship and I request that this certificate may be registered by the commissioners of your Lordship. (GDR/350/95)

678 Lydbrook, St Briavels hundred. 2 Apr 1829 (8 Apr 1829). *Primitive Methodist.* I John Challinor of Pillowell in the hundred of 'St Breavels' certify that a chapel and premises at 'Lidbrook' in the hundred of St Briavels, now in the holding or occupation of Primitive Methodists, are intended to be a place of religious worship and I request you to register the same and request a certificate thereof for which shall be taken no more than two shillings and six pence. (GDR/350/101)

679 Cinderford, St Briavels hundred. 22 July 1829 (23 July 1829). I Aaron Goold of Bilson certify that a meeting-house at Cinderford in the Forest of Dean, hundred of 'St Briavells', is intended forthwith to be a place of religious worship and I require you to register the same and request a certificate thereof. (GDR/350/104)
Note. This may be the room adapted by a union of Baptists, Independents and Methodists, as described by Horlick, *A visit to the Forest of Dean* 29. For Aaron Goold, colliery manager and businessman, *see* VCH 5, esp. 380, 403.

680 Joyford, Dean Forest, St Briavels hundred. 28 Oct 1829 (31 Oct 1829). *Wesleyan.* I Thomas James of Coleford certify that a building called the Wesleyan Chapel at Joyford, Forest of Dean, hundred of St Briavels, is intended forthwith as a place of religious worship and I require you to register the same and request a certificate thereof. (GDR/350/105)

681 Bream's Eaves, Newland. 30 Mar 1833. I Jacob Robbins of 'Bream Eves' in the parish of Newland certify that my dwelling house is intended forthwith to be a place of religious worship and I require you to register the same and request a certificate thereof. J Robinson, minister. (GDR/350/138)
Note. Certifier and signature differ.

682 Yorkley, Newland. 10 Sept 1836 (3 Oct 1836). *Primitive Methodist.* I Richard Kear of Yorkley in the parish of Newland certify that a new chapel at Yorkley, now in the holding of a congregation of protestants called Primitive Methodists, 'are' to be a place of religious worship and I request you to register the same and request a certificate thereof for which shall be taken no more than two shillings and six pence. (GDR/350/200-1)

683 Drybrook, St Briavel's hundred. 30 May 1837 (30 May 1837). *Bible Christian Connexion.* I Robert Hurley of Woodside in the parish of 'Woollastone' [Woolaston] certify that a chapel and premises at Drybrook in the hundred of St Briavels, now in the holding and occupation of the Bible Christians Connexion, are to be a place of religious worship and I request you to register the same and request a certificate thereof for which shall be taken no more than two shillings and six pence. (GDR/350/209)
Note. For Bible Christians in the Forest *see VCH Glos* 5, 398-9.

684 Viney Hill, St Briavels hundred. 27 Feb 1838 (29 Mar 1838). I William Gailes of Viney Hill in the hundred of 'St Breavels' certify that my house and premises in Viney Hill, now in [my] holding and occupation, are to be a place of religious worship and I request you to register the same and request a certificate thereof for which shall be taken no more than two shillings and six pence. (GDR/350/221)

685 Lydbrook. 21 Mar 1838 (registered 29 Mar 1838, GDR/350/221). I John Richard of Hereford in the parish of Saint Martyn in the county of Hereford certify that a chapel and premises at Lydbrook, now in the holding and occupation of Thomas Jordan, Robert Wall, William Davies, Joseph Hatton, John Hatton, are intended to be a place of religious worship, and I request you to register the same and request a certificate thereof, for which shall be taken no more than two shillings and sixpence. (GDR N2/1)

Note. The only printed form found in the Gloucester records. The form has 'Lydbrook in the parish of [blank]'.

686 Joyford, St Briavels hundred 10 Dec 1840 (18 Dec 1840). I James Hall of Joyford in the hundred of St Briavels, certify that my house and premises at Joyford, now in [my] holding and occupation, are to be a place of religious worship and request you to register the same and request a certificate thereof for which shall be taken no more than two shillings and six pence. (GDR/350/267)

687 Cinderford. 25 Jan 1842 (26 Jan 1842). I George Wood Rodway of Stroud Road, Gloucester, dissenting minister, certify that a room at Cinderford in the Forest of Dean, now occupied by Mr William Rhodes, is intended forthwith to be a place of religious worship and I request you to register the same and request a certificate thereof. (GDR/350/290)

688 St Briavels village. (6 Jan 1844). *Baptist.* We [named below] certify that a dwelling house in the village of 'St Braivels', now in the occupation of William Jenkins of the said village, labourer, is intended forthwith to be a place of religious worship by dissenters of the Baptist persuasion and we require you to register the same and request a certificate of the same. Moses Philpin, James Williams, Edward Johnson. (GDR/350/329)

689 [Viney Hill], East Dean. 9 Nov 1844 (16 Nov 1844). I Richard Ems of the parish of 'Lidney' certify that the dwelling house and premises at 'the Vinehill' in the parish of East Dean, now in the holding and occupation of William Davis, is intended to be a place of religious worship and I request you to register the same and request a certificate thereof for which shall be taken no more than two shillings and six pence. (GDR/350/351)

690 St Briavels parish. 20 Nov 1845 (22 Nov 1845). *Baptist.* We [named below] certify that a building in the parish of St Briavels, in the possession or occupation of John Mercy, [is] intended to be a meeting-house for religious worship by dissenters of the denomination of Baptists, and we request that this certificate may be registered in the commissary's court of your Lordship. Thomas Nicholson, E E Elliott, James Ridler. (GDR/350/364)

691 Ellwood, West Dean. 23 Jan 1846 (2 Feb 1846). *Primitive Methodist.* I Robert Langford of Monmouth in the county of Monmouth certify that a chapel and premises at Ellwood in the parish of West Dean, now in the holding and occupation of the Primitive Methodists, are intended to be a place of religious worship and I request you to register the same and request a certificate thereof for which shall be taken no more than two shillings and six pence. Witness Edmund Rawlings. (GDR/350/368)

Note. A certificate for Ellwood, West Dean with dates 23 Nov 1854 (9 Dec 1854) (D7007/2) states 'I William Jones of Ellwood in the township of West Dean certify that a certain building known by the name of Ellwood Chapel, is forthwith intended to be used by a denomination called Primitive Methodists. William Jones, trustee'.

692 The Lonk, West Dean. 23 Feb 1846 (24 Feb 1846). [*Primitive Methodist*]. I Robert Langford of Monmouth, Monmouthshire, certify that a house and premises at The Lonk in the parish of West Dean, now in the holding and occupation of Charles Williams, are intended to be a place of religious worship and I request you to register the same and request a certificate thereof for which shall be taken no more than two shillings and six pence. Witness Edmund Rawlings. (GDR/350/369)

Note. The Lonk is north of Coleford, adjoining Berry Hill.

693 Littledean Hill, St Briavels hundred. 16 Mar 1846 (16 Mar 1846). I George Halliday of Cheltenham certify that the house of Thomas Beddis and premises at 'Littledeanhill in the hundred of St Brevels', now in [his] holding and occupation, are intended to be a place of religious worship and I request you to register the same and request a certificate thereof for which shall be taken no more than two shillings and six pence. (GDR/350/372)

Note. Littledean Hill was partly in Littledean, partly in Lea Bailey tithing and partly in Cinderford.

694 Whitecroft, Newland. (27 Sep 1848). House & premises of John Morgan. Henry Webb. [RG/31/2 has 'Farm house' and 'Dean Forest']. (Q/RNp/4)

695 Viney Hill, Awre. (19 May 1849). Dwelling house occupied by John Phelps. Joseph Hyatt. [RG/31/2 has 'Viney Hill, Dean Forest']. (Q/RNp/4)

696 Littledean Hill, Flaxley. (15 May 1850). Meeting-house. Aaron Goold [RG/31/2 has 'Littledean Hill, Dean Forest' and Aaron Gould of Bilson']. (Q/RNp/4)

697 West Dean. (18 Jun 1850). House & premises occupied by Joseph Jones. Robert Esam Farley. [RG/31/2 has 'Dean Forest']. (Q/RNp/4)

698 Littledean Hill. (1 Nov 1850). Chapel. Samuel Wesley [RG/31/2 has 'of Littledean Hill, Dean Forest']. (GA Q/RNp/4)

699 'Bream in Newland'. (14 Jan 1851). House occupied by Thomas Hill. William Baker. [RG/31/2 has 'Bream, Dean Forest' and 'William Baker [of] Monmouth, minister'.] (Q/RNp/4)

700 St Briavels, Dean Forest. 3 Jan 1852. House. P G Johnson, St Briavells. (RG/31/2 f.126/r)

DEERHURST

701 Deerhurst [and elsewhere?]. 1672. *Congregational.* Licence recorded 25 July 1672 to 'Thomas Hemings of 'Dearhurst' to be a General Congregational teacher'. (LT/538)

702 Apperley [Deerhurst]. 23 Aug 1785 (25 Aug 1785; registration GDR/319A/23).'This is to certify that we [named below, dissenters] intend to hold a meeting for the public worship of Almighty God in the dwelling house of Thomas Margrett in the parish of Deerhurst'. Thomas Margrett (mark), James Nind, 'Jhon' [John] Margrett, Miliora Nind, Lawrence Clayton, James Park, William Hatcher (mark), Richard Cue. (GDR/N2/1)

Note. This certificate uses very abbreviated words like 'Al: Gd', which have been expanded here, implying a copy made for a temporary record. Every line of script roughly underlined, the whole crossed through. [*see* illus., lxxiv]

703 Apperley, Deerhurst. 25 Aug 1785 (25 Aug 1785; registration GDR/319A/23). This is to certify your Lordship that we [named below, dissenters] intend to hold meeting for the public worship of Almighty God in the dwelling house of John Healing in the tithing of Apperley in the parish of Deerhurst. 'We therefore pray that this certificate may be entered in your Lordship's Registry according to an act of parliament made and appointed in that behalf in the reign of King William and Queen Mary.' John Healing, Hannah Healing, Sarah Randle, William Hemming, Robert Smith, Peter Oakley. (GDR/N2/1)

Note. Paper crossed through. [*see* illus., lxxiv]

704 Apperley, Deerhurst. 1 Apr 1802 (17 July 1802). This is to certify that we [named below] intend to hold a meeting for the public worship of Almighty God in the chapel of

Apperley in the parish of Deerhurst. We therefore pray that this certificate may be entered in your Lordship's registry. Joseph Healing, James Trenfield, John Margrett, Joseph Davis, James Price snr, James Price jnr. (GDR/319A/312)

705 Apperley, Deerhurst. 1 Apr 1804 (17 July 1804). This is to certify that we [named below] intend to hold a meeting for the publick worship of Almighty God in the 'Chappel of Apperley' in the parish of Deerhurst. We therefore pray that this certificate may be entered in your Lordship's registry. Thomas Healing, James Trenfield, John Margrett, Joseph Davis, James Price Senr, James Price (GDR/334B/437)

706 Deerhurst Walton, Deerhurst. 2 November 1822 (2 Nov 1822). I Abraham Harris of Gloucester Row, Tewkesbury, late hosier, certify that a tenement situated at Walton Hill in the parish of Deerhurst Walton, now in the occupation of John Meredith, is intended forthwith to be a place of religious worship and I hereby request you to register the same. (GDR/344/39v)

707 Deerhurst. 24 Oct 1823 (28 Oct 1823). I Abraham Harris of Gloucester Row, Tewkesbury, master hosier, certify that a tenement situated at Deerhurst, now in the occupation of John Fowler, is intended forthwith to be a place of religious worship and I request you to register the same. (GDR/344/117r)

708 Deerhurst. 19 Nov 1828 (19 Nov 1828). [*Particular Baptist: see* **1721**]. We certify that the dwelling house now in the occupation of William Hale in the parish of Deerhurst is henceforth intended to be a place of religious worship and we therefore request that this certificate may be registered in the consistory court of the diocese. Daniel Trotman, Tewkesbury, Thomas Randall. (GDR/350/95)

709 Apperley, Deerhurst. 2 June 1838. I Daniel Browett of the Leigh certify that the house of Richard Robbins and premises in Apperley in the parish of Deerhurst are to be a place of religious worship and I request you to register the same and request a certificate thereof. (GDR/350/226)

710 Deerhurst. 2 June 1838 (2 June 1838). I Daniel Browett of the Leigh certify that the house of William Hopkins and premises at Deerhurst, now in [his] holding and occupation, are to be a place of religious worship and I request you to register the same and request a certificate thereof for which shall be taken no more than two shillings and six pence. (GDR/350/227)

711 Walton Hill, Deerhurst. 31 Oct 1840 (6 Nov 1840). I Daniel Browett of the parish of the Leigh certify that the house of William Done and premises at Walton Hill in the parish of Deerhurst, now in [his] holding and occupation, is to be a place of religious worship and I request you to register the same and request a certificate thereof for which shall be taken no more than two shillings and six pence. (GDR/350/260)
Note.: Rubric is 'Leigh' but the house is in Deerhurst.

712 Deerhurst. 5 May 1841 (29 May 1841). I John Hill of Twigworth St Catherine certify that the house of William Margaret and premises at Deerhurst, in [his] holding and occupation, are to be a place of religious worship and I request you to register the same and request a certificate thereof for which shall be taken no more than two shillings and six pence. (GDR/350/281)

DIDBROOK

713 Didbrook. 22 July 1824 (23 July 1824). I George Nash certify that a dwelling house occupied by me in the village of Didbrook in the parish of Didbrook is intended forthwith to be a place of religious worship and I require you to register and record the same, and request a certificate thereof. Witness John Lomas (GDR/344/135v)

714 Didbrook. 15 Mar 1829 (25 Mar 1829). I James Reeve of the parish of Didbrook, farmer, certify that a house occupied by me is intended forthwith to be a place of religious worship and I hereby require you to register and record the same and request a certificate thereof. (GDR/350/101)

715 Didbrook. 2 Mar 1832 (3 Mar 1832). I Thomas Osborne of Cheltenham, minister of the Gospel, certify that a house in the parish of Didbrook, now in the occupation of William White, is intended forthwith to be a place of religious worship and I request you to register the same and request a certificate thereof. (GDR/350/125)

DIDMARTON

716 Didmarton. 28 May 1838 (9 June 1838). [*Primitive Methodist: see* **254**]. I Joseph Preston of Brinkworth, Wiltshire, certify that a house and premises in Didmarton, now in the holding and occupation of Rowland Hill, are to be a place of religious worship and request you to register the same and request a certificate thereof for which shall be taken no more than two shillings and six pence. Witness John Excell (GDR/350/228)

717 Didmarton. (26 May 1843). I Benjamin Rees of Chippenham certify that a dwelling house at Didmarton, occupied by Jessa Mills, is intended to be used herewith as a place of religious worship and request you to register the same. (GDR/350/321)
Note. Rubric has 'Chippenham'.

DOWN HATHERLEY

718 [Down] Hatherley. 24 Nov 1827 (1 Dec 1827). We certify that the dwelling house of Thomas Smith in the parish of Hatherley is intended forthwith to be a place of religious worship and we require you to register the same and request a certificate thereof. Thomas Smith, Jacob Stanley. (GDR/350/77-8)

719 [Down] Hatherley. 10 May 1838 (12 May 1838). *Wesleyan.* I Thomas Moss of Gloucester certify that the house of William Boyce, labourer, in the parish of Hatherley, is forthwith to be a place of religious worship and require you to register the same and request a certificate thereof. Thomas Moss, Weslyan Minister. (GDR/350/225)

DOYNTON

720 Doynton. (29 July 1811). We [named below] certify that a house in the occupation of William Amos in the parish of Doynton is set apart for the public worship of Almighty God and request that the same be registered and a certificate granted accordingly. Paul Rose, minister, William Amos, Samuel Nichols. (GDR/334B/364)

721 Doynton. 13 Sept 1813 (15 Sept 1813). We [named below] certify that a room in the occupation of Richard Wakely Spry in the parish of Doynton is set apart for the public worship of Almighty God and request that the same may be registered and a certificate granted. Paul Rose, minister, Richard Wakely Spry, Samuel Nichols. (GDR/334B/343)

722 Doynton. 30 Oct 1834. *Baptist.* We whose names are subscribed certify that a building in the parish of Doynton, occupied by George Bateman, is intended to be a place for the public worship of Almighty God by dissenters called Baptists and we require the same to be registered and a certificate granted. George Bateman, James Dimond, Edward Fox, Henry Liles, John Jackson, Edward Hancock, John Seaman, Charles Chapel Davis. (GDR/350/160)

DUMBLETON

723 Dumbleton. 10 June 1813 (11 Jun 1813). I Ann Archer of Dumbleton certify that my dwelling house in the parish of Dumbleton is intended forthwith to be a place of religious worship and I require you to register the same and request a certificate thereof. Witness James Tracy, James Bale. (GDR/334B/344)

DUNTISBOURNE ABBOTS

724 Upper Duntisbourne [Abbots?]. 13 July 1818 (25 July 1818). I Henry Hawkins of Eastcomb in the parish of Bisley, minister, certify a building or stone kitchen in the parish of 'Upper Dunsbourn', in the occupation of Robert Burch, is forthwith to be used for religious worship and require you to register the same. Witness Henry Dowling. (GDR/334B/277)

725 Duntisbourne Abbots. (3 Dec 1842). I John Belcher of the parish of 'Duntisbourn' Abbots certify that a building in the said parish, in the occupation of Samuel Painter, is intended to be used as a chapel for religious worship and request that this certificate may be registered. (GDR/350/307)

726 Duntisbourne [Abbots?]. 21 Jan 1843 (26 Jan 1843). I George Obern of Cirencester certify a house and premises at 'Duntisbourn', occupied by James Kilminster, is intended to be used for religious worship and and I request you to register the same and request a certificate thereof for which shall be taken no more than two shillings and six pence. (GDR/350/313)

DURSLEY

727 'Dursty' [Dursley]. 1672. *Congregational.* Application by Owen Davies for 'Francis Ham[m] of Dursty' as a Congregational minister at his own house; licence recorded 10 June 1672 for him and his house in 'Durston'. (LT/372, 509, 510)
Note. His name is given as Francis Haine in Evans, *As mad as a hatter!* 30; see **2035** for licence to Francis Hayne with no place named.

728 Dursley. (Trinity 1704). Thomas Young's house. (Q/SO/3/521)

729 Dursley. 17 February 1755. These are to certify that some [dissenters] intend to hold a meeting in the dwelling house of Nathaniel Parry in the parish of Dursley, and desires it may be registered. John Dando, John Shatford, Thomas Browning, John Higgins, John Shipway, Nathaniel Parry, James Perrett. (GDR/292A/7)
Note. Dando was a hat-maker; monument in United Reformed Church 'Tabernacle'. Shatford was a yeoman, and Perrett a broadweaver (Evans, 69, 71; *Nonconformist Chapels* (RCHM) 81).

730 Dursley. 14 Sept 1760. We [named below] certify your Lordship that we and some others intend to hold a meeting for the worship of Almighty God in a house in the parish of Dursley lately erected for that purpose and desire it may be registered. Thomas Mercer, William King, Christopher Brown, Samuel Griffin, John Dando, William Vine. (GDR/292A/15)
Note. The first Dursley Tabernacle. Revd George Whitefield, chaplain to the Rt Hon. Countess of Huntingdon, clerk, headed the list of trustees. (Evans, 71; *Nonconformist Chapels* (RCHM) 81)

731 Dursley. 5 October 1779 (19 Oct 1779). We being [dissenters] intend to hold a meeting for the worship of Almighty God in the dwelling house of Samuel Griffin, baker, in the parish of Dursley and pray that this certificate may be registered in your Lordship's Consistory Court. William Brooksbank, Samuel Griffin, John Sansum, John Trotman, William Bendall, Richard Stiff, James Purchas, Thomas Tyndall, Richard Hitchins. (GDR/292A/224)

732 Dursley. 20 Oct 1799 (11 Nov 1799). We [named below] certify that we have a chapel in Dursley for religious worship and pray that the said chapel may be recorded as a place of meeting. Samuel King, William Vizard, John Howard, John Sansum, Thomas Wall, William Elliott, William Hardwick, William Underwood, John Cook. (GDR/319A/286-7)

733 Dursley. 17 Feb 1810 (17 Feb 1810). We [named below] certify that the Tabernacle in the parish of Dursley is appropriated for the public worship of Almighty God and request that the same may be registered and a certificate be granted. William Bennett, dissenting minister, William Smith, Thomas Trotman, Thomas Tyndall, James Taylor, Joseph Packer, John Packer. (GDR/334B/389)

734 Dursley. 1 Jan 1839 (16 Jan 1839). We certify that a chapel or buildings with vestry room adjacent to Parsonage Street, called 'the Dursley Tabernacle', is appropriated and used for religious purposes and request it may be registered. William Harris, Joseph Packer, John Trotman, Thomas Trotman, trustees. (GDR/350/234)
Note. Signatories all trustees.

735 Dursley. (24 Jun 1851). Building. H Smith. (RG/31/2/f.126/r)
Note. No diocesan record of this certificate.

736 Dursley. (8 Jan 1852). House. J Bendall [of] Dursley. (RG/31/2 f.126/r)

DYMOCK

737 Dymock. 1672. *Presbyterian.* Licence recorded to John Giles to be a Presbyterian teacher in his house in Dymock and for the house. (LT/517)

738 Dymock. 1672. Licence recorded 22 July 1672 for the house of John Hawkins in Dymock. (LT/531)

739 Dymock.1672. Licence recorded 22 July 1672 for the 'howse' of John White in Dymock. (LT/531]

740 Dymock. 6 Dec 1819 (11 Dec 1819). *Methodist.* I Richard Allen, Methodist preacher, certify that a house in the parish of Dymock, occupied by Paul Grabham, is intended forthwith to be a place of religious worship and require you to register the same and request a certificate thereof. (GDR/334B/249)

741 Dymock. 6 Dec 1820 (9 Dec 1820). I James Bethel of 'Gosley' [Gorsley], dissenting minister, certify that a malthouse, now in the possession of John Chadwick, in the village of Dymock is intended forthwith to be a place of religious worship and require you to register the same. Thomas Bethell, William Pugh. (GDR/334B/229)
Note. James Bethell's name is not included in the list of signatures.

742 Dymock. 26 Jan 1822 (26 Jan 1822). I James Bethell of Gorsley, dissenting minister, certify that a messuage now the property and in possession of John Boulton, carpenter, near the village of Dymock and in the parish of Dymock, is forthwith to be a place of religious worship. James Bethell, John Weaver. (GDR/344/15v)

743 Dymock. 21 Feb 1825 (24 Feb 1825). I Thomas Shepherd of Ledbury in county of Hereford certify that a dwelling house of James Gabb of Dymock is intended forthwith to be a place of religious worship and hereby require you to register and record the same, and request a certificate thereof. (GDR/350/33)

744 Dymock. 8 Feb 1834 (8 Feb 1834). I John Jones in the parish of Dymock certify that I purpose to use one room in a house in the parish of Dymock in [my] possession for the purpose of religious worship and which is intended to contain a congregation exceeding 20 persons. John Jones (mark). (GDR/350/145)

745 Broom's Green, Dymock. 14 Apr 1834 (19 Apr 1834). I Thomas Kington of the Hill, in the parish of 'Castle Froome', Herefordshire, certify that the house of Joseph Holden and premises at 'Brooms Green' in the parish of Dymock, now in [his] holding and occupation, are intended to be a place of religious worship and request you to register the same and request a certificate thereof. (GDR/350/150)

746 Oak Bottom, Dymock. 30 Sept 1836 (20 Oct 1836). I Christopher Bown of the Greenhouse, Dymock certify that the house of James Collins and premises at Oak Bottom in the parish of Dymock, now in the holding and occupation of Benjamin Warr, are to be a place of religious worship and request you to register the same and request a certificate thereof for which shall be taken no more than two shillings and six pence. (GDR/350/201)

747 Broom's Green, Dymock. 28 Apr 1838 (28 Apr 1838). *United Brethren* [*Moravian*]. I Charles Price of the Hill in the parish of 'Castle Froome' in the county of Hereford certify that the Chapel of United Brethren and premises at 'Broom Green' in the parish of Dymock, now in the holding and occupation of the said United Brethren, are to be a place of religious worship and request you to register the same and request a certificate thereof for which shall be taken no more than two shillings and six pence. (GDR/350/224)

748 Allwood Green, Dymock. [blank] Nov 1838 (25 Nov 1838). I Joshua Wade of Ledbury in the county of Hereford certify that a dwelling house at Allwood Green in the parish of Dymock, now in the occupation [of] Mark Whittingslow, is intended forthwith to be a place of religious worship and I hereby require you to register and record the same and request a certificate thereof. (GDR/350/238)

749 Dymock. 25 May 1839 (25 May 1839). I Thomas Kington of Dymock in the parish of Dymock certify that the house of Hannah Pitt and premises at Dymock, now in [her] holding and occupation, are to be a place of religious worship and I request you to register the same and request a certificate thereof for which shall be taken no more than two shillings and six pence. (GDR/350/240)

750 Dymock. 14 Apr 1842 (15 Apr 1842). [*Bible Christian see* **1989**]. I John Knight of Ruardean certify that the house and premises at and in the parish of Dymock, and now in the holding and occupation of Richard Hayes, is to be used as a place of religious worship and I request you to register the same and request a certificate thereof for which shall be taken no more than two shillings and six pence. (GDR/350/295)

751 Dymock. 20 Jan 1844 (20 Jan 1844). I William Palmer of the parish of Dymock certify that a dwelling house, in the occupation of Edmund Tilley, called the Lower Cross in the village of Dymock is intended forthwith to be a place of religious worship and I require you to register the same and request a certificate thereof. (GDR/350/330)

DYRHAM

752 Hinton, Dyrham. 25 Feb 1830 (17 Mar 1830). *Independent*. We [named below] certify that a building at Hinton in the parish of Dyrham is intended to be a chapel for religious worship by dissenters of the denomination of Independents, and we humbly pray that the dwelling, now in the occupation of David Sparrow, may be registered and a certificate granted. William Gregory, George Baker, Roger Willcocks, John Williams. (GDR/350/108)

753 Dyrham. 7 Apr 1842 (9 Apr 1842). I hereby certify that the premises occupied by Elizabeth Hacker in the parish of Dyrham will hereafter be occupied as a place of religious worship and request that the same may be registered accordingly. D J Shaw, Bishop's Street, Bristol. (GDR/350/295)

EASTINGTON

754 Eastington. 9 Mar 1763. Some [dissenters] intend to hold a meeting for the worship of God in their way in the dwelling house of John Whetmour in the parish of Eastington. We therefore pray that this may be recorded in your court. William Heyward, John Whitmore, Henry Mace. (GDR/292A/57)

755 Eastington. 10 July 1795. We [named below] are desirous to have a house in the parish of Eastington, now occupied by John Pride, tenant, set apart for religious worship and humbly desire that your Lordship may record the same in your Court. R Rogers, Thomas Wiles, Jos. Fairthorne. (GDR/319A/210)
Note. Entry squeezed in at bottom of page and names difficult to read.

756 Eastington. 1 Feb 1802 (6 Feb 1802). These are to certify that some of His Majesty's subjects intend to hold a meeting for the worship of Almighty God in a house in the occupation of Richard Hewlett in Eastington. We therefore pray that this certificate may be registered. William Hardwick, Samuel Evans, Richard Hewlett, Thomas Hardwick, Thomas Hayward. (GDR/N2/1)
Note. No record in Diocesan Act Book or RG/31/2.

757 Nupend, Eastington. 21 May 1803 (21 May 1803). These are to certify that some [dissenters] intend to hold a meeting for the worship of Almighty God in a house belonging to Thomas French of Nuppend in the parish of Eastington. We therefore pray that this certificate may be registered. William Hardwick, James Warner, C F Davis, R V Clutterbuck, Isaac Brian. (GDR/319A/321)

758 Eastington. 15 Sept 1823 (26 Sept 1823). I Joseph Cook of Nupend in the parish of Eastington certify that a house and premises at Nupend in the parish of Eastington, and now in [my] holding and occupation, are intended to be a place of religious worship and I hereby request you to register the same and I request a certificate thereof for which shall be taken no more than two shillings and sixpence. (GDR/344/114v)

759 Westend, Eastington. 1 Apr 1826 (3 Apr 1826). We, Joseph Hall, Daniel Clutterbuck, Joseph Cook of Westend in the parish of Eastington, certify that a chapel and premises at Westend in the parish of Eastington, and now in the holding and occupation of [the above 3], Trustees, are intended to be a place of religious worship and we request you to register the same, and request a certificate thereof for which shall be taken no more than two shilings and sixpence. Joseph Hall, Daniel Clutterbuck, Joseph Cook. (GDR/350/55)

760 Alkerton, Eastington. 11 Apr 1845 (31 May 1845). I, the undersigned David Apperley of Rodborough, clothier, certify that a messuage at Alkerton in the parish of Eastington, now in the occupation of George Barnard, is used and intended to be used as a place of religious worship and I request you to register the same and request a certificate thereof for which shall be taken no more than two shillings and six pence. (GDR/350/358)

EASTLEACH MARTIN

761 Eastleach [Martin]. 2 July 1775 (7 July 1775). *Baptist*. Some [dissenters] called Baptists intend to hold a meeting for the worship of Almighty God at the house occupied by William Eyles in the parish of Eastleach and therefore pray that this certificate may be duly registered. William Taylor, Charles Hooke, John Edmonds, Isaac Saliss, John Preston, James Andrew, Joseph Price, Samuel Baskerville, Thomas Davis, William Eyles, John Thomas, William Ebsworth, Isaac Taylor, John Porter, Robert Barratt, Jonathan Cull, John Lock, Henry Thomson, John Taylor, Richard Ebsworth, Benjamin Price, William Baker. (GDR/292A/182)
Note. VCH Glos 7, 61 places this meeting in Eastleach Martin.

762 Eastleach Martin. 30 Jan 1789 (9 Feb 1789; registration GDR/319A/93). *Baptist*. 'These are to certify that some of His Majesty's subjects called Baptists intend to hold a meeting for the worship of Almighty God at a house occupied by William Eyles in the parish of Eastleach Martin and therefore pray that this certificate may be duly registered.' William Eyles, Jonathan Cull, Thomas Burdin, Richard Bantin, Thomas Cook, William Bantin, William Ebsworth, John Parker, Francis Bunting, William Barett. (GDR/N2/1)
Note. Crossed through.

763 Eastleach Martin. 30 June 1811 (31 July 1811). *Baptist*. These are to certify that some dissenters called Baptists intend to hold a meeting for the worship of Almighty God in a barn occupied by William Eyles in the parish of Eastleach Martin and pray that this certificate may be duly registered according to the Act of Toleration. William Eyles, Charles Hooke, William Hooke, Henry Thompson, Daniel Williams. (GDR/334B/363)

EASTLEACH TURVILLE

764 Eastleach [Turville]. 22 Mar 1813 (2 Apr 1813). I Isaac Purkis of 'Leachlade', minister of the Gospel, certify that a barn in the parish of 'East Leach', in the occupation of John Tovey, is intended forthwith to be a place of religious worship and I require you to register the same. Isaac Purkis, minister, William Wentworth. (GDR/334B/347)
Note. VCH Glos 7, 68 places this meeting in Eastleach Turville.

765 Eastleach Turville. 9 Dec 1824 (23 Dec 1824). We [named below] certify that a house occupied by John Baker in the village of Eastleach Turville in the parish of Eastleach Turville will henceforth be a place of worship. John Baker, Robert Brown, Thomas Baker. (GDR/350/27)

766 Eastleach Turville. 26 Sept 1827 (23 Oct 1827). I Benjamin Baker of Eastleach in the parish of Eastleach Turville certify that a dwelling house and premises at Eastleach in the parish of Eastleach Turville, now in the holding and occupation of Thomas Baker, are intended to be a place of religious worship and I request you to register the same, and I request a certificate thereof for which shall be taken no more than two shillings and sixpence. Benjamin Baker (GDR/350/74)

EBRINGTON

767 Ebrington. 12 Apr 1811 (29 Apr 1811). This is to certify that the dwelling house of Hannah Cornell in the parish and village of Ebrington is set apart for the public worship of

God and we require that the same house be registered. James Gartrell, Jonathan Kershall, Hannah Cornell, William Keyte, William Mace. (GDR/334B/365)

768 Ebrington. 12 Jan 1819 (20 Jan 1819). This is to certify that an house in the village of Ebrington, in the occupation of William Neal, is intended forthwith to be a place of religious worship and request you to register the same. Samuel Taylor, William Neal, John Huggins. (GDR/334B/269)

769 Ebrington. 9 Dec 1840 (15 Dec 1840). I William Roberts of Ebrington, miller, certify that the house of William Canniford, schoolmaster, in the parish of Ebrington is forthwith to be a place of religious worship and I require you to register the same and request a certificate thereof. (GDR/350/265)

EDGEWORTH
770 Edgeworth. 9 May 1817 (12 May 1817). I Henry Hawkins of 'Eastcomb' in the parish of Bisley, minister, certify that a building or dwelling house or kitchen in the parish of Edgeworth, now in the occupation of Stephen Ford, shop keeper, is intended forthwith to be used as a place of religious worship and require you to register the same. Witness Job Gardner. (GDR/334B/297)

ELBERTON
771 Elberton. (Michaelmas 1689). 'Eberton', Jonathan Tovey's barn. (Q/SO/3/522)

ELKSTONE
772 Elkstone. 31 July 1818 (1 Aug 1818). I Henry Hawkins of 'Eastcombs' in Bisley, minister, certify that a certain building or parlour in the parish of Elkstone, now in the occupation of Robert Bompass, clothier, is intended forthwith to be used as a place of religious worship and I require you to register the same. Witness Richard Davis. (GDR/334B/277)

773 Elkstone. 11 February 1822 (13 Feb 1822). I Henry Hawkins of Eastcombe in the parish of Bisley, minister, certify that a building or kitchen in the parish of Elkstone, and now in the occupation of Thomas Moss, labourer, is intended forthwith to be a place of religious worship. And I hereby require you to register the same. Witness Henry Hawkins snr Stroud. (GDR/344/16v)

774 Cockleford, Elkstone. 30 Dec 1828 (9 Jan 1829). I William Shurmer his mark X labourer, certify that a house in Cockleford in the parish of Elkstone occupied by me is intended forthwith to be a place of religious worship and I hereby require you to register and record the same and request a certificate thereof. (GDR/350/98)

775 Elkstone. 24 Jan 1829 (26 Jan 1829). I Thomas Davis of Winstone, gentleman, certify that a building or dwelling house in the occuaption of Richard Kilmaster is intended forthwith to be a place of religious worship and I require you to register the same. Witness S B Gibbons, Thomas Davis. (GDR/350/98)

ELMORE
776 Elmore. 20 Mar 1817 (21 Mar 1817. I William Bishop, minister in the city of Gloucester, certify that a dwelling house in the parish of Elmore, occupied by Zechariah Greening, is intended forthwith to be used as a place of religious worship and I require you to register the same. (GDR/334B/301)

777 Elmore. 15 Oct 1819 (15 Oct 1819). I James Wood of Norfolk Buildings [Spa, South Hamlet] certify that a dwelling house in the parish of Elmore, occupied by Elizabeth Pockett, is to be forthwith a place of religious worship and request you to register the same. (GDR/334B/253)
Note. See VCH 4, 164-7, Gell & Bradshaw Directory 1820, Pigot 1830 for Norfolk Buildings.

778 Elmore. 22 Sept 1820 (28 Sept 1820). I James Grimes of Westgate Street in the city of Gloucester certify that a dwelling house in the parish of Elmore, occupied by Robert Watts, labourer, is to be forthwith a place of religious worship and request you to register the same. (GDR/334B/232)

779 Elmore. 19 July 1821 (20 July 1821). I Joseph Vick of Westgate Street, Gloucester, certify that a dwelling house in the parish of Elmore, occupied by John Hardwicke, is intended forthwith to be a place of religious worship and I request you to register the same. (GDR/334B/216)

780 Elmore. 13 Aug 1831 (13 Aug 1831). I James Grimes of the city of Gloucester certify that a dwelling house in the parish of Elmore, occupied by Elizabeth Spiers, on the banks of the Severn, is intended forthwith to be a place of religious worship and I hereby request you to register the same. (GDR/350/118)

781 Elmore. 6 Sept 1836 (8 Sept 1836). I James Grimes of Southgate Street, Gloucester, mercer, certify that a schoolroom in the parish of Elmore, the property of Jeremiah Hawkins of Elmore, is to be forthwith a place of religious worship and request you to register the same. (GDR/350/199)

ELMSTONE HARDWICKE
782 Elmstone Hardwicke. (5 Apr 1850). House occupied by George Yeend. Benjamin Browne [RG/31/2 has 'Benjamin Browne, Tewkesbury']. (Q/RNp/4)

783 Elmstone Hardwicke. (15 Jun 1850). [*Wesleyan*]. Dwelling house belonging to Charles Holder. John Evans. [RG/31/2 has 'John Evans, Tewkesbury Wesleyan minister']. (Q/RNp/4)

ENGLISH BICKNOR
784 English Bicknor. 15 Jan 1818 (19 Jan 1818). I William Lowe of 'New Ware' [New Weir] in the parish of English Bicknor, cordwainer, certify that my dwelling house in the parish of English Bicknor is intended to be used as a place of religious worship and require you to register the same. Witness J E Richards, Whitchurch, Samuel Anthony. (GDR/334B/286)
Note. New Weir was the name of a settlement at Symonds Yat (*VCH Glos* 5, 105).

785 English Bicknor. 25 Sept 1823 (26 Sept 1823). *Baptist (or Particular Baptist: see* **648**). I William Williams of Ryeford [Herefordshire], Baptist minister, certify that a dwelling house in the occupation of Thomas Frowen, labourer, in the parish of English Bicknor is intended forthwith to be a place of religious worship and I require you to register the same. (GDR/344/114v)

786 English Bicknor. 3 Sept 1827 (8 Sept 1827). I James Tuffley of English Bicknor certify that my dwelling house is intended forthwith to be a place of worship and require you to register the same. James Tuffley (mark). Witness Thomas Wright (GDR/350/71)

EYFORD

Eyford was regarded as extra-parochial by the 16th century, because the church had been allowed to disappear, for example in Bishop Benson's survey of the diocese, and sometimes was included with Upper Slaughter, with which it was merged in 1935 (VCH Glos 6, 76).

787 Eyford. Dec 1807 (3 Dec 1807). We [named below] have set apart the house of John Bateman of Eyford in the parish of Stow for the public worship of Almighty God and pray the same may be registered. Jer. Brettell, John Bateman, Henry Collett, Edward Baker, William Dowman, James Etheridge, 'Cat. [blank]'. (GDR/334B/417)

FAIRFORD

788 Fairford. (Epiphany 1723/24). *Baptist*. It is ordered by this court that the new built house lately erected and built in the town of Fairford be licensed and allowed for the Protestant dissenters in and near the said town called Baptists to assemble and meet together in for the worship of God in their way. (Q/SO/4/465)

789 Fairford. 6 Aug 1731. These are to certify you that [dissenters] intend to hold a meeting in the dwelling house of James Lambe esq in the parish of Fairford for the worship of God in their way and pray that it may be registered. Richard Adey, Nathaniel Washbourn, William Still, Richard Houlton. (GDR/279a/246)

790 Fairford. undated. (registered Easter 1740, Q/SO/6/f.176v). *Quaker*. 'We with others the King's Protestant subjects called Quakers intend to hold a meeting in a house in Fairford, the which we desire may be recorded.' Thomas Maddock, John Maddock. (Q/SR/1740/B/8)

791 Fairford. (Michaelmas 1744). *Independent*. It is ordered by this court that the new built house in the parish of Fairford be licensed and allowed for [dissenters] called Independents to assemble and meet together in for the worship of Almighty God in their way pursuant to a petition and request now made. (Q/SO/7/f.83ᵣ)

792 Fairford. 11 Feb 1820 (18 Feb 1820). These are to certify that some dissenters intend to hold a meeting for the worship of Almighty God at the house occupied by George Wentworth. We, in the parish of Fairford, pray that this certificate may be registered. Jacob Betterton, George Wentworth. (GDR/334B/248)

793 [Milton End], Fairford. 17 Sept 1823 (19 Sept 1823). We [named below] request 'his Lordship the Bishop of Gloster to grant for the publick worship of Almighty God and for the preaching of his most Holy Word' a licence in a dwelling house, now in the occupation of Jacob Cowley, situate in Mill Townend [Milton End] in the parish of Fairford. Jacob Cowley, William Mills, Elijah Savory, Ð James Jeall. (GDR/344/114r)
Note. Milton End was a tithing in the west of the parish, and included the mill which seems to have given the area its name, rather than 'the middle ton' as suggested by Smith, 1964. Mill Townend is presumed to be this tithing and may represent an earlier form of the name.

794 Fairford. 20 Oct 1834 (30 Oct 1834). *Independent & Baptist*. We [named below] humbly certify that the house of Miss Elizabeth Frances Kimber, in her occupation, in the town of Fairford, is intended to be a place of religious worship by dissenters comprised of Independents and Baptists, and we request the same may be registered. Frederick Brown, Edmund Smith, George Hawes, Isaac Teall, Albert Brown, Thomas Carpenter, William Fowles, John Aycliffe. (GDR/350/158-9)

795 Fairford. 28 Sept 1835 (30 Sept 1835). *Baptist & Independent*. We [named below] humbly certify that the house or premises of Frederick Brown, known as Church Acre

Cottage, in the parish of Fairford, is intended to be a place of religious worship by dissenters comprised of Baptists and Independents, and we request the same may be registered. Frederick Brown, John Cowley, John Cowley jnr, Charles Webb, William Fowler, Charles Bond, William Bowles, Thomas Carpenter. (GDR/350/179)

796 Fairford. 21 Dec 1841 (22 Dec 1841). I John William Peters of Quenington certify that a room and premises at Fairford, now in [my] occupation, are intended to be a place of religious worship and I request you to register the same and request a certificate thereof. (GDR/350/287)

797 Fairford. (6 Nov 1851). House and premises occupied by Charles Evans. Edmund Rawlings [RG/31/2 has of Highworth]. (Q/RNp/4)

798 Fairford. (6 Nov 1851). House & premises occupied by Isaac Reeves. Edmund Rawlings [RG/31/2 has of Highworth]. (Q/RNp/4)

FALFIELD
Falfield was a tithing and chapelry in Thornbury parish.
799 Falfield. (Epiphany 1696/7). *Presbyterian [& Independent].* Daniell Iles's house. [RG/31/6 has 'Falfield, Thornbury', and 'Presbyterian and Independent'] (Q/SO/3/522)
Note. This entry for Falfield and the preceding one for Blakeney **322** are difficult to disentangle.

800 Falfield. 13 Nov 1813 (16 Nov 1813). We [named below] certify that we intend to meet for the worship of Almighty God in an upper room over an outhouse belonging to William Dorney, yeoman, at Falfield in the parish of Thornbury and pray that this certificate may be registered. William Dorney, James Eley, John Day, Thomas Eley, John Greenwood, John Shepperd, George Cossham, John Nick, Geroge M Hey, John Lane. (GDR/334B/340) [*see* illus., xv]

FARMINGTON
801 Farmington. 24 Feb 1836 (4 Mar 1836). I Caleb Joynes of the parish of Farmington certify that a dwelling house in [my] occupation is intended to be forthwith a place of religious worship and I require you to register the same and request a certificate thereof. (GDR/350/192)

FILTON
Diocese of Bristol from 1542
802 Filton. 21 May 1811 (13 May 1811). *Independent.* We [named below] dissenters of the Independent denomination have set apart a house or building, now in the occupation of J B Hillier, in the parish of Filton for the worship of Almighty God and we pray that the same building may be registered and a certificate granted us. J B Hillier, Nathaniel Pugsley, John Foster, J Gardner, Joseph Riller, Joseph Dodge, Thomas Hicks minister. (EP/A/45/2/43-4)
Note. Dates as recorded.

803 Filton. 17 Aug 1821 (17 Aug 1821). I William Aver of the city of Bristol certify that a house in Filton in the diocese of Bristol and county of Gloucester, occupied by Samuel Merrott and James Davies, is forthwith to be a place of religious worship and require you to register the same and require a certificate thereof. (EP/A/45/2/139-40)

FLAXLEY

804 Mousell, Flaxley. (23 Dec 1850). House belonging to Willing Guilding. Samuel Wesley [RG/31/2 adds of Littledean]. (Q/RNp/4)

Note. Land known as 'Mousel' was recorded in 1591 in a detached part of Flaxley. A Strict Baptist chapel was listed under Flaxley in 1876 (*VCH Glos* 5, 139, 149).

FRAMPTON COTTERELL

805 Frampton Cotterell. 28 July 1795 (3 Aug 1795). *Independent.* We [named below] certify that an house just built, known by the name of Zion chapel in the parish of Frampton Cotterel, on a piece of ground called or known by the name of Brockeridge Close, is intended to be a place of meeting for religious worship and we request it may be registered in the Bishop's Court. John Hey, minister of the Independent Meeting in Castle Green, Bristol, Thomas Humphris and Joseph Hawkins, two of the trustees for said chapel. (GDR/319A/211)

FRAMPTON ON SEVERN

806 Frampton on Severn. 6 Apr 1756. *Independent.* Some of His Majesty's Protestant Independent subjects intend to hold a meeting for the worship of Almighty God in a house, garden or orchard adjoining thereunto, now in the possession of Thomas King, in the parish of 'Frampton upon Severn' and pray it may be registered. Thomas Holder, Thomas King, Christopher Brown, Edward Evans, Samuel Collins. (GDR/292A/12)

807 Frampton on Severn. 13 Apr 1757. [RG/31/2 has registered 18 Apr 1757]. *Independent.* Some of His Majesty's Protestant Independent dissenting subjects intend to hold a meeting for the worship of Almighty God in a house, or any of the courts adjoining thereunto or belonging to the said house, now in the possession of Edward Evans, in the parish of 'Frampton upon Severn' and pray it may be registered. Samuel Collins, Thomas King, Edward Evans. (GDR/292A/26)

808 Frampton on Severn. 14 Mar 1776 (16 Mar 1776). *Independent.* We and some others of His Majesty's Protestant dissenting subjects called Independents intend to hold a meeting for the worship of Almighty God in a house lately erected for that purpose, called by the name of the 'Brethertons Chappel', in the parish of 'Frampton upon Severn' and 'prays' it may be registered in your Lordship's Court. William Young, Richard Bond, John Smith, Thomas King. (GDR/292A/196)

Note. See **811**.

809 Fromebridge Mills, Frampton on Severn. 18 Oct 1820 (18 Oct 1820). I certify that the premises occupied by Robert Johnson at 'Froombridge Mills' in the parish of 'Frampton upon Severn' will hereafter be a place of religious worship. Adam Nightingale, minister. (GDR/334B/231)

810 Frampton on Severn. 19 Nov 1823 (20 Nov 1823). I Joseph Greening of Frampton-upon-Severn, being a clock and watchmaker, certify that a tenement in the parish of 'Frampton-upon-Severn', which tenement I at present hold and occupy, is intended forthwith to be a place of religious worship and I require you to register the same and request a certificate thereof. (GDR/344/118v)

811 Frampton on Severn. 29 Dec 1825 (30 Dec 1825). [*Independent: see* **3506**] I William Richardson of Frampton on Severn, dissenting minister, certify that a building in the parish of Frampton on Severn, called the 'Brethren Chapel', is intended to be continued to be a

place of religious worship (a former certificate being lost) and I hereby require you to register the same. (GDR/350/50)
Note. See **808**.

812 Frampton on Severn. 29 Sept 1826 (30 Sept 1826). [*Wesleyan Methodist: see* **608**]. This is to certify that the dwelling house of George Keys at 'Frampton upon Severn' is intended forthwith to be a place of religious worship and I require you to register the same, and request a certificate thereof. (GDR/350/59)

FRETHERNE

813 Fretherne. 12 Apr 1808 (13 Apr 1808). These are to certify that some 'being protestant' intend to hold meetings for the worship of Almighty God in the dwelling house and barn belonging to and in the occupation of Anthony Ely and on the land adjoining and round about the same to the extent of one hundred yards, in the parish of Fretherne. We pray that this certificate may be registered. William Worthington, George Pegler, Anthony Ely, John Ely, James Warner, William Hardwick. (GDR/334B/417-16)

FROCESTER

814 Frocester. 9 Apr 1824 (10 Apr 1824). *Baptist.* 'Please to take notice that we [named below] who are dissenters of the Baptist persuasion "whish" to set apart for religious worship a dwelling house of Mrs Barnes in the parish of Frocester and wish to have it licensed for that purpose. James Cousins, William Baffin, John Alder, Thomas Lusty, Peter King, John King [of] 'King Stanly', pastor & deacons [recorded against bracketted names]. (GDR/344/132v)
Note. RG/31/2 lists first five names 'of' King's Stanley but not John King; registration 9 Apr 1824.

GLOUCESTER CITY

The 11 ancient parishes in Gloucester city are listed here together with their out-parishes where named: Barton Street, Kingsholm, Longford, Tuffley, Twigworth and Wotton, and the extra-parochial areas of Littleworth, North Hamlet, South Hamlet and the vill of Wotton. Twigworth, which see, became a parish in 1844. The certificates specify the relevant parish in most cases. See Introduction xxiv–xxv.

815 Gloucester. 1672. *Congregational.* Owen Davies applied for licence to James Forbes, Congregational minister of the city of Gloucester, for the house of 'Samson Bacon' in Gloucester; licence recorded 22 May 1672 for the house of 'Sampson Baker' and repeated for 'Samson Baron'; licence received by Owen Davies 1 June 1672. (LT/371, 389, 490, 491)
Note. For James Forbes *see* Introduction xlviii–xlix.

816 Gloucester. 1672. *Congregational.* Licence recorded 10 June for the house of John Wall in Gloucester Congregational Meeting. (LT/502)

817 Gloucester. 1672. *Congregational.* Licence recorded for the house of Elizeas Hatheway of the city of Gloucester and to 'Elizeas Hatheway Congregational teacher at his house'. (LT/578)

818 Gloucester. 1672. *Independent.* Licence recorded for the house of Francis Yaats of the city of Gloucester'. (LT/584)

819 Longford, Gloucester. 1672. *Congregational.* Application by Owen Davies for licence to 'John Badger' [Congregational minister] preacher at Thomas Bishop's house in Longford; licence recorded to 'John Badgett' 22 May 1672; licence received 1 June 1672 for 'John Badgett for himself in Thomas Bishop's house in Longford'. (LT/371, 388, 490)

820 Longford, Gloucester. 1672. *Congregational.* Application by Owen Davies for 'Thomas Cole's ditto'; licence recorded 22 May 1672 for the house of Thomas Cole in Longford, 'Gloucester Congregational Meeting'; licence received 1 June 1672 for Thomas Cole and house. (LT/371, 389, 490)
Note. Application for 'Thomas Cole's ditto' with other references suggests that Thomas Cole, like John Badger, was a Congregational minister but could mean that John Badger also preached there.

821 Gloucester. 11 Oct 1725. *Congregational.* This is to certify that dissenters called 'Congregationall' intend to hold a meeting for the worship of God in their way at the dwelling house of Abraham Smith in Southgate Street (next door to the *Sign of the Three Cups*) in this city, and pray that it may be recorded. Daniel Bryan, Joseph Everard, Martin Lloyde. (GDR/279a/123)
Note. For Joseph Everard *see* **197**.

822 [Littleworth] Gloucester. 24 Apr 1728. These are to certify you that [dissenters] intend to hold a meeting for the worship of Almighty God in their way in the dwelling house of John Riddall in the Southgate Street in Gloucester and pray that it may be registered. Martin Lloyd, Joseph Everard, John Ashmeade. (GDR/279a/195)
Note. Southgate Street was also known as Littleworth (*VCH Glos* 4, 383). For Joseph Everard *see* **197**.

823 St Mary de Crypt [Gloucester]. 14 Sept 1736. These are to certify you that some [dissenters] intend to hold a meeting for the worship of God in their way in the dwelling house of Martin Lloyd in the parish of St Mary de Crypt. Martin Lloyd snr, Nathaniel Brock, Joseph Everard, Edward Cowcher. (GDR/284/56)
Note. For Joseph Everard *see* **197**.

824 North Hamlet, Gloucester city. 28 May 1739. These are to certify your Lordship that some [dissenters] intend to meet together for the worship of Almighty God in the dwelling house of one Richard Sherriff, staymaker, in the 'North Hamlett near the Common Jail or Prison called the Castle' and therefore desire the same may be registered. Joseph Everard, Martin Lloyd. (GDR/284/100)
Note. For Joseph Everard *see* **197**.

825 Gloucester. 3 Dec 1739. This is to certify your Lordship that the house of Mr John Garn, weaver, in the Eastgate street of the city of Gloucester, is intended to be used by some [dissenters] for their religious worship and pray that the said house may be registered. Martin Lloyd, Jacob Lumbard, Nathaniel Brock (GDR/284/101)

826 Holy Trinity, Gloucester. 19 Mar 1741/42. These are to certify your Lordship that some [dissenters] intend to hold a meeting for the worship of God at the house of John Garn, weaver, in the Catherine Wheel Lane [now Berkeley Street] in the parish of the Holy Trinity in the city of Gloucester, therefore we pray that it may be registered. John Crofts, Thomas Bingham jnr, John Radnall (GDR/284/127)

827 St Mary de Lode [out-parish], Gloucester. 1 Mar 1743/44 (24 Mar 1743/44). *Independent.* These are to certify your Lordship that [dissenters] commonly called Independents intend to hold a meeting for the worship of Almighty God at the dwelling house of Isaac Gardner in Barton Street in 'the hamlett of St Mary de Load' and therefore desire it may be registered. Isaac Gardner, James Bingley, Matthew Donaldson, Thomas Garn. (GDR/284/159)

828 St Owen, Gloucester. 9 Jan 1768. We [named below] being Protestant dissenters humbly request that the Hall commonly called Cordwainers Hall in Saint Owen's parish in the city of

Gloucester be recorded as a place of public worship of Almighty God. Samuel Baskervile, John Brown, Thomas Garn, Richard Adey, Thomas Squire, Robert Neill. (GDR/292A/106)

829 St Mary de Lode, Gloucester. 24 Dec 1788 (24 Dec 1788; registration GDR/319A 90). *Lady Huntingdon's Connexion* [RG/31/2 states *Wesleyan*]. We [named below] certify that a building belonging to Lady Huntingdon in the parish of St Mary de Lode in the city of Gloucester is appropriated, set apart and used for religious worship by a congregation of [dissenters] and we hereby desire that the same may be registered. W Taylor minister, Samuel Horseman, Js. Clarke, John Skinner, William Collins, Robert Lloyd, John Ballinger, John Daniele, John Ballinger, William Price. (GDR/N2/2)
Note. Signatures appear to be originals and scribe the minister. Certificate crossed through. Entered in GDR 319A with rubric 'St Mary's Square, Gloucester'.

830 St John the Baptist, Gloucester. (28 Jun 1790) [RG/31/2 states *Wesleyan*]. These are to certify that we with others intend to hold a meeting for the worship of Almighty God in a building lately erected and set apart for that purpose in the Lower Northgate Street in the parish of St John the Baptist in the city of Gloucester and pray it may be registered in your Lordship's Court. Joseph Davis, George Conibere, James Lee, James Collins, Robert Conibere, Robert Wells. (GDR/319A/102)

831 St Michael, Gloucester. 11 Dec 1794 (11 Dec 1794). We [named below] certify that a building belonging to Reverend Joshua Dickenson, William Washbourn and others in the parish of St Michael in the city of Gloucester is appropriated set apart and used for religious worship and we desire that the same may be registered. John Tremlett, R Chandler, W Washbourn, Moshach Charlton, Powell Chandler, George Washbourn. (GDR/319A/201-2)
Note. Barton Street recorded in rubric.

832 St Catherine's, Gloucester. 28 Mar 1811 (29 Mar 1811). We [named below] certify that the dwelling house of Thomas Newcombe, near the east end of Catherine St. in the parish of St Catherine's and city of Gloucester, be set apart for the public worship of Almighty God and request the same may be registered. William Knox, Thomas Proband, John Deane, Thomas Hayns, John Duck. (GDR/334B/367)

833 St Michael, Gloucester. 21 July 1813 (23 July 1813). [*Baptist: see note*]. I George Box Drayton of the city of Gloucester, surgeon, certify that a building commonly called a Meeting-house situated in the New Inn Lane in the parish of St Michael in the city of Gloucester is intended forthwith to be a place of religious worship and require you to register the same. G B Drayton, R Whittard, J Tippetts; Witness R Whittard. (GDR/334B/344)
Note. A group of Baptists newly settled in Gloucester initially met here. George Box Drayton became the minister in 1820, and provided the money to build a chapel in Parkers Row, *see* **838**. (*VCH Glos* 4, 321). *See also* **517**.

834 St Mary de Lode, Gloucester. 16 Dec 1814 (16 Dec 1814). I Thomas Perks of the city of Gloucester, 'taylor', certify that part of a tenement in Leather Bottle Lane in the parish of St Mary de Lode in the city and county of Gloucester, in the occupation of Daniel Bryant, is intended forthwith to be a place of religious worship and require you to register the same. (GDR/334B/333)

835 St Aldate, Gloucester. 9 Mar 1816 (9 Mar 1816). [*Methodist: see* **179**]. I Daniel Campbell of Gloucester certify that the house of John Dean in the parish of St Aldate's in the city of Gloucester is intended forthwith to be a place of religious worship and require you to register the same and request a certificate thereof. Daniel Campbell, minister. (GDR/334B/322)

836 St Mary de Crypt, Gloucester. 9 Mar 1816 (9 Mar 1816). [*Methodist, see* **179**]. I Daniel Campbell of Gloucester certify that the house of Thomas Jeffs in the parish of St Mary de Crypt in the city of Gloucester is forthwith to be a place of religious worship and require you to register the same and request a certificate thereof. (GDR/334B/322)

837 St Mary de Grace, Gloucester. 12 Nov 1816 (13 Nov 1816). I William Jones certify that a messuage in the parish of St Mary de Grace, St John Lane in the city of Gloucester, occupied by Thomas Hawkins, is intended forthwith to be used as a place of religious worship and require you to register the same and request a certificate thereof. (GDR/334B/309)

838 St Michael, Gloucester. 4 May 1821 (7 May 1821). [*Baptist: see note*]. I George Box Drayton of the city of Gloucester, surgeon, certify that a newly erected chapel in the parish of St Michael in the city of Gloucester, in a row called Parkers Row, is intended forthwith to be used as a place of religious worship and require you to register the same. (GDR/334B/222)
Note. See also **849**, **867**. GA D4373/3/2 gives registration date 11 May 1821. GA D4373/3 file also includes (3/5) agreement with Mr Joseph Simms, 24 May 1847, to build a Baptist chapel, school room and offices in Parkers Row, Gloucester; and (3/8) note dated 1851 re Dean and Chapter leases imposing covenant not to build any dissenting chapel or brothel. For George Box Drayton *see* **517**.

839 St Nicholas, Gloucester. 6 Oct 1821 (6 Oct 1821). We [named below] certify that the dwelling house and premises occupied by Elizabeth Brooks on the Quay in the parish of St Nicholas in the city of Gloucester is set apart for the public worship of Almighty God and we request the same may be registered. John Gibbons, Elizabeth Brooks, John England Smart, Thomas Parry. (GDR/334B/213)

840 Longford, St Mary de Lode, Gloucester. 19 Jan 1822 (19 Jan 1822). I William Barber of Longford Hamlet in the parish of St Mary de Lode certify that my dwelling house as aforesaid is intended forthwith to be a place of religious worship and I require you to register the same and require a certificate thereof. (GDR/344/15r)

841 St Mary de Lode, Gloucester. 2 Mar 1822 (2 Mar 1822). We [named below] 'do heare' certify that the dwelling house of 'William Niblitt' in the parish of 'St Mary de Loude in the city of Glocester' has opened for the religious worship of Almighty God for certain of His 'Magystes' subjects commonly called Protestant 'decentas' and we request that the same may be registered. William Niblett, John Thurston, J Gibbins. (GDR/344/19r)

842 St Michael Gloucester. 6 Mar 1822 (7 Mar 1822). We [named below] certify that the dwelling house and 'primiss' occupied by John Brown, in Barton Street in the parish of 'St. Mickles' is opened for the religious worship of Almighty God and we request the same may be registered. John Brown, Elizabeth Brown, Elizabeth Jackson. (GDR/344/19v)

843 St Catherine, Gloucester. 7 Mar 1822 (7 Mar 1822). We [named below] certify that the dwelling house and premises, occupied by Thomas Hayward, in the parish of St Catherine in the city of Gloucester is opened for the publick worship of Almighty God. Thomas Hayward (mark), Elizabeth Hayward, John Gibbins. (GDR/344/19v)

844 St Nicholas, Gloucester. 13 Mar 1822 (12 Mar 1822). We [named below] do certify that the dwelling house and premises occupied by John Powell in the parish of 'St. Nickols' in the city of Gloucester is set apart for the public worship of Almighty God and we request the same may be registered. John Thurston, John Pool, John Powell. (GDR/344/20v)
Note. Dates as recorded.

845 St Mary de Lode, Gloucester. 19 Mar 1822 (19 Mar 1822). We [named below] certify that the premises belonging unto William Thomson in the parish of St. Mary de Lode in the city of 'Glocester' is set apart for the public worship of Almighty God and we request the same may be registered. William Thomson, John Gibbins, John Thurston. (GDR/344/20v)

846 Barton St Michael, Gloucester. 22 Apr 1822 (23 Apr 1822). I William Ulett of 'Out Hamlet of Barton St Michaelĺs' certify that my dwelling house is forthwith to be a place of religious worship and I hereby require you to register and record the same, and request a certificate thereof. (GDR/344/22r)

847 St Catherine, Gloucester. 15 July 1823 (16 July 1823). I William Cook of the city of Gloucester certify that a tenement, now in the occupation of Nathaniel Perkins, in the parish of Saint Catherine in the city of Gloucester, is intended forthwith to be a place of religious worship and I do hereby require you to register the same. Henry Cook, William Cooke, Nathaniel Perkins. (GDR/344/110v)
Note. William Cook/Cooke as recorded.

848 St Michael, Gloucester. (19 July 1823). We the undersigned certify that a room in the parish of St. Michael in the city of Gloucester, occupied by John Hatch, is intended to be a place for the Annual Union Meeting of the Gloucester Sunday School Teachers, when a form of religious worship will be used, and we hereby request you to register the same. James Grimes, William Wheeler. (GDR/344/111r)

849 Barton St Michael, Gloucester. 27 Oct 1823 (27 Oct 1823); registration GDR/344/117v). [*Baptist: see* **517**]. I George Box Drayton of the city of Gloucester, surgeon, certify that a building newly erected near Barton Terrace in the out hamlet of St Michael is intended forthwith to be a place of religious worship and I hereby require you to [register] the same. GDR/344/117v)
Note. See also **838**, **867**. GA D4373/8/1 is an original certificate, endorsed on the back '27 October 1823 I hereby certify that this certificate was duly registered in the Consistory Court of the Lord Bishop of Gloucester pursuant to the statute by me. Thomas Gardner Registrar.' The file also contains a certificate for registering a school room lately erected at Barton End Front Terrace, *see* **867**, and a bill and specification for building a school room and other papers relating to Barton End school. For George Box Drayton *see* **517**.

850 Gloucester. 3 Dec 1823 (5 Dec 1823). I, W Wheeler of the city of Gloucester, draper, certify that a warehouse in the Island in the city aforesaid, now in the occupation of Mr R. Jones, owner, is intended forthwith to be a place of religious worship and I require you to register and record the same and request a certificate thereof. (GDR/344/119v)

851 Littleworth [Gloucester] 21 Feb 1824 (21 Feb 1824). I Francis Collier, minister, certify a house of Sabey Wingate in the hamlet of Littleworth to be a place of religious worship and request you to register the same and request a certificate thereof. (GDR/344/129r)
Note. Littleworth and South Hamlet were extra-parochial but small parts were included in some Gloucester parishes. (*VCH Glos* 4, 382.)

852 Longford [Gloucester]. 3 June 1824 (3 June 1824). I John Ford of city of Gloucester certify that a barn and field adjoining thereto in Longford near the city of Gloucester, now in the occupation of Mr Joseph Page, hallier, is intended forthwith to be a place of religious worship and I require you to register and record the same, and request a certificate thereof. (GDR/344/133r)

853 Gloucester. 5 June 1824 (5 June 1824). I John Ford city of Gloucester certify that a piece of ground 'lately plan'd out for building', near the London Road in the city of Gloucester, and now in occupation of John Bowyer, is intended forthwith to be a place of religious worship and I require you to register the same, and request a certificate thereof. (GDR/344/133v)

854 St Mary de Lode, Gloucester. 12 June 1824 (12 June 1824). I John Drew of the city of Gloucester certify that part of a warehouse, the property of Charles Greenwood Thompson, in Archdeacon Lane in the parish of St Mary de Lode, is intended forthwith to be a place of religious worship and I require you to register the same. Charles Greenwood Thompson; witness Joseph Taylor. (GDR/344/133v)

855 St Mary de Lode, Gloucester. 8 Sept 1825 (8 Sept 1825). I Henry Cook of St Mary de Lode certify that a dwelling house in the same parish, now in my own occupation, is intended forthwith to be a place of religious worship and I require you to register the same, and request a certificate thereof. Witness Thomas Jones (GDR/350/44)

856 Gloucester. 22 Dec 1830 (10 Jan 1831). I Colin Campbell, Captain the Royal Navy, residing at the Spa near the city of Gloucester, certify that a lower room, part of a Counting House or Office of Messrs Sturge & Co, on the western side of the basin of the Gloucester and Berkeley canal, is intended forthwith to be a place of religious worship and I require you to register the same. (GDR/350/113)

857 Longford [Gloucester]. 27 Aug 1831 (27 Aug 1831). I Job Bown of the city of Gloucester certify that a dwelling house in the hamlet of Longford, occupied by Thomas Cook snr, is intended to be forthwith a place of religious worship and I request you to register the same. Thomas Cook, Job Bown. (GDR/350/119)

858 South Hamlet, Littleworth [Gloucester]. 2 Feb 1832 (4 Feb 1832). I Job Bown of the city of Gloucester certify that a dwelling house in the 'South Hamlet of Littleworth', occupied by James Nelmes, is intended to be forthwith a place of religious worship and I request you to register the same. James Nelmes (mark), Job Bown. (GDR/350/123)
Note. On Littleworth, see **851** above.

859 St Aldate, Gloucester. 17 July 1832 (19 July 1832). I Job Bown of the city of Gloucester certify that a dwelling house in the parish of St Aldate in the city of Gloucester, occupied by [me], is intended to be forthwith a place of religious worship and I request you to register the same. (GDR/350/131)

860 St John the Baptist, Gloucester. 24 Nov 1832 (26 Nov 1832). I Job Bown of the city of Gloucester certify that a room in Worcester Street in the parish of St John's in the city of Gloucester, occupied by Thomas Cox, is intended to be forthwith a place of religious worship and I hereby request you to register the same. Job Bown, Thomas Cox (GDR/350/135)

861 White Friars, St Mary de Crypt, Gloucester. 30 May 1836 (30 May 1836). *Friends (Quaker).* I John Fowler of the city of Gloucester in the parish of St Michael certify that the meeting-house and premises in the White Friars in the city of Gloucester, in the parish of St Mary de Crypt, 'is' to be a place of religious worship by an assembly or congregation of Friends commonly called Quakers and I request you to register the same and request a certificate thereof for which shall be taken no more than two shillings and six pence. John Fowler, a Trustee. (GDR/350/196)

862 Gloucester. 24 Apr 1837 (25 Apr 1837). I William Worth of Gloucester, preacher of the Gospel, certify that the dwelling house in the occupation of William Hore in Barton Terrace in the city of Gloucester is forthwith to be a place of religious worship and require you to register the same and request a certificate thereof. (GDR/350/208)

863 St John the Baptist, Gloucester. 22 Aug 1839 (22 Aug 1839). This is to certify that the School Room of Mr James Ricketts in Oxford Street in the parish of St John the Baptist in the city of Gloucester is set apart for the religious worship of Almighty God and we require you to register the same. James Ricketts, Richard Cordwell. (GDR/350/243)

864 Longford, St Catherine, Gloucester. 24 Jan 1840 (24 Jan 1840). I Isaac Cooke of St John the Baptist in the city of Gloucester certify that a house in the hamlet of Longford in the parish of St Catherine near the city, in the occupation of Samuel Gwillim, is forthwith to be a place of religious worship and request you to register the same and request a certificate thereof. (GDR/350/249)

865 St Mary de Grace, Gloucester. 4 Apr 1840 (4 Apr 1840). I Charles Jones of the parish of St Mary de Crypt in Gloucester certify that a room in a building in Bull Lane in the parish of St Mary de Grace in the city of Gloucester, is forthwith to be a place of religious worship and I require you to register the same and request a certificate thereof. (GDR/350/251-2)

866 St Mary de Lode, Gloucester. 28 May 1840 (30 May 1840). I William Hall of the city of Gloucester certify that a dwelling house in Sweetbriar Street in the outhamlet of St Mary de Lode, occupied by William Cottreall, stone mason, is forthwith to be a place of religious worship and I request you to register the same. (GDR/350/254)

867 Barton End [Gloucester]. 10 Oct 1840 (21 Oct 1840). [*Baptist: see* **838**]. I George Wood Rodway of Stroud Road, Gloucester, dissenting minister, certify that a room lately erected at Barton End at a place called the Front Terrace, and now occupied as a school room, is intended forthwith to be a place of religious worship and I request you to register the same and request a certificate thereof. (GDR/350/258)
Note. See also **849**. GA D4373/8/1/3 is an original certificate, endorsed '21 October 1840 Registered and Recorded in the Registry of the Lord Bishop of Gloucester and Bristol at Gloucester pursuant to the statute'. Thomas Holt N.P. [Notary Public] Registrar.'

868 St Mary de Lode [Gloucester]. 1 Dec 1840 (1 Dec 1840). I John Horlick of the parish of Norton certify that the house of Thomas Taylor and premises at 'Kings Holm' in the parish of St Mary de Lode, now in [his] holding and occupation, are a place of religious worship and I request you to register the same and request a certificate thereof for which shall be taken no more than two shillings and six pence. (GDR/350/265)
Note. Possibly identical with the Revd John Horlick, Forest of Dean preacher. *See* Introduction lxv.

869 St John the Baptist, Gloucester. 6 Nov 1841 (6 Nov 1841). I John Siddaway of Gloucester certify that a room called the Democratic Assembly Room in Worcester Street in the parish of St John the Baptist in the city of Gloucester, now in the occupation of John Hay, is forthwith to be a place of religious worship and I require you to register the same and request a certificate thereof. (GDR/350/284)

870 St John [the Baptist], Gloucester. 15 Dec 1841 (15 Dec 1841). I Thomas Smith of the parish of Cheltenham certify that the house or building in 25 Alvin Street in the parish of St John, Gloucester, is to be a place of religious worship and I require you to register the same and request a certificate thereof. (GDR/350/286)

871 St Nicholas, Gloucester. 22 July 1846 (22 July 1846). I George Halliday of Gloucester in the parish of St Nicholas in the city of Gloucester certify that a room and premises in Davenport Yard in the Westgate Street in the parish of St Nicholas, now in [my] holding, are intended to be a place of religious worship and I request you to register the same and request a certificate thereof for which shall be taken no more than two shillings and six pence. (GDR/350/377)

872 St Michael, Gloucester. 28 June 1847 (30 June 1847). *Baptist.* This is to certify that a room in the premises, No 1 Russell Terrace, Clarence Street, in the parish of St Michael in the city of Gloucester is set apart for the public worship of Almighty God for certain [dissenters] commonly called Baptists and we hereby require you to register the same in your court. Richard Cordwell, John Browning. (GDR/350/388)

873 Barton St Michael, Gloucester. (27 Oct 1847). [*Wesleyan*]. Schoolroom and preaching house, Victoria Street. Edward Jennings [RG/31/2 has 'Edward Jennings Wesleyan minister']. (Q/RNp/4)

874 Holy Trinity, Gloucester. (1 Jan 1848). Room occupied by James Tummey. Henry Webb. (Q/RNp/4)
Note. RG/31/2 states that the room was in Westgate Street, and that Webb was of Chalford Hill.

875 St Michael, Gloucester. (4 Mar 1848). Building occupied by Henry Webb. Henry W[ebb] [torn]. (Q/RNp/4)
Note. RG/31/2 states building in Eastgate Street, and Henry Webb of Chalford Hill.

876 [St Catherine] Gloucester. (29 Mar 1848). House, No 13 St Catherine's Street. James B[ayliss] [torn; RG/31/2 confirms name]. (Q/RNp/4)
Note. RG/31/2 states house in Cross Keys Lane, and James Bayliss of Cheltenham.

877 Barton St Michael, Gloucester. (13 Oct 1849). House, No 3 Victoria Street, Gloucester. James Bayliss. (Q/RNp/4)

878 Gloucester. (25 June 1850). Round House, Worcester Street. John Thurston. (Q/RNp/4)
Note. RG/31/2 gives registration date 18 June 1850.

879 Kingsholm St Catherine. (14 Dec 1850). House or building occupied by Thomas Salcomb. Thomas Salcomb. (Q/RNp/4)
Note. RG/31/2 has 'Kingsholm near Gloucester' and certifier as James Bayliss of Painswick.

880 Barton St Mary [St Mary de Lode, Gloucester]. (7 Mar 1851). Newly erected building known as Ebenezer school. John Thurston. (GA Q/RNp/4)

881 Holy Trinity, Gloucester. (10 May 1851). Building known by the name of the Mechanics room, Playhouse Passage. James Wiltshire and Samuel Jeffs [RG/31/2 has of Gloucester]. (Q/RNp/4)

GREAT BARRINGTON

882 Great Barrington. 13 July 1804 (23 July 1804). *Baptist.* This is to certify that a room in an house in the occupation of Mr Barnabus Collett in the village of Great Barrington is to be a place of worship for dissenters of the Baptist denomination. We therefore request that the same may be registered. John Smith, minister, Barnabas Collett, Joseph Collett, William Eden. (GDR/334B/436)

883 Great Barrington. 29 Oct 1839 (2 Nov 1839). I John Bryan of Burford, Oxfordshire, certify that a house or building in the village of Great Barrington, occupied by William Ridler alias Halborough, labourer, is forthwith to be a place of religious worship and I require you to register the same and request a certificate thereof. (GDR/350/245)

884 Great Barrington. 7 Dec 1839 (Dec 1839). I Samuel Jones, dissenting minister of Burford, Oxfordshire, certify that a dwelling house in the village of Great Barrington, occupied by John Case, labourer, is forthwith to be a place of religious worship and I require you to register the same and request a certificate thereof. (GDR/350/246)

GREAT RISSINGTON

885 Great Rissington. 5 July 1797 (5 July 1797). We the undersigned request your Lordship to cause to be registered in your court the house of John Mason of Great Rissington. John Wood, Henry Hanks, John Wood, Benjamin Henderson. (GDR/319A/254)

GRETTON

Gretton was a chapelry in Winchcombe.

886 Gretton. 17 May 1815 (19 May 1815). I Samuel Lear of 'Winchcomb', minister of this Gospel, certify that a meeting-house at Gretton in the parish of 'Winchcomb' is intended forthwith to be a place of religious worship and I require you to register the same and request a certificate thereof. (GDR/334B/328)

Note. For Samuel Lear s*ee* **240**.

GUITING POWER

887 Guiting Power. 16 Nov 1797 (18 Nov 1797). We [named below] certify that we intend to meet for the worship of Almighty God in a house occupied by Samuel Etheridge in the parish of Guiting Power and pray that this certificate may be registered. Samuel Etheridge, John Wood, John Rowland, John Reynolds, Benjamin Henderson, John Stait. (GDR/319A/258)

888 Guiting Power. 27 Oct 1815 (15 Nov 1815). We [named below] certify that we intend to meet for the worship of Almighty God in the dwelling house of William Robins, cooper, in the parish of Guiting Power and pray that this certificate may be registered in your Lordship's registry. William Bradley, William Rowlands the elder, Henry Collett, Robert Rowland, George Morton, William Rowlands, Clemon Walter, William Robbins, Thomas Wood, Edward Robbins, Thomas Robbins, William Collett, William H Jones. (GDR/334B/325)

Note. Robbins with 2 b's in the signature.

889 Guiting Power. 21 Dec 1824 (24 Dec 1824). We whose names are herunto subscribed certify that we intend to meet for the worship of Almighty God in a room adjoining the dwelling house of Joseph Acock, schoolmaster, in the parish of Guiting Power and pray that this certificate may be registered. Joseph Acock, Joseph Midwinter, Job Maisey, Edward Robins, William Dearlove, William Robbins, William Collett, Isaac Wood, George Norton, Richard Collett. (GDR/350/27)

890 Guiting Power. 14 Jan 1841 (30 Jan 1841). [*Baptist}.* We [named below] certify that we intend to meet for the worship of Almighty God in a building called the Baptist Chapel in the parish of Guiting Power and pray that this certificate may be registered. Joseph Acock, Edward Wood, George Norton, Joseph Midwinter, Edward Wood Guiting, Henry Draper. (GDR/350/272)

HANHAM

Hanham was a chapelry in Bitton parish.

891 Hanham. (Easter 1709). *Baptist.* Samuell Harvey's house. (Q/SO/3/520)

892 Hanham. 13 Feb 1828 (26 Mar 1828). [*Wesleyan Methodist: see note*]. I Joseph Marsh of Kingswood near Bristol certify that a new chapel in the village of Hanham is intended forthwith to be a place of religious worship and I require you to register the same and request a certificate thereof. (GDR/350/86)

Note. Munden, 20.7 has return from Wesleyan Methodist chapel, date of erection 1827. *See also* Hanham Street below.

893 Hanham. 3 Feb 1843 (3 Feb 1843). I Charles Marsh of the city suburbs of Gloucester, in the parish of Longford, certify that a chapel and premises at Hanham, parish of Bitton, are intended to be a place of religious worship and I request you to register the same and request a certificate thereof for which shall be taken no more than two shillings and six pence. (GDR/350/314)

894 Hanham. (9 Nov 1850). *Wesleyan Methodist.* Chapel, Hanham Street. Charles Clay [RG/31/2 has of Bitton]. (Q/RNp/4)
Note. For Charles Clay *see* **120**.

HARDWICK
Hardwicke was a chapelry in Standish parish.
895 Hardwick. 14 Oct 1815 (14 Oct 1815). [*Methodist, see* **179**]. I Daniell Campbell of Gloucester, minister, certify that the house of James Walkley in the parish of Hardwick is intended forthwith to be a place of religious worship and require you to register the same and request a certificate thereof. (GDR/334B/325)

896 Hardwick. 18 Apr 1817 (18 Apr 1817). I William Bishop, minister of the city of Gloucester, certify that a dwelling house in the parish of Hardwick, the property of William Prosser, gunsmith in the city of Gloucester, and occupied by Martha Hale, is intended to be forthwith used as a place of religious worship and request you to register the same. (GDR/334B/299)

897 Hardwick. 6 Oct 1820 (7 Oct 1820). I Joseph Burrows of Stroud [RG/31/2 has 'cordwainer'] certify that a messuage or tenement in the parish of Hardwick, in the occupation of James Walkley as tenant to J Ravenell, is intended forthwith to be a place of religious worship and require you to register the same. Witness Henry Hawkins of Stroud. (GDR/334B/231)

HARESFIELD
898 Haresfield. 16 Mar 1743/44 (24 Mar 1743/44). *Independent.* These are to certify that some dissenters of the denomination commonly called 'Independant' intended to hold a meeting for the worship of Almighty God at the dwelling house of George White in the village and parish of Haresfield and therefore we pray that the said house may be duly registered. Thomas Jenkins, William Hogg, William Bayly, John Rudhall. (GDR/284/158)
Note. This was the first diocesan record giving the date of registration as well as the date the certificate was signed.

899 Haresfield. 4 Sept 1784 (4 Sept 1784; registration GDR/319A/13). We with some others [dissenters] intend to hold a meeting for the worship of Almighty God at the house of John Hodges in the parish of Haresfield and pray it may be registered. William Hogg, William White, Isaac Grimes, John Hodges, John Sutton, Samuel Vick. (GDR/N2/1)
Note. One of a bundle of five certificates, all very worn and crossed through.

900 Haresfield. 7 June 1809 (9 Jun 1809). These are to certify that some dissenters intend to hold a meeting for the worship of Almighty God in a house, in the occupation of Daniel Short, in the parish of Haresfield. We pray that this certificate be registered. William Hardwick, Thomas Trinder, Daniel Short, Ann Short, William Short, Charles Jeens, Elijah Morgan, William Short (mark). (GDR/334B/401)

Note. 'Trinder' not well written but Thomas Trinder named in the certificate for Berkeley which followed, and William Hardwick signed both.

901 Haresfield. 19 July 1823 (21 July 1823). I William Cooke of the city of Gloucester certify that a tenement, now in the occupation of Charles Avery, in the parish of Haresfield is forthwith to be a place of religious worship and I hereby require you to register the same. William Cooke, Charles Avery. (GDR/344/111v)

902 Haresfield. 16 Dec 1823 (17 Dec 1823). I Joseph Burroughs of Stroud in the county of Gloucester, cordwainer, certify that a building in the parish of Haresfield belonging to John Edwards, and late in the occupation of Samuel Williams as his tenant, is to be a meeting-house for religious worship and I request that this certificate may be registered. (GDR/344/121v)

903 Haresfield. 10 June 1832 (12 June 1832). I Job Bown of the city of Gloucester certify that a dwelling house, now in the occupation of Charles Avery, in the parish of Haresfield is intended forthwith as a place of religious worship and I hereby require you to register the same. Job Bown, Charles Avery. (GDR/350/129)

HARTPURY
904 Hartpury. 18 Nov 1814 (18 Nov 1814). [*Methodist: see* **178**]. I John Chettle of Gloucester, minister, certify that the house of William Hatch in the parish of Hartpury is intended forthwith to be a place of religious worship and require you to register the same and request a certificate thereof. (GDR/334B/334)

905 Hartpury. 13 Mar 1817 (15 Mar 1817). [*Methodist, see* **179**]. I Daniel Campbell of Gloucester, minister, certify that the house of Jeremiah Mann in the parish of Hartpury is intended forthwith to be used as a place of religious worship and require you to register the same and request a certificate thereof. (GDR/334B/304)

906 Hartpury. 24 June 1819 (25 Jun 1819). I William Phelps of Hartpury certify that the now dwelling house of John Oakey in the parish of Hartpury is intended forthwith to be a place of religious worship and require you to register the same and require a certificate thereof. (GDR/334B/259)

907 Hartpury. 12 October 1822 (12 Oct 1822). I William Phelps, yeoman, of Hartpury certify that a dwelling house in the village of 'Blackersend' in the parish of Hartpury, and in the occupation of William Francis, is intended forthwith to be a place of religious worship and I hereby require you to register and record the same and request a certificate thereof. (GDR/344/38r)
Note. Possibly Blackwell's Green End.

908 Hartpury. 7 December 1822 (27 December 1822). I Francis Collier of Gloucester, minister of the Gospel, certify that the dwelling house of William Powell of the parish of Hartpury is intended forthwith to be a place of religious worship, and require you to register the same and request a certificate thereof. (GDR/344/40v)

909 Hartpury. 28 Mar 1838 (29 Mar 1838). *Wesleyan.* I Thomas Moss of Gloucester certify that the house of Henry Brunsdon in the parish of Hartpury, labourer, is forthwith to be a place of religious worship and I require you to register the same and request a certificate thereof. Thomas Moss, Weslyan minister. (GDR/350/222)

910 Hartpury. (7 Mar 1851). House and premises occupied by Thomas Geers. John Thurston. (Q/RNp/4)

HAWKESBURY

Hillesley, Tresham, Kilcot, Settlewood, Upton and Wast were tithings; Hillesley 'was a very considerable village and once had a chapel, by 1779 converted into tenements for the poor' (Rudder, 482). Tresham, which see, and Little Badminton, were chapelries annexed to Hawkesbury.

911 Kilcot, Hawkesbury. (Trinity 1724). *Baptist.* It is ordered by this court that the dwelling house of William Worlock situate in 'Killcoate in the parish of Hawksbury' be licensed and allowed for [dissenters] called Baptists to assemble and meet together in for the worship of God in their way according to their petition for that purpose filed and allowed. (Q/SO/5/f.12v)

Note. Rubric has 'Killcoate file'.

912 Hillesley, Hawkesbury. (Michaelmas 1734). *Baptist.* It is ordered by this court that the new house late built at 'Hillsley in the parish of Hawksbury' be licensed and allowed for [dissenters] called Baptists 'resideing' in and near here to assemble and meet together in for the worship of Almighty God in their way according to their petition for that purpose now filed and allowed. (Q/SO/6/f.19v)

913 Hawkesbury. 1 Mar 1787 (22 Mar 1787). We [named below] certify that we intend to meet for the worship of Almighty God in the dwelling house of Nathaniel Gowin at Hawkesbury and pray that this certificate may be registered. William Hitchman, Joseph Rodway, Nathaniel Gowin, Nathaniel Rodway, James Dutton, John Boulton, Isaac Joyne, Thomas Joyne, William Boulton, John Pitt, John Dutton, Henry Box. (GDR/319A/60)

914 Hawkesbury. 30 Mar 1811 (15 Apr 1811). *Baptist.* We [named below] being dissenters of the Baptist persuasion certify that a chapel or meeting-house is erected and built in the parish of Hawkesbury and is to be set apart and used as a place of religious worship of Almighty God, pray that this certificate may be registered. Richard Boulton, Nathaniel Gowen, Thomas Limbrick, William Thompson, William Harrison, Nathaniel Rodway, Moses Stinchcomb, William Brookes, Samuel Chappell. (GDR/334B/365)

915 Inglestone common, Hawkesbury. 30 June 1818 (7 July 1818). I Stephen Hopkins of the parish of 'Woottonunderedge' certify that the house and garden of Matthew Hopkins of Inglestone Common in the parish of Hawkesbury is intended forthwith to be used as a place of religious worship and require you to register the same and request a certificate thereof. [Signed] in the presence of Thomas Wright. (GDR/334B/278)

916 Hillesley, Hawkesbury. 31 Mar 1823 (12 Apr 1823). *Baptist.* These are to certify that some [dissenters] called by the name of Baptists intend to hold a meeting for the worship of God in a building, now used as a malthouse, at Hillesley in the parish of Hawkesbury, belonging to John Gunter, yeoman, during the time that their usual place of worship is enlarged and rebuilt, and desire it may be registered in your Court. John Gunter, James Dutton, Joseph Arthurs, Charles Purnell, William Winter. (GDR/344/108r)

917 Hillesley, Hawkesbury. 17 June 1824 (18 June 1824). *Baptist.* These are to certify your Lordship that some [dissenters] called Baptists intend to hold a meeting for the worship of God in a building recently erected for that purpose at 'Hillsley' in the parish of Hawkesbury, and desire it may be registered in your Court. Joseph M Chapman, James Dutton, John Gunter, Edward Hopkins. (GDR/344/134r) [*see* illus., title page]

918 Hawkesbury. 9 Dec 1824 (11 Dec 1824). *Methodist.* This is to certify that the house and premises now in possession of Edward Tocknell in Hawkesbury Hither Town is appointed for religious worship to be from henceforth there performed by a congregation of Protestants of the Methodist denomination. Edward Tocknell, George Hale, William Dutton, James Warriner. (GDR/344/134r)

919 Upton, Hawkesbury. 10 Feb 1826 (30 Mar 1826). I William Rodway of the tithing of Upton in the parish of Hawkesbury, farmer, certify that the house I now occupy is intended occasionally to be a place of religious worship and I require you to register the same. (GDR/350/54)

920 Upton, Hawkesbury. 24 Mar 1835 (24 Mar 1835). I William Boulton of the tithing of Upton in the parish of Hawkesbury, labourer, certify that the house I now occupy is occasionally to be a place of religious worship and I require you to register the same. (GDR/350/168)

921 Hawkesbury. 1 Jan 1836 (2 Jan 1836). *Wesleyan Methodist.* I Aquila Barber, Wesleyan minister of the Wesleyan Methodist congregation in the parish of Hawkesbury, certify that the house of Mr William Tuck of the same parish is intended forthwith to be a place of religious worship and require you to register the same and request a certificate thereof. (GDR/350/187)

922 Inglestone Common, Hawkesbury. 24 May 1839 (25 May 1839). *Wesleyan.* I William White of 'Wotton under Edge' certify that a chapel on 'Ingleston' Common known by the name of Wesleyan Chapel in the parish of Hawkesbury is to be a place of religious worship and I require you to register the same and request a certificate thereof. Witness Robert Clark. (GDR/350/241)

923 Upton, Hawkesbury. 29 Jan 1844 (2 Feb 1844). *Primitive Methodist.* I Robert Moore of Sherston Magna, Wiltshire, certify that a meeting-house and premises at 'Hawkesbury Upton in the parish of Hawkesbury Upton', now in the holding and occupation of the Primitive Methodist Connexion, are intended to be used a place of religious worship and I request you to register the same and request a certificate thereof for which shall be taken no more than two shillings and six pence. (GDR/350/333)

924 Hawkesbury. (4 Nov 1850). Chapel or meeting-house. James Carter & others. (Q/RNp/4)
Note. RG/31/2 gives registration date 9 Nov 1850.

925 Hawkesbury. (13 May 1852). House. Allen Goulter, Hawkesbury, farmer. (RG/31/2 f.126/r)

HAWLING
926 Hawling. 6 Dec 1811 (20 Dec 1811). We [named below] certify that a house in the parish of Hawling, the property of Jane Cooke and in the possession of Thomas Cooke, is to be used for the worship of Almighty God and we beg the same may be registered. Samuel Lear, John Rowland, William Newman, Charles Hammands, William Cooke. (GDR/334B/357)
Note. This certificate repeated exactly, including the dates, but house both owned and occupied by Jane Cooke. For Samuel Lear *see* **240**.

HAZLETON
927 Hazleton. 7 Feb 1835 (7 Feb 1835). I James Smith of Cheltenham certify that a dwelling house in the parish of Hazleton occupied by Mary Draper, shopkeeper, is intended to be used for a place of religious worship and I request you to register the same. Witness Charles Channon, James Hughes (GDR/350/162)

HENBURY

Diocese of Bristol from 1542. King's Weston, Lawrence-Weston, Redwick, Northwick, Aust, Stowick and Aylminton (alias Edminton) were tithings in the parish.

928 King's Weston [Henbury]. (Easter 1690). Quaker Meeting-house. (Q/SO/3/522)

929 King's Weston [Henbury]. (Michaelmas 1707). A house erected for Quakers. (Q/SO/3/520)

930 Redwick, Henbury. 25 Oct 1816 (2 Nov 1816). *Wesleyan.* We, residing in [Redwick in the parish of Henbury] 'wishes to have preaching by Mr Wesley's minister; that no person or persons should take any advantage of us we claim a licence'. Endorsed 'Robert Petheram wishes his house to be licensed for the above use'. Robert Petheram, James Rosser, Thomas Hignell, Stephen Hignell, Thomas Moseley, Henry Hall. (EP/A/45/2/106)

931 Compton, Henbury. 27 Nov 1818 (30 Nov 1818). I Betty Carter of Compton Greenfield in the parish of Henbury certify a building belonging to my dwelling house is to be used as a place of religious worship and I require you to register the same and require a certificate thereof. Betty Carter (mark); witness Mary Carter, Enoch Williams jnr (EP/A/45/2/114)
Note. Betty Carter seems to have been mistaken in the parish or did the clerk who wrote the certificate add 'Greenfield' to Compton in error?

932 Hatton, Henbury. 24 Jan 1825 (1 Feb 1825). *Baptist.* We [named below] being dissenters of the Baptist denomination have set apart a dwelling house, now in occupation of John Gibbs, at Hatton in the parish of Henbury and pray the said house may be registered and a certificate granted. Richard Thompson, Thomas Brown, Thomas Underwood, James Skinner. (GDR/350/31)

933 Charlton, Henbury. 27 July 1826 (3 Aug 1826). *Independent.* 'May it please your Lordship to to grant unto us [named below] dissenters of the Independent denomination a certificate for a house at Charlton in the parish of Henbury for the worship of Almighty God'. We pray that the same may be registered and a certificate granted us. B Hillier, Samuel Wade, Robert Hadfield, John Williams, Roger Willcocks, minister, J M Humberstone, Isaac Parsons, James Chard. (EP/A/45/2/229)

934 Henbury. 30th Nov 1827 (7 Dec 1827). *Baptist.* We [named below] certify that a building in the parish of Henbury in the possession of John Caribe is intended to be a chapel for religious worship by Protestants of the denomination of Baptists and we request that this certificate may be registered in the Consistory Court of your Lordship. Henry Tripp, Thomas Underwood, Richard Thompson, James Skinner. (GDR/350/79)

935 Hallen, Henbury. 9 Aug 1828 (9 Aug 1828). *Baptist.* We certify that a building at Hallen in the parish of Henbury is to be used for religious worship by dissenters of the denomination of Baptists. We request that this certificate may be registered. William Parsons, Henry Tripp. (EP/A/45/2/252)

936 Hallen Academy, Henbury. 22 Nov 1847 (18 Nov 1847). *Wesleyan Methodists.* We [named below] certify that a building known as the Schoolroom of Hallen Academy at Hallen in the parish of Henbury, in the oocupation of Mr Maynard, is to be used for religious worship by dissenters of the denomination of Wesleyan Methodists and request that this certificate may be registered. Thomas Maynard, Henry L Gibbs, George Hewett. (EP/A/45/3/431)
Note. One of two certificates with original signatures bound together into book and paginated in sequence but not pasted. But date '22' inserted against November 1847 does not match registration date.

937 Redwick, Henbury. 21 Mar 1851 (11 Apr 1851). *Wesleyan Methodist*. We [named below] certify that a building in the occupation of John Norris of Redwick and known as a Wesleyan Methodist chapel in the parish of Henbury is to be used for religious worship by dissenters of the denomination of Wesleyan Methodists and we request that this certificate may be registered. Richard Williams, Henry Curnock, Jane 'C' Norris. (EP/A/45/4/59)
Note. Pasted in. Signed. Jane Norris appears to have signed her Christian name only and Richard Williams, who appears to have written the certificate, added a symbol like 'C' and her surname. RG/31/2 has 'Robert' Williams but name quite clear in certificate.

938 Compton, Henbury. 28 Apr 1851 (1 May 1851). *Wesleyan Methodist*. I Mary Morgan certify that premises now held by me at Compton in the parish of Henbury is forthwith to be a place of religious worship by a congregation of Wesleyan Methodists and I request you to register the same and request a certificate thereof. Mary Morgan, Samuel Mountain, George Distin, Charles Garlick. (EP/A/45/4/82)
Note. Pasted in sideways.

HEWELSFIELD
Hewelsfield was a chapelry in Lydney parish. Most of Brockweir was in Hewelsfield parish, and entries are all included here.
939 Brockweir, Hewelsfield. 14 Apr 1813 (28 Apr 1813). I George Birley of Newport in the county of Monmouth certify that a house now in the possession of William Hopkin in 'Brockware in the parish of Ewersfield' is intended forthwith to be a place of religious worship and require you to register the same and request a certificate thereof. George Birley, William Hopkin. (GDR/334B/345)

940 Hewelsfield. 18 Apr 1818 (28 Apr 1818). I William Miles of Hewelsfield, cordwainer, certify a building messuage or tenement, together with its court thereof, 'where I reside at, being my own premises in Hewelsfield, is intended' forthwith to be used as a place of religious worship and require you to register the same. (GDR/334B/281)

941 Brockweir Common, Hewelsfield. 21 June 1819 (25 Jun 1819). [RG/31/2 states *Methodist*]. I William Brocklehurst of Newport, county of Monmouth, minister of the Gospel, certify that a newly erected building or chapel situated on 'Brockwear' Common in the parish of Hewelsfield is intended forthwith to be used as a place of religious worship and require you to register the same and request a certificate thereof. (GDR/334B/258)

942 Brockweir, Hewelsfield. 25 May 1821 (5 June 1821). I John Williams, cordwainwer, 'certify that a building, messuage or tenement (commonly called the Backhouse) where I reside at, (Charles Jackson, shipwright, owner) at Brockwear on the back parish of Hewelsfield' is intended forthwith to be a place of religious worship and require you to register the same. (GDR/334B/221)

943 Hewelsfield. 10 July 1922 (30 July 1822). I Daniel Edwards of Alvington, Officer of Excise, certify that a building together with its court and yard thereof (called Zion Chapel) at Hewelsfield in the parish of Hewelsfield (William Miles late owner but now the property of the said Church) is intended forthwith to be a place of religious worship and I hereby require you to register the same. (GDR/344/34r)

944 Brockweir, Hewelsfield [RG/31/2 notes Dean Forest]. 17 Sept 1825 (21 Sept 1825). [*Congregational: see* **671**] I John Parkyn, minister, [Tintern] Abbey, certify that a house in the village of 'Brookweir in the parish of Hewesfield', in the occupation of Oliver Worgin, is intended forthwith to be a place of religious worship and I require you to register and record the same. John Parkyn, minister, Oliver Worgin, occupier. (GDR/350/46)

945 Brockweir, Hewelsfield. 7 May 1832 (7 May 1832). *United Brethren [Moravian].* I, C J Ramftler certify that a house in the hamlet of 'Bokwear' in the parish of Hewisfield', in the occupation of John Pritchard, is intended forthwith to be a place of religious worship and I hereby require you to register and record the same and request a certificate thereof. C J Ramftler, Moravian Minister for Bristol; John Pritchard householder, William Syner householder, James Watkins. (GDR/350/127)

946 Hewelsfield [RG/31/2 names place as 'Bowspring']. 15 Jan 1844 (9 Feb 1844). *Wesleyan.* I Henry V Olver of Monmouth, Wesleyan minister, certify that a house in the occupation of Henry Kilson in the parish of 'Hueldsfield' is intended forthwith to be a place of religious worship and I hereby require you to register the same and request a certificate thereof. (GDR/350/334)

947 Brockweir, Hewelsfield [RG/31/2 notes 'Dean Forest']. 14 Oct 1846 (15 Oct 1846) [Q/RNp/4 has 13 Oct 1846]. *Wesleyan.* I James Meadmore of Monmouth town, county of Monmouth, certify that a building by the name of Salem or Wesleyan Chapel in Brockwear in the parish of Hewelsfield is intended to be a place of religious worship and I require you to register the same and request a certificate thereof. (GDR/350/380-1)

HILL

948 Hill. 18 Apr 1817 (29 July 1817). We [named below] certify that we intend to meet for the worship of Almighty God in the dwelling house now in the occupation of John Lewis at Hill in the parish of Hill and pray that this certificate may be registered. Thomas Eley, John Lewis, Robert Long, Anne Lewis, Hester Riddiford, Thomas Lewis, Robert Hopkins, Jacob Clutterbuck. (GDR/334B/294)

HORFIELD

Diocese of Bristol from 1542

949 Horfield. 1672. *Presbyterian.* Application for licence to Edward Hancocke of Horfield; application by James Innes jnr for Mr Edward Hancock, general teacher; licence recorded 10 May 1672 for Edward Hancocke of Horfield to be a general Presbyterian teacher; licence received 12 June 1672 by Owen Davies for 'Edward Hancox' and his house. (LT/357, 364, 401, 483)

950 Horfield. 5 Oct 1839 (7 Oct 1839). *Baptist.* We [named below] certify that a dwelling house in the occupation of Jabez Fletcher, cooper, in the parish of Horfield is to be used for religious worship by dissenters of the denomination of Baptists and we request that this certificate may be registered. Jabez Fletcher, Thomas Clifford Dudley, William Lane. (EP/A/45/2/593)

951 Horfield. 16 Apr 1846 (22 Apr 1846). *Wesleyan Methodists.* We [named below] trustees, certify that a building newly erected and known as Mount Zion chapel in the parish of Horfield, in our occupation, is to be used for religious worship by dissenters of the denomination of Wesleyan Methodists and we request that this certificate may be registered. Henry Hodges, John [blank], Richard Friske, J Russom, Stephen Fisher, Henry Curnock, Robert Blake, G Richards, Richard Williams, Joseph Jenkin, James Giles. (EP/A/45/3/389)

HORSLEY

See also Nailsworth which was partly in Horsley.

952 [Horsley]. 1672. *Congregational.* Application by Owen Davies for licence for Thomas Webb's house in 'Horsey'; licence recorded 10 June 1672 for the house of Thomas Webb in 'Horsey for Congregational'; licence received by Owen Davies 12 June 1672. (LT/372, 401, 509)

953 [Horsley].1672. *Congregational.* Application for licence by Owen Davies for Widow Elizabeth Bird's house in 'Horsey'; licence recorded 10 June 1672 for the house of Elizabeth Bird in 'Horsey'; licence received by Owen Davies for 'Ellis Byrd's house'. (LT/372, 401, 509)

954 [Horsley]. 1672. *Congregational.* Application for licence by Owen Davies to 'Will Tray of Horcy' as a Congregational minister at his own house. (LT/372)

955 Horsley. (Epiphany 1707/8). *Baptist.* William Harding's house. (Q/SO/3/520)

956 Horsley. (Epiphany 1732/33). *Anabaptist.* It is ordered by this court that the house of William Smith, broadweaver, in the parish of Horsley be registered and allowed to be a Meeting-house for the worship of Almighty God by [dissenters] called 'Ana Baptists' and that Thomas Flower be registered and allowed to be their teacher or preacher, he having now in open court taken and subscribed the oaths of allegiance, supremacy and abjuration and subscribed the Articles of Religion pursuant to the statute in that case made and provided. (Q/SO/5/f.185v)
Note. Rubric has 'Horsley Meeting-house Tho Flower preacher'.

957 Horsley. 6 June 1735. These are to certify you that some [dissenters] intend to hold a meeting for the worship of God in their way in the dwelling house of Stephen Box in the parish of Horsley, therefore we desire that it may be recorded. Martin Lloyd, Joseph Fownes, Martin Lloyd jnr. (GDR/284/38)

958 Horsley. 14 July 1746 (registered Michaelmas 1746, Q/SO/7/f.128r). *Baptist [Independent: see note].*'To the Worshipful the bench of Justices, their humble petitioners sheweth: That the dwelling house of Francis Hoskinson in the parish of Horsley was licenced above 30 years ago for a Baptist congregation there to assemble and there to worship God according to the laws of the land but the licence being lost and we being willing to act according to law do petition your worships to grant us a new licence there to meet and you will highly oblige your humble petitioners and servants.' Francis Hopkins, John Marttin, Nathaniel Mildwaters, William Hoskins. (Q/SR/1746/D 3)
Note. For possible first registration *see* **955** (Epiphany 1707/8). The registration in the Quarter Sessions Order book named 'Independents'.

959 Horsley. 5 June 1756. *Baptist.* 'We whose names are hereunder subscribed do in the name of many others of His Majesty's loyal subjects under the denomination of Baptists, meeting in the parish of Horseley under your cognizance, humbly petition a licence for the houses and place where we meet to worship God in, according to the dictates of our conscience, having by some accident lost a former licence to us granted for that purpose, which favour will be gratefully received by us that continue to pray for the protection and happiness of His Majesty's person and government.' Samuel Bowen, George Haines, Thomas Powell, James Loakier [?Lockier], Daniel Cook. (GDR/292A/12)
Note. The second petition referring to a lost licence for the Baptist congregation.

960 Horsley. 13 Dec 1816 (21 Dec 1816). We [named below] being resident in the parish of Horsley and its neighbourhood, are desirous of making use of the ground floor of the house of Mary Heaven in the village of 'Dawmead' [Downend] for religious worship. We therefore request that your Lordship would order the regular entry in your court of this our intention to meet in the said premises for the purpose already specified. William Clements, Isaac Paine, John Webb, John Seale, Daniel Window, William Window. (GDR/334B/307) *Note.* 'Dawmead' appears to be a copying error from the original certificate. The meeting was probably the beginning of the Wesleyan congregation who built a chapel in 1820 (*VCH Glos* 11, 183).

961 Nupend, Horsley. 12 July 1818 (30 July 1818). I James Rickards of Nupend in the parish of Horsley, clothworker, certify that my dwelling house at Nupend is intended forthwith to be used as a place of religious worship and require you to register the same. (GDR/334B/277)

962 Downend, Horsley. 15 May 1821 (21 May 1821). We, Isaac Bushell, yeoman of Downend in the parish of Horsley, and Thomas Edkins, dissenting minister of Nailsworth, certify that a house at Downend in the occupation of Isaac Bushell is intended forthwith to be a place of religious worship and require you to register the same. Isaac Bushell (mark) of Horsley, Thomas Edkins, Nailsworth. (GDR/334B/221)

963 Horsley. 6 June 1821 (6 Jun 1821). I certify that the premises occupied by Thomas Bushell in the parish of Horsley will be hereafter used as a place of religious worship. Adam Nightingale, minister (GDR/334B/220)

964 Horsley. 6 June 1821 (6 Jun 1821). I certify that the premises occupied by Thomas Manning in the parish of Horsley will hereafter be used as a place of religious worship. Adam Nightingale. (GDR/334B/220)

965 Downend, Horsley. 7 Mar 1822 (8 Mar 1822). I Richard Wintle [RG/31/2 has 'of Horsley'] certify that a building or chapel recently erected at Downend in the parish of Horsley is intended forthwith to be a place of religious worship. And I require you to register and record the same. Richard Wintle, officiating minister. Witness Stephen Hopkins. (GDR/344/20r)

966 Horsley. 20 Sept 1824 (22 Sept 1824). I Thomas May of Horsley certify that a tenement now in the occupation of Thomas Gazard in the parish of Horsely is intended forthwith to be a place of religious worship and I hereby require you to register the same. Witness Thomas Sansom. (GDR/344/137r)

967 Nupend, Horsley. 12 July 1828 (12 July 1828). I Thomas Cox of Nupend, labourer, certify that my dwelling house at Nupend in the parish of Horsley is intended forthwith to be a place of religious worship and I require you to register the same. (GDR/350/92)

968 Downend, Horsley. 4 Dec 1834 (6 Dec 1834). I Thomas Sansum of 'Dowenend' in the parish of Horsley, confectioner, certify that my dwelling house in Downend is intended forthwith to be a place of religious worship and I require you to register the same. Witness George Shermer, James Moore. (GDR/350/161)

969 Shortwood, Horsley. 27 June 1837 (27 June 1837). We, Edward Barnard and Henry Bliss of Nailsworth in the parish of Minchinhampton certify that Shortwood Meeting-house in the parish of Horsley is and is intended to be a place of religious worship and we request you to register the same and request a certificate thereof. (GDR/350/210)

HORTON

970 'Harton' [Horton?]. 1672. *Anabaptist*. Licence recorded 5 Sept 1672 to 'James Nobbs of Harton in Glocestersh to be an Anabapt teacher at his one [own] house there'. (LT/559)

971 Horton. 9 July 1798 (1 Aug 1798). We [named below] certify that we intend to meet for the worship of Almighty God in the dwelling house of Mr William Gibbs in the parish of Horton and pray that this certificate may be registered. William Gibbs, John Prout, Thomas Ferebee, Charles Power, James Nash, George Hendy, Abraham Warner. (GDR/319A/268)

972 Horton. 6 Dec 1802 (22 Dec 1802). In pursuance of an act of parliament we [named below] desire that the house of John Prout, yeoman, called or known by the Lands House, be registered for the worship of God and religious exercise for protestant dissenting subjects. John Brown, John Prout, Robert Hobbs, Thomas Cooper. (GDR/N2/1)
Note. No record in Diocesan Act Book or RG/31/2. John Brown was an Independent minister in Rodborough in 1799, *see* **1471**.

973 Horton. 30 June 1818 (7 July 1818). I Stephen Hopkins of the parish of 'Woottonunderedge' certify that the house of Robert Hobbs in the parish of Horton is intended forthwith to be used as a place of religious worship and require you to register the same and request a certificate thereof. [Signed] in the presence of Thomas Wright. (GDR/334B/278)

974 Horton. 24 May 1839 (25 May 1839). [*Wesleyan see* **922**]. I William White of Wotton-under-Edge certify that the house of Mr Giles Beard in the parish of Horton is to be a place of religious worship and require you to register the same and request a certificate thereof. Witness Robert Clark. (GDR/350/241)

975 Horton. [-] Feb 1841 (12 Feb 1841). I David Kent of Cirencester certify that a house and premises in the parish of Horton, now in the holding and occupation of James Maul, are to be a place of religious worship and request you to register the same and request a certificate thereof for which shall be taken no more than two shillings and six pence. (GDR/350/273)

976 Horton. 27 Nov 1843 (29 Nov 1843). I David Kent of Sherston Magna, Wiltshire, certify that a house and premises at Horton in the parish of Horton, now in the holding and occupation of William Drew, are to be a place of religious worship and I request you to register the same and request a certificate thereof for which shall be taken no more than two shillings and six pence. (GDR/350/324)

HUNTLEY

977 Huntley. 1672. *Presbyterian*. Application for licence 31 May 1672 by John Juxon to 'Mr Thomas Smith of Huntley of the presbyterian perswation'; licence received 12 June 1672 by Owen Davies for Thomas Smith and his house, Gloucestershire, also for Thomas Smith at Thomas Bradeley's house [no place indicated]; three further records of licence, including 5 Sept 1672 to 'Thomas Smith of 'Huntly' to be a Presbyterian teacher'. (LT/385, 401, 404, 514, 553)
Note. See also Ruardean for Thomas Smith; entry for Huntley probably refers to **1485**, 'an outhouse belonging to Thomas Bradley of Ruarden'.

978 Huntley. 20 Nov 1798 (1 Dec 1798). These are to certify that we [named below] with others intend to hold a meeting for the worship of Almighty God in the dwelling house of William Fowle, yeoman, in the parish of Huntley and pray it may be registered. Edmund

Shaw, William Fowle (mark), John Simmons, Henry Stoke, Job Jeffs, Joseph Vernon. (GDR/319A/272)

979 Huntley. 23 October 1822 (23 Oct 1822). I John Powell of the parish of Huntley, mason, certify that a tenement in the parish of Huntley, now in my occupation, is intended forthwith to be a place of religious worship and I hereby request you to register the same. Witness S Miles. (GDR/344/38v)

980 Huntley. 23 Feb 1838 (23 Feb 1838). I Richard Clinton of the parish of Huntley certfiy that my house and premises in Huntley, now in [my] holding and occupation, are to be a place of religious worship and request you to register the same and request a certificate thereof for which shall be taken no more than two shillings and six pence. (GDR/350/219)

981 Huntley. (12 Oct 1847). House called White Hall. John Holder [RG/31/2 has 'dissenting minister']. (Q/RNp/4)

982 Huntley. (11 May 1850). [*Baptist*]. House occupied by Thomas Hulbert. Henry Clement Dawes [RG/31/2 has 'H C Davies of Longhope, Baptist Minister']. (Q/RNp/4)

IRON ACTON

983 [Iron] Acton. 1 May 1753. Some [dissenters] intend to hold a meeting for the worship of Almighty God in the dwelling house of Isaac Naish in the parish of Acton, maltster, and therefore desire the same may be registered. Joseph Everard, John Ashmeade, Martin Lloyd. (GDR/284/226)
Note. For Joseph Everard *see* **197**. Benson's survey of the diocese noted a number of dissenters (6 Presbyterians, 2 Anabaptists, 2 Quakers) in Iron Acton in 1735 to 1750 (*Benson* 2.15) but none at this date in Acton Turville (2.23).

984 Iron Acton. 28 Nov 1799 (13 Jan 1800; registration GDR/319A/289-90). In pursuance of an act of parliament we [named below] desire that the house of Giles Coates in the parish of Iron Acton may be registered among the records of the Bishop's Court as a house set apart for the worship of God and religious exercise. John Varlow, Daniel Fugill, James Davies, Thomas Rolph, Joseph Smith, Thomas Stiff, Giles Coates. (GDR/N2/1)

985 Iron Acton. 11 June 1810 (14 Jun 1810). *Methodist.* We [named below], being trustees of the Methodist Chapel lately erected at Iron Acton, certify that the chapel is appropriated for the purpose of the public worship of Almighty God and we require that the same may be registered and a certificate granted. William Pearce, William Curtis, John Knapp, Edward Curtis, John Hodgson, William Dixon. (GDR/334B/383)

986 Iron Acton. 14 Mar 1814 (19 Mar 1814). I John Parsons of the parish of Iron Acton certify that a building, occupied by me as a dwelling house in the principal street of Iron Acton, is intended forthwith to be a place of religious worship and require you to register the same. John Parsons, John Drew, Bartholomew Fugill, William Gibbs. (GDR/334B/339)

987 Stover, Iron Acton. 31 Oct 1839 (22 Nov 1839). *Independent.* May it please your Lordship to grant unto us [named below], being dissenters of the Independent denomination, a certificate for a chapel called Hope Chapel at Stover in the parish of Iron Acton for the worship of Almighty God. And we pray that the said chapel may be registered in your court and a certificate granted. Thomas Haynes, dissenting minister, Joseph Foote, Thomas White, Jonathan Gibbs, William Holloway, Joseph Rider, John Ivey, Samuel Pullin, James Bessell. (GDR/350/246)

KEMERTON
In Worcestershire since 1931

988 Kemerton. 10 Apr 1800 (registered 15 Apr 1800, Q/SO/12/113). [RG/31/6 states *Quaker*]. This is to certify to His Majesty's Justices of the Peace at the Quarter Sessions of the Peace, holden at the Booth Hall in Gloucester on Tuesday in the week next after the close of Easter in the year 1800 [15 Apr], that it is the desire of the inhabitants of the parish of Kemerton that ["those quarters over the parlour and kitchen of" *deleted*] the dwelling house of Mr. Charles Bidlake, apothecary, in Wing Lane in the parish of Kemerton be licensed according to the Act of Toleration and that the same be registered and a certificate thereof granted. William Mumford, Joseph Barney, Thomas Thornberry, Thomas Dudfield, John Purson, Joseph Troughton, Charles Bidlake. (Q/SR/1800/B/15)

989 Kemerton. 20 Feb 1809 (21 Feb 1809). We [named below] being inhabitants of the parish of 'Kemmerton' request that the dwelling house of William Pace in the same parish 'be licenced and registered in your Lordship's court as set apart for a place of religious worship agreeable to the act of parliament that grants and secures to protestant dissenters this privilege and do grant a certificate thereof.' Thomas Pace, Anthony Bearn, Thomas Wright, William Pratt. (GDR/334B/408)

990 Kemerton. 10 Aug 1816 (17 Aug 1816). [*Methodist, see* **179**]. I Daniel Campbell of Gloucester, minister, certify that the house of Jonah Gannaway in the parish of Kemerton and county of Worcester is intended forthwith to be a place of religious worship and I require you to register the same and request a certificate thereof. (GDR/334B/317)
Note. For Daniel Campbell *see* **179**.

991 Kemerton. 7 Feb 1817 (8 Feb 1817). I Jonathan Williams of Gloucester, minister, certify that the house of Thomas Mumford in the parish of 'Kemmerton', Gloucestershire, is intended forthwith to be used as a place of religious worship and require you to register the same and request a certificate thereof. (GDR/334B/305)

992 Kemerton. 4 Mar 1820 (21 Mar 1820). I Benjamin Andrews of Tewkesbury certify that a certain chapel adjacent to the premises of William Mumford in the village of Kemerton is intended forthwith to be a place of religious worship and require you to register the same and request a certificate thereof. (GDR/334B/245)

993 Kemerton. 26 Dec 1843 (1 Jan 1844). I Joseph Earnshaw of the borough of Tewkesbury certify that a building, usually called the 'Wesleyan Chapel' in the parish of Kemerton, is intended forthwith to be a place of religious worship and I require you to register the same and request a certificate thereof. (GDR/350/327)

KEMPLEY

994 Kempley. 24 Oct 1816 (29 Oct 1816). I Abraham Watmough [RG/31/2 has 'Whatmough'] of Newent, minister of the Gospel, certify that a dwelling house, belonging to and in the occupation of Daniel Hook of Kempley, is intended forthwith to be a place of religious worship and require you to register the same and request a certificate thereof. (GDR/334B/310)

995 Kempley Green, Kempley. 20 Feb 1836 (20 Feb 1836). I Thomas Kington of the Hill in the parish of 'Castle Froome', Herefordshire, certify that the house of Richard Phelps and premises at Kempley Green in the parish of Kempley are intended to be a place of religious worship and request you to register the same and request a certificate thereof for which shall be taken no more than two shillings and six pence. (GDR/350/189)

996 Kempley. (26 Jun 1852). House. Thomas Catterick [of] Ledbury. (RG/31/2/ f.126/v)

KEMPSFORD
Welford was a tithing in Kempsford

997 Welford, Kempsford. 12 Mar 1799 (16 Mar 1799). *Baptist.* These are to certify that some of His Majesty's subjects called Baptist intend to hold a meeting for the worship of Almighty God at the dwelling house of Robert Gearing of 'Whelford' in the parish of Kempsford and therefore pray that this certificate may be duly registered. Daniel Williams, James Andrews, John Smith, William Hooke, Henry Thomson, Jacob Betterton, John Kent, Charles G Thomson, Charles Hooke, John Thomas, Benjamin Thomas, John Purbrick; Molly Betterton, Priscilla Smith, Amelia Stephenson, Mary Bosbery, Mary Thomson, Jane Thomson, Sarah Gardner, Sarah Hooke, Ann 'Salip' [Saliss?], Mary Hooke. (GDR/319A/279) [*see frontispiece*]

Note. The men's names are set out in a first column, the women's in a second column. A registration for Kempsford listed in RG/31/2 for 23 Nov 1798 appears to have been for Tewkesbury. *See* **1719**.

998 Welford, Kempsford. 20 Aug 1820 (20 Sept 1820). *Independent.* We [named below] certify that some dissenters commonly called Independents intend to hold a meeting for divine worship in a certain erection or building standing on the ground belonging to the house in the occupation of Mr Isaac Vines, yeoman, 'Wilford', in the parish of Kempsford, and request that this certificate be registered. Joseph Jefferis [RG/31/3 has of Kempsford], church minister, Isaac Wane deacon, John Bason deacon, William Wane, Isaac Vines yeoman, John Kent, Thomas Kent, Henry Wheeler, John Caswell. (GDR/334B/232)

999 Welford, Kempsford. Dec 1825 (20 Jan 1826). We the undersigned certify that a house at 'Whelford' in the parish of Kempsford in the occupation of William Harrison will henceforth be used as a place of religious worship. J W Lowrie, John Jefferis Church, William Thomas, John Reynolds. (GDR/350/51)

1000 Kempsford. 25 Mar 1836 (25 Mar 1836). *Baptist.* I David Wassell of Fairford, Baptist minister, certify that a house in the parish of Kempsford is intended forthwith as a place of religious worship and I require you to register the same and request a certificate thereof. (GDR/350/194)

1001 Welford, Kempsford. 20 June 1840 (23 June 1840). [*Primitive Methodist: see* **254**]. I Joseph Preston of Brinkworth, Wiltshire, certify that a house and premises at Welford in the parish of Kempsford, now in the holding of James Pool, are to be a place of religious worship and I request you to register the same and request a certificate thereof for which shall be taken no more than two shillings and six pence. Witness R Hill. (GDR/350/255)

1002 Horcott, Kempsford. 4 Jan 1841 (14 Jan 1841) I the undersigned certify that a building or chapel belonging to me at 'Horcutt' in the parish of Kempsford is forthwith to be a place of religious worship and require you to register the same. John Kent. (GDR/350/272)

1003 Dunfield, Kempsford. 27 Dec 1844 (28 Dec 1844). I Thomas Boulton of Cirencester certify that a house and premises at Dunfield in the parish of Kempsford, now in the holding and occupation of John Peart, are to be a place of religious worship and I request you to register the same and request a certificate thereof for which shall be taken no more than two shillings and six pence. (GDR/350/355)

1004 Dunfield, Kempsford. (27 Nov 1849). House occupied by Edward Hawkins. John Court. (Q/RNp/4)

1005 Whelford, Kempsford. (27 Nov 1849). House occupied by James Legg. John Fleetwood Lewis. (Q/RNp/4)

KING'S STANLEY

1006 King's Stanley. 1672. *Presbyterian*. Licence recorded 10 Aug 1672 for the house of Sam Smith at 'Kingstanley'. (LT/551)

1007 King's Stanley. (Epiphany 1689/90). 'King Stanley, Stanly Court'. (Q/SO/3/522)

1008 King's Stanley. 6 Dec 1715. [*Anabaptist: see note*]. Benjamin Britton of 'King Stanley' dissenting preacher took oaths of allegiance and supremacy. Q/SO/4/[8]
Note. Benjamin Britton was the Anabaptist minister in the Evans list.

1009 King's Stanley. 17 Nov 1795 (18 Nov 1795). *Anabaptist*. We [named below], being Protestant dissenters under the denomination of 'Anna Baptists' and housekeepers dwelling in or near King's Stanley certify that we intend to set apart the dwelling house of Mrs Ann Hayward and request that this our certificate may be recorded and the entry therof duly certified. James Golding, Isaac Lusty, John Webster, Thomas Warton bachelor, Levi Ash (mark), Joseph Legg, Samuel Vick, John Bird. (GDR/319A/222)

1010 King's Stanley. Aug 1805 (3 Aug 1805). We [named below] certify that we with others intend to meet for the worship of Almighty God at the house in the court before the house of Mr John Tennells in the parish of 'Kingstanley' and we request that this certificate may be registered. Joseph Sling, Thomas Clutterbuck, Phillip Burroughs, John Neale. (GDR/334B/430)

1011 [King's] Stanley. 28 May 1807 (28 May 1807). We [named below] have set apart the house of John Wells in the parish of Stanley for the publick worship of Almighty God and we desire the same may be registered. Jer. Brettell, John Wells, Thomas Wells, Peter Roberts, John Oakeley, Thomas Wells jnr, John [blank]. (GDR/334B/422)

1012 King's Stanley. 20 Mar 1817 (21 Mar 1817). This is to certify that a house now in the occupation of Mary Bowden, widow, in the parish of 'King Stanley', is intended to be opened as a place of religious worship and request it may be registered and a certificate granted. Stephen Davis, minister, Isaac Brewer, Charles Cains, John Jones. (GDR/334B/300)
Note. RG/31/2 has 'Henry Davis, minister' instead of Stephen Davis here and in Stonehouse. *See* **1596**.

1013 King's Stanley. 25 Feb 1820 (28 Feb 1820). *Baptist*. Please to take notice that we [named below] of the Baptist persuasion wish to set apart for religious worship a room in the dwelling house of John Trueman in the parish of 'King Stanley' and wish to have it licensed for that purpose. James Cousins pastor, Thomas Lusty, Samuel Hudson deacons, John Truman, John Alder, John Iddles, James Ratcliffe, George Baker, George Lusty. (GDR/334B/246)

1014 King's Stanley. 25 Jan 1822 (26 Jan 1822). *Baptist*. Please to take notice that we the undersigned of the Baptist persuasion wish to set apart for religious worship a room adjoining the dwelling house of John Briant in the parish of 'Kingstanley' and wish to have it licensed for that purpose. James Cousins, pastor; Thomas Lusty, William Biffen, Robert Briant, John Alder deacons; John Briant, John Wood, David Little, William Burroughs, John Burroughs, John Baker, Joseph Pegler, Richard Pegler. (GDR/344/16r)

1015 King's Stanley. 12 February 1822 (13 Feb 1822). *Baptist*. Please to take notice that we who are Protestant dissenters of the Baptist persuasion wish to set apart for religious worship the dwelling house of Robert Holder in the parish of 'King Stanley' and wish to have it licensed for that purpose. James Cousins, pastor; Thomas Lusty, William Biffen, Robert Briant, John Alder, deacons; Robert Holder, William Jones, Daniel Hobbs, Giles Lusty, Luke Lusty, Joseph Alder, Charles Parsons, Anthony Alder. (GDR/344/17v)

1016 King's Stanley. 22 Jan 1823 (25 Jan 1823). *Baptist.* Please to take notice that we the undersigned who are of the Baptist persuasion wish to set apart for religious worship the dwelling house of Daniel Hobbs in the parish of 'Kingstanley' and wish to have it licensed for that purpose. James Cousins pastor, Thomas Lusty, William Biffen, Robert Briant deacons, Daniel Hobbs, John Wood, David Little, William Burroughs, John Burroughs, John Baker, Joseph Pegler, Richard Pegler. (GDR/344/41v)

1017 King's Stanley. 16 Mar 1825 (17 Mar 1825). *Baptist.* Please to take notice that we the undersigned of the Baptist persuasion wish to set apart for religious worship the dwelling house of James Bidmead in the parish of 'Kingstanley' and wish to have it licensed for that purpose. James Bidmead, Thomas Nait, Nathaniel Bryant; James Cousins, pastor; Thomas Lusty, William Biffin, Robert Bryan deacons; Anthony Alder, Nathaniel Heaven, George Baker, William Burroughs, John Alder, John Baker. (GDR/350/34)

1018 King's Stanley. 18 Mar 1825 (19 Mar 1825). I Thomas James of 'Kingstanley' certify that a dwelling house and premises in the parish of 'Kingstanley', now in [my] holding and occupation, are intended to be used as a place of religious worship and I do hereby request you to register and record the same, and I hereby request a certificate thereof for which shall be taken no more than 2 shillings and 6 pence. (GDR/350/35)

1019 King's Stanley. 4 May 1825 (7 May 1825). I Thomas James of 'Kingstanley' certify a dwelling house and premises at 'Kingstanley', now in [my] holding and occupation, are intended to be used as a place of religious worship and I request you to register and record the same, and request a certificate thereof for which shall be taken no more than 2 shillings and 6 pence. Witnesses: John Walkely (mark), John Clissold (mark) William James (mark), Thomas Sislinton, William Waters (mark), Thomas James (mark). (GDR/350/40)

1020 King's Stanley. 31 Jan 1828 (2 Feb 1828). I Thomas Lacey of 'KingStanley' certify that my house and premises at 'Kingstanley', now in [my] holding and occuaption, are intended to be a place of religious worship and I hereby request you to register the same and request a certificate thereof for which shall be taken no more than two shillings and six pence. (GDR/350/81)

1021 King's Stanley. 20 Mar 1828 (22 Mar 1828). I Charles Hawthorne of the town of Stroud certify that a dwelling house in the occupation of Thomas Thomas in King's Stanley is intended forthwith to be a place of religious worship and I require you to register the same and request a certificate thereof. (GDR/350/85)

1022 Stanley End, King's Stanley. 20 July 1835 (21 July 1835). I William Hobbs of 'Kingstanley' certify that a dwelling house and premises at 'Stanleys End' in the parish of Kingstanley, now in the holding and occupation of Thomas Stephens, are to be a place of religious worship and I request you to register the same and request a certificate thereof for which shall be taken no more than two shillings and six pence. Thomas Stephens (mark), William Hobbs (mark). (GDR/350/177)
Note. Rubric noted 'Stanleyend'.

1023 King's Stanley. 15 Mar 1836 (23 Apr 1836). I James Baker of Stroud certify that a dwelling house and premises at Kingstanley', now in the holding and occupation of Jacob

Smith, are to be a place of religious worship and I request you to register the same and request a certificate thereof for which shall be taken no more than two shillings and six pence. James Baker, Jacob Smith. (GDR/350/195)

1024 King's Stanley. 27 Nov 1841 (4 Dec 1841). *Baptist.* We [named below] certify that a building in the parish of 'Kingstanley' is forthwith to be a place of religious worship by dissenters of the Baptists denomination and require you to register the same and request a certificate thereof. James Cousins, minister, John King, Peter King, Nathaniel Heaven. (GDR/350/285)

1025 [?Dudbridge], King's Stanley. 6 Dec 1842 (6 Dec 1842). The undersigned David Apperley of Cainscross, clothier, certifies that a messuage in 'Dewbridge' in the parish of Stanley, late in the occupation of Franklin, is used and intended to be used as a place of religious worship and request you to register the same and request a certificate thereof for which shall be taken no more than two shillings and six pence. (GDR/350/308)

KINGSCOTE
Kingscote was a chapelry in Beverstone parish (for which there are no dissenters' meeting-house certificates). Part was in Newington Bagpath; see **1270***.*

1026 Kingscote. 22 Jan 1821 (23 Jan 1821). I certify that the premises occupied by Nathaniel Pritchard in the parish of Kingscote will hereafter be a place of religious worship. Adam Nightingale, minister. (GDR/334B/229)

1027 Kingscote. 13 May 1837 (13 May 1837). I Aquila Barber of Dursley, preacher of the Gospel, certify that a dwelling house in the occupation of James Hinks of Kingscote is intended forthwith to be a place of religious worship and I require you to register the same and request a certificate thereof. (GDR/350/208)

KINGSWOOD *near* WOTTON-UNDER-EDGE
Kingswood near Wotton under Edge was a parish in Wiltshire until 1832 for parliamentary purposes, and until 1844 for civil purposes. As this parish was surrounded by Gloucestershire, six dissenters' meetings were registered in the bishop of Gloucester's Act Books and one in the Quarter Sessions. Two early certificates were registered at Wiltshire Quarter Sessions and were calendared in Wiltshire MHC; for completeness, they are included here. The bishop's Registry usually noted the county, distinguishing Kingswood in Wiltshire from Kingswood near Bristol, which was a hamlet in Oldland tithing in the parish of Bitton, which see.

1028 Kingswood. 18 Apr 1699. The dwelling house of Nathaniel Coopye of Kingswood. William Griffin, Nathaniel Foord, Thomas Bence, Francis Foord. (W&SA A/110 E1699)
Note. Recorded in *Wilts. MHC 77E.*

1029 Kingswood. 14 Apr 1702. A new built house in Kingswood (near adjoining the now dwelling house of Nathaniel Cooper). Nathaniel Ford, Daniel Ford, Nathaniel Cooper, John Furnell jnr. (W&SA A/250)
Note. Recorded in *Wilts. MHC 127.*

1030 Kingswood. 6 Dec 1715. [*Presbyterian: see note*]. Richard 'Adye' of Kingswood, dissenting preacher, took oaths of allegiance and supremacy in 1715. (Q/SO/4/[9])
Note. Richard Addy was Presbyterian minister in Evans list and moved to Gloucester 1729.

1031 Kingswood. 22 July 1772 [?1773] (8 Aug 1773). *Independent.* We and some others called Independents intend to hold a meeting for the worship of Almighty God in the dwelling house of Sarah Fernly in the parish of Kingswood and desires it may be registered. William Young, Michael James, John Rugg, Paul Rowles. (GDR/292A/158)

1032 Kingswood, Wilts. (12 Dec 1798). These are to certify that we [named below] with others intend to 'hould' a meeting for the worship of Almighty God in the dwelling house of Robert Gainer in the parish of Kingswood in the county of Wilts. Robert Gainer, William Lovett, Joseph Short. (GDR/319A/273)

1033 Kingswood, Wilts. (12 Dec 1798). These are to certify that we [named below] with others intend to 'hould' a meeting for the worship of Almighty God in the workshop of Sara Mower in the parish of Kingswood in the county of Wiltshire and pray it may be registered. Robert Gainer, William Dinton, William Morton, William Lovett, Abraham Cornock (mark), Joseph Short. (GDR/319A/272)
Note. Registrar General's return is calendared in *Wilts. MHC 548C.*

1034 Kingswood. 1 Feb 1802 (8 Feb 1802). 'We [named below] being housekeepers within the parish of Kingswood do hereby beg leave to certify your Lordship that we are protestant dissenters and of the number of his Majesty's most loyal subjects and that we have set apart a messuage or tenement in Kingswood aforesaid, late in two tenements and in the occupation of George Flower and Thomas Bailey, the property of Robert Gainer of Kingswood aforesaid, dyer, for the public worship of Almighty God in our way and manner. And we humbly pray that this our certificate may be allowed and registered.' Robert Gainer, Nathaniel Long, William Robinson, Joseph Croome, William Heaven. (GDR/N2/2)
Note. No record in Diocesan Act Book or RG/31/2.

1035 Kingswood, Wilts. 23 Oct 1807 (24 Oct 1807). These are to certify that some dissenters intend to hold a meeting for the worship of Almighty God in a house belonging to Richard Baker in the parish of Kingswood, Wilts. We pray that this certificate be registered. Richard Baker, T Pinder, Thomas Aynes, John Balser, T Palser, George Hopkins, W Summers. (GDR/334B/419-18)

1036 Kingswood. 16 Aug 1821 (25 Aug 1821). We, William Alexander Long, James Counsell and John Millman of the parish of Kingswood, clothiers, certify that the new building erected in this village for a meeting-house, with the vestry, which has the churchyard on the east and south side, the land of Messrs John and Thomas Carpenter on the north side and a road from the churchyard on the west side, is intended forthwith to be a place of religious worship and require you to register the same. (GDR/334B/214)

LECHLADE

1037 Lechlade. (registered Michaelmas 1741, Q/SO/7/f.14r). *Quaker.* 'We with others the King's Protestant subjects called Quakers 'desires' a house in the town of Lechlade may be recorded and licenced for to meet and worship Almighty God.' Thomas Elkerton, William Humphris. (Q/SR/1741/D/1)

1038 Lechlade. 2 Sept 1783 (29 Sept 1783). We [named below] certify that we have set apart a house occupied by Mr Stephen Smith in the parish of 'Letchlade' as a place of meeting for religious worship and pray that the said house may be recorded as a place of meeting pursuant to an act of parliament. Stephen Smith, Edward Smith, William Lifeley, John Hamblin, William Golding, Richard Allsup, Richard Banting, Abraham Goulding, Elizabeth Goulding, Mary Allsup, Mary Gallaway, Lifely Golding, Esther Smith. (GDR/N2/1)
Note. One of a bundle of five certificates, all very worn and crossed through. Men's names in column 1 and women's names in column 2. The Registrar has entered 'reg. 29th Sept 1783' very clearly. But on the reverse side is the note '1784 Cert to be ent.' And underneath in a bold hand 'Entd' [Entered]. Identical wording to this certificate, including all the names of certifiers, is in GDR/319A/13, but dated 2 Sept 1784 and registered 29 Sept 1784. RG/31/2 also has date 1784. It appears that the certificate was copied or resubmitted.

1039 Lechlade. 22 Aug 1802 (23 Aug 1802). These are to certify that some [dissenters] intend to hold a meeting for the worship of Almighty God at the house occupied by John Edgington in the parish of 'Letchlade' and pray that this certificate may be duly registered. William Eyles, minister, William Puffett, Richard Bartin, John Edgington, James Hall, Godfrey Hey, Richard Woodward, John Bassones, William Kerby. (GDR/319A/316-7)

1040 Lechlade. 22 May 1811 (28 May 1811). We [named below] certify that a house in the occupation of Isaac Purkins in the parish of 'Leachlade' is intended to be used as a place of religious worship and request that it may be registered and a certificate granted. Isaac Purkins [RG/31/2 has 'Perkins'], William Collier Ward, John Wane, Jacob Betterton. (GDR/334B/364)
Note. RG/31/2 has registration 22 May 1811.

1041 Lechlade. 24 Oct 1817 (25 Oct 1817). [*Baptist*]. We [named below] certify that a house lately erected in Pudding Lane in the town of 'Leachlade', belonging to W Fox esq, John Ward, A Flint, B Thomas, W Thomas, Jacob Betterton is intended as a place of worship and we request that it may be registered. Jonathan Wane, William Wane, Henry Loveday, Samuel Wood, William Newbury, B Thomas. (GDR/334B/291) [*see* illus., xiv]

1042 Lechlade. 22 Nov 1843 (23 Nov 1843). I Joseph Campind of 'Brodwell' in the parish of Broadwell, Oxfordshire, certify that a house and premises at Lechlade now in the holding and occupation of William Boulton, are to be a place of religious worship and I request you to register the same and request a certificate thereof for which shall be taken no more than two shillings and six pence. (GDR/350/323-4)

1043 Little London, Lechlade. 22 Apr 1845 (2 May 1845). I John Wheeler of 'Leachlade' certify that a house in Little London, 'Leachlade', is to be forthwith a place of religious worship and I request you to register the same. (GDR/350/358)

LECKHAMPTON
1044 Leckhampton. 4 Apr 1835 (30 Apr 1835). I James Gill of Cheltenham certify that a dwelling house in the occupation of Edward Long in the parish of Leckhampton is intended forthwith to be a place of religious worship and require you to register the same and request a certificate thereof. (GDR/350/172)

[THE] LEIGH
1045 Leigh. (7 Feb 1810). *Methodist.* We [named below] beg leave to inform your Lordship that a house in the occupation of Martha Vernon, widow, in the parish of Leigh is to be used for the religious worship of Almighty God by dissenters commonly called Methodists and request that the same may be registered and certificate given accordingly. James Finch, Martha Vernon, Samuel Vernon (mark), Ann Vernon (mark), Samuel Brooks (mark), James Fussell. (GDR/334B/393)

1046 Leigh. 24 May 1819 (25 May 1819). I Benjamin Andrews of Tewkesbury certify that the dwelling house of James Finch in the parish of Leigh is intended forthwith to be a place of religious worship and require you to register the same and require a certificate thereof. (GDR/334B/259)

1047 Leigh. 13 May 1826 (13 May 1826). [*Methodist: see* **1399**]. I James Blackett, minister of the Gospel in the city of Gloucester, certify that the dwelling house of Joshua Weaver in the parish of Leigh is intended forthwith to be a place of religious worship and require you to register and record the same and request a certificate thereof. (GDR/350/56)

1048 Leigh. 19 Sept 1837 (20 Sept 1837). I Thomas Kington, of the Hill, in the parish of 'Castle Froome' in the county of Hereford certify that the house of Samuel Browett and premises at the Leigh in the parish of Leigh and now in [his] holding and occupation are to be a place of religious worship and I request you to register the same and request a certificate thereof for which shall be taken no more than two shillings and six pence. (GDR/350/214)

1049 Leigh. 22 Jan 1838 (23 Jan 1838). I certify that a room, occupied by me as a schoolroom in the parish of Leigh, will forthwith be a place of religious worship and request the same to be registered and I require a just certificate of the same. Dennis Potter, William Crofton Moat. (GDR/350/219)

1050 Leigh. 19 Mar 1841 (20 Mar 1841). I John Hill of Twigworth St Catherine certify that the house of Joseph Baylis and premises in the parish of Leigh, now in [his] occupation, are to be a place of religious worship and request you to register the same and request a certificate thereof for which shall be taken no more than two shillings and six pence. (GDR/350/277)

1051 Leigh. (16 Mar 1849). Wesleyan Methodist chapel. James Heaton. (Q/RNp/4)
Note. RG/31/2 has James Heaton of Tewkesbury.

LEIGHTERTON

1052 Leighterton. 10 Jan 1834 (20 Feb 1834). We the undersigned, being trustees of a meeting-house in the parish of Leighterton, certify that it is intended forthwith to be a place of religious worship and we require you to register the same. Levi Chandler, John Bowen, William Taylor (GDR/350/146)

LEMINGTON

1053 Lemington. 19 Nov 1836 (19 Nov 1836). I John Mann of Moreton [-in-Marsh] parish certify that a dwelling house in the occupation of Richard Linsey in the parish of 'Leamington' is to be a place of religious worship and require you to register the same and request a certificate thereof. (GDR/350/203)

LEONARD STANLEY

1054 Leonard Stanley. 14 July 1802 [RG/31/2 has registered 17 July 1802]. We [named below] certify that we with others intend to meet for the worship of Almighty God at the house and in the Court before the house of Mr Thomas Brewer in the parish of Leonard Stanley and request that this certificate may be registered and that certificate of the same be granted. James Williams, Joseph King, Thomas Brewer, Joseph Blackwell, Nathaniel Cook. (GDR/319A/313)

1055 Leonard Stanley. 12 Feb 1805 (12 Feb 1805). These are to certify that some dissenters intend to hold a meeting for the worship of Almighty God in a house in the occupation of Richard Bamford in the parish of Leonard Stanley. We pray that this certificate may be registered. William Hardwick, Elijah Morgan, James Warner, James Howell. (GDR/334B/435)

1056 Leonard Stanley. 18 Sept 1807 (19 Sept 1807). These are to certify that some dissenters intend to hold meetings for the worship of Almighty God in a house belonging to Jonah Smith in the parish of Leonard Stanley. We pray that this certificate may be registered. William Hardwick, Jonah Smith, James Warner, Thomas Pinder, William Dixon, William Curry. (GDR/334B/419)

1057 Leonard Stanley. 20 Jan 1814 (20 Jan 1814). *Methodist.* I Joseph Baker of Leonard Stanley certify that a building known by the name of the Methodist Chapel in Leonard Stanley is intended forthwith to be a place of religious worship and require you to register the same and request a certificate thereof. Joseph Baker of Leonard Stanley (mark), John Chettle, minister. (GDR/334B/340)
Note. For John Chettle *see* **178**.

LITTLE BARRINGTON
1058 Little Barrington. 30 Mar 1840 (31 Mar 1840). I John Bryan of Burford in the county of Oxford, certify that a house or building in the village of Little Barrington, occupied by David Chipperfield, papermaker, is forthwith to be a place of religious worship and require you to register the same and request a certificate thereof. (GDR/350/251)

LITTLE COMPTON
Little Compton was transferred to Warwickshire in 1844.
1059 Little Compton. 27 February 1822 (1 Mar 1822). We do hereby certify that a house in the parish of Little Compton in the occupation of Mr. Peter Bartlett will henceforth be a place of religious worship. Peter Bartlett, William Wheeler, Thomas Goffe. (GDR/344/18v)

1060 Little Compton. 2 Dec 1833 (9 Dec 1833). I Charles Hunt of Little Compton certify that a house in my own occupation is intended to be forthwith a place of religious worship and I hereby request you to register the same. (GDR/350/142)

1061 Little Compton. 18 Apr 1843 (21 Apr 1843). I Richard Phillips of Little Compton certify that a building at Little Compton 'and now in occupation and holding as a place of religious worship, and intended to be used as a place of religious worship', request you register the same and request a certificate thereof for which shall be taken no more than two shillings and six pence. (GDR/350/319)

LITTLE RISSINGTON
1062 Little Rissington. Epiphany, 10 Jan 1715/16. John Reynolds of Little Rissington, dissenting preacher, took oaths of allegiance and supremacy and abjuration. (Q/SO/4/[13])

1063 Little Rissington. 13 Nov 1779 (8 Jan 1780). We being [dissenters] intend to meet for the worship of Almighty God in the dwelling house of Edward Reynolds, maltster, in the parish of Little Rissington and therefore pray that this certificate may be registered. William Wilkins, Thomas Reynolds, Robert Rowland, Edward Reynolds, Thomas Hanks, Robert Maysey, Charles Maisey, Thomas Gatten, William Kitchen. (GDR/292A/225)

1064 Little Rissington. 25 Mar 1812 (31 Mar 1812). We [named below] certify that a dwelling house in the occupation of Richard Cooper at Little Rissington is intended to be used for religious worship. Richard Cooper, William Truby, Stephen Reynolds, Jeremiah Cresser, Charles Mayse [?Maysey], John Truby. (GDR/334B/354)

1065 Little Rissington. 12 June 1820 (1 July 1820). *Baptist.* We [named below] certify that a certain building in the parish of Little Rissington, in the possession and occupation of Richard Cooper, is to be used as a chapel for religious worship by dissenters of the denomination of Baptists and request that this certificate may be registered. Richard Cooper, Edward Truby, John Truby, Jeremiah Cresser, Samuel Perry, William Truby. (GDR/334B/240)

LITTLE SODBURY

1066 Little Sodbury. 10 Sept 1832 (11 Sept 1832). I Richard Monk of Chipping Sodbury, tailor and draper, certify that a certain tenement in the parish of Little Sodbury, now occupied by Thomas Fry, is intended forthwith to be used as a place of religious worship and I hereby require you to register the same. (GDR/350/134)
Note. Rubric stated 'Chipping Sodbury'.

LITTLEDEAN

1067 Littledean. 1672. Licence recorded 25 July 1672 for John Braine's house at 'Little Dean'. (LT/540)

1068 Littledean. 28 Nov 1724. *Independent*. These are to certify that there is to be a meeting of Protestant dissenters (called Independents) for the worship of God in the town of 'Little Dean' and at the house of Mary Watkins, widow, and this our certificate we humbly desire may be registered in either of your courts. Samuel Philipps, Richard Burkin, John Watkins. (GDR/279a/94)
Note. Rubric has 'Dean Parva'.

1069 Littledean. 8 Mar 1803 (9 Mar 1803). [*Independent*]. We [named below] certify that an house in the occupation of Samuel Morgan in the parish of Littledean is intended to be set apart and used as a place of religious worship and we request your Lordship that this certificate may be registered and a certificate granted for such. Richard Stiff, Thomas Abenhall, James Hooper.
[on left of signatures:] 'March 9th 1803 I do hereby certify that this certificate was this day duly registered in the Registry of the Lord Bishop of Gloucester by me.' (GDR/N2/1)
Note. Certificate very faded. No record in Diocesan Act Book or RG/31/2, despite note above. For Richard Stiff *see* **324**.

1070 Littledean. 5 June 1805 (12 Jun 1805. *Independent*. This is to certify that an house, the property of James Hyatt in the town of 'Little Deane', is to be set apart and used as a place of religious worship by [dissenters] of the Independent denomination. And we request that this certificate may be registered. Richard Stiff, William Moore, William Moore, Thomas Abraham, James Hooper. (GDR/334B/431)
Note. The name William Moore is written twice in original. For Richard Stiff *see* **324**.

1071 Littledean. 13 Jan 1815 (20 Jan 1815). I John Wright of Newent certify that the house of James Reese of 'Little Dean in the parish of Little Dean' is intended forthwith to be a place of religious worship and I require you to register the same and request a certificate thereof. (GDR/334B/331)

1072 Littledean. 13 Jan 1815 (20 Jan 1815). I John Wright of Newent certify that the house of David Robert Lindeford in the parish of 'Little Dean' is intended forthwith to be a place of religious worship and I require you to register the same and request a certificate thereof. (GDR/334B/331)

1073 Littledean, hundred of St Briavels. 12 July 1820. (13 July 1820). We certify that part of a messuage or tenement at 'Little Deane in the hundred of St Brevils', in the occupation of Nathaniel Wakeford, commonly called the Club Room, is intended forthwith to be a place of religious worship and we request you to register the same. Nathaniel Wakeford, W Wakeford, Titus Pritchard; witness George Wakeford. (GDR/334B/239)

1074 Littledean, hundred of St Briavels. 13 Feb 1821 (15 Feb 1821). We certify that a new place of worship in the village and parish church of 'Little Dean in the hundred of St Briavils' is intended forthwith to be used as such and we request you to register the same. Titus Pritchard, Nathaniel Wakeford, William Cooper. (GDR/334B/228)

1075 Littledean. 13 Sept 1823 (15 Sept 1823). This is to certify that the dwelling house of Benjamin Beard, Silver Street, 'Little Dean', is intended forthwith to be used as a place of religious worship; and I require you to register the same and hereby request a certificate thereof. Benjamin Beard. (GDR/344/113v)

1076 Littledean. 9 Jan 1824 (10 Jan 1824). [*Wesleyan Methodist: see* **608**]. I Isaac Denison of Little Dean certify that the dwelling house of George Bynon at Littledean is intended forthwith to be a place of religious worship and I require you to register the same and request a certificate thereof. And I hereby request a certificate thereof. (GDR/344/126r)

1077 Woodside, Littledean. 26 Oct 1846 (27 Oct 1846). I James Single of Littledean Woodside in the parish of East Dean certify that the house of Thomas Witehorne and premises at Littledean, now in [his] holding and occupation, are intended to be a place of religious worship and I request you to register the same and request a certificate thereof for which shall be taken no more than two shillings and six pence. (GDR/350/383)
Note. Littledean Woodside lay partly in Cinderford, Lea Bailey, and Littledean (*VCH Glos* 5, 306).

LONG MARSTON
1078 Long Marston. 21 May 1817 (8 May 1817). I Thomas Gibbs of Long Marston certify that a dwelling house belonging to Frances Brooks of Offenham, now in the occupation of Mary Mealin, is intended forthwith to be used as a place of religious worship and require you to register the same and request a certificate thereof. (GDR/334B/298)

1079 Long Marston. 16 Nov 1824 (17 Nov 1824). I John Thurston, minister of Wellesbourne in the county of Warwick, certify that the house in the possession of Henry Matthews in the parish of Long Marston is set apart for the public worship of Almighty God and we do hereby require you to register the same. (GDR/350/23)

LONGBOROUGH
1080 Longborough. (Easter 1700). 'Longborow', Robert Collett's house. (Q/SO/3/521)

1081 Longborough. (26 Apr 1798). *Independent.* This is to certify that a house in the parish of Longborough in the occupation of Joseph Acock snr, mason, and in the street of the said parish, is to be used as a place of religious worship by dissenters of the Independent denomination. We therefore request that the said house may be registered and a certificate granted accordingly. John Mann, James Rodway, John Kendall, Joseph Acock, Anthony Collett. (GDR/319A/266)

1082 Longborough. 30 June 1811 (18 Sept 1811). We [named below] have set apart the house of Jane Walford of the parish of Longborough for the public worship of Almighty God and desire the same may be registered. George Thornton, John Hobbs, William Dowman, Daniel Wallford, Richard Day, Isaac Day, George Green. (GDR/334B/362)

1083 Longborough. 16 Nov 1831 (19 Nov 1831). I John Greyhurst of Longborough in the parish of Longborough certify that my house and premises at Longborough, now in [my] holding and occupation, are intended to be used as a place of religious worship and I request you to register the same and request a certificate thereof for which shall be taken no more than two shillings and six pence. John Greyhurst (mark), William Coxhead, Boaz Tripp. (GDR/350/112)

1084 Banks Fee, Longborough. 29 Jan 1832 (20 Feb 1832). I John Greyhurst of Banks Fee, a hamlet of Longborough in the parish of Longborough, certify that my house and premises at Banks Fee now in [my] holding and occupation, are intended to be used as a place of religious worship and I hereby request you to register the same and request a certificate thereof for which shall be taken no more than two shillings and six pence. John Greyhurst (mark), Charles Smith, Thomas Mason (mark). (GDR/350/124)

1085 Longborough. 22 Feb 1836 (25 Feb 1836). I James Morish of Cheltenham certify that a dwelling house and premises at Longborough, now in the holding and occupation of Charles Lowe of Longborough, labourer, are to be a place of religious worship and request you to register the same and request a certificate thereof for which shall be taken no more than two shillings and six pence. James Morish, Charles Lowe. (GDR/350/190)

1086 Banks Fee, Longborough. 24 Mar 1838 (26 Mar 1838). I William Robbins of Banksfee in the parish of Longborough certify that a dwelling house and premises at 'Bankfee', now in [my] holding and occupation, are to be a place of religious worship and request you to register the same and request a certificate thereof for which shall be taken no more than two shillings and six pence. (GDR/350/220)

1087 Longborough. 24 Oct 1840 (31 Oct 1840). I Francis H Green of the parish of Moreton certify that a dwelling house in the occupation of William Green in the parish of Longborough is forthwith to be a place of religious worship and request you to register the same and request a certificate thereof. (GDR/350/259)

1088 Longborough. (15 Dec 1849). Building or chapel. Benjamin Harris Cowper. (Q/RNp/4)

LONGHOPE
1089 Longhope. 1672. *Presbyterian*. Licence recorded for the house of Hannah Weale at Longhope. (LT/526)

1090 [Longhope]. 1672. *Congregational.* Application by Owen Davies for licence to Thomas Smith to be a congregational minister at his own house in 'Hope'; licence recorded 10 June 1672 as 'teacher'. (LT/372, 509)

1091 Longhope. (Trinity 1710). *Presbyterian*. Richard Birkin's house. (Q/SO/3/520)

1092 Little London, Longhope. (17 Apr 1799). This is to certify that a house in the occupation of John Hayward in the village of Little London in the parish of Longhope is intended to be opened as a place of worship. We therefore request that the said house may be registered. Stephen Phipps minister, John Hayward occupier, John Stephens, Nathaniel Vaughan. (GDR/319A/280)

1093 Longhope. 25 Sept 1807 (7 Oct 1807). We [named below] have set apart a newly erected chapel in the parish of Longhope for the public worship of Almighty God and desire the same may be registered. John Brettell, William Macklow, Jonathan Parry, Joseph Rodge, John Spencer, James Coleman, Thomas Dayer. (GDR/334B/418)

1094 Longhope. 19 July 1823 (19 July 1823). [*Baptist: see* **517**]. I George Box Drayton of the city of Gloucester, surgeon, certify that a tenement in the parish of Longhope, now in the occupation of James Bowkite, is intended forthwith to be a place of religious worship and I require you to register the same. (GDR/344/111r)
Note. For George Box Drayton *see* **517**.

1095 Little London, Longhope. 12 Jan 1824 (12 Jan 1824). [*Baptist: see* **517**]. I George Box Drayton of Gloucester, surgeon, certify that a newly erected building called a meeting-house in the parish of Longhope, and at a place called Little London, is intended forthwith to be a place of religious worship and I desire you to register the same. (GDR/344/126v)
Note. For George Box Drayton *see* **517**.

1096 Longhope. 24 Jan 1829 (27 Jan 1829), I John Horlick, dissenting minister, certify that the dwelling house in the occupation of John Parry, farmer, is intended forthwith to be used as a place of religious worship and I require you to register the same. John Horlick, minister, John Parry, farmer. (GDR/350/99)
Note. For Revd John Horlick *see* Introduction and **1489**.

1097 Longhope. 1 Feb 1840 (5 Jan 1840). *Wesleyan.* I Thomas Moss of Gloucester, Wesleyan minister, certify that a messuage in the occupation of John Constance of Longhope, wood turner, is forthwith to be a place of religious worship and I request you to register the same and request a certificate thereof. (GDR/350/249)

1098 Longhope. (16 Oct 1847). Zion chapel. Henry Clement Davies. (Q/RNp/4)

LONGNEY
1099 Longney. 17 Nov 1819 (17 Nov 1819). I James Wood of Norfolk Buildings [Spa, South Hamlet, Gloucester] certify that a room in the parish of Longney, belonging to Mary Sims, widow, is intended to be forthwith a place of religious worship and request you to register the same. (GDR/334B/250)

1100 Longney. 19 May 1838 (19 May 1838). I James Grimes of the city of Gloucester, gentleman, certify that a dwelling house in the parish of Longney occupied by Daniel Ellis is to be forthwith a place of religious worship and request you to register the same. (GDR/350/225)

1101 Longney. 9 May 1839 (9 May 1839). I Robert Stratford of the city of Gloucester certify chapel or meeting-house in the parish of Longney is to be forthwith a place of religious worship and request you to register the same. (GDR/350/239)

LOWER SLAUGHTER
Lower Slaughter was annexed to the parish of Bourton-on-the-Water.
1102 Lower Slaughter. 21 Dec 1715. [*Anabaptist: see note*]. Joshua Head of Lower Slaughter, dissenting preacher, took oaths of allegiance and supremacy and made declaration against transubstantiation. (Q/SO/4/[10])
Note. Joshua Head was named as Anabaptist minister at Bourton-on-the-Water [**346**] in Evans list.

1103 Lower Slaughter. 16 Dec 1824 (31 Dec 1824). We [named below] certify that a building used as a dwelling house in the occupation of William Rowlands at Lower Slaughter is intended to be used for religious worship and we request that this certificate may be registered. Richard Prosser, William Rowlands, John Reynolds. (GDR/350/29)
Note. On page 29: '57 certificates of Divine Worship registered in the year 1824'

1104 Lower Slaughter. (8 Oct 1850). Cottage or dwelling house occupied by William Bowles. William Bowles. (Q/RNp/4)

LOWER SWELL

1105 Lower Swell. 17 Mar 1809 (21 Mar 1809). We [named below] have set apart the house of John Bateman in the parish of Lower Swell for the 'publick' worship of Almighty God and desire that the same may be registered. John Bateman, Henry Collett, Charles Upstone, Elizabeth Wilks, William Danman, William Banning, Ann Blizard, John Hobs. (GDR/334B/404)

1106 Lower Swell. 23 Dec 1826 (13 Jan 1827). *Wesleyan.* I Solomon Whitworth of Chipping Norton, Oxfordshire, certify that a dwelling house, now in the occupation of Hannah Gardener, in the parish of Lower Swell is intended forthwith to be used as a place of religious worship and I require you to register and record the same and require a certificate thereof. Solomon Whitworth, Wesleyan Minister (GDR/350/61)

LYDNEY

Aylburton and Hewelsfield, which see, were chapelries in Lydney. St Briavel's, also a chapelry in Lydney, is included under Dean Forest.

1107 Lydney. 17 Dec 1796 (13 Jan 1797). *Independent.* This is to certify that a house in the parish of 'Lidney', now in the occupation of Mrs Ann Gill, is intended to be a place of worship for dissenters of the Independent denomination and request that the said house may be registered. William Bishop, minister, Ann Gill, John Cooper. (GDR/319A/247)
Note. RG/31/2 has registration 21 Dec 1796.

1108 Newerne, Lydney. (17 Feb 1804). This is to certify that the dwelling house of Mrs Sarah Stephens in 'Newarn' in the parish of' Lidney' is to be a place of public worship. We [named below] request that the same may be registered and a licence granted. Isaac Skynner [RG/31/2 has 'of Lydney'], minister, S Huntley, M Dyer, William Thomas, William Roberts, Richard Stiff, Nathaniel Wakeford, Jenney Lee Wakeford, William Cooper, Elizabeth Cooper, John Cooper, William Moss, John Williams. (GDR/334B/440)
Note. For Richard Stiff *see* **324**.

1109 Lydney. 3 Oct 1816 (10 Oct 1816). *Wesleyan Methodist.* This is to certify that in the house of George Morgan in the parish of 'Lidney' the religious worship of Almighty God is intended to be performed by those commonly called Wesleyan Methodists and we require that the same may be registered. William Brocklehurst, minister, William Edwards, James Jones, Henry Collins. (GDR/334B/312)

1110 Lydney. 23 Dec 1816 (27 Dec 1816). *Methodist.* This is to certify that in the house of Samuel Nash in the parish of Lydney the religious worship of Almighty God is intended to be preformed by those commonly called Methodists and we require that the same may be registered. William Brocklehurst, minister, William Edwards, James Jones, Samuel Nash, Christopher Morris. (GDR/334B/307)

1111 Lydney. 1 June 1819 (1 Jun 1819). *Baptist.* We [named below] certify that a certain building in the parish of Lydney, rented by, and in the occupation of, John Trotter jnr, is intended forthwith to be a place of religious worship by dissenters of the denomination of Baptists, and request that a certificate may be registered. John Trotter jnr, Christopher Pain, John Watkins. (GDR/334B/260)
Note. Watkins was an officer of excise in Lydney: Horlick, *A visit to the Forest of Dean* (c.1832) 44.

1112 Lydney. 12 Oct 1824 (28 Dec 1824). I Thomas Edwards of 'Lidney' certify that my dwelling house and premises in the parish of 'Lidney', now in [my] holding and occupation, 'is' intended to be used as a place of religious worship and I do hereby request you to register and record the same, and I hereby request a certificate thereof for which no more that 2 shillings and 6 pence shall be taken. (GDR/350/28)

1113 Upper Forge, Lydney. 30 June 1827 (5 July 1827). I William Bond of Lydney Upper Forge in the parish of Lydney certify that my dwelling house at Upper Forge, now in [my] holding and occupation, 'are' intended to be a place of religious worship and I request you to register the same and request a certificate thereof for which shall be taken no more than two shillings and six pence. Witness Richard Keen, Henry Morse, William Bond. (GDR/350/69)

1114 Lydney. 14 July 1837 (15 July 1837). *Baptist.* We [named below] certify that a building in Lydney Street in the parish of Lydney, in the possession or occupation of Revd Edward Edkins Elliott and others (and called or known by the name of Lydney Baptist Meeting-house) is to be a chapel for religious worship by dissenters of the denomination of Baptists and we request that this certificate may be registered in the Commissary's court of your Lordship. Thomas Nicholson, William Adams, William Spires. (GDR/350/212)

1115 Lydney. 17 Apr 1844 (18 Apr 1844). [*Baptist*]. I Charles Phelps of Burton Street in the parish of Cheltenham certify that the Old Baptist Chapel and premises at Lydney, now in the holding and occupation of John Richards, are to be a place of religious worship and I request you to register the same and request a certificate thereof for which shall be taken no more than two shillings and six pence. (GDR/350/341)

1116 Newerne, Lydney. (14 Mar 1851). *Methodist.* Building called or known by the name of the Methodist meeting-house. Thomas Imm and others. (Q/RNp/4)

MAISEMORE
1117 Maisemore. 18 Aug 1820 (19 Aug 1820). I James Wood of Norfolk Buildings [Spa, South Hamlet, Gloucester] certify that a dwelling house in the parish of Maisemore, occupied by Thomas Sparrow, carpenter, is intended to be forthwith a place of religious worship and I request you to register the same. (GDR/334B/236)

1118 Maisemore. 9 June 1827 (9 May 1827). We the undersigned certify that a dwelling house in the parish of Maisemore, occupied by William Clarke, is intended to be forthwith a place of religious worship and we request you to register the same. Samuel Franklin, Robert Homan. (GDR/350/66)
Note. Dates of certificate and registration do not agree.

MANGOTSFIELD
Diocese of Bristol from 1542
1119 Mangotsfield. (Easter 1725). *Baptist.* It is ordered by this court that the dwelling house of John Betts in the parish of Mangotsfield be licensed and allowed for [dissenters] called Baptists living in and about Mangotsfield to assemble and meet together for the worship of God in their way according to their petition for the purpose filed and allowed. (Q/SO/5/f.26r)
Note. Rubric has 'Mangotsfield Meeting-house lycensed'.

1120 Mangotsfield. (8 Feb 1794). We [named below] signify to the Register of the Bishop's Court that a house in the occupation of Thomas Jones in the parish of

Mangotsfield is intended to be a place of religious worship. And we desire the Register of the Bishop's court to record the same. Thomas Jones, Robert Kendall, William Tugill. (GDR/319A/164)

1121 Mangotsfield. (1 Sep 1794). We [named below] signify that a building in the parish of Mangotsfield is intended to be used for the worship of the Almighty God and we desire the register of our court to record the same. William Mannering, J Jones, Thomas Burchell, John Smith, John Burchell, H Burchell. (GDR/319A/187)

1122 Morend, Mangotsfield. 20 Nov 1795 (Epiphany 1796). *Quaker*. 'These are to certify that we [named below] and others being dissenters called Quakers have agreed and do intend to assemble and meet together from time to time for religious worship at the present dwelling house of the undersigned Thomas Rutter at Morend in the parish of Mangotsfield and we desire that this certificate may be recorded or registered. Thomas Rutter, George Webb, Thomas Harding, John Wilmott. (Q/SO/11/f.267r)
Note. Text has 'recorded or registered'. Names repeated in text and also underneath certificate.

1123 Downend [as in heading], Mangotsfield. 28 Mar 1804. These are to certify your lordship that we [named below] with others intend to hold a meeting for the worship of Almighty God in a building set apart for that purpose in the parish of Mangotsfields, and pray [it] may be registered. Thomas Young, John Burchell, Thomas Emett, Samuel Gerrish surgeon, Joseph Gibbs, James Green. (EP/A/45/1/346)

1124 Mangotsfield. 10 Nov 1806 (13 Dec 1806). *Methodist*. We [named below] beg leave to certify to your lordship that a room in a house occupied by George James, coal miner, in Mangotsfield is set apart for the worship of Almighty God by a society of dissenters commonly called Methodists, and request the same may be registered and a certificate of the same given accordingly. George James, Thomas Llewellin, William Chilcott, Stephen Davis, William Kemmery, James Green. (EP/A/45/1/401)

1125 Mangotsfield. 27 Apr 1811 (6 May 1811). *Independent*. We [named below] being dissenters of the Independent denomination have set apart the lowest room or ground floor of a tenement or dwelling house, now in the occupation of William Mabberly, in the parish of Mangotsfield, for the worship of Almighty God, and pray that the apartment of the dwelling house or tenement may be registered and a certificate granted. William Mabberly, Joseph Orchard, Thomas Farrington, Samuel Wade, W Vaughan, John Nicholas, W Wrintmore, Robert Padfield, John Gibbs, Howell Jones, Thomas Edward, William Darcy, Robert Ward, minister. (EP/A/45/2/43)

1126 Mangotsfield 27 May 1813 (2 Aug 1813). We [named below] certify that a building in Mangotsfield Street in the parish of Mangotsfield is intended forthwith to be a place of religious worship and require you to register the same. Josh Seager, William Thomas, John Prosser, Joseph Barber, Robert Ware, John Nicholas, minister. (EP/A/45/2/63-4)

1127 Mangotsfield. Jan 1828 (11 Jan 1828). *Independent.* We [named below] certify that a building in the parish of Mangotsfield is intended to be used as a chapel for religious worship by dissenters of the denomination of Independent and we request that this certificate may be registered. Robert Padfield, John Gardiner, S Wade, Roger Wilicocks [*sic*], Isaac Parsons, John Williams. (EP/A/45/2/236-37)

1128 Soundwell, Mangotsfield. 31 Jan 1851 (1 Feb 1851). *Wesleyan Methodist*. I Charles Clay of Kingswood Hill in the parish of Bitton certify that a building at Soundwell called the Wesleyan Methodist School Room and preaching house, near the turnpike road leading

from Kingswood Hill to Downend in the parish of Mangotsfield, is intended to be used as a place of religious worship and request a certificate thereof. (EP/A/45/4/49)
Note. Certificate pasted in and signed. For Charles Clay *see* **120**.

MARSHFIELD

1129 Marshfield. 1672. *Presbyterian.* Licence recorded 20 Apr 1672 to John Fox of Marshfield to be a Presbyerian teacher in any licensed place. (LT/443)

1130 Marshfield. 1672. *Presbyterian.* Application by John Hickes for licence to Mr George Seele in Marshfield, Presbyterian teacher; the parish house thereof commonly called the Church house, to be licensed as desired; licence recorded 22 July 1672 for the house of George Steele at Marshfield. (LT/329, 529)

1131 Marshfield. 1672. *Presbyterian.* Licence recorded 16 May 1672 for the house of John Gostlett in Marshfield, Gloucester. Presbyterian meeting place. (LT/487)
Note. See 'house of Thomas Goslett esq' in next entry on different date.

1132 Marshfield. 1672. *Presbyterian.* Licence twice recorded 25 July 1672 for the house of Thomas Goslett esq in Marshfield. (LT/536, 541)

1133 Marshfield. 1672. *Presbyterian.* Application for licence for the house of John Gloster esq of 'Marshfeeld'. (LT/357)

1134 Marshfield. (Easter 1690). *Quaker.* Meeting-house. (Q/SO/3/522)

1135 Marshfield. (Epiphany 1699/1700). *Independent.* Charles Rudder's house. (Q/SO/3/521)

1136 Marshfield. 9 Dec 1715. [*Presbyterian: see note*]. Robert Patterson of Marshfield, dissenting preacher, took oaths of allegiance and supremacy. (Q/SO/4/[10])
Note. 'Patterson' named on Evans list as Presbyterian minister at Marshfield after George Seale deceased.

1137 Marshfield 4 July 1753 (registered Trinity 1753, Q/SO/8/f.72v). *Presbyterian.* 'We his Majesties Protestant subjects dissenting from the Church of England called Presbyterians [named below] being inhabitants of the town and parish of Marshfield … Do hereby humbly certify that the house or edifice lately erected in the town of Marshfield aforesaid, on a piece of ground which was late parcel of the messuage of John Tiley the younger of Marshfield aforesaid, maltster, is intended to be a place of worship of a congregation or assembly for religious worship … and pray that the same may be recorded in pursuance of the said act.' William Hands, John Oland, Henry White, Daniel Taylor, George Bennett, John Harford, Daniel Oland, William Bryan, Thomas Miller, Joseph White, Thomas Osborne, J Shapland, Thomas Barnes, Seale Emerson, John Felto. (Q/SR/1753/C/23)
Note. Original signatures but none recorded in Q/SO/8.

1138 Marshfield. 11 June 1764. *Baptist.* 'We [named below] being His Majesty's Protestant subjects desenting [*sic*] from the Church of England called Baptists do hereby certify that we intend to make use of the dwelling house of Michael Ferrice in the town of Marshfield … as a place of meeting for religious worship and pray that the said house may be recorded …' Joseph Sheppard, John Betts, Thomas Burcheley, Jos. Francom, Isaac Stephens, James Godfrey, Benjamin Kendall, Caleb Sheppard, Thomas Britton. (Q/SR/1764/C3)
Note. Not in QS order book nor in RG/31/6.

1139 Marshfield. 20 Dec 1791 (29 Dec 1791). *Independent.* 'We [named below] being Protestant dissenting subjects, Independent perswasion, having sett apart a place for the worship of Almighty God in the possession of Mrs Martha Oland, widow, of Marshfield in the diocese of Gloucester have in pursuance thereof presented this memorial requesting the same may be registered in the Bishop's Court that we may enjoy the benefits of the Acts in that case made and provided and worship God according to the dictates of our own Consciences and without any molestation'. John Hey, minister, Thomas Stibbs, James Ranger, William Ranger, Joseph Ranger, Daniel Taylor, William Small (mark). (GDR/319A/133) [*see* illus., lxxvi]

1140 Marshfield. 25 Oct 1802 (10 Nov 1802). We [named below] certify that a chapel belonging to the Revd George Bourne, Mr Christopher Stibbs, and certain other trustees is intended to be used for religious worship. George Bourne, Thomas Stibbs, Christopher Stibbs. (GDR/N2/1)
Note. No record in Diocesan Act Book or RG/31/2, but registration date noted on certificate itself.

1141 Marshfield. 12 July 1830 (17 July 1830). I Charlotte Hulbert of Marshfield certify that a dwelling house in my possession at Marshfield is set apart for the public worship of God and require you to register the same. Witness John Turner. (GDR/350/111)

1142 Marshfield. (7 Aug 1848). *Independent.* Chapel. Charles Bodman and others. (Q/RNp/4)
Note. RG/31/2 has 'J Bond'.

1143 Marshfield. (19 Aug 1848). Room in the dwelling house of George England. George England. (Q/RNp/4)

MARSTON SICCA
1144 Marston Sicca. 21 Mar 1807 (21 Mar 1807). We [named below] of the parish of Marston Sicca certify 'to the Rt Reverend the Lord Bishop of Gloucester, or to his Vicar General in spirituals or whomsoever it doth or may concern' that the dwelling house of John Gibbs in the parish of Marston Sicca is designed and set apart for the religious worship of Almighty God. Thomas Gibbs, William Mander, William Pardoe, John Winter, Daniel Smith, John Lancaster. (GDR/334B/424-3)

1145 Marston Sicca. (27 Dec 1848). Dwelling house of William Mander. Thomas Gibbs and others. (Q/RNp/4)

MEYSEY HAMPTON
1146 Meysey Hampton. (Trinity 1702). *Anabaptist.* 'Maysey Hampton', Henry Moulder's house. (Q/SO/3/521)

1147 Meysey Hampton. 25 Nov 1715. *Baptist.* William Moulder of 'Mayseyhampton', Baptist dissenter, took oaths of allegiance and supremacy. (Q/SO/4/[7])

1148 Meysey Hampton. (Easter 1734). *Baptist.* It is ordered by this court that the dwelling house of William Moulder in 'Maysey' Hampton be and is hereby licensed and allowed for [dissenters] called Baptists to assemble and meet together in, for their worship of Almighty God in their way, according to their petition or request for that purpose now made to this court. (Q/SO/6/f.8r)

1149 Meysey Hampton. 28 July 1788 (17 Oct 1788; registration GDR/319A/84-5). 'This is to certify that we [named below] intend to hold a meeting for the worship of Almighty God in the dwelling house of Richard Trueman in the parish of 'Maiseyhampton'. We therefore pray that this certificate may be entered in your Lordships Registry.' Joseph Jack,

Thomas Drake, John Price, Richard Truman, Thomas Short (mark), Thomas Greenwood (mark). (GDR/N2/1)

Note. Certificate crossed through. Written out on the back of a piece of paper with the start of a record of 'Gloucestershire Militia 1788' and with a certificate for Cirencester *see* **550**.

1150 Meysey Hampton. 8 Dec 1812 (23 Dec 1812). This is to certify that we [named below] intend to hold a meeting for the worship of God in the dwelling house of Thomas Millar in the town and parish of 'Mazyhampton'. We pray that this certificate may be entered in your Lordship's registry. George Moorhouse, Joseph Tuck, Thomas Miller, John Allen, Robert Wheeler. (GDR/334B/350)

1151 Meysey Hampton. 11 February 1822 (26 Feb 1822). We do hereby certify that a house at 'Maizyhampton' now in the occupation of the Revd J.H. Lewrie will henceforth be a place of religious worship. Thomas Clarke, Revd J H Lewrie, Mary Clarke, Harriett Miller. (GDR/344/18r)

1152 Meysey Hampton. 23 Sept 1833 (24 Sept 1833). *Baptist.* We [named below] certify that a building in the parish of Maisey Hampton in the possession of William Thomas is to be a chapel for religious worship by dissenters of the denomination of Baptists and we request that this certificate may be registered in the Commissary's Court of your Lordship. Daniel White, William Thomas, David Wassell. (GDR/350/142)

MICKLETON

1153 Mickleton. 24 Mar 1812 (26 Mar 1812). *Wesleyan connexion.* This is to certify that the dwelling house of William Neal in the village and parish of Mickleton is set aside for the public worship of God by the ministers and people in 'connexion' with the late Revd John Wesley and we request that the said house be registered. William Neal, Josh Trotman, James Gartrell, Richard Martin, Robert Paynes. (GDR/334B/355)

1154 Mickleton. 11 Dec 1819. I, W H L Eden of Evesham in the county of Worcester certify that a house now in the possession of Joseph Wheatley at Mickleton is intended forthwith to be used as a place of religious worship and require you to register the same and request a certificate thereof. William Henry Loxdale Eden. (GDR/334B/241)

Note. The name of the place in the rubric has been corrected from Evesham to Kemerton but the certificate text says meeting at Mickleton.

1155 Hidcote, Mickleton. 6 June 1821 (15 Jun 1821). *Methodist.* I Joseph Bowes [signature 'Bower'], Methodist minister of Evesham in Worcestershire, certify that a dwelling house in the hamlet of 'Hitcoat' in the parish of Mickleton and in the occupation of Thomas Beavington, is forthwith to be a place of religious worship and require you to register the same and request a certificate thereof. (GDR/334B/219)

1156 Hidcote [Mickleton]. (10 Jun 1852). Cottage. Owen Corbett, Campden. (RG/31/2 f126/v)

Note. The only other certificate for Hidcote, **1155** *above,* was for the part in Mickleton parish, but as no parish was named for this second one, it could have been in Ebrington.

MINCHINHAMPTON

See also Nailsworth, which was partly in Minchinhampton, and Rodborough, which was a chapelry in Minchinhampton.

1157 Forwood [Minchinhampton]. (Michaelmas 1699). *Anabaptist.* Giles Mason's house. (Q/SO/3/521)

1158 Minchinhampton. (Trinity 1723). *Independent.* It is ordered by this Court that the dwelling house of Samuel King in 'Minchin Hampton' in a street there called the Westend be licensed and allowed for dissenters called Independents to assemble and meet in for the worship of God according to the petition for that purpose filed and allowed 'and that Richard Rawlins be lycensed and admitted to be the teacher or preacher there.' (Q/SO/4/455)

1159 Minchinhampton. 11 Jan 1727/28. *Baptist.* These are to certify you that [dissenters] (called Baptists) intend to hold a meeting for the worship of God in their way in the house of Joseph Freeman in the parish of 'Michin Hampton', near 'Sinkley farme', and pray that it may be recorded. John Blake, Joseph Freeman, Jacob Mower. (GDR/279a/190)

1160 Minchinhampton. (Trinity 1731). *Quaker.* It is ordered by this court that [dissenters] called Quakers residing in and about Minchinhampton be licensed and allowed to assemble and meet together for the worship of God in their way in the dwelling house of Daniel Fowler in Minchinhampton. (Q/SO/5/f.164r)
Note. Rubric has 'Quakers Minchinhampton Meeting-house lysenced'.

1161 Well Hill, Minchinhampton. 20 June 1735. These are to certify you that [dissenters] intend to hold a meeting for the worship of Almighty God in the dwelling house of Edward Danford, a chandler, on or near a place called and known by the name of Well Hill in the town and parish of Minchinhampton and desire the same may be registered. Nathaniel Brock, Martin Lloyd, Joseph Everard. (GDR/284/39)
Note. For Joseph Everard *see* **197**.

1162 Minchinhampton. 7 Apr 1739. These are to certify your Lordship that some dissenters intend to hold a meeting for the worship of God in their way in the dwelling house of Thomas King in a street known by the name of the Westend in the Town of Minchinhampton. We therefore pray that it may be registered. Martin Lloyd, Martin Lloyd jnr, John Harmar. (GDR/284/100)

1163 Well Hill, Minchinhampton. 7 Nov 1743. These are to certify that [dissenters] intend to hold a meeting for the worship of God at the dwelling house of Thomas Adams, lastmaker, on or near a place called and known by the name of Well Hill in the town and parish of 'Minchin Hampton' and desire the same may be registered. Thomas Jones, William Hogg, William Jones, John Bingham. (GDR/284/156)

1164 Minchinhampton. 23 June 1746. *Quakers.* We and others of 'the King's Protestant subjects called Quakers' desires the Market House in Minchinhampton may be recorded for the use and worship of Almighty God.' Christopher Young, Henry Wilkins, William Humphris. (GDR/284/173) [*see* illus., xiii]

1165 Minchinhampton. 24 June 1746. These are to certify your Lordship that some [dissenters] intend to hold a meeting for the worship of God in a house belonging to John Vick in the town of Minchinhampton and desire the same may be registered. Martin Lloyd, William Hogg, Henry Restall. (GDR/284/173)

1166 Minchinhampton. 6 Feb 1761. *Independent.* We [named below] humbly desire that the house wherein William Knight now resides in the parish of Minchinhampton be registered for a place of divine worship in the Protestant dissenting way. John Hoskins, Thomas Mercer, Joseph Dee, John Fords, James Lockier, William Kirby. (GDR/292A/16)

1167 Minchinhampton. 1 Oct 1765. *Baptist.* 'We do hereby most humbly desire your Worships that a house lately erected in the town of Minchin-Hampton which was built for the purpose of and intended to be a place of divine worship for a congregation called Baptists may be licenced and registered among the records of your Court.' Benjamin Francis, William Clissold, John Trevor, Thomas Mercer. (Q/SR/1765/D)

Note. This petition is exactly the same as that registered in GDR/319A/285-6 dated 20 Oct 1799 and registered on 26 Oct 1799. The four signatories are the same, which suggesrs this petition has been misdated or re-registered in the Bishop's court.

1168 Minchinhampton. 26 Mar 1792 (17 Apr 1792). *Independent.* We [named below] dissenters under the denomination of Independents and housekeepers dwelling in or near the town of Minchinhampton certify that we intend to set apart the dwelling house of Mr William Casey in the town of Minchinhampton for the service and worship of Almighty God and we request that this certificate may be recorded in your Lordship's Registry and the entry thereof duly certified. James Golding, Samuel Wood, William Jeens, William Smart, William Canter, John Griffin, Thomas Wright, John Swain, Morris Rowe. (GDR/319A/135)

1169 Minchinhampton. 25 Oct 1799 (26 Oct 1799). *Baptists.* We [named below], dissenters under the denomination of Baptists and housekeepers dwelling in and near the town of 'Minchin Hampton', intend to set apart the dwelling house of Miss Mary Cambridge in the town of 'Minchin Hampton' for the service and worship of Almighty God, and we request that this our certificate may be recorded in your Lordship's Registry and the entry thereof duly certified. Benjamin Francis, Thomas Islint, both ministers; James Golding, Joshua Handcock, Richard Monk, William Jeens, William Clissold, Samuel Wood, Thomas Flower. (GDR/319A/285-6)

1170 Minchinhampton. 19 Nov 1802 (20 Nov 1802). We humbly desire that the room over the Market House in the town of Minchinhampton be registered for a place of divine worship by some [dissenters]. Orlando A Jeary, minister, Thomas Dangerfield, Richard Monk, James Kibble, Samuel Wood, William Clift. (GDR/N2/1) [*see* illus, xxiii]

Note. No record in Diocesan Act Book or RG/31/2.

1171 Littleworth, Minchinhampton. 11 Apr 1809 (11 Apr 1809). These are to certify that some dissenters intend holding a meeting for the worship of Almighty God in a building erected for that purpose in the village of Littleworth in the parish of 'Hampton' [Minchinhampton]. We pray that this certificate be registered. William Blagborne, Thomas Cooper, Josh. Hort jnr, Benjamin Dudbridge, David Burford, James Clifft. (GDR/334B/403)

1172 Brimscombe, Minchinhampton. 11 Apr 1809 (11 Apr 1809). These are to certify that some dissenters intend holding a meeting for the worship of Almighty God in a building erected for that purpose in the village of 'Brimpscomb in the parish of Hampton' [Minchinhampton]. We pray that this certificate be registered. William Blagborne [RG/31/2 has of Littleworth], William Webb, Eliza Baker, Sarah Lees, Sarah Bretler, James Willis, Thomas Ellis. (GDR/334B/403)

1173 Box, Minchinhampton. 13 Oct 1813 (6 Nov 1813). This is to certify that a house in the occupation of Sarah Manfield at the Box in the parish of Minchinhampton is to be a place of religious worship. We request that the house may be registered and a certificate granted accordingly. Christopher Pain, minister, James Thomas, George Thomas, William Osborne, William Clissold. (GDR/334B/341)

1174 Minchinhampton. 19 Feb 1820 (19 Feb 1820). This is to certify that an house in the occupation of Daniel Davis in the Market street in the town of Minchinhampton is to be a place of religious worship and request that it may be registered. John Rees, minister of Rodborough Tabernacle, Daniel Davis. (GDR/334B/247)

1175 Littleworth, Minchinhampton. 19 Feb 1820 (19 Feb 1820). This is to certify that an house and paddock, about half an acre of land, in the occupation of William Peach Cooper esq, at Littleworth in the parish of Minchinhampton, is to be a place of religious worship and request that the same may be registered. John Rees, minister of Rodborough Tabernacle; W P Cooper of Littleworth. (GDR/334B/247)

1176 Hampton Common, Minchinhampton. 24 July 1820 (26 July 1820). This is to certify that two acres of ground situate on Hampton Common, the centre of which two acres is the place commonly called 'Whitfields [Whitefield's] Tump', is to be appropriated occasionally as a place of religious workship and we request that it may be registered. John Rees, minister of 'Rodboro' Tabernacle; Thomas Edkins, minister of Forest Green Meeting; James Thomas, inhabitant of parish of Hampton, George Thomas, inhabitant of parish of Hampton. (GDR/334B/238)
Note. George Thomas's name is followed by 'Do Do'. It is assumed this related to 'inhabitant of Hampton' against previous name.

1177 Littleworth, Minchinhampton. 21 Oct 1820 (25 Nov 1820). This is to certify that an house in the occupation of Mary Clift, widow, at Littleworth in the parish of Minchinhanpton is to be a place of religious worship and I request you to register the same. Seth A Morris, minister of Littleworth Chapel, Mary Clift (mark). (GDR/334B/230)

1178 Minchinhampton. 11 February 1822 (13 Feb 1822). This is to certify that the premises now in the occupation of Mr. J B Foxwell, called Dye House Mills, in the parish of Minchinhampton is to be a place of religious worship and we request it may be registered. John Rees, minister of Rodborough Tabernacle, John Burford Foxwell, Thomas Williams. (GDR/344/17r)

1179 Minchinhampton. 20 Oct 1823 (25 Oct 1823). [*Methodist: see* **1399**]. I James Blackett, minister of the Gospel, of Stroud certify that a house in the occupation of Mr Richard Heath in 'Mincinhampton' is forthwith to be a place of religious worship and require you to register the same and request a certificate thereof. (GDR/344/117r)
Note. Rubric refers to Stroud.

1180 Box, Minchinhampton. 12 Mar 1824 (15 Mar 1824). I John Evins of Box in the parish of Minchinhampton certify that a dwelling house and premises in Box in Minchinhampton in [my] holding and occupation are intended forthwith to be a place of religious worship and I require you to register the same and request a certificate thereof for which shall be taken no more than two shillings and sixpence. (GDR/344/131v)

1181 Minchinhampton. 6 June 1824 (5 July 1824). I certify that the premises occupied by Daniel Bingel in the parish of Minchinhampton will be hereafter a place of religious worship. 'Please to send it by the bearer'. Samuel Park, minister. (GDR/344/134v)

1182 Walls Quarry, Minchinhampton. 22 Mar 1825 (22 Mar 1825). I Robert Higginbottin of Walls Quarry in Minchinhampton certify that [a] house and premises at Walls Quarry in the parish of Minchinhampton in [my] holding and occupation are to be a place of religious worship and I request you to register the same, and request a certificate thereof for which shall be taken no more than two shillings and six pence. (GDR/350/36)

1183 Box, Minchinhampton. 17 Nov 1825 (18 Nov 1825). I James Harris of Box in the parish of 'Hampton' certify that my dwelling house and premises at Box in the parish of

Minchinhampton now in [my] holding and occupation are to be a place of religious worship and I request you to register the same, and request a certificate thereof for which shall be taken no more than two shillings and six pence. (GDR/350/49)

1184 Hyde Court, Minchinhampton. 22 Dec 1826 (30 Dec 1826). We [named below] with others in the parish of Minchinhampton and its vicinity, being desirous of enjoying according to our own views the worship of God among ourselves, have opened a room in a dwelling house at Hyde Court in the parish of Minchinhampton devoted to religious uses. This therefore our wish that your Lordship would order an entry to be made of the above-mentioned place of worship. B R Pilly, John Heskins, S E Francis, Joshua Dunn snr, John Balllinger, Joseph Wear. (GDR/350/61)

1185 Pinfarthing, Minchinhampton. 20 Dec 1828 (20 Dec 1828). I John [RG/31/2 has 'James'] Weels of Pinfarthing, in the parish of Minchinhampton, weaver, certify that my dwelling house in Pinfarthing is intended forthwith to be a place of religious worship and I require you to register the same. John Woodward, William Woodward. (GDR/350/97)

1186 Minchinhampton. 23 Dec 1831 (24 May 1832). We [named below] humbly desire the house wherein Richard Earle now resides in the parish of Minchinhampton be registered for a place of divine worship. Joseph Dunn, George Dickinson, Robert Daniells, Richard Earle, Samuel Hill, William Freeman, Samuel Hill, Peter Ford. (GDR/350/128) *Note.* The name Samuel Hill is written twice.

1187 Minchinhampton. 4 Sept 1835 (5 Sept 1835). *Wesleyan.* I Paul Orchard of the town of Stroud, Wesleyan minister, certify that a house in the town and parish of Minchinhampton is intended forthwith to be a place of religious worship and I require you to register the same and request a certificate thereof. (GDR/350/178)

1188 Minchinhampton. 19 Sept 1837. *Baptist.* We whose names are undersigned being residents in the parish of Minchinhampton certify that the building commonly called the Baptist Meeting-house in Tetbury Street in [the] town of Minchinhampton, in the holding of John Hopkins esq of Nailsworth and others as trustees, is to be a place of religious worship and I request you to register the same and request a certificate thereof for which shall be taken no more than two shillings and six pence. Joseph Dunn, Isaac Paine, Samuel Wood, Astin Franklin, Daniel Filpot, Francis Mayo. (GDR/350/217)

1189 Walls Quarry, Minchinhampton. 24 Apr 1838 (7 Sept 1838). *Primitive Methodist.* I Thomas Hill of Moor's Farm in the parish of Rodborough certify that a 'Chappel' and premises at Walls Quarry in the parish of MInchinhampton, now in the holding and occupation of the Primitive Methodist Society, are to be a place of religious worship and I request you to register the same and request a certificate thereof for which shall be taken no more than two shillings and six pence. (GDR/350/230)

1190 Box, Minchinhampton. 13 Oct 1841 (15 Oct 1841). [*Primitive Methodist: see* **254**]. I Joseph Preston of Brinkworth, Wilts, certify that a house and premises at Box in the parish of Minchinhampton, now in the holding and occupation of Ann Sansome, are to be a place of religious worship and I request you to register the same and request a certificate thereof for which shall be taken no more than two shillings and six pence. Witness George Oborn. (GDR/350/283)

1191 Minchinhampton. (6 July 1849). House in Watledge Lane belonging to Nathaniel Dean. James Willard Cummings [RG/31/2 has of Cheltenham]. (Q/RNp/4)

MINETY

Most of Minety formed a detached part of Gloucestershire until 1844 when it was transferred to Wiltshire. From 1836 the diocese of Gloucester and Bristol included some north Wiltshire parishes. The following two certificates registered in Gloucester diocesan records presumably relate to Minety in Gloucestershire.

1192 Minety. 18 Mar 1812 (26 Mar 1812). This is to certify that we [named below] intend to hold a meting for the worship of God in the dwelling house of Eli Cove in the parish of Minety and we pray that this certificate may be entered in your Lordship's Registry. George Moorhouse, James Ames, Eli Cove. (GDR/334B/354)
Note. See Wilts. MHC 730 where the RG return has been related to Minety, Wilts.

1193 Minety. 2 Mar 1822 (19 Apr 1822). We do hereby certify that a house at 'Minty' in Gloucestershire, now in the occupation of the Revd J W Lowrie, will henceforth be a place of religious worship. James Wr. Lowrie, William Stanly, John Hicks. (GDR/344/22r)
Note. See Wilts. MHC 999B where the RG return has been related to Minety in Wilts.

MINSTERWORTH

1194 Minsterworth. 1672. *Presbyterian.* Licence recorded 5 Sept 1672 for the house of Isaac Williams at Minsterworth. (LT/561)

1195 Minsterworth. 28 Dec 1814 (28 Dec 1814). I John Cullen of Gloucester, minister, certify that the house of William Pugh in the parish of Minsterworth is intended forthwith to be a place of religious worship and require you to register the same and request a certificate thereof. (GDR/334B/332)

1196 Over, Minsterworth. 24 Feb 1834 (24 Feb 1834). I James Grimes of the city of Gloucester certify that a dwelling house at Over in the parish of Minsterworth, occupied by William Preen, labourer, is intended to be forthwith a place of religious worship and I request you to register the same. James Grimes (GDR/350/146)

1197 Minsterworth. 20 Nov 1838 (20 Nov 1838). I William Viner Ellis the undersigned certify that a dwelling house in the parish of Minsterworth in the occupation of Mary Hawkins is forthwith to be a place of religious worship and I request you to register the same and request a certificate thereof. (GDR/350/234)

1198 Minsterworth. 18 Sept 1845 (18 Sept 1845). I John Hall of the parish of St John Baptist in the city of Gloucester certify that a Chapel recently erected in the parish of Minsterworth is intended forthwith to be a place of religious worship and I require you to register the same and request a certificate thereof. (GDR/350/361)

1199 Naight, Minsterworth. (26 Feb 1851). Room or building occupied by Richard Clifford. John Thurston. (Q/RNp/4)

MISERDEN

1200 The Camp, Miserden. 13 Jun 1797 (19 Jun 1797). We [named below] and others intend to use the dwelling house of Daniel Sellen at the Camp in the parish of 'Miserdine' as a place for the worship of Almighty God and request the same may be registered in your Lordship's court. Daniel Selten, W Jenkins, W Williams, William Pickersgill. (GDR/319A/253)

1201 Miserden. 12 Oct 1816 (19 Oct 1816). I William Shelmerdine of Stroud, minister, certify that the house of John Brooks in the parish of 'Miserdine' is forthwith to be a place of religious worship and require you to register the same and request a certificate thereof. (GDR/334B/311)

1202 Miserden. 12 Mar 1817 (18 Mar 1817). I John Rees, dissenting minister of Rodborough Tabernacle, certify that a dwelling house situated in a place called the Camp, occupied by William Ireland in the parish of Miserden, is to be forthwith used as a place of religious worship and require you to register the same. (GDR/334B/302)

1203 Camp, Miserden. 2 Jan 1818 (3 Jan 1818). I William Shelmerdine of Stroud, minister, certify that the house of Peter Herbert of the Camp in the parish of Miserden is intended forthwith to be used as a place of religious worship and require you to register the same and request a certificate thereof. (GDR/334B/288)

1204 Miserden. 29 Sept 1834 (4 Oct 1834). I Thomas Davis of Winstone, gentleman, certify that a building or meeting-house at the Camp in the parish of Miserden, belonging to Peter Herbert, is intended forthwith to be a place of religious worship and I require you to register the same. Witness Peter Herbert jnr. (GDR/350/157)

MITCHELDEAN

1205 Mitcheldean. 19 Nov 1715. [*Independent: see note*]. Owen Davis, dissenting preacher at 'Michel Deane', took oaths of allegiance and supremacy. (Q/SO/4/[4])
Note. Owen Davis, Independent minister, listed in Mitcheldean and Abenhall in Evans list. *See* **127**.

1206 Mitcheldean. 19 Apr 1728. [*Independent: see note*]. These are to certify you that [dissenters] intend to hold a meeting for the worship of God in their way in the dwelling house of Mr Samuel Philips, minister in the town of Mitcheldean and pray it may be registered. William Lodge, Jacob Lumbard, Godfrey Fownes. (GDR/279a/194)
Note. First use of the word 'registered' rather than 'recorded'. Horlick, *A visit to the Forest of Dean* stated that Mitcheldean Independent chapel, Mr Philips, minister, was the most ancient dissenting interest in the Forest. *But see* **1205**.

1207 Mitcheldean. 12 May 1775. *Independent*.
Note. Householders in Mitcheldean included in this certificate but meeting place in Ruardean. *See next entry and Ruardean* **1486** *for text.*

1208 Mitcheldean. 7 Jan 1782 (registered Epiphany 1782, Q/SO/10/f.38r). *Independent*.
Note. Householders in Mitcheldean included in this certificate but meeting place in Ruardean. *See previous entry and Ruardean* **1487** *for text.*

1209 Mitcheldean. 11 Dec 1797 (13 Dec 1797). We [named below] require that the house of John Powell of 'Michael Deane' be licensed for the purpose of divine worship. John Powell, John Milles, William Griffiths, William Pearce. (GDR/319A/259-60)

1210 Mitcheldean. 27 Aug 1816 (20 Sept 1816). *Wesleyan Methodist.* I Abraham Watmough [RG/31/2 has 'Whatmough'] of Newent, minister of the Gospel, certify that a chapel or building in the parish of Mitcheldean, belonging to the Wesleyan Methodists, is intended forthwith to be a place of religious worship and require you to register the same and request a certificate thereof. (GDR/334B/313)

1211 Mitcheldean. 28 Jan 1824 (26 Feb 1824). I Edward Howe of 'Michel Dean' certify that my dwelling house and appurtenances thereto belonging is intended forthwith to be a place of religious worship and I require you to register the same and request a certificate thereof. (GDR/344/129r)
Note. Spelling of date: 'twenty heightth' January 1824.

1212 Mitcheldean. (12 Jan 1847). *Independent* chapel. John Horlick [RG/31/2 has 'of Ruardean']. (Q/RNp/4)
Note. For John Horlick *see* Introduction and **1489**. [*see* illus., xvii]

MORETON VALENCE

1213 Moreton Valence. 23 Sept 1741. These are to certify your Lordship that some [dissenters] intend to hold a meeting for the worship of God in the house of William Fowler, called Moreton Hill Farm, in the parish of Moreton Valence. We therefore pray it may be registered. Martin Lloyd, Joseph Everard, Jacob Lumbard, Nathaniel Brock. (GDR/284/117)
Note. For Joseph Everard *see* **197**.

1214 Moreton Valence. 30 Nov 1805 (30 Nov 1805). *Independent.* We [named below] certify that a house in the occupation of Joseph Haithorne in the parish of 'Moreton Vallence' in the hundred of Whitstone is intended to be a place of religious worship by [dissenters] of the Independent denomination and we request that it may be registered and a certificate granted accordingly. William Richardson, minister, Thomas Vick, Joseph Haithorne, John Pope. (GDR/334B/429)

1215 Moreton Valence. (20 Dec 1810). We [named below] certify that a house in the occupation of Joel Ford in the parish of 'Morton Valence' is intended to be used as as a place of religious worship and we request that it may be registered and a certificate granted accordingly. William Richardson, Joel Ford, William Ravenhill, John Reynolds. (GDR/334B/369)

1216 Epney, Moreton Valence. 17 Oct 1846 (28 Oct 1846) [registered 20 Oct 1846, Q/RNp/4]. I William Longney of the parish of Longney certify that a dwelling house at Epney in the parish of Moreton Valance, occupied by William Davis, mariner, is intended to be forthwith a place of religious worship and I require you to register the same. (GDR/350/381)

MORETON-IN-MARSH
Moreton-in-Marsh was a chapelry in Bourton-on-the-Hill parish.
1217 Moreton-in-Marsh. 28 Apr 1796 (13 May 1796; registration GDR/319A/234-5). We [named below, dissenters] certify that a building in the town of Moreton in the Marsh, late in occupation of Thomas Keen, is appropriated and set apart for divine worship by a number of dissenters and we request that the same may be entered. John Proctor, Samuel Rawlings, William Rawlings, Samuel Callow, George Newman, William Mayo, Edward Churchill. Endorsed 'copy of cert'. (GDR/N2/1)
Note. Certificate crossed through.

1218 Moreton-in-Marsh. 30 June 1817 (5 July 1817). *Independent.* I John Mann, dissenting minister of Moreton in the Marsh, certify that my school in [Moreton] is intended forthwith to be used as a place of religious worship by a congregation of the Independent denomination, and I request you to register the same. J Mann, S Rawlings, J Horne. (GDR/334B/295)

1219 Moreton-in-Marsh. 29 Sept 1817 (3 Oct 1817). *Independent.* I John Mann, dissenting minister of Moreton in the Marsh, certify that a new meeting-house in the parish is intended forthwith to be a place of religious worship by a congregation of the Independent denomination, and require you to register the same. J Mann, Edward Careless, Samuel Rawlings. (GDR/334B/293-2)
Note. Ink marks over Edward Careless's name are probably from closing the book with the ink wet.

1220 Moreton-in-Marsh. 2 Nov 1831 (19 Nov 1831). I Joseph Joiner of Moreton-in-Marsh certify that my house and premises at Moreton-in-Marsh, now in [my] holding and occupation, are intended to be forthwith a place of religious worship and I request you to register the same and request a certificate thereof for which shall be taken no more than two shillings and six pence. Joseph Joiner (mark), Boaz Tripp, Thomas Keen, George Wheeler. (GDR/350/121-2)

1221 Moreton-in-Marsh. 11 July 1836. I James Baker of Chipping Norton certify that a dwelling house in the occupation of John Jewell is forthwith to be a place of religious worship and require you to register the same and request a certificate thereof. (GDR/350/198)

1222 Moreton-in-Marsh. 22 Oct 1846 (22 Oct 1846). I Joseph Lander, dissenting minister, certify that a tenement in the parish of Moreton in the occupation of George Davis, is intended forthwith to be a place of religious worship and I require you to register the same. (GDR/350/382)

NAILSWORTH

Nailsworth was a settlement on the edge of the parishes of Avening, Horsley and Minchinhampton, and certificates which relate to Nailsworth may possibly be found under those parishes. Nailsworth parish was created in 1892 All registrations naming Nailsworth are collected here..

1223 Nailsworth. 1672. *Presbyterian.* Application for licence to Mr John Fox for a barn belonging to Mr Crag in Hornisham in Wiltshire, a barn in Nailsworth (LT noted this entry was 'At the back [of a sheet with entries for elsewhere in the country] written the reverse way'); record 12 Apr 1672 of the barn of - - in 'Nailesworth' licensed to be a Presbyterian meeting place'. (LT/223, 430)

Note. A second record covered the licence application for Mr Cray's house in Hornisham, Mr John Fox in Marshfield a general licence, and a house in Nailsworth. (LT/255)

1224 Nailsworth. (Easter 1690). *Quaker.* Meeting-house. (Q/SO/3/522) [*see* illus., xii]

1225 Nailsworth [RG/31/6 has only Avening]. (Michaelmas 1705). An house formerly built for Quakers. (Q/SO/3/521)

1226 Nailsworth [RG/31/6 has only Avening]. (Trinity 1708). *Presbyterian.* Thomas Small's house. (Q/SO/3/520)

1227 Nailsworth [RG/31/6 has only Avening]. (Trinity 1708). *Presbyterian.* Where Dr Giles dwelt. (Q/SO/3/520)

1228 Nailsworth [RG/31/6 has only Avening]. (Trinity 1708). *Presbyterian.* George Small's house. (Q/SO/3/520)

1229 Nailsworth. 6 Dec 1715. [*Independent: see note*]. Joseph Allen of Nailsworth, dissenting preacher, took oaths of allegiance and supremacy. (Q/SO/4/[8])

Note. Joseph 'Allein' listed as Independent minister in Evans list.

1230 Nailsworth, Avening. 7 Jan 1754. *Independent.* These are to certify your Lordship that some dissenting Independent subjects intend to hold a meeting for the worship of Almighty God at the house of John Croome's in Nailsworth in the parish of Avening and therefore we pray your Lordship that the said house may be duly registered. Edward Shipway, Thomas Stanly, Henry Restall, John Hooper. (GDR/284/232)

1231 The Corner, Nailsworth, Horsley. 30 Mar 1770. 'We [named below] do humbly petition the Reverend Father the Lord Bishop of Gloucester to grant us licence and leave for to meet in the dwelling house of Samuel Warner, built with stone and timber, in the place called the Corner in Nailsworth in the parish of Horsley for a meeting-house for some of His Majesty's protestant dissenters to worship God according to the direction of their conscience and the Act of Toleration in that case made.' Daniel Clift, Matthew Archer, Nathaniel Browning, Joseph Ricketts (mark), Caleb Brooke, Thomas Gazzard, John Dyer (mark). (GDR/292A/139)
Note. Date in rubric but not in certificate nor in RG/31/2.

1232 Nailsworth, Minchinhampton. 18 Mar 1797 (21 Mar 1797). This is to certify that a house in the occupation of William Boggs at Nailsworth in the parish of Minchinhampton is intended to be used as a place of worship and request it may be registered in your Lordship's court. William Boggs, minister, William Boggs, occupier, George Thomas, James Thomas. (GDR 319A/251)

1233 Nailsworth, Horsley. 12 Feb 1818 (16 Feb 1818). I William Davis of Nailsworth in the parish of Horsley, dyer, certify that my dwelling house in Nailsworth in the parish of Horsley is intended forthwith to be used as a place of religious worship and I require you to register the same. (GDR/334B/284)

1234 Nailsworth, Avening. 25 February 1822 (26 Feb 1822). We certify that a house at Nailsworth in the parish of Avening (erected for the purpose) will be henceforth a place of religious worship and we request that it may be registered. Thomas Edkins, James Thomas, James Thomas. (GDR/344/18v)
Note. James Thomas's name recorded twice.

1235 Nailsworth. 7 June 1826 (7 June 1826). *Unitarian.* I Henry Edward 'House' [Howse] jnr of the city of Bath, Secretary of the Somerset, Gloucestershire and Wiltshire Unitarian Missionary Association, certify that the dwelling house of Thomas Sweet in Nailsworth is intended forthwith to be a place of religious worship and I require you to register the same and request a certificate thereof. H E Howse jnr. (GDR/350/57)
Note. The certifier's name is written here as 'House' but 'Howse' in signature and subsequent entries.

1236 Nailsworth. 30 June 1827 (2 July 1827). I Thomas Smith, joiner and cabinet maker, certify that a room in the house in which I reside in Nailsworth is intended forthwith to be a place of religious worship and require you to register the same and request a certificate thereof. Witness Matt Harding, Thomas Smith. (GDR/350/67)

1237 Nailsworth. 12 Jan 1841 (12 Jan 1841). I the undersigned Thomas Sampson of Nailsworth, grocer, certify that a messuage in Nailsworth, late in the occupation of William Ball, is used and is intended to be used as a place of religious worship and I request you to register the same and request a certificate thereof for which shall be taken no more than two shillings and six pence. (GDR/350/271)

1238 Nailsworth, Avening. 10 Apr 1843 (11 Apr 1843). I David Apperley of Cainscross, clothier, certify that a messuage at Nailsworth in the parish of Avening, in the occupation of Mrs Holmes, is intended to be a place of religious worship and I request you to register the same and request a certificate thereof for which shall be taken no more than two shillings and six pence. (GDR/350/318)

NAUNTON

1239 Naunton. 2 Jan 1779 (9 Jan 1779). His Majesty's protestant dissenting subjects do hereby certify that we intend to hold a meeting for the worship of Almighty God in the dwelling house of Robert Rowland, taylor, in the parish of Naunton and therefore pray that this certificate may be registered. William Rowland, John Steel (mark), Richard Reynolds, John Hanks, John Preston, Joseph Hitchman, Robert Hanks, George Wood, Samuel Perry, William Fox. (GDR/292A/214)

1240 Naunton. 26 Jun 1784 (3 July 1784; registration GDR/292A/261). We [named below] certify to your lordship that we intend to meet for the worship of Almighty God in the dwelling house of Richard Reynolds, blacksmith, in the parish of Naunton and pray that this certficate may be registered. Samuel Fox, Robert Hanks, Jeremiah Cresser, William Hitchman, John Steel, Robert Parry, Richard Dalby, Barnabas Collett, John Hanks, Thomas Henderson, Samuel Eldridge. (GDR/N2/1)
Note. One of a bundle of five certificates, all very worn and crossed through.

1241 Naunton. 26 Oct 1797 (3 Nov 1797). We [named below] certify that we intend to meet for the worship of Almighty God in a house erected by us for this purpose in the parish of Naunton and therefore pray that this certificate may be registered. William Fox, Robert Rowland sen., John Reynolds, Samuel Palmer, William Portlock, William Rowland, Joseph Combs, John Buller, Edward Reynolds, Thomas Biddle, James Savery, Robert Noyse, William Wood, Edward Wood, William Wilkins, Thomas Stait, Samuel Etheridge, Robert Pinchin, Henry Collett, James Goodman. (GDR/319A/256)

1242 Naunton. 18 Jan 1830 (18 Jan 1830). I James Smith of Cheltenham certify that a dwelling house in the parish of Naunton occupied by Charles Hicks, labourer, is intended to be forthwith a place of religious worship and I request you to register the same. (GDR/350/107)

1243 Naunton. 20 Mar 1841 (Mar 1841). *Methodist.* I James Lancaster of Chipping Norton, Oxon., certify that the house of Stephen Stiles In the parish of Naunton is forthwith to be a place of religious worship and require you to register the same and request a certificate thereof. James Lancaster, Methodist minister. (GDR/350/278)

1244 Naunton. 16 Mar 1846 (20 Mar 1846). I William Everiss of Cheltenham certify that a dwelliing house at Naunton, occupied by John Buller, is intended to be forthwith a place of religious worship and I request you to register the same. (GDR/350/374)

NEWENT

1245 Newent. 20 Apr 1779 (28 Apr 1779). We intend to meet and assemble on the 29th day of April now instant for the public worship of Almighty God in a dwelling house in Newent, now in the occupation of Mary Ballinger, and that such dwelling house is intended to be set apart for the same purpose in future, which we desire may be registered in your Lordship's office. William Beale, James Prosser, William Morgan, Samuel Warburton, John Malvern, Thomas Wood. (GDR/292A/220)
Note. Date specified for first meeting.

1246 Newent. (12 Apr 1792). These are to certify that we [named below] with others intend to hold a meeting for the worship of Almighty God in a building in Culver Street in the town of Newent and pray it may be registered. Richard Cue, Michel Baldwin, James Vaughan, Danniel Baldwin, Benjamin Acton, George Jaynes, William Jones, James Prosser. (GDR/319A/134-5)

1247 Newent. 27 Mar 1805 (11 Apr 1805). [*Methodist: see* **166**]. We [named below] have set apart a house, the property of Mr Thomas Warne in Culver Street, Newent, for the worship of Almighty God and request it may be registered. Thomas Dayer, William Davis, George Bradley, William Gatfield, J M Byron, minister, R Connibere [Conibere], Thomas Fearnley, Samuel Jeffs. [Noted at the bottom] 'Registered 1 April 1805 in the Consistory Court of the bishop by me Thomas Rudge Registrar'. [In pencil on the back, not very distinct:] 'J Padfield Birtsmorton bank.' (GDR/334B/432)

Note. GA D2689/1/5/1 appears to be an original certificate, preserved amongst the records of the Gloucester Methodist Circuit. The date of registration recorded on the certificate is 1 April but the diocesan record is clearly 11 April. The same house was registered again under date 19 May 1808, with a different set of certifiers. See following entry.

1248 Newent. 6 May 1808 (19 May 1808). We [named below] have set apart a house the property of Mr Thomas Warne in Culver Street, Newent, for the worship of Almighty God and request it may be registered. Jer. Brettell, William Gatfield, Charles Malvern, Elizabeth Warne, Sarah Peters, Leda Hope. (GDR/334B/416)

1249 Newent. 24 Apr 1816 (25 Apr 1816). [*Methodist, see* **179**]. I Daniel Campbell of Gloucester, minister, certify that the house of William Nelms in the parish of Newent is intended forthwith to be a place of religious worship and require you to register the same and request a certificate thereof. (GDR/334B/319)

1250 Newent. 3 Dec 1818 (12 Dec 1818). I Richard Allen, minister of the Gospel, of Newent, certify that a house in the occupation of Daniel Robins, cordwainer, in the town of Newent is intended forthwith to be a place of religious worship and require you to register the same and request a certificate thereof. (GDR/334B/270)

1251 Clifford's Mine [Mesne], Newent. 11 Mar 1819 (13 Mar 1819). I Richard Allen of Newent certify that a room belonging to Thomas Warn of Newent, situate in Cliffords Mine in the parish of Newent, is intended forthwith to be a place of religious worship and require you to register the same and request a certificate thereof. (GDR/334B/265)

Note. Clifford's Mesne or Mine wood adjoined Clifford's Mesne on the lower slopes of May Hill. *VCH Glos* 12, 10.

1252 Newent. 26 Feb 1819 (24 Mar 1819). [*Baptist: see* **648**]. I William Williams, dissenting minister of Ryeford [Herefordshire], certify that a certain messuage, now in the occupation of Samuel Baldwin, woodcutter, in the parish of Newent, is intended forthwith to be a place of religious worship and require you to register the same. William Williams, James Hart. (GDR/334B/264)

1253 Newent. 15 Apr 1819 (17 Apr 1819). [*Baptist: see* **648**]. I John Williams of Ryeford [Herefordshire] [RG/31/2 has of Newent], dissenting minister, certify that a messuage now in the occupation of Mr Samuel Reynolds in Culver Street in the parish of Newent is intended forthwith to be a place of religious worship and require you to register the same. William Williams, James Bethill. (GDR/334B/263)

1254 Brand Green, Newent. 8 Mar 1820 (9 Mar 1820). *Methodist.* I Richard Allen, Methodist preacher of the Ledbury Circuit certify that a house at 'Bran Green' in the parish of Newent, occupied by John Davies, is intended forthwith to be a place of religious worship and require you to register the same and request a certificate thereof. (GDR/334B/245)

1255 Malswick, Newent. 14 Sept 1820 (16 Sept 1820). I William Nelmes, labourer, of Malswick in the parish of Newent certify that a room in the possession of William

Richardson in the parish of Newent is intended forthwith to be a place of religious worship and require you to register the same and request a certificate thereof. (GDR/334B/233)

1256 Brand Green, Newent. 14 Sept 1820 (16 Sept 1820). I Thomas Wood, labourer, of Brand Green in the parish of Newent certify that my dwelling house in the parish of Newent is intended forthwith to be a place of religious worship and require you to register the same and request a certificate thereof. 'T W'. (GDR/334B/233)

1257 Gorseley, Newent. 25 Nov 1823 (28 Nov 1823). *Baptist.* I Thomas Jones of 'Gorsely', Baptist minister, certify that a dwelling house in the occupation of Benjamin Jones, Excise Officer, in the parish of Newent is intended forthwith to be a place of religious worship and I require you to register the same. (GDR/344/119r)

1258 Newent. 16 Oct 1824 (16 Oct 1824). I George Jones, minister of the Gospel of the town of Newent, certify a dwelling house, occupied by Benjamin Deakin in the town of Newent, waterman, is intended forthwith to be a place of religious worship and I require you to register the same, and request a certificate thereof. (GDR/344/138v)

1259 Newent. 1825 (19 Mar 1825). I James Webb of the town of Newent certify that a dwelling house, occupied by Benjamin Hodges in the parish of Newent, labourer, is intended forthwith to be a place of religious worship and I require you to register the same, and request a certificate thereof. (GDR/350/35)

1260 Newent. 24 Aug 1825 (7 Sept 1825). I Robert Winfield, minister of the Gospel of the town of Newent, certify that a chapel, the property of James Webb, nail manufacturer of Newent, is intended forthwith to be a place of religious worship, and I require you to register the same, and request a certificate thereof. (GDR/350/44)

1261 Newent. 25 Feb 1828 (26 Feb 1828). I, G H Roper Curzon, certify that the dwelling house of Mary Drinkwater in the parish of Newent is intended forthwith to be a place of religious worship, and I require you to register the same. G H Roper Curzon, Mary Drinkwater. (GDR/350/84)

1262 Newent. 2 Oct 1829 (10 Oct 1829). I John Glass, minister, certify that a dwelling, now in the occupation of John Tranter in the parish of Newent, is intended forthwith to be a place of religious worship, and I require you to register the same and request a certificate thereof. John Glass, John Tranter (mark). (GDR/350/105)

1263 Brand Green, Newent. 1 Dec 1835 (1 Dec 1835). I Thomas Kington of the Hill in the parish of 'Castle Froome', Herefordshire, certify that the house of William Davis and premises at 'Bran Green' in the parish of Newent, now in [his] holding and occupation, are intended to be a place of religious worship, and require you to register the same and request a certificate thereof for which shall be taken no more than two shillings and six pence. (GDR/350/184)
Note. This certificate was entered twice in the Act Book, identically worded.

1264 Kent's Green, Newent. 20 Feb 1836 (20 Feb 1836). I Thomas Kington of the Hill in the parish of 'Castle Froome', Herefordshire, certify that the house of Richard Lewis and premises at 'Pent Kents Green' in the parish of Newent, now in [his] holding and occupation, are intended to be a place of religious worship and I request you to register the same and request a certificate thereof for which shall be taken no more than two shillings and six pence. (GDR/350/190)

1265 Kilcot, Newent. 18 Mar 1836 (19 Mar 1836). I Thomas Kington of the Hill in the parish of 'Castle Froome', Herefordshire, certify that the house of William Peart and premises at 'Killcot' in the parish of Newent, now in [his] holding and occupation, are intended to be a place of religious worship, and require you to register the same and request a certificate thereof for which shall be taken no more than two shillings and six pence. (GDR/350/193)
Note. Kilcot was a tithing of Newent.

1266 Newent. 7 Sept 1844 (7 Sept 1844). I Joseph Hyatt of the city of Gloucester certify that a room, lately used as schoolroom by Abraham Lauder, teacher, and being the property of William Nicholls, carpenter, in the parish of Newent, is intended to be forthwith a place of religious worship and I request you to register the same. (GDR/350/347)

1267 Newent. (11 May 1848). House occupied by Nicholas Eyzingbarth, Church Street, Newent. James Bayliss [RG/31/2 has of Cheltenham]. (Q/RNp/4)

1268 Clifford's Mesne, Newent. (10 May 1851). House or building occupied by James Apperley. James Bayliss. (Q/RNp/4)

NEWINGTON BAGPATH
Bagpath was a separate estate joined with Newington to form the parish. Part was associated with Kingscote, which see, a chapelry in Beverstone parish; Owlpen, which see, was a chapelry in Newington Bagpath.
1269 Bagpath [Newington Bagpath]. 8 Jan 1806 (22 Feb 1806). We [named below, dissenters] in the parish of Bagpath and its neighbourhood, 'are desirious of using the liberty of our own conveniences in religious worship and we have for this purpose engaged the house of Richard Webb, labourer, which house we intend applying to the aforesaid use (that is to say) as much of it as is called the kitchen, and we therefore wish your Lordship would order the regular entry in your court of the above mentioned apartment according to the authorized liberty of His Majesty's dissenting subjects for the use here specified and none others.' Nathaniel Lloyd, Richard Webb, William Austin, Josh Evans, William Body, James Woodward, William Martin, Daniel Lloyd. (GDR/334B/428)

1270 Newington Bagpath, Kingscote. 30 Mar 1844 (1 Apr 1844). I Robert Moore of Sherston Magna, Wiltshire, certify that a house and premises at Newington Bagpath in the parish of Kingscote, now in the holding and occupationn of Moses Boddey, are intended to be a place of religious worship and I request you to register the same and request a certificate thereof for which shall be taken no more than two shillings and six pence. (GDR/350/338)

NEWLAND
The parish was formed before 1200 out of assarts in the Forest, and consisted of 22 detached parts as well as three larger ones, the centres of the tithings of Coleford, Newland and Clearwell. Coleford has been separately listed, see above. Clearwell, though larger than Newland village and with a small part, Clearwell Meend, in Dean Forest, was largely in Newland parish and is included here. Other places where a dissenting meeting was noted, in detached settlements nominally in Newland, or in settlements with some parts in the Forest, are placed with extra-parochial areas under Dean Forest. Minor settlements may not always have been named. See Dean Forest: Bream and Bream's Eaves, Ellwood, Joyford, Pillowell, Whitecroft, Yorkley.
1271 [Clearwell, Newland]. 1672. *Congregational.* Application by Owen Davies for a licence to 'John Skiner' [Skinner] preacher at his own house in 'Clonwell'; licence

recorded 10 June 1672 for the house of 'John Skiner' in 'Clanwell', Gloucester Congregational Meeting Place and for 'John Skiner' to be a Congregational teacher in his house in 'Clonwell'; licence received by Owen Davies 12 June 1672. (LT/380, 401, 507) *Note.* A comment in LT/3, 839 claims this was a Baptist meeting. John Skinner may be the man who signed two letters in 1653, one to Oliver Cromwell on behalf of the Gathered Churches of Herefordshire and Gloucestershire, and specifically for Weston-under-Penyard, and included three signatories for Dymock, and another to a church in Hexham, signed amongst others by William Skinner 'for the church baptized in the Forest of Dean'. (Stanley (1912) 117-20; *VCH Glos* 5, 396). He was an ejected minister.

1272 Newland. Epiphany, 10 Jan 1715/16. Thomas Lane, lecturer of Newland, took oaths of allegiance and supremacy. (Q/SO/4/[12])

1273 Newland. (7 Aug 1811). We [named below] humbly request to cause to be registered the dwelling house of William Blanch in the parish of Newland as set apart for the purpose of the worship of Almighty God by certain dissenters. William Blanch, William Trotter, George Dow, Benjamin Greening, Anne Dell [possibly her mark above name] in the presence of D Phillips and Thomas Turner. (GDR/334B/363)

1274 Newland. (7 Aug 1811). We [named below] humbly request [the Bishop etc] to cause to be registered the dwelling house of Richard Jones in the parish of Newland as set apart for the purpose of the worship of Almighty God by certain dissenters. Richard Jones, Roger Hopkins, James Powell, Martha Trotter, in the presence of D Phillips and J Bigham. (GDR/334B/362)

1275 Redbrook, Newland. 4 Dec 1811 (6 Dec 1811). We [named below] desire to have registered for the public worship of Almighty God a room in the occupation of John Tyler situated in Redbrook in the parish of Newland. William Woodall, John Tyler, John Bell, John Deverell. (GDR/334B/358)

1276 Newland. 15 Mar 1813 (16 Mar 1813). We [named below] have set apart and appropriated for the public worship of Almighty God a room in the occupation of Timothy Smith, situated in Clay Lane in the parish of Newland. William Woodall, Thomas Nash, James Smith, John Tyler. (GDR/334B/348)

1277 Newland. 22 Dec 1814 (2 Jan 1815). *Methodist.* This is to certify that [in] the house of Jeptha James in the parish of Newland the religious worship of Almighty God is intended to be preformed by those commonly called Methodists and we request that the same may be registered. John James, William Kear, Joseph Priest, George James. (GDR/334B/332)

1278 Newland. 28 Nov 1815 (5 Jan 1816). *Wesleyan Methodist.* This is to certify that [in] a vacant house near 'Lidney', belonging to John James esq., in the parish of Newland, the religious worship of Almighty God is intended to be performed by [dissenters] commonly called Methodists, and we require that the same may be registered. William Brocklehurst, William Edwards, John Tyler, Philip Tyler. (GDR/334B/323)

1279 Newland. 30 Oct 1818 (9 Nov 1818). *Baptist.* We [named below] certify that a dwelling house at Five Acres in the parish of Newland, in the occupation of Mr John Worgan, is intended to be used occasionally as a place of religious worship by dissenters of the denomination of Baptists, and request that this certificate may be registered. George Harris, James Trotter, Thomas Turner. (GDR/334B/272)

1280 Clearwell, Newland. 30 Oct 1818 (9 Nov 1818) *Baptist.* We [named below] certify that a dwelling house at Clearwell in the parish of Newland, in the occupation of Mr John

Trotter snr, is intended to be used occasionally as a place of religious worship by dissenters of the denomination of Baptists, and we request that this certificate maybe registered. James Teague, Peter Teague, George Trotter. (GDR/334B/273)

1281 Newland. 30 Oct 1818 (9 Nov 1818). *Baptist.* We [named below] certify that a certain dwelling house situated at 'Wainalls Hill' [RG31/2 has Winnalls Hill] in the parish of Newland, in the occupation of Mr John Trotter, is to be used occasionally as a place of religious worship by dissenters of the denomination of Baptists, and request that this certificate may be registered. John Fry, John Trotter, James Thomas. (GDR/334B/272)

Note. VCH Glos 5, 135 notes that Wynols Hill House [or Winnals Hill House], where John Trotter lived, was in Coleford. *See also* **1280** above.

1282 Clearwell, Newland. 20 Nov 1818 (21 Nov 1818). I John Fry, minister of the town of 'Colford', certify that a dwelling house at Clearwell in the parish of Newland, in the occupation of William Constant, is intended forthwith to be a place of religious worship and require you to register the same. (GDR/334B/271)

1283 Lower Redbrook, Newland. 4 Jan 1819 (29 Jan 1819). *Wesleyan.* I Joseph Hunt of Monmouth, Wesleyan minister, certify that the school room belonging to Henry Pewtner in Lower Redbrook in the parish of Newland is intended forthwith to be a place of religious worship and require you to register the same and require a certificate thereof. Joseph Hunt, Henry Pewtner, John Vale, Thomas Jones. (GDR/334B/269)

Note. The Wesleyan chapel was a converted barkhouse. *See VCH Glos* 5, plate 33.

1284 Clearwell, Newland. 3 Aug 1819 (6 Aug 1819). I John Fry, minister of Coleford, certify that a dwelling house at Clearwell in the parish of Newland, in the occupation of Joseph Beachs, is intended forthwith to be a place of religious worship and I request you to register the same. (GDR/334B/256)

1285 Newland. 28 Apr 1820 (6 May 1820). I William Evans, of Coleford Lane in the tithing of Coleford, certify that my dwelling house, in the parish of Newland, is intended forthwith to be a place of religious worship and require you to register the same and request a certificate thereof. (GDR/334B/243)

1286 Whitecliff, Newland. 3 Mar 1826 (9 Mar 1826). [*Congregational: see* **671**]. I John Parkyn, minister, certify that a dwelling in 'White Clift' in the parish of Newland, in the occupation of Samuel Steel, is intended forthwith to be a place of religious worship and require you to register the same and request a certificate thereof. Samuel Steel (mark), John Parkyn. (GDR/350/52)

1287 Newland. 24 Apr 1827 (5 July 1827). I George Morgan of Weatcroft in the hundred of St Briavels certify that my dwelling house in the parish of Newland is intended forthwith to be a place of religious worship and I require you to register the same and request a certificate thereof. Witness James Johnson, Joshua Harrison. (GDR/350/68)

NEWNHAM

1288 Newnham. 20 Nov 1792 (20 Nov 1792). We the underwritten certify that we and some others intend to hold a meeting for the worship of Almighty God in a house of Sarah Leonards in the town and parish of Newnham and we desire it may be registered in your court. David Williams, John Hartland, William Playne, Samuel Playne. (GDR/319A/143)

1289 Newnham. 20 Jan 1797 (20 Jan 1797) [*Countess of Huntingdon's Connexion: see note*]. We [named below] request your Lordship to cause to be registered a house belonging to John Adey in the parish of Newnham for the worship of Almighty God. Robert McAll, minister, John Adey, Samuel Daniell, William Dyer. (GDR/319A/248)

Note. Robert McAll was a minister of the Countess of Huntingdon's Connexion. See also **641**.

1290 Newnham. 13 Nov 1814 (14 Nov 1814). [*Wesleyan connexion: see note*]. I John Wright of Newent, minister, certify that the house of John and Sarah Marshall in the town and parish of Newnham is intended forthwith to be used as a place of religious worship and I require you to register the same and request a certificate thereof. (GDR/334B/334)

Note. RG/31/2 gives St Briavels as the place for a certificate with this date and certifier. Bright, 6, suggests this house was licensed for the Wesleyan Connexion.

1291 Newnham. 30 May 1822 (1 June 1822). I Thomas Stevenson, dissenting minister, certify that the dwelling house occupied by John Hall at Harem in the parish of Newnham is intended forthwith to be a place for religious worship and I require that you will register the same. (GDR/344/31v)

Note. Certificate signed at Ebley. 'Harem', possibly The Haie, or Hall Farm, but Bright, 6, suggests it was a house in the neighbourhood of what was (c. 1953) Arams Farm.

1292 Newnham. 28 June 1823 (2 July 1823). May it please your Lordship, I Isaac Bridgman of the parish of Ruardean respectfully inform your Lordship that a house in the lower part of the town and parish of Newnham, now in the possession of Mr. Nicholas Hawkey, is to be henceforth a place of religious worship and I respectfully request that the same be duly entered into the Registry of your Lordship's diocese. (GDR/344/109v)

Note. Rubric refers to Ruardean. For Isaac Bridgman *see* **210**.

1293 Newnham. 21 Nov 1823 (22 Nov 1823). I Isaac Bridgman, now residing at the Wood Side Cottage near Blakeney , certify that a house, now in the occupation of Mr. John Thomas, in the town and parish of Newnham is intended forthwith to be a place of religious worship and I require you to register and request a certificate thereof. (GDR/344/119r)

Note. For Isaac Bridgman *see* **210**.

1294 Newnham. 9 Sept 1825 (9 Sept 1825). We [named below] certify that a building or dwelling house in the occupation of Mr John Niblett, Main Street, in the parish of 'Newnham upon Severn', is intended forthwith to be a place of worship and we request you to register the same. David Frain, minister; John Niblett occupier; William Clark witness. (GDR/350/45)

1295 Newnham. 16 Oct 1825 (18 Oct 1825). We [named below] certify that a building or dwelling house in the occupation of Mr Joseph Thomas, farmer, in the parish of Newnham, is intended forthwith to be a place of religious worship and we request you to register the same. David Frain, minister; Joseph Thomas, occupier; William Clark, witness. (GDR/350/48)

1296 Newnham. 3 Aug 1826 (4 Aug 1826). I William Bishop, minister in the city of Gloucester and trustee of the chapel now erected in the road which leads from Newnham to Little Dean, in the occupation as trustees of Revd William Bishop, Revd John Lewis, Revd John Burder, Revd Thomas Edkins and others, [certify that it] is intended forthwith to be a place of religious worship and I desire you to register the same. (GDR/350/56)

Note. For John Burder *see* **292 & 1655**.

1297 Newnham. 29 Mar 1838 (29 Mar 1838). *Wesleyan*. I William Moss of Gloucester certify that the house of Daniel Harding, labourer, in the parish and town of Newnham, is forthwith to be a place of religious worship and require you to register the same and request a certificate thereof. Thomas Moss, Weslyan minister. (GDR/350/220)

Note. Names of certifier and signature are different.

NORTH CERNEY

1298 North Cerney. 27 July 1808 (28 July 1808). This is to certfy that we [named below] intend to hold a meeting for the worship of Almighty God in the dwelling house of John Trinder in the parish of North Cerney. We pray that this certificate may be entered. Thomas Broadsmith, William Dyke, John Trinder, William Tynson, Daniel Belcher (mark), Giles Tombs. (GDR/334B/415)

1299 Calmsden, North Cerney. 12 Oct 1811 (14 Oct 1811). *Independent.* This is to certify that a house in the occupation of Thomas Fry in the village of 'Calmsdown' in the parish of North Cerney is intended 'to be a licence' as a place of public worship of dissenters of the Independent denomination. We request that the house may be registered. Stephen Phillips, minister; T Fry occupier; Timothy Barnes, William Price, William Palmer. (GDR/334B/361-60)

1300 North Cerney. 19 Apr 1816 (20 Apr 1816). I Henry Hawkins of Eastcomb in the parish of Bisley certify that a certain building or kitchen in the parish of North Cerney is intended forthwith to be a place of religious worship and require you to register the same. Witness Daniel White. (GDR/334B/319)

1301 Woodmancote, North Cerney. (9 Jan 1841). I Peter Herbert of Chalford, Bisley, printer's joiner, certify that a building at Woodmancote in the parish of North Cerney, in the occupation of Joseph Dickes, is to be used as a chapel for religious worship and I request that this certificate may be registered in your Lordship's court. (GDR/350/270)

NORTH NIBLEY

1302 [?North] Nibley. (Michaelmas 1691). 'Nibley', John Burroughs house. (Q/SO/3/522)

1303 North Nibley. 21 Apr 1744. *Baptist.* Some [dissenters] known by the name of Baptists intend to hold a meeting for the worship of God in the dwelling house of Richard Tipping in the parish of North Nibley and prays it may be registered. John Mittchell, Edward Cowcher, Martin Lloyd. (GDR/284/161)

1304 North Nibley. 1 Jan 1748/49. Some [dissenters] intend to hold a meeting for the worship of God in the dwelling house of George Nelmes in the parish of North Nibley and desire it may be registered. John Stratford, Thomas Browning, John Dando, Thomas Higgins. (GDR/284/199)
Note. Old and new style year indicated in original.

1305 Forthay, North Nibley. 8 June 1755. The house of Henry Carpenter at 'Foretay' in the parish of North Nibley, yeoman, 'is a convenient place for meeting for divine worship and it is the desire of the said Henry Carpenter and of several of His Majesty's Protestant dissenting subjects thereabouts that the said house should be recorded at your Court'. Daniel Summers, Thomas Buckland, William Nelmes. (GDR/292A/9)

1306 Forthay, North Nibley. 31 Jan 1788 (Epiphany 1788). We [named below], householders in the parish of North Nibley, at an adjournment at the Kings Head, city of Gloucester, Saturday 16 Feb 1788, intend to set apart a convenient part of the dwelling house, now in the occupation of Richard Stratford, at Forthay in the parish of North Nibley and humbly request that this certificate may be entered and inrolled and a licence thereupon granted. Josiah Hancock, George Owen, Thomas Hancock, Josiah Hancock, John Gazzard, Robert Curnock. (Q/SO/10/f.280r)
Note. Names written in a different or much larger hand but not signatures.

1307 [North] Nibley. (3 Sept 1804). We [named below] certify that the house of Grace Jones in the parish of Nibley is appropriated to the purpose of religious worship and pray that it may be registered. Thomas Talboys, John Webb, James Walter, James Walter jnr, William Williams. (GDR/334B/435)

1308 Stinchcomb, North Nibley. (19 Nov 1806). We [named below] certify that the house of Thomas Summers in 'Stanchcomb' in the parish of North Nibley is appropriated for the purpose of the 'publick' worship of Almighty God and we require the same may be registered and a certificate be granted. Thomas Summers, Joseph Turner, Richard Barrett, John Chappell, William Summers, Joseph Cornock. (GDR/334B/425)
Note. RG/31/2 has registered 6 Dec 1806.

1309 North Nibley. 22 Sept 1807 (26 Sept 1807). We [named below] do make known to your Lordship that a house at Spinkham [?Spuncombe] Bottom in the parish of North Nibley, in the occupation of Richard Cox, is appropriated and set apart for the purpose of worshipping God and performing religious duties therein and we desire that the same may be registered. James Organ, William Elliott, Stephen Brown (mark), W B Wiltshaw, minister, Sarah Daniel (mark). (GDR/334B/420)
Note. The word 'minister' is above the name W B Wiltshaw in this entry but see **384**.

1310 North Nibley. Feb 1809 (17 Feb 1810). We [named below] humbly certify that the Tabernacle in the parish of North Nibley is appropriated for the public worship of Almighty God and request that the same may be registered and a certificate thereof granted. William Bennett, minister, William Austin, Thomas Powell, Harry Randall, Jacob Organ, Cornelius Gazon, James Organ. (GDR/334B/388)
Note. Date Feb 1809 with blank for day.

1311 Waterley Bottom, North Nibley. 1 Mar 1822 (11 May 1822). I Peter Bird certify that my dwelling house at 'Watterley' Bottom in the parish of North Nibley is intended forthwith to be a place of religious worship. Witness Thomas Thomas, M A Thomas. (GDR/344/page 3 (from rear))
Note. No return to RG.

NORTHLEACH
1312 Northleach. 1 Mar 1796 (4 Mar 1796; registration GDR/319A/230). *Independent.* This is to certify that the longest room in the house of Mr John Cook, carrier, in Northleach, is intended to be used for dissenters of the Independent denomination, which room is now in the occupation Mr William Wilson of Chedworth. We therefore request that the said room may be registered. Christopher Pain, William Wilson, Daniel Wilson, John Wilson, Richard Broad. Endorsed on back 'copy of certificate Mar 4 1796'. (GDR/N2/1)

1313 Northleach 14 July 1798 (1 Aug 1798) [RG/31/2 has '*Independent* chapel']. This is to certify that a new chapel or meeting-house lately erected in a piece of ground called the Antelope Close in Northleach, and of which the Revd William Wilkins of Bourton, the Revd William Bishop of Gloucester and others are trustees, is intended to be a place of worship. We request that the new Chapel may be registered and a certificate granted accordingly. Christopher Pain, minister, William Bishop, John Wilson, Thomas Ashwin, trustees. (GDR/319A/267)
Note. William Bishop was an Independent minister in 1796 (Hine 5).

1314 Northleach. 6 Mar 1821 (21 Apr 1821). I William Woodall of the village of Chalford, minister of the Gospel, certify that the dwelling house of Mary Hathaway, baker, in the town of Northleach is intended forthwith to be a place of religious worship and require you to register the same and request a certificate thereof. William Woodall, Justinian Hathaway, Charles Barton, Thomas Turfery. (GDR/334B/223)

1315 Northleach. 7 June 1827 (8 June 1827). I Charles Hawthorne of the town of Stroud certify that a chapel in the town and parish of Northleach is intended forthwith to be a place of religious worship and I require you to register the same and request a certificate thereof. (GDR/350/65)

NORTON
1316 Norton. 9 June 1815 (9 Jun 1815). I John Cullen of Gloucester, minister, certify that the house of John Sadler in the parish of Norton is intended forthwith to be a place of religious worship and require you to register the same and request a certificate thereof. (GDR/334B/328)

1317 Norton. 22 June 1816 (24 June 1816). [*Methodist, see* **179**]. I Daniel Campbell of Gloucester, minister, certify that the house of Robert Mann in the parish of Norton, is intended forthwith to be a place of religious worship and I require you to register the same and request a certificate thereof. Witness Jeremiah Grant. (GDR/334B/318)

1318 Norton. 6 Mar 1824 (6 Mar 1824). I Francis Collier of Gloucester, minister of the gospel, certify that a dwelling house in Norton, now in the occupation of Thomas Curtis, is intended to be a place of religious worship and I require you to register the same and request a certificate thereof. (GDR/344/129v)

1319 Norton. 18 Jan 1836 (18 Jan 1836). I William Worth of Gloucester, preacher of the Gospel, certify that a room in the parish of Norton is intended forthwith to be a place of religious worship and require you to register the same and request a certificate thereof. (GDR/350/187)

1320 Norton. 10 Aug 1838 (11 Aug 1838). I Christopher Bourn of the Green House in the parish of Dymock certify that the house of George Courtice and premises at Norton, now in [his] holding and occupation, are to be a place of religious worship and I request you to register the same and request a certificate thereof for which shall be taken no more than two shillings and six pence. (GDR/350/229)

1321 Norton. 10 July 1841 (10 July 1841). I William Wheeler of the parish of St Michaels in the city of Gloucester certify that a chapel, recently erected in the parish of Norton near the Green, is forthwith to be a place of religious worship and require you to register the same and request a certificate thereof. (GDR/350/282)

NOTGROVE
1322 Notgrove. (Easter 1705). *Anabaptist.* Jane Evans, widow, house. (Q/SO/3/521)

1323 Notgrove. (Trinity 1727). *Baptist.* It is ordered by this court that the dwelling house of William Preston at Notgrove be hereby licensed for [dissenters] called Baptists to assemble and meet together for the worship and service of God in their way and that John Poulson be licensed and allowed to be preacher there. (Q/SO/5/f.77v)
Note. Rubric records 'Notgrove meeting-house lysenced'; RG/31/6 has 'Nutgrove'.

1324 Notgrove. 3 June 1740. Some [dissenters] intend to hold a meeting for the worship of Almighty God in their way in the dwelling house of William Preston in the parish of

Notgrove and therefore we pray that it may be recorded. John Harmar, John Wickham, Matthew Smith. (GDR/284/110)

1325 Notgrove. 23 May 1784 (25 May 1784; registration GDR/292A/260). We [named below] certify to your lordship that we intend to meet for the worship of Almighty God in the Folley Farm House in the parish of Notgrove and therefore pray that this certificate may be registered.' William Rowland, Richard Reynold, William Wood, Robert Rowland, John Preston, James Roberts, Joseph Collett. (GDR/N2/1)
Note. One of a bundle of five certificates, all very worn and crossed through.

1326 Notgrove. 23 Aug 1802 (27 Sep 1802). We [named below] certify that we intend to meet for the worship of Almighty God in the dwelling house of James Roberts, farmer, in the parish of Notgrove and pray that this certificate may be registered. William Rowlands [RG/31/2 has of Notgrove], William Roberts, James Roberts, John Wood, Edward Wood, Henry Collett, William Portlock, John Rowlands, Edward Reynolds, John Butler. (GDR/319A/318)

1327 Notgrove. 23 Jan 1825 (8 Feb 1825). We [named below] certify that we intend to meet for the worship of Almighty God in the dwelling house of Richard Gardner, labourer, in the parish of Notgrove and that this certificate may be entered in your Lordship's Registry. Richard Alcock, Isaac Wood, Joseph Alcock, Richard Collett, Edward Robins. (GDR/350/32)

NYMPSFIELD

1328 Nympsfield. 1672. *Baptist.* Licence recorded for the Widow Pegler's house and 28 Oct 1672 for Thomas Evans 'of the Baptist perswasion' to teach at the Widow Pegler's house. (LT/573)

1329 'Nymphsfield'. (Epiphany 1689/90). *Anabaptist.* Widow Kedd's house. (Q/SO/3/522)

1330 Nympsfield. (Epiphany 1730/1). *Quaker.* It is ordered by this court that [dissenters] called Quakers living in or near the parish of Nympsfield be licensed and allowed to meet and assemble together for the worship of God in their way in the dwelling house of Henry Wilkins in Nympsfield. (Q/SO/5/f.150v)

1331 Nympsfield. 15 Dec 1739. Some [dissenters] intend to hold a meeting for the worship of Almighty God in their way in the dwelling house of Martha Warner in the parish of Nympsfield and therefore pray that it may be registered. Samuel Warner, William Hoskins, John Rudge. (GDR/284/102)

1332 Nympsfield. 12 Feb 1779 (22 Feb 1779). His Majesty's protestant subjects dissenting from the Church of England certify that we have set apart a house, occupied by Edward Poulton, in the parish of 'Nymphsfield' as a place of meeting for religious worship and pray that the said house may be recorded as a place of meeting. Daniel Wilkins, W. Burford, Samuel Poulton, Ann Poulton, Edward Poulton. (GDR/292A/216)

1333 Nympsfield. 13 July 1809 (15 July 1809). We [named below] being dissenters in the parish of Nympsfield and its neighbourhood are desirous of enjoying the liberty of our own consciences in worshipping God amongst ourselves and we have for that purpose hired the house of John Burford which house is wholly devoted to religious uses and it is our wish your Lordship would order an entry in your court. Thomas Flint, Aaron Smith, Edward

Mitchell, William Gainey, Isaac Brooks, Samuel Ford, John Sent, John Sutton. (GDR/334B/399)

1334 Nympsfield. 5 Nov 1813 (6 Nov 1813). We [named below] with others in the parish of Nympsfield and its vicinity, being desirous of enjoying according to our own views the worship of God amongst ourselves, have erected and set apart a chapel or meeting-house in the parish of Nympsfield wholly devoted to religious uses. It is therefore our wish that your Lordship would order an order to be made of the above mentioned place of worship. William Winterbotham, Thomas Clift, Thomas Flint, Samuel Enock Francis, Thomas Cooke, Edward Mitchel, Isaac Brookes, Lindsey Winterbotham, William Laney, Samuel Ford, John Lute, John Hoskins, Edward Barnard, Cornelius Blackwell. (GDR/334B/342)

ODDINGTON

1335 Oddington. 1672. *Congregational.* Application by Owen Davies for licence for William Baker's house in Oddington; licence recorded 10 June 1672; received 12 June 1672 by Owen Davies. (LT/372, 401, 509)

1336 Oddington. 1672. *Congregational.* Application by [Stephen] Ford for 'A licence for Mr William Troy. And a house in Odington in Gloscestershire. And the Town Hall in the Borrough of Chipping Norton in Oxfordshire. The people Congregationall'; licence recorded 9 May 1672 to William Troy to be a Congregational teacher in his house in 'Odington', and for his house. Congregational meeting place; received 1 June 1672 by Owen Davies for 'William Tray' at his own house in Oddington. (LT/218, 389, 473)
Note. William Tray had been ejected in 1662.

1337 Oddington. (Michaelmas 1707). *Quaker.* Richard Haydon's house. (Q/SO/3/520)

1338 Oddington. 12 Apr 1798 (17 Apr 1798). We [named below] certify that we intend to meet for the worship of Almighty God in the dwelling house of Josiah Hill, threadmaker, in the parish of Oddington, and pray that this certificate may be registered. James Radway, John Baker, Richard Margetts, Josiah Hill, R Farmer, Thomas Smith. (GDR/319A/265)

1339 Oddington. 12 Aug 1823 (13 Aug 1823). Baptist. I William Collett of Oddington certify that a certain room in the parish of Oddington aforesaid, in the occupation of John Gordon, farmer, is intended forthwith to be used as a place of religious worship by an assembly or congregation of Protestants of the Baptist denomination and I require you to register the same accordingly and hereby request a certificate thereof. (GDR/344/112r)

1340 Oddington. 17 Nov 1845 (24 Dec 1845). We [named below] certify that we intend to meet for the worship of Almighty God in the dwelling house of George Campin in the parish of Oddington, and pray that this certificate may be registered in your Lordship's Registry. Joseph Acock, John Gorton, George Campin, Richard Phillips, Benjamin Clift, Jethro Hemmings. (GDR/350/365)

OLD SODBURY
Chipping Sodbury, which see, was a chapelry in Old Sodbury.

1341 Old Sodbury. 2 June 1807 (3 Jun 1807). We [named below] certify that we intend to meet for the worship of Almighty God in the dwelling house of Mr James Reed in the parish of Old Sodbury and pray that this certificate may be registered. James Reed, Samuel Arthurs, Elias Isaac, Thomas Arthurs, Thomas Ferebee, Charles Power, Stephen Sallis, Abraham Warner, John Vick. (GDR/334B/422-1)

1342 Old Sodbury. 17 Sept 1819 (20 Sept 1819). *Baptist.* I William Southwood of Chipping Sodbury, Baptist minister, certify that a room in a house occupied by John Garraway in the parish of Old Sodbury is intended forthwith to be a place of religious worship and I require you to register the same. (GDR/334B/255)

1343 Old Sodbury. (22 Dec 1827). We [named below] certify that we intend to set apart the dwelling house belonging to James Reed in the parish of Old Sodbury for the service and worship of Almighty God and request that this our certificate may be recorded in your Lordship's Register and the entry thereof duly certified. James Reed, Thomas Mealing, Thomas Brookes, Thomas Light, John Garraway, Samuel Isaac, Moses Search, Sampson Lockstone, Moses Stinchcombe. (GDR/350/80)

1344 Old Sodbury. 24 Jan 1844 (30 Jan 1844). I William Pearce of Chipping Sodbury, chemist, certify that a Chapel at Old Sodbury is intended forthwith to be used as a place of religious worship and I require you to register the same. (GDR/350/331)

OLDBURY ON THE HILL
1345 Oldbury on the Hill. (Epiphany 1729/30). *Quaker.* It is ordered by this court that [dissenters] called Quakers residing in and near 'Oldbury upon the Hill' be licensed and allowed to assemble and meet together in the house of John Mapsons in Oldbury 'to performe Worship to Almighty God in their way according to their petition.' (Q/SO/5/f.128r)

OLDBURY-ON-SEVERN
Oldbury on Severn was a tithing and chapelry in Thornbury parish.
1346 Oldbury. 1 Oct 1810 (4 Oct 1810). We [named below] certify that the house of Mary Hopkins in the tithing of Oldbury in the parish of Thornbury is intended to be used for the occasional worship of Almighty God which we desire may be registered. Obed Pitcher, Thomas Trayhern, Absolom Riddeford, Henry Bidden, John Croome, James Higgs. (GDR/334B/380-79)

1347 Oldbury. 7 June 1842 (18 June 1842). *Wesleyan.* I James Bartholomew, minister of Thornbury, certify that a chapel in the village of Oldbury in the parish of Thornbury, the property of Wesleyan Methodist Conference, is intended forthwith to be a place of religious worship and require you to register the same and request a certificate thereof. (GDR/350/299)

OLDLAND
Oldland was a chapelry in Bitton parish.
1348 Oldland. 26 Jun 1796 (16 July 1796; registration GDR/319A/236). *Independent.* This is to certify that a large building known and called by the late Revd Mr Whitfield's Room at Kingswood in the hamlet of 'Oland' in the parish of Bitton is a place of worship for dissenters of the Independent denomination. We therefore request that it may be registered in your Lordship's Court and a certificate granted accordingly.' Thomas Williams, minister; Aaron Brain, John Tippett, Edward Jones. (GDR/N2/1)
Note. Crossed through, endorsed 'copy of certificate July 16th 1796'.

1349 Oldland Common, Bitton. 22 Jan 1812 (28 Jan 1812). *Independent.* We [named below], dissenters of the Independent denomination, have erected and set apart a certain building or meeting-house at Oldland Common in the parish of Bitton for the worship of Almighty God and pray that the said building or meeting-house may be registered and a certificate granted. William Mooles, Samuel Wade, John Bailey, Robert Ward, William Wrintmore, John Nicholson, John Johnston, John Gibbs, minister. (GDR/334B/356)

1350 Oldland Common, Bitton. 25 Apr 1846 (30 Apr 1846). *Independent.* May it please your Lordship to grant unto us [named below] being dissenters of the Independent denomination, a certificate for a house or tenement, now in the possession of Mr George Short at Oldland Common, in the parish of Bitton for the worship of Almighty God and we pray that the same may be registered and a certificate granted. George Short, James Davis, John David, James Williams, William Stibbs. (GDR/350/375)
Note. Registration originally entered was 15 May but then crossed out and 30 April substituted.

1351 Longwell Green, Oldland. (9 Nov 1850). *Wesleyan* Methodist chapel. Charles Clay. (Q/RNp/4)
Note. For Charles Clay *see* **120**.

1352 Oldland. (23 Nov 1850). [*Wesleyan*]. Building called the Cock Road School. Charles Clay [RG/31/2 has of Bitton]. (Q/RNp/4)
Note. For Charles Clay *see* **120**.

1353 Oldland Common, Bitton. (2 Dec 1850). House and premises occupied by Samuel Long. Edward Foizey. (Q/RNp/4)

OLVESTON
Diocese of Bristol from 1542. Tockington was a hamlet in the parish. Alveston, which see, was a chapelry annexed to Olveston.
1354 Olveston. (Easter 1690). *Quaker.* Meeting-house. (Q/SO/3/522)

1355 Tockington [Olveston]. (Trinity 1701) *Presbyterian.* A new erected house. (Q/SO/3/521)

1356 Olveston. (Epiphany 1706/7). *Quaker.* A house erected for Quakers. (Q/SO/3/520)

1357 Tockington, Olveston. 7 Nov 1806 (13 Dec 1806). *Methodist.* We [named below] beg leave to certify that a room in a house occupied by William Gardinor, shoemaker, in Tockington in the parish of Olveston, is set apart for the worship of Almighty God by a congregation of dissenters commonly called Methodists and request that the same may be registered and a certificate of the same given accordingly. William Gardner, Edward Dunn, William Cummings, Guy Sinderbury, John Bishop, John Mashall, David Cooke. (EP/A/45/1/402)

1358 Olveston. 10 May 1810 (30 July 1810). *Methodist.* We [named below] beg leave to certify that the house and court yard adjoining, occupied by William Kersleake, grocer at 'Olvestone', is set apart for the public worship of Almighty God by a congregation of dissenters commonly called Methodists and request that the same may be registered. William Kersleak, John Freem, Edward Dunn, Thomas Curtis, William Gardner, James Burford, Isaac Brooks, William Niblett, John Olive, Thomas Freem. (EP/A/45/2/35)

1359 Olveston. 23 Feb 1821. *Methodist.* I William Jones of Thornbury, Methodist minister, certify that a building or meeting-house in the village and parish of Olveston is forthwith to be a place of religious worship and I require you to register the same and request a certificate thereof. William Jones; 'witness to the signature of William Jones, F J Councell'. (EP/A/45/2/139)

1360 Olveston. 12 Feb 1851 (12 Feb 1851). *Wesleyan Methodist.* I Henry Dodd certify that premises now held by me in Haw Lane, parish of Olveston, are intended to be

forthwith a place of religious worship by a congregation of Wesleyan Methodists and I request you to register the same and request a certificate thereof. (EP/A/45/4/53).
Note. Certificate pasted in and signed.

OWLPEN
Owlpen was a chapelry in Newington Bagpath parish. The name was sometimes written 'Wolpen' or 'Woolpen' (EPNS Glos II 245)

1361 [?Owlpen]. 1672. *Presbyterian.* Licence recorded 5 Sept 1672 to Thomas Jennings of 'Woollon in Glocstersh to be a Presbyterian teacher'. (LT/560)

1362 [?Owlpen]. 1672. *Presbyterian.* Licence recorded for the house of . . . Smith of 'Woollan in Glocstersh'. (LT/560)
Note. Thomas Jennings (*see* previous entry) probably preached at this house.

1363 Owlpen. (Easter 1702). *Presbyterian.* 'Jo:' Ady's house. [RG/31/6 has Joseph]. (Q/SO/3/521)

1364 Owlpen. (Michaelmas 1702). *Anabaptist.* 'Woolpen', William Martin's house. (Q/SO/3/521)
Note. RG/31/6 has 'Owlpen'.

OXENHALL
1365 Oxenhall. 24 Oct 1816 (29 Oct 1816). I Abraham Watmough [RG/31/2 has Whatmough] of Newent, minister of the Gospel, certify that the dwelling house in the parish of Oxenhall, in the occupation of Joseph Taylor, labourer, is intended forthwith to be a place of religious worship and I require you to register the same and request a certificate thereof. (GDR/334B/310)

1366 Shaw Common, Oxenhall. 20 Feb 1836 (20 Feb 1836). I Thomas Kington of the Hill in the parish of 'Castle Froome', Herefordshire, certify that the house of William Rogers and premises at Shaw Common in the parish of 'Oxonhall', now in [his] holding and occupation, are to be a place of religious worship and I request you to register the same and request a certificate thereof for which shall be taken no more than two shillings and six pence. (GDR/350/188)

1367 Three Ashes, Oxenhall. 4 Oct 1845 (4 Oct 1845). I Joseph Stratford of the parish of Newent certify that the cottage, in the occupation of John Apperley, at Three Ashes in the parish of Oxenhall is to be a place of religious worship and I request you to register the same and request a certificate thereof for which shall be taken no more than two shillings and six pence. (GDR/350/362)

OXENTON
1368 Oxenton. (26 Mar 1851). Room in a cottage occupied by Joseph Allsop. Jonas Radford & others. (Q/RNp/4)

PAINSWICK
1369 Painswick. 1672. *Congregational.* Application by Owen Davies for 'Francis Hariss and his house Payneswick Herefford shyre'; licence recorded 10 June 1672 to 'Francis Harry' to be a Congregational teacher in his house in Painswick, Hereford and for the house. (LT/401, 507)
Note. This is taken to be Painswick in Gloucestershire. *See* Thornbury **1737** for a similar case.

1370 Painswick. 10 Apr 1716. Samuel Seavell of Painswick dissenting preacher, took oaths of allegiance, supremacy and abjuration of 1 Geo I. (Q/SO/4/496)

1371 Painswick. (Epiphany 1689/90). The Town Hall. (Q/SO/3/522)

1372 Painswick. (Easter 1690). *Quaker.* Meeting-house. (Q/SO/3/522)
Note. There was a Quaker burial in Painswick of 'Ales, wife of Walter Humphries' on 22 Jan 1657, as recorded on a ledger slab.

1373 Painswick. (Easter 1705). *Anabaptist.* James Davis's house. (Q/SO/3/521)

1374 Painswick. (Michaelmas 1705.) *Presbyterian.* A new erected house. (Q/SO/3/521)

1375 Painswick. 22 Aug 1726. *Baptist.* This is to certify that [dissenters] (called Baptists) intend to hold a meeting for the worship of God in their way in the house of Thomas Hutson near Mr Adams in Painswick and pray that it may be recorded. Robert Mill, Thomas Jones, Thomas Cook, Jacob Mower. (GDR/279a/145)

1376 Painswick. [1729; entry between 15 July 1729 and 7 Nov 1729]. This is to certify that [dissenters] intend to hold a meeting for the worship of God in the house of John Stephens near the Market House in 'Paynswick' and pray that it may be recorded. John Stephens. (GDR/279a/216)

1377 Painswick. 10 June 1732. [Dissenters] intend to hold a meeting for the worship of God in their way in the house of John Stanley's near Mr Nathaniel Adams's in Painswick. We therefore pray it may be recorded in your Court. Robert Mill, Thomas Jones, William Fisher. (GDR/284/4)

1378 Painswick. 11 May 1734. Some [dissenters] intend to hold a meeting for the worship of God in their way in the dwelling house of Thomas Rogers in the town of Painswick and therefore desire that it may be recorded. Martin Lloyd, Joseph Fownes, Martin Lloyd jnr. (GDR/284/32)

1379 Painswick. 20 May [1735; entry between 29 Apr 1735 and 6 June 1735]. Some [dissenters] intend to hold a meeting for the worship of God in their way in the dwelling house of Henry Reu in the town of Painswick, therefore we desire it may be recorded. Joseph Everard, John Harmar, Martin Lloyd. (GDR/284/37)
Note. For Joseph Everard *see* **197**.

1380 Painswick. 23 Dec 1738. Some dissenters in and about the town of Painswick intend to hold a meeting for the worship of God in their way in the house of Mary Gardner, the widow of Luke Gardner, deceased, near the *Falcon* in the town and desire it may be regstered. Martin Lloyd, Joseph Everard, William Lodge jnr. (GDR/284/98)
Note. For Joseph Everard *see* **197**. RG/31/2 has 'Martin Lloyd (and others) of Wotton-under-Edge' but ditto marks in the column relating to the residence of the certifier may have been an error.

1381 Painswick. 24 Feb 1739/40. Some [dissenters] intend to hold a meeting for the worship of God in their way in a dwelling house of William Fisher's in the town of Painswick. We therefore pray it may be recorded. Thomas Jones, John Mitchel, Ambrose Huett [Hyett]. (GDR/284/109)

1382 Painswick. 22 Apr 1741. Some [dissenters] intend to hold a meeting for the worship of God in their way in a dwelling house of Richard Gardner's belonging to the town of Painswick. We therefore pray that this may be recorded. John Mitchel, Ambrose Huett, William Fisher. (GDR/284/116)

1383 Sheepscombe, Painswick. 22 Sept 1741. Some [dissenters] intend to hold a meeting for the worship of God at the house of Robert Clissold, broadweaver, in the tithing of 'Sheepscomb' in the parish of Painswick. We pray your Lordship that it may be registered. Robert Clissold, John Bowley, Thomas Stanly, Henry Wrenn, John Cook. (GDR/284/120)

1384 Painswick. 11 July 1743. Some [dissenters] intend to hold a meeting for the worship of God in their way in the dwelling house of Thomas Gardner in the parish of Painswick. We pray that it may be recorded. John Mitchell, Ambros[e] Huett [Hyett], Thomas Cook. (GDR/284/155)

1385 Painswick. 10 Dec 1747. *Independent.* Some dissenting Independent subjects intend to hold a meeting for the worship of Almighty God at the house of William Knights in the town of Painswick near the upper Market House and we pray that the house may be duly registered. William Hogg, John Cook, Daniel Cook, Thomas Hadley. (GDR/284/194)

1386 Painswick. 30 July 1751 (2 Aug 1751). *Baptist.* Some dissenting subjects of the Baptist denomination intend to hold a meeting for the worship of God in the dwelling house of Thomas Mace in the parish of Painswick. We pray that this certificate may be entered in your register. Thomas Jones, Thomas Mace, Thomas Woodfield, Thomas Solloman. (GDR/284/212)

1387 Painswick. 14 Aug 1756. *Baptist.* Some dissenting subjects of the Baptist denomination intend to hold a meeting for the worship of God in the dwelling house of Richard Gardner in the parish of Painswick. We pray that this certificate may be entered in your Register. Richard Gardner, Thomas Jones, Thomas Woodfield, Thomas Geleman. (GDR/292A/14)
Note. See entry for Bisley **276**, where Thomas Jelleman made his mark.

1388 Painswick. 27 May 1759. *Baptist.* Some [dissenters] of the Baptist denomination intend to hold a meeting for the worship of God in the dwelling house of Thomas Jones in the parish of Painswick. We therefore pray that this certificate may be entered in your register. Thomas Jones, Thomas Skinner, Thomas Jeleman, Thomas Woodfield. (GDR/292A/47)

1389 Painswick. 27 Apr 1768. These are to certify your Lordship that some [dissenters] intend to hold a meeting for the worship of God in their own way in or at the dwelling House of Thomas Horlick in the parish of Painswick. We therefore pray that this may be recorded in your Court. Benjamin Morgan, Robert Horlick, Thomas Horlick, Henry Mace. (GDR/292A/117)

1390 Painswick. 2 Oct 1774. Some [dissenters] intend to hold a meeting for the worship of God in their way in or at the dwelling house of Robert Horlick in the parish of Painswick. We therefore pray that this may be recorded. William Hayward, Henry Mace, Robert Horlick, Thomas Wiggall. (GDR/292A/177)

1391 Painswick. 2 Sep 1794 (4 Sep 1794). *Quakers.* These are to certify that we [named below] with divers others being people called Quakers intend to hold a meeting for the worship of Almighty God in the dwelling house of Daniel Roberts in the town of Painswick and give this notice that the place of our meeting may be known to and registered in the Consistory court and also request a certificate thereof. Daniel Merrell, Robert Hinton, Daniel Roberts. (GDR/319A/187-8)

1392 Painswick. 27 Nov 1798 (28 Nov 1798). [*Independent: see Intro., lxv*]. We [named below] certify that we intend to meet for the worship of Almighty God in a house occupied by Samuel Wood in the parish of Painswick and pray that this certificate may be registered. John Skinner, Samuel Wood, Cornelius Winter, William Richardson. (GDR/319A/271)

1393 Edge, Painswick. 31 Mar 1804 (31 Mar 1804). *Independent.* We [named below] certify that a dwelling house and court situated at the Edge in the parish of Painswick, now occupied by Priscilla King 'gent' [gentlewoman], is set apart and to be used for the religious worship for dissenters called Independents and desire that the same may be registered. Thomas Sims, John Skinner, John Stephens. (GDR/334B/439)
Note. No RG return.

1394 Painswick. 25 June 1804 (30 June 1804). *Independent.* This is to certify that a house at Buddings in the parish of Painswick, in the occupation of Mr Daniel Papps, is to be a place of worship for dissenters of the Independent denomination and we request that the said house may be registered and a certificate granted accordingly. Orlando Augustus Jeary, minister, Thomas Rice, John Harris, Daniel Papp [*sic*]. (GDR/334B/438)

1395 Painswick. 22 Feb 1809 (24 Feb 1809). These are to certify that some dissenters intend to hold a meeting for the worship of Almighty God in a building erected for that purpose in the town and parish of Painswick. We pray that this certificate be registered. William Baylis, Thomas Ward, John Baylis, Robert Arundell, John Jones, Robert Wright, John Jacob, Thomas Smith, William Niblett, Richard Perrott. (GDR/334B/407)

1396 Painswick. 4 Feb 1817 (4 Feb 1817). I William Shelmerdine of Stroud, minister, certify that the house of Henry Wyatt in the parish of Painswick is intended forthwith to be used as a place of religious worship and require you to register the same and request a certificate thereof. (GDR/334B/305)

1397 Sheepscombe, Painswick. 17 Nov 1817 (22 Nov 1817). I William Shelmerdine of Stroud, minister, certify that the house of Sarah Taylor of Sheepscombe in the parish of Painswick is intended forthwith to be used as a place of religious worship and require you to register the same and request a certificate thereof. (GDR/334B/289)

1398 Painswick. 2 Sept 1820 (2 Sept 1820). I Samuel Meredith of the Edge near Painswick, being a farmer, certify that a certain tenement in the parish of Painswick which I at present hold, is forthwith to be a place of religious worship and require you to register the same and request a certificate thereof. (GDR/334B/235)

1399 Sheepscombe, Painswick. 4 Oct 1821 (6 Oct 1821). *Methodist.* I James Blackett, Methodist minister of Stroud, certify that a dwelling house, in the occupation of William Wager, carpenter, in Sheepscombe in the parish of Painswick, is intended forthwith to be a place of religious worship and require you to register the same and request a certificate thereof. (GDR/334B/212)

1400 Painswick. 10 Mar 1824 (25 Mar 1824). I William Roberts of the parish of Painswick certify that my dwelling house and premises, now in my occupation are to be a place of religious worship and I require you to register the same, and request a certificate thereof for which shall be taken no more than two shillings and sixpence. (GDR/344/131v)

1401 Painswick. 17 Sept 1824 (18 September 1824). I William Roberts of Painswick certify that my dwelling house and premises in the parish of Painswick are to be a place of religious worship and assembly and I require you to register the same, and request a certificate thereof for which shall be taken no more than two shillings and six pence. (GDR/344/137r)

1402 Edge, Painswick. 18 Nov 1824 (18 Nov 1824). I William Wager of Edge in the parish of Painswick certify that a house and premises at Edge, now in [my] holding and occupation, are to be a place of religious worship and I request you to register a the same, and request a certificate thereof for which shall be taken no more than two shillings and sixpence. (GDR/350/23)

1403 Sheepscombe, Painswick. 29 Mar 1825 (29 Mar 1825). We [named below] certify [that a] house now in the occupation of Mr William Wager at Sheepscombe in the parish of Painswick is intended forthwith to be a place of religious worship and I require you to register the same, and request a certificate thereof. Richard Heath, William Baglin. (GDR/350/37)

1404 Painswick. (30 May 1827). *Independent.* We the undersigned of the Independent denomination beg respectfully to inform your Lordship that a house or building and premises now in the occupation of Daniel Hammon, situate at *The Bull*, in the parish of Painswick is to be henceforth a place of religious worship and we respectfully request that the same be duly entered in the Registry of your Lordship's diocese. Daniel Hammon, Samuel Lewis, Thomas Gillman, John Hooper, Richard Clissold. (GDR/350/64)

1405 Small's Mill, Painswick. (30 May 1827). *Independent.* We the undersigned of the Independent denomination beg respectfully to inform your Lordship that a certain house or building and premises, now in the occupation of Matthew Rice at Small's Mill, in the parish of Painswick is to be henceforth a place of religious worship and we respectfully request that the same be duly entered in the Registry of your Lordship's diocese. Matthew Rice, Thomas Gillman, Thomas Burnett, William Cratchley, Paul Hawkins Gardner, John Neal. (GDR/350/64-5)

1406 Painswick. 8 Sept 1827 (8 Sept 1827). I Charles Vick certify that my dwelling house and premises in the parish of Painswick are to be a place of religious worship and I request you to register and record the same and request a certificate thereof. (GDR/350/72)

1407 Painswick. 18 Oct 1827 (20 Oct 1827). I Samuel Gardner of the parish of Painswick certify that my dwelling house and premises in the parish of Painswick, now in my own occupation, are to be a place of religious worship and I request you to register and record the same and request a certificate thereof for which shall be taken no more than two shillings and six pence. (GDR/350/74)

1408 Painswick. 13 June 1829 (13 June 1829). I Samuel Meredith of Painswick Edge in the parish of Painswick certify that house and premises in 'George's' [George] Court, Painswick, now in [my] holding and occupation, are to be a place of religious worship and I request you to register the same and request a certificate thereof for which shall be taken no more than two shillings and six pence. (GDR/350/103)

1409 Painswick. 29 Sept 1830 (2 Oct 1830). I William Guy of Painswick certify that my dwelling house and premises in 'Tibwell' [Tibbiwell] Lane, Painswick, is intended henceforth to be a place of religious worship and I request you to register the same and request a certificate thereof. (GDR/350/112)

1410 Sheepscombe, Painswick. 16 Apr 1833 (17 Apr 1833). I Henry Hawkins of Sheepscombe House in the parish of Painswick, gentleman, certify that a certain building adjoining my dwelling house, now in my occupation, is intended forthwith to be used as a place of religious worship and I require you to register the same. (GDR/350/139)

1411 Sheepscombe, Painswick. 10 June 1836. *Particular or Calvinist Baptist.* I Peter King of Dudbridge Mill in the parish of Rodborough, mealman, certify that a meeting-house at Sheepscomb in the parish of Painswick is intended to be used, occupied and enjoyed as and for a place of public religious worship for the service of God by a society or congregation of dissenters called Particular or Calvinistic Baptists and request that this certificate may be registered in the consistory court of your Lordship. (GDR/350/197)

1412 Painswick. 6 Sept 1844 (6 Sept 1844). I William Hamlett of the *Bull* in Wick Street in the parish of Painswick, certify that a house and premises at the *Bull* in [my] occupation are to be a place of worship and I request you to register the same and request a certificate thereof for which shall be taken no more than two shillings and six pence. (GDR/350/347)

1413 Painswick. (19 Feb 1850). House and premises of Daniel Spring, 35, Friday Street. Daniel Spring. (Q/RNp/4)

1414 Sheepscombe, [Painswick]. (26 July 1850). House and premises, 'Sheepscomb'. William Richings [RG/31/2 has 'Richins']. (Q/RNp/4)

1415 Painswick. (5 Oct 1850). House or building occupied by William Holder, Gloucester Street. James Bayliss [RG/31/2 has of Gloucester]. (Q/RNp/4)

1416 Sheepscombe, Painswick. (27 Feb 1851). Room in a void mill and premises. William Richins. (Q/RNp/4)

PAUNTLEY
1417 Pauntley. 15 Dec 1726. These are to certify that [dissenters] intend to hold a meeting for the worship of God in their way in the parish of Pauntley 'at the house known by the name of Crooks in part whereof William Warr doth now dwell and pray that it may be registered.' William Lodge, Martin Lloyd, Joseph Everard. (GDR/279a/161)
Note. For Joseph Everard *see* **197**.

1418 Pauntley. 13 May 1740. Some [dissenters] intend to hold a meeting in the house of Mr William Fincher known by the name of Crooks in the parish of Pauntley and therefore desire that it may be registered. Martin Lloyd, Martin Lloyd jnr, John Summers. (GDR/284/109)

1419 Pauntley. 17 June 1814 (17 Jun 1814). I John Wright of Newent, minister, certify that a field called Colley Hill [RG/31/2 has 'Cally'], the property of John Stokes esq, in the parish of Pauntley, is intended forthwith to be a place of religious worship and I require you to register the same and request a certificate thereof. (GDR/334B/337)

1420 Pauntley .6 May 1819 (8 May 1819). I Richard Allen of Newent certify that a house in the parish of Pauntley, occupied by William Cole, is intended forthwith to be a place of religious worship and I require you to register the same and request a certificate thereof. (GDR/334B/261)

PEBWORTH
1421 Pebworth. (Trinity 1695). *Presbyterian.* John Gray's house. (Q/SO/3/522)
Note. RG/31/6 has registration Epiphany 1696.

1422 Pebworth. (Michaelmas 1695). *Presbyterian.* Thomas Cooper's house. (Q/SO/3/521)

1423 Pebworth. 22 Aug 1817 (28 Oct 1817). I Benjamin Holmes, minister, certify that a house in the parish of Pebworth, now in my possession, is intended forthwith to be used as a place of religious worship and assembly and require you to register the same. (GDR/334B/290)

1424 Broad Marston, Pebworth. 14 Oct 1818 (13 Nov 1818). I Thomas Kinchin of Broad Marston certify that my dwelling house is intended forthwith to be a place of religious worship and require you to register the same and request a certificate thereof. (GDR/334B/271)

1425 Pebworth. 20 Feb 1841 (11 Mar 1841). I David Comforth of Evesham certify that a chapel in the village and parish of Pebworth is forthwith to be a place of religious worship and I require you to register the same and request a certificate thereof. (GDR/350/275)

PITCHCOMBE
1426 Pitchcombe. (10 Sept 1742). These are to certify your Lordship that some [dissenters] intend to hold a meeting for the worship of God at the house of William Hogg at the upper end of 'Pitchcomb village in the parish of Pitchcomb' and therefore we pray your Lordship that the said house may be duly registered. John Hogg, Thomas Jenkins, William Hogg, Thomas Bingham. (GDR/284/141)

1427 Pitchcombe. 16 Oct 1802 (30 Oct 1802). *Independent.* We [named below] certify that a certain dwelling house and court at 'Pichcomb', now occupied by Jeremiah Franklin, stone mason, is set apart and intended to be used by a congregation of [dissenters] called Independents and to desire the same may be registered. Thomas Sims, William Bennett, Samuel Franklin, John Stephens. (GDR/N2/1)
Note. The last name is difficult to read. No record in Diocesan Act Book or RG/31/2.

1428 Pitchcombe. (30 May 1827). *Independent.* We [named below] of the Independent denomination beg respectfully to inform your Lordship that a certain house or building and premises, now in the occupation of George Hewling, in the parish of Pitchcombe is to be henceforth a place of religious worship and we respectfully request that the same be duly entered in the Registry of your Lordship's diocese. Thomas Gillman, William John Russean, Thomas Pack, Richard Jeffries. (GDR/350/64)

PRESTBURY
1429 Prestbury. 14 Mar 1798 (29 Mar 1798). These are to certify that we [named below] have taken a house in the town and parish of Prestbury, the property of William Burrows of the said town, and certify the same at the request of and by the desire of the said William Burrows to the intent that the same may be registered and a certificate thereof given. William Burrows, Hugh H Williams, Thomas James, Caleb Fisher, Samuel Preston. (GDR/319A/264)

1430 Prestbury 11 May 1810 (19 May 1810). [*Baptist: see* **517**]. These are to certify that we [named below] have taken a house in the town and parish of Prestbury, the property of Catherine James, and certify the same at the request and by the desire of the said Catherine James and several others to the court to the intent that the same may be registered as a place of Divine Service and public worship and a certificate thereof be given. Hugh H Williams, Griffith Williams, George Gibbs, Benjamin Wells, William Groe, J B Drayton. (GDR/334B/385)

1431 Prestbury. 2 June 1825 (15 June 1825). We the undersigned certify that a house and the land belonging thereto in the parish of Prestbury, the property of Charles Carpenter, is intended to be a place of religious worship and we request you to register the same. Charles Carpenter (mark); witness J Beckingsale, James Hyett, Henry Rogers. (GDR/350/42)

1432 Prestbury. 10 Feb 1826 (10 Feb 1826). I Jacob Boobyer of Windsor Terrace, Cheltenham, certify that a certain dwelling house in the parish of Prestbury occupied by John Stonham, carpenter, is intended to be forthwith a place of religious worship and I request you to register the same. (GDR/350/51)

1433 Prestbury. 12 May 1826 (13 May 1826). We [named below], dissenters and householders, beg leave to inform your Lordship that we intend opening the house of William Simpson in the parish of Prestbury for the purpose of divine worship and request that it may be registered. Henry Lucy, James Hughes, Joseph Wellington, William Potter, Joseph Collins. (GDR/350/55)

1434 Prestbury. 30 May 1834 (2 June 1834). I James Smith of Cheltenham certify that a dwelling house in the parish of Prestbury, taken for the purpose, is intended to be forthwith a place of religious worship and I request you to register the same. Witness James Hughes, Joseph Leonard. (GDR/350/151)

1435 Prestbury. 5 Dec 1836 (12 Dec 1836). I James Merchant of the parish of Prestbury certify that a messuage or tenement, occupied by me, in the village and parish of Prestbury, to be forthwith a place of religious worship and I request you to register the same. (GDR/350/203)

1436 Prestbury. 14 Sept 1838 (15 Sept 1838. *Wesleyan.* I John Mowan of Cheltenham certify that a dwelling house in the occupation of Robert Onslow in the parish of Prestbury is forthwith to be a place of religious worship and require you to register the same and request a certificate thereof. John Mowan, Weslyan minister. (GDR/350/230)

1437 Prestbury. (7 Nov 1851). Room in a dwelling house of David Fidoe. Isaac Bell and others. [RG/31/2 has J Smith as certifier]. (Q/RNp/4)

PUCKLECHURCH
The chapelry of Westerleigh, which see, was in Pucklechurch.
1438 Pucklechurch (Easter 1690). *Quaker.* Meeting-house. (Q/SO/3/522)

1439 Pucklechurch. 7 Nov 1816 (9 Nov 1816). *Independent.* We [named below], dissenters of the Independent denomination, have set apart the lower rooms or ground floor of a tenement or dwelling house, now in the occupation of Hannah Clark, in the parish of Pucklechurch, for the worship of Almighty God and pray that the apartments of the said tenement or dwelling house may be registered. John Gardner, minister, George W Sage, John Godwin, Joseph Rider, William Rake, J Wade, J Hoskins, William Huxtable. (GDR/334B/309)

1440 Pucklechurch. 19 Mar 1818 (23 Mar 1818). *Independent.* We [named below] of the Independent denomination have set apart the upper rooms of a certain tenement or intended dwelling house, at present unoccupied, belonging to John Osborne in the parish of Pucklechurch for the worship of Almighty God and pray that the apartments of the said tenement may be registered and a certificate granted us. Thomas Edwards, minister, John

Foster, Samuel Wade, George W Sage, John Williams, Robert Padfield, William Chandler. (GDR/334B/283)

1441 Pucklechurch. 28 Jan 1840 (18 Apr 1840). *Independent.* May it please your Lordship to grant unto us [named below] being dissenters of the Independent denomination, a certificate for a house or tenement, now in the occupation of Mr S Bruton, in the village of Pucklechurch for the worship of Almighty God. And we pray that the same may be registered in your court and a certificate granted. Stephen Bruton, John Rafill, Thomas Mealing, Thomas W Hammond, Henry Mealing, William Jollyman, John Jones, James Tayler, James Bissell. (GDR/350/252)

QUEDGLEY
1442 Quedgley. 14 July 1814 (15 July 1814). [*Methodist: see* **178**]. I John Chettle of Gloucester, minister, certify that the house of James Rodway in the parish of Quedgley is intended forthwith to be a place of religious worship and require you to register the same and request a certificate thereof. (GDR/334B/336)

QUENINGTON
1443 Quenington. 7 February 1822 (26 Feb 1822). We certify that a house in 'Quinnington', now in the occupation of the Revd Mr. Lewrie, will henceforth be a place of religious worship. Henry Wheeler, Edward West, Revd J H Lewrie. (GDR/344/18r)

1444 Quenington. 4 Apr 1834. [*Baptist*]. I Jenkin Thomas of Cheltenham certify and declare that I intend to open a certain room or building (heretofore used as a wood barn) belonging to me, near a dwelling house in my occupation, in the parish of 'Quinnington', as a place of public worship. (GDR/350/149)
Note. Jenkin Thomas was a Baptist minister in Cheltenham (*VCH Glos* 7, 128).

1445 Quenington. 8 July 1835 (11 July 1835). I Revd John William Peters of 'Quennington' certify that [my] building or chapel is intended forthwith to be a place of religious worship and I request you to register the same and request a certificate thereof. (GDR/350/176)
Note. Revd Peters resigned as rector of Quenington in 1834 (*VCH Glos* 7, 128).

1446 'Quennington'. (6 Nov 1851). House and premises occupied by Richard Archer. Edmund Rawlings [RG/31/2 has of Highworth]. (Q/RNp/4)

QUINTON
Transferred 1931 to Warwickshire.
1447 Quinton. 1 Jun 1799 (15 July 1799). This is to certify that an house in the parish of Quinton, in the occupation of George Hughes, flaxdresser, and in the public street, is intended to be a place of religious worship. We therefore request that the house may be registered and a certificate granted accordingly. John Higgins, William Kings, Richard Rogers, William Hughes, Samuel Salmon, Thomas Hale. (GDR/319A/281)

1448 Upper Quinton, Quinton. 14 May 1823 (17 May 1823). I Samuel James Housman of Eastgate Street in the city of Gloucester certify that a newly erected meeting-house in the hamlet of Upper Quinton in the parish of Quinton is intended to be forthwith a place of religious worship and I do hereby request you to register the same. (GDR/344/108v)

RANDWICK
Randwick was a chapelry in Standish parish.

1449 Randwick. 5 Jan 1758. Some [dissenters] intend to hold a meeting for the worship of God in the dwelling house of William Vine in the parish of Randwick and desire it may be registered. William Vine, Giles Chapman, James Chapman (mark), Mary Vine, Esther Barfoote (mark). (GDR/292A/34)

1450 Randwick. 24 Mar 1798 (24 Mar 1798). This is to certify that a large building, lately erected at the bottom of Voxmore Field near to Ebley, in the parish of Randwick is intended to be opened and occupied as a place of worshiip. We therefore request that it may be registered and a certificate granted accordingly. James Hogg, Stephen Clissold, William Crockford, John Allgood. (GDR/319A/264)

1451 Oxlinch, Randwick. 13 Jun 1802 (30 July 1802). We [named below] certify that a certain building at Oxlinch in the parish of Randwick, now occupied by James Browning, broadweaver, is intended to be used for religious worship. William Bennett, John Hiscox, Thomas Sims, Samuel Cooper, William Harries. (GDR/319A/314-5)

1452 Westrip, Randwick. 30 Jun 1802 (31 July 1802). We [named below] certify that we with others intend to meet for the worship of Almighty God in the house and in the court before the house of Abigail Walker at 'Westrup' in the parish of Randwick and we request that this certificate may be registered and that a certificate of the same might be granted. John Morley, Francis Holmes, William Walker, Isaac Brewer, William Lacey. (GDR/319A/315)

1453 Randwick. 22 Feb 1809 (24 Feb 1809). [*Methodist: see note*]. These are to certify that some dissenters intend to hold a meeting for the worship of Almighty God in a building erected for that purpose in the village and parish of Randwick. We pray that this certificate may be registered. Rowles Scudamore [RG/31/2 has 'of Randwick'], Francis Holmes, Walter Watkins, T Watkins, William Reece, Charles Lewis. (GDR/334B/408-9)
Note. GA D2770 contains the following Declaration: 'These are to Certify that [at the Quarter Sessions at the Boothall, in Gloucester, on Tuesday, in the week next after the Feast of Thomas à Becket - i.e., on 4 Jan 1809] William Knee personally appeared in open court, and then and there as a person in or pretending to Holy Orders and as a preacher or teacher of a Congregation of dissenting Protestants, took the Oaths and made and subscribed the Declaration appointed to be taken made and subscribed by an Act of Parliament' [19 Geo III c44] intituled An act for the further Relief of Protestant Dissenting Ministers and Schoolmasters'. This licence was preserved in the records of Stroud Methodist Circuit, series 'Randwick'. [*See* illus., xxii]

1454 Randwick. 7 Oct 1824 (7 Oct 1824). I Peter Chew in the parish of Painswick certify that my dwelling house and premises in the parish of Randwick is intended to be a place of religious worship and I request you to register the same, and request a certificate thereof for which shall be taken no more than two shillings and six pence. (GDR/344/137v)

1455 Randwick. 20 Jan 1825 (22 Jan 1825). I Stephen Critchley of Randwick certify that a dwelling house and premises at Randwick, now in [my] occupation, are intended to be used as a place of religious worship and I request you to register the same, and request a certificate thereof for which shall be taken no more than two shillings and six pence. (GDR/350/30)

1456 Oxlinch, Randwick. 9 Feb 1827 (10 Feb 1827). I Charles Hawthorne of the town of Stroud certify that a dwelling house in the occupation of Thomas Niblett in 'Oxlynch' in the parish of Randwick is intended forthwith to be a place of religious worship and require you to register the same and request a certificate thereof. (GDR/350/62)

1457 Randwick. 8 Oct 1835 (10 Oct 1835). I James Baker of Stroud certify that a dwelling house and premises at Randwick in the parish of Randwick, now in the holding and occupation of Joseph Bassett, are intended to be used to be used as a place of religious worship and I hereby request you to register and record the same and request a certificate thereof. Joseph Bassett (mark). (GDR/350/180)

1458 Randwick. 11 Apr 1840 (13 Apr 1840). I Benjamin Parsons of Ebley in the parish of Randwick certify that the school room near Ebley Chapel in the parish of Randwick, held in trust by Peter King, Samuel Sims, A S Marling and others, is to be forthwith a place of religious worship and I request you to register the same. (GDR/350/252)

1459 Randwick. 23 Jan 1843 (31 Jan 1843). I John Coxhead of Stroud certify that a meeting-house or chapel and premises at Randwick, now in the holding and occupation of the following Trustees: Peter Fluck, Joseph Fluck, Daniel Oxley, are intended to be a place of religious worship and I request you to register the same and request a certificate thereof for which shall be taken no more than two shillings and six pence. (GDR/350/313)

1460 Oxlynch, Randwick. 31 Jan 1846 (7 Feb 1846). I John Cooper Grimes of the parish of Stonehouse certify that a dwelling house at 'Oxlinch' in the parish of Randwick, occupied by Thomas Pearce, carpenter, is intended to be forthwith a place of religious worship and I request you to register the same. (GDR/350/385)

RANGEWORTHY
1461 Rangeworthy. (Trinity 1689). *Presbyterian.* William Moxham's barne. (Q/SO/3/522)

1462 Rangeworthy. (Easter 1706). *Presbyterian.* 'Raingworthy. Jo: Rodman's house'. [RG/31/6 has Joseph]. (Q/SO/3/520)

1463 Rangeworthy. (Trinity 1723). *Presbyterian.* It is ordered by this court that the new built house in the parish of Rangeworthy be licensed and allowed for dissenters called presbyterians to assemble and meet for the worship of God in their way according to the petition for that purpose filed and allowed.' (Q/SO/4/455)

1464 Rangeworthy. 11 July 1764. We [named below] certify that we have set apart a house occupied by Thomas Andrews in the parish of 'Raingworthy' as a place of meeting for religious worship. And pray that the said house may be recorded in your Office as a place of meeting. John Stichell, Daniel Wilkins, William Wilsh, William Arundell, John Thrupp, Edward Bizzey, Charles Rainger. (GDR/292A/64)

ROCKHAMPTON
1465 Rockhampton. 7 Dec 1715. *Quaker.* John Clarke of Rockhampton, dissenting minister gave the solemn affirmation to William Baker (Frenchay) and William Burton (Thornbury), schoolmasters and Quakers. (Q/SO/4/[9])

RODBOROUGH
Rodborough was a chapelry in Minchinhampton parish.
1466 Rodborough. (Easter 1701). *Presbyterian.* Simon Knight's house. (Q/SO/3/521)

1467 Rodborough. 10 Apr 1716. William Betterly of Rodborough, dissenting preacher, took oaths of allegiance, supremacy and abjuration of 1 Geo I. (Q/SO/4/496)

1468 Rodborough. 13 Mar 1748/49. *Independent.* Some [dissenters] intend to hold a meeting for the worship of God in a house adjoining to the house of William Stone, now in the possession of William Bidmead, in the parish of Rodborough and prays it may be registered. John Hooper, William Bidmead, Samuel Trotman. (GDR/284/203)

Note. This certificate corresponds to the first meeting-house of George Whitefield's followers who 20 years later built the Tabernacle 'somewhere near' (*A Memorial of Nonconformity,* 5).

1469 Rodborough. 30 May 1777 (28 June 1777). We humbly request that the dwelling house of William Antill in the parish of Rodborough be registered for a place for divine worship in the protestant dissenting way. Benjamin Francis, William Clissold, John Heskins, Edward Bliss, William Antill, Richard Clutterbuck, Evan Davies, John Hill, Daniel Pegler, Thomas Antill snr. (GDR/292A/205)

1470 Rodborough. 18 Mar 1797 (23 Mar 1797). This is to inform your lordship that a house in the parish of Rodborough, in the occupation of Mrs Martha Clutterbuck, is intended to be a place of religious worship and request that it may be registered in your Lordship's court. Robert Heath, minister, Martha Clutterbuck, John Harris, John Wood, Robert Leighton, Samuel Stephens, Henry Webb, Edward Dicks, Charles Reinget. (GDR/319A/251)

1471 Rooksmore, Rodborough. 16 May 1799 (22 Jun 1799). *Independent.* This is to cerify that an house at Rooksmore in the parish of Rodborough, now in the occupation of Mr John Harris, is intended to be a place of worship for dissenters of the Independent denomination and we request that the said house may be registered and a certificate granted accordingly. John Brown, minister, Thomas Rice, John Harris. (GDR/319A/280-1)

1472 Rodborough. 12 Mar 1817 (18 Mar 1817). *Independent.* I John Rees, dissenting minister of Rodborough Tabernacle, certify that a certain dwelling house situated at the Back path in the parish of Rodborough, occupied by John Poulston, is intended to be forthwith used as a place of religious worship and I request you to register the same. (GDR/334B/302)

1473 Rooksmore, Rodborough. 29 June 1822 (29 June 1822). This is to certify that an house and premises, now occupied by Mr. Samuel Stephens, in Rooksmore in the parish of Rodborough is intended to be a place of religious worship by a congregation of Protestants and we request that it may be registered. John Rees, minister of Rodborough Tabernacle. (GDR/344/32v)

1474 Rodborough. 4 Apr 1823. We [named below] beg respectfully to inform your Lordship that a house in the parish of Rodborough, occupied by James Clissold, is intended to be a place of religious worship and we request your Lordship to cause the same to be duly entered in the Registry of your Lordship's Diocese. Thomas Gough, John Wood. Signed James Clissold. (GDR/344/108r)

1475 Bowbridge, Rodborough. 30 Mar 1827 (23 June 1827). I William Gouldin [RG/31/2 has 'Golding'] of Bowbridge in the parish of Rodborough certify that my house and premises at Bowbridge in the parish of Rodborough, now in [my] holding and occupation, are intended to be a place of religious worship and I request you to register the same and request a certificate thereof for which shall be taken no more than two shillings and six pence. (GDR/350/66-7)

1476 Rodborough. 11 Sept 1833 (11 Sept 1833). *Baptist & Independents.* This is to certify that a building lately erected by me in the Summer House Garden in the Butter Row, parish of Rodborough, is about to be used as a place of religious worship by a congregation of dissenters consisting chiefly of persons of the Independent and Baptist denomination and I request you to register the same. Joseph Partridge. (GDR/350/141)

1477 Rodborough. 22 June 1835 (22 June 1835). I John Webb of Bagpath in the parish of Rodborough certify that a dwelling house, occupied by me, is intended forthwith to be a place of religious worship and I request you to register the same and request a certificate thereof. Witness George Webb. (GDR/350/175)

1478 Bowl Hill, Rodborough. 8 Oct 1835 (10 Oct 1835). I James Baker of Stroud certify that a dwelling house and premises at 'Bowell' [Bowl] Hill in the parish of Rodborough, now in the holding and occupation of David Hirld, are to be a place of religious worship and I hereby request you to register the same and request a certificate thereof for which shall be taken no more than two shillings and six pence. Witness David Hirld. (GDR/350/181)

1479 Bowl Hill, Rodborough. 13 Apr 1844 (15 Apr 1844). We [named below] certify that a building at Bowl Hill in the parish of Rodborough, now occupied as a British School Room, is intended to be used as a chapel for religious worship and we request that this certificate may be duly registered. Benjamin Backhouse, W Major Paull, Andrew Gammon. (GDR/350/339)

RODMARTON
1480 Rodmarton. 26 Feb 1796 (14 June 1796; registration GDR/319A/235). *Independent.* Whereas we [named below] being dissenters of the Independent denomination, have set apart a house in the parish of 'Rodmartin', now in the occupation of Hannah Liddington, for the worship of Almighty God 'we humbly intreat that the same might be registered in your Lordship's Consistorial Court.' William Griffin minister [RG/31/2 has 'of Rodmarton'], Richard Shipway, Thomas Shipway, Richard Liddington, John Walker, Nathaniel Tanner, Thos Ockle. (GDR/N2/1)
Note. Very well written, crossed through, endorsed on the back 'Registrar's Office' and 'Copy of Certificate June 14th 1796'.

1481 Culkerton, Rodmarton. 27 Feb 1819 (6 Mar 1819). I Philip Rawlings, licensed teacher, Park Street, Cirencester, certify that a dwelling, occupied by Samuel Woodrup [*sic*], labourer, in Culkerton, parish of Rodmarton, is intended forthwith to be used as a place of religious worship and I request you to register the same and request a certificate thereof. Philip Rawlings, Samuel Woodroffe, William Woodroffe, John Wallis, Thomas Ireland, Robert Clapton, John Evans. (GDR/334B/265)

1482 Culkerton, Rodmarton. 28 May 1838 (9 June 1838). [*Primitive Methodist*]. I Joseph Preston of Brinkworth, Wiltshire, certify that a house and premises at Culkerton in the parish of Rodmarton, now in the holding and occupation of William Ellison, are to be a place of religious worship and I request you to register the same and request a certificate thereof for which shall be taken no more than two shillings and six pence. Witness John Excell (GDR/350/228)
Note. For Joseph Preston and John Excell *see* **254**.

ROEL
1483 Roel. 15 Nov 1779 (15 Jan 1780; registration GDR/292A/226). We [named below] certify that we intend to hold a meeting for the worship of Almighty God in the dwelling house of William Coles, husbandman, being a house in an extra-parochial place called 'Rowell Farm'. We pray that this certificate may be registered'. Benjamin Beddome,

William Palmer, George Gorton, Robert Rowland. 'This certificate was registered in the Consistory Court of the Lord Bishop of Gloucester by me Thomas Rudge, Deputy registrar'. (GDR/N2/1)

RUARDEAN
See also Lydbrook, Dean Forest.

1484 Ruardean. 1672. *Congregational.* Licence recorded 10 June 1672 to 'John Cheapman' for his house in 'Rewerden'; licence received by Owen Davies 12 June 1672 for 'John Chapman' and his house 'Rerwarden, Glostershire'. (LT/401, 507)
Note. A comment in LT/3, 839 claims this was a Baptist meeting.

1485 Ruardean. 1672. *Presbyterian.* Application by John Juxon, 31 May 1672 for licence to Mr Thomas Smith, of Huntley in Gloucestershire of 'the presbiterian perswasion', and for an outhouse belonging to Thomas Bradley of 'Ruarden'; licence recorded 10 June 1672 to Thomas Smith to be a Presbyterian in Thomas Bradley's outhouse in 'Burden', Gloucestershire, and 5 Sept 1672 for the house of Thomas Bradley of 'Ruarden' and for Thomas Smith of Huntley to be a Presbyterian teacher. (LT/385, 507, 553)
Note. See also Thomas Smith in Huntley **977**.

1486 Ruardean. 12 May 1775. *Independent.* We [named below] being dissenters commonly called Independents, householders of the town and parish of Mitcheldean, certify that we design to hold a meeting at or in the dwelling house of Richard Matthews in the parish and near the town of Ruardean, called the *Crooked Inn,* for the worship of Almighty God, humbly petitioning the Reverend Father in God Lord Bishop of the diocese to grant his Lordship's leave, and this our certificate may be registered in his Lordship's Register Office, that we thereby may enjoy the liberty without interruption granted by the statute in that case made and provided. Josiah Vaughan, Thomas Partridge, Richard Miller, Nathaniel Vaughan. (GDR/292A/179)
Note. Rubric states 'Mitchel Dean', but premises in Ruardean. Briefly mentioned under Micheldean **1207**.

1487 Ruardean. 7 Jan 1782 (registered Epiphany 1782, Q/SO/10/f.38r). *Independent.* 'We [named below] being Protestant dissenters commonly called Independents and of the number of His Majesty's loyal subjects, householders in the towns and parishes of Mitchel Dean and Ruardean . . . certify to this court that we do intend to set apart a dwelling house, lately inhabited by one Joseph Evans, deceased, (the property and freehold of Mr Terrott) in the town and parish of Ruardean . . . for the service and worship of Almighty God and we request that this our certificate may be recorded and a licence thereupon granted'. Thomas Partridge, Mary Gough, James Teague, William Pearce, Richard Miller, Nathaniell Vaughan, Betty Clark, Esther Miller, Rachel Annats. (Q/SR/1782/A 29)
Note. An original signed certificate: the men's signatures are on the left hand side and the women's on the right hand side beneath the text. Briefly mentioned under Micheldean **1208** above.

1488 Ruardean. 24 Feb 1798. *Independent.* This is to certify that a chapel newly erected in the village of Ruardean is intended to be a place of worship for diissenters of the Independent denomination. We request that the said chapel may be registered. S Phillips, minister; Thomas Partridge, John Bennett, John Rudge, Joseph Eadey, James Cook, Joseph Blanch, Henry Smart, Thomas Bennett, Thomas Meek, James Bennett, John Evans, Charles Lewis, John Vaughan. (GDR/319A/263)

1489 Ruardean. 27 Aug 1808 (3 Sept 1808). *Independent.* This is to certify that a house in the occupation of Joseph Blanch, coal miner, in the parish of Ruardean is to be used for religious worship for dissenters of the Independent denomination. We therefore request that the said house may be registered. John Horlick, minister; Joseph Blanch, John Bennett, Jacob Chivers. (GDR/334B/412)

Note. For Horlick *see* Introduction lxv and **1096**. *See also Mitcheldean* **1212** and references in **654**, **679**, **868**, **1111**, **1206**.

1490 Ruardean. 13 Sept 1823 (15 Sept 1823). This is to certify that the dwelling house of Joseph Hood (in the Square), Ruardean, is intended forthwith to be a place of religious worship and I require you to register the same and hereby request a certificate thereof. John Taylor. (GDR/344/113v)

1491 [Crooked End], Ruardean. 9 June 1828 (28 June 1828). I William Lawry, minister, certify that a chapel (the property of Mary Cook, Varnister) at 'Crooker' in the parish of Ruardean is intended forthwith to be a place of religious worship and hereby require you to register and record the same and request a certificate thereof. William Lawry, Mary Cook. (GDR/350/91)

RUDFORD
1492 Rudford. 8 Aug 1818 (11 Aug 1818). I Jonathan Williams of Gloucester, minister, certify that the house of Henry Stock in the parish of Rudford is intended forthwith to be used as a place of religious worship and require you to register the same and request a certificate thereof. (GDR/334B/276)

ST BRIAVELS *For parish see Dean Forest*

SAINTBURY
1493 Saintbury. 18 September 1822 (20 Sept 1822). I Robert Storley of Saintbury certify that my dwelling house, the property of [-] West esq is intended forthwith to be a place of religious worship and I require you to register the same. Robert Storley (mark), witness George Jayne, dissenting minister, Peter Haines. (GDR/344/37v)

SANDHURST
1494 Sandhurst. (25 May 1810). *Methodist.* We [named below] beg leave to certify that a house in the occupation of George Gears in the parish of Sandhurst is intended to be used for the worship of Almighty God by dissenters commonly called Methodists and we request that the same may be entered in your Lordship's Registry and a certificate of the same granted accordingly. George Gears, Joseph Drinkwater [RG/31/2 has of Sandhurst], Peter Drinkwater, Paul Drinkwater, Thomas Drinkwater. (GDR/334B/384)

1495 Sandhurst. 29 Mar 1817 (29 Mar 1817). We [named below] residing in the parish of Sandhurst certify that we are desirous of meeting for religious worship in the dwelling house of William Brawn [Sandhurst] i.e. in the kitchen, which apartment your Lordship will be pleased to have registered. William Brawn snr, William Brawn jnr. (GDR/334B/299)

1496 Sandhurst. 15 Feb 1819 (15 Feb 1819). We [named below], residing in the parish of Sandhurst and its neighbourhood, are desirous of meeting for religious worship in the dwelling house of William Harris in the said parish i.e. in the kitchen of the said house, which appartment your Lordship will be pleased to have registered. William Perkes [RG/31/2 has of Sandhurst], Thomas Mark, William Harris (mark), James Hollister. (GDR/334B/266)

1497 Sandhurst. (28 May 1850). House and premises occupied by John Tarling. John Thurston. (Q/RNp/4)

SAPPERTON

1498 Frampton [Mansell], Sapperton. 21 Mar 1804 (27 Mar 1804) We [named below] have agreed to set apart for the public worship of Almighty God a dwelling house, now in the holding or occupation of Samuel Jones, at Frampton in the parish of Sapperton and desire that the same may be registered. Jer. Brettell, Hugh Ransom, William Lewis, Samuel Jones, William Hale, William Smith, William Wood, William Gurner. (GDR/334B/440)

1499 Sapperton. *Independent.* 2 November 1822. We [named below] certify that a building in the parish of 'Saperton', in the occupation of James Whiting, is intended to be a place for religious worship by dissenters of the denomination of Independents and we request that this certificate may be registered in the Consistory Court of your Lordship. William Wild, minister. (GDR/344/39r)

SAUL

Saul was a chapelry in Standish parish.

1500 Framilode, Saul. 10 June 1825 (11 June 1825). I William Richardson of Frampton upon Severn, dissenting minister, certify that a tenement at Framilode in the parish of Saul, in the occupation of William James, labourer, is intended forthwith to be a place of religious worship and I do hereby require you to register and record the same. (GDR/350/41)

1501 Framilode [Saul]. 5 Dec 1829 (9 Dec 1829). I William Richardson of Frampton on Severn, minister, certify that a building or tenement at 'Framelode', in the occupation of William James, labourer, is intended forthwith to be a place of religious worship and I hereby request you to register the same. William James, William Richardson (GDR/350/106)

1502 Framilode, Saul. 30 May 1836 (30 May 1836). I John James Waite of the city of Gloucester certify that a house, in the occupation of Thomas Williams, at Framilode Mills in the parish of Saul are intended to be a place of religious worship and I hereby request you to register the same and request a certificate thereof. James Waite (mark). (GDR/350/196-7)

1503 Framilode, Saul. 16 July 1842 (23 July 1842). I William Lewis of Frampton on Severn, dissenting minister, certify that a tenement at Framilode in the parish of Saul, in the occupation of Mary Nurse, is forthwith to be a place of religious worship and I require you to register the same. (GDR/350/301)

1504 Framilode, Saul. 1 Jan 1845 (4 Jan 1845). I William Lewis of Frampton on Severn, dissenting minister, certify that a tenement at Framilode in the parish of Saul, in the occupation of William Andrews, waterman, is intended forthwith to be a place of religious worship and I require you to register the same. (GDR/350/356)

1505 Saul. (10 Sep 1850). Tenement. William Lewis. (Q/RNp/4)

1506 'Framilode in Saul'. (16 May 1851). Premises known as the British schoolroom. George Knight. (Q/RNp/4)

SEVENHAMPTON

1507 Brockhampton, Sevenhampton. 9 Mar 1813 (12 Mar 1813). I Susan Wood of Brockhampton in the parish of Sevenhampton certify that my dwelling house is intended to be used as a place of religious worship and require you to register the same and request a certificate thereof. (GDR/334B/348)

1508 Brockhampton, Sevenhampton. 24 Jan 1833 (26 Jan 1833). I James Smith of Cheltenham certify that a dwelling house at Brockhampton in the parish of Sevenhampton, occupied by Michael Cook, labourer, is intended forthwith to be a place of religious worship and I request you to register the same. James Smith, James Hughes, Benjamin Leach. (GDR/350/137)

1509 Brockhampton [Sevenhampton]. 30 May 1834 (2 June 1834). I James Smith of Cheltenham certify that a building at Brockhampton in the parish of Sevenhampton called Bethel Chapel is intended to be forthwith a place of religious worship and I request you to register the same. James Smith, witness James Hughes, Joseph Leonard. (GDR/350/152)

1510 Sevenhampton. (25 May 1850). Premises occupied by George Coombs. John Lewis, William Charles Chambers. (Q/RNp/4)

SHENINGTON
Transferred to Oxfordshire in 1844.
1511 Shenington. 30 Nov 1815 (9 Dec 1815). I John Arnold of 'Shennington', blacksmith, certify that a shop, now in my occupation, is intended forthwith to be a place of religious worship and require you to register the same and request a certificate thereof. John Arnold, blacksmith, signed in the presence of John Saden. (GDR/334B/324)

1512 Shenington. 7 May 1818 (12 May 1818). *Methodist.* I John Cullen of Banbury, minister, certify that house of John Arnold in the parish of Shenington, is intended forthwith to be used as a place of religious worship and require you to register the same and request a certificate thereof. John Cullen Methodist minister. (GDR/334B/280)

1513 Shenington. 23 July 1819 (24 Nov 1819). *Methodist.* I John Cullen of Banbury, Methodist minister, certify that a chapel in the parish of 'Shennington' is intended forthwith to be a place of religious worship and require you to register the same and request a certificate thereof. (GDR/334B/250)

SHIPTON MOYNE
1514 Shipton [Moyne]. 1672. *Presbyterian.* Licence recorded 16 July 1672 to William Hodges to be a presbyterian teacher in the house of Widow Hodges at Shipton, and for the house of Widow Hodges; also recorded 18 Nov 1672. (LT/527, 573)
Note. LT suggested Shipton Moyne; and see next entry.

1515 Shipton Moyne. 6 Dec 1715. [*Presbyterian: see note*]. John Oldham of Shipton Moyne, dissenting preacher, took oaths of allegiance and supremacy. (Q/SO/4/[8])
Note. 'Oldham' named as Presbyterian minister in 'Shipton or Wotton underedge' in Evans list. He was ejected from curacy at Shipton Moyne in 1662.

SHIPTON OLIFFE
1516 Shipton Oliffe. 14 July 1773 (20 July 1773). *Baptist.* Some [dissenters] called Baptists intend to hold a meeting for the worship of Almighty God at the dwelling house of John Swinford in the parish of 'Shipton Oliff' and therefore pray that this certificate may be duly registered in your Court according to the Act of Toleration. Edward Grifin, Bety Grifin, Sabrah Grifin, Sarah Grifin, Maray Grifin, Mary Wood, Hanah Wood, Mary Tiling, Rebaco Cadle, John Grifin, Thomas Pain, Benjamin Preston, Mary Preston snr, Samuel Dunscombe, Hester Swinford, Ann Wood, Benjamin Wood, Thomas Swinford, Edund

Grifin, Mary Grifin jnr, James Cadle, Mary Pain, Mary Preston jnr, Charles Wood, John Swinford. (GDR/292A/157-8)

Note. This certificate was entered again on p171 and crossed out, with a note: 'entered before on page 79' [i.e. folio 79/p157]. The copy contains 24 signatures, not in the same order, recording Mary not Maray Grifin, but omitting Mary Wood.

1517 Shipton Oliffe. 9 Mar 1837 (10 Mar 1837). I Samuel Franklin of Cheltenham certify that a dwelling house in the parish of Shipton Oliffe, occupied by Charles Cooper, labourer, is to be forthwith a place of religious worship and I request you to register the same. (GDR/350/207)

SHIPTON SOLLARS
1518 Shipton Sollars. 7 Feb 1835 (7 Feb 1835). I James Smith of Cheltenham certify that a dwelling house in the parish of 'Shipton Solars', ocuupied by John Smith, labourer, is intended to be forthwith used as a place of religious worship and I hereby request you to register the same. Witness Charles H Channon, James Hughes. (GDR/350/163)

SHIREHAMPTON
Shirehampton was a chapelry in Westbury-on-Trym and became a parish in 1844.
1518a Shirehampton. 18 Jun 1762 (21 Jun 1762). We [named below] being some dissenters certify that we intend to make use of a house situate at 'Shirehamton' in the parish of 'Westbury upon Trym', now in the possession of Nicholas Fennick, as a place of religious worship and pray that the same may be registered. James Rogers, John Colston, Mary Saunders, Kath Harris, Francis George, Mary Rogers, John Williams, Mary Sutton, Ann Camlin, Benjamin Ramner, Samuel Poe, Mary Fay. (EP/A/45/1/28)

1518b Shirehampton. 15 Dec 1818 (24 Dec 1818). I Nicholas Thomas of Shirehampton in the parish of Westbury, Gloucestershire, certify that a room in my house in the village [of] Shirehampton is forthwith to be a place of religious worship and I require you to register the same and require a certificate thereof. Witness Robert Edbrooke. (EP/A/45/2/116)

SHURDINGTON
Shurdington was a chapelry in Badgeworth parish; for Little Shurdington see Badgeworth.
1519 Shurdington. 26 July 1825 (31 July 1825). We [named below] certify that a house and garden in the parish of Shurdington, the property of Joseph Shill, is intended forthwith to be a place of religious worship and we request you to register the same. John Blackwell, Joseph Shill, Jo Hips (mark), George Moulder (mark), George Blackwell, Thomas Fisher (mark), James Hyett. (GDR/350/43)

1520 Shurdington. 14 Jan 1833. These are to certify that we the undersigned in the behalf of ourselves and others have engaged a certain tenement or house in the parish of Shurdington, the property of John Bullock of the same place, and occupied by George Blackwell as tenant, which tenement or house is intended by and with the consent of the above named to be used for the purpose of public worship or divine service. And we request that the house may be registered and duly entered on the records of the Consistory Court and that a certificate thereof be given to us. George Blackwell, Isaac Jones, Baynham Coopey, William Holliday, George Long, Richard Gregory, Thomas Strong, William Yeates. (GDR/350/136)

1521 Shurdington. (26 Mar 1851). Room in a cottage occupied by James Organ. Jonas Radford and others. (Q/RNp/4)

SIDDINGTON

1522 Siddington. 17 Jan 1822 (1 Feb 1822). [*Methodist: see* **1399**]. I James Blackett, minister of the Gospel at Stroud, certify that a dwelling house at Siddington, in the occupation of Daniel Smith, is intended forthwith as a place of religious worship and I require you to register and hereby request a certificate thereof. (GDR/344/16r)

1523 Siddington. 19 Apr 1822 (2 May 1822). We hereby certify that a hay loft and barn at Siddington, now in the occupation of the Revd J W Lowrie, will henceforth be a place of religious worship. Revd James Walter Lowrie, John Bramble, James Maysey (mark). (GDR/344/23r)

1524 Siddington. 22 Dec 1827 (26 Dec 1827). We [named below] certify that a certain newly erected building in the parish of Siddington is intended forthwith to be a place of religious worship and we require you to register the same. Mark Drury, dissenting minister, William Wilkins, Rachel Cook, James Brasington, John Box, Sarah Box. (GDR/350/80)

1525 Siddington. 26 Mar 1838 (26 Apr 1838). *Independent.* We [named below] certify that a building in the parish of Siddington, in the possession of William Wilkins, is to be a place of religious worship by dissenters of the denomination of Independents and request that this certificate may be registered. William Wilkins, Ann Wilkins, Hanah Fluss [Flux], Rachel Cook, Jonah Habgood. (GDR/350/223)
Note. Hanah Flux recorded in mid-19th century censuses.

1526 Siddington. 30 Dec 1839 (1 Jan 1840). I John Goodwin of Cirencester certify that a house and premises in the parish of Siddington, now in the holding and occupation of John See, are to be a place of religious worship and I request you to register the same and request a certificate thereof for which shall be taken no more than two shillings and six pence. John Goodwin, John See. (GDR/350/247-8)

1527 Siddington. 7 June 1842 (9 June 1842). [*Primitive Methodist: see* **254**]. I Joseph Preston of Brinkworth, Wilts, certify that a chapel and premises at Siddington, Wilts, now in the holding and occupation of James May, are intended to be a place of religious worship and I request you to register the same and request a certificate thereof for which shall be taken no more than two shillings and six pence. (GDR/350/298)

SISTON

1528 Siston. 3 Oct 1760 (registered Michaelmas 1760, Q/SO/8/f.246v). *Presbyterian.* We [named below] certify that we intend to make use of the house of Isaac Sommeril in the parish of Siston as a place of meeting for religious worship, and pray that the said house may be recorded as a place of meeting for [dissenters] (Presbyterians) from the Church of England. William Prockter, William Lewis, Joseph Harris, Isaac Summerhill, Christopher Wise, David Thomas, Joseph Graft, Samuel Tippett, Richard Monk, Nathaniel Williams. (Q/SR/1760/D/19)
Note. Certificate crossed through.

1529 Warmley Tower, Siston. 25 Nov 1811 (28 Nov 1811). *Wesleyan Connexion.* Whereas we [named below] being in the connexion of the late Revd John Wesley, deceased, have appropriated and set apart a building, known by the name of the Methodist Preaching House, at the Warmley Tower in the parish of Siston for the worship of Almighty God, we request that the same may be registered. Joseph Bowes, Robert Janes, William Johnson, Robert Kitch, James Parker, Thomas Clark, John Peacock, Francis Monton. (GDR/334B/359-58)

SLIMBRIDGE

1530 Slimbridge. 21 Dec 1796 (3 Jan 1797). We [named below] certify that we have set apart a house, now occupied by John Warner, in the parish of Slimbridge as a place of meeting for religious worship and pray that the said house may be recorded. William Archard, Richard King, William Huntley. (GDR/319A/247)

1531 Slimbridge. 9 Feb 1797 (13 Feb 1797). We [named below] certify that we have set apart a barn, now occupied by William Archard jnr, in the parish of Slimbridge as a place of meeting for religious worship and pray that the said house or barn may be recorded. William Archard jnr, Richard King, Joseph Sims jnr, Samuel King snr. (GDR/319A/249)

1532 Slimbridge. 6 Nov 1797 (8 Nov 1797). We [named below] certifiy that we have set apart a house, now occupied by William Huntley, in the parish of Slimbridge as a place of meeting for religious worship and pray that the said house may be recorded as a place of meeting. Richard King, William Archard jnr, William Huntley, Samuel King snr. (GDR/319A/257)

1533 Slimbridge. (20 Aug 1808). We [named below] certify that 20 yards of ground, extending every way from the corner where the Slimbridge highway crosses the Gloucester and Bristol turnpike road, is appropriated for the purpose of the public worship of Almighty God and we require that the same may be registered. Hester King, William Worthington, John Jenkins, Thomas Pinder, William Dixon, J Answorth. (GDR/334B/414)

1534 Slimbridge. (20 Aug 1808). We [named below] certify that the barn, the court and the orchard of Hester King in the parish of Slimbridge is appropriated for the pupose of the public worship of Almighty God and require that the same may be registered. Hester King, William Worthington, John Jenkins, Thomas Pinder, J Answorth, W Dixon. (GDR/334B/414)

1535 Cambridge, Slimbridge. 25 Aug 1808 (27 Aug 1808). We [named below] certify that we have set apart a chapel at Cambridge in the parish of Slimbridge as a place of meeting for religious worship and pray that the said chapel may be recorded. William Orchard, Benjamin Smith, John Warner, William Huntley, Richard Mallett, Joseph Bick. (GDR/334B/413)

1536 The Warth, Slimbridge. 31 Dec 1825 (18 Jan 1826). I John Barnett of Dursley certify that a house and premises at 'Wath' in the parish of Slimbridge, now in the holding and occupation of William Thornwell, are intended to be used as a place of religious worship and I hereby request you to register and record the same, and I hereby request a certificate thereof. (GDR/350/50)

SNOWSHILL

1537 Snowshill. 20 Dec 1812 (2 Jan 1813). I Stephen Stanley of Snowshill, labourer, certify that a certain building messuage or tenement, being myself proprietor and also occupier, is intended forthwith to be used as a place of religious worship and require you to register the same. Stephen Stanley, Mary Stanley, David Taylor, Elizabeth Brain. (GDR/334B/349)

1538 Snowshill. 6 Jan 1818 (2 Feb 1818). I Stephen Stanley of Snowshill, labourer, certify that a certain building, messuage or tenement in the parish of Snowshill, the property of William Sharp of Stanton, mason, and in my possession, is intended forthwith to be used as a place of religious worship and require you to register the same. Witness John Morris. (GDR/334B/286)

1539 Snowshill. 16 Nov 1824 (17 Nov 1824). I John Thurston, minister of Wellesbourne in the county of Warwick, certify that the house in the possession of William Hall in the parish of 'Snow hill' is set apart for the public worship of Almighty God and require you to register the same. (GDR/350/22)

1540 Snowshill. 9 Dec 1840 (5 Jan 1841). I Stephen Stanley of the parish of Snowshill certify that my house in Snowshill is forthwith to be a place of religious worship and require you to register the same and request a certificate thereof. Witness Thomas Jennings. (GDR/350/269)

SOUTH CERNEY

1541 South Cerney. 19 May 1810 (24 May 1810). This is to certify that we [named below] intend to hold a meeting for the worship of Almighty God in the dwelling house of John Turk in the parish of 'South Surney'. We pray that this certificate may be entered in your Lordship's Registry. John Rogers, Thomas Morgan, John Turk (mark), William Hall, Thomas Atkins, Edward Herbert. (GDR/334B/385)
Note. Clerk underlined 'Surney' lightly in pencil.

1542 South Cerney. 20 November 1821 (28 Nov 1821). We certify that a house at South Cerney, now in the occupation of the Revd J Walter Lowrie, will henceforth be a place of religious worship. Walter Lowrie, Philip Bramble, Elizabeth Tayler, Henery Antold. (GDR/344/Page 1 from rear)
Note. No RG return. Certificate apparently re-written in Apr 1822.

1543 South Cerney. 25 Apr 1822 (2 May 1822). We the undersigned certify that a house or shop and kitchen at South Cerney, now in the occupation of the Revd J Walter Lowrie, will henceforth be a place of religious worship. Revd J W Lowrie, Elizabeth Taylor, Henry Arnold. (GDR/344/23r)

1544 South Cerney. 29 Sept 1824 (8 Oct 1824). We [named below] certify that a house, stable and cottage at South Cerney, now in the occupation of Revd J W Lowrie will henceforth be used as a place of religious worship. J W Lowrie, J Hooper, S Habgood, William Wilkins. (GDR/344/138r)

1545 South Cerney. (28 July 1849). *Primitive Methodist* chapel. George Lee [RG/31/2 has of Cirencester]. (Q/RNp/4)

SOUTHROP

1546 Southrop. 30 Sept 1835 (2 Oct 1835). I John William Peters certify that the dwelling house of Joseph Emblin in his occupation in the parish of Southrop near Fairford is intended to be a place of worship and I request that the same may be registered accordingly. (GDR/350/180)

1547 Southrop. (27 Nov 1849). House occupied by William Mustow. John Fleetwood Lewis. (Q/RNp/4)

STANDISH

Standish parish contained three chapelries, Hardwick, Randwick and Saul, which see.

1548 Putloe [Standish]. (Michaelmas 1702). *Anabaptist.* 'Putlo', Virgil Cripps house. (Q/SO/3/521)

1549 Standish. 2 June 1764. *Baptist.* Some [dissenters] intend to hold a meeting for the worship of God in their way in the dwelling house of John Merrett in the parish of

Standish. We therefore pray that this may be recorded. James Drewett Baptist minister [RG/31/2 has James 'Brewett']; Robert Day Browning, Samson Browning, William Motley (mark), Thomas Haglet, John Merrett, Elizabeth Motley (mark). (GDR/292A/63)

STANTON
The modern spellings are Stanton in the north of the county and Staunton in the west of the county but in the past the spellings were not so distinghised. Lewis's Topographical Dictionary confused them. See Staunton below.
1550 Stanton. 23 Mar 1824 [entry in GDR 350 has 22 Mar] (24 Apr 1824). I Edward Rosser of Stanton in the parish of Stanton certify that my house and premises 'is' intended forthwith to be a place of religious worship and require you to register the same, and request a certificate thereof. Revd Samuel Heath. (GDR/344/130r)

1551 Stanton. 4 Apr 1843 (24 Apr 1843). I George Wood Rodway of Gloucester, dissenting minister, certify that a building near the road in Stanton, adjoining Robert Shills' garden, is intended to be a place of religious worship and I request you to register the same and request a certificate thereof. (GDR/350/320)

STANWAY
1552 Stanway. 17 Feb 1835 (20 Feb 1835). I William Harris of the parish of Stanway certify that my house in Stanway is intended forthwith to be a place of religious worship and I request you to register the same and request a certificate thereof. Witness David Taylor, William Taylor. (GDR/350/165)

STAPLETON
Diocese of Bristol. Fishponds became a parish in 1869 (Youngs 173).
1553 Stapleton 8 May 1779 (13 May 1779). *Independent.* We [named below] being part of a congregation of dissenters certify that an house situate in the parish of Stapleton in your lordship's diocese now in the possession of Mr John Hall is set apart for a meeting place of a congregation under the denomination of Independents. We desire the same may be registered in your lordship's court. James Harding, John Colston, John Gwyer, Dan Wait, Hugh Saunderson. (EP/A/45/1/105)

1554 Fishponds, Stapleton. 18 Jun 1802 (21 Jun 1802). We [named below] being part of a congregation of dissenters certify that part of a certain dwelling house at 'the Fish Ponds' within the parish of Stapleton now in the occupation of Richard Hoare is set apart for and to be used as a place of meeting for religious worship. We therefore desire that the same may be registered in your lordship's court. Thomas Parker, Lucian Brown, Thomas Smith, Charles Stone, John King, Richard Hoare, Isaac James. (EP/A/45/1/323-24)

1555 Stapleton. 4 Mar 1806 (8 Mar 1806). We [named below] being part of a congregation of dissenters certify that a certain building situate near Stapleton Bridge in the parish of Stapleton in the occupation of Martha Randole sp[inste]r is to be set apart as a place of religious worship of Almighty God. We desire the same may be registered. Martha Randole [RG/31/2 has 'Randal'], Thomas Howland, Henry Hobbs, John Flock, John King, Thomas Rainford, George Highfield, Henry Collings, Thomas Saunders, William Fish, James White. (EP/A/45/1/360)

1556 Fishponds, Stapleton. 21 Nov 1810 (13 Mar 1811). *Wesleyan.* Whereas we [named below] dissenting from the Church of England, and in the connection of the late Revd John Wesley, deceased, have appropriated and set aside a house called the Methodist Preaching Society belonging to Daniel Smith snr, gardener, in the village of Fishponds in the parish of Stapleton, for the worship of Almighty God, [we] request that the same may be registered. Thomas Smith jnr, Thomas Smith snr, 'Zechrah' Porter, Robert Hopton, Joseph Flook jnr, Joseph Flook snr, John Watkins, Richard Ponting, Charles Middleton, Moses Garland, Daniel Smith. (EP/A/45/2/41)

1557 Upper Stapleton, [rubric states Fishponds], Stapleton. 22 July 1814 (3 Aug 1814). *Baptist.* I John Vernon of Downend, Gloucestershire, Baptist minister, certify that the house of Thomas Tyler, Upper Stapleton in the parish of Stapleton, is forthwith to be a place of religious worship and I require you to register the same and request a certificate thereof.
'I Thomas Tyler certify that I fully approve of having my house appropriated to the above purpose. Witness my hand 25 July 1814'. (EP/A/45/2/84)

1558 Stapleton. 26 Sept 1815 (14 Nov 1815). I Peregrine Phillips, living at No 34 Milk Street in the city of Bristol, tailor, certify that a building messuage or tenement in the parish of Stapleton near the *Bell Inn* in Stapleton Street, late in the possession of [-] Lock but now void and about to be occupied by David Jones, is forthwith to be a place of religious worship and require you to register the same. (EP/A/45/2/100)

1559 Frenchay, Stapleton. 14 Jan 1831 (18 Jan 1831). *Baptist.* We [named below] certify that a dwelling house in Frenchay, a hamlet in the parish of Stapleton, in a part of the hamlet called Frenchay Vale, adjoining Mr Hobbes's Iron Foundry, and now in the occupation of William Kelson, is to be used for religious worship by dissenters of the denomination of Baptists and we request that this certificate may be registered in the Commissary's Court of your Lordship. Thomas S Crisp, John Ford, John Eyres. (GDR/350/113)

1560 Stapleton. 6 Jan 1834 (15 Feb 1834). *Baptist.* We [named below] certify that a building called Stapleton chapel in the parish of Stapleton is to be used for religious worship by dissenters of the denomination of Baptists and we request that this certificate may be registered. John Battershill, James Clift, William Howell. (EP/A/45/2/402)

1561 Stapleton. 26 Mar 1841 (29 Mar 1841). *Wesleyan Methodist.* We [named below] certify that a school room in the occupation of Mark Whitwill, and known as Freeland Buildings School Room, in the parish of Stapleton is to be used for religious worship by dissenters of the denomination of Wesleyan Methodist and we request that this certificate may be registered. Mark Whitwill, Thomas West, George Hobbs. (EP/A/45/3/34)

1562 Stapleton. 21 May 1850 (25 May 1850). *Baptist.* I George J[oseph] Bompas certify that a room in the house in which I reside in the parish of Stapleton is to be a place of religious worship by dissenters of the denomination of Baptists and I request that this certificate may be registered. George J Bompas [Joseph inserted after the copy of the certificate was written]. (EP/A/45/4/27)
Note. Certificate pasted in. Probably signed.

1563 Fishponds, Stapleton. 7 Nov 1850 (8 Nov 1850). *Wesleyan Methodist.* I Charles Clay of Kingswood Hill in the parish of Bitton certify that a building at Fishponds called the Wesleyan Methodist chapel in the parish of Stapleton is used and henceforth to be used as a place of religious worship and I require you to register the same and request a certificate thereof. (EP/A/45/4/43)
Note. For Charles Clay *see* **120**.

1564 Fishponds, Stapleton. 3 Nov 1850 (9 Nov 1850). *Wesleyan Reformers.* 'We the undersigned do make an application to the Registrar of the Register Office, Broad Street, Bristol, to grant a licence for preaching in a premises belonging to Mr Job Smith, Fishponds, as a Wesleyan Reformers Chapel, situated at Fishponds in the parish of Stapleton in the county of Gloucester. Signed our hands November 3th 1850.' John Webber, Joseph Ball, Joseph Watts, Jacob Monks, John Garland, Daniel King, Job Smith, owner of the premises, John Purdy, chapel steward, John Ball, treasurer. (EP/A/45/4/42)
Note. Written in a very large hand, quite legibly. May be original signatures. One of four certificates pasted in to volume, two to a side turned sideways. [*see* illus., xix]

1565 Fishponds, Stapleton. 17 Dec 1851 (31 Dec 1851). *Baptist.* We, George Joseph Bompas and George Kerry, certify that the Fishponds Baptist chapel in the parish of Stapleton is to be a place of religious worship by dissenters of the denomination of Baptists and we request that this certificate may be registered. George Kerry, minister, George J Bompas, deacon. (EP/A/45/4/120a)
Note. Loose sheet inserted in volume but not pasted in. Signed.

STAUNTON

Richard Morgan, a preacher for Lady Huntingdon's Connexion in Staunton in St Briavel's hundred, was said by Horlick in 'A visit to the Forest of Dean' to have introduced the gospel there. See also Stanton above, the spelling of which name was sometimes 'Staunton'.

1566 Staunton. 7 Oct 1796 (14 Oct 1796; registration GDR/319A/239). We the undersigned request your Lordship to be so obliging as register in your office a room in the house of Thomas Powell in the parish of Staunton for the purpose of divine worship. John Watts [RG/31/2 has of Staunton], George Dew, James Powell, John Parry. (GDR/N2/1)
Note. The surnames suggest connections with the area west of the Severn at this date rather than with Stanton in the Cotswolds. Many members of the Powell family are recorded in Nonconformist registers in the Forest of Dean.

1567 Staunton. 13 Feb 1815 (2 Mar 1815). *Independent.* We [named below] certify that the house of Richard Morgan at Staunton is set apart and appropriated for religious worship for dissenters commonly called Independents. We request that the house may be registered and a certificate of the same be given. J Griffiths, minister, George Dew, Richard Morgan, Thomas Weston, Charles Morgan, John Harris, Charles Vaughan, Thomas Stead, James Lewis, George White, George Richards, John Griffiths. (GDR/334B/330)

1568 Staunton. 17 May 1824 (17 May 1824). I Richard Morgan of Staunton request that my dwelling house, now in my own occupation, is intended forthwith to be used as a place of religious worship and I do hereby require you to register and record the same, and hereby request a certificate thereof. Witness Charles Smallridge. (GDR/344/133r)

1569 [Staunton]. 6 May 1825 (6 May 1825). I Richard Morgan of 'Stanton' certify that a dwelling house and premises, now in [my] occupation is intended to be a place of religious worship and require you to register the same. (GDR/350/39)
Note. An identically-worded certificate follows on the same page, but substituting George Morgan as occupier.

1570 Staunton. 8 Apr 1832 (16 Apr 1832). I Daniel Ricketts, certify that a building or tenement in the parish of Staunton, being myself occupier, is intended to be forthwith a place of religious worship and I request you to register the same. Witness John Sharp, Thomas Sharp. (GDR/350/126)

STAVERTON

1571 Staverton. 8 Dec 1834 (8 Dec 1834). I, D Latimer St Clair of Staverton, certify that a dwelling house at Staverton is intended forthwith to be a place of religious worship and I request you to register the same. (GDR/350/162)

1572 Staverton. 2 May 1835 (2 May 1835). I William Bullock of Leckhampton certify that a dwelling house, in the occupation of William Lewis, in the parish of Staverton is intended to be forthwith a place of religious worship and I hereby require you to register the same and request a certificate thereof. (GDR/350/173)
Note. It appears this certificate may have been entered twice, with the buildings further described, on 20 June. *See following entry.*

1573 Staverton. 20 June 1835 (20 June 1835). I William Bullock of Leckhampton certify that a dwelling house, outbuildings and premises adjoining and belonging thereto, in the occupation of William Lewis, in the parish of Staverton, are intended forthwith to be a place of religious worship and I require you to register the same and request a certificate thereof. (GDR/350/175)

1574 Staverton. 11 Sept 1835 (12 Sept 1835). I John Edward Lea of the city of Gloucester certify that a dwelling house, in the occupation of Hannah Butt, in the parish of Staverton is intended forthwith to be a place of religious worship and require you to register the same and request a certificate thereof. (GDR/350/178)

STINCHCOMBE

1575 Stinchcombe. 1672. *Independent.* Licence recorded 3 February 1672/3 to James Forbes Independent teacher in the barn of Charles Eliot of 'Stinchcomb'. (LT/584)

1576 Stinchcombe. (Easter 1690). *Quaker.* 'Stinchcomb', Meeting-house. (Q/SO/3/522)

1577 Stancombe [Stinchcombe]. (Michaelmas 1691). *Quaker.* Meeting-house. (Q/SO/3/522)

1578 Stancombe [Stinchcombe]. (Trinity 1706). *Quaker.* 'Stancomb', Elizabeth Chiltenham's house. (Q/SO/3/520)

1579 Stancombe, Stinchcombe. (Easter 1731). *Presbyterian.* It is ordered by this court that [dissenters] called presbyterians living in or near the parish of 'Stinchcome' be licensed and allowed to meet together in the dwelling house of Moses Tiller in 'Stanscombe'. (Q/SO/5/f.157r)
Note. Rubric has 'Stancombe Meeting-house lycensed'; Stancombe Farm and park were in Stinchcombe (Smith 2, 250).

1580 Stancombe, Stinchcombe. 25 July 1746. Some [dissenters] intend to hold a meeting for the worship of God in the dwelling house of Mary Chiltenham in 'Stancomb' in the parish of Stinchcombe and desire it may be registered. John Higgins, William Williams, John Shipway, Matthew Hale, James Fisher. (GDR/284/174)

1581 Stinchcombe. 21 July 1767. Some [dissenters] intend to hold a meeting for the worship of Almighty God at the dwelling house of John Brown, wire drawer, in the parish of 'Stinchcomb', and desire that the same may be registered. Daniel Trotman, John Brown, John Browning. (GDR/292A/101)

STOKE GIFFORD

Diocese of Bristol from 1542

1582 Stoke Gifford. (Epiphany 1742/3). *Quaker.* It is ordered by this court that the dwelling house of Joseph Player in the parish of Stoke Gifford be licensed and allowed for [dissenters] called Quakers to assemble and meet together in for the worship of Almighty God in their way 'pursuant to to a request now made to this court for that purpose and the form of the statute in that case made and provided'. (Q/SO/7/f.52r)

1583 Stoke Gifford. 21 May 1843 (10 June 1843). [*Wesleyan*]. I William Griffith of Downend near Bristol, Wesleyan Minister, certify that a dwelling house or cottage in the parish of Stoke Gifford now in the occupation of Giles Lawrence, labourer, is to be forthwith a place of religious worship and I require you to register the same and request a certificate thereof. (EP/A/45/3/157)

STOKE ORCHARD

Stoke Orchard was a chapelry in Bishop's Cleeve parish.

1584 Stoke Orchard. (Easter 1690). *Quaker.* 'Stoak' Orchard, Meeting-house. (Q/SO/3/522)

1585 Stoke Orchard. 28 July 1821 (28 July 1821). I Benjamin Andrews of the Borough of Tewkesbury certify that a dwelling house in the parish of Stoke Orchard in the occupation of Joseph Barnes, day labourer, is intended forthwith to be a place of religious worship and I require you to register the same and request a certificate thereof. (GDR/334B/215)

1586 Stoke Orchard. 12 Dec 1840. I James Smith of Cheltenham certify that a house in the occupation of Daniel Harris, carpenter, at Stoke Orchard in the parish of Bishop's Cleeve, is intended to be forthwith a place of religious worship and I request you to register the same. Witness John Whitmore, Samuel Fisher (GDR/350/264)

1587 Stoke Orchard. 7 Jan 1842 (8 Jan 1842). I Charles Channor of Cheltenham certify that a house in the occupation of Daniel Harris, carpenter, at Stoke Orchard in the parish of Bishop's Cleeve, is intended to be forthwith a place of religious worship and I request you to register the same. Witness Charles Henry Channon, Samuel Trinder, John Whitmore. (GDR/350/288)

STONE

Stone was a chapelry in Berkeley parish.

1588 Stone. 19 Aug 1786 (26 Sept 1786; registration GDR/319A/55). 'We [named below] certify that we intend to meet for the worship of Almighty God in a dwelling house of William Oldland at Stone in the parish of Berkeley and pray that this certificate may be registered.' Thomas Symmons, Thomas Jones, Daniel Long, Joseph Heaven, Samuel Creed, William Howen, William Oldland [written 'Oland' but crossed out and 'Oldland' inserted], John Tipping. (GDR/N2/1 41)

1589 Stone. 14 Feb 1800 (27 Feb 1800; registration GDR/319A/291). 'We [named below] certify that we intend to meet and assemble for the purpose of publickly worshipping Almighty God in the dwelling house of William Mower in the tything of Stone in the parish of Berkeley and we desire the same may be registered.' William Mower, Thomas James, James Eley, William Jones. (GDR/N2/1)

STONEHOUSE

Cainscross was in Stonehouse; it became a separate parish from 1838, created from parts of the parishes of Stonehouse, Randwick and Stroud, with Ebley, Dudbridge, parts of Pakenhill and Westrip, but certificates are listed here.

1590 Haywards End, Stonehouse. 23 July 1802 (31 July 1802). We [named below], certify that we with others intend to meet for the worship of Almighty God at the house and in the court before the house of Nathaniel Biddle at Haywards End in the parish of Stonehouse, request that this certificate may be registered and that a certificate of the same might be granted. O A Jeary, minister [Orlando Augustus], James Stephens, John Anteel, Daniel Fowler, John Aldridge, Richard Glover, John Wood. (GDR/319A/316)

1591 Stonehouse. 2 February 1807 (7 Feb 1807). We [named below] certify that a large upper room in the north east end of the clothing factory, in the occupation of Messrs Cooper and Wathen, in the parish of Stonehouse is set apart and intended to be used as a place of religious worship and we request that it may be registered and a certificate granted accordingly. Thomas Cooper, S E Francis, S Stephens, T Watkins. (GDR/334B/424)

1592 Stonehouse. (30 Nov 1808). We [named below] certify that the house and the court in front of the house of 'Lewellin' Powell in the parish of Stonehouse is appropriated for the pupose of the public worship of Almighty God and we require that the same may be registered and a certificate granted. Lewellin Powell, Sarah Powell, Richard Haines, William Worthington, Jacob Burford, William Willis, Richard Burford (mark). (GDR/334B/411)

1593 Stonehouse. (18 Mar 1809). We [named below] certify that we with others intend to meet for the worship of Almighty God at the malthouse of Nathaniel Gardner and in the court before the malthouse in Stonehouse and request that this certificate may be registered and a certificate of the same may be granted. Revd John Brown [RG/31/2 has 'of Stonehouse], John Stephens, Nathaniel Biddle, John Elliott, James Jeens, Francis Hawlings. (GDR/334B/405)

1594 Stonehouse. 7 Sept 1811 (20 Sept 1811). We [named below] certify that we with others intend to meet for the worship of Almighty God in a house or building erected for that purpose on the premises of Elizabeth Hyde and in the court before the building, in the parish of Stonehouse, request that this certificate may be registered and a certificate of the same may be granted. John Brown, minister, James Hoff, John Knight, Isaac Brewer, John Stephen, John Ellis, Nathaniel Biddle, Nathaniel Gardner, James Jeens, Francis Hewlings. (GDR/334B/361)

1595 Stonehouse. (2 Nov 1811). We [named below] certify that the dwelling house of Richard Haines in the parish of Stonehouse is appropriated for the public worship of Almighty God and request that the same be registered and a certificate of the same be granted. John Hodgson, Joseph Griffiths, Thomas H Walker, Luke Haywood, Richard Haines, John Harris. (GDR/334B/360)

1596 Stonehouse. 21 June 1817 (24 June 1817). This is to certify that a house, now in the occupation of Joseph Poulston, in the parish of Stonehouse, is intended to be opened as a place of worship. We request it may be registered. Stephen Davis, minister, John Clayfield, Joseph Poulston, William Vick. (GDR/334B/295)

Note. RG/31/2 has 'Henry Davis, minister' rather than Stephen Davis here and in Stonehouse, *see* **1012**; registration misread as 14 June 1817.

1597 Stonehouse. 20 June 1823 (21 June 1823). We [named below] certify that we with others intend to meet for the worship of Almighty God in a chapel or house erected for that purpose on a piece of land, lately purchased by Mr Nathaniel Gardner of J H Sheppard esq, in the parish of Stonehouse, and request that this certificate may be registered and that a certificate of the same may be granted. Nathaniel Gardner, George Spearing, Isaac Brewer, James Stephens, J W James, minister, John Elliot, B[enjami?]n Jones, James Jeens, Joseph King. (GDR/344/109v)

1598 Westrip, Stonehouse. 5 Nov 1823 (8 Nov 1823). I Charles Harrison of Westrip in the parish of Stonehouse certify that a house and premises at Westrip in the parish of Stonehouse, now in [my] holding and occupation, are to be a place of religious worship and I request you to register the same and request a certificate thereof for which shall be taken no more than two shillings and sixpence. (GDR/344/118v)

1599 Ryeford, Stonehouse. 5 Mar 1824 (25 Mar 1824). I John Clissold of 'Ryford' in the parish of Stonehouse certify that a dwelling house and premises in 'Ryford' in Stonehouse, and now in [my] holding and occupation, are intended to be a place of religious worship and require you to register the same. And I hereby request a certificate thereof for which shall be taken no more than two shillings and sixpence. (GDR/344/132v)

1600 Westrip, Stonehouse. 10 June 1825 (10 June 1825). [*Methodist: see* **1399**]. I James Blacketts of the city of Gloucester certify that a dwelling house, in the occupation of John Butcher, in Westrip in the parish of Stonehouse is intended forthwith to be a place of religious worship and I require you to register the same, and request a certificate thereof. (GDR/350/41)

1601 Cainscross, Stonehouse. 23 Dec 1826 (23 Dec 1826). *Countess of Huntingdon's Connexion.* I Benjamin Parsons, minister of the Countess of Huntingdon's Chapel, Ebley, certify that a building at 'Cains Cross' in the parish of Stonehouse, owned and occupied by John Mozeley, is to be used for the worship of God and I request you to register the same. (GDR/350/60)

1602 Cainscross, Stonehous.e 10 Apr 1843 (11 Apr 1843). I David Apperley of Cainscross, clothier, certify that a messuage at Cainscross in the parish of Stonehouse, in the occupation of John Flight, is to be a place of religious worship and I request you to register the same and request a certificate thereof for which shall be taken no more than two shillings and six pence. (GDR/350/319)

STOW-ON-THE-WOLD

1603 Stow [-on-the-Wold]. (Easter 1690). *Quaker.* 'Stow'. Meeting-house. (Q/SO/3/522)

1604 Stow [-on-the-Wold]. (Easter 1700). *Baptist.* 'Stow'. A new erected house. (Q/SO/3/521)

1605 Stow-on-the-Wold. 21 Dec 1715. James Smith and Caleb Brooks of Stow, dissenting preachers, took oaths of allegiance and supremacy and made declaration against transubstantiation. (Q/SO/4/[10])

1606 Stow [-on-the-Wold]. 25 July 1736 (reg'd Trinity 1736, Q/SO/6/f.80, specifying '*Baptist*']. 'These are to certify his Majesty's Justices of the peace for the said county at their General Sessions held att the Boothall in the city of Gloucester for the county aforesaid That we whose names are subscribed together with other his Majesty's well-affected subjects being Protestant dissenters do meet for the performance of religious worship at the house of Mr

Thomas Sandford in 'Stowe' which house we desire may be registred (for the purpose aforesaid) as required in an act of parliament made in the first year of the reign of the late King William and Queen Mary by the last clause of the said act. In witness whereof we have hereunto set our hands the 25th day of July in the year of our Lord 1736.' Thomas Rooke, William Franks, Anthony Fletcher, William Hall, Robert Perry, Joseph Marsh. (Q/SR/1736/C/18)

Note. The names appear to be actual signatures.

1607 Stow-on-the-Wold. 4 Sept 1765. Some [dissenters] intend to hold a meeting for the worship of Almighty God in the house of John Kimble in Stow-on-the-Wold and desires the same may be registered according to the Act of Toleration. Alexander Payne, Harry Collet, William Ellis, Ralph Ellis, James Horseman. (GDR/292A/84)

1608 Stow-on-the-Wold. 4 July 1772. Some [dissenters] intend to hold a meeting for the worship of Almighty God at the house of Mary Collett in Stow-on-the-Wold and desire the same may be registered according to the Act of Toleration. Harry Collett, Jos. Morse, Ann Fox, Alexander Payne, Mary Payne, Jane Blizzard, Jane Dyer. (GDR/292A/157)

1609 Stow-on-the-Wold. 12 Apr 1798 (17 Apr 1798). *Baptist.* We [named below] certify that we intend to meet for the worship of Almighty God in a house in the parish of 'Stow' belonging to the Society of Baptists in the said parish and its environs and therefore pray that this certificate may be registered. R Farmer, Josiah Hill, John Baker, Richard Margetts, Thomas Smith, Samuel Perry. (GDR/319A/265)

1610 Stow-on-the-Wold. 16 Aug 1814 (23 Sept 1814). I William Ebsworth of 'Stow on the Would' certify that a building lately erected in Sheep Street in 'Stow on the Would' is intended forthwith to be a place of religious worship and require you to register the same and request a certificate thereof. William Ebsworth, gentleman. (GDR/334B/335)

1611 Donnington, Stow [-on-the-Wold]. 14 Apr 1815 (20 Apr 1815). I William Ebsworth of Stow-on-the-Wold, gent, certify that a messuage or tenement in the hamlet of Donnington in the parish of 'Stow on the Would', now in the occupation of John Cowley, labourer, is intended forthwith to be a place of religious worship and require you to register the same and request a certificate thereof. (GDR/334B/329)

1612 Donnington, Stow [-on-the-Wold]. 22 Oct 1819 (25 Oct 1819). *Methodist.* I John Mason of Chipping Norton in the county of Oxford, Methodist minister, certify that the house of John Day, Donnington hamlet of 'Stow', is intended forthwith to be a place of religious worship and I require you to register the same and require a certificate thereof. (GDR/334B/252)

1613 Maugersbury, Stow 31 May 1830 (31 May 1830). I Robert Roff of Stow certify that a dwelling house in the parish of Maugersbury, in the occcupation of Robert Gorten, farmer, is intended forthwith to be a place of religious worship and I request you to register the same. (GDR/350/110)

1614 Maugersbury [Stow-on-the-Wold]. 9 July 1842 (13 July 1842). I Robert Roff of Stow-on-the-Wold certify that a building called Ebenezer Chapel in the hamlet of Maugersbury is forthwith to be a place of religious worship and I request you to register the same. (GDR/350/300)

1615 Donnington, Stow-on-the-Wold. 13 Dec 1845 (24 Dec 1845). We [named below] certify that we intend to meet for the worship of Almighty God in a room pertaining to premises belonging to George Haines of Chipping Campden, being in Donnington in the parish of Stow-on-the-Wold, and we therefore pray that this certificate may be registered. Joseph Acock, George Butler, John Harris, Richard Askill, George Pierce, William Jones, William Teal. (GDR/350/364)

1616 Stow-on-the-Wold. (4 Mar 1852). Cottage. J M Hunt Stow. (RG/31/2 f.126/r)

STRATTON
1617 Stratton. 1672. *Congregational.* Application by Owen Davies for Giles Hancox' house in 'Stretton'; licence recorded 10 June 1672. (LT/372, 509)

1618 Stratton. 29 May 1823 (18 June 1823). I John Willis of Chipping Norton in the county of Oxford certify that a tenement, now in the occupation of Robert Lovett, in the parish of Stratton is intended forthwith to be a place of religious worship and require you to register the same and require a certificate thereof. (GDR/344/108v/109r)

1619 Stratton. 16 Oct 1835 (21 Oct 1835). *Wesleyan.* I Paul Orchard, Wesleyan minister of the town of Stroud, certify that a house in the village and parish of Stratton is intended forthwith to be a place of religious worship and I require you to register the same and request a certificate thereof. (GDR/350/182)

STROUD
The eastern division of Stroud (or Stroudwater) contained the tithings of Upper Lypiatt, Lower Lypiatt and Steanbridge, and included Stroud town, the hamlets of Thrupp and Bourne and part of Brimscombe; the western divison of Paganhill tithing contained the villages or hamlets of Paganhill, Ruscombe and Whiteshill. (VCH Glos 11, 99-100).

1620 Stroud. (Epiphany 1689/90). [*Presbyterian: see note*]. 'Strowd Water', Robert Viner's barn. (Q/SO/3/522)
Note VCH Glos 11, 140 states that this was a Presbyterian meeting.

1621 Bourne, [Thrupp, Stroud]. (Epiphany 1710/11). *Quaker.* Henry Showell's house. [RG/31/6 has Richard Showell] (Q/SO/3/520)

1622 Stroud. 29 Dec 1715. [*Independent: see note*]. Richard Rawlin of 'Strowd', dissenting preacher, took oaths of allegiance and supremacy. (Q/SO/4/[10])
Note. Richard Rawlin named as Independent minister in Stroudwater in Evans list.

1623 Stroud. [1725; entry between 11 Dec 1725 and 10 Jan 1725/26]. *Congregational.* This is to certify that [dissenters] (called 'Congregationall') intend to hold a meeting for the worship of God in their way in the dwelling house of William Ricketts in the upper end of the town of 'Strowd' and pray it may be recorded. Martin Lloyd, Thomas Beale, Thomas Bingham, William Lodge. (GDR/279a/135)

1624 Stroud. 2 June 1732. These are to certify you that [dissenters] intend to hold a meeting for the worship of God in their way in the dwelling house of Daniel Bingham and pray it may be recorded. Joseph Everard, Martin Lloyd, Samuel Bryan. (GDR/284/4)
Note. For Joseph Everard *see* **197**.

1625 Stroud. 11 May 1734. Some [dissenters] intend to hold a meeting for the worship of God in their way in the dwelling house of Daniel Elland in the upper end of the town of Stroud and therefore desire that it may be recorded. Martin Lloyd, Joseph Fownes, Martin Lloyd jnr. (GDR/284/31)

1626 Stroud. 16 Jan 1739/40. These are to certify you that some dissenters intend to hold a meeting for the worship of Almighty God in their way in the dwelling house of the Revd Mr Thomas Jenkins at the upper end of the town of Stroud and therefore desire it may be registered in your court. Martin Lloyd, Martin Lloyd jnr, Joseph Crofts. (Q/SR/1740/A 4)
Note. Registration not found in QS or RG/31/6.

1627 Lower Lypiatt, Stroud. 28 Apr 1741. Some dissenters intend to hold a meeting for the worship of God at the house of Alice Cox widow in that part of 'Lower Lippate tything called Quarhouse' in the parish of Stroud and therefore we pray that the said house may be registered. Thomas Jenkins, William Watkins, Robert Blake, William Dikerson (mark), John Blake, James Wheatley. (GDR/284/116)
Note. RG/31/2 has registration 22 Apr 1741.

1628 Stroud. 24 Sept 1764. *Independent.* We whose names are subscribed being Independent Protestant dissenters intend to make use of a house erected for that purpose in a place called the Acre Edge in the parish of Stroud as a place of religious worship of Almighty God, and desire you'll be pleased to license the same. Alexander Mather, John Hooper, John Grime, William Sainger, Samuel Grime, Edward Bizzey, William Arundell. (GDR/292A/67)

1629 Paganhill, Stroud. 3 Oct 1799 (4 Oct 1799). We certify that a building at Paganhill in the parish of Stroud now occupied by John Tanner, wheelwright, is intended to be used for religious worship. William Harris, James Deane, John Tanner, Edward Holmes, Francis Holmes. (GDR/319A/283)

1630 Ruscombe, Stroud. 17 July 1802 (17 July 1802). This is to certify that a house at Ruscomb in the parish of Stroud, now occupied by Richard Browning, clothworker, is intended to be used for religious worship and that a certificate of the same might be granted. John Boulder, William Bennett, John Stephens, Thomas Sims. (GDR/319A/312-3)

1631 Stroud. 5 Dec 1805 (8 Dec 1805). We with some others intend to hold a meeting for the worship of Almighty God at the house of John Knight in the parish of Stroud and pray it may be registered. William Harris [RG/31/2 has of Stroud], minister, Isaac Brewer, John Mather, Thomas Newcomb, Joseph Browning, Thomas Sims, John Knight, Samuel Cooper, William Lacey. (GDR/334B/429)

1632 Stroud. 3 Apr 1807 (6 Apr 1807). We [named below] certify that a certain building in the Meeting Street, Stroud, lately occupied by Henry Lewellin as tenant and now in the possession of Revd William Harries, is to be used for religious worship. William Harries, Edward Humpage, L Harries. (GDR/334B/423)
Note. RG/31/2 has registered 18 Apr 1807.

1633 Paganhill, Stroud. 7 Sept 1810 (8 Sept 1810). We [named below], inhabitants and householders of the tithing of 'Pagan Hill' in the parish of Stroud, request that a newly erected house in Bread Street in the tithing of 'Pagan Hill', now in the occupation of Charles Offley, may be registered in your Lordship's court as a place for divine worship to be used as such by us being dissenters. Thomas Ellary, William Workman, Thomas Sims, Thomas Smith, John Knight, Joseph Browning. (GDR/334B/382)

1634 Stroud. 6 Apr 1813 (8 Apr 1813). I John Burder, minister of the town of Stroud, certify that a building commonly called the Assembly Room, belonging to the *George Inn* in the town of Stroud, occupied and owned by Mr Thomas Hall, is intended forthwith to be a place of religious worship and require you to register the same. (GDR/334B/346)

Note. For John Burder *see* **292** & **1655**.

1635 Paganhill, Stroud. 10 Feb 1817 (21 Feb 1817). We [named below] inhabitants and householders in the tithing of Pagan Hill request that a newly fitted-up house in the village of 'Paken Hill', now in the occupation of Charles Affley, may be registered as a place of divine worship. John Knight, Thomas Ellary, William Mayo, James Wilkins, Thomas Holmes, Edward Holmes. (GDR/334B/304)

1636 Thrupp, Stroud. 12 Mar 1817 (18 Mar 1817). I John Burder, minister of Stroud, certify that a certain dwelling house at 'Thrup' in the parish of Stroud, occupied and owned by Joseph Clutterbuck, is intended to be forthwith used as a place of religious worship and I request you to register the same. (GDR/334B/301)
Note. For John Burder *see* **292** & **1655**.

1637 Ruscombe, Stroud. 6 July 1819 (7 July 1819). I Samuel Smith of Ruscombe, being by trade a cloth weaver, certify that a tenement in the parish of Stroud, which I at present hold and occupy, is intended forthwith to be a place of religious worship and require you to register the same and request a certificate thereof. (GDR/334B/257)

1638 Whiteshill, Stroud. July 1820 (4 July 1820). I John Gilbert of 'White's Hill', being a day labourer, certify that a certain tenement in the parish of 'Stroud Water', which I at present hold and occupy, is intended forthwith to be a place of religious worship and I require you to register the same and request a certificate thereof. John Gilbert (mark). (GDR/334B/240)

1639 Whiteshill [Stroud]. 23 Feb 1821 (24 Feb 1821; registration GDR/334B/227). I John Norgrove of 'Whites Hill near Stroudwater', being a book seller, certify that a tenement at 'Whites Hill' in the parish of Stroudwater, which I hold and occupy, is intended forthwith to be a place of religious worship and I require you to register the same.
'24 February 1821 I do hereby certify that this certificate was duly registered in the Consistory Court.' (GDR/N2/1)
Note. A very neatly written certificate, formerly folded in two. On reverse of one side 'to the Right Reverend the Lord Bishop of Gloucester'.

1640 Stroud. 28 June 1822 (29 June 1822). This is to certify that the premises now in the occupation of Mr. Thomas Newcomb and Mr. Thomas Rice, known by the name of Bowbridge Mills in the parish of Stroud [are] intended to be a place of religious worship and we request that 'it' may be registered. John Rees, minister of Rodborough Tabernacle, Thomas Newcomb, Thomas Rice. (GDR/344/32v)

1641 Stroud. 6 September 1822 (7 Sept 1822). I Benjamin Barnfield of Stroud, clothier, certify that a clothing mill, dwelling house and premises in the parish of Stroud, now in my own occupation as tenant thereof to Thomas Holbrow esquire, or in the occupation of Timothy Matthews my undertenant, and commonly known by the name of Badbrook Mill, is intended forthwith to be a place of religious worship and require you to register the same. (GDR/344/37v)

1642 Stroud. 22 Sept 1823 (26 Sept 1823). I James Bonser of Stroud in the parish of Stroud certify that a chapel and premises at Stroud, now in [my] holding and occupation are intended to be a place of religious worship and I request you to register the same and request a certificate thereof for which shall be taken no more than two shillings and sixpence. (GDR/344/114r)
Note. First mention of fee in this register.

1643 Ebley, Stroud. 5 Nov 1823 (8 Nov 1823). I George Worston of Ebley in the parish of Stroud certify that a house and premises at Ebley in the parish of Stroud, and now in [my] holding and occupation, are intended to be a place of religious worship and I hereby request you to register and record the same and request a certificate thereof for which shall be taken no more than two shillings and sixpence. (GDR/344/118r)

1644 Middle Lypiatt, Stroud. 7 Nov 1823 (8 Nov 1823). I John Burder dissenting minister of the town of Stroud certify that a building situate at Middle Lypiatt in the parish of Stroud, owned by Mrs Leversage and at present occupied by John Ford, is intended to be a place of religious worship and I request you to register the same. (GDR/344/118r)

Note. For John Burder *see* **292** & **1655.**

1645 Stroud. 29 June 1824 (30 June 1824). *Baptist.* We [named below] certify that a meeting-house in Stroud is intended to be used by dissenters of the Baptist denomination and request that this certificate may be registered in the Commissary's Court. Henry Hawkins snr, Henry Hawkins jnr. (GDR/344/134r)

1646 Ruscombe, Stroud. 1 Oct 1824 (2 Oct 1824). I William Chandler of Ruscomb in the parish of Stroud certify that my dwelling house and premises at 'Ruscomb', now in my own occupation, are to be a place of religious worship and I require you to register the same, and request a certificate thereof for which shall be taken no more than two shillings and six pence. (GDR/344/137v)

1647 Stroud. 7 Oct 1784 (7 Oct 1824). I William Edwards of Stroud certify that my dwelling house and premises in the parish of Stroud are intended to be a place of religious worship and I request you to register the same, and request a certificate thereof for which shall be taken no more than two shillings and six pence. (GDR/344/138r)

1648 Stroud. 19 Oct 1824 (20 Oct 1824). This is to certify that a dwelling house situated on Stroud Hill in the parish of Stroud, owned by Paul Hawkins Fisher esq, at present inhabited by Thomas Damsel, is intended to be forthwith a place of religious worship and to request that you will register the same. John Burden [Burder], Protestant dissenting minister at Stroud. (GDR/344/139r)

Note. For John Burder *see* **292** & **1655**.

1649 Stroud. 5 Nov 1824 (6 Nov 1824). I Mary Mills of the parish of Stroud certify that my dwelling house and premises in the parish of Stroud [are] intended to be used as a place of religious worship and I request you to register the same, and request a certificate for which shall be taken no more than two shillings and six pence. (GDR/350/20)

1650 Paganhill, Stroud. 23 July 1825 (23 July 1825). This is to certify that a house at Paganhill in the parish of Stroud, occupied by Samuel Underwood and owned by Mrs Bird, is intended to be forthwith a place of religious worship and I request that you will register the same. John Burder protestant dissenting minister at Stroud. (GDR/350/43)

Note. For John Burder *see* **292** & **1655**.

1651 Stroud. 12 Oct 1825 (12 Oct 1825). [*Primitive Methodist? see note*] We [named below] of the parish of Stroud certify that our chapel and premises in the parish of Stroud are intended to be used as a place of religious worship and we request you to register and record the same and we request a certificate for which shall be taken no more than two shillings and six pence. [Signed by all those named]. Edward Hogg, James Hogg, William Hopson, John Paine, William Richards, Richard Paris, Nathaniel Thomas, Thomas Mills,

William Gardner, Henry Reeves, Joseph Chandler, John Thomas, James Aldridge. (GDR/350/47)

Note. The Primitive Methodist Western Mission was in Stroud in 1823, but the church was said by Tonks to commence in 1827, and became part of the Brinkworth Circuit. (Tonks 29, 63). Bishop Bethel's Visitation book (1825) records Ranters' [Primitive Methodist] chapel (see Appendix X*).* In 1829 a register of baptisms was started (D3187 1/4/1). Chapel built on north side of Parliament Street 1836, *see* **1658**.

1652 Stroud. 31 Oct 1826 (1 Nov 1826). I John Burder, dissenting minister at Stroud, certify that a certain dwelling house in Silver Street, Stroud, owned by Mr Robert Hughes, occupied by Mr Joseph Browning, is intended forthwith as a place of religious worship and I request you to register the same. (GDR/350/59)

Note. For John Burder *see* **292** & **1655**.

1653 Stroud. 10 Feb 1827 (10 Feb 1827). I Charles Hawthorne of the town of Stroud certify that a shop, in the occupation of Mr Charles Peaty, is intended forthwith to be a place of religious worship and require you to register the same and request a certificate thereof. (GDR/350/62)

1654 Stroud. 8 Oct 1827. I Thomas Hill of the parish of Stroud certify that my dwelling house and premises in the parish of Stroud, now in my own occupation, are intended to be a place of religious worship and require you to register the same and request a certificate thereof. (GDR/350/73)

1655 Thrupp, Stroud. 15 Apr 1828 (16 Apr 1828). *Independent.* I John Burder, dissenting minister at Stroud, certify that a dwelling house at 'the Thrup' in the parish of Stroud, owned by William Clutterbuck Chambers esq, and occupied by Robert Stephen, is intended forthwith to be a place of religious worship by a congregation of the Independent denomination and I request you to register the same. (GDR/350/87)

Note. This is the only reference to John Burder as a minister of an Independent congregation. He refers to himself as a 'Protestant dissenting minister' [*see* **1650**]; in Stroud Hill [**1656**] a building was certified by John Burder for Independents and Congregationalists, while in Thrupp in Stroud [**1657**] the building was for Independents and Baptists. *VCH Glos* 11, 140-41 assumes he was a Congregationalist. He appears to have been a non-denominational dissenting minister. *See also* **292**.

1656 Stroud Hill, Stroud. 10 July 1833 (12 July 1833). *Independent and Congregational.* This is to certify that a building lately erected on Stroud Hill in the parish of Stroud, on land which lately belonged to Joseph Watts, is about to be used as a place of religious worship by persons of the Independent or Congregational denomination and I request you to register the same. John Burder. (GDR/350/140)

Note. For John Burder *see* **292** & **1655**.

1657 Thrupp, Stroud. 11 Mar 1834 (14 Mar 1834). *Independent and Baptist.* This is to certify that a certain building in Tanners Row, Thrupp, parish of Stroud, occupied by Mrs Stephens and owned by Mr John Joel Tanner, is intended to be used by a congregation partly of the Independent and partly of the Baptist denomination and I request you to register the same. John Burder, dissenting minister at Stroud. (GDR/350/148)

Note. For John Burder *see* **292** & **1655**.

1658 Stroud. 5 May 1837. [*Primitive Methodist? see note*]. I James Baker [RG/31/2 has Charles Baker] of Stroud in the parish of Stroudwater certify that a meeting-house or chapel and premises at Stroudwater, now in the holding and occupation of the following trustees: James Moreland, James Whitfield, Job Davis, Charles Gardner, William Ind, John Gardner, John Clissold, James Hiatt [?Hyatt], Humphrey Gould, Thomas Chandler,

Thomas Dowle, are to be a place of religious worship and I request you to register the same and request a certificate thereof for which shall be taken no more than two shillings and six pence. (GDR/350/213)

Note. Chapel built 1836 on north side of Parliament Street by Primitive Methodists. *VCH Glos* 11, 141.

1659 Stroud. 17 July 1837. I John Burder, dissenting minister of Stroud, certify that a building or meeting-house in Meeting Street in the parish of Stroud, called the Old Meeting or the Old Chapel, is and is to be a place of religious worship and I request you to register the same and request a certificate thereof. (GDR/350/213)

Note. For John Burder *see* **292** & **1655**.

1660 Stroud. 14 Sept 1837 (26 Sept 1837). *Congregational or Independent.* This is to certify that a building in a street sometimes called Union Street in the parish of Stroud is to be a chapel for religious worship by dissenters of the denomination of Congregationalists or Independents and I request you to register the same. John Burder, dissenting minister. (GDR/350/215) [*see* illus., xvi]

Note. For John Burder *see* **292** & **1655**.

1661 Stroud. 28 Apr 1840 (2 May 1840). I George Shermer of the Thrupp in the parish of Stroud certify that a house in Middle Street, Stroud, is forthwith to be a place of assembling together of Christians in the name of the Lord Jesus Christ and I require you to register the same. George Shermer, William Foster. (GDR/350/253)

1662 Stroud. 14 Nov 1840. I John Siddaway of Gloucester, in the parish of St John the Baptist, certify that the house of James Clissold and premises at Stroud in the parish of Stroud, now in [his] holding and occupation, is to be a place of religious worship and I request you to register the same and request a certificate thereof for which shall be taken no more than two shillings and six pence. (GDR/350/261)

1663 Stroud. 12 Feb 1841 (12 Feb 1841). I William Ind of Stroud certify that my house and premises at Stroud in the parish of Stroud, now in [my] holding and occupation, are to be a place of religious worship and I request you to register the same and request a certificate thereof for which shall be taken no more than two shillings and six pence. (GDR/350/273)

1664 Stroud. 26 Apr 1841 (26 Apr 1841). I John Harris of Stroud certify that my room and premises at Stroud, now in [my] holding and occupation, are to be a place of religious worship and I request you to register the same and request a certificate thereof for which shall be taken no more than two shillings and six pence. (GDR/350/279)

1665 Stroud. 17 Jan 1842 (18 Jan 1842). *Congregational & Baptist.* This is a certificate that a certain building near the turnpike [at] Bowbridge near Stroud, owned by Mr Joseph Partridge is intended to be a place of religious worship by dissenters of the Congregational and Baptist denomination and I request you to register the same 'agreeably to act of parliment'. John Burder, dissenting minster Stroud. (GDR/350/289)

Note. For John Burder *see* **292** & **1655**.

1666 Stroud. 9 Aug 1843 (10 Aug 1843). I John Coxhead of Stroud certify that a room and premises in the holding and occupation of Samuel Wynn and John Coxhead, are intended to be a place of religious worship and I request you to register the same and request a certificate thereof for which shall be taken no more than two shillings and six pence. (GDR/350/322)

1667 Stroud. 4 Jan 1844 (5 Jan 1844). I Richard Coles of the parish of Randwick certify that a house and premises in the parish of Stroud, now in [my] holding and occupation, are intended to be a place of religious worship and I request you to register the same and request a certificate thereof for which shall be taken no more than two shillings and six pence. Witness Henry Harris, Cainscross nr Stroud. (GDR/350/328)

1668 Stroud. 8 Feb 1844 (9 Feb 1844). I John Coxhead of Stroud certify that a dwelling and premises at Stroud, now in the holding and occupation of Peter Older, are intended to be a place of religious worship and I request you to register the same and request a certificate thereof for which shall be taken no more than two shillings and six pence. (GDR/350/336)

1669 Stroud. 9 July 1844 (11 July 1844). I John Fletcher of Stroud certify that a house and premises at Stroud, now in the holding and occupation of John Coxhead, are intended to be a place of religious worship and I request you to register the same and request a certificate thereof for which shall be taken no more than two shillings and six pence. (GDR/350/344)

1670 Stroud. (2 Feb 1848). [*Independent*]. Room in a house in Dyers Court. William Wheeler [RG/31/2 has Independent minister of Stroud]. (Q/RNp/4)

1671 Brimscombe, [Stroud]. (18 Nov 1851). Dwelling house occupied by Samuel Clutterbuck. Samuel Clutterbuck [RG/31/2 has 'Samuel Clutterbuck Brimscombe gentleman']. (Q/RNp/4)

SWINDON (near Cheltenham)
1672 Swindon. 21 February 1822 (22 Feb 1822). We [named below] respectfully give notice to your Lordship that we intend opening a room for public worship in the house where James Jones now resides in the parish of Swindon. Thomas Newman, Stanbridge White [RG/31/2 has Thomas White], Henry Lucy, John Jones, James Edward. (GDR/344/18r)

1673 Swindon. 20 Jan 1834 (23 Jan 1834). I James Smith of Cheltenham certify that a dwelling house in the parish of Swindon, occupied by Philip Weaver, labourer, is intended forthwith to be a place of religious worship and I request you to register the same and request a certificate thereof. Witness Charles Channon, Jacob Cowly. (GDR/350/145)

TAYNTON
1674 Taynton. 12 Dec 1797 (13 Dec 1797). We [named below] require that the house of John Simmons in the parish of 'Tainton' be licensed for the purpose of divine worship. William Macklow, John Harris, John Spencer, John Simmons. (GDR/319A/260)
Note. John Simmons was noted in an Abstract of Wesleyan Trusts in the Ledbury Circuit as the donor of a plot in 1820 on which May Hill chapel in Taynton was built . (Information from J E C Peters, Malvern, quoting Hereford CRO AL29/11).

1675 Taynton. 2 May 1802 (8 May 1802). We [named below] intend to meet for the worship of Almighty God at the house of John Broadstock in the parish of Taynton and pray that the house may be registered and that a copy of the same might be granted. Richard Thomas, minister, John Broadstock, James Partridge, Samuel Wall, James Turner, George Brown, Abraham Smith, Thomas Turner. (GDR/319A/310)

TEMPLE GUITING
1676 Barton, Temple Guiting. (Easter 1700). *Baptist*. William Wood's house;. (Q/SO/3/521)

1677 Kineton, Temple Guiting. 6 Oct 1736. Some [dissenters] intend to hold a meeting for the worship of Almighty God in their way in the dwelling house of Thomas Dowdeswell of 'Keynton' [Kineton] in the parish of Temple Guiting, therefore we desire that it may be registered in your office. Thomas Dowdeswell, Joseph Everard, Martin Lloyd. (GDR/284/60)
Note. For Joseph Everard *see* **197**.

1678 Temple Guiting. (4 Jun 1803). We [named below] have set apart a house in the occupation of Mr Thomas Hudson in the parish of Temple Guiting for the worship of Almighty God and hereby request it may be registered. John Butterman, Thomas Dowty, Thomas Hudson, Charles Hammond, John Hobbs, John Etheridge, William Robins, George Fry. (GDR/319A/321)

TETBURY
1679 Tetbury. 1672. *Congregational and Presbyterian.* Application 29 May 1672 by Owen Davies for licence to Jonathan Smith [Congregational minister] of 'Tedbury' at his own house; licence received by Owen Davies 1 June 1672 for Jonathan Smith and house; but licence recorded 29 May 1672 for the house of Jonathan Smith in Tetbury 'Gloucester Presbyterian meeting place' and for Jonathan Smith to be a Congregational teacher. (LT/372, 388, 497, 498)

1680 Tetbury. 1672. *Presbyterian.* Licence recorded 22 July 1672 for the house of Mary Cradock 'at Tidbury, Gloc'. (LT/529)

1681 Tetbury. (Easter 1690). Mr Beeby's Lecture. (Q/SO/3/522)

1682 Tetbury. (Easter 1690). *Quaker.* Meeting-house. (Q/SO/3/522)

1683 Tetbury Upton. (Trinity 1695). *Presbyterian.* 'Tetburys Upton, Jo: Wicks's house' [RG/31/6 has Joseph]. (Q/SO/3/521)

1684 Tetbury. (Trinity 1705). A house built near the 'Chiping Croft'. (Q/SO/3/521)

1685 Tetbury. (Trinity 1706). *Independent.* Matthew Beale's house. (Q/SO/3/520)

1686 Tetbury. (Epiphany 1706/7). *Quaker.* A house erected for Quakers. [RG/31/6 has Epiphany 1705] (Q/SO/3/520)

1687 Tetbury. (Epiphany 1710/11). *Presbyterian.* William Poole's house. (Q/SO/3/520)

1688 Tetbury. (Epiphany 1710/11). *Presbyterian.* Daniell Birt's house. (Q/SO/3/520)

1689 Tetbury. 6 Dec 1715. [*Presbyterian: see note*]. Thomas Jones of Tetbury, dissenting preacher, took oaths of allegiance and supremacy. (Q/SO/4/[8])
Note. Thomas Jones was named as the Presbyterian minister in the Evans list.

1690 Tetbury. (Michaelmas 1724). *Presbyterian.* It is ordered by the court that the dwelling house of Daniel Bennett in Tetbury be licensed and allowed for [dissenters] called presbyterians to assemble and meet together for the worship of God in their way according to their petition for the purpose filed and allowed. (Q/SO/5/f.18r)
Note. Rubric has 'Tetbury meeting-house'.

1691 Tetbury. (Trinity 1725). *Baptist.* It is ordered by this court that the new built house in Tetbury be licensed and allowed for [dissenters] called Baptists residing in and near Tetbury to assemble and meet together in for the worship of God in their way according to their petition for that purpose filed and allowed. (Q/SO/5/f.30r)

Note. Rubric has 'Tetbury meeting-house'.

1692 Tetbury. (Easter 1732.) *Quaker.* It is ordered by this court that [dissenters] called Quakers be licensed and allowed to assemble and meet in the Market House at Tetbury. (Q/SO/5/f.175v)

1693 Tetbury. 13 Oct 1732. *Baptist.* We His Majesty's dissenting subjects called Baptists design to hold a meeting for the worship of God in our way in the dwelling house of Samuel Woodman in the West Street in Tetbury which we pray may be recorded. Nathaniel Overbury, Daniel Bennets, Samuel Woodman. (GDR/284/8)

1694 Tetbury. [1737] [undated; entry between 27 May 1737 and 10 Sept 1737]. *Baptist.* We [dissenters] called Baptists design to hold a meeting for the worship and service of God in their way in the house of Boman [?Benjamin] Holiday in Tetbury which we humbly pray may be recorded. Nathaniel Overbury, Daniel Bennett, John Freem, Michael Ferritt, Samuel Woodward. (GDR/284/74)

1695 The Green, Tetbury. [1758] (undated; entry between 26 Aug 1758 and 10 Oct 1758). *Congregational.* We [named below] and others of the Congregational persuasion intend to hold a meeting or meetings for the worship of Almighty God in the dwelling house, belonging to one Edward Brown and late in the occupation of the Revd Mr David Edwards, and being in a place called the Green in the market town of 'Tedbury' and therefore pray that the same may be registered. Jonathan Hickcox, Martin Lloyd, Cove Lloyd, Thomas Barrow, John Hobbs, Isaac Browning, 'Hiz.' Thomson, Martin Browning. (GDR/292A/38)

1696 Tetbury. 22 Apr 1765. *Independent.* Some [dissenters] commonly called Independents intend to hold a meeting for the worship of Almighty God in and at the dwelling house of Cove Lloyd, woolstapler, being in a street called Gloucester Street in the town and parish of Tetbury and desire this said certificate may be registered. Joseph Ayre, Nathaniel Leonard, Thomas Poole, Martin Lloyd, William Webb, Thomas Barrow. (GDR/292A/83)

1697 The Green, Tetbury. 25 Feb 1766. Some [dissenters] intend to hold a meeting for the worship of Almighty God at the dwelling house of Thomas Barrow, a woolcomber, in a place called the Green in the town and parish of Tetbury and therefore desire that the same may be registered in your Court. Thomas Barrow, Martin Lloyds, Cove Lloyd, Isaac Browning. (GDR/292A/90)

1698 Tetbury. 25 Feb 1766. Some [dissenters] intend to hold a meeting for the worship of Almighty God at the dwelling house of Joseph Ayre, gentleman, in Gumstool Street in the town and parish of Tetbury and therefore desire that the same may be registered in your Court. Joseph Ayre, Thomas Barrow, Martin Lloyd, Cove Lloyds, Isaac Browning. (GDR/292A/91)

1699 Tetbury. 6 Mar 1766. *Presbyterian.* Some [dissenters] intend to hold a meeting for the worship of Almighty God at the meeting-house standing and being at the bottom of a hill, or near a place called the Chipping Croft in the town and parish of Tetbury going under the denomination of Presbyterians and therefore desire that the same may be registered in your Court according to the Act of Toleration. Joseph Ayre, Thomas Barrow, Martin Lloyd, Henry Thomson, Richard Houlday, Isaac Browning, Cove Lloyd, Nathaniel Lloyd, Giles Hobbs, Samuel Hobbs, Nathaniel Barrow. (GDR/292A/91)

1700 Tetbury. 17 June 1777 (18 June 1777). *Baptist.* We [named below] dissenters of the Baptist denomination meeting in a house erected for religious worship in a court in the street called the 'Churchstreet' in Tetbury desire to have the said house recorded as a place for religious worship. Joseph Burchell, Nathaniel Overbury, William Overbury: Thomas West, Thomas Wear, John Overbury. (GDR/292A/204)

1701 Tetbury. 10 Mar 1779 (15 Mar 1779). *Independent.* We with some others [dissenters] called Independents intend to hold a meeting for the worship of Almighty God in the house of Martin Lloyd in the parish of Tetbury. Therefore we desire that this certificate may be registered. William Young, James Thompson, Martin Lloyd, James Thompson jnr. (GDR/292A/218)

1702 Tetbury. 7 Apr 1780 (8 Apr 1780). *Independent.* We with some others [dissenters] called Independents intend to hold a meeting for the worship of Almighty God in the house lately occupied by John Giles in the parish of Tetbury, therefore we desire that this certificate may be registered. John Glover, Martin Lloyd, James Thompson, Henry Blake. (GDR/292A/227)

1703 Tetbury. 31 Mar 1791 (1 Apr 1791). *Independents.* Whereas the underwritten with some others called Independents intend holding a meeting for the worship of Almighty God in the house lately occupied by Mr Thomas Wickes in the parish of Tetbury, we desire that this certificate may be registered. Thomas Baily, John Rainger, John Keynton, James Thompson. (GDR/319A/124-5)

1704 Tetbury. 15 May 1816 (18 May 1816). I Martin Lloyd of Tetbury, woolcomber, certify that a tenement, being part of a building in the Long Street in the parish of Tetbury, now in the occupation of W Thomas Young, is intended forthwith to be a place of religious worship and require you to register the same. Martin Lloyd, Jeremiah Grant, Milburn Crew, Thomas Phillips, William Keynton. (GDR/334B/318)

1705 Tetbury. 16 June 1823 (18 June 1823). *Tent Methodists.* May it please your Lordship, I John Barnet of the parish of Dursley request to inform your Lordship that a house and premises adjoining, in the parish of Tetbury, the property of Samuel Lamb and in the joint occupation of the said Samuel Lamb and John Bigland, is set apart by protestants denominated Tent Methodists for the public worship of Almighty God and I request the same may be entered in your Lordship's Registry and a certificate granted accordingly. John Barett. (GDR/344/109r)
Note. Discrepancy between surname in text and in signature, but see also following certificate.

1706 Tetbury. 2 July 1823 (5 July 1823). *Independent or Tent Methodists.* I John Barnett of Dursley certify that a piece of waste land called Cuttal Bottom, occupied by Mr John Benjamin, in the parish of Tetbury is intended forthwith to be a place of religious worship by Protestants of the denomination of Independent or Tent Methodists, and I require you to register the same and request a certificate thereof. (GDR/344/110r)

1707 Tetbury. 7 Oct 1826 (14 Oct 1826). We the undersigned inhabitants of Tetbury certify that a house and premises in Cirencester Street, Tetbury, formerly in possession of John Baldwin, tawer, but now void, will be henceforth a place of religious worship. Thomas Ashton, minister, William Dyke, Thomas Trotman, Edward Turrell. (GDR/350/60)

1708 Tetbury. 16 Sept 1828 (18 Sept 1828). I James Stancombe of Tetbury certify that a large room, the property of Mr John Sealey snr, in the town and parish of Tetbury and near

the *Angel Inn*, is forthwith to be a place of religious worship and I require you to register the same. James Stancombe, John Sealey snr, proprietor, Thomas Trotman, James Pope, John Haynton, Martin Lloyd, J Hill, John Cave. (GDR/350/93)
Note. Names are not clear.

1709 Tetbury. 7 Mar 1842 (26 Mar 1842). I John Prior [RG/31/2 has of Sherston] certify that the room, in the occupation of John Howell, at Tetbury is intended to be a place of religious worship and require you to register the same and require a certificate thereof. (GDR/350/294)
Note. 'Wilts' written in margin and 'Sherston near Malmesbury' added to signature.

1710 Tetbury. 7 Dec 1842 (7 Dec 1842). I John M Collard certify that a room, in the occupation of Edward Edwards, at Tetbury is intended to be a place of religious worship and require you to register the same and require a certificate thereof. (GDR/350/309)

1711 Tetbury. 7 Mar 1844 (6 Mar 1844). We [named below] certify that a room in a dwelling house in the parish of Tetbury, called the dwelling house of William Barnes, [is] intended to be a place of religious worship and we request that this certificate may be registered. James Head, James Smart, Richard Pinnell, William Barnes. (GDR/350/336)
Note. Dates as entered.

1712 Tetbury. (14 Dec 1848). Room belonging to Mary Warn [RG/31/2 has 'An old room']. John M Collard. (Q/RNp/4)

TEWKESBURY
1713 Tewkesbury. 1672. *Congregational.* Application by Owen Davies for Thomas Skey at his house in 'Tewxbery'; licence recorded 29 May 1672 for Thomas Skey to be a Congregational teacher at his house and for his house, 'Gloucester Congregational meeting place, Teuxbury'; received by Owen Davies 12 June 1672. (LT/372, 389, 498)

1714 Tewkesbury. 1672. *Congregational.* Application by Owen Davies for Henry Collett [Congregational minister] at his house in 'Tewxbery'; licence recorded 29 May 1672 for Henry Collett to be a Congregational teacher at his house and for his house, 'Gloucester Congregational meeting place, Teuxbury'; licence received by Owen Davies 12 June 1672. (LT/372, 389, 498)
Note. Henry Collett was perhaps ejected from Claydon in Suffolk. (Skea 162).

1715 Tewkesbury. 1672. *Congregational.* Application by Owen Davies for William Davison of 'Tewxbery' [Congregational minister] at his owne howse; licence recorded for William Davison in his house in 'Teukesbury' 10 June 1672, and for his house; received by Owen Davies 12 June 1672. (LT/372, 401, 509, 510)
Note. William Davison was ejected rector of Notgrove.

1716 Tewkesbury. (Easter 1690). *Quaker.* 'Teuxbery', Meeting-house. (Q/SO/3/522)

1717 Tewkesbury. 25 Apr 1746. Some [dissenters] intend to hold a meeting for the worship of Almighty God at the house of Samuel Wells in Guest Lane in Tewkesbury and desire the same may be registered. Thomas Walker, Samuel Moore, Samuel Wells. (GDR/284/172)

1718 Tewkesbury. (17 Jan 1777). 'At this session Mr John Cole of the Barton Street in the said borough of Tewkesbury in pursuance of the statute made in the first year of the Reign of their late Majestys King William and Queen Mary delivered into Court a Certificate in the words following - I the underwritten John Cole of the Barton Street in the Town and

Borough of Tewkesbury aforesaid in the county of Gloucester do certify that a house situated lying and being in the said Barton Street … is appropriated to and for Religious Worship and which was lately purchased of me for the purpose aforesaid'. (QT/SO/1)

1719 Tewkesbury. 23 Nov 1798 (24 Nov 1798). *Independent.* A house now in the occupation of Mr Edward Laight in the High Street of Tewkesbury is intended to be a place of worship for dissenters of the Independent denomination. And we request that the said house may be registered and a certificate granted accordingly. Thomas Spilsbury, minister, Edward Laight, William Haynes. (GDR/319A/271)
Note. It appears that in copying this entry for Tewkesbury in the return to the Registrar General, the name of Whelford (Kempsford), on the facing page, was copied in error against the Tewkesbury details.

1720 Tewkesbury. 1 Apr 1805 (11 Apr 1805). [*Methodist: see* **166**]. We [named below] have set apart a house in Guest Lane, Tewkesbury, for the worship of Almighty God and request that the same may be registered. James M Byron, minister, Thomas Fearnly, James Nind, Roberts Wells, George Sperry, Samuel Collins, John Collins, Richard Collins, William Vevers jnr, John Pace, Robert Smith. (GDR/334B/433)

1721 Tewkesbury. 3 June 1805 (11 Jun 1805). *Particular Baptist.* We [named below] certify that a building newly erected on premises lately appertaining to the *Star and Garter* Inn in Barton Street in the borough of Tewkesbury is to be occupied as a place of religious worship by the denomination of Particular Baptists and request that the clerk of the court be desired to register the same. Daniel Trotman, minister, Samuel Jones, Thomas Craddick, John Pearce, William Loyd, Peter Oakley, Abraham Harris, Thomas Holland. (GDR/334B/432)
Note. Daniel Trotman was ordained minister of the Baptist church in Tewkesbury in September 1803, having come from Crockerton, in Wilts. (GA D4944 1/2)

1722 Tewkesbury. (18 July 1806). *Quaker.* 'Isaac Butterfield, Nathaniel Hartland and Joseph Russell, three of the people called Quakers, did by writing under their hands certify that a building lately erected with a plot of ground adjoining and appurtenances belonging thereto situate in Barton Street within the said Borough were intended to be used as a place of religious worship by the Society of Friends called Quakers being Protestants dissenting from the established church of England (In pursuance of the Act of Toleration 1 W. c. 18.)'. (QT/SO/2)

1723 Tewkesbury. (19 Oct 1821). The Revd Henry Welsford a dissenting teacher of the said Borough of Tewkesbury certified that a certain messuage or tenement situate in the Back Avon Street in the said borough in the occupation of Mary Collins was intended forthwith to be used as a place of religious worship and required the same to be registered. (QT/SO/2)

1724 Tewkesbury. (19 Oct 1821). The said Henry Welsford certified that a certain messuage or tenement situate in Collins's Alley in the High Street in the said borough in the occupation of Samuel Spicer was intended forthwith to be used as a place of religious worship by an assembly or congregation of Protestants and required the same to be registered and the same was ordered to be registered and recorded. (QT/SO/2)

1725 Tewkesbury. (19 Oct 1821). The said Henry Welsford certified that a certain messuage or tenement situate in St Mary's Lane in the Church Street in the said borough in the occupation of George Greenaway was intended forthwith to be used as a place of religious worship by an Assembly or congregation of Protestants and required the same to be registered and the same was ordered to be registered and recorded. (QT/SO/2)

1726 Tewkesbury. 9 Jan 1823 (9 Jan 1823). I Ann Wilkes of the parish of Tewkesbury certify that my dwelling house in the parish of Tewkesbury is intended forthwith to be a place of religious worship and I require you to register the same and request a certificate thereof. (GDR/344/41r)

1727 Tewkesbury. (1 Jan 1828). We [named below] certify that a building in the parish of Tewkesbury, in the possession or occupation of James Wood, Thomas D Lewis, James B Lewis, W Lloyd, James Nind, Robert Groves, W Knight and others as trustees, is to be a chapel for religious worship and request that this certificate may be registered in the Commissary's Court of your Lordship. Henry Welsford, James Wood, William Freeman. (GDR/350/81)

1728 Tewkesbury. 16 Feb 1828 (16th Feb 1828). I James Long of Tewkesbury certify that a house and premises at Tewkesbury, in [my] holding and occupation, are to be a place of religious worship and I request you to register the same and request a certificate thereof. Witness Benjamin Bond, Thomas Meredith, George Meredith. (GDR/350/83)

1729 Tewkesbury. 8 Feb 1837 (8 Feb 1837). I John Tharm of the parish of Tewkesbury certify that a house and premises in High Street in the borough of Tewkesbury, in the holding and occupation of Mr Joseph Dean and Mr Edward Huntley, are to be a place of religious worship and I request you to register the same and request a certificate thereof for which shall be taken no more than two shillings and six pence. (GDR/350/205)

1730 Tewkesbury. 9 Jan 1838 (13 Jan 1838). I William Beaham of Tewkesbury certify that a house and premises at Tewkesbury, now in the holdings and occupation of Mr Thomas Townley, in the Bank Alley of the 'Borrow' of Tewkesbury is to be a place of religious worship and I request you to register the same and request a certificate thereof for which shall be taken no more than two shillings and six pence. William Beaham, William Beasley. (GDR/350/218)

1731 Tewkesbury. (25 Oct 1839). 'It was certifed to the court that a certain tenement or dwelling house situate in the Orchard Court in the said Borough and in the occupation of Mary Parker widow was thenceforth intended to be used as a place of religious worship by a congregation of Protestants'. [RG/31/8 records Henry Welsford as certifier] (QT/SO/3)

1732 Tewkesbury. (25 Oct 1839). 'It was certifed to the court that a certain tenement or dwelling house situate in the Mill Bank in the said Borough in the occupation of James Stephens was thenceforth intended to be used as a place of religious worship by a congregation of Protestants'. [RG/31/8 records Henry Welsford as certifier] (QT/SO/3)

1733 Tewkesbury. (25 Oct 1839). 'It was certifed to the court that a certain tenement or dwelling house situate at the back of the High Street fronting the Oldbury Field in the said Borough and in the occupation of John Ursell was thenceforth intended to be used as a place of religious worship by a congregation of Protestants'. [RG/31/8 records Henry Welsford as certifier] (QT/SO/3)

1734 Tewkesbury. (21 Oct 1848). House in Potters Yard, Barton Street occupied by John Matty. John Matty. (Q/RNp/4)

1735 Workhouse Alley, Barton Street, Tewkesbury. (26 Jun 1849). House occupied by William Wilkes. (Q/RNp/4) *299*

1736 Church Street, Tewkesbury. (4 Sep 1850). House. John Eyles. (Q/RNp/4)

THORNBURY

Oldbury, Kington, Morton and Falfield were tithings in Thornbury. Falfield and Oldbury-on-Severn were chapelries, which see.

1737 Thornbury. 1672. *Presbyterian*. Licence recorded for the house of Thomas Collins of Thornbury in Herefordshire. (LT/572)
Note. This is probably Thornbury in Gloucestershire. Compare Painswick **1369** which was also placed in Herefordshire.

1738 Thornbury. (Easter 1690). *Quaker*. Meeting-house. (Q/SO/3/522)

1739 Thornbury. (Michaelmas 1695). *Quaker*. A new erected house. (RG/31/6 f.72/v)
Note. This licence is not recorded in Q/SO/3/and the order of the entries is slightly different from the Registrar General's returns though in all other entries there is a close correspondence in the information given.

1740 Morton, Thornbury. (Trinity 1700). *Presbyterian*. Daniel Iles's house. (Q/SO/3/521)

1741 Thornbury. (Trinity 1702). *Quaker*. A new erected house. (Q/SO/3/521)

1742 Thornbury. 7 Dec 1715. *Quaker*. William Burton, schoolmaster in Thornbury, gave the solemn affirmation. (Q/SO/4/[9])

1743 Thornbury. 23 Oct 1747 (28 Mar 1748 'entered'). Some [dissenters] intend to hold a meeting for the worship of Almighty God at the dwelling house of one John Rawlings in the parish of Thornbury and therefore desire the same may be registered. John Rawlings, George Lane, Leonard Rodman, James Tyler, Thomas Beswick (GDR/284/194)

1744 Lower Moreton, Thornbury. 21 Feb 1748/49. *Presbyterian.* Some [dissenters] called Presbyterians intend to hold a meeting for the worship of God in the dwelling house of Joan Lawrence, widow, in Lower Moreton in the parish of Thornbury and pray it may be registered. Martin Lloyd, Joseph Everard, James Bingley. (GDR/284/202)
Note. For Joseph Everard *see* **197**.

1745 Thornbury. 10 July 1752 (13 July 1752). Some [dissenters] intend to hold a meeting for the worship of God in the dwelling house of John Whitfield in the parish of Thornbury. We therefore pray that this certificate may be entered in your Register. Thomas Bissex (mark), George Lane, Leonard Rodman, James Tyler. (GDR/284/218)

1746 Thornbury. 15 Mar 1756. *Independent.* Some [dissenters] called by the name of Independents intend to hold a meeting for the worship of God in the house called the Greenhouse in the town amd parish of Thornbury and desire it may be registered. Thomas Webb [RG/31/2 has Thomas Webb [of] Temple Guyting], Joseph Knight, John Johnson, Thomas Adams, William Uite [*sic*], Andrew Whitefield, Richard Scarlett. (GDR/292A/11)

1747 Thornbury. 28 July 1789 (1 Aug 1789; registration GDR/319A/95). *Baptist.* These are to certify that some [dissenters] called by the name of Baptists intend to hold a meeting in a house lately erected for that purpose in the town and parish of Thornbury and desire it may be registered. James Eley, Danel Reed, William Reed, John Shepherd, Thomas Shepherd. (GDR/N2/1)
Note. Crossed through; the first Shepherd name entered as Sheppard and firmly altered.

1748 Thornbury. 2 Sep 1794 (4 Sep 1794). *Quaker.* These are to certify that we [named below] with divers others being people called Quakers intend to hold meetings for the worship of Amighty God in the dwelling house of Robert Young, yeoman, in the town and parish of Thornbury, and give this notice that the place of our meeting may be known and registered and also request a certificate thereof. John Player, Samuel Lewis, Robert Young, Thomas Cole. (GDR/319A/188)

1749 Lower Moreton, Thornbury. 27 Nov 1805 (29 Nov 1805). We [named below] certify that we intend to meet and assemble for the purpose of publicly worshipping Almighty God in the dwelling house of Edward Lippiatt of Lower Moreton in the tithing of Moreton in the parish of Thornbury and we desire the same may be registered. John Sheppard, Edward Lippiatt, James Eley, William Jones, James Gundey, John Parslow. (GDR/334B/430)

1750 Thornbury. 11 Sept 1826 (15 Sept 1826). I Thomas Palmer, minister in Thornbury, certify that a building or chapel now erected in the town and parish of Thornbury, on the north side of Nelms Street, and in the occupation as trustees of the Revd John Leifchild, John Hensley, John Godwin, all of Bristol, William Ralph esq, Daniel Pitcher, George Motley, John Lane, all of Thornbury, Revd John Angell, James Birmingham, James Tayler, John Glanville, Thomas Tyndall of Dursley, Stephen Hignell Wickwar, Revd Charles Daniel, John Cook, George Long, William Long, James Counsell, John Millman, all of Kingswood, Samuel Long of Charfield, Revd John Lewis, 'Wottonunderedge', is intended forthwith to be a place of religious worship and require you to register the same. (GDR/350/58)

1751 Thornbury. (1 Jan 1852). Large room. John Garrett [of] Olveston. (RG/31/2 f.126/r)

TIBBERTON
1752 Tibberton. 3 Mar 1821 (5 Mar 1821). I William Phelps of the parish of Tibberton certify that the now dwelling house of William Parsons is intended forthwith to be a place of religious worship and require you to register the same and require a certificate thereof. (GDR/334B/225)

TIDENHAM
1753 Tiddenham. 5 June 1820. *Methodist.* I Benjamin Taylor of Chepstow in the county of Monmouth certify that the dwelling house of Thomas Saunigar in the parish of Tidenham is intended forthwith to be a place of religious worship and require you to register the same and request a certificate thereof. Benjamin Taylor, Methodist preacher. (GDR/334B/242)

1754 Tidenham. 17 Aug 1824 (17 Aug 1824). I Francis Metherall of Tidenham hereby certify that a certain barn situate in the parish of Tidenham, in the occupation of Isaac Williams, baker, is intended forthwith to be a place of religious worship and require you to register the same, and request a certificate thereof. Witness Mrs Wood. (GDR/344/136r)

1755 Tidenham. 16 Dec 1828 (18 Dec 1828). I William Williams of Chepstow, Monmouthshire, certify that a house in the parish of Tidenham, now in the occcupation of William Watkins, is intended forthwith to be a place of religious worship and require you to register the same and require a certificate thereof. (GDR/350/97)

1756 Beachley, Tidenham. 18 June 1831 (7 July 1831). I William Williams of Chepstow in the county of Monmouth, draper, certify that a house in the village of 'Bachley' in the parish of Tidenham, now in the occupation of William Luce, is intended forthwith to be a place of religious worship and require you to register the same and request a certificate thereof. (GDR/350/116)

1757 Woodcroft, Tidenham. 2 Jan 1844 (2 Jan 1844). We whose names are underwritten certify that a room at Woodcroft in the parish of Tidenham, called the Reading Room, is intended to be a place of religious worship 'by Protestants and Protestant dissenters' and we request that this certificate may be registered. George Dougles, Thomas Jones, Walter S Thomas. (GDR/350/329)

Note. RG/31/2 has 'Dean Forest' under place name.

1758 Bowspring, Tidenham. 15 Jan 1844 (9 Feb 1844). *Wesleyan.* I Henry V Olver of Monmouth, dissenting minister of Monmouth in the county of Monmouth, certify that the Wesleyan Chapel at Bowspring in the parish of Tidenham, is intended forthwith to be a place of religious worship and I require you to register the same and request a certificate thereof. (GDR/350/335)

TIRLEY

1759 'Turley'. (Trinity 1689). William Arnold's house. (Q/SO/3/522)

1760 'Turley'. (Easter 1690). *Quaker.* Meeting-house. (Q/SO/3/522)

1761 'Turley'. (Easter 1700). *Presbyterian.* Thomas Cole's house. (Q/SO/3/521)

1762 'Turley'. (Trinity 1702). *Quaker.* Thomas Cole's house. (Q/SO/3/521)

1763 Tirley. 15 Jan 1813 (16 Jan 1813). We [named below] certify that a house in the parish of Tirley, now occupied by Joseph Davies, is intended to be used henceforth as a place of divine worship, which we desire may be registered. Richard Jeffes, William Smith, Joseph Davis [Davies in text], William Herbert, James Peters, Charles Peters, Josiah Hopkins, John Cooper. (GDR/334B/349)

1764 Tirley. 6 Sept 1816 (13 Sept 1816). We [named below] certify that a piece of building in the parish of Tirley, now in the occupation of Josiah Hopkins as owner thereof, and made use of for a Sunday school, is intended forthwith to be a place of religious worship which we desire may be registered. Richard Jeffs, Josiah Hopkins, Joseph Davis, Joseph Paine, George Hodges, David Newman, James Peters. (GDR/334B/314)

1765 Tirley. 9 Oct 1816 (10 Oct 1816). [*Methodist, see* **179**]. I Daniel Campbell of Gloucester, minister, certify that an outhouse of Josiah Hopkins in the parish of 'Turley' is intended forthwith to be a place of religious worship and require you to register the same and request a certificate thereof. Witness Jeremiah Grant. (GDR/334B/312)

1766 Tirley. 11 Aug 1821 (11 Aug 1821). I Josiah Hopkins of the parish of Tirley certify that a Temple is erected on Zions Hill on my premises for divine worship. I require you to register the same and request a certificate thereof. (GDR/334B/214)

1767 Tirley. 19 Sept 1837 (20 Sept 1837). I Thomas Kington, of the Hill, in the parish of 'Castle Froome' in the county of Hereford, certify that a room of Richard Hogg and premises at Tirley in the parish of Tirley, now in [his] holding and occupation, are to be a place of religious worship and I request you to register the same and request a certificate thereof for which shall be taken no more than two shillings and six pence. (GDR/350/215)

1768 Tirley. 3 Apr 1839 (5 Apr 1839). I Christopher Borne [RG/31/2 has 'Bourne'] of the Greenhouse in the parish of Dymock certify that the chapel and premises at Tirley in the parish of Tirley, now in the holding and occupation of Richard Hogg, are to be a place of religious worship and I request you to register the same and request a certificate thereof for which shall be taken no more than two shillings and six pence. (GDR/350/238)

TODDINGTON

1769 Newtown, Toddington. 22 July 1824 (23 July 1824). I John Clee certify that a dwelling house occupied by me in Newtown, 'Toddinton', is intended forthwith to be a place of religious worship and I require you to register the same. I hereby request a certificate thereof. Witness John Lomas. (GDR/344/135v)

Note. A copying error in GDR350 has 'Tredington'. Judge (1912) has a reproduction of John Clee's hand-written certificate.

1770 Toddington. 14 Apr 1834 (16 Apr 1835). I Francis Constant of the parish of Toddington certify that my house in Toddington is intended forthwith to be a place of religious worship and require you to register the same and request a certificate thereof. Witness William Pardington, Benjamin Hunt. (GDR/350/169)

1771 Newtown, Toddington. 1 Feb 1836 (2 Feb 1836). I James Morish of Cheltenham certify that a dwelling house and premises at Toddington 'New Town' in the parish of Toddington, now in the holding and occupation of John Hunt, labourer, are intended to be a place of religious worship and I request you to register the same and request a certificate thereof for which shall be taken no more than two shillings and sixpence. James Morish, John Hunt. (GDR/350/188)

TODENHAM

1772 Todenham. 9 Sept 1818 (14 Sept 1818). I John Mason of Chipping Norton in the county of Oxford certify that the house of William Newbury in the parish of 'Todingham' is intended forthwith to be used as a place of religious worship and require you to register the same and require a certificate thereof. (GDR/334B/276)

TORMARTON

1773 Tormarton. (29 Mar 1852). House Daniel Mossop [of] Hawkesbury. (RG/31/2 f.126/r)

TORTWORTH

1774 Tortworth. 2 Jan 1843 (2 Jan 1843). I Joseph Hyatt of Gloucester, dissenting minister, certify that a house in the parish of Tortworth, on the left side of the entrance to Tortworth Court, and formerly used as a Lodge but now as a school room, is intended forthwith to be licensed as a place of religious worship and require you to register the same and request a certificate thereof. (GDR/350/310)

1775 Tortworth. 3 Feb 1844 (3 Feb 1844). I Joseph Hyatt of Gloucester, dissenting minister, certify that a house recently erected in the parish of Tortworth is intended forthwith to be used as a place of religious worship and I request you to register the same and request a certificate thereof. (GDR/350/333)

TREDINGTON

1776 Tredington. May 1809. 'Treddington cert registered May 1809 but by mistake sent out before it was copied'. (GDR/334B/401).

1777 Tredington. 22 July 1822 (23 July 1822). I Francis Collier, minister of Gloucester, certify that the dwelling house of John Robins of 'Treddington' is intended forthwith to be a place of religious worship and require you to register the same. (GDR/344/33v)

1778 Tredington. 17 May 1828 (17 May 1828). [*Particular Baptist: see* **1721**]. We certify that the dwelling house, now in the occupation of John Healing, in the parish of Tredington is henceforth intended to be a place of religious worship and request that this certificate may be registered. D Trotman, Tewkesbury, T Blandy, Tewkesbury. (GDR/350/88)

TRESHAM
Tresham was a chapelry in Hawkesbury parish.
1779 Tresham. 25 Mar 1816 (29 Mar 1816). I Stephen Hopkins of 'Woottonunderedge' certify that the house of William Willis of Tresham in the parish of Hawkesbury is intended forthwith to be a place of religious worship and require you to register the same and request a certificate thereof. Stephen Hopkins, J Rickards. (GDR/334B/321)

1780 Tresham. 31 Jan 1818 (9 Feb 1818). I Stephen Hopkins of 'Woottonunderedge' certify that the house of George Showell of Tresham in the parish of Hawkesbury is intended forthwith to be used as a place of religious worship and require you to register the same and request a certificate thereof. Signed in the presence of Robert Hopkins. (GDR/334B/285)

1781 Tresham. 4 Dec 1846 (9 Dec 1846). I James Franckum of Tresham in the parish of Hawkesbury, labourer, certify that a house belonging to me in Tresham is intended occasionally to be used as a place of religious worship and I require you to register the same. (GDR/350/384)

1782 Tresham. (9 Dec 1847). House belonging to Samuel Franckum. Samuel Franckum. (Q/RNp/4)

TURKDEAN
1783 Turkdean. 15 Sept 1830 (17 Sept 1830). I James Whitworth of the town of Stroud, minister of the Gospel, certify that a cottage, in the occupation of William Townsend, in the parish of 'Turk's Dean' is intended forthwith to be a place of religious worship and require you to register the same and request a certificate thereof. (GDR/350/110)

1784 Turkdean. 18 Feb 1835 (5 Mar 1835). *Wesleyan.* I Paul Orchard of the town of Stroud certify that a house in Turkdean is intended forthwith to be a place of religious worship and require you to register the same and request a certificate thereof. Paul Orchard, Wesleyan minister. (GDR/350/166)

1785 Turkdean. 15 May 1835 (15 May 1835). I William Bullock of Leckhampton certify that a dwelling house, in the occupation of George Draper, in the parish of 'Turk Dean' is intended forthwith to be used as a place of religious worship and require you to register the same and request a certificate thereof. (GDR/350/174)

1786 'Turk Dean'. 23 Apr 1852. House. John Kirk [of] Cheltenham, Wesleyan minister. (RG/31/2 f.126/r)

TWIGWORTH
Twigworth, a hamlet which had a medieval chapel, was divided beween the parishes of St Catherine and St Mary de Lode, and became a parish in 1844 (VCH Glos 4, 382).
1787 Twigworth. 24 Nov 1827. I Marshall Claxton of Gloucester, minister, certify that the now dwelling house of John Hill in the hamlet of Twigworth is intended forthwith to be a place of religious worship and require you to register the same and require a certificate thereof. (GDR/350/75-7)
Note. No signature.

1788 Twigworth. 24 Nov 1827 (1 Dec 1827). We certify that a room in the dwelling house of John Hill in the hamlet of Twigworth is intended forthwith to be used as a place of religious worship and I hereby require you to register the same and require a certificate thereof. John Hill, Jacob Stanley. (GDR/350/77)

TWYNING

1789 Twyning. 5 July 1804 (5 July 1804). *Particular Baptist.* We [named below] certify that the dwelling house of Mr Daniel Merrett in the parish of 'Twinning' is intended to be occupied as a place of religious worship by the denomination of Particular Baptists. And we request that the clerk of the court may be desired to register the same. Daniel Trotman, minister, Daniel Merrett, Peter Oakley, Samuel Jones, John Merrell, William Lloyd, George Purser, John Turner, William Straford. (GDR/334B/437)

1790 Twyning. 14 Oct 1813 (19 Oct 1813). [*Methodist: see* **178**]. I John Chettle of Gloucester, minister, certify that the dwelling house of James Price, hosier, in the parish of 'Twinning near Tewkesbury' is intended forthwith to be a place of religious worship and require you to register the same and request a certificate thereof. (GDR/334B/342)

1791 Twyning. 3 July 1821 (4 July 1821). I Abraham Harris of Gloucester Row, Tewkesbury, late hosier, certify that a tenement in the parish of 'Twining' in the occupation of John Purser is intended forthwith to be used as a place of religious worship and require you to register the same. (GDR/334B/217)

1792 Twyning. 29 Sept 1828 (29 Sept 1828). We certify that the dwelling house now in the occupation of Philip Roberts in the parish of 'Twynning' is henceforth intended to be a place of religious worship and we therefore request that this certificate may be registered. D Trotman, Tewkesbury, Richard Warder, Tewkesbury. (GDR/350/94)

1793 Twyning. 14 Jan 1837 (8 Feb 1837). I John Tharm of the parish of Tewkesbury certify that a house and premises in the parish of 'Twynning', now in the holding and occuaption of Mr James Price, are to be a place of religious worship and I request you to register the same and request a certificate thereof for which shall be taken no more than two shillings and six pence. (GDR/350/206)

1794 Twyning. 4 May 1838 (5 May 1838). We certify that the dwelling house now in the occupation of John Booth in the parish of Twyning is henceforth to be a place of religious worship and I request you to register the same. Daniel Trotman, Tewkesbury, Thomas Talmersh, Tewkesbury. (GDR/350/224)

1795 Twyning. 24 May 1838 (24 May 1838). We humbly certify that the dwelling house and other premises, now in the occupation of Joseph Passey, in the parish of Twyning is henceforth to be a place of religious worship and request that this certificate may be registered in the Consistory court of the diocese. Robert Dickson, Tewkesbury, Thomas Talmash, Tewkesbury. (GDR/350/226)

1796 Twyning. 20 Nov 1840 (21 Nov 1840). We certify that the dwelling house, now in the occupation of John Booth, in the parish of Twyning is henceforth to be a place of religious worship and we therefore request that this certificate may be registered. Daniel Trotman, Tewkesbury, Thomas Talmash, Tewkesbury. (GDR/350/264)

1797 Twyning. 12 Dec 1842 (17 Dec 1842). We certify that the dwelling house, now in the occupation of Joseph Pagsey, in the parish of Twyning is henceforth intended to be a place of religious worship and request that this certificate may be registered. William Knight, Richard Jarman. (GDR/350/309)

TYTHERINGTON

1798 Tytherington. 2 Jan 1790 (2 Jan 1790). *Arminian.* These are to certify that some [dissenters] called by the name of 'Armenians' intend to hold a meeting for the worship of God in the dwelling house of William Pullen in the parish of Tytherington and desire it may be registered. Moses Tyler, Benjamin Stephens, Elias Summers. (GDR/319A/99)
Note. See following certificate.

1799 Tytherington. (Michaelmas 1790). *Methodist.* We whose names are hereunto subscribed for ourselves and others called by the name of Methodists certify that we have set apart part of the dwelling house of William Pullen in the parish of Tytherington for the worship of Almighty God in their way, and we pray that this certificate may be entered and enrolled of Record pursuant to the statute in that case made & provided. James Werrett, Thomas Andrews, Mark Werrett, William Roach, Christopher Andrews, John Alpass. (Q/SO/11/f.330r)
Note. RG/31/6 recorded William Pullen as certifier. *See previous entry.* Names written in a different or much larger hand than the certificate but not signatures. Elaborate rubric 'A certificate of the Methodists of Tytherington having set apart a building there for Public Worship, recorded'.

1800 Tytherington. 27 Mar 1811 (3 Apr 1811). We [named below] certify that the house of Thomas Bidgood in the parish of Tytherington is intended to be used for the occasional worship of Almighty God which we desire may be registered accordingly. John Croome, Henry Pinden, Thomas Morgan, Thomas Bidgood, Obed[iah] Pitcher, Enoch Pinden. (GDR/334B/367)

1801 Tytherington. 14 Sept 1832 (15 Sept 1832). I William Jarman Cross of Thornbury, disssentling minister, certify that I purpose to use two rooms in a house in the possession of Thomas Addis in 'Titherington' for the purpose of religious worship and which is intended to contain a congregation exceeding 20 persons. (GDR/350/134)

1802 Tytherington. 10 Oct 1839 (11 Oct 1839). I the undersigned William Jarman Cross of Thornbury, dissenting minister, certify that I purpose to use a room in the house in the possession of Henry Curtis in the parish of Tytherington for the purpose of religious worship and is to contain a congregation exceeding 20 persons. (GDR/350/244-5)

ULEY

1803 Uley. 1672. *Presbyterian.* Licence recorded for the house of Mary Torry of Uley. (LT/581)

1804 'Uly'. (Trinity 1703.) *Presbyterian.* Maurice Dancy's house. [RG/31/6 has 'Dauncey'] (Q/SO/3/521)

1805 Uley. (Trinity 1707). *Anabaptist.* 'Jos:' Hancock's house [RG/31/6 has Joseph]. (Q/SO/3/520)

1806 Uley. (Easter 1724). It is ordered by this court that the dwelling house of John Fisher in Uley be hereby licensed for [dissenters] residing in and about the parish of Uley to assemble and meet together in for the worship of God in their way. (Q/SO/4/484)

1807 Uley. (Michaelmas 1727). It is ordered by this court that the dwelling house of George Dauncey in Uley be licensed and allowed for [dissenters] inhabiting in and about that parish to meet together in. (Q/SO/5/f.83v)
Note. Rubric has 'Uley meeting-house'.

1808 Uley. (Epiphany 1736/7). *Baptist.* It is ordered by this court that the dwelling house of 'Aron Smith' in the parish of Uley be licensed and allowed for [dissenters] called Baptists to assemble and meet together for the worship of Amighty God in their way. (Q/SO/6/f.97v)

1809 Uley. 13 Dec 1776 (21 Dec 1776). We [named below] certify that we intend on Sunday the 22nd day of this Instant Dec to meet and assemble for the publick worshipping of Almighty God in a dwelling house in a place called Garlick's Court in the parish of Uley, late in the occupation of Thomas Hill but now vacant, and that such dwelling house is intended to be set apart for the same purpose in future which we desire may be registered. J Thomas, John Pope, William Minett, Thomas Cummings, Joseph Minett, Isaac Danford, Edward Jackson, Samuel Souls, Charles Whittard. (GDR/292A/201)

1810 Uley. 2 July 1791 (6 July 1791). We [named below] request that the house newly erected, named the Union Chapel, in the parish of Uley be registered for a place of divine worship. James Harris, Daniel Lloyd, George Harris, Nathaniel Lloyd. (GDR/319A/126-7)

1811 Uley. (18 Apr 1807). We [named below] certify that the house of Michael Robbins in the parish of Uley is appropriated for the worship of Almighty God and we require the same may be registered and a certificate be granted. William Austin [RG/31/2 has of Uley], Daniel French jnr, Isaac Exel, Abel Robbins, Michael Robins, N Exel, John Millard, William Robbins. (GDR/334B/423)

1812 Uley. (14 Nov 1807). We [named below] certify that the the the house of Toby Hurcombe in the parish of Uley is appropriated for the purpose of the public worship of Almighty God and we require the same may be registered. Toby 'Hurcomb', Thomas Talboys, John Talboys, Thomas Pinder, William Dixon. (GDR/334B/418-7)

1813 Uley. (20 Aug 1808). We [named below] certify that the dwelling house of Charles Norris in the parish of Uley is appropriated for the purpose of the public worship of Almighty God and we require the same may be registered and a certificate of the same be granted. Charles Stephen, Daniel French, John Wilkins, Charles Norris, William Curry. (GDR/334B/415-14)

1814 Uley.19 June 1818 (20 June 1818). I Samuel Park certify that a certain building in the parish of Uley [in my occcupation] is intended forthwith to be used as a place of religious worship and I require you to register the same. Samuel Park, Peter Powell, James Fisher, Joseph Tilley, Daniel Ricketts, Joseph Evans, Thomas Hill. (GDR/334B/279)

1815 Uley. 9 Jan 1819 (30 Jan 1819). I Edward Jackson certify that a building in the parish of Uley [in my occupation] is intended forthwith to be a place of religious worship and I require you to register the same. Edward Jackson, E J Blackwell, Joseph Trull, William Taylor, Joel Brian, James Dangerfield, William Souls, William Baglin. (GDR/334B/268)

1816 Uley. 17 May 1820 (31 May 1820). *Independent.* We [named below] certify that a building in the parish of Uley, in the possession and occupation of Edward Austin, is intended to be used as a chapel for religious worship by dissenters of the denomination of Independents and we request that this certificate may be registered. R Taylor, minister;

William Austin, proprietor; Edward Austin, tenant; George Dauncey, Thomas Freeman. (GDR/334B/242)

1817 Uley. 15 Jan 1820 (15 Jan 1820). *Methodist.* I certify that a new building, called the New Methodist Chapel, in the parish of Uley is intended to be used as a place of religious worship by those commonly called Methodists, and I request that the same may be registered. Elijah Morgan, minister. (GDR/334B/249)

1818 Uley. 29 Sept 1838 (11 Oct 1838). *Baptist.* I Edward Webb of the parish of Uley, Baptist minister, certify that a building called Bethesda Chapel at Clap Yate Lane in the parish of Uley is forthwith to be a place of religious worship and I require you to register the same and request a certificate thereof. (GDR/350/233)

1819 Uley. 29 Nov 1844 (14 Dec 1844). We [named below] certify that a room in the dwelling house in the parish of Uley, called the dwelling house of Ann Wilkins, is intended to be a place of religious worship and we request that this certificate may be registered in the consistory court. William Barnett, John Boulton, Ann Wilkins. (GDR/350/352)

UPLEADON
1820 Upleadon. 24 June 1828 (24 June 1828). I Marshall Claxton of the city of Gloucester certify that a house, now in the occupation of Joseph Smith, in the parish of Upleadon is intended forthwith to be a place of religious worship and I require you to register the same and request a certificate thereof. Witness Joseph Smith. (GDR/350/90)

1821 Upleadon. 30 Aug 1834 (30 Aug 1834). I Richard Merrett in the parish of Upleadon certify that I purpose to use one room in a house in the parish of Upleadon, in [my] possession, for the purpose of religious worship and which is intended to contain a congregation exceeding the number of 20 persons. (GDR/350/156)

UPPER SLAUGHTER
See also Eyford, sometimes regarded as attached to Upper Slaughter.
1822 Upper Slaughter. 21 Dec 1715. John Collett of Upper Slaughter, dissenting preacher, took oaths of allegiance and supremacy. (Q/SO/4/[10])

1823 Upper Slaughter. 10 Mar 1841 (13 Mar 1841). I William Collett of Stow-on-the-Wold certify that a cottage in the parish of Upper Slaughter, in the occupation of William Yearp, shoemaker, is forthwith to be a place of religious worship and I request you to register the same. (GDR/350/276)

1824 Upper Slaughter. 9 July 1842 (13 July 1842). I William Collett of Upper Slaughter certify that a house in Upper Slaughter, in the occupation of Thomas Collett, farmer, is forthwith to be a place of religious worship and I request you to register the same. (GDR/350/300)

UPTON ST LEONARDS
1825 Upton St Leonards. 9 Sept 1740. Some [dissenters] intend to hold a meeting for the worship of Almighty God in their way in the dwelling house of William Wathern, shoemaker, in the parish of Upton St Leonards, therefore desires it may be registered. Martin Lloyd snr, Samuel Bryan, Joseph Everard. (GDR/284/111)
Note. For Joseph Everard *see* **197**.

1826 Upton St Leonards. (27 Oct 1792). These are to certify that we with others intend to hold a meeting for the worship of Almighty God in the dwelling house of William Wathen in the parish of Upton St Leonards and pray it may be registered in your Lordship's Court. Thomas Higgs, Benjamin Wathan, William Wathan, Henery Turner, Benjamin Rivers, William Cooke jnr. (GDR/319A/142)

1827 Upton St Leonards. (9 Aug 1802). We [named below, dissenters] have set apart a house occupied by Mr John Woodcock in Upton St Leonards for the worship of Almighty God and humbly request it may be registered. Richard Gower, Henry Tombs, John Woodcock, Thomas Wells, William Higgs, Benjamin ?Walker [?Wathan], William Turner, John Turner. (GDR/N2/1)
Note. Benjamin's surname inserted through the gg of Higgs; no record in Diocesan Act Book or RG/31/2.

1828 Upton St Leonards. 27 Dec 1805 (3 Feb 1806). [*Methodist: see* **166**]. We [named below] have 'separated' a house, the property of Henry Tombs, in the parish of Upton St Leonards for the public worship of Almighty God and request it may be registered. Henry Tombs, William Kilby, Benjamin Wathen, Henry Drinkwater, J M Byron, minister, William Turner, John Turner, Thomas Wells. (GDR/334B/428)

1829 Upton St Leonards. 9 July 1809 (14 July 1809). *Methodist.* We [named below] beg leave to certify that a chapel lately erected in the parish of Upton St Leonards is set apart for the worship of Almighty God by dissenters commonly called Methodists and we request that the same may be registered and a certificate of the same given. Henry Tombs, William Turner, John Turner, Benjamin Wathen, William Witcombe, Henry Drinkwater. (GDR/334B/399)

WAPLEY & CODRINGTON
1830 Wapley & Codrington. 7 Apr 1835 (8 Apr 1835). I, J C Norgrove, dissenting minister of Chipping Sodbury, certify that a tenement in the parish of Wapley & Codrington, now occupied by John Evans, is intended to be forthwith a place of religious worship and require you to register the same. John Corban Norgrove. (GDR/350/168)

1831 Wapley & Codrington. 18 Sept 1847 (25 Sept 1847). *Independent.* May it please your Lordship to grant unto us [named below], dissenters of the Independent denomination, a certificate for a house belonging to Mr Daniel Carter in the parish of Wapley and Codrington for the worship of Almighty God and we pray that the same may be registered and a certificate granted us. William Holloway, William Shipp, William Matthews, John Evans, George Lawrence. William Stephens. (GDR/350/385-6)

WELFORD-ON-AVON
The main part of Welford-on-Avon, south of the Avon, was in Gloucestershire, and part, north of the river, was in Warwickshire.
1832 Welford [-on-Avon]. 22 Sep 1798 (1 Oct 1798). We [named below] request that a room in the dwelling house of Matthew Mills in the parish of 'Wellford' be set apart for the worship of Almighty God and we desire the same may be registered. Matthew Mills, William Sale, William Harris, James Mills, Thomas Nickolls, George Allcock. (GDR/319A/270)

1833 Welford [-on-Avon]. 24 Sep 1798 (1 Oct 1798). We [named below] request that a room in the dwelling house of Abraham Commander of the parish of 'Wellford' be set apart for the worship of Almighty God and we desire the same may be registered.

Abraham Commander, Henry Matthews, Thomas Adkins, Richard Boyce, William Harris, James Mills. (GDR/319A/269-70)

1834 Welford [-on-Avon]. 14 Dec 1816 (27 Dec 1816). I Mary Parker of 'Wellford' certify that a certain house and buildings adjoining, now in my possession occupied by me, is intended forthwith to be used as a place of religious worship and require you to register the same. Mary Parker, Thomas Tibbaths Smith, Thomas Adams, John Tasker. (GDR/334B/306)

1835 Welford [-on-Avon]. 16 Feb 1826 (18 Feb 1826). I John Thurston, minister, certify that the house and barn of William Harris are intended forthwith to be set aside for the public worship of Almighty God and we require you to register the same. (GDR/350/52)

1836 Welford [-on-Avon]. (30 Nov 1849). House occupied by John Court. John Court. (Q/RNp/4)

WESTBURY-ON-TRYM
Diocese of Bristol. Now part of Bristol. Redland was a chapelry; Shirehampton, which see, was a tithing and chapelry and became an ecclesiastical parish in 1844.
1837 Westbury [on Trym]. (Epiphany 1706/7). *Quaker.* A house erected for Quakers. [RG/31/6 confirms Westbury-on-Trym]. (Q/SO/3/520)

1839 Westbury-on-Trym. 14 Sept 1792 (22 Sept 1792). We [named below] being part of a congregation of dissenters humbly certify that a new erected building, in a street called Portland Street within the parish of 'Westbury upon Trym' is intended, set apart for and to be used as a place of meeting for religious worship. We desire that the same may be registered in your lordship's court. Samuel Bradburn, minister, James Davis, Edward Jones, William Chitty, George Surway, James Davies, Thomas Tennant, John Hall jnr, John Hall snr, James Ewer, William Davies, William Hartland, William Moore, John Powell, John Moore, F Morrish, Robert Boley. (EP/A/45/1/246)

1840 Westbury-on-Trym. 9 Sept 1801 (15 Sept 1801). We [named below] certify that a certain dwelling house situate at Westbury-on-Trym now in the occupation of George Brooks, carpenter, is to be used as a place of meeting for religious worship. And we request that the said may be registered. George Brooks, Philip Williams, William Vaughan, Joseph Woolcott, George Beachem, Isaac Price. (EP/A/45/1/289)

1841 Westbury-on-Trym. 9 May 1807 (12 Jun 1807). We [named below] desire that a room or meeting-house now erecting and building on premises belonging to Philip Williams in the parish of Westbury-on-Trym may be registered among the records of this diocese as a meeting-house set apart for the worship of God and religious exercise. Philip Williams, Amos Tavener, Isaac Price, John Hughes, William Taylor, Samuel Griffith. (EP/A/45/1/407)

1842 Westbury-on-Trym. 13 Mar 1811 (28 Mar 1811). In pursuance of an act of parliament we [named below] desire that the room or meeting-house now building, on a spot of ground purchased of Mr William Favill, at 'Westbury upon Trym' may be registered as a meeting-house set apart for the worship of God and religious exercise. James Holmes, Amos Tavener, George Brooks, Samuel Harris, John Taylor, Morgan Thomas, John Phillimore, John Millard, John Holmes, William Vaughan. (EP/A/45/2/41-2)

1844 Westbury-on-Trym. 16 Jan 1845 (17 Jan 1845). I William Lane, dissenting minister, residing in the parish of 'Westbury upon Trym', and the persons [named below] desire to have the house of a poor blind man named Francis Garraway, in Chalk Lane in the said village or parish of 'Westbury upon Trym', licensed as a place of divine worship. William Lane, Francis Garraway (mark), Elisabeth Fletcher, Amos Tavener, Henry Nichols, James Adams. (EP/A/45/3/326)

1845 Westbury-on-Trym. 10 Mar 1845 (11 Mar 1845). I William Lane, dissenting minister residing in the parish of 'Westbury upon Trym'and the persons [named below] desire to have the house in which I dwell in The Butts, in the said village or parish of 'Westbury upon Trym', duly licensed as a place of divine worship. William Lane, Elizabeth Fletcher, Amos Tavener, Joel Tavener, Henry Nichols, James Adams. (EP/A/45/3/353-54)

1846 Westbury-on-Trym. 10 June 1846 (11 June 1846). *Baptist*. We [named below] certify that a building in the parish of Westbury in the county of Gloucester is to be used as a chapel for religious worship by dissenters of the denomination of Baptists and we request that this certificate may be registered. Samuel Brewer Wearing, Isaac Dainton, John Shoard, John Henry Cuzner, Henry Lee, George Vowles jnr. (EP/A/45/3/397)

WESTBURY-ON-SEVERN

1847 Elton, Westbury [-on-Severn]. (Easter 1690). *Quaker*. 'Elton in Westbury', Meeting-house. [RG/31/2 confirms Westbury-on-Severn]. (Q/SO/3/522)

1848 Westbury [-on-Severn]. 5 Jan 1810 (6 Jan 1810). These are to certify that some dissenters intend to hold meetings for the worship of Almighty God in the dwelling house, occupied and belonging to Mr William Mayo, in the parish of Westbury. We pray that this certificate be registered. William Hardwick, Samuel Lear, Anthony Ely, George Pegler, William Ely. (GDR/334B/394)
Note. For Samuel Lear *see* **240**.

1849 [?Chaxhill], Westbury-on-Severn. 3 May 1814 (10 Jun 1814). I William Hardwick of the parish of Eastington, clothier, certify that a messuage or tenement situated in 'Chacks' in the parish of 'Westbury-upon-Severn', in the occupation of Josiah Coleman, carpenter, is intended forthwith to be a place of religious worship and require you to register the same and request a certificate thereof. Witness W Flint. (GDR/334B/338)

1850 Northwood, Westbury-on-Severn. 9 Dec 1816 (20 Dec 1816). *Independent*. We [named below] certify that an house in the occupation of Richard Hart, situated in a common field called the Newlands, near the lower end of Ley-Park, in the tithing of Northwood in the parish of Westbury-upon-Severn', is intended to be used as a place of religious worship for dissenters of the Independent denomination, and we request that the same may be registered. Richard Hart of Northwood, Thomas Constance of Westbury, John Hart (mark). (GDR/334B/308)

1851 Rodley, Westbury–on-Severn. 3 Apr 1819 (8 Apr 1819). I John Wilkins of Westbury certify that the dwelling house of William Bright, waterman, in the tithing of Rodley in the parish of Westbury-on-Severn is intended forthwith to be a place of religious worship and I require you to register the same and request a certificate thereof. John Wilkins, John Wilkins, John Gough. (GDR/334B/264)
Note. John Wilkins' name appears twice.

1852 Westbury [-on-Severn]. 31 Aug 1819 (4 Sept 1819). I certify that the premises occupied by Benjamin Coleman in the parish of Westbury will hereafter be a place of religious worship. John Pyer, minister. (GDR/334B/255)

1853 Westbury-on-Severn. 11 Apr 1820 (11 Apr 1820). I certify that the premises occupied by Richard Ryder in the parish of Westbury-upon-Severn will hereafter be a place of religious worship. Adam Nightingale, a minister. (GDR/334B/243)

1854 Rodley, Westbury–on-Severn. 7 Sept 1820 (9 Sept 1820). I certify that a piece of land called Okles, occupied by Thomas Roan, in the parish of Westbury-on-Severn in the tithing of Rodley will hereafter be a place of religious worship. David Comforth, minister. (GDR/334B/235)

1855 Rodley, Westbury-on-Severn. 24 Feb 1821 (24 Feb 1821). [*Methodist: see* **166**]. I, W Wheeler of the city of Gloucester, linen draper, certify that a chapel erected at Rodley in the parish of Westbury-on-Severn is intended forthwith to be a place of religious worship and require you to register the same and require a certificate thereof. W Wheeler, James M Byron, minister. (GDR/334B/226)

1856 Silver Street, Westbury-on-Severn. 15 Nov 1824 (16 Nov 1824). We [named below] certify a building or dwelling house, in the occupation of Thomas Constance, tailor, Silver Street, in the parish of Westbury-upon-Severn is intended forthwith to be a place of religious worship and I request you to register the same. David Pearce, minister, Thomas Constance, occupier, William Clark. (GDR/350/21)

1857 Westbury [-on-Severn]. 4 Dec 1827 (4 Dec 1827). We [named below] certify that a building or dwelling house, in the occcupation of James Critchley, in the parish of Westbury is intended forthwith to be a place of religious worship and I request you to register the same. Joseph Saunders, witness; David Pearce, minister; James Critchley, occupier. (GDR/350/78)
Note. Names have been altered and are not clear. RG/31/2 has David Rain minister.

1858 Walmore Hill, Westbury [-on-Severn]. 28 Nov 1829 (1 Dec 1829). I John Watts of 'Walmers Hill' in the parish of Westbury, land drainer, certify that my dwelling house at 'Walmers Hill' is intended forthwith to be a place of religious worship and I require you to register the same. (GDR/350/106)

1859 Adsett, Westbury-on-Severn. 4 June 1838 (11 June 1838). *Independent.* We [named below], being inhabitant householders residing in the parish of Westbury-on-Severn, certify that a building called Ebenezer Chapel in the tithing of Adsett in the parish of Westbury-on-Severn, in the occupation of Josiah Coleman, John Wilkins and others, is to be used and set apart for the public worship of Almighty God by dissenters 'known by the name of Nonconformists or Independents' and require the same to be duly registered and a certificate granted. John Wilkins jnr, Joseph Thomas, Thomas Roberts. (GDR/350/226)

WESTCOTE
1860 Westcote. 6 July 1800 (22 Aug 1800; registration GDR/319A/300-1.) We [named below] certify that part of the building called a malthouse, in the occupation of Thomas Midwinter, in the parish of 'Westcott' is intended to be used for religious worship. And we require the same to be registered. William Hambidge, William Sutton, Laurence Mace. (GDR/N2/1)

WESTERLEIGH
A chapelry in Pucklechurch, which early had a civil identity but did not become an ecclesiastical parish until 1886 (Youngs 190).

1861 [?Westerleigh]. 1672. *Presbyterian*. Licence recorded for the house of Richard Parker of 'Westerby', Gloucestershire. (LT/570)

Note. This entry is with a group of Shropshire licences. A second entry (for William Jordan) in Westerby, Leicestershire was included with others for that county (LT/518).

1862 Westerleigh. (Michaelmas 1691). *Quaker.* [Meeting-house]. (Q/SO/3/522)

1863 Westerleigh. 17 Apr 1727. These are to certify that [dissenters] intend to hold a meeting for the worship of God in their way in the parish of Westerleigh in the house of Thomas Roberts of Westerleigh and pray that it may be registered. Alexander Griffiths, James Smith, Richard Hale. (GDR/279a/168)

1864 Westerleigh. 11 Dec 1794 (13 Dec 1794). We [named below] signify that a building in the parish of Westerleigh is intended to be used for the religious worship of Almighty God and we desire the register to record the same. William Offer, Mary Offer, James Jones. (GDR/319A/202)

1865 Kindleshire, Westerleigh. 25 Nov 1810 (Nov 1810). *Methodist*. We [named below] commonly called Methodists have appropriated and set aside a room on the ground floor of a dwelling house of Mary Fugill, widow, the present occcupier, at Kindleshire in the parish of Westerleigh, for the worship of Almighty God. We request that the same be registered. Joseph Bowes, Edward Smith, Charles Edwards, John Webb, Walter Fugill, John A Lomas. (GDR/334B/371)

1866 Westerleigh. 11 Nov 1811 (13 Nov 1811). *Wesleyan Connexion.* We [named below] being in the connection of the late Revd John Wesley, deceased, have appropriated and set aside all the rooms on the ground floor of a house, now in the occupation of John Roach, labourer, in the village and parish of Westerleigh, for the worship of Almighty God and request that the same may be registered. Joseph Bowes, Stephen Frankcombe, William Pullin, Sarah Bryant, John Roach (mark), George Croome, John Crew, John Whatley, James Green. (GDR/334B/359)

1867 Westerleigh. 27 Mar 1816 (29 Mar 1816). I George Wilton Sage of the city of Bristol, timber merchant, certify that a certain building or tenement situated in Westerleigh Street in the parish of Westerleigh, lately occupied by John Canick, is forthwith to be used as a place of religious worship and require you to register the same. G W Sage, Thomas Edward, minister, Joseph Ridler, Robert Padfield, Samuel Taylor. (GDR/334B/320)

1868 Nibley, Westerleigh. 8 June 1822 (22 June 1822). *Independent.* We [named below] being dissenters of the Independent denomination have set apart a certain tenement or dwelling house, lately occupied by George Carter, at Nibley within the parish of Westerleigh for the worship of Almighty God and we pray that the said tenement may be registered and a certificate granted us. Thomas White, James Lane, William Britton, Daniel Gibbs, Jonathan Gibbs, Joseph Rider, Daniel Townsend, Samuel Pullen, William Russell. (GDR/344/32r)

1869 Westerleigh. 10 Sep 1832 (11 Sept 1832). I William Pearce of Chipping Sodbury, chemist and druggist, certify that a tenement in the parish of Westerleigh, now occupied by George Luton, is intended forthwith to be a place of religious worship and I require you to register the same. (GDR/350/133)

Note. Rubric gives 'Chipping Sodbury'.

1870 Westerleigh. 18 Oct 1836 (1 Nov 1836). *Independent.* May it please your Lordship to grant unto us [named below] of the Independent denomination a certificate for a house or tenement, now in the possession of Mr J M Humberstone, in the parish of Westerleigh for the worship of Almighty God, and we pray that the same may be registered in your court and a certificate granted. J M Humberstone, John Jack, dissenting minister, William Wait, William Iles, V Gibbs, James Bessell, Samuel Wade, John Gardner. (GDR/350/202-3)

1871 Westerleigh. 13 June 1844 (17 June 1844). *Independent.* May it please your Lordship to grant unto us [named below] being dissenters of the Independent denomination, a certificate for a building called the Tabernacle in the parish of Westerleigh for the worship of Almighty God and we pray that the same building may be registered in your court and a certificate granted us. William Shipway, Edmund Stiff, George Close, William Gibbs, J M Humberstone, Joseph Lydiard. (GDR/350/343)

1872 Westerleigh. 18 Sept 1847 (25 Sept 1847). May it please your Lordship to grant unto us [named below] being dissenters of the Independent denomination, a certificate for the lower part or ground floor of a house or tenement now in the occupation of Mr George Bryant in the parish of Westerleigh for the worship of Almighty God and we pray that the same may be registered and a certificate granted us. Stephen Gibbs, William Sherborne, Richard Iles, J M Humberstone, George Close, Gregory Nicholls. (GDR/350/390)

WESTON-ON-AVON

1873 Weston-on-Avon. 30 Jan 1791 (17 Feb 1791). We [named below] request that a room in the dwelling house of Caleb Adkins in the parish of 'Weston-upon-Avon' be set apart for the worship of Almighty God and desire that the same may be registered. Caleb Adkins, Richard Boyce, Thomas Nickolls, Matthew Mills, William Sale, George Mills. (GDR/319A/121-2)

WESTON-SUB-EDGE

1874 Weston-sub-Edge. 28 Jan 1819 (10 Feb 1819). I Joseph Wheatley of the village and parish of 'Weston Subage', certify that the dwelling house, now in the occupation of John Steel, husbandman, in the village and parish of Weston Subedge, is intended forthwith to be a place of religious worship and require you to register the same and request a certificate thereof. Witness John Steel (mark). (GDR/334B/267)

1875 Weston-sub-Edge. 4 June 1829 (9 June 1829). *Baptist.* We [named below] certify that the dwelling house, occupied by William Gardner, in the parish of 'Weston Subedge' is intended to be used as a place of religious worship by a congregation of the Baptist denomination and we require you ro register the same and request a certificate thereof. William Elliott, William Gardner. (GDR/350/102)

1876 Weston-sub-Edge. 9 Apr 1835 (17 Apr 1835). *Wesleyan.* I John Wevill of Evesham, Wesleyan minister, certify that a dwelling house (at present unoccupied) at 'Weston Subedge', belonging to Robert Smith, is intended forthwith to be a place of religious worship and I require you to register the same and request a certificate thereof. John Wevill, Robert Smith. (GDR/350/171)

WESTONBIRT

1877 Weston[birt]. 1 May 1753. His Majesty's Protestant dissenting subjects intend to hold a meeting for the worship of Almighty God at the dwelling house of John Ball in the parish of Weston and desire the same may be registered. Martin Lloyd, Robert Smily, Henry Dodge. (GDR/284/226)

Note. There is just one reference to Robert Smily in the GA genealogical database; he was an overseer at Westonbirt in 1751. Bishop Benson's survey of the diocese 1735-1750 noted three Presbyterians in Westonbirt (2.27) and one in Weston Subedge (10.32).

1878 Westonbirt. 20 Nov 1773 (10 Dec 1773). His Majesty's Protestant dissenting subjects intend to hold a meeting for the worship of Almighty God at the dwelling house of Arthur Woodroffe in the parish of 'Weston Birt', and desire the same may be registered. Thomas Bamford, James Thompson, Cove Lloyd, John Cox. (GDR/292A/171)

1879 Westonbirt. 21 November 1821 (28 Nov 1821). *Independent.* We [named below] certify that a building in the parish of 'Weston Birt', now in the occupation of Mr George Ball, is intended to be a place of religious worship by dissenters of the denomination of Independents. George Bubb, Isaac Ashley, William Dyke, Thomas Mann, George Bubb, Isaac Ashley, William Dyke, Thomas Mann. (GDR/344/Page 1 (from rear))
Note. No return to RG. George Bubb listed twice.

WHITMINSTER *alias* WHEATENHURST
1880 Wheatenhurst. 26 Apr 1781 (2 May 1781). We have set apart a house, now occupied by John Clutterbuck, in the parish of Whitminster or Wheatenhurst as a place of meeting for religious worship and pray that the said house may be recorded as a place of meeting. N Butler, Edward Rogers, Samuel Cratchley, John Clutterbuck (mark). (GDR/292A/234)

1881 Whitminster. 26 Nov 1803 (28 Nov 1803). These are to certify that some dissenters intend to hold a meeting for the worship of Almighty God in the house in the occupation of Richard Golding in the parish of Whitminster. We therefore pray that this certificate may be registered. William Hardwick, James Warner, William Williams, H Ransom. (GDR/334B/441)

1882 Wheatenhurst. 23 May 1805 (1 Jun 1805). These are to certify that some [dissenters] intend to hold meetings for the worship of Almighty God in a house in the occupation of William Short in the parish of Wheatenhurst. We pray that this certificate may be registered. William Hardwick, James Warner, Elizabeth Morgan, Hannah Critchley. (GDR/334B/431)

1883 Wheatenhurst. 22 Jan 1821 (23 Jan 1821). I certify that the premises occupied by Hannah Brewer in the parish of Wheatenhurst will hereafter be a place of religious worship. William Hardwick, Adam Nightingale, minister. (GDR/334B/229)

WHITTINGTON
1884 Whittington. 29 Oct 1812 (6 Nov 1812). We [named below] beg leave to certify that a house in the parish of Whittington called Crawford, in the possession of John Humphries and late of Robert Miflin, the property of Mary Fisher of Winchcomb, is intended to be used for the worship of Almighty God and request the same to be registered. John Roberts, John Staite, Thomas Slatter, Thomas Fisher, James Bate, Joseph Smith, Thomas Howman. (GDR/334B/351)
Note. Signed at Winchcombe.

WICK AND ABSON
Abson was a chapelry in Pucklechurch parish. Wick was a hamlet in Abson.
1885 Wick and Abson. 1 Oct 1760. (registered Michaelmas 1760, Q/SO/8/f.246v) *Presbyterian.* We [named below] certify that we intend to make use of the house of Henry Pearce in the parish of 'Wick and Opsom' [written above in different hand 'Wick and Abston']

as a place of meeting for religious worship and pray that the said house may be recorded at the said sessions as a place of meeting for His Majesty's dissenting subjects (Presbyterians) from the Church of England. Michael Thomas, Robert Stobel, William Thomas, William Jefferis, Thomas Jefferis, Henry Pearce, Thomas Pearce, Isaac Wilmott. (Q/SR/1760/D 16)
Note. The last three names appear to be written by the same hand; the others appear to be signatures.

1886 Wick & Abson. (Michaelmas 1760). *Presbyterian.* It is ordered by this court that the house of Henry Pearce is hereby licensed and allowed for dissenters called Presbyterians to assemble and meet together pursuant to a petition and request. (Q/SO/8/f.246v)
Note. Rubric has 'Wick and Abston'.

1887 Wick, Wick & Abson. 28 Oct 1810 (14 Nov 1810). *Methodist.* Whereas we [named below] being in the connexion of the late Revd John Wesley deceased, have appropriated and set apart that new building called the Methodist Chapel at Bridgeyate [or Bridge Yate] in the parish of 'Wick in Apson' for the worship of Almighty God, we request that the same may be registered. Joseph Bowes, Thomas Jefferies, Robert Kitch, William White, Thomas Clark, Thomas Potter, John Davis, William Johnson, Henry Wilmott, John A Lomas. (GDR/334B/379-78)

1888 Wick, Wick & Abson. 4 Mar 1822 (7 Mar 1822). I Jane Jefferis of Wick in the parish of Wick & Abson certify that my dwelling house now in my occupation is forthwith to be a place of religious worship and require you to register the same. (GDR/344/20r)

1889 Wick, Wick & Abson. 16 Nov 1835 (2 Dec 1835). *Independent.* May it please your Lordship to grant unto us [named below] being dissenters of the Independent denomination a certificate for the lower part or ground floor of a house or tenement, now in the occupation of Mr J Elmes, in the village of Wick in the parish of Wick and Abson for the worship of Almighty God. And we pray that the same may be registered in your Court and a certificate granted us. Joseph Elmes, John Jack, minister of Castle Green Chapel, John Gardner, Samuel Meade, James Bessell, James Weeks, Robert Padfield, James Chard, John Jones. (GDR/350/186)

1890 Wick, Wick & Abson. 16 Nov 1837 (22 Nov 1837). *Independent.* May it please your Lordship to grant unto us [named below] being dissenters of the Independent denomination, a certificate for a chapel called The Tabernacle in the village of Wick in the parish of Wick and Abson for the worship of Almighty God and we pray that the said chapel may be registered and a certificate granted to us. James Taylor, minister; John Gardner, Samuel Wade, John Jones, James Bessell, Harford Jones. (GDR/350/216)

WICKWAR

1891 Wickwar. 1672. *Presbyterian.* Licence recorded 30 Sept 1672 to Thomas Wortham to be a Presbyterian teacher at the house of Henry Mounsell of 'Wickwarr'. (LT/568)

1892 Wickwar. (Michaelmas 1711). Thomas Bishop's house. (Q/SO/3/520)

1893 Wickwar. 18 May 1728. These are to certify that [dissenters] intend to hold a meeting for the worship of Almighty God in their way in the dwelling house of Richard Griffith of Wickwar and pray that it may be registered. Richard Griffith, Thomas Hamonds, Nathaniel Washbourn. (GDR/279a/196)

1894 Wickwar. 2 May 1734. His Majesty's Protestant dissenting subjects do intend to hold a meeting in the dwelling house of Rice Griffith. Rice Griffith, John Sommers, William Hobbs, William Jones (GDR/284/31)

1895 Wickwar. 20 Feb 1744/45 (3 May 1745 'entered'). We [named below] being Protestant dissenters do hereby give notice that we do intend to hold a meeting for the worship of God in the dwelling house of John Taylor in the town of Wickwar and pray that it may be registered. Joseph Mason, John Taylor, Thomas Hale jnr, William Rutherford, William Burnell, Thomas London, Thomas Bishop. (GDR/284/166)

1896 Wickwar. 1 Jan 1766. His Majesty's Protestant subjects dissenting from the Church of England certify that we have set apart a house occupied by Daniel Wilkins in Wickwar parish as a place of religious worship and pray that the said house may be recorded in your Office as a place of meeting. Thomas Hale, Daniel Wilkins, John White, William Vearly, Richard Rowles. (GDR/292A/90)

1897 Wickwar. 8 Feb 1780. These are to certify that we and some others [dissenters] intend to hold a meeting for the worship of Almighty God in a house, yard or whatever thereto belongs, formerly the property of Daniel Wilkins, in the parish of Wickwar and 'prays' it may be registered. Nicholas Bick, William Canter, Nicholas Smith, James Sumner, William Jones, Martin Wennat (mark). (GDR/N2/1) [*see* illus., xxi]
Note. Appears to have original signatures.
Certificate is not well written, and was probably re-written five weeks later. A certificate for a meeting in the same house, dated 17 Mar 1780, was registered on 8 Apr 1780 (GDR/292A/228); three certifiers were the same, but William Jones and Martin Wennat were replaced by N Butler (listed first) and Nicholas Bick (listed last). This was the version in RG/31/2.

1898 Wickwar. (19 May 1794). These are to certify that we [named below] with others intend to hold a meeting for the worship of Almighty God in the dwelling house of Nicholas Bick in the parish of Wickwar and pray it may be registered in your Lordship's Court. Nicholas Bick, James Taylor (mark), John Short, Edward Pinnell, Joseph Short, William Lovell, James Croome. (GDR/319A/182-3)

1899 Wickwar. 27 Aug 1816 (2 Sept 1816). We, William Heath, gentleman, Moses Amos, cooper, John Chandler, victualler, James Tanner, 'taylor', Thomas Phillips, 'sadler', Joseph Amos, cooper, of the parish of Wickwar certify that a meeting-house and vestry, on the east side of the street and nearly opposite the market house, in the parish of Wickwar is intended forthwith to be a place of religious worship and require you to register the same. (GDR/334B/315)
Note. An original copy of this certificate in GA/24615/17 has the signatures of certifiers and an endorsement by the deputy registrar of Gloucester diocese that the certificate was duly registered in the Consistory Court.

1900 Wickwar. (16 Feb 1828). We [named below] certify that we intend to set apart the dwelling house, belonging to William Baker, in the parish of Wickwar for the service and worship of Almighty God and request that this our certificate may be recorded and the entry thereof duly certifed. Moses Stinchcombe, William Baker, Charles Webber, Thomas Dawes, James Jones, Charles Stinchcombe, Thomas Stafford. (GDR/350/82)

WILLERSEY

1901 Willersey. (Michaelmas 1689). [RG/31/6 has *Anabaptist*]. William Davison, minister, and in Cambden [Chipping Campden; 'Davidson' in RG/31/6]. (Q/SO/3/522)

1902 Willersey. 16 Nov 1824 (17 Nov 1824). I John Thurston, minister of Wellesbourne in the county of Warwick, certify that the house in the possession of William Garne in the parish of Willersey is set apart for the public worship of Almighty God and require you to register the same. (GDR/350/22)

Note. Common phrase is 'register and record' but 'and record' is crossed out.

1903 Willersey. 13 Dec 1824 (12 Feb 1825). I William Gibbs of Willersey, silk throwster, certify that a room adjoining my dwelling house is intended forthwith to be a place of religious worship and require you to register the same, and request a certificate thereof. (GDR/350/33)

1904 Willersey. 22 Sept 1828 (27 Sept 1828). I John Davis of Willersy, weaver, certify that a building or tenement, being myself occupier and Mr William Garn proprietor, is intended forthwith to be a place of religious worship and I request you to register the same. Witness Joseph Parry, Henry Elliott, John Davis. (GDR/350/94)

1905 Willersey. 15 Feb 1838 (17 Apr 1838). *Wesleyan.* I John Crowe of the borough of Evesham, Wesleyan minister, certify that the dwelling house of Richard Knight in the parish of Willersey is forthwith to be a place of religious worship and require you to register the same and request a certificate thereof. (GDR/350/223)

WINCHCOMBE
Gretton, which see, was a chapelry in Winchcombe. There had been a chapel at Greet, in ruins by 1735, but it was not regarded as a chapelry.

1906 Winchcombe. 1672. *Presbyterian.* Licence recorded 10 Aug 1672 for the house of Mary Parnell of 'ffinchcombe in Glorsh'. (LT/550)

1907 Winchcombe. 1672. *Congregational.* Application by Owen Davies for William Beckett [Congregational minister] of 'Winchcome' at his owne house; licence recorded 10 June 1672 for the house of William Beckett; licence received by Owen Davies for William Beckett and his house 12 June 1672. (LT/372, 401, 509)

1908 Winchcombe. (Easter 1709). *Quaker.* James Mason's house. (Q/SO/3/520)

1909 Winchcombe. 7 Dec 1764. *Independent.* 'We whose names are under subscribed being Independent Protestant dissenters are desirous to make use of a room near the *George Inn*, and in the possession of John and Benjamin Wood, in the town of 'Winchcomb' as a place of religious worship of Almighty God and desire you would be pleased to license the same according to laws.' William Becket, James Dobbins, Benjamin Wood, James Cull, William Tovey, William Dudfield. (GDR/292A/67)

1910 Winchcombe. 12 June 1775 (12 June 1775). *Baptist.* Some of His Majesty's Protestant dissenting subjects called Baptists intend to hold a meeting for the worship of Almighty God at the dwelling house of William Thorndell in the parish of 'Winchcomb' and therefore pray this certificate may be duly registered. William Thorndell, Elizabeth Thorndell, William Thomson, Jos. Thomson, Thomas Thomson, Ann Thomson, James Simpson, Edward Thomson, Thomas Ashwin, Thomas Fisher, 'Filliph [?Phyllis] Allen (her mark). (GDR/292A/181)

1911 Winchcombe. 3 Jan 1786 (19 Jan 1786; registration GDR/319A/49). 'We certify that we intend to use the dwelling house of Mr John Havens, now in the possession of Mr John Staite and others, in 'Winchcomb' as a place for the public worship of Almighty God and we do "Demand" a certificate of the same being registered.' John Staite, Samuel Chadborn, William Burrows. (GDR/N2/1)
Note. The inverted commas round 'Demand' in the records suggest the clerk was commenting ironically on the wording.

1912 Winchcombe. (29 Oct 1795). We [named below] and others in the borough of 'Winchcomb' certify that we intend to use for the worship of Almighty God a house in Cow Lane, otherwise Colslane, in the Borough, which has been purchased for the said purpose and is now in the possession of John Staite and others of the borough, and we request that the same be registered. William Fisher, John Fisher, John Staite, Thomas Slatter. (GDR/319A/220)

1913 Winchcombe. 13 Feb 1805 (21 Feb 1805). We [named below] certify that a building at 'Winchcomb', now occupied by Mr Thomas Jordan, is intended to be used for religious worship. T Jordan, John Powderhill, Henry Kane. (GDR/334B/434)
Note. Signature is T Gordan.

1914 Winchcombe. 9 Feb 1806 (13 Mar 1806). We [named below] certify that a certain building at 'Winchcomb', now occupied by Mr Charles Mason, is intended to be used for religious worship. Charles Mason, John Powderhill, Thomas Jordan, William Bleby. (GDR/334B/427)

1915 Winchcombe. 31 Mar 1806 (3 Apr 1806). We [named below] certify that a building in 'Winchcomb', occupied by Mr John Powderhill, is intended to be used for religious worship. Charles Mason, Edward Mason, Robert Crawford, John Powderhill, Thomas Jordan, Benjamin Beckett. (GDR/334B/427)

1916 Winchcombe. 15 Mar 1810 (24 Mar 1810). We [named below] certify that the dwelling house, now in the occupation of Samuel Fisher, Ails Street [?Hailes Street], 'Winchcomb', is intended to be used as a place of religious worship and request that the clerk of the court be desired to register the same. Samuel Fisher, Thomas Fisher, Thomas Hatter, Samuel Greening. (GDR/334B/387)

1917 Winchcombe. 3 May 1810 (5 May 1810). We [named below] certify that a building at 'Winchcomb', now occupied by Mr John Mason, is intended for religious worship. John Roberts, John Mason, William Tovey, Benjamin Beckett. (GDR/334B/387)

1918 Winchcombe. 5 May 1810 (5 May 1810). We [named below] certify that a building at 'Winchcomb', now occupied by Mr John Roberts, is intended to be used for religious worship. John Roberts, P Coussins, John Mason, Benjamin Beckett. (GDR/334B/386)

1919 Winchcombe. 5 May 1810 (5 May 1810). We [named below] certify that a building at 'Winchcomb', now occupied by Mr W Tovey, is intended for religious worship. Thomas Ashwood, John Roberts, William Tovey snr, John Jones. (GDR/334B/386)

1920 Winchcombe. 28 May 1810 (29 May 1810). We [named below] beg leave to certify that a house, in the occupation of Penelope Coussins, in Winchcombe is intended to be used for the worship of Almighty God and request that the same may be entered in your Lordship's Registry and a certificate granted accordingly. Penelope Coussins, Joseph Smith, John Roberts, Thomas Slatter, John Staite. (GDR/334B/384)

1921 Winchcombe. 25 June 1810 (5 July 1810). We [named below] beg leave to inform your Lordship that a loft, in the possession of Fisher & Co, tanners, in 'Winchcomb' is intended to be used for the worship of Almighty God and request that the same may be entered in your Lordship's Registry and a certificate given accordingly. Thomas Fisher, John Staite, Thomas Howman, Thomas Slatter, John Roberts, John Mason. (GDR/334B/383)

1922 Greet, Winchcombe. 23 Nov 1810 (5 Dec 1810). We [named below] beg leave to certify that a house at Greet in the parish of 'Winchcomb', the property of Mr Thomas Fisher of 'Winchcomb', is intended to be used for the worship of Almighty God, request the same to be registered. Thomas Fisher, Thomas Howman, John Abbott. (GDR/334B/371)

1923 Winchcombe. 28 Dec 1810 (31 Dec 1810). We [named below] certify that the chapel, now in the possession of Samuel Fisher and others, in the High Street at Winchcombe, called Zion Chapel, is intended to be used as a place of religious worship and we request that the clerk of the court be desired to register the same. Samuel Fisher, Samuel Etheridge, Samuel Greening, George Timbrell. (GDR/334B/369)

1924 Winchcombe. 21 October 1821 (2 Feb 1822). I Thomas Dowty of Cheltenham, minister of the Gospel, certify that a house, in the occupation of James Tovey, linen weaver, in Gloucester Street in the parish of 'Winchcomb' is intended forthwith to be a place of religious worship and I require you to register the same and request a certificate thereof. (GDR/344/16v)
Note. Registered almost 3 months after certificate signed.

1925 Winchcombe. 14 Jan 1823 (17 Jan 1823). I John Hughes Adams of 'Winchcomb', minister of the Gospel, certify that a house, in the occupation of William Tovey, in the parish of 'Winchcomb' is intended forthwith to be a place of religious worship and I require you to register the same and request a certificate thereof. (GDR/344/41r)

1926 Winchcombe. 12 July 1824 (13 July 1824). I Richard Osman of the town of Winchcomb certify that my house in the said town is intended forthwith to be a place of religious worship and I require you to register the same, and request a certificate thereof. Witness William Smith, Samuel Greening. (GDR/344/135r)

1927 Winchcombe. 14 Nov 1827 (19 Nov 1827). I John Mullis, labourer, of the parish of Winchcombe certify that a house in the parish of Winchcombe, occupied by me, is intended forthwith to be a place of religious worship and require you to register the same and request a certificate thereof. John Mullis (mark). (GDR/350/75)

1928 Greet, Winchcombe. 11 Mar 1828 (13 Mar 1828). I David Sifton of the hamlet of Greet in the parish of Winchcombe certify that a house in the said hamlet, occupied by me, is intended forthwith to be a place of religious worship and require you to register the same and request a certificate thereof. (GDR/350/85)

1929 Greet, Winchcombe. 9 Mar 1829 (16 Mar 1829). *Baptist.* I Thomas Hartley of the hamlet of Greet in the parish of 'Winchcomb' certify that my house in the hamlet of Greet is intended forthwith to be used as a place of religious worship by an assembly or congregation of the Baptist denomination and require you to register the same and request a certificate thereof. Witness John Mills, Thomas Hartley. (GDR/350/100)

1930 Greet, Winchcombe. 9 Sept 1829 (17 Sept 1829). I William Hughes of the hamlet of Greet in the parish of 'Winchcomb' certify that my house in the hamlet of Greet is intended forthwith to be a place of religious worship and I request you to register the same and request a certificate thereof. Witness John Mills, William Hughes. (GDR/350/104)

1931 Winchcombe. 29 Nov 1832 (3 Jan 1833). I Ann Swinburn of Corndean Hall in the parish of 'Winchcomb' certify that a room in my possession in the town of Winchcomb, now used as infant schoolroom, is intended forthwith to be a place of religious worship and

I require you to register the same and request a certificate thereof. Witness John Mills. (GDR/350/135)

1932 Winchcombe. 27 Sept 1843 (29 Sept 1843). *Baptist.* I Thomas Littleton, Baptist minister in the parish of Cheltenham, certify that a chapel in North Street in the parish of 'Winchcomb' is forthwith to be used as a place for religious worship of dissenters of the Baptist denomination, and I request you will register the same. (GDR/350/322)

WINSON
Winson was a chapelry in Bibury parish.
1933 Winson. 3 Apr 1823. This is to certify the premises, now in the occupation of Richard Wheels, called [blank], in the parish of Winson is intended to be a place of religious worship and we request it may be registered. Thomas Turfery, Thomas Coles, Richard Wheeler. (GDR/344/42r)

1934 Winson. 26 Nov 1842 (30 Nov 1842). I George Obern of Cirencester certify that a house and premises at Winson, now in the holding and occupation of James Lewis, are intended to be a place of religious worship and I request you to register the same and request a certificate thereof for which shall be taken no more than two shillings and six pence. (GDR/350/304)

1935 Winson. 27 Feb 1843 (6 Mar 1843). *Baptist.* We [named below] certify that a dwelling house in the parish of Winson in the possession or occupation of Richard Smith is intended to be used as a meeting-house for religious worship by dissenters of the denomination of Baptists and we request that this certificate may be registered. Robert Coles, William Coles, Edward Coles. (GDR/350/316)
Note. VCH Glos 7, 42 notes meeting in Winson before 1800 and refers to the new-built house of 1754 in Arlington and the Baptist chapel NW of Green rebuilt in 1839 (*Baptist account book 1834-1853 GA D2751/8).*

WINSTONE
1936 Winstone. 18 Apr 1816 (20 Apr 1816). I Henry Hawkins of Eastcomb in the parish of Bisley, minister, certify that a building or barn in the parish of Winstone, now in the occupation of Sarah Turk, spinster, is intended forthwith to be a place of religious worship and require you to register the same. Witness Thomas Hind. (GDR/334B/320)

WINTERBOURNE
Diocese of Bristol from 1542. Frenchay was created an ecclesiastical parish in 1836.
1937 Frenchay [Winterbourne]. (Easter 1690). *Quaker.* 'French hay'. Meeting-house. (Q/SO/3/522)
Note. Records of a Quaker Meeting begin in 1654, and the first Meeting-house was erected in 1673 (Vinter, 1963).

1938 Hambrook, [Winterbourne]. (Easter 1704). *Presbyterian.* Edward Bergis's house. 'Hambrooke'. (Q/SO/3/521)
Note. RG/31/6 has 'Hambrook, Winterbourne' and 'Edward Bergess'.

1939 Frenchay [Winterbourne]. (Easter 1704). *Presbyterian.* 'French Hay', Mr William Browne's house. (Q/SO/3/521)

1940 Winterbourne. (Easter 1704). *Presbyterian.* Timothy Davis's house. (Q/SO/3/521)

1941 Frenchay [Winterbourne]. (Epiphany 1706/7). *Quaker.* 'French Hay', a new built house for Quakers. (Q/SO/3/520)

1942 Frenchay [Winterbourne]. 7 Dec 1715. Thomas Tyler of Frenchay, dissenting minister, took oaths of allegiance and supremacy. (Q/SO/4/[9])
Note. Joseph Tyler was named in Evans list.

1943 Frenchay [Winterbourne]. 7 Dec 1715. *Quaker.* William Baker, schoolmaster at Frenchay, gave the solemn affirmation. (Q/SO/4/[9])

1944 Hambrook, Winterbourne. (Epiphany 1723/4). *Presbyterian.* It is ordered by this court that the dwelling house of Robert Albright in the tithing of Hambrook in the parish of Winterbourne be and is hereby licensed and allowed for [dissenters] called Presbyterians to assemble and meet in for the worship of God in their way according to the petition for that purpose filed. (Q/SO/4/471)
Note. The same meeting place was recorded in the same words in the Trinity 1724 Quarter Sessions (Q/SO/5/f12v) with the exception of the name of the owner or occupier, there given as Robert Abbotts, and the form endorsed 'filed and allowed'; rubric is 'Hambrook Meeting-house'. The first petition may, therefore, have been incorrect.

1945 Winterbourne. 6 Oct 1760 (registered Michaelmas 1760, Q/SO/8/f.247r). [*Presbyterian* noted in Quarter Sessions record]. We [named below] certify that we intend to make use of a house, occupied by John Amoss, feltmaker, in the parish of Winterbourne as a place of meeting for religious worship and do pray that the said house may be recorded at the said sessions as a place of meeting for subjects dissenting from the Church of England.' John Amos, John Good, Gabriel Amoss, Thomas Amoss, John Webb jnr, Thomas Day, Thomas Hawkins, John Rogers, Joseph Hathaway, Thomas Russel, John Well snr, William Pagler snr, William Pagler jnr, George Pagler (mark). (Q/SR/1760/D 20)

1946 Winterbourne. 15 Jan 1796 (29 Jan 1796; registration GDR/319A/229). *Methodist.* 'We [named below] being Protestant subjects in some things dissenting from the Church of England, having sett apart a room or building called the Methodist chapel in the parish of Winterbourne as a place for the public worship of Almighty God, desire that the same may be registered.' Charles Atmore, William Hartland, William Pullin, John Morgan, William Burrough, Thomas Young, Thomas Morgan. (GDR/N2/1)
Note. Endorsed 'Copy of cert for divine worship. 29 Jan 1796 Ent'd.'

1947 Winterbourne. 18 Nov 1797 (28 Dec 1797). *Independent.* We [named below] being dissenters of the Independent denomination have set apart a dwelling house now in the occupation of John Hutton, cordwainer, in the parish of Winterbourne, for the worship of Almighty God and we pray the said dwelling house may be registered and a certificate granted us. James Mathias, James Thatcher, George Tavender, Robert Jones, John Pullin, Thomas Maggs, Je. Evans. (EP/A/45/1/270)

1948 Winterbourne. 24 Oct 1804. These are to certify your lordship that we [named below] with others intend to hold a meeting for the worship of Almighty God in the dwelling house of Ann Fugill in the parish of Winterbourne and pray it may be registered. Ann Fugill, Valentine Ward, William Pearce, Joseph Fugill, Bartholomew Fugill, George Crooss [*sic*], Robert Lowe, Samson Evans. (EP/A/45/1/350)

1949 Winterbourne. 18 Apr 1808 (18 May 1808). *Methodist.* We [named below] beg leave to certify to your lordship that a room in a house occupied by George Cross, shoemaker, situate in 'Sturdy-Hill' [?Sturden] in the parish of Winterbourn is set apart for the worship of Almighty God by a congregation of dissenters commonly called Methodists and request the same may be registered and a certificate of the same given accordingly.

George Cross, James Lackington Brice, William Curtis, Bartholomew Fugill, William Pearce, Edward Curtis. (EP/A/45/1/415)

1950 Pye Corner, Winterbourne. 22 Dec 1811 (26 Dec 1811). *Wesleyan Connexion. Wesleyan* Whereas we [named below] dissenting from the Church of England and in the connection of the late Revd John Wesley deceased have appropriated and set apart all the rooms on the ground floor of the dwelling house, now in the occupation of Samuel Monks, quarrier, at Pye Corner in the parish of Winterbourne, for the worship of Almighty God, we request that the same may be registered. Joseph Bowes, Thomas Dodd, Samuel Monks (mark), Edward Smith, John Sellin, Henry Wooderoff, William Pullin. (EP/A/45/2/60-1)

1951 Winterbourne. 9 Apr 1813 (10 Apr 1813). *Independent.* May it please your Lordship to grant unto us [named below], being dissenters of the Independent denomination, a certificate for the lower part or ground floor of a house or tenement, now in the occupation of Mr Henry Tripp, in the parish of Winterbourne, for the worship of Almighty God. And pray that [it] may be registered and a certificate granted. Robert Padfield, John Gardner, William Merintmore, minister, Henry Tripp, Joseph Rider, Samuel Wallis, Thomas Edwards. (GDR/334B/345)

1952 Whiteshill, Winterbourne. 16 Aug 1816 (19 Aug 1816). We [named below] certify that a certain meeting-house situated on 'White's Hill' in the parish of Winterbourne is intended forthwith to be a place of religious worship and require you to register the same. Joseph Wickwick, Nathaniel Good of Hambrook, John Forster, John Godwin, John Gardner. (GDR/334B/316)

1953 Frenchay, Winterbourne. 14 Aug 1817 (14 Aug 1817). I Thomas Williams of Bristol certify that a house and premises at Frenchay in the parish of Winterbourne occupied by Mary Kilby is intended forthwith to be a place of religious worship and I require you to register the same and request a certificate thereof. Thomas Williams; witness James Wood, Josh Vickery.
'I, Deputy Registrar of the bishop of Bristol, do hereby certify that a certificate of which the above is a true copy was this day delivered to me to be registered and recorded pursuant to the act of parliament therein mentioned [52 George III An act to repeal certain acts and amend other acts relating to religious worship and assemblies and persons teaching or preaching therein]. 14 Aug 1817. (EP/A/45/2/108-9)

1954 Whiteshill, Winterbourne. 16 Feb 1833 (27 Feb 1833). *Independents.* We [named below] certify that a building called White's Hill chapel in the parish of Winterbourne is intended to be used as a chapel for religious worship by dissenters of the denomination of Independents, and we request that this certificate may be registered. John Pendock, Winterbourne, Charles Jefferis Bryant, Winterbourne, John Godwin, Richard Hensley. (EP/A/45/2/384)
Note. RG/31/2 has 'Jonathan Penduck'.

1955 Frenchay, Winterbourne. 9 Feb 1839 (9 Feb 1839). I Evan Parry, minister of Downend in the county of Gloucester, certify that a room in the village of 'French Hay' in the parish of Winterbourne, the property of Robert Johnson esq, is intended forthwith to be a place of religious worship and I require you to register the same and request a certificate thereof. E Parry. (EP/A/45/2/574)

1956 Winterbourne Down, Winterbourne. 30 Mar 1843 (31 Mar 1843). *Wesleyan.*
I William Griffith of Downend, parish of Mangotsfield, Wesleyan minister, certify that a building usually called the Infant school at Winterbourne Down in the parish of

Winterbourne is intended forthwith to be a place of religious worship and I require you to register the same and request a certificate thereof. William Griffith, Downend near Bristol. (EP/A/45/3/155).

Note. Long endorsement by registrar referring to bishop of Gloucester and Bristol.

1957 Winterbourne Down, Winterbourne. 4 May 1843 (6 May 1843). I John Godwin of Charlotte Street in the parish of St George in the city of Bristol certify that a dwelling house on Winterbourne Down in the parish of Winterbourne, in the occupation of Francis Rowland, hatter, is about to be used as a place of religious worship by dissenters and I request you to register the same and request a certificate thereof. (EP/A/45/3/156)

1958 St John, Frenchay, Winterbourne. 3 Mar 1845 (7 Mar 1845). *Presbyterian.* I Henry Edward Howse of Frenchay in the county of Gloucester, gentleman, certify that part of a messuage at Frenchay in the parish of St John is intended forthwith to be a place of religious worship and I require you to register the same, and request a certificate thereof. Witness Samuel Walker, minister of Presbyterian chapel, Frenchay. (EP/A/45/3/353)

1959 Winterbourne. 15 Nov 1847 (18 Nov 1847). I Robert Payne, thatcher, of the parish of Frampton Cotterell, dissenting minister, certify that a tenement in the parish of Winterbourne, occupied by Samuel Grant, gardener, is intended forthwith to be a place of religious worship and I request you to register the same. (EP/A/45/3/429)

Note. Not clear if Thatcher is occupation or surname. One of two loose certificates bound into book but not pasted and paginated in sequence, with signatures. It is the first of what became the practice of pasting or binding in loose certificates, including the one printed form (for Bedminster 2 Mar 1847) similarly bound in. *See* **2048**.

1960 Watley's End, Winterbourne. 6 Feb 1851 (8 Feb 1851). *Wesleyan Methodist.* I George Lewton the younger of Watley's End in the parish of Winterbourne certify that premises now held by me are iintended to be forthwith a place of religious worship by a congregation of Wesleyan Methodists and I request you to register the same and request a certificate thereof. (EP/A/45/4/51)

Note. Certificate pasted in and signed. RG/31/2 has surname 'Luton', but name and signature both quite clear on document.

1961 Winterbourne Down, Winterbourne. 10 Oct 1851 (17 Oct 1851). *Wesleyan Methodists.* I John Sperring of Winterbourne Down in the parish of Winterbourne certify that premises now held by me at Winterbourne Down are intended to be used forthwith as a place for religious worship by a congregation of Wesleyan Methodists and I request you to register the same and request a certificate thereof. (EP/A/45/4/98)

Note. Certiificate pasted in and signed if written by Sperring.

WITHINGTON

1962 Withington. 3 June 1818 (17 June 1818). I John Rodgers of Cirencester, licensed teacher, certify that a dwelling house in the occupation of Richard Smith in the parish of Withington is intended forthwith to be a place of religious worship and I request you to register the same and request a certificate thereof. (GDR/334B/279)

1963 Withington. 5 Apr 1819 (1 May 1819). I Philip Rawlings licensed teacher of the parish of Cirencester certify that a dwelling house occupied by John Perin of the parish of Withington is intended forthwith to be a place of religious worship and I request you to register the same and request a certificate thereof. Philip Rawlings, John Fox Perkin, Hannah Smith, Joseph Smith, Jane Slade, Thomas Mason, Richard Smith, Edmon Ryman, Ann Ryman. (GDR/334B/262)

1964 Withington. 4 Mar 1823 (8 Mar 1823). I Henry Hawkins of Eastcomb in the parish of Bisley, dissenting minister, certify that a building or kitchen situated in the parish of Withington, now in the occupation of William Banford, labourer, is intended forthwith to be a place of religious worship and require you to register the same. Witness Thomas Davis. (GDR/344/41v)
Note. Rubric has Eastcomb.

1965 Withington. 13 Aug 1836 (13 Aug 1836). We, Samuel Franklin and Joseph Aldan Gardiner of Cheltenham, certify that a dwelling house in the parish of Withington, occupied by Sarah Bishop, is forthwith to be a place of religious worship and I request you to register the same. Samuel Franklin. (GDR/350/199)

1966 Foxcote, Withington. 1 Jan 1841 (1 Jan 1841). *Baptist.* I John Bridgeman in the parish of Charlton Kings certify that a building, known by the name of Baptist Chapel, at Foxcote in the parish of Withington is to be a place of religious worship and I request you to register the same and request a certificate thereof. (GDR/350/268)

1967 Withington. 24 Feb 1841 (24 Feb 1841). I John Bridgeman of Charlton Kings certify that a cottage at Withingon, rented by William Dyer for the purpose, is to be a place of religious worship and require you to register the same and request a certificate thereof. (GDR/350/275)
Note.: Rubric has Charlton Kings.

WOODCHESTER
1968 Woodchester. 30 July 1758. We [named below] humbly desire that the house, wherein Mary Cowell now resides, in the parish of Woodchester be registered for a place of divine worship in the Protestant dissenting way. Benjamin Francels, William Webb, William Shurmur, William Rede, William Churches. (GDR/292A/37)

1969 Woodchester. 16 July 1792 (17 July 1792). *Independent.* We [named below] dissenters under the denomination of Independents and housekeepers, dwelling in or near Woodchester, certify that we intend to set apart the dwelling house of Mr William Merrit in Woodchester for the service and worship of Almighty God and request that this our certificate may be recorded in your Lordship's Registry and the entry thereof duly certified. James Golding, William Merrit, James Peters, Thomas Lewis, Robert Leighton, Thomas Powell snr, Richard Hill, Samuel Summers, Samuel Stevens, James Lewis. (GDR/319A/138-9)

1970 Frogmarsh, Woodchester. 29 Mar 1796 (2 Apr 1796; registration GDR/319A/231-2). *Independent.* 'We [named below] under the denomination of Independents and dwelling in or near Woodch[torn edge] certify that we intend to set apart a dwelling house of Mr Samuel Stephens sit[uate] at Frogmarsh near Woodchester and do request that this our certificate may be recorded.' William Griffin, James Golding, Thomas Portlock, Samuel Stephens, William Marling, Thomas Hile, Thomas Lewis, Robert Leighton, John Harris. (GDR/N2/1)
Note. crossed through. Endorsed on back 'Ent' and date.

1971 Woodchester. 18 May 1802 (30 July 1802). *Independent.* We [named below] being dissenters under the denomination of Independents and housekeepers dwelling in and near Woodchester certify that we intend to set apart the dwelling house of Mrs Anna Webb at Woodchester for the service and worship of Almighty God and request that our certificate may be recorded and the entry thereof duly certified. Elijah King, John Cooper, Thomas

Cooper, James Weight, William Marling, Samuel Stephens, Thomas Lewis, Robert Leighton. (GDR/319A/314)

1972 Woodchester. 10 Dec 1802 (11 Dec 1802). *Independent.* This is to certify that a house, in the occupation of Mary Saunders, is intended to be used as a place of worship for dissenters of the Independent denomination. We therefore require that it may be registered. Christopher Pain, minister; Dan Richards, George Thomas, Edward Bliss, James Thomas. (GDR/N2/1)
Note. No record in Diocesan Act Book or RG/31/2 though certificate has a note 'entered.

1973 Woodchester. 31 Jan 1812 (8 Feb 1812). We [named below] being householders of the parish of Woodchester certify to the Right Reverend the Lord Bishop of Gloucester and any other person whom it doth and may concern that a certain 'house Gough' [of Thomas?] of the parish of Woodchester is by and with his consent set apart for the religious worship of Almighty God by dissenters. Thomas Gough, Robert Lughton, William Keene, William Harling, John Whatley, Nathan Halliday, John Essex. (GDR/334B/356)

1974 Woodchester. 13 Oct 1813 (6 Nov 1813). This is to certify that a house in the occupation of William Chivers in the parish of Woodchester is intended to be a place of religious worship. We request that [it] may be registered and a certificate granted accordingly. Christopher Pain, minister; William Chivers, James Thomas, George Thomas, William Osborne, William Clissold. (GDR/334B/341)

1975 Woodchester. 3 Aug 1820 (8 Aug 1820). This is to certify that an house in the occupation of Mr Robert Leighton in the parish of Woodchester is intended to be a place of religious worship and we request that it may be registered. John Rees, minister of Rodborough Tabernacle, Robert Leighton. (GDR/334B/237)

1976 Woodchester. 17 July 1821 (18 July 1821). I certify that the premises occupied by Samuel Miles in the parish of Woodchester will be hereafter used as a place of religious worship. Adam Nightingale, minister. (GDR/334B/216)

1977 Woodchester. 3 Apr 1824 (7 Apr 1824). I Samuel French of the parish of Woodchester certify that my dwelling house and premises in Woodchester, and now in my own occupation, are intended to be a place of religious worship and I require you to register the same. And request a certificate thereof for which shall be taken no more than two shillings and sixpence. (GDR/344/132v)

1978 Woodchester. 30 Oct 1825 (5 Nov 1825). I Nathaniel Beard of Woodchester, clothworker, certify that a tenement in the parish of Woodchester, which I at present hold and occupy, is intended forthwith to be a place of religious worship and I require you to register the same, and request a certificate thereof. Nathaniel Beard (mark), Samuel French, Thomas Cole. (GDR/350/49)

1979 Woodchester. 5 Mat 1827 (7 May 1827). *Unitarian.* I Henry Edward Howse jnr, late of the parish of 'Lyncomb and Widcombe', Somerset, and now residing at Nailsworth, secretary to the Somerset, Gloucestershire and Wiltshire Unitarian Missionary Association, certify that part of a dwelling house belonging to Mary Boulton in Woodchester is intended forthwith to be a place of religious worship and require you to register the same and request a certificate thereof. (GDR/350/63)

WOOLASTON

1980 Woolaston. 27 Jan 1802. We [named below] certify that the dwelling house of William Jones of the parish of Woolaston is set apart for the public worship of Almighty God by a congregation of Protestant dissenters and we require that this certificate be registered. William Jones, John Sydser [followed by symbol like an 'H' which may indicate his mark], John Osborn, Mary Osborn. (GDR/N2/1)
Note. No record in Diocesan Act Book or RG/31/2.

1981 Woolaston Common, Woolaston. 21 Nov 1809 (7 Dec 1809). We [named below] have set apart and appropriated for the public worship of Almighty God a dwelling house, in the occupation of William Barber, situated in 'Wooliston Common and parish of Wooliston' and request that the same may be registered and a certificate granted. John Williams, William Cook, William Barber, Moses Fisher, John Grant. (GDR/334B/395)

1982 Woolaston.16 Oct 1818 (3 Nov 1818). [RG/31/2 has *Methodist*]. I William Brocklehurst of the town of Newport, Monmouthshire, certify that the house of Simon Reekes of the parish of 'Woollaston' is intended forthwith to be a place of religious worship and I require you to register the same. William Brocklehurst, minister. (GDR/334B/273)

1983 Woolaston. 23 Dec 1824 (28 Dec 1824). I Edward Martin of the parish of 'Wollaston' certify that a part of my dwelling house in the aforesaid parish is intended forthwith to be a place of religious worship and I require you to register the same. Edward Martin, David Thomas, minister. (GDR/350/28)

1984 Netherend, Woolaston. 1 Jan 1825 (7 Jan 1825). I William Long of the parish of 'Wollaston' certify that a house at Netherend in my possession is intended forthwith to be a place of religious worship and I require you to register the same, and request a certificate thereof. (GDR/350/30)

1985 Woolaston. 5 Mar 1830 (8 Mar 1830). *Independent*. We [named below] certify that a certain building, in the occupation of John Thomas, is intended to be used as a meeting-house for religious worship by a congregation of the denomination of Independents and request that this certificate may be registered. John Thomas, Thomas Freeman. (GDR/350/107)

1986 Woolaston. 24 May 1830 (28 May 1830). I John Glass, minister, certify that a dwelling house now in the occupation of Joseph Lewis is intended forthwith to be a place of religious worship and require you to register the same and request a certificate thereof. John Glass, Joseph Lewis (mark). (GDR/350/109)

1987 Woolaston. 22 Jan 1833. I William Derrick of Coln Mill in the parish of 'Wollaston' certify that my house is intended to be used as a place of religious worship and require you to register and record the same and request a certificate thereof. John Robinson, William Derrick. (GDR/350/138)

1988 Woolaston. 30 Jan 1837 (31 Jan 1837). I Thomas Wilkins, teacher, certify that a dwelling house in the occupation of Thomas James in the parish of 'Woolastone' is forthwith intended as a place of religious worship and require you to register the same and request a certificate thereof. (GDR/350/205)

1989 Woodside, Woolaston. 15 Apr 1842. *Bible Christian*. I John Knight of Ruardean certify that the Bible Christian Chapel at Woodside in the parish of Woolaston to be used as a place of religious worship and I request you to register the same and request a certificate thereof for which shall be taken no more than two shillings and six pence. (GDR/350/296)

1990 Woodside, Woolaston. 8 May 1844. *Bible Christian.* I John Knight of Ruardean certify that the Bible Christian Chapel at Woodside, in the parish of Woolaston, to be a place of religious worship and I request you to register the same and request a certificate thereof for which shall be taken no more than two shillings and six pence. (GDR/350/344)

WOTTON-UNDER-EDGE
Sinwell & Bradley, Simondshall & Combe, and Wortley were tithings in Wotton-under-Edge.
1991 Wotton-under-Edge. 1672. *Presbyterian.* Licence recorded to Edward Hancock to be a Presbyterian teacher at the house of Samuel Wallington at the Headborough of 'Wotton underedg'. (LT/568)

1992 Sinwell & Bradley [Wotton-under-Edge]. (Epiphany 1689/90). 'Sinwell and Bradly', Thomas Crow's outhouse. (Q/SO/3/522)

1993 Wotton-under-Edge. (Epiphany 1697/8). 'Wottonunderedge', Stephen Hunt's house. (Q/SO/3/521)

1994 Wotton-under-Edge. (Epiphany 1701/2). *Presbyterian.* 'Wottonunderedge', q new erected house. (Q/SO/3/521)

1995 Wotton-under-Edge. (Easter 1709). *Quaker.* 'Wottonunderedge', Sampson Cary's house. (Q/SO/3/520)

1996 Nind, Wotton-under-Edge. (Epiphany 1710/11). *Presbyterian.* 'Nind in Wottonund.' [?Thomas] Slade's house. (Q/SO/3/520)

1997 Wortley [Wotton-under-Edge]. (Epiphany 1710/11). *Presbyterian.* 'Jo:' Munday's house [RG/31/6 had Joseph]. (Q/SO/3/520)

1998 Wotton-under-Edge. (Trinity 1725). *Quakers and Protestant Dissenters.* 'It is ordered by this court that the Town Hall or room over the market house in 'Wooton under Edge' be licensed and allowed for [dissenters] called Quakers to assemble and meet together for the worshipp of God in their way or for such other lawfull meeting as they shall think proper. And it is further ordered that the dwelling house of John Wallington known by the name or signe of the *Crown* in 'Wooton under Edge' aforesaid be also licensed and allowed for dissenters to assemble and meet together in if they shall think propper so to do according to their petition for that purpose filed and allowed.' (Q/SO/5/f.30r)

1999 Wotton-under-Edge. [Nov 1726; entry between 10 Nov 1726 and 28 Nov 1726]. *Congregational.* This is to certify that [dissenters] called congregational intend to hold a meeting for the worship of Almighty God in the house of Edward Grimes in the parish of 'Wottonunderedge' and pray that it may be recorded. (GDR/279a/158)
Note. A fuller Latin rubric than usual for this entry: 'cert[ificat]um domus pro cultu divino apud Wottonunderedge' [certificate of house for divine worship at Wottonundedge]. No signatories.

2000 Wotton-under-Edge. [Nov 1726; entry between 28 Nov 1726 and 1 Dec 1726]. *Congregational.* This is to certify that his Majesty's protestant subjects called congregational intend to hold a meeting for the worship of Almighty God in their way in the house of Joseph Parry in the parish of 'Wottonunderedge' and pray that it may be recorded. (GDR/279a/159)

Note. Similar format to previous entry. No signatories.

2001 Old Town, Wotton-under-Edge. 22 Dec 1737. Some [dissenters] intend to hold a meeting for the worship of God in their way in a place called the meeting-house in the Old Town in Wotton-under-Edge, 'therefore we desire it may be recorded in your Office'. Godfrey Fownes, Sam Bryan, Martin Lloyd. (GDR/284/80)

2002 Wotton-under-Edge. 22 Dec 1737. Some [dissenters] intend to hold a meeting in their way for the worship of God in the dwelling house of Thomas Bayley in the street called High Street in the town of Wotton-under-Edge, 'therefore we desire that it may be recorded in your Office'. Godfrey Fownes, Sam Bryan, Martin Lloyd. (GDR/284/80)

2003 Wotton-under-Edge. 18 Dec 1759. *Congregational.* [Dissenters] of the Congregational persuasion intend to hold a meeting for the worship of Almighty God at the dwelling house of William Driver, a broadweaver in the town and parish of 'Wottonunderedge', and desire that the same may be registered. William Tallamy, Joseph Everard, George Vine, Joshua Vine, John Jennings. (GDR/292A/55-6)

Note. For Joseph Everard *see* **197**.

2004 Wotton-under-Edge. 24 Mar 1764. *Congregational.* [Dissenters] of the Congregational persuasion intend to hold a meeting for the worship of Almighty God at the dwelling house of Richard 'Dawneses', weaver, in the parish of 'Wootonunderedge' and desires the same may be registered. James Davies, George Vine, Thomas Dauncy, Robert Wright. (GDR/292A/63)

2005 Wotton under Edge. 1 Apr 1767. [Dissenters] intend to assemble together to worship Almighty God in the dwelling house of Michael James in the parish of 'Wooton underedge', 'a member of the Church of England', and desire the same may be registered. Thomas Lapley, Samuel Bark, Charles Long, Robert Knight, Paul Rowles. (GDR/292A/101)

2006 Wotton-under-Edge. 21 Nov 1771. *Independent.* We [named below] certify that we, called Independents, intend to hold a meeting for the worship of Almighty God in a house in a field called the Acre near Bear Lane in the parish of 'Wotton underedge' lately erected for that purpose and desire it may be registered. Thomas Lapley, William Young, Thomas Mercer, James Sommers, Joel Spencer, Samuel Park. (GDR/292A/147) [*see* illus., xvi]

2007 Wotton-under-Edge. (3 Sept 1804). We [named below] certify that the house of John Dyer in the town of 'Wottonunderedge' is appropriated to the purpose of religious worship and pray that the same may be registered. T Palser, John Palser, George Hopkins, J Dyer, Edward Wade, Hugh Ransom. (GDR/334B/436)

2008 Coombe, Wotton-under-Edge. 3 Aug 1815 (8 Aug 1815). I Stephen Hopkins of 'Wottonunderedge' certify that the house of Samuel Holloway at 'Comb' at 'Wottonunderedge' is forthwith to be a place of religious worship and require you to register the same and request a certificate thereof. (GDR/334B/327)

2009 Wotton-under-Edge. 17 Apr 1818 (22 Apr 1818). I Daniel Cooke of 'Huntinford Mill' in the parish of 'Wottonunderedge', gig man, certify that the tenement now occupied by me near the Mill is occasionally to be used as a place of religious worship and require you to register the same. (GDR/334B/281)

2010 Wotton-under-Edge. 5 Oct 1818 (12 Oct 1818). I Stephen Hopkins of the parish of 'Wottonunderedge' certify that a chapel lately erected, together with the land thereunto adjoining, near the Chipping in the parish of 'Wottonnderedge', and vested in the hands of Joseph Rodway, William Perrin and others, is forthwith to be a place of religious worship and require you to register the same and request a certificate thereof. Signed in the presence of Robert Hopkins. (GDR/334B/275)

2011 Wotton-under-Edge. 10 Aug 1819 (10 Aug 1819). I Stephen Hopkins of the parish of 'Wottonunderedge' certify that a field or plot of ground commonly called Merry Haven, now in the occpation of Richard Cornwall, adjoining the road leading from the town of 'Wottonunderedge' to the tithing of Bradley in the said parish, is intended forthwith to be a place of religious worship and require you to register the same and request a certificate thereof. Witness Robert Hopkins. (GDR/334B/256)

2012 Wotton-under-Edge. 12 July 1827 (12 July 1827). I Matthew Harding, minister of the Gospel, certify that the dwelling house of Lydia Rose in Wotton-under-Edge is intended forthwith to be a place of religious worship and require you to register the same and request a certificate thereof. Witness Thomas Smith, Matthew Harding.
'Certificate to be addressed to Harding at the Post Office.' (GDR/350/70)
Note. One of the few indications of the use of messengers to convey certificates to and from the court.

2013 Wotton-under-Edge. 11 Sept 1828 (11 Sept 1828). I certify that my dwelling house, No3 Locum Well, 'Wottonunderedge', is intended forthwith to be a place of religious worship and require you to register the same and request a certificate thereof. Clement Mingay Syder. (GDR/350/93)

2014 Wotton-under-Edge. 24 Apr 1830 (24 Apr 1830). This is to certify that a room in the parish of Wotton-under-Edge in occupation of John Forsbury on the Cloud Walk in the parish is to be a place of religious worship and we request that the room may be registered and a certificate granted. John Forsbury, William Hall, John Powell. (GDR/350/108)

2015 Old Town, Wotton-under-Edge. 8 Dec 1837 (13 Dec 1837). *Presbyterian.* We [named below] certify that a building at the Old Town called Old Town Meeting-house in the parish of 'Wottonunderedge', in the possession or occupation of David Thomas and trustees, is to be a chapel for religious worship by dissenters of the Presbyterian denomination and request that this certificate may be registered. John Aycliffe, James Palser, John Palser, householders. (GDR/350/217)

2016 Wotton-under-Edge. 26 Apr 1841 (26 Apr 1841). I Isaac Shelton of 'Wottonunderedge' certify that my room and premises at 'Wottonunderdge', now in [my] holding and occupation, are to be a place of religious worship and I request you to register the same and request a certificate thereof for which shall be taken no more than two shillings and six pence. (GDR/350/278-9)

2017 Wotton-under-Edge. 3 Mar 1842 (11 Mar 1842). I William James of 'Wottonunderedge' certify that a building called the Tabernacle at 'Wottonunderedge' is to be a place of religious worship and require you to register the same. William James, one of the managers of the Tabernacle. (GDR/350/291)

2018 Holywell, Wotton-under-Edge. 18 Mar 1842 (19 Mar 1842). I William Strange of Wotton underedge', dyer, certify that an upper room belonging to me at Holywell on the parish of 'Wotton underedge' is intended occasionally to be used and I require you to register the same. (GDR/350/293)

2019 Coombe, Wotton-under-Edge. 6 Apr 1842 (30 Apr 1842). I Joseph Wheeler of Coombe, 'Wotton underedge', miller, certify that a cottage belonging to me at Coombe is occasionally to be a place of religious worship and require you to register the same. (GDR/350/296)

2020 Bradley Green, Wotton-under-Edge. 21 Nov 1842 (2 Dec 1842). I Samuel Long, of Cromhall, snr, certify that a cottage belonging to me at Bradley Green in the parish of 'Wottonunderedge' is occasionally to be a place of religious worship and require you to register the same. (GDR/350/305)

2021 Wotton-under-Edge. 21 Nov 1842 (2 Dec 1842). I John Palser of 'Wottonunderedge' certify that a room belonging to me in the house, No 4 Gloucester Row, in the parish of 'Wottonunderedge', is occasionally to be a place of religious worship and require you to register the same. (GDR/350/305)

2022 Wotton-under-Edge. 21 Nov 1842 (2 Dec 1842). I Thomas Moody of 'Wottonunderedge', labourer, certify that a house I now occupy is occasionally to be a place of religious worship and require you to register the same. (GDR/350/306)

2023 Wotton-under-Edge. 30 Nov 1842 (2 Dec 1842). I Samson Rymer, of Wottonunderedge, labourer, certify that a house I now occupy is occasionally to be a place of religious worship and require you to register the same. (GDR/350/306)

2024 Wotton-under-Edge. 15 July 1844 (16 July 1844). I Richard Knill of 'Wottonunderedge', minister of the Tabernacle, certify that a building called "The British Schools" at Wottonunderedge is to be a place of religious worship and I require you to register the same. Richard Knill, of the Committee of the British School. (GDR/350/345)

2025 Wotton-under-Edge. 4 Feb 1845 (5 Feb 1845). *Wesleyan.* I Maurice Britton of Dursley certify that a building, named the Weselyan Chapel, at Haw Street in the parish of 'Wottonunderedge' is intended forthwith to be a place of religious worship and I require you to register the same and request a certificate thereof. (GDR/350/357)

2026 Sinwell, Wotton-under-Edge. 16 Mar 1846 (2 Mar 1846). I Mary Dauncey of Sinwell in the parish of 'Wottonunderedge' certify that a cottage belonging to me at Sinwell is occasionally to be a place of religious worship and require you to register the same. (GDR/350/371)

2027 Wotton-under-Edge. (7 Nov 1848). House of Daniel Pope. 'Wottonunderedge'. Job Salter. (Q/RNp/4)

2028 Wotton-under-Edge. (30 Nov 1850). House occupied by George Thatcher. Bradley Road, 'Wottonunderedge'. George Thatcher. (Q/RNp/4)

2029 Wotton-under-Edge. (6 May 1851). Building called the British schoolroom. 'Wottonunderedge'. William Woodward. (Q/RNp/4)

YATE
2030 Yate. (Michaelmas 1699). William Pullen's house. (Q/SO/3/521)

2031 Yate. 6 Dec 1715. [*Presbyterian: see note*]. Rice Griffiths of Yate, dissenting preacher, took oaths of allegiance and supremacy. (Q/SO/4/[8])
Note. Rice Griffiths [?Rhys] was the Presbyterian minister in Yate and Wickwar in the Evans list. A meeting was licensed in one Rice Griffiths' house in Wickwar in 1734, *see* **1894**.

2032 Yate. 9 Oct 1817 (16 Oct 1817). *Baptist.* I Ezra Horlick of Chipping Sodbury, Baptist minister, certify that a tenement in the parish of Yate, occupied by James Chambers, is intended forthwith to be a place of religious worship and I require you to register the same. (GDR/334B/291)

2033 Yate. 17 Nov 1817 (20 Nov 1817). *Baptist.* I Ezra Horlick of Chipping Sodbury, Baptist minister, certify that a certain room in the possession of Mrs Alpass in the parish of Yate, is intended forthwith to be a place of religious worship and I require you to register the same. (GDR/334B/290)

2034 Yate. 27 Sept 1819 (28 Sept 1819). *Baptist.* I William Southwood of Chipping Sodbury, Baptist minister, certify that a certain room in a house occupied by Rebecca Shipp in the parish of Yate is intended forthwith to be used as a place of religious worship and I require you to register the same. W Southend. (GDR/334B/254)
Note. Signature does not match minister's name.

PLACES NOT KNOWN

2035 NK (1672). 'Francis Hayne and his house Gloster shyr', noted by Owen Davies. (LT/401)
Note. He may have been the Congregtional minister licensed in Dursley; *see* **727**.

2036 NK. (1672) *Presbyterian.* 'Licence to John Wilsebye Pr teacher att his owne house att . . . in Glocestersh'. (LT/584)
Note. John Wilsebye (Wilsby), Presbyterian, was recorded preaching in Birmingham, Warwickshire, in the Episcopal returns 1669 (Skea 268).

OUT COUNTY

DORSET

To make the new diocese of Bristol more viable, Dorset parishes were removed from the diocese of Salisbury in 1542 and attached to Bristol diocese. The Archdeacon of Dorset carried out most registrations of dissenters meeting-houses, but a few were recorded in the Bristol Diocesan Register of Records. These parishes were restored to the diocese of Salisbury in 1836.

2037 Melcombe Regis, Dorset. 25 Feb 1774 (5 Mar 1774). *Independent.* We [named below] certify that a house in the town of Melcombe Regis, Dorset, is intended or set apart for a meeting place of dissenters under the denomination of Independents. We desire the same may be registered. William White, minister, William Johns, Edward Barrett, Munday Dyer, Joseph Keatt, Robert Miller, Daniel Kingsbury. (EP/A/45/1/91)

2038 Wimborne Minster, Dorset. 23 June 1786. *Baptist.* These are to certify that we [named below] being dissenters under the denomination of Baptist, housekeepers in the town of Wimborne Minster, Dorset, have set apart and appointed the house of Joseph Howard in the town for public service and worship of Almighty God and desire that this our request may be recorded and a certificate thereupon granted. Joseph Apsey, William Bartlett, Robert Howard, Joseph Howard, Richard Wareham, William Harding, Richard Wearam, William Wareham. (EP/A/45/1/157)

2039 Wareham, Dorset. 28 Mar 1789 (7 Apr 1789). We [named below] have appointed a house belonging to Ephraim Dean in the town of Wareham in the parish of Lady St Mary as a place for public worship of Almighty God and desire the same might be registered and a copy thereof granted to us. William White, Thomas Lamb, John Budden, Samuel Tuck, Stephen Bird, Walter Gray, Samuel Tuck jnr, William Baker, John Cox, John Gray. (EP/A/45/1/181)

2040 Corfe Mullen, Dorset. 11 Jan 1790 (13 Jan 1790). *Independent.* We [named below] humbly certify that an house in the parish of Corfe Mullen, Dorset, now in the possession of Mr John Apsey, is intended or set apart for a meeting place of dissenters under the denomination of Independents. We request and desire the same may be registered. George Apse, William Harding, Matthew Meadus, William Cove, Thomas Bishop. (EP/A/45/1/181-82)

2041 Wimborne Minster, Dorset. 12 Nov 1792 (20 Dec 1792). These are to certify that we [named below] have appointed a building known by the name of the New Chapel, lately erected in Chapel Lane, in the town and parish of Wimborne Minster, Dorset, as a place for the exercise of the worship of Almighty God and desire the same may be entered in the Bishop's Court and a copy thereof granted to us. John Duncan, William Ward Wright, Christopher Vey, Joseph Bowles. (EP/A/45/1/248)

2042 Dalwood, Dorset. 20 Sept 1799 (26 Sept 1799). We [named below] certify that a certain building in the parish of Dalwood, Dorset, and now in the occupation of Mr Henry French, is intended to be used for religious worship. Henry French, John Newton, William Pratt, James French, George Shipped, Richard Gile. (EP/A/45/1/280)

SOMERSET

BEDMINSTER

The northern part of Bedminster in Somerset was included in the parliamentary constituency of Bristol in 1832, following the first Parliamntary Reform Act. The city and county boundary of Bristol included the same area as the constituency after the Municipal Corporations Act of 1835, and likewise the combined diocese of Gloucester and Bristol in 1836. The rest of the parish remained in the diocese of Bath & Wells until 1845, when it was transferred to the diocese of Gloucester and Bristol.

2043 Bedminster. 19 June 1828 (not registered). I James Wood of No 32 High Street, Bristol, chemist & druggist, certify that a building in Langton Street in the parish of Bedminster in the diocese of Bristol is forthwith to be a place of religious worship and I require you to register the same and request a certificate thereof. James Wood. (EP/A/45/2/243)

Note. This entry crossed out and endorsed 'mistake not in the diocese of Bristol'. An Independent chapel in Bedminster erected 1828 recorded in Munden, 20.39.

2044 Maesbury, [Bedminster, Somerset] 1 Nov 1831 (19 Nov 1831). I Charles Cosier of 'Mazebury' in the parish of 'Mazebury' certify that my house and premises at 'Mazebury', now in [my] holding and occupation, are intended to be a place of religious worship and I request you to register the same and request a certificate thereof for which shall be taken no more than two shillings and six pence. Charles Cosier (mark), Boaz Tripp, Richard Harkell. (GDR/350/119-20)

Note. Maesbury is the site of an Iron Age hillfort high on the Mendip Hills and Maesbury Road is today is railway station in Bedminster.

2045 Bedminster. (11 Apr 1846 (14 Apr 1846). *Independent.* We [named below] certify that a building known as Mill Lane chapel in Mill Lane in the parish of Bedminster in the borough of the city of Bristol is to be used for religious worship by dissenters of the denomination of Independents and we request that this certificate may be registered. Henry Kingdon, William Maxey, Simon Dumble. (EP/A/45/3/387)

2046 Bedminster. 11 Apr 1846 (14 Apr 1846). *Independent.* We [named below] certify that a dwelling house in Sargent Street in the parish of Bedminster in the borough of the city of Bristol, in the occupation of Elizabeth Webb, is to be used for religious worship by dissenters of the denomination of Independents and we request that this certificate may be registered. Elizabeth Webb, William Hatrell, Henry Kingdon. (EP/A/45/3/388)

2047 Bedminster Down, Bedminster. 2 June 1846 (4 June 1846). *Baptist.* We [named below] certify that the dwelling house belonging to George Poole, on Bedminster Down in the parish of Bedminster in the county of Somerset, is to be used as a chapel for religious worship by dissenters of the denomination of Baptists and we request that this certificate may be registered. William Hicks, George Spile, James Davies, J N Hawtin. (EP/A/45/3/396)

2048 The Parrock, Bedminster. 2 Mar 1847 (2 Mar 1847). I William Goss, of the Parrock in the parish of Bedminster in the county of Somerset, certify my dwelling house and premises now in [my] holding and occupation, are to be a place of religious worship and I request you to register the same and request a certificate thereof for which shall be taken no more than 2 shillings and 6 pence. (EP/A/45/3/415)

Note. This is the first and only printed form encountered.

2049 Bedminster. 25 Sept 1850 (27 Sept 1850). *Wesleyan Methodists.* We (named below] certify that a building known as the British School, in Back Lane in the parish of

Bedminster in the borough ot the city of Bristol, is to be used for religious worship by dissenters of the denomination of Wesleyan Methodists and we request that this certificate may be registered. Isaac Rider, Bedminster, Capper Pass, Bedminster, William Cheese, Bedminster, William Mears, Bedminster, George Colbrook, Bedminster, John Smith, Bedminster, Thomas Jenkins Bedminster, Isaac Knight, Samuel Regnald, Bedminster. (EP/A/45/4/36)

Note. Sheet pasted in book and may be original signatures.

2050 Bedminster. 17 Dec 1850 (18 Dec 1850). *Independent.* We [named below] certify that a building known as Sargent Street chapel, in the parish of Bedminster in the borough of the city of Bristol, is to be used for religious worship by dissenters of the denomination of Independents and we request that this certificate may be registered. Henry Kingdon, William Quick, H B Osborne, Henry Hodson, John Llewellin, William Hatsell (Hatrell?]. (EP/A/45/4/46)

Note. Names difficult to read. Certificate pasted in. Signed.

WILTSHIRE

Parishes in the deaneries of Cricklade and Malmesbury were in the diocese of Gloucester & Bristol from 1837: dissenters meeting-house certificates for these parishes were recorded in GA/GDR/350.

The certificates are calendared in Wilts. MHC in chronological order. Three records not calendared are given in a fuller version here. Other certificates in the Gloucester & Bristol diocesan records are listed (with some small additions) with the appropriate reference to the Wiltshire volume.

Kingswood near Wotton-under-Edge, a parish surrounded by Gloucestershire, was in Wiltshire but was transferred to Gloucestershire in 1844. The majority of certificates were registered by the bishop of Gloucester and Bristol, and all are included above with Gloucestershire parishes.

2051 Poulton. (27 Dec 1836). 'To Revd John Cullen, Independent Minister, Fairford. Whereas it hath been certified to the right Reverend Father in God, Thomas by Divine Permission Lord Bishop of Salisbury, that a house in the parish of Poulton in the county of Wilts and in his Lordship's diocese is intended forthwith to be used as a place of religious worship by an assembly or congregation of protestant dissenters, I do hereby certify, that the same hath been registered and recorded in the Court. Edward Davies Registrar.' (GA D3187/1/3/21)

Note. This printed form is in an envelope with various other items re mortgages etc. in Gloucestershire Archives. *See Wilts. MHC 1477.*

2052 Purton, [Wilts.]. 6 Jan 1842 (8 Jan 1842). *[Primitive Methodist].* I Joseph Preston of Brinkworth, Wilts certify that a house and premises at Purton 'Dorset' now in the holding and occupation of Robert Lordis is intended to be a place of religious worship and I request you to register the same and request a certificate thereof for which shall be taken no more than two shillings and sixpence. Witness E Preston. (GDR/350/287-8)

Note. Very difficult hand. See *Wilts. MHC 1584,* where Chandler, using the RG return, leaves this place as unidentified. Joseph Preston of Brinkworth was a Primitive Methodist evangeliser, and both Purton and Wootton Bassett (now Royal Wootton Bassett), 4 miles away, were on the Brinkworth Prinitive Methodist circuit. (Tonks 49, 78.) The name read as 'Dorset' may be 'Bassett'. *See Wilts. MHC 1614* where the occupier of the chapel a year later is named as William Driffield, described as 'the finest preacher ever in the [Brinkworth] Circuit and he wore top boots'. (Tonks, 88) Purton Primitive Methodist chapel was converted from a cottage in 1843. VCH Wilts. 18, 284; Wiltshire Community History: Primitive Methodist Chapel, Purton. (*https://history.Wiltshire.gov.uk/ community/getchurch.php?id=548*).

2053 Tisbury. (30 Jan 1851). House and premises of Richard Russell. Richard Russell. (Q/RNp/4)

Poole [Keynes]. 5 Oct 1838 (8 Oct 1838). (GDR/350/231) *Wilts. MHC 1518.*

Oaksey. 6 Oct 1838 (8 Oct 1838). (GDR/350/232) *Wilts. MHC 1520.*

Luckington. 6 Oct 1838 (8 Oct 1838). (GDR/350/233) *Wilts. MHC 1519.*

Highworth. 27 Jan 1839 (31 Jan 1839). (GDR/350/235) *Wilts. MHC 1526.*

Moredon, Rodborne Cheny. 8 Mar 1839 (25 Mar 1839). (GDR/350/236) *Wilts. MHC 1528*

Sutton Benger. 11 Mar 1839 (18 Mar 1839). (GDR/350/236) *Wilts. MHC 1531.*

Swindon. 8 Mar 1839 (25 Mar 1839). (GDR/350/237) *Wilts. MHC 1529.*

Wroughton. 23 Apr 1839 (29 Apr 1839). (GDR/350/237) *Wilts. MHC 1534.*

Dauntsey, Brinkworth. 23 Mar 1839 (23 May 1839). (GDR/350/239-40) *Wilts. MHC 1533*

Stratton St Margaret [RG 31/2 has Upper Stratton]. 6 June 1839 (7 June 1839). [*Note: Congregational*]. (GDR/350/242) *Wilts. MHC 1539.*

Ashton Keynes. 6 June 1839 (7 June 1839). (GDR/350/242) *Wilts. MHC 1538.*

Broad Blunsdon [Highworth]. 24 July 1839 (26 July 1839). (GDR/350/243) *Wilts. MHC 1543.*

Corston. 2 Mar 1840 (19 Mar 1840). (GDR/350/250) *Wilts. MHC 1549.*

Ashton Keynes. 26 Apr 1840 (28 Apr 1840). (GDR/350/255) *Wilts. MHC 1555.*

Hook, Lydiard Tregoze. 25 Aug 1840 (28 Aug 1840). (GDR/350/257) *Wilts. MHC 1562.*

Grittleton. 10 Nov 1840 (13 Nov 1840). (GDR/350/261) *Wilts. MHC 1567.*

Hook, Lydiard Tregoze. 13 Nov 1840 (16 Nov 1840). (GDR/350/262) *Wilts. MHC 1568.*

Pinkney, Sherston. 15 Dec 1841 (22 Dec 1841). (GDR/350/286) *Wilts. MHC 1582.*

Cricklade. 12 Feb 1842 (16 Feb 1842). (GDR/350/290) *Wilts. MHC 1586.*

Sherston. 5 Apr 1842 (7 Apr 1842). (GDR/350/294) *Wilts. MHC 1588.*

Malmesbury. 13 May 1842 (13 May 1842). (GDR/350/297) *Wilts. MHC 1589.*

Sopworth. 21 Sept 1842 (24 Sept 1842). (GDR/350/302-3) *Wilts. MHC 1597.*

Hullavington. 9 Jan 1843 19 Jan 1843. (GDR/350/311) *Wilts. MHC 1607.*

Thornend, Christian Malford. 9 Jan 1843 [10 Jan 1843]. [*Note: Witness John Hyatt.*] (GDR/350/310) *Wilts. MHC 1608.*

Stanton St Quinton. 3 Feb 1843 (6 Feb 1843). (GDR/350/315) *Wilts. MHC 1612.*

Purton. 23 Feb 1843 (28 Feb 1843). (GDR/350/315) *Wilts. MHC 1614.*

Swindon. 12 June 1843 (21 June 1843). (GDR/350/321) *Wilts. MHC 1627.*

Startley [Starkley], Summerford Magna. 25 Nov 1843 (27 Nov 1843). (GDR/350/324) *Wilts. MHC 1634.*

Nettleton. 27 Nov 1843 (29 Nov 1843). (GDR/350/325) *Wilts. MHC 1635.*

Hullavington. 30 Nov 1843 (2 Dec 1843). (GDR/350/326) *Wilts. MHC 1636.*

Sherston. 29 Jan 1844 (2 Feb 1844). (GDR/350/332) *Wilts. MHC 1641.*

Swindon. 14 Mar 1844 (16 Mar 1844). (GDR/350/337) *Wilts. MHC 1643.*

Castle Combe. 7 May 1844 (9 May 1844). (GDR/350/342) *Wilts. MHC 1648.*

Inglesham. 8 Apr 1845 18 Apr 1845. (GDR/350/356) *Wilts. MHC 1667.*

Chippenham. 13 Nov 1845 (14 Nov 1845). (GDR/350/363) *Wilts. MHC 1675.*

Nettleton. May 1846 (4 June 1846). (GDR/350/376) *Wilts. MHC 1690.*

Nettleton. (30 Nov 1848). Chapel [*Note: newly erected on the premises of William Strange*]. Samuel Stubbins. (Q/RNp/4) *Wilts. MHC 1717.*

Eastcott, Swindon. 2 Mar 1849 (5 Mar 1849). (GDR/350/551) *Wilts. MHC 1723.*

APPENDIX 1

A LIST OF THE EARLIEST REGISTRATIONS AT THE GLOUCESTERSHIRE QUARTER SESSIONS

This list is at the back of the third Quarter Sessions Order book (GA Q/SO/3) - see Introduction, xxxvi. Places and names as headed in the original have been transcribed exactly; contractions in the Distinctions column have been expanded.

[page/order]	[cert no]	Places	Names	Distinctions
522/1	344	Bourton on the Water	Jo: Johnsons Barne	Dissenters Trinity 1688
522/2	1759	Turly	Wm Arnolds House	Dissenters Trinity 1689
522/3	345	Bourton on the Water	Tho: Colletts house	protestant Dissenters Epiphany 1689
522/4	1620	Strowd Water	Ro: Viners barn	
522/5	1373	Painswick	The Town Hall	
522/6	193	Avening	at the Forest Green	
522/7	540	Cirencester	Giles Watkins house	
522/8	1992	Sinwell & Bradly	Tho: Crows outhouse	
522/9	1007	King Stanly	Stanly Court	
522/10	1329	Nymphsfield	Widdow Kedds house	Anabaptists Epiphany 1689
522/11	493	Cambden	Wm Davison minister	- Michaelmas 1689
522/12	1901	Willersey		
522/13	771	Ebberton	Jonat: Toveys barn	protestant Dissenters Michaelmas 1689
522/14	1461	Ramgeworthy	Wm Moxham's barne	Presbyterians Trinity 1689
522/15	600	Colford	Ri: Benfeilds house	- Michaelmas 1689
522/16	1224	Nailsworth		Meeting houses for Quakers Easter 1690
522/17	1682	Tetbury		
522/18	541	Cirencester		
522/19	494	Broad Cambden		
522/20	1603	Stow		
522/21	426	Cheltenham		
522/22	1584	Stoak Orchard		

522/23	1716	Tewksbury		
522/24	1760	Turley		
522/25	1847	Elton in Westbury p.		
522/26	601	Cover in Newland p.		
522/27	1738	Thornbury		
522/28	1354	Olveston		*(Quakers Easter 1690 continued)*
522/29	928	Kings Weston		
522/30	1937	French hay		
522/31	1438	Pucklechurch		
522/32	1134	Marshfield		
522/33	508	Sodbury		
522/34	1576	Stinchcomb		
522/35	1372	Painswick		
522/36	1681	Tetbury	Mr Beebys Lecture	
522/37	219	Badgworth	Tho: Lawrence's barn	protestant Dissenters Easter 1690
522/38	407	Charlton Kings	Wm Welch's house	
522/39	408		Ri: Kench's house	
522/40	1577	Stancomb	-	Qakers (sic) Michaelmas 1691
522/41	1862	Westerleigh	-	
522/42	177	Ashleworth	Daniel Dobbins house	
522/43	319		James Baylys house	
522/44	320	Blakeney	Nicholas Billingleys Cl	protestant Dissenters Michaelmas 1691
522/45	321		Edmond Brownes	
522/46	1302	Nibley	John Burroughs house	
522/47	318	Blakeney	Ansel Naish's house	
522/48	227	Grafton	Dan: Dobbins house	Quakers Epiphany 1692
522/49	322	Blakeney	Philllip Pare's house	Presbyterians & Independents Epiphany 1693
522/50	799	Falfeild	Daniell Iles's house	Presbyterians Epiphany 1696
522/51	1421	Pebworth	John Grays house	
522/52	495	Chiping Cambden	~~Eliz: Popes house~~ Mary Wells house	Presbyterians Trinity 1695
522/53	627	Honibourne	Eliz: Peters house	

521/54	1683	Tetburys Upton	Jo: Wicks's house	Presbyterians Trinity 1695
521/55	1422	Pebworth	Tho: Coopers house	Presbyterians Michaelmas 1695
521/56	127	Abenhall	Wm Vaughans house called the Bear House	Presbyterians Michaelmas 1695
521/57	392	Bisley p Chalford	a new erected house	Presbyterians Trinity 1696
521/58	427	Cheltenham	Wm Ballingers house	Anabaptists Easter 1697
521/59	1993	Wottonunderedge	Steph: Hunts house	protestant Dissenters Epiphany 1697
521/60	509	Chiping Sodbury	Mans house	Quakers Michaelmas 1698
521/61	428	Cheltenham	Jo: Ballingers house	Anabaptists Easter 1698
521/62	194	Avening	Jo: Giffins house	Anabaptists Michaelmas 1699
521/63	1157	Horwood	Giles Masons house	Anabaptists Michaelmas 1699
521/64	510	Chiping Sodbury	Nathll Bennetts house	Anabaptists Michaelmas 1699
521/65	2030	Yate	Wm Pullens house	- Michaelmas 1699
521/66	1135	Marshfield	Char: Rudders house	Independents Epiphany 1699
521/67	300	Bitton	Jos: Roswells house	Independents Epiphany 1699
521/68	1740	Morton. Thornbury p	Danll Iles's house	Presbyterians Trinity 1700
521/69	1604	Stow	a new erected house	Baptists Easter 1700
521/70	1080	Longborow	Ro: Collett's house	- Easter 1700
521/71	1676	Barton in Temple Guit. p	Wm Woods house	Baptists Easter 1700
521/72	247	Beaveston	Jo: Shipways house	Presbyterians Easter 1700
521/73	228	Beckford	Benj: Bayleys house	Presbyterians Easter 1700
521/74	1761	Turley	Tho: Coles house	Presbyterians Epiphany 1700
521/75	1466	Rodborough	Simon Knights house	Presbyterians Easter 1701
521/76	1355	Tockington	a new erected house	Presbyterians Trinity 1701
521/77	419	Chedworth	Tho: Robert's house	Quakers Trinity 1701
521/78	1994	Wottonunderedge	a new erected house	Presbyterians Epiphany 1701

521/79	346	Bourton on the Water	a new erected house	Baptists Trinity 1701
521/80	372	Bromsberrow	Jo: Stocks house	protestant Dissenters Easter 1702
521/81	1363	Owlpen	Jo: Adys house	Presbyterians Easter 1702
521/82	429	Cheltenham	Jos: Kears house	Anabaptists Trinity 1702
521/83	1762	Turly	Tho: Coles house	Quakers Trinity 1702
521/84	622	Coln Allwins	Gil: Phettiplace's house	Quakers Trinity 1702
521/85	1741	Thornbury	a new erected house	Quakers Trinity 1702
521/86	1146	Maysey Hampton	Hen: Moulders house	Anabaptists Trinity 1702
521/87	301	Bitton	a new house on Jeffreys Hill	Presbyterians Michaelmas 1702
521/88	1548	Putlo	Virgil Cripps house	Anabaptists Michaelmas 1702
521/89	1364	Woolpen	Wm Martins house	Anabaptists Michaelmas 1702
521/90	195	Avening	Abr: Hicks's house	Presbyterians Epiphany 1702
521/91	232	Berkeley	Margt Alcotts mill house	Presbyterians Epiphany 1702
521/92	233		Ri: Clarks house	
521/93	381	Cam	Jam: Sanachers house	Presbyterians Trinity 1703
521/94	1804	Uly	Maur: Dancys house	Presbyterians Trinity 1703
521/95	430	Cheltenham	a new erected house lying towards Alston	Quakers Michaelmas 1703
521/96	431		Jo: Drewetts certificates a new built house for Quakers	Quakers Epiphany 1703
521/97	382	Cam	a new built house for Presbyterians	Presbyterians Epiphany 1703
521/98	1939	French Hay	Mr Wm Brownes house	Presbyterians Easter 1704
521/99	1940	Winterbourne	Tim: Davis's house	Presbyterians Easter 1704
521/100	1938	Hambrooke	Edw: Burgis's house	Presbyterians Easter 1704
521/101	728	Dursley	Tho: Youngs house	protestant Dissenters Trinity 1704
521/102	1371	Painswick	James Davis's house	Anabaptists Easter

				1705
521/103	1322	Notgrove	Jane Evans wid house	Anabaptists Easter 1705
521/104	302	Bitton	The Goat house T: Baylys	protestant Dissenters Trinity 1705
521/105	1684	Tetbury	a house built near the Chiping Croft	protestant Dissenters Trinity 1705
521/106	234	Berkeley	Wm Hawks's house	Presbyterians Michaelmas 1705
521/107	1374	Painswick	a new erected house	Presbyterians Michaelmas 1705
521/108	1225	Nailsworth	an house formerly built for Quakers	- Michaelmas 1705
520/109	248	Bibury	Tho: Pooles house	Independents Easter 1706
520/110	1462	Raingworthy	Jo: Rodmans house	Presbyterians Easter 1706
520/111	1685	Tetbury	Matthew Beales house	Independents Trinity 1706
520/112	1578	Stancomb	Eliz: Chiltenhams house	Quakers Trinity 1706
520/113	1941	French Hay	a new built house for	Quakers Michaelmas 1706
520/114	1686	Tetbury	a house erected for	Quakers Epiphany 1706
520/115	1356	Olveston	a house erected for	Quakers Epiphany 1706
520/116	1837	Westbury	a house erected for	Quakers Epiphany 1706
520/117	929	Kings Weston	a house erected for Quakers	protestant Dissenters Michaelmas 1707
520/118	331	Heyden	Eliz: Hallings house	protestant Dissenters Easter 1707
520/119	1805	Uley	Jos: Hancocks's house	Anabaptists Trinity 1707
520/120	235	Alkington [Berkeley deleted]	a new erected house	Presbyterians Epiphany 1708
520/121	161	Arlingham	Sarah Daniells house	Presbyterians Michaelmas 1708
520/122	1226		Tho: Smalls house	
520/123	1227	Nailsworth	& where Dr Giles dwelt	Presbyterians Trinity 1708
520/124	1228		& George Smalls house	
520/125	1337	Oddington	Ri: Haydons house	Quakers Michaelmas

				1707
520/126	955	Horsley	Wm Hardings house	Baptists Epiphany 1707/8
520/127	229	Grafton	Alice Baylis house	Presbyterians Easter 1709
520/128	891	Hannam	Samuell Harveys house	Baptists Easter 1709
520/129	1908	Winchcomb	James Masons house	Quakers Easter 1709
520/130	1995	Wottonunderedge	Sampson Carys house	Quakers Easter 1709
520/131	542	Cirencester	the Weavers Hall	Anabaptists Easter 1709
520/132	1091	Longhope	Richd Birkins house	Presbyterians Trinity 1710
520/133	511	Chiping Sodbury	a house in Hounds Lane	Baptists Trinity 1709
520/134	432	Cheltenham	Edwd Nicholls's house	Anabaptists Michaelmas 1710
520/135	1996	Nind in Wottonund. p	?Thos Slades house	
520/136	1997	Wortley	Jo: Mundays house	Presbyterians Epiphany 1710/11
520/137	1687	Tetbury	Wm Pooles house	
520/138	1688		Daniell Birts house	
520/139	1621	Bourne	Henry Showells house	Quakers Epiphany 1710
520/140	1892	Wickwarr	Tho: Bishops house	protestant Dissenters Michaelmas 1711

APPENDIX 2

SUMMARY OF THE ANSWERS TO QUESTION 17 IN BISHOP CHRISTOPHER BETHEL'S
SURVEY OF THE DIOCESE OF GLOUCESTER 1825 (see Introduction, xlvi).[1]

No. in volume	Parish	Nonconformists
Campden Deanery		
1	Beckford	One - RC
2	Ashton Underhill	None
3	Alderton	One - Anabaptist
4	Ashton Somerville	None
5	Aston Subedge	None
6	Battsford	None
7	Bourton on the Hill	None
8	Moreton in Marsh	One - Independent
9	Buckland	Licensed house - Revivalists
10	Chipping Campden	Two - Baptists & Wesleyan Methodists
11	Clifford Chambers	None
12	Didbrook cum Pinnock	None
13	Hayles chapel	None
14	Horsington	None
15	Dumbleton	None
16	Hinton on the Green	None
18	Kemmerton	One - Wesleyan Methodists
18	Lemington	None
19	Long Marston	Ranters or Revivalists
20	Mickleton cum Ebrington	Licensed house at Mickleton - Wesleyans; ditto at Ebrington - Baptists
21	Pebworth	One - Wesleyan Methodists
22	Preston upon Stour	None
23	Quinton	Two licensed houses – Wesleyans & Revivalists
24	Saintbury	None
25	Shenington	Licensed room - Methodists
26	Stanton	None
27	Snowshill	None
28	Stanway	None
29	Toddington with Stanley Portlarge	None
31	Todenham	One licensed house – Wesleyan Methodists
32	Welford	Methodists, Ranters
33	Weston Subedge	None
34	Weston upon Avon	None

---

[1] GDR/383. Parish names are as given in the original. The layout of entries has been standardised.

35	Great Washbourne	None
36	Willersey	None
37	Wormington	None
38	Peculiar Childs Wickham	None

Cirencester Deanery

39	Cirencester	Four - Quakers; Unitarians; Baptists; Methodists
40	Driffield	None
41	Harnhill	None
42	Amney Crucis	None
43	Amney Peter	None
44	Amney Mary or Ashbrook	None
45	Baunton	None
46	Badgendon	None
47	Chedworth	One of old date - Independents
48	Coates	Licensed house - Calvinists
49	Coln St Dennis	None
50	Coln Rogers	One - Baptists.
51	Compton Abdale	None
52	Daglingworth	None
53	Duntsbourne Abbotts	In a cottage - Methodists
54	Duntsbourne Rouse	None
55	Farmington	None
56	Hampnett	None. One RC family
57	Stowell	Chapel to Hampnett [for most answers] see Hampnett
58	North Cerney	None
59	North Leach	One chapel almost deserted - Independents. One licensed room - Wesleyans
60	Preston	None
61	Rendcombe	None
62	Siddington St Peter and Mary	A person calling himself a missionary
63	South Cerney	Home missionary
64	Stratton	None

Dursley Deanery

65	Rockhampton	None
66	Berkeley	Three small places but the vicar knows nothing of their tenets
67	Stone	None
68	Beverstone	None
69	Kingscote	One - Wesleyans
70	Cam	One - Independents
71	Coaley	One chapel - Wesleyan; two licensed rooms - Independents
72	Dursley	Three - Calvinists; Wesleyan Methodists; Tent Methodists

73	Frampton upon Severn	One - Independents
74	Hill	None
75	Kingswood Wilts	Old Protestant Dissenters. Many go to the meeting because they have no seats in the church
76	Lasborough	None
77	Newington Bagpath	None
78	Owlpen	None
79	North Nibley	Two at least - Wesleyans and Whitfieldians
80	Slimbridge	One - Independents
81	Stiinchcombe	meetings in houses – Wesleyans and Calvinists
82	Thornbury	Three – Wesleyans; Baptists; Quakers
83	Falfield	One Wesleyan
89	Oldbury on Severn	None
90	Uley	Three – Baptists; Independents; Wesleyans
91	Woozleworth	None
92	Wooton under Edge	Five - Rowland Hill; Independents; Baptists; Methodists; Wesleyans

Fairford Deanery

93	Kempsford	None
94	Coln St Aldwyns	None
95	Down Ampney	None
96	East Leach Martin	None
97	East Leach Turville	Licensed house Baptists
98	Fairford	Two - Baptists & Independents
99	Hatherop	A R. Catholic chapel
100	Letchlade	One - Baptist
101	Maysey Hampton	A Licensed house - Calvinists
102	Marston Maysey	None
103	Quennington	None
104	Southrop	None

Forest Deanery

104 *sic*	Abinghall	One - Independents
105	Awre	L Hoare-Bridgeman
106	Blaisdon	None
107	Bromsberrow	None
108	Churcham with Bully	Chapel at Birdwood - Wesleyans
109	Dean Michell	Two – Wesleyan; Independent
110	Dean Parva	Two – Independents; Wesleyans
111	Dymock	None
112	English Bicknor	Licensed house - Baptists
113	Flaxley	None
114	Huntley	None
115	Kempley	None
116	Lea	Licensed house - Baptists
117	Longhope	Two – Baptists; Wesleyans
118	Lydney with Ailburton Chapel	Two - Baptists; Wesleyans
119	St Briavells	One - Bryanites

120	Hewelsfield	One - Independents
121	Minsterworth	One - Methodists
122	Newent	One - Wesleyan Methodists
123	Newland	Many: Baptists; Wesleyans; Ranters; Bryanites; Bridgeman
124	Colford Chapel	One - Baptists. Licensed House - Wesleyans
125	Bream	None
126	Newnham	Two - Independents; Bridgeman.
127	Oxenhall	None
128	Pauntley	One - Wesleyan Methodists
129	Preston	None
130	Ruardean	One - Independents
131	Rudford	None
132	Staunton	Two licensed houses
133	Taynton	One three miles from church - Wesleyan Methodists
134	Tibberton	None
135	Tiddenham	One licensed house - Brianites
136	Upleadon	None
136 *sic*	Westbury on Severn	One - Wesleyan Methodists
137	Wollastone	Itinerant teacher occasionally
138	Alvington	as Wollastone
139	Christ Church in the Forest	Licensed house at Joyford - Methodists
140	Holy Trinity	meetings in cottages
141	St Pauls	chapel of Methodists

Gloucester Deanery

142	Arlingham	One - Wesleyan
143	Ashelworth	None
144	Barnwood	None
145	'Brookthrop'	Licensed house - Wesleyans
146	Churchdown	Two - Wesleyans; Lady Huntingdon
147	Elmore	One - Independents who have a S[unday] S[chool]
149	Fretherne	One - Wesleyans
150	Harescombe	None
151	Pitchcombe	One – Wesleyans; Curate doubts it being now used as a place of worship
152	Haresfield	Two houses - Methodists
153	Hartpury	Catholic chapel. Methodists meet in a house
154	Hempstead	None
155	Lassington	None
156	Longney	None
157	Maisemore	None
158	Matson	None
159	Moreton Valence	None
160	Norton	None. A Methodist School chiefly attended from other parishes
161	Quedgley	None

162	Sandhurst	None
163	Standish	None
164	Hardwicke	Licensed house - Baptists
165	Randwick	Two - Lady Huntingdon; Wesleyans at Ebley
166	Saul	None
167	Upton St Leonards	One - Wesleyans
168	Whaddon	None
169	Wheatenhurst	Licensed room - Wesleyans
170	Great Witcombe	None
171	St Aldate GC	None
172	St John Baptist	Chapel in Lower Northgate St - Wesleyans
173	St Michael with St Mary Le grace	One - Baptists
174	St Mary le Crypt with St Owen & All Saints	One - Independents
175	St Nicholas	One - Wesleyan Methodists
176	St Mary le Lode with Holy Trinity	Two - Lady Huntingdon; Ranters
177	St Catherines	None
178	Christ Church	None

Hawkesbury Deanery

179	Siston	One small chapel but many of the inhabitants attend those in adjoining parishes being nore inclined to dissenting than Church interest
180	Alderley	None
181	Badminton Gt and Little	None
182	Bitton	One - Whitfieldians
183	Hanham	parts visited by itinerants
184	Oldland	One - Wesleyans
185	Holy Trinity in Bitton	Three Methodist chapels; one Tabernacle; one Baptist chapel; one Moravian; two seceders from Wesleyans besides innumerable preaching houses - Kingswood
186	Boxwell cum Leighterton	None
187	Charfield	None
189	Cold Ashton	None
190	Cromhall	None
191	Daynton or Doynton	[Q17 omitted]
192	Didmarton	None
192 *sic*	Oldbury on the Hill	None
193	Doddington	None
194	Dyrham	None
195	Frampton Cotterell	Two – Whitfieldian; Wesleyans
196	Hawkesbury	2 Particular Baptists
197	Tresham	None
198	Horton	One - Wesleyans
199	Iron Acton	One - Wesleyan Methodists
200	Marshfield	Independents - Unitarians

201	Pucklechurch	Licensed house - Independents
202	Abson chapel	One - Belonging to Methodists
203	Westerleigh	One - Independents
204	Rangeworthy	Two - Independents; Methodists
205	Old Sodbury	None
206	Chipping Sodbury	One - Baptists
207	Little Sodbury	None
208	Tormarton	None
209	West Littleton	None
210	Acton turville	None
211	Tortworth	None
212	Tytherington	None
213	Wapley	None
214	Weston Birt	None
215	Wickwar	Two – Wesleyans; Calvinists
216	Yate	None

Stonehouse Deanery

217	Frocester	Licensed house
218	Nympsfield	1 Baptist
219	Avening	Three - Baptists
220	Nailsworth	[No reply]. 'An unconsecrate chapel. The village situated in three parishes: Avening, Minchinhampton & Horsley'
221	Bisley	Two Baptist; one Independent; four Methodist in Bisley
222	Chalford chapel	
223	Brimpsfield	None
224	Cranham	None
225	Cherington	None
226	Cowley	None
227	Cubberley	One - Independent
228	Eastington	Two – Wesleyans; Ranters
229	Edgeworth	None
230	Elkstone	None
231	Horsley	Three - Quakers; Baptists; Wesleyans
232	Minchinhampton	One Baptist. Three Wesleyans.
233	Rodborough	A large chapel capable of containing 1200. Whitfieldians
234	Miserden	One licensed house in Camp Hamlet – Methodists
235	Painswick	Two - Independents; Wesleyans.
236	Shepscombe	None
237	Rodmarton	None
238	Sapperton	Licensed house at Frampton
239	Shipton Moyne	None
240	Stanley Leonard	One - Wesleyans
241	Stanley Regis	One chapel – Baptists; three licensed houses - Calvinists; Wesleyans; Ranters
242	Stonehouse	One chapel - Independents. Licensed houses – Wesleyans; Ranters.

243	Stoud	Four - Independents; Methodists; Baptists; Ranters; besides licensed rooms
244	Tetbury	Two - Independents; Baptists
245	Syde	None
246	Winstone	One - Methodists
247	Woodchester	None

Stow Deanery

248	Little Rissington	Licensed house - Baptists.
249	Aston Blank	None
250	Addlestrop	None
251	Broadwell	Licensed house - Wesleyans
252	Barrington Great	None
253	Barrington Little	None
254	Bleddington	None
255	Bourton on the Water	One - Baptists
256	Clapton chapel	None
257	Slaughter Lower chapel	None
258	Compton Little	Licensed house - Baptists
259	Condicote	None
260	Guiting Lower	None
261	Guiting Temple	None
262	Halling	One - Wesleyans
263	Hazleton	None
264	Yanworth or Emsworth	None
265	Longborough cum Seasincote	A licensed cottage
266	Naunton	One - Baptists
266 *sic*	Notgrove	None
267	Oddington	One licensed house - Baptists
268	Great Rissington	None
269	Rissington Wick	None
270	Salperton	None
271	Shipton Sollars [and Oliffe crossed through]	None
272	Shireborne	None
273	Windrush	None
274	Upper Slaughter	None
275	Stow-on-the-Wold	Two - Baptists; Wesleyan Methodists
276	Sutton under Brailes	None
277	Swell Upper	None
278	Swell Lower	None
279	Turkdean	None
280	Westcote	None
281	Widford	None

'No CXLVIII [148] has been accidentally omitted – therefore I shall number the next benefice CCLXXXI [281]'

Winchcombe Deanery

281 *sic*	Tewkesbury	Wesleyan Methodists. Independents. Baptists. Quakers.
282	Prestbury	None
283	Winchcomb	One of long standing - Sabbatarian Baptists
284	Badgeworth	One in the parish - Methodists
285	Shurdington	See Badgeworth
286	Bishop's Cleeve	None
287	Stoke Orchard	None
288	Brockworth	Licensed cottage - Methodists
289	Charlton Abbotts	None
290	Charlton Kings	None
291	Colesbourn	None
292	Cheltenham	Baptists. Independents. Methodists. Quakers. R. Catholic. Lady Huntingdon. One nameless.
293	Trinity Church	see Cheltenham
294	Corse	None
295	Deerhurst	One in the hamlet of Appeley - Independents
296	Dowdeswell	None
297	Down Hatherley	None
298	Elmstone Hardwick	None
299	Forthampton	None
300	Hasfield	None
301	Leckhampton	None
302	Lye or Leigh	Methodists meet occasionally in a private house
303	Oxenton	None
304	Sevenhampton	None
305	Staverton	None
306	Tyrley	see Staverton
307	Swindon	None
308	Tirley or Tyrley	Methodists chapel now disused
309	Treddington	None
310	Twining	A few meet in a cottage. Baptists and Methodists
311	Walton Cardiffe	None
312	Whittington	None
313	Winchcombe with Gretton and Sudely	Two - Baptists; Wesleyans
314	Gretton	
315	Sudeley	
316	Withington	Cottage. Methodists
317	Woolstone	None

Bibury Peculiar

318	Barnsley	None
319	Bibury	[blank]
320	Winson chapel	[blank]
321	Aldsworth	'None. No dissenter in the parish'

INDEX OF PERSONS

Roman numerals refer to the Introduction; Arabic numerals refer to entry serial numbers.

Richard 1327, 1382, 1387
Samuel 1407
Sarah 997
Thomas 849
William 272, 1651, 1875, 1357–8
 William M 411–2, 451,
Garland, John 1564
 Moses 1556
Garlick, Charles 938
Garn (Garne), John 825–6
 Thomas 827–8
 William 1902, 1904
Garraway, Francis 1844
 John 1342–3
Garrett (Garritt), Charles 186
 John 1751
Gartrell, James 767, 1153
Gatfield, William 1247–48
Gatten, Thomas 1063
Gatward, Joseph 15
Gay, Thomas 639
Gazard (Gazzard), John 1306
 Thomas 966, 1231
Gazon, Cornelius 1310
Gearing, Robert 997
Gears (Geers), George 1494
 Thomas 910
Geden, John 531
Gegg, Thomas 594–5
Geleman, Thomas 1387 *and see* Jellyman
George I xxxvi
George, Francis 1518a
Gerrard, G W 57
Gerrish, Emerson 303
 Samuel 1123
Gibbins (Gibbons), John (J) 839, 841, 843, 845
Gibbons, Samuel 459
 S B 775
 Sarah 574
Gibbs, Daniel 109, 1868
 George 16, 259, 1430
 Henry L 936
 John 932, 1125, 1349
 Jonathan 987, 1868
 Joseph 1123
 Stephen 1872
 Thomas 1078, 1144, 1145
 V 1870
 William 433, 971, 986, 1903, 1871
Gibson, Richard 379
Gifford (Jifford), Andrew 9
Gilbert, John 1638
 Thomas 326
Gile, Richard 2042
Giles, Dr 1227
 James 951
 John 737, 1702
Gill, Ann 1107

 James 265, 462, 1044
Gillard, George 441
Gillespie, Robert 547
Gilliam, John 435
Gillies, John 105
Gillman (Gilman), Daniell 281
 Francis 68
 John 547
 Thomas 1404–5, 1428
Glanville, John 1750
Glass, John 1262, 1986
Gloster, John 1133
Glover, John 1702
 Joseph 452
 Richard 1590
Glyde, James 29
Godfrey, James 1138
Godwin, Christopher (Chris) 116
 John 107, 1439, 1750, 1952, 1954, 1957
Goffe, Thomas 1059
Golding, James 1009, 1168–9, 1969–70
 Lifely 1038
 Richard 1881
 William 1038, 1475
Good, John 1945
 Nathaniel 1952
Goodland, Sarah 574
Goodman, James 1241
 Mary Ann 15
Goodwin, Benjamin 156
 John 557, 1526
Goold (Gould), Aaron 679, 696
Gordon, John 1339
Gorton, George 1483
 John 1340
 Robert 1613
Goss, William 2048
Gostlett Goslett), John 1131
 Thomas 1132
Gough, John 1851
 Mary 1487
 Thomas 105, 1474, 1973
 William 181
Gould, George 28
 Humphrey 1658
 S 101
 William 628, 629
Gouldin, William *see* Golding 1475
Goulding, Abraham 1038
 Elizabeth 1038
Goulter, Allen 925
 James 129, 130
Gower, Richard 257, 1827
Gowin, Nathaniel 913–4
Grabham, Paul 740
Graft, Joseph 1528
Grant, Jeremiah 22, 1317, 1704, 1765
 John 1981

INDEX OF PLACES

(in Gloucestershire unless otherwise indicated)

Roman numerals refer to the Introduction; Arabic numerals refer to entry serial numbers.

INDEX OF SELECTED SUBJECTS

Roman numerals refer to the Introduction; Arabic numerals refer to entry serial numbers.

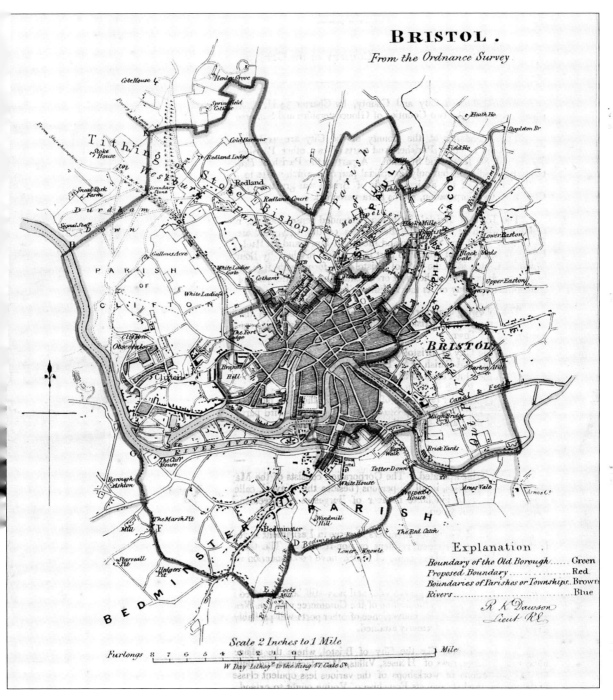

Bristol area parishes, 1832 *(BA: reproduced with permission)*

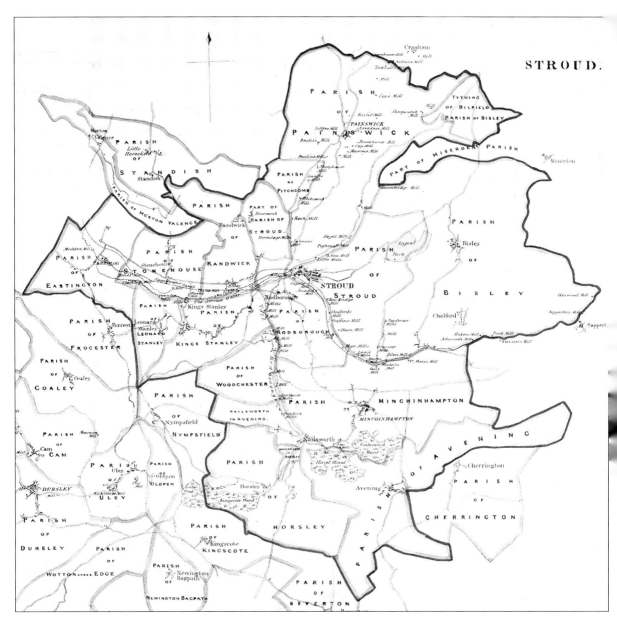

Stroud area parishes, 1832 *(GA: reproduced with permission)*

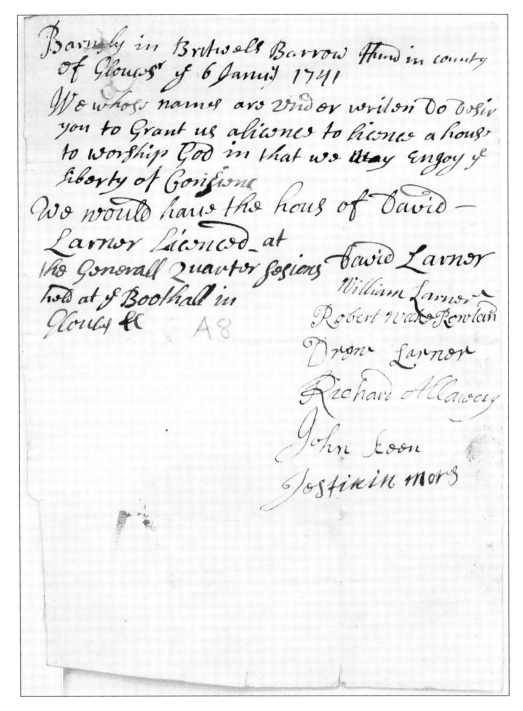

A certificate for Barnsley [**223**] preserved in the Gloucester Quarter Sessions papers, very probably in the hand of David Larner, the first signatory.   *GA*

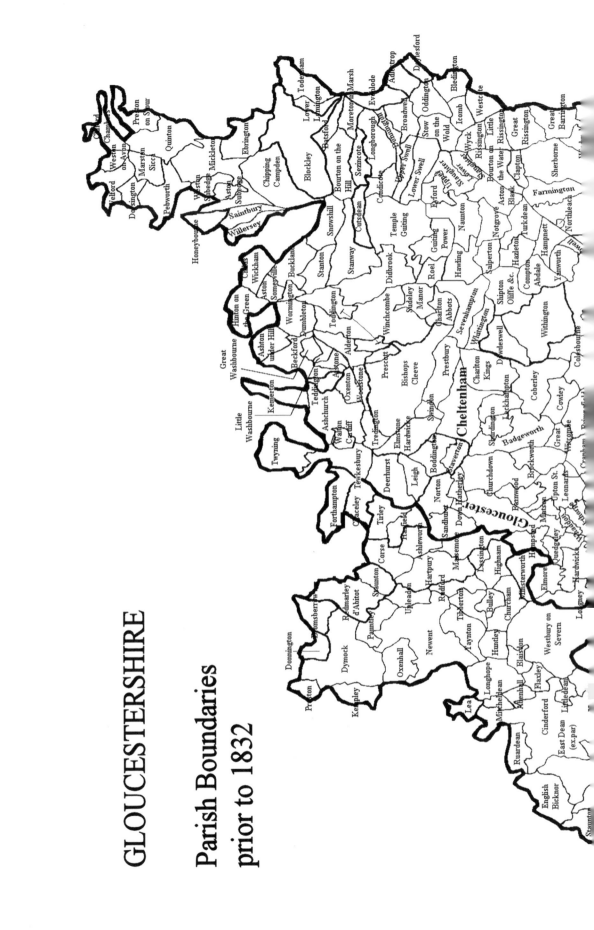

GLOUCESTERSHIRE

Parish Boundaries
prior to 1832